Communications
in Computer and Information Science　　　1567

More information about this series at https://link.springer.com/bookseries/7899

Balasubramanian Raman ·
Subrahmanyam Murala · Ananda Chowdhury ·
Abhinav Dhall · Puneet Goyal (Eds.)

Computer Vision and Image Processing

6th International Conference, CVIP 2021
Rupnagar, India, December 3–5, 2021
Revised Selected Papers, Part I

 Springer

Editors
Balasubramanian Raman
Indian Institute of Technology Roorkee
Roorkee, India

Subrahmanyam Murala
Indian Institute of Technology Ropar
Ropar, India

Ananda Chowdhury
Jadavpur University
Kolkata, India

Abhinav Dhall
Indian Institute of Technology Ropar
Ropar, India

Puneet Goyal
Indian Institute of Technology Ropar
Ropar, India

ISSN 1865-0929   ISSN 1865-0937 (electronic)
Communications in Computer and Information Science
ISBN 978-3-031-11345-1   ISBN 978-3-031-11346-8 (eBook)
https://doi.org/10.1007/978-3-031-11346-8

Preface

The sixth edition of the International Conference in Computer Vision and Image Processing (CVIP 2021) was organized by the Indian Institute of Technology (IIT) Ropar, Punjab, India. CVIP is a premier conference focused on image/video processing and computer vision. Previous editions of CVIP were held at IIIT Allahabad (CVIP 2020), MNIT Jaipur (CVIP 2019), IIIT Jabalpur (CVIP 2018), and IIT Roorkee (CVIP 2017 and CVIP 2016). The conference has witnessed extraordinary success with publications in multiple domains of computer vision and image processing.

In the face of COVID-19, the conference was held in virtual mode during December 3–5, 2021, connecting researchers from different countries around the world such as Sri Lanka, the USA, etc. The team—composed of Pritee Khanna (IIIT DMJ), Krishna Pratap Singh (IIIT Allahabad), Shiv Ram Dubey (IIIT Sri City), Aparajita Ojha (IIIT DMJ), and Anil B. Gonde (SGGSIET Nanded)—organized an online event with flawless communication through Webex. Moreover, the publicity for the submission of research articles by Shiv Ram Dubey (IIIT Sri City), Deep Gupta (VNIT Nagpur), Sachin Chaudhary (PEC Chandigarh), Akshay Dudhane (MBZUAI, Abu Dhabi, UAE), and Prashant Patil (Deakin University, Australia) made CVIP 2021 a great success, with the overwhelming participation of about 110 researchers. Also, the efficient teamwork by volunteers from IIT Ropar and PEC Chandigarh helped to overcome the challenges of virtual communication, thus resulting in the smooth running of the event.

CVIP 2021 received 260 regular paper submissions that went through a rigorous review process undertaken by approximately 500 reviewers from different renowned institutes and universities. The technical program chairs, Puneet Goyal (IIT Ropar), Abhinav Dhall (IIT Ropar), Narayanan C Krishnan (IIT Ropar), Mukesh Saini (IIT Ropar), Santosh K. Vipparthi (MNIT Jaipur), Deepak Mishra (IIST Trivandrum), and Ananda S. Chowdhury (Jadavpur University), coordinated the overall review process which resulted in the acceptance of 97 research articles.

The event was scheduled with one plenary talk and two keynote talk sessions each day. On the very first day, the event commenced with a plenary talk on "AI for Social Good" by Venu Govindaraju (State University of New York at Buffalo, USA) followed by the keynote talks by Shirui Pan (Monash University, Australia) and Victor Sanchez (University of Warwick, UK). On second day, Tom Gedeon (Curtin University, Australia) guided the audience with a plenary talk on "Responsive AI and Responsible AI". The keynote talks by Vitomir Štruc (University of Ljubljana, Slovenia) and Munawar Hayat (Monash University, Australia) enlightened the audience with informative discussion on computer vision. The last day of the conference, with the informative plenary talk on "Cognitive Model Motivated Document Image Understanding" by Santanu Chaudhury (IIT Jodhpur) and the keynote talk by Sunil Gupta (Deakin University), gave a deep insight to the audience on AI and its applications.

CVIP 2021 presented high-quality research work with innovative ideas. All the session chairs were invited to vote for four different categories of awards. For each award, three papers were nominated depending on the novelty of work, presentation skills, and the reviewer scores. Four different awards were announced: the IAPR Best Paper Award, the IAPR Best Student Paper Award, the CVIP Best Paper Award, and the CVIP Best Student Paper Award.

Also, CVIP 2021 awarded Prabir Kumar Biswas (IIT Kharagpur) with a CVIP Lifetime Achievement Award for his remarkable research in the field of image processing and computer vision. The awards were announced in the valedictory ceremony by General Co-chair Balasubramanian Raman (IIT Roorkee).

All the accepted and presented papers from CVIP 2021 are published in this volume in Springer's Communications in Computer and Information Science (CCIS) series. The proceedings of all previous editions of CVIP have also been successfully published in this series, and the papers are indexed by ISI Proceedings, EI-Compendex, DBLP, SCOPUS, Google Scholar, Springer link, etc. The organizers of the next event have given us a glimpse of their plan for CVIP 2022 at VNIT Nagpur: https://vnit.ac.in/cvip2022/.

December 2021

Balasubramanian Raman
Subrahmanyam Murala
Ananda Chowdhury
Abhinav Dhall
Puneet Goyal

Organization

Patron

Bidyut Baran Chaudhuri   ISI Kolkata, India

General Chairs

Venu Govindaraju	State University of New York at Buffalo, USA
Mohamed Abdel-Mottaleb	University of Miami, USA
Rajeev Ahuja	IIT Ropar, India

General Co-chairs

Balasubramanian Raman	IIT Roorkee, India
Javed N. Agrewala (Dean Research)	IIT Ropar, India

Conference Chairs

Subrahmanyam Murala	IIT Ropar, India
Satish Kumar Singh	IIIT Allahabad, India
Gaurav Bhatnagar	IIT Jodhpur, India
Sanjeev Kumar	IIT Roorkee, India
Partha Pratim Roy	IIT Roorkee, India

Technical Program Chairs

Santosh Kumar Vipparthi	MNIT Jaipur, India
Abhinav Dhall	IIT Ropar, India
Narayanan C. Krishnan	IIT Ropar, India
Deepak Mishra	IIST Trivandrum, India
Ananda S. Chowdhury	Jadavpur University, India
Puneet Goyal	IIT Ropar, India
Mukesh Saini	IIT Ropar, India

Conference Convenors

Sachin Chaudhary	PEC Chandigarh, India
Pritee Khanna	IIIT DMJ, India

Krishna Pratap Singh	IIIT Allahabad, India
Shiv Ram Dubey	IIIT Allahabad, India
Aparajita Ojha	IIIT DMJ, India
Anil B. Gonde	SGGSIET Nanded, India

Publicity Chairs

Shiv Ram Dubey	IIIT Allahabad, India
Deep Gupta	VNIT Nagpur, India
Akshay Dudhane	MBZUAI, Abu Dhabi, UAE
Prashant W. Patil	Deakin University, Australia

Website Chairs

| Sachin Chaudhary | PEC Chandigarh, India |
| Prashant W. Patil | Deakin University, Australia |

International Advisory Committee

Luc Van Gool	ETH Zurich, Switzerland
B. S. Manjunath	University of California, USA
Vishal M. Patel	Johns Hopkins University, USA
Richard Hartley	ANU, Australia
Mohammed Bennamoun	University of Western, Australia
Srinivasa Narasimhan	Carnegie Mellon University, USA
Daniel P. Lopresti	Lehigh University, USA
Victor Sanchez	University of Warwick, UK
Fahad Shahbaz Khan	MBZUAI, Abu Dhabi, UAE
Junsong Yuan	State University of New York at Buffalo, USA
Chenliang Xu	University of Rochester, USA
Xiaojun Chang	Monash University, Australia
Sunil Gupta	Deakin University, Australia
Naoufel Werghi	Khalifa University, Abu Dhabi, UAE
C.-C. Jay Kuo	University of Southern California, USA
Salman Khan	MBZUAI, Abu Dhabi, UAE
Hisham Cholakkal	MBZUAI, Abu Dhabi, UAE
Santu Rana	Deakin University, Australia
Zhou Wang	University of Waterloo, Canada
Paul Rosin	Cardiff University, UK
Bir Bhanu	University of California, Riverside, USA
Gaurav Sharma	University of Rochester, USA
Gian Luca Foresti	University of Udine, Italy

Mohan S. Kankanhalli   National University of Singapore, Singapore
Sudeep Sarkar   University of South Florida, USA
Josep Lladós   Autonomous University of Barcelona, Spain
Massimo Tistarelli   University of Sassari, Italy
Kiran Raja   NTNU, Norway
Alireza Alaei   Southern Cross University, Australia
Ankit Chaudhary   University of Missouri – St. Louis, USA
Ajita Rattani   Wichita State University, USA
Emanuela Marasco   George Mason University, USA
Thinagaran Perumal   Universiti Putra Malaysia, Malaysia
Xiaoyi Jiang   University of Münster, Germany
Paula Brito   University of Porto, Portugal
Jonathan Wu   University of Windsor, Canada

National Advisory Committee

P. K. Biwas   IIT Kharagpur, India
Sanjeev Kumar Sofat   PEC Chandigarh, India
Debashis Sen   IIT Kharagpur, India
Umapada Pal   ISI Kolkata, India
Chirag N. Paunwala   SCET Surat, India
Sanjay Kumar Singh   IIT (BHU) Varanasi, India
Surya Prakash   IIT Indore, India
A. S. Chowdhury   Jadavpur University, India
S. N. Singh   IIT Kanpur, India
K. R. Ramakrishnan   IISC Bangalore, India
Sushmita Mitra   ISI Kolkata, India
Puneet Gupta   IIT Indore, India
Somnath Dey   IIT Indore, India
M. Tanveer   IIT Indore, India
O. P. Vyas   IIIT Allahabad, India
G. C. Nandi   IIIT Allahabad, India
Aparajita Ojha   IIIT Jabalpur, India
U. S. Tiwari   IIIT Allahabad, India
Sushmita Gosh   Jadavpur University, India
D. S. Guru   University of Mysore, India
B. H. Shekhar   Mangalore University, India
Bunil Kumar Balabantaray   NIT Meghalaya, India
Munesh C. Trivedi   NIT Agartala, India
Sharad Sinha   IIT Goa, India

Reviewers

Aalok Gangopadhyay	IIT Gandhinagar, India
Abhimanyu Sahu	Jadavpur University, India
Abhinav Dhall	IIT Ropar, India
Abhirup Banerjee	University of Oxford, UK
Abhishek Sharma	IIIT Naya Raipur, India
Abhishek Sinha	Indian Space Research Organization, India
Adarsh Prasad Behera	IIIT Allahabad, India
Ahmed Elnakib	Mansoura University, Egypt
Ajita Rattani	Wichita State University, USA
Akshay Dudhane	IIT Ropar, India
Albert Mundu	IIIT Allahabad, India
Alireza Alaei	Southern Cross University, Australia
Alok Ranjan Sahoo	IIIT Allahabad, India
Amar Deshmukh	RMDSSOE, India
Amit Singhal	NSUT, India
Amitesh Rajput	BITS Pilani, India
Anamika Jain	IIIT Allahabad, India
Anand Singh Jalal	GLA University, India
Ananda Chowdhury	Jadavpur University, India
Angshuman Paul	IIT Jodhpur, India
Anil Kumar	MANIT Bhopal, India
Anirban Mukhopadhyay	IIT Gandhinagar, India
Anjali Gautam	IIIT Allahabad, India
Ankit Chaudhary	University of Missouri – St. Louis, USA
Ankur Gupta	IIT Roorkee, India
Anoop Jacob Thomas	IIIT Tiruchirappalli, India
Anshul Pundhir	IIT Roorkee, India
Ansuman Mahapatra	NIT Puducherry, India
Anuj Rai	IIT, Ropar, India
Anuj Sharma	PEC Chandigarh, India
Anukriti Bansal	LNMIIT Jaipur, India
Anup Nandy	NIT Rourkela, India
Anupam Agrawal	IIIT Allahabad, India
Anurag Singh	NIT Delhi, India
Aparajita Ojha	IIIT Jabalpur, India
Arindam Sikdar	Jadavpur University, India
Arnav Bhavsar	IIT Mandi, India
Aroof Aimen	IIT Ropar, India
Arun Chauhan	IIIT Dharwad, India
Arya Krishnan	IIITMK, India
Ashish Khare	University of Allahabad, India

Ashish Mishra	Jaypee Institute of Information Technology, India
Ashish Phophalia	IIIT Vadodara, India
Ashish Raman	NIT Jalandhar, India
Ashutosh Kulkarni	IIT Ropar, India
Asish Mishra	IIST, India
Avadh Kishor	Graphic Era University, India
Ayatullah Faruk Mollah	Aliah University, India
B. H. Shekar	Mangalore University, India
B. N. Chatterji	IIT Kharagpur, India
B. Surendiran	NIT Pondicherry, India
Babu Mehtre	IDRBT Hyderabad, India
Badri Subudhi	IIT Jammu, India
Balasubramanian Raman	IIT Roorkee, India
Balasubramanyam Appina	IIITDM Kancheepuram, India
Bibal Benifa	IIIT Kottayam, India
Bikash Sahana	NIT Patna, India
Bini Aa	IIIT Kottayam, India
Binsu C. Kovoor	Cochin University of Science and Technology, India
Bir Bhanu	University of California, Riverside, USA
Bishal Ghosh	IIT Ropar , India
Brijraj Singh	Sony Research, India
Buddhadeb Pradhan	NIT Jamshedpur, India
Bunil Balabantaray	NIT Meghalaya, India
Chandra Prakash	NIT Delhi, India
Chandra Sekhar	IIIT Sri City, India
Chandrashekhar Azad	NIT Jamshedpur, India
Chinmoy Ghosh	Jalpaiguri Government Engineering College, India
Chirag Paunwala	SCET Surat, India
Chiranjoy Chattopadhyay	IIT Jodhpur, India
D. Guru	Mysore University, India
Daniel Lopresti	Lehigh University, USA
Debanjan Sadhya	ABV-IIITM Gwalior, India
Debashis Sen	IIT Kharagpur, India
Debi Dogra	IIT Bhubaneswar, India
Debotosh Bhattacharjee	Jadavpur University, India
Deep Gupta	VNIT Nagpur, India
Deepak Ranjan Nayak	NIT Jaipur, India
Deepankar Adhikari	IIT Ropar, India
Deepika Shukla	National Brain Research Centre, India
Dileep A. D.	IIT Mandi, India
Dilip Singh Sisodia	NIT Raipur, India

Dinesh Vishwakarma	Delhi Technological University, India
Dipti Mishra	IIIT Allahabad, India
Diptiben Patel	IIT Gandhinagar, India
Durgesh Singh	IIITDM Jabalpur, India
Dushyant Kumar Singh	MNNIT Allahabad, India
Earnest Paul Ijjina	NIT Warangal, India
Ekjot Nanda	PEC Chandigarh, India
Emanuela Marasco	George Mason University, USA
G. C. Nandi	IIIT Allahabad, India
G. Devasena	IIIT Trichy, India
Gagan Kanojia	IIT Gandhinagar, India
Garima Sharma	Monash University, Australia
Gian Luca Foresti	University of Udine, Italy
Gopa Bhaumik	NIT Sikkim, India
Gopal Chandra Jana	IIIT Allahabad, India
Gourav Modanwal	IIT (BHU) Varanasi, India
Graceline Jasmine	VIT University, India
Gurinder Singh	IIT Ropar, India
H. Pallab Dutta	IIT Guwahati, India
Hadia Kawoosa	IIT Ropar, India
Hariharan Muthusamy	NIT Uttarakhand, India
Harsh Srivastava	IIIT Allahabad, India
Hemant Aggarwal	University of Iowa, USA
Hemant Kumar Meena	MNIT Jaipur, India
Hemant Sharma	NIT Rourkela, India
Himadri Bhunia	IIT Kharagpur, India
Himansgshu Sarma	IIIT Sri City, India
Himanshu Agarwal	Jaypee Institute of Information Technology, India
Himanshu Buckchash	IIT Roorkee, India
Hrishikesh Venkataraman	IIT Sri City, India
Indra Deep Mastan	LNMIIT Jaipur, India
Irshad Ahmad Ansari	IIITDM Jabalpur, India
Ishan Rajendrakumar Dave	University of Central Florida, USA
J. V. Thomas	ISRO Bangalore, India
Jagat Challa	BITS Pilani, India
Jagdeep Kaur	NIT Jalandhar, India
Jasdeep Singh	IIT Ropar, India
Javed Imran	IIT Roorkee, India
Jayant Jagtap	SIT Pune, India
Jayanta Mukhopadhyay	IIT Kharagpur, India
Jaydeb Bhaumik	Jadavpur University, India
Jayendra Kumar	NIT Jamshedpur, India

Jeevaraj S	ABV-IIITM Gwalior, India
Jignesh Bhatt	IIIT Vadodara, India
Joohi Chauhan	IIT Ropar, India
Josep Llados	Computer Vision Center Barcelona, Spain
Juan Tapia	Hochschule Darmstadt, Germany
K. M. Bhurchandi	VNIT Nagpur, India
K. R. Ramakrishnan	IISc Bangalore, India
Kalidas Yeturu	IIT Tirupati, India
Kalin Stefanov	Monash University, Australia
Kapil Mishra	IIIT Allahabad, India
Kapil Rana	IIT Ropar, India
Karm Veer Arya	IIITM Gwalior, India
Karthick Seshadri	NIT Andhra Pradesh, India
Kaushik Roy	West Bengal State University, India
Kaustuv Nag	IIIT Guwahati, India
Kavitha Muthusubash	Hiroshima University, Japan
Kiran Raja	NTNU, Norway
Kirti Raj Bhatele	RJIT, BSF Academy, India
Kishor Upla	NIT Surat, India
Kishore Nampalle	IIT Roorkee, India
Komal Chugh	IIT Ropar, India
Koushlendra Singh	NIT Jamshedpur, India
Krishan Kumar	NIT Uttarakhand, India
Krishna Pratap Singh	IIIT Allahabad, India
Kuldeep Biradar	MNIT Jaipur, India
Kuldeep Singh	MNIT Jaipur, India
Lalatendu Behera	NIT Jalandhar, India
Lalit Kane	UPES Dehradun, India
Liangzhi Li	Osaka University, Japan
Lyla Das	NIT Calicut, India
M. Srinivas	NIT Warangal, India
M. Tanveer	IIT Indore, India
M. V. Raghunath	NIT Warangal, India
Mahua Bhattacharya	IIIT Gwalior, India
Malaya Dutta Borah	NIT Silchar, India
Malaya Nath	NIT Puducherry, India
Mandhatya Singh	IIT Ropar, India
Manish Khare	DA-IICT, India
Manish Okade	NIT Rourkela, India
Manisha Verma	Osaka University, Japan
Manoj Diwakar	Graphic Era University, India
Manoj Goyal	Samsung, India

Manoj K. Arora	BML Munjal University, India
Manoj Kumar	Babasaheb Bhimrao Ambedkar University, India
Manoj Kumar	GLA University, India
Manoj Rohit Vemparala	BMW Group, Germany
Manoj Singh	UPES, India
Mansi Sharma	IIT Madras, India
Massimo Tistarelli	University of Sassari, Italy
Michal Haindl	UTIA, Czech Republic
Mohammed Javed	IIIT Allahabad, India
Mohan Kankanhalli	National University of Singapore, Singapore
Mohit Singh	MNIT Jaipur, India
Monika Mathur	IGDTUW, India
Monu Verma	MNIT Jaipur, India
Mridul Gupta	Purdue University, USA
Mrinal Kanti Bhowmik	Tripura University, India
Muhammad Kanroo	IIT Ropar, India
Muneendra Ojha	IIIT Allahabad, India
Munesh C. Trivedi	NIT Agartala, India
Murari Mandal	National University of Singapore, Singapore
Muzammil Khan	MANIT Bhopal, India
N. V. Subba Reddy	Manipal Institute of Technology, India
Naga Srinivasarao Kota	NIT Warangal, India
Nagendra Singh	NIT Hamirpur, India
Nagesh Bhattu	NIT Andhra Pradesh, India
Namita Mittal	MNIT Jaipur, India
Namita Tiwari	NIT Bhopal, India
Nancy Mehta	IIT Ropar, India
Nand Kr Yadav	IIIT Allahabad, India
Nanda Dulal Jana	NIT Durgapur, India
Narasimhadhan A. V.	NITK Surathkal, India
Navjot Singh	NIT Allahabad, India
Navjot Singh	IIIT Allahabad, India
Nayaneesh Kumar	IIIT Allahabad, India
Neeru Rathee	MSIT, India
Neetu Sood	BRANIT, India
Neha Sahare	SIT Pune, India
Nehal Mamgain	Woven Planet, India
Nibaran Das	Jadavpur University, India
Nidhi Goel	IGDTUW, India
Nidhi Saxena	VIT University, India
Nilkanta Sahu	IIIT Guwahati, India

Nishant Jain	Jaypee University of Information Technology, India
Nitin Arora	IIT Roorkee, India
Nitin Kumar	NIT Uttarakhand, India
Nitish Andola	IIIT Allahabad, India
Oishila Bandyopadhyay	IIIT Kalyani, India
Om Prakaah	HNB Garhwal University, India
P. V. Sudeep	NIT Calicut, India
P. V. Venkitakrishnan	ISRO Bangalore, India
Pankaj Kumar	DA-IICT, India
Pankaj Kumar Sa	NIT Rourkela, India
Pankaj P. Singh	CIT, India
Parmeshwar Patil	SGGSIET Nanded, India
Parth Neshve	SVIT Satara, India
Partha Pakray	NIT Silchar, India
Parveen Kumar	NIT Uttarakhand, India
Paula Brito	University of Porto, Portugal
Piyush Kumar	NIT Patna, India
Poonam Sharma	VNIT Nagpur, India
Poornima Thakur	IITDM Jabalpur, India
Prabhu Natarajan	DigiPen Institute of Technology, Singapore
Prabhu Natarajan	University of Technology and Applied Sciences - Al Mussanah, Oman
Pradeep Kumar	Amphisoft, India
Pradeep Singh	NIT Raipur, India
Praful Hambarde	IIT Ropar, India
Prafulla Saxena	MNIT Jaipur, India
Pragati Agrawal	NIT Bhopal, India
Pragya Dwivedi	MNNIT Allahabad, India
Prashant Patil	Deakin University, Australia
Prashant Shukla	IIIT Allahabad, India
Prashant Srivastava	University of Allahabad, India
Prateek Keserwani	IIT Roorkee, India
Pratik Chattopadhyay	ITI (BHU) Varanasi, India
Pratik Narang	BITS Pilani, India
Pratik Shah	IIIT Vadodara, India
Pratik Somwanshi	IIT Jodhpur, India
Praveen Kumar Chandaliya	MNIT Jaipur, India
Praveen Sankaran	NIT Calicut, India
Praveen Tirupattur	University of Central Florida, USA
Pravin Kumar	IIIT Allahabad, India
Prerana Mukherjee	Jawaharlal Nehru University, India

Pritee Khanna	IITDM Jabalpur, India
Pritpal Singh	National Taipei University of Technology, Taiwan
Priya Kansal	Couger, Japan
Priyanka Singh	DA-IICT, India
Priyankar Choudary	IIT Ropar, India
Puneet Gupta	IIT Indore, India
Puneet Kumar	IIT Roorkee, India
Pushpendra Kumar	MANIT Bhopal, India
R. Malmathanraj	NIT Trichy, India
Rachit S. Munjal	Samsung, India
Ragendhu S. P.	IITM Kerala, India
Rahul Dixit	IIIT Pune, India
Rahul Kumar	IIT Roorkee, India
Rajeev Srivastava	IIT (BHU) Varanasi, India
Rajendra Nagar	IIT Jodhpur, India
Rajet Joshi	SIT Pune, India
Rajitha Bakthula	MNNIT Allahabad, India
Rajiv kumar Tripathi	NIT Delhi, India
Rajlaxmi Chouhan	IIT Jodhpur, India
Rameswar Panda	MIT-IBM Watson AI Lab, USA
Ramya Akula	University of Central Florida, USA
Ravindra Kumar Soni	MNIT Jaipur, India
Ridhi Arora	IIT Roorkee, India
Ripon Patgiri	NIT Silchar, India
Rishav Singh	NIT Delhi, India
Rohit Gupta	University of Central Florida, USA
Rohit Mishra	IIIT Allahabad, India
Rubin Bose S.	Madras Institute of Technology, India
Rukhmini Bandyopadhyay	University of Texas, USA
Rukhmini Roy	Jadavpur University, India
Rupam Bhattacharyya	IIIT Bhagalpur, India
Rusha Patra	IIIT Guwahati, India
S. H. Shabbeer Basha	IIT Sri City, India
S. K. Singh	IIT (BHU) Varanasi, India
S. N. Tazi	RTU, India
S. Sumitra	IIST, India
Sachin Chaudhary	IIT Ropar, India
Sachin Dube	MNIT Jaipur, India
Sachit Rao	IIIT Bangalore, India
Sahana Gowda	BNMIT Bangalore, India
Sambhavi Tiwari	IIT Allahabad, India
Sandeep Kumar	NIT Delhi, India

Sandesh Bhagat	SGGSIET Nanded, India
Sanjay Ghosh	University of California, San Francisco, USA
Sanjeev Kumar	IIT Roorkee, India
Sanjoy Pratihar	IIIT Kalyani, India
Sanjoy Saha	Jadavpur University, India
Sanoj Kumar	UPES, India
Santosh Kumar	IIIT Naya Raipur, India
Santosh Kumar Vipparthi	MNIT Jaipur, India
Santosh Randive	PCCOER Pune, India
Saravanan Chandran	NIT Durgapur, India
Saroj Kr. Biswas	NIT Silchar, India
Satendra Singh	IIT Jodhpur, India
Sathiesh Kumar V.	Madras Institute of Technology, India
Satish Singh	IIIT Alahabad, India
Satya Jaswanth Badri	IIT Ropar, India
Satya Prakash Sahu	NIT Raipur, India
Satyasai Jagannath Nanda	MNIT Jaipur, India
Satyendra Chouhan	MNIT Jaipur, India
Satyendra Yadav	NIT Meghalaya, India
Saugata Sinha	VNIT Nagpur, India
Saurabh Kumar	Osaka University, Japan
Sebastiano Battiato	Università di Catania, Italy
Shailza Sharma	Thapar Institute of Engineering and Technology, India
Shanmuganathan Raman	IIT Gandhinagar, India
Sharad Sinha	IIT Goa, India
Shashi Poddar	CSIR, India
Shashi Shekhar Jha	IIT Ropar, India
Shashikant Verma	IIT Gandhinagar, India
Shekhar Verma	IIIT Allahabad, India
Shirshu Verma	IIIT Allahabad, India
Shitala Prasad	NTU Singapore, Singapore
Shiv Ram Dubey	IIIT Allahabad, India
Shivangi Nigam	IIIT Allahabad, India
Shreya Ghosh	Monash University, Australia
Shreya Goyal	IIT Jodhpur, India
Shreya Gupta	MANIT Bhopal, India
Shrikant Malwiya	IIIT Allahabad, India
Shruti Phutke	IIT Ropar, India
Shubham Vatsal	Samsung R&D, India
Shubhangi Nema	IIT Bombay, India
Shyam Lal	NIT Karnataka, India

Shyam Singh Rajput	NIT Patna, India
Skand Skand	Oregon State University, USA
Slobodan Ribaric	University of Zagreb, Croatia
Smita Agrawal	Thapar Institute of Engineering and Technology, India
Snehasis Mukherjee	Shiv Nadar University, India
Somenath Das	IISc, India
Somnath Dey	IIT Indore, India
Sonali Agarwal	IIIT Allahabad, India
Soumen Bag	IIT Dhanbad, India
Soumendu Chakraborty	IIIT Lucknow, India
Sourav Pramanik	New Alipore College, India
Sri Aditya Deevi	IIST, India
Srimanta Mandal	DA-IICT, India
Subhas Barman	Jalpaiguri Government Engineering College, India
Subrahamanian K. S. Moosath	IIST, India
Subrahmanyam Murala	IIT Ropar, India
Sudhakar Kumawat	Osaka University, Japan
Sudhakar Mishra	IIIT Allahabad, India
Sudhish George	NIT Calicut, India
Sudipta Banerjee	Michigan State University, USA
Sukwinder Singh	NIT Jalandhar, India
Sule Yildirim-Yayilgan	NTNU, Norway
Suman Deb	NIT Surat, India
Suman Kumar Maji	IIT Patna, India
Suman Mitra	DA-IICT, India
Sumit Kumar	IIIT Allahabad, India
Suneeta Agarwal	MNNIT Allahabad, India
Suraj Sawant	COEP, India
Suranjan Goswami	IIIT Allahabad, India
Surendra Sharma	Indian Institute of Remote Sensing, India
Suresh Raikwar	Thapar Institute of Engineering and Technology, India
Suresh Raikwar	GLA University, India
Surya Prakash	IIT Indore, India
Sushil Ghildiyal	IIT Ropar, India
Sushmita Mitra	ISI Kolkata, India
Susmita Ghosh	Jadavpur University, India
Suvidha Tripathi	LNMIIT, India
Suvidha Tripathi	IIIT Allahabad, India
Swalpa Kumar Roy	Jalpaiguri Government Engineering College, India
Swarnima Singh Gautam	IIIT Allahabad, India

T. Veerakumar	NIT Goa, India
Tandra Pal	NIT Durgapur, India
Tannistha Pal	NIT Agartala, India
Tanushyam Chattopadhyay	TCS Pune, India
Tarun Chaudhary	NIT Jalandhar, India
Tasneem Ahmed	Integral University Lucknow, India
Thinagaran Perumal	Universiti Putra Malaysia, Malaysia
Tirupathiraju Kanumuri	NIT Delhi, India
Trilochan Panigrahi	NIT Goa, India
Tripti Goel	NIT Silchar, India
U. S. N. Raju	NIT Warangal, India
U. S. Tiwary	IIIT Allahabad, India
Umapada Pal	ISI Kolkata, India
Umarani Jayaraman	IITDM Kancheepuram, India
Umesh Pati	NIT Rourkela, India
Upendra Pratap Singh	IIIT Allahabad, India
Varsha Singh	IIIT Allahabad, India
Varun P. Gopi	NIT Tiruchirppalli, India
Vibhav Prakash Singh	NIT Allahabad, India
Vibhav Prakash Singh	MNNIT Allahabad, India
Vibhor Kant	BHU Varanasi, India
Vidhya Kamakshi	IIT Ropar, India
Vijander Singh	NSIT Delhi, India
Vijay Kumar Yadav	IIIT Allahabad, India
Vijay N. Gangapure	Government Polytechnic Kolhapur, India
Vijay Semwal	MANIT Bhopal, India
Vinit Jakhetiya	IIT Jammu, India
Vinti Agarwal	BITS Pilani, India
Vishal Satpute	VNIT, India
Vishwambhar Pathak	BIT Jaipur, India
Vishwas Rathi	IIT Ropar, India
Viswanath P.	IIIT Sri City, India
Vivek Singh Verma	Ajay Kumar Garg Engineering College, India
Vivek Tiwari	IIIT Naya Raipur, India
Vivekraj K.	IIT Roorkee, India
Vrijendra Singh	IIIT Allahabad, India
W. Wilfred Godfrey	IIIT Gwalior, India
Watanabe Osamu	Takushoku University, Japan
Wei-Ta Chu	National Cheng Kung University, Taiwan
Xiaoyi Jiang	University of Münster, Germany
Zhixi Cai	Monash University, Australia
Ziwei Xu	National University of Singapore, Singapore

Contents – Part I

Contents – Part II

Classification of Brain Tumor MR Images Using Transfer Learning and Machine Learning Models

LillyMaheepa Pavuluri$^{(\boxtimes)}$ and Malaya Kumar Nath

Department of ECE, National Institute of Technology Puducherry, Karaikal 609609, India
pmaheepa@gmail.com, malaya.nath@gmail.com

Abstract. Brain tumors are the extra buildup of cells in the regions of brain. Any unwanted mass in the brain tissues is termed as tumor. Glioma, meningioma and pituitary tumors are the three main types of tumors. All the tumors are dangerous and cause severe damage when not treated. Proper diagnostic methods include tumor viewing using MR images among other imaging techniques. But, the manual identification of the tumor from MR images requires more time and error prone. Therefore classification of brain tumors requires the development of an effective method. Deep learning has methods have proved to be efficient in classification and identification tasks by using feature extraction methods.

In this paper deep transfer learning technique has been used for multi class tumor classification on the publicly available dataset. Eleven pretrained networks are used and experimented for a learning rates of $1e-2$, $1e-3$ and $1e-4$ and sgdm, adam, rmsprop as optimizers. Further the same networks are experimented using classifiers support vector machine (SVM), k nearest neighbor (KNN) and decision tree (DT) for varied learning rates and optimizers. Inception-v4 network has observed an highest overall accuracy of 98.1% with KNN for a learning rate of $1e-4$, 25 epoch and rmsprop as optimizer. The highest overall accuracy without the integration of classifiers is observed as 96.5% for resNet-50 with a learning rate of $1e-4$ and rmsprop as optimizer. It is observed that the proposed method has observed higher accuracy with the integration of classifiers. Performance metrices used other than accuracy include precision, F1 score, micro F1 score.

Keywords: Brain tumor · MR image · CNN · Pretrained network · Classification

1 Introduction

Many important body functions, such as, emotions, vision, thought, speech, and movement are controlled by the brain. Human brain is made up of billions of cells. The cycle for destruction of old cells and growth of new cells occurs continuously. The abnormal growth of cells forms unwanted tissues or growth. This unwanted growth in the regions of brain is called as brain tumor. Brain tumors increase the intracranial pressure causing damage in the tissues, headaches, vomiting and other symptoms. These tumors can be

B. Raman et al. (Eds.): CVIP 2021, CCIS 1567, pp. 1–9, 2022.
https://doi.org/10.1007/978-3-031-11346-8_1

cancer causing. There are two categories of brain tumors, primary and secondary. Any type of tumors can be benign or malignant. A benign tumor does not contain cancer cells and do not spread to the other regions of the brain. But, malignant tumor contains cancer cells and spreads to other regions of the brain. There are various primary type of tumors. Among them, glioma, meningioma and pituitary tumors are the most common type of tumors.

Further, based on the characteristics of the tumors, world health organization (WHO) classified tumors into four different grades. These grades are assigned based on the appearance of the tissues and brain cells. A tumor is identified as grade I if the tissue is benign with normal brain cells. The growth of the tumor is slow. In grade II tumors, the tissue is observed as malignant and cells with less various from the normal cells. Grade III and grade IV tumor tissue is malignant and the cells are abnormal. Grade IV tumors are known as glioblastomas multiforme (GBM). Grade I and grade II are also termed as low grade gliomas (LGG) and grade III and IV are called as high grade gliomas (HGG). To identify these tumors in brain locations proper image viewing techniques are required. There are various imaging techniques to view and study the tumor location, shape and size. Computer tomography (CT) scanning, X-rays, magnetic resonance imaging (MRI), positron emission tomography (PET) and ultrasound scanning (US) are few among them. In these, MR imaging is the most common and preferred one.

MRI provides high resolution images of the brain regions. It has four modalities, T1, T1c, T2 and fluid image resonance (FLAIR). These modalities are taken at different times with different parameters. Therefore it is easier to identify the abnormalities. Each modalities highlight the different regions like, fat content, cerebrospinal fluid, tumor borders and grey matter. These high dimensional images are obtained in three different views axial, coronal and sagittal. Axial view image is obtained by separating the plane into top and bottom. Image taken by dividing the plane into front and back is termed as coronal and sagittal view divides the plane into left and right planes. The identification and detection of abnormalities or tumors from these images is a very difficult task because of varying size, shape, location and texture of the tumors. It takes a great amount of time to detect tumors from these images. It is also erroneous. To avoid these a proper tumor identification and detection methods are required.

In the past few years, with the advancements in the field of image processing, neural networks, deep learning and artificial intelligence (AI) many traditional and conventional methods have been developed for the accurate identification and classification of tumors. In recent years, convolutional neural networks (CNN), have shown an effective performance in the classification tasks. The design and modelling of these networks from scratch has been used and found to be effective. In the recent years, usage of the CNNs designed for a different classification task has proved to be efficient with the transfer learning techniques. So, in this work with the help of brain MR images, a method for classification of brain tumors using such convolutional neural network models has been proposed.

The layout of this paper is arranged as follows: The literature review is given in Sect. 2. The proposed methodologies are discussed in Sect. 3. The experiential results and discussions are presented in Sect. 4. Finally, this work is concluded in Sect. 5.

2   Literature Review

The diagnosis of the brain tumor involves various tumor imaging techniques. The study of the tumor characteristics from these requires a lot of time and the identification is error prone with human eye. Therefore, researchers used many deep learning techniques for classification and identification of the tumor. Recently, transfer learning techniques has been used for the classification. Swati et.al. [8] has proposed the novel method to classify the brain MR images using transfer learning and block wise fine tuning the images. The entire architecture of the VGG 19 model is divided into six blocks and the learning parameters for the fine tuning are set for each block. The authors have used CE-MRI dataset for their work and obtained an accuracy of 94.82%.

Deepak et al. [3] has classified three types of tumors using the concept of deep transfer learning. GoogleNet network has been used for the classification. Three types of brain tumors has been classified. Figshare dataset has been used. The features are extracted using the pretrained network by modifying the last three layers of the network. The fully connected network layer in the basic architecture has been replaced with the new layer to match to the size of the input. The network is fine tuned by training it with the MRI images from the dataset. Classifiers softmax, SVM and KNN are used to improve the accuracy of the network and obtained a 97% with SVM and 98% with KNN and 92.3% with just the network. The dataset is obtained from figshare and the performance measures used are precision, recall, F-score and specificity. Authors have also given misclassification rate for better understanding.

Khan et al. [5] used transfer learning technique to compare the proposed CNN model with VGG-16, resNet-50 and inception-v3 models with the proposed CNN model. The CNN model has 8 convolutional layers along with max pooling, fully connected layers. Authors have used other pre trained networks and obtained 90% for VGG-16, 93% for inception-v3 and on resNet-50, 92% whereas the CNN model proposed scored a higher accuracy of 100% on the dataset from kaggle.

Rehman et al. [7] conducted three studies using alexNet, googLeNet and VGGNet for the classification of the tumor types. Further authors used transfer learning techniques like fine tuning, data augmentation and freezing using the MRI slices of the brain tumor dataset at figshare. Authors obtained a accuracy of 98.69% for classification of the tumors.

Ahmet et al. [4] modified the last five layers of ResNet-50 and added ten new layers and obtained an accuracy of 97.2%. AlexNet, ResNet50, InceptionV3, googleNet and denseNet201 models were also used for the classification task.

Yang et al. [10] used alexNet and googleNet networks were trained and fine tuned and observed an increase in the performance of the classification task. In 2018, Khawaldeh et al. [6] has used modified alexNet on MRI images obtained from the Cancer imaging archive (TCIA) and obtained an accuracy of 91.16%. Talo et al. [9] has used resNet34 model for deep feature extraction along with data augmentation, fine tuning and the proposed model obtained an 100% accuracy on a smaller dataset.

In this work various pretrained networks are used for brain tumor classification along with various classifiers. Before feeding the data to the classifier the images are preprocessed. All the models are evaluated and explored with varied parameters and layers. Further the classification performances are evaluated and compared. The CNN architectures discussed above are represented in systematic way in the Table 1. The table provides the architecture used along with the technique, dataset and performance of each method to provide relevant information about the methodologies.

Table 1. Literature review

Author	Architecture (Technique)	Dataset	Accuracy	Remarks
Khawaldeh et al. [6]	Modified AlexNet	TCIA 4069 2D image samples	91.16%	–
Yang et al. [10]	GoogLeNet	ClinicalTrails.gov 499 HGG , 368 LGG	94.5%	–
Deepak et al. [3]	GoogLeNet	Figshare 1426 glioma, 708 meningioma 930 pitutary tumor images	98%	–
Talo et al. [9]	ResNet34	Harvard Medical School Datat 27 normal, 513 abnormal	100%	–
Swati et al. [8]	VGG-19 & Blockwise fine tuning	CE-MRI 1426 glioma, 708 meningioma 930 pitutary tumor images	94.82%	-
Rehman et al. [7]	VGG-16 & Fine tuning	Figshare	98.69%	–
Ahmet et al. [4]	Modified ResNet50	Obtained from Kaggle 98 no tumor , 155 tumor images	97.2%	Small dataset
Khan et al. [5]	CNN	Obtained from Kaggle 158 malignant, 98 bening tumor images	100%	Small dataset

3   Working Model

In this paper the brain tumor classification is performed in two different method. In the first method the MRI images are given as input to the pretrained networks and classified into four classes. The details of the method are given in Sect. 3.1. In the second method the MRI images are given as input to the pretrained networks and classified using different classifiers. This method is explained in Sect. 3.2. The dataset used for evaluating the classification performance are described in Sect. 3.3. The performance measures are represented in Sect. 3.4.

3.1   Proposed Method-1

This method mainly consists of two blocks - MR image database and the pretrained network for classification as shown in Fig. 1. The MR images are used for training and testing the pretrained networks. The details about the MR image database has been mentioned in Sect. 3.3. From the total MR images 80% is used for training, the rest 20% is used for testing. These images are classified by various pretrained networks (alexNet, googleNet, inception-v3, ResNet-18, ResNet-50, ResNet-101, inceptionresNet-v2, shuffleNet, squeezeNet, mobileNet and xception) into four different classes such as glioma, meningioma, no tumor and pituitary tumor. The classification is performed for different hyperparameters (learning rates, optimizers, epoch). In this case the learning rates are considered to be 1e-2, 1e-3, 1e-4. This method uses stochastic gradient descent (sgdm), adaptive moment estimation (adam), root mean square propagation (rmsprop) as optimizers for 25 epochs. For each class various performance measures such as, precision, recall, F1-score, micro F1-score and accuracy has been computed.

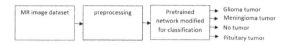

Fig. 1. Proposed method-1 for tumor classification from MR images.

3.2 Proposed Method-2

This method uses pretrained networks (alexNet, googleNet, inception, ResNet-18, ResNet-50, ResNet-101, inceptionresNet-v2, shuffleNet, squeezeNet, mobileNet and xception) for extraction of features with different classifier (SVM, KNN and DT). The block diagram is represented in Fig. 2. It consists of three main blocks, input images, feature extraction by pretrained networks and classification of MR images using classifiers. The same input images mentioned in proposed method-1 are used in 80%, 20% from total images for training and testing purpose. The pretrained networks are used for training the network and the features are extracted at a particular layer (other than last 5 layers). The extracted features are classified using the classifiers for varied learning rates, optimizers and epochs as mentioned in the above section. Performance measures accuracy, precision, recall, F1-score, micro F1 score are calculated.

Fig. 2. Tumor classification by pretrained network and classifiers.

3.3 Datasets

The methods discussed above have been applied to the publicly available database in kaggle [1] and figshare [2]. The database available in kaggle consists of a total of 3,264 images in .png format. The images are obtained in greyscale. The total images are divided into 2,870 training images and 394 testing images. Further, the images are divided into four different classes, glioma tumor, meningioma tumor, no tumor and pituitary tumor. The training set consists of 826 glioma, 822 meningioma, 395 no tumor and 827 pituitary tumor images. The testing set consists of 100 glioma, 115 meningioma, 105 no tumor and 74 pituitary images.

Figshare Dataset: This database is mostly used for classification purposes. The database consists of 3064 MR images of brain obtained form 233 patients with glioma, meningioma and pituitary tumors. The obtained MR images are T1ce weighted and in .mat format. The size of each file is 512×512 obtained in three different views axial, coronal and sagittal. There are 1426 glioma, 708 meningioma and 930 pituitary tumor files. All the files are preprocessed as shown in the Fig. 3.

Initially the .mat files are converted into grey scale images in .png format. Intensity normalization is performed to scale to a minimum value of 0 and a maximum value of 1. The grey scale values are replicated into three RGB channels. Further the images are resized to match to the input size of the pretrained networks. The images are divided randomly into training and testing sets. The training set consists of 1286 glioma, 573 meningioma 791 pituitary images. The testing set consists of 138 tumor images in all the classes of the testing set.

Fig. 3. Data preprocessing steps.

3.4 Performance Metrices

The classification performance of the networks have been computed by precision, recall, F1-score, micro F1 score and accuracy. These measures are computed based on true positive (TP), true negative (TN), false positive (FP) and false negative (FN) values. The description of individual performance measures are represented in Table 2. For better classification the performance metric values should attain the maximum value.

Table 2. Performance measures

Name	Representation	Range
Accuracy (Acc)	$\frac{TP+TN}{TP+FP+FN+TN}$	[0–100]
Precision (Pre)	$\frac{TP}{TP+FP}$	[0–100]
Recall	$\frac{TP}{TP+FN}$	[0–100]
F1-score	$2 \times \frac{Precision*Recall}{Precision+Recall}$	[0–100]
Micro F1-score	$2 \times \frac{Total\,precision*Total\,recall}{Total\,precision+Total\,recall}$	[0–100]

where, TP-true positive, FP-false positive, TN-true negative, FN-false negative

4   Results and Discussions

Initially, the pre trained network architecture is chosen. The architecture of the model is modified to match the size of the input data given. The classification layer, fully connected layer are modified to the input size. Further, the network model is analyzed for any type of errors. As the next step, the dataset path is chosen and given to the network as the input. For training the network, the training parameters like learning rate, optimizers, batch size, epoch are given. Sgdm, adam and rmsprop are used as optimizers. The network is trained for learning rates of $1e-2$, $1e-3$ and $1e-4$. The confusion matrix is obtained after training the network for 25 epochs.

A similar procedure has been followed for training the network with the integration of the classifier. Initially the network is chosen and the input data is given. A particular layer other than the last three layers of the network has been selected and the classifier is integrated for the classification purpose. Classifiers SVM, KNN and decision tree has been employed for this method. After the integration of the classifiers, the network parameters, learning rate, batch size, epoch, and other training parameters are given and the network is trained. Confusion matrix is obtained and the performance metrices are calculated.

All the eleven pretrained networks have been trained and their performance metrices are calculated in a similar manner. Further, accuracy of all the networks is summarized and compared in the table 3. It is observed the highest accuracy obtained is 96.5%. It is obtained for resNet-50, for a learning rate of $1e-4$. The optimizer used is rmsprop. In the same way, all the eleven networks after the integration of classifiers have been trained and performance is evaluated. The accuracies obtained are presented in table 4. It is noted that inception v3 network, with KNN as classifier has obtained highest accuracy of 98.3%. The optimizer used is rmsprop with a learning rate of $1e-4$. Further, to evaluate the class imbalance in the dataset and to not rely just on the accuracy of the network micro F1 score has been calculated for every network in both the proposed methods.

Table 3. Pretrained network performance

Pre trained network	Epoch	Learning rate	Optimizer	Accuracy(%)	Micro F1 score	Macro F1 score
ResNet-18	25	1e−4	adam	95.3	95.27	95.97
AlexNet	25	1e−4	rmsprop	89.7	89.96	90.50
GoogLeNet	25	1e−4	adam	95.5	95.43	96.05
Inception	25	1e−4	adam	94.6	94.57	95.32
ResNet-50	25	1e−4	rmsprop	**96.5**	96.49	96.85
InceptionresNet-v2	25	1e−2	Sgdm	95.6	95.62	96.20
ShuffleNet	25	1e−4	rmsprop	93.7	93.70	94.62
SqueezeNet	25	1e−4	rmsprop	92.1	92.14	93.37
MobileNet	25	1e−3	rmsprop	93.5	93.53	93.87
ResNet-101	25	1e−2	rmsprop	94.1	94.06	94.92
ResNet-101	25	1e−4	rmsprop	94.1	94.06	94.90
Xception	25	1e−4	adam	96.0	95.97	96.50

Table 4. Performance of pretrained network integrated with classifiers

Pre trained network	Classifier	Epoch	Learning rate	Optimizer	Accuracy(%)	Micro F1	Macro F1 score
ResNet-18	SVM	25	1e−3	sgdm	98.1	98.08	98.17
ResNet-18	SVM	25	1e−4	rmsprop	98.1	98.08	98.17
AlexNet	KNN	25	1e−4	rmsprop	97.4	97.37	97.57
GoogLeNet	SVM	25	1e−4	rmsprop	96.3	96.28	96.65
Inception	KNN	25	1e−4	rmsprop	**98.3**	98.24	98.47
ShuffleNet	SVM	25	1e−3	adam	97.7	97.72	97.90
ShuffleNet	KNN	25	1e−3	rmsprop	97.7	97.72	97.57
MobileNet	SVM	25	1e−2	sgdm	97.7	97.72	97.55
ResNet-50	SVM	25	1e−4	adam	97.2	97.19	96.97
SqueezeNet	SVM	25	1e−3	sgdm	97.0	97.01	96.92

5 Conclusions

Brain tumors pose a serious threat to life. There are different types of brain tumors, among them the most common type is glioma. Other tumor types include meningioma and pituitary. Glioma tumors are life threatening and are dangerous when not treated. Therefore a proper diagnostic method is required for proper identification of the tumors. MRI, CT, US and PET are few of the tumor viewing techniques. Among them MRI is most commonly used as it provides four modalities highlighting the different regions of the brain. But manual identification and classification of the tumors from these modalities is time consuming and error prone. Therefore automatic or semi automatic methods are preferred. In the recent years, deep learning architectures has proved to be efficient in the identification and classification tasks. In this work such deep learning architectures are employed for the classification of the brain tumor images. The datasets used are obtained from kaggle and figshare website. Four classes are present in the first dataset whereas three tumor classes are present in the latter. The images are preprocessed and used for training and testing of the deep network architectures. All the deep network architectures are experimented for learning rates of 1e−2, 1e−3 and 1e−4 with sgdm, adam, rmsprop as optimizers for 25 epochs and 96.5% accuracy is observed as highest with resNet-50 network for a learning rate of 1e−4 and rmsprop as the optimizer. The same procedure has been followed for all the networks. Further, SVM, KNN and decision tree classifiers are integrated with the networks and inception-v3 network has obtained 98.3% accuracy for a learning rate of 1e−4 with rmsprop as the optimizer. But, the accuracy can further be improved by following few pre processing techniques and combining the extracted features from two networks.

References

1. https://github.com/sartajbhuvaji/brain-tumor-classification-dataset
2. Cheng: Figshare brain tumor dataset (2017). https://doi.org/10.6084/m9.figshare.1512 427.v5
3. Deepak, S., Ameer, P.: Brain tumor classification using deep CNN features via transfer learning. Comput. Biol. Med. **111**, 103345 (2019). https://doi.org/10.1016/j.compbiomed.2019. 103345. https://www.sciencedirect.com/science/article/pii/S001048251930214

4. Çinar, A., Yildirim, M.: Detection of tumors on brain MRI images using the hybrid convolutional neural network architecture. Med. Hypotheses **139**, 109684 (2020). https://doi.org/10.1016/j.mehy.2020.109684
5. Khan, H.A., Jue, W., Musthaq, M., Musthaq, M.U.: Brain tumor classification in mri image using convolutional neural network. Math. Biosci. Eng. **17**(5), 6203–6216 (2020). https://doi.org/10.3934/mbe.2020328
6. Khawaldeh, S., Pervaiz, U., Rafiq, A., Alkhawaldeh, R.: Noninvasive grading of glioma tumor using magnetic resonance imaging with convolutional neural networks. Appl. Sci. **8**, 27 (2017). https://doi.org/10.3390/app8010027
7. Rehman, A., Naz, S., Razzak, M.I., Akram, F., Imran, M.: A deep learning-based framework for automatic brain tumors classification using transfer learning. Circuits Syst. Signal Process. **39**(2), 757–775 (2019). https://doi.org/10.1007/s00034-019-01246-3
8. Swati, Z.N.K., et al.: Brain tumor classification for MR images using transfer learning and fine-tuning. Comput. Med. Imaging Graph. **75**, 34–46 (2019). https://doi.org/10.1016/j.compmedimag.2019.05.001
9. Talo, M., Baloglu, U.B., Yıldırı, Ö., Rajendra Acharya, U.: Application of deep transfer learning for automated brain abnormality classification using MR images. Cogn. Syst. Res. **54**, 176–188 (2019). https://doi.org/10.1016/j.cogsys.2018.12.007
10. Yang, Y., et al.: Glioma grading on conventional MR images: a deep learning study with transfer learning. Front. Neurosci. **12**, 804 (2018). https://doi.org/10.3389/fnins.2018.00804

Deep-TDRS: An Integrated System for Handwritten Text Detection-Recognition and Conversion to Speech Using Deep Learning

Bisakh Mondal, Shuvayan Ghosh Dastidar$^{(\boxtimes)}$, and Nibaran Das

Jadavpur University, Kolkata, India
sgd030@gmail.com, nibarandas@jadavpuruniversity.in

Abstract. Development of complete OCR for handwritten document (HOCR) is a challenging task due to a wide variation in writing styles, cursiveness, and contrasts in captured text images. We introduce a new three-staged pipeline process consisting of a) text detection, b) text recognition, c) text to speech conversion for the development of successful HOCR of multi-line document and converting them to speech. We have considered two state of the art object detection deep neural networks, EfficientDet and Faster R-CNN (Region based Convolutional Neural Network) followed by Weighted Boxes Fusion to obtain bounding boxes among all sentence wise text instances in the document. The detected text instances (image) are passed on to a hybrid CNN-RNN(CNN-Recurrent Neural Network) to obtain the recognized texts after appropriate training. The recognized text instances are provided as inputs to a state of the art TTS (Text to Speech) model DeepVoice3 for converting the text to speech which gets compiled as an audio book. The developed handwritten text detection and recognition model is comparable with the state of the art.

Keywords: OCR · Object detection · Sequence modelling · Neural networks

1 Introduction

Recognition of handwritten text is an evolving research area with many papers coming out in this domain [18]. The success of convolutional neural networks (CNNs) in the domain of computer vision led to the formation of different hybrid architectures consisting of convolutional layers for recognition of handwritten text in document images as well as scene text images. Moreover, many competitions are evolved in recent times for the fast and efficient models development in

---

B. Mondal and S. G. Dastidar—These authors contributed equally to this work.

B. Raman et al. (Eds.): CVIP 2021, CCIS 1567, pp. 10–20, 2022.
https://doi.org/10.1007/978-3-031-11346-8_2

these areas. Unlike printed text, where the texture and fonts are uniforms, handwritten text comprises of different styles, sizes and textures that make it difficult for recognition. Earlier character segmentation based models [18] fail miserably to recognize handwritten texts. Many researchers consider OCR of handwritten text as a solved problem, but successful handwritten text detection and recogntion is still a challenging task to the researcher. In this paper, we provide Deep-TDRS, an integrated system consisting of a three staged pipelined approach for recognizing handwritten text documents and finally converting them to speech i.e. audiobooks. The major contributions of the paper are:

- Providing an efficient way of localizing handwritten text instances by using two state of the art object detection deep neural networks like EfficientDet [25] and Faster R-CNN [21] and also analyzing their relative performance.
- Image level sentence formation from the localized text or word instances using clustering based approach to mitigate the loss in recognition. It helps to incorporate those word instances that have been missed by the object detection module.
- An attention based OCR system consisting of a hybrid CNN-RNN model is used here to predict the possible words from the obtained text instances, followed by an isolated post-processing language modelling network to generate the final predictions.
- The DeepVoice3 [20] TTS model is utilized for generation of speech from the generated text.

The complete pipeline is summarised in Fig. 1 showing the different stages.

2   Related Works

Present approach is divided into three stages - handwritten word detection and clustering, recognition, and converting them to speech. There has been ample research in each of these fields [15,18]. A large number of methods have been developing on dealing with the problem of text detection and recognition [27]. Generally, text is represented with edges, strokes, CCs (Connected Components) and texture [27] and their combinations. Earlier, texture based methods-[6,8,11] were used to detect text regions in word using various image processing techniques such as Wavelet Coefficients and Adaptive Mean Shift algorithm. However these methods are computationally expensive and take a lot of time on processing whole images. Region based methods [10,19] first extract text based features through edge detection, clustering and various other heuristic rules such as MSER (Maximally Stable Extremal Regions). The paper [16] used image processing techniques such as Hough transforms to detect lines after binarization and connected components extraction. Deng et al. [4] used instance segmentation and linking of characters to detect the text instances without location regression. Dutta et al. [5] used an encoder-decoder architecture for pixelwise segmentation of text instances. Textboxes [13] is an end to end network which is capable of detecting and recognising text instances in natural scene text images in a single pass. In [1], Bluche et al. proposed a method of Multi-Dimensional Long Term Short Memory (MDLSTM) with attention and CTC(Connectionist Temporal Classification) loss for recognition of handwritten text. [12] uses recursive convolutional neural networks with attention for OCR of scene text images. These methods infer that a multi RNN model with attention can be a good recognition framework.

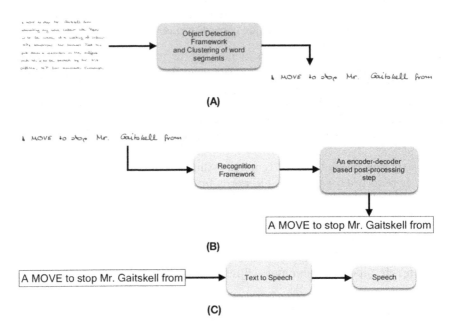

Fig. 1. The complete flowchart of the proposed method. In (A), the document containing handwritten text is passed on to a object detection framework which outputs word bounding boxes, which are clustered to form sentence wise bounding boxes. (B) shows the recognition process of the detected sentences in the document which is done by a recognition framework followed by a pre-processing step. (C), the recognised sentence is converted into speech by a text to speech model.

3   The Proposed Pipeline

Previous research works [18] have shown less focus on a complete pipeline for handwritten text detection and recognition, which we introduce in this paper. It comprises of i) Object detection network for creating bounding boxes of text instances, ii) A hybrid CNN-RNN based custom hybrid recognition model with attention which can perform character level text recognition from handwritten images, iii) An efficient post processing LSTM(Long Short Term Memory) model, and finally iv) the convolutional model with attention for text-to-speech synthesis.

3.1   Detection System

Object detection model is one of the prime necessities for recognition system especially when the recognition to be performed in a full page document and the individual words are very small in size compared to the document. The feature size of the individual words being very low, it becomes difficult for even recurrent neural networks like LSTM and GRU [3] (Gated Recurrent Units) to keep track of long short term dependencies trained from the feature map of the convolutional network. Thus without the presence of any object detection module, the recognition system fails miserably. In this context, we have considered numerous experiments on various state of the art object detection models - EfficientDet [25] and Faster R-CNN [21] and compared their performance with respect to FPS (Frames per Second) and mAP(mean average precision).

EfficientDet. EfficientDet [25], a computationally efficient highly accurate object detection model is considered as one of our Object Detection network. It involves the work on scaling neural networks EfficientNet [24] and incorporating a novel bi-directional feature network (BiFPN) and is able to achieve state of the art accuracies even being 9x times smaller than the previous models. They do several optimizations architecture wise such as taking dethwise separable convolutions and a fast-normalized fusion method. Their BiFPN is both lightweight and more accurate than previous FPN such as PANet. They achieve a mAP(mean average precision) of 52.2 on the COCO test dataset [14]. For our purposes we have considered using the EfficientDet-D5 for recognizing and making bounding boxes around the text instances.

Faster R-CNN. [21] is a state of the art object detection network that introduced a region-proposal network(RPN) that shares convolutional features with the detection framework. We have used a backbone of ResNet-50 in the framework, which acts as a feature extractor. They solve the problem of variable number of bounding boxes by taking different sizes of anchors across the image and considering the top most anchors and rejecting others by Non-Maximum Supression(NMS).

The details for making line bounding boxes is shown in Algorithm 1. The input bounding boxes are sorted according to their y_{min} co-ordinate.

3.2   Recognition System

Traditional Optical Character Recognition (OCR) system mainly focuses on scanned printed documents [7] but here it involves handwritten text which is unconstrained due to no fixed fonts and also hugely challenging due to the visual artifacts such as cluttered background, distortion, blur etc. Considering the faster yet effective performance with less computational penalty, we have considered an attention based recognition system [26] which consists of a hybrid CNN-RNN architecture in which images get processed through the CNN first then the RNN to predict the possible text captured through the detection model.

In the present work, we took advantage of the Inception-V3 [23] as the feature extractor of the model takes huge advantage from a lots of architectural change which include small factorized convolution for higher computation efficiency, convolution with different sized parallel kernels to create a feature vector of different receptive fields. The authors also introduced spatial factorization into asymmetric convolution while keeping the same receptive field - a nxn Conv2D layer can be replaced by a $1xn$ layer followed by $nx1$ layer which is highly effective for this purpose when we are focusing on a computationally efficient pipeline. Still, a question arises, from how deep we should consider, after careful observation and study shown by Yosinski et al. [28], we have used an architecture comprises of 4 basic convolution layers of filter size 3×3 and 1×1 and 3 InceptionA, shown in Fig. 2(A), blocks which uses 1×1, 3×3 and 5×5 kernels in parallel and concatenates the results.

An attention based RNN, for which we have used customized GRU [3], has been integrated after the feature extracting CNN. It takes the encoded feature vector spatially weighted by an attention mask as shown in Fig. 2(B), where the attention energies are computed by,

$$\alpha_{t,i,j} = softmax(V^T tanh(encoder\_outputs + s_t)) \tag{1}$$

where s_t is the hidden state of RNN at timestep t. Now the RNN takes the feature vector i.e. $f_{i,j,c}$ is weighted with attention mask along with the one hot vector of the previous character, c_{t-1},

$$output, s_t = RNN \left(W_a \left(\sum \alpha_{t-1,i,j} f_{i,j,c} \right) + W_c C_{t-1}, s_{t-1} \right) \tag{2}$$

We are taking the most likely character from the RNN prediction using greedy decoding.

3.3   Post Processing

Post processing is an integral part of an recognition system especially when the captured text needs to be accurate and here it is passed to a Text to Speech (TTS) model for audio synthesis. The recognition system being character level, penalize less computation overhead on the final fully connected softmax layer but fails to predict some of the crucial characters on which the meaning of the word varies. So post processing is necessary and in the present work we have worked with 2 different approaches i.e.

- Post OCR Correction using Edit Distance
- Post OCR Correction using seq2seq model

Edit Distance is a very generic way of computing the similarity between two words and finding the Minimum Edit Distance (MED) required for two words to be exactly same. Here in correction post OCR, edit distance is used for

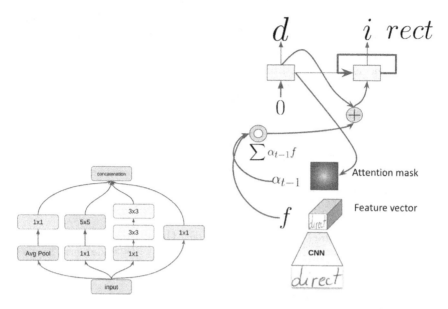

Fig. 2. In *(A)*, the InceptionA block is shown. *(B)* shows the operation of the the attention based recognition process.

finding the nearest match which in our case is one or two edits away from the OCR prediction. Here single edit signifies removal of one character or swapping of adjacent two characters or addition of one character or addition of a single character. It uses simple probability to calculate the possibility of the predicted word to be replaced by a word that has the highest count and has maximum MED of two, came from a millions words public book excerpt, *Project Gutenberg.*

Sequence to Sequence model which is often abbreviated as seq2seq is quite popular in complex language problems such as language generation, machine translation, captioning etc. It's basically an encoder-decoder architecture where in our case both encoder and decoder are LSTM and stacked LSTM respectively, which takes the prediction of the OCR. The encoder reads it sequentially and creates a internal state or context vector with cell state. Then for decoder, the very last output of the encoder gets repeated and passed through the stacked LSTM sequentially where for each timestamp on top of it a time-distributed dense or fully connected layer is attached which predicts one of the characters from the vocabulary.

3.4 Text to Speech

Text to Speech (TTS) models convert written language into human speech. These systems first transform text into a compact audio representation, and then convert this representation into audio using an audio waveform synthesis method called vocoder. For our purposes we have used the fully convolutional attention based neural text to speech system DeepVoice3 [20]. Their model allows parallel computation and is able to scale to large amount of audio data. The architecture consists of an encoder, decoder and a converter which predicts final vocoder parameters from the decoder hidden states. For the present work, we have used their pretrained model trained on LJSpeech [9] dataset for converting the text generated by the recognition framwork into speech.

Algorithm 1: Algorithm for merging word bounding boxes

Data: bboxes in the form xmin, ymin , xmax, ymax

Function makeLineBboxes(*bboxes , threshold*)**:**

    sortedBoxes = sortBboxes(bboxes)　　　　　　　　`/* sorting helper */`

    xyTup = calXYbbox(sortedBoxes[0])　　`/* update bbox helper */`

    lineBboxes = [ ]

    for *box ∈ bboxes* **do**

        if *isSameLine(xyTup, box ,threshold)* **then**

            xyTup = calXYTup(box, xyTup)　　　　`/* update xyTup */`

        else

            lineBboxes.append(xyTup)

            xyTup = calXYTup(box)　　　　　　`/* new line bbox */`

        end

    end

    postProcess(lineBboxes)　　　　`/* helper process function */`

    return lineBoxes

end

Function isSameLine(*xyT, bbox, threshold*)**:**

    sizeExt = threshold * (xyT[3] - xyT[1])

    return isInside(bbox , xyT, sizeExt)

end

Helper Functions

isInside(bbox, xyT, size): Checks the bbox is withing the range of xyT and additional size calculated according to a threshold.

calXYTup(bbox, xyTup:Optional): Takes in box and an optional input *XYTup* : the forming line bounding box and returns the updated *XYTup* based on the current bbox

postProcess(lineBboxes): Takes in line bboxes and post processes them to eliminate error boxes by rejecting boxes of width less than the mean of all boxes excluding the last box, which is followed by WBF [22] to avoid duplicate boxes.

---

4   Training Details

4.1   Dataset

For training of the pipeline we have considered the use of publicly available IAM dataset 3.0 [17]. IAM dataset contains of word wise annotated handwritten pages. There are 1539 scanned handwritten pages by 657 different authors, 115,320 labelled and isolated words. Such a huge number of sample space enabled us to train our object detection framework to detect handwritten text instances in document images and recognition framework on annotated words as well. Splitting of dataset on train, validation and test has been performed as per the image IDs provided by IAM dataset.

4.2 Implementation

We have used the Pytorch framework for implementation. Augmentations such as random brightness and random contrast were also added to the images during training. We further used the Stochastic Gradient Descent(SGD) optimizer with nesterov momentum of 0.95 and a learning rate of 0.005. We have also used weight decay of 0.001 for training purposes. For training of the object detection networks, the images were resized to 512 in case of EfficientDet and the bounding boxes were transformed by a factor of $Img_{resized}/Img_{original}$. For post processing the predictions or the detected bounding boxes an algorithm called weighted boxes fusion (WBF) [22] was used. WBF, instead of considering the bounding boxes with the maximum score and IoU threshold, it constructs the averaged or a fusion of the predicted bounding boxes. For the training of OCR we took the words cropped around the ground truth bounding box, mapped with the provided word annotation. One of our important contribution lies in the post-processing system where instead of training the language model in a new dataset we are training the model using the prediction of the OCR with the same ground truth in parallel completely isolatedly as discussed in Subsect. 3.3.

5   Experimental Results and Analysis

This section consists of the list of experiments performed to analyse the performance of different deep neural networks with respect to handwritten text detection, text recognition and post-processing.

5.1   Detection

The two object detection frameworks, EfficientDet and Faster R-CNN are trained on the IAM offline dataset. The training is done only the images labelled "ok". For efficientDet the images are resized to a size of 512. For evaluation purposes, we have considered using the last 500 pages of the dataset, when the image ids are taken in alphabetical order. The performance of the object detection networks can be summarized in Table 1. It can be inferred that Faster R-CNN performs well providing a greater mAP(mean average precision) score however it is very slow, reflected in the FPS (frames per second), due to its FPN(Feature Pyramid Network) network, which makes it unfavourable for it's use in real life applications such as ours (Fig. 3).

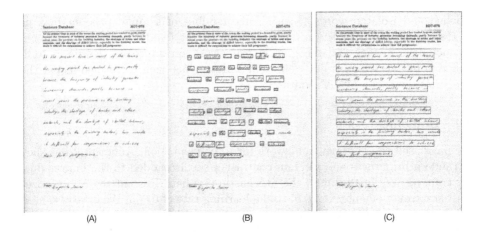

(A)   (B)   (C)

Fig. 3. (A), (B) and (C) shows the detection results on one of the images on the test set. **A.** shows the input image, **B.** shows the detected word wise bounding boxes, and **C.** shows the merged line bounding boxes.

Table 1. A. Performance of the object detection networks on IAM offline dataset. **B.** Performance of the Recognition framework on IAM offline dataset.

Network	mAP	FPS
EfficientDet	58.15%	5.9
Faster R-CNN	71.84%	0.52

Network	CER(in %)	Word level accuracy (in %)
CNN-LSTM (ours)	8.14	**65.86**
CNN-GRU (ours)	**8.21**	65.33
Chung et al. [2]	8.5	—

5.2   Recognition and Post Processing

The recognition framework is trained on the labelled sentences as per the IAM splits, followed by applying Gaussian blur and adaptive threshold with kernels of 7×7 and 13×13 respectively for 150 epochs. For inferencing, we are considering two metrics, one for measuring the total characters that has been correctly predicted irrespective of the parent word, another for measuring the total predicted words that has been an exact match with the annotated label. The performance has been summarized in Table 1. Even the character error rate (CER) of our model surpasses the state of the art sophisticated character level single word recognition system [1]. Observing their individual performance, the smaller performance gap between LSTM and GRU, GRU is a better trade off in real life scenario for being computationally more efficient.

6   Conclusion

In this paper, we have introduced a pipeline for converting handwritten text in a document into speech. The system comprises of an object detection phase for extraction of the sentences in the text document which undergoes a recognition module followed by post-processing, where they are converted into text. The predicted text instances are then converted into speech using the TTS model. In our results, we have used computationally efficient models like EfficientDet for detection purposes and have achieved satisfactory performance by the hybrid CNN-RNN model for text recognition. To the best of our knowledge, the proposed architecture is first of this kind where text to speech conversion has been done from full paged handwritten text documents. In the future, more better performance in terms of detection and recognition can be obtained by improving the model architectures. The proposed pipeline being computationally efficient may be considered for development of real life applications and can be extended along with other non-Latin scripts.

References

1. Bluche, T., Louradour, J., Messina, R.: Scan, attend and read: end-to-end handwritten paragraph recognition with mdlstm attention (2016)
2. Chung, J., Delteil, T.: A computationally efficient pipeline approach to full page offline handwritten text recognition (2020)
3. Chung, J., Gulcehre, C., Cho, K., Bengio, Y.: Empirical evaluation of gated recurrent neural networks on sequence modeling. arXiv preprint arXiv:1412.3555 (2014)
4. Deng, D., Liu, H., Li, X., Cai, D.: Pixellink: detecting scene text via instance segmentation (2018)
5. Dutta, Ket al.: Multi scale mirror connection based encoder decoder network for text localization. Pattern Recogn. Lett. **135**, 64 – 71 (2020). https://doi.org/10.1016/j.patrec.2020.04.002, http://www.sciencedirect.com/science/article/pii/S0167865520301227
6. Dutta, K., Das, N., Kundu, M., Nasipuri, M.: Text localization in natural scene images using extreme learning machine. In: 2019 Second International Conference on Advanced Computational and Communication Paradigms (ICACCP), pp. 1–6 (2019)
7. Fast, B.B., Allen, D.R.: OCR image preprocessing method for image enhancement of scanned documents. uS Patent 5,594,815 (1997)
8. Gllavata, J., Ewerth, R., Freisleben, B.: Text detection in images based on unsupervised classification of high-frequency wavelet coefficients. In: Proceedings of the 17th International Conference on Pattern Recognition, 2004, ICPR 2004, vol. 1, pp. 425–428 (2004). https://doi.org/10.1109/ICPR.2004.1334146
9. Ito, K., Johnson, L.: The lj speech dataset (2017). https://keithito.com/LJ-Speech-Dataset/
10. Jain, A.K., Bin Yu: Automatic text location in images and video frames. In: Proceedings Fourteenth International Conference on Pattern Recognition (Cat. No.98EX170), vol. 2, pp. 1497–1499 (1998). https://doi.org/10.1109/ICPR.1998.711990
11. Kim, K.I., Jung, K., Kim, J.H.: Texture-based approach for text detection in images using support vector machines and continuously adaptive mean shift algorithm. IEEE Trans. Pattern Anal. Mach. Intell. **25**(12), 1631–1639 (2003). https://doi.org/10.1109/TPAMI.2003.1251157
12. Lee, C.Y., Osindero, S.: Recursive recurrent nets with attention modeling for OCR in the wild (2016)

13. Liao, M., Shi, B., Bai, X., Wang, X., Liu, W.: Textboxes: a fast text detector with a single deep neural network (2016)
14. Lin, T.-Y., et al.: Microsoft COCO: common objects in context. In: Fleet, D., Pajdla, T., Schiele, B., Tuytelaars, T. (eds.) ECCV 2014. LNCS, vol. 8693, pp. 740–755. Springer, Cham (2014). https://doi.org/10.1007/978-3-319-10602-1_48
15. Liu, L., Ouyang, W., Wang, X., Fieguth, P., Chen, J., Liu, X., Pietikäinen, M.: Deep learning for generic object detection: a survey. Int. J. Comput. Vision **128**(2), 261–318 (2020)
16. Louloudis, G., Gatos, B., Pratikakis, I., Halatsis, C.: Text line detection in handwritten documents. Pattern Recogn. **41**(12), 3758 – 3772 (2008). https://doi.org/10.1016/j.patcog.2008.05.011, http://www.sciencedirect.com/science/article/pii/S0031320308001775
17. Marti, U.V., Bunke, H.: The IAM-database: an English sentence database for offline handwriting recognition. Int. J. Doc. Anal. Recogn. **5**, 39–46 (2002). https://doi.org/10.1007/s100320200071
18. Memon, J., Sami, M., Khan, R.A., Uddin, M.: Handwritten optical character recognition (OCR): a comprehensive systematic literature review (SLR). IEEE Access **8**, 142642–142668 (2020). https://doi.org/10.1109/ACCESS.2020.3012542
19. Neumann, L., Matas, J.: A method for text localization and recognition in real-world images. In: Kimmel, R., Klette, R., Sugimoto, A. (eds.) ACCV 2010. LNCS, vol. 6494, pp. 770–783. Springer, Heidelberg (2011). https://doi.org/10.1007/978-3-642-19318-7_60
20. Ping, W., et al.: Deep voice 3: scaling text-to-speech with convolutional sequence learning (2018)
21. Ren, S., He, K., Girshick, R., Sun, J.: Faster r-cnn: towards real-time object detection with region proposal networks (2016)
22. Solovyev, R., Wang, W., Gabruseva, T.: Weighted boxes fusion: ensembling boxes for object detection models (2020)
23. Szegedy, C., Vanhoucke, V., Ioffe, S., Shlens, J., Wojna, Z.: Rethinking the inception architecture for computer vision. In: Proceedings of the IEEE Conference on Computer Vision and Pattern Recognition, pp. 2818–2826 (2016)
24. Tan, M., Le, Q.V.: Efficientnet: rethinking model scaling for convolutional neural networks (2020)
25. Tan, M., Pang, R., Le, Q.V.: Efficientdet: scalable and efficient object detection (2020)
26. Wojna, Z., et al.: Attention-based extraction of structured information from street view imagery. In: 2017 14th IAPR International Conference on Document Analysis and Recognition (ICDAR), vol. 1, pp. 844–850. IEEE (2017)
27. Ye, Q., Doermann, D.: Text detection and recognition in imagery: a survey. IEEE Trans. Pattern Anal. Mach. Intell. **37**(7), 1480–1500 (2015). https://doi.org/10.1109/TPAMI.2014.2366765
28. Yosinski, J., Clune, J., Bengio, Y., Lipson, H.: How transferable are features in deep neural networks? In: Advances in Neural Information Processing Systems, pp. 3320–3328 (2014)

Computer Aided Diagnosis of Autism Spectrum Disorder Based on Thermal Imaging

Kavya Ganesh[1], Snekhalatha Umapathy[2]([⊠]) [iD], and Palani Thanaraj Krishnan[1,2]

[1] Department of Biomedical Engineering, College of Engineering and Technology,
SRM Institute of Science and Technology, Chennai, India
[2] Department of Electronics and Instrumentation Engineering,
St. Joseph College of Engineering, Anna University, Chennai, India
sneha_samuma@yahoo.co.in

Abstract. Autism Spectrum Disorder is a fast-growing area of study in the field of neurodevelopmental sciences. It is widely recognized that individuals with ASD have emotional processing impairments which ultimately leads to the inability to recognize facial expressions. The aim of the study was as follows: (1) To compare the facial skin temperature for different emotions namely happiness, sadness and anger using thermal imaging by doing a comparison between autistic and non-autistic children; (2) To develop a CAD tool which comprises of segmentation using K-means algorithm, GLCM feature extraction and classification using SVM. A number of 30 autistic and 30 non-autistic subjects were considered for the study. The thermography approach was used to acquire the temperature of the many facial regions such as eyes, cheek, forehead, and nose while the subjects were asked to react to the projected formats. The mean temperature difference between the autistic and non-autistic individuals in the nose region for the emotion happy, anger and sad is 2.77%, 12.7%, and 13% respectively. The accuracy obtained by classifying the thermal images of the autistic and non-autistic children using SVM classifier was found to be 88% respectively compared to random forest (73%) and Naïve bayes classifier (66%). The Dense-net 121 provided better accuracy of 89.47% compared to the other machine learning classifiers. Thermography is a diagnostic approach used to acquire temperature differences with high resolution. The computer-aided diagnostic tool can be a reliable and an enduring method in the diagnosis of the autistic individuals.

Keywords: Autism spectrum disorder · Thermal imaging · Machine learning

1 Introduction

Autism Spectrum Disorder is a neuropsychological and a developmental disorder that corresponds to a continuum of conditions implying obstacles in social communication and interaction followed by difficulties in non-verbal communication and speech. The term "Spectrum" reflects the large variance in incidence, severity and symptoms. The restricted, repetitive and standardized behavioral pattern in ASD individuals exists as a hurdle in communication and socialization. Emotion is a state of consciousness or a key factor which influences every action. It is a subjective condition which is a response to an external stimulus. The identification of emotions stands as a challenge to the autistic individuals due to the significance in complication in their facial muscular control. Hence, acquiring the facial skin temperature of an autistic individual will pave the way for a thorough understanding of the physiological process. Physical responses and physiological stimuli play a crucial role in the identification of emotions which can be carried out through several modalities. There are several non-invasive or invasive procedures for the assessment of the effective state of the autistic individuals. Though these procedures are intended to be non-invasive, these approaches lead to a deviation in the emotion of an autistic individual due to the placing of sensors that leads to mere distraction. Therefore, thermography being a novel, reliable and a non-contact technique has been inculcated in the study to acquire facial skin temperature. The "fight or flight or freeze" reaction induces variations in the autonomic nervous system that modulates the cutaneous temperature. Using the infrared camera, the particular thermal variation can be precisely observed [1]. This recognition method is independent of the external illumination conditions since only the heat generated by the object is detected by the thermal sensors. It has been demonstrated that a range of emotions stimulates thermal responses [2]. Fear, for example, is associated with a decrease in temperature of the cheeks [3]. However, the fluctuations in the temperature will not be visible with the naked eye hence, it is imperative to foster and investigate segmentation algorithms for detection and classification. Segmentation plays a momentous role in medical image analysis. A number of segmentation methods namely edge-based segmentation [4], Region-based segmentation [5] and cluster-based segmentation and neural network based. From the mentioned segmentation techniques, one of the common techniques is cluster-based methods. The K-means algorithm is a vector quantization method which is used to partition the observations into a number of clusters. This hard segmentation algorithm is used on a higher scale since it is computationally easier to implement in comparison with that of other clustering techniques. k-means clustering is a unsupervised learning based clustering techniques which aims to detect the number of clusters specified by the user which are depicted by their centroids. The advantages of k-means clustering techniques are simple to implement, assured convergence by minimizing the sum of squared error as an objective function, easily adaptable to new applications, fast and computational cost is less. Grey level co-occurrence matrix is one of the renowned methods for statistical feature analysis [6]. A range of structural features can be processed using the Support Vector Machine after obtaining the statistical features [7]. SVM is a widely used classifier since it reduces the computational intricacy and enhances the efficiency of the classification. To the best of our knowledge, there has been no study executed to acquire the facial skin temperature for varied emotions (happiness, sadness, and anger) using the thermal imaging modality in autism. The aim of the study was as follows (1) To compare the facial skin temperature for different emotions namely happiness, sadness and anger using thermal imaging by doing a comparison between autistic and non-autistic children (2) To develop a CAD tool which comprises of segmentation using k-means algorithm, GLCM feature extraction and classification using various machine learning classifier and convolution neural network like Dense net 121.

2 Related Works

Autism Spectrum Disorder is a significant issue, which has been discussed on a wide scale since there is a spike in the number of individuals impacted by these neuropsychiatric disorders. These groups of autistic individuals are described as having impairments in social communication and interaction. They also suffer emotional instabilities which stand as an obstacle in socialism. Therefore, identifying their emotions will pave the foundation for the autistic groups to develop stronger socialising skills. Chaddad et al. [8] analysed the texture characteristics by utilizing the Grey Level Co-Occurrence Matrix as a method of characterizing variations between the developmental control individuals and the autistic individuals. They implemented the SVM classifier and the Random-forest classifier to define the most discriminatory characteristics and use these characteristics to classify the autistic and developmental control subjects. Ingalhalikar et al. [9] presented a framework for producing a quantitative pathological marker that promotes diagnosis and offers a promising biomarker for neuropsychological disorders such as Autism Spectrum Disorder. This paradigm was achieved by inculcating Support Vector Machine to construct high-dimensional non-linear classification which recognise the underlying structure of pathology using various regional, atlas-oriented characteristics extracted from the data through Diffusion Tensor Imaging. Bosl et al. [10] demonstrated that the transformed multi-scale entropy calculated on the premise of EEG resting data can be used in the form of a biomarker for the normal development of the brain to distinguish developing children from a class of children with elevated risk of Autism Spectrum Disorder. A multiclass support vector machine algorithm was used for the classification of normally developing children and children at elevated risk. In our study, a graphical user interface format of different emotions (happiness, anger, sadness) was projected from a screen and the subjects were asked to react to the emotions. The normal subjects reacted to every emotion displayed but the autistic individuals showed an unresponsive facial expression. Hence, the particular region of interest in the face of the individuals were obtained by a comparison between the normal and autistic.

3 Methodology

3.1 Study Design and Population

The study was confirmed by the Ethical Clearance Committee and is been approved. Every patient involved in this study signed the informed consent form. Included groups involve the autistic children and normal children within the range of 5–10 years. A total of 30 autistic children and 30 normal children were selected for the study. The ratio of male and female in the group of autistic children as well normal children is 1:1. The subjects recruited for the study were chosen according to the present Diagnostic and statistical Manual of Mental Disorders, assessed by the Autism Diagnostic Interview-Revised and reviewed by the social communication questionnaire. This research excluded participants with illness such as cold, cough, fever, respiratory infections, and diarrhea.

3.2 Thermal Image Acquisition Procedure

In accordance with the standard approach instructed by the International Academy of Clinical Thermology, the thermal imaging acquisition procedure was carried out. The subjects involved in the study were advised to take away any metallic or non-metallic ornaments worn. The children were seated in an air-conditioned room having a temperature of 20 °C for a duration of 15–20 min at a humidity rate of 40 to 45%. The subjects were then called separately and were seated away from the projection screen at a distance of 1.5 m. Every child was time-bound to a 10–15 min duration and were asked to react to the animated graphics interchange displaying various emotions (Anger, sadness and happiness). The child was positioned at a distance of 1.5 m from the thermal camera. The procedure took place within a duration of 5 min for every individual. The facial thermal images were procured using the FLIR SC 305 version. It is composed of 320 × 240 resolution along with 8x wide zoom lens. The lens size is 18mm with a manual and automatic focus. The camera is boosted with a long wave imagery efficiency and comprises of an uncooled bolometer detector. The thermal camera is designed to evaluate a temperature range of −2 °C–120 °C with a 2 °C accuracy and 0.05 °C sensitivity. Using FLIR software (2.0 version), the obtained data was analysed. Once the thermal images were acquired, the average skin temperature for the various regions namely the eyes, cheeks, forehead and nose were calculated.

3.3 Thermal Image Segmentation Algorithm

The thermal image segmentation was executed for the obtained facial images by the application of the K-means algorithm. The K-Means is a machine learning segmentation algorithm which forms the limited number of clusters by parting the data in accordance with the features of the image [11]. This partitioning technique assembles the data taking in consideration of the intimacy of each data in accordance with the Euclidean distance [12].

The algorithm is described as follows:

1. The facial thermal image is taken as the input.
2. The conversion of the RGB thermal image to HSV is executed. When a colour depiction and the need for the separation of the colour components from intensity plays an essential role, the HSV is much preferable and favourable than an RGB colour model.
3. The initial centroids are assigned with a value of K = 3
4. The least possible distance amidst the centroid and the input pixel was found after which the clustering was executed.
5. The three centroids were updated considering the mean values of the HSV points.
6. Until a high number of iterations were achieved, the steps 1–5 were repeated.

3.4 Statistical Feature Extraction

The statistical features of the segmented images are obtained by performing the Grey-level co-occurrence matrix method [1]. The GLCM method gives a high level of information regarding the inter-pixel correlation of an investigated texture and provides statistical features of the neighbouring pixels in an image. The features such as mean, standard deviation, entropy, skewness, variance, contrast, energy, RMS, autocorrelation, cluster prominence, cluster shade, sum of squares, sum of average, sum of variance, difference entropy, measure of correlation and maximum probability were obtained from the thermal images extracted by the following method (Table 1):

Table 1. Represents the GLCM features and the formulas

GLCM feature	Formula
Mean	$\sum x \sum y x Q(x, y)$
Standard Deviation	$\left(\sum_{x=0}^{N-1} \sum_{y=0}^{N-1} (x - \mu)^2 q(x, y)\right)^{1/2}$
Skewness	$\frac{(\sum (Q(x,y) - \mu)2/N)}{\sigma 3}$
Contrast	$\sum_{x=0} \sum_{x=0} x, y^2 Q x, y^2 Q_{x+y}$
Kurtosis	$\sum [[Q(X, Y) - \mu)^4 /N)/\sigma^4)$
Energy	$\sum_{x,y=0} (q_{xy})^2$
RMS	$\sqrt{\frac{1}{n} \sum_{x=1}^{np} (u(x) + d)^2}$
Autocorrelation	$\sum_{x=0} \sum_{y=0} \frac{(x-\mu)(y-\mu)Q(x,y)}{\sigma x_{\sigma y}}$
Cluster Prominence	$\sum_{X=0}^{G-1} \sum_{X=0}^{G-1} (x + y - \mu u - \mu v)^4 Q(x, y)$
Cluster Shade	$\sum_{X=0}^{G-1} \sum_{X=0}^{G-1} (x + y - \mu u - \mu v)^3 Q(x, y)$
Sum of squares/variance	$\sum_x \sum y (x - \mu)^2 q(x, y)$
Sum average	$\sum_{X=0}^{2G-2} x Q_{x+y} + (x)$
Sum variance	$\sum_{x=2}^{Ng} (x - [\sum_{x=2}^{Ng} x Q_{u+v(x)}])$
Difference entropy	$\sum_{X=0}^{G-1} P_{u+v}(x) log P_{u+v}(u))$
Information measure of correlation	$\frac{Huv - Huv1}{max(Hu, Hv)}$
Entropy	$\sum x \sum y Q(x, y) log (Q(x, y))$

Oriented FAST and rotated BRIEF (ORB) constructs the multi-scale image pyramid and employs FAST algorithm to determine the key points in the images of interest. The FAST measures the key points based on the intensity brightness around the areas of interest[13]. Then Harris corner measure is used to find the peak points among the N detected points. The peak points are determined based on movement of windows over the image and identify the area which produce large variations.

3.5 Machine Learning and Deep Learning Classifier

3.5.1 Support Vector Machine

SVM is a supervised learning algorithm which is a consolidation of machine learning, optimized algorithm and kernel-based techniques. This classifier is highly chosen since it curtails the training error and elevates the accuracy during testing even for unfamiliar data. Hyper plane is been constructed in higher dimensions to perform SVM classification [14]. The decision plane is termed as the hyper plane. A group of data is been distinguished from one type of group to another by the decision plane. The decision boundary is been given by the support vectors which further determines the classes through marginal separation. This kernel-based algorithm escalates the boundary between the data and the class through the removal of unwanted data from the dataset [15]. Therefore, we have in-cooperated the RBF kernel function to classify the given groups of data. The RBF kernel is given as follows:

$$K(x_a, x_b) = \exp(-\gamma ||x_a - x_b||^2), \ \gamma > 0 \tag{1}$$

where x_a and x_b has been considered as the dataset to be trained. x_a is been considered as the feature vectors which represents the observations and the x_b is a representation of the labels for the observations. A hyperplane was then recognized to classify the one group of data (labelled as +1) from the other group of data (labelled as −1). The data of the group of normal individuals is termed as +1 and the data of the group of autistic individuals is termed as −1.

3.5.2 Random Forest Classifier

Random forest classifier functions based on multiple decision tree and prediction based on voting results. The algorithm initialized with selection of random samples from the data set and building the decision tree for every sample present in the data set [16]. The prediction result is obtained from each decision tree and voting is carried out for every anticipated result. The final result is predicted based on the majority vote possessed by the particular decision tree. This classifier is a non-parametric based classifier in which complexity increases as the number of training samples increases.

3.5.3 Naïve Bayes Classifier

Naïve bayes classifier is a supervised machine learning model which functions on massive volume of training data. It uses bayes rule with an assumption that each attributes are independent [16]. The classifier check for the presence of particular feature of the class is correlated to the existence of any other feature in the class variable. It is a simple linear function which exhibits low variance to generalize the hidden data based on its training set and hence prevents from over fitting of data.

3.5.4 Dense Net 121

Dense net 121 is a CNN based architecture which performs multi-layer feature concatenation [16]. It consists of four dense blocks which contains 6, 12, 24, 16 layers. Each layer acquires additional inputs from preceding layer and transfers its own feature maps to all the successive layers. The advantage of Dense net 121 are reduces vanishing-gradient problems, reinforce feature propagation, boost the feature reuse and considerably lowers the number of parameters.

3.6 Statistical Analysis

The analysis of the data was achieved by using the SPSS software package version (SPSS Inc., Chicago, IL, USA). The student t-test was executed to obtain the significance in the facial regions by calculating the average temperature of the surface. The student t-test was further performed to obtain the significant features acquired by the GLCM feature extraction.

4 Results

The aim of the study was to characterize two groups namely the autistic and non-autistic Subjects on the basis of the average skin temperature for different emotions namely happiness, sadness and anger. To showcase the reactions procured while the Subjects were reacting for the various projections; the thermal imaging camera was used to obtain the images of the Subjects. The FLIR tool was used to acquire the maximum, minimum and average temperature of the various regions from the acquired images.

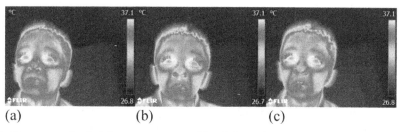

Fig. 1. Represents the facial temperature considered for various emotions namely (a) sad, (b) happy and (c) anger in an autistic child

Figure 1 - A represents the various temperature regions considered for the emotion sad in an autistic child, (b) depicts the various temperature regions considered for the emotion happy in an autistic child, (c) is a representation of the various temperature regions considered for the emotion anger in an autistic child.

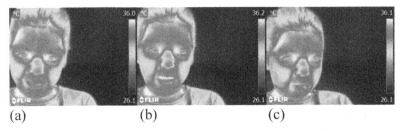

Fig. 2. Represents the facial temperature considered for various emotions namely (a) sad, (b) happy and (c) anger in a normal child.

Figure 2 - (a) represents the various temperature regions considered for the emotion sad in a normal child, (b) depicts the various temperature regions considered for the emotion happy in a normal child, (c) is a representation of the various temperature regions considered for the emotion anger in a normal child.

It was observed that for the emotion – happiness, there was an increase in temperature in the cheek, eye and nose region in the case of the autistic Subjects in comparison with that of the non-autistic Subjects. In the case of the emotion – anger, there was an increase in temperature in the eye, cheek and nose region. And for the emotion sad, there was an increase in temperature in the cheek and nose region respectively. Table 2 indicates the average temperature and the obtained significance for the various facial regions in the autistic and non-autistic Subjects for the different emotions namely happy, anger and sad.

Table 2. Average temperature measured for different facial regions for a population of N = 60

	Regions				
		Forehead	Eye	Cheek	Nose
Happy	Normal	35.8 ± 0.49	36.3 ± 1.1	33.2 ± 1.4	30.9 ± 2.3
	Autism	35.8 ± 0.49	36.8 ± 0.9	33.5 ± 0.7	35.45 ± 1
	Significance	0.836	0.11	0.2	1.17E-13
Anger	Normal	35.4 ± 0.5	36.5 ± 0.7	33.1 ± 1.3	31.03 ± 2.3
	Autism	35.7 ± 0.8	36.9 ± 0.4	33.4 ± 0.6	35.5 ± 0.8
	Significance	0.75	0.001	0.25	7.61E-14
Sad	Normal	35.4 ± 0.8	36.6 ± 0.6	33.9 ± 1.1	31.0 ± 2.2
	Autism	35.8 ± 0.8	36.8 ± 0.6	33.7 ± 0.8	35.6 ± 0.8
	Significance	0.33	0.35	0.004	3.72E-15

The measurement of the mean skin temperature at the nose region for the emotion happy (35.45 ± 1) for the autistic subjects was indicatively higher in than that of normal subjects (30.9 ± 2.3). For the emotion anger, the mean skin temperature in the nose region for autistic subjects (35.5 ± 0.8) has a significant increase than that of non-autistic subjects (31.03 ± 2.3). In the case of the emotion – sad, there is a significant increase in mean skin temperature in the nose region for the autistic subjects (35.6 ± 0.8) than that of normal subjects (31.02 ± 2.2) respectively. Mean temperature difference between the autistic and non-autistic subjects in the nose region for the emotion happy, anger and sad is 2.77, 12.7 and 13 respectively.

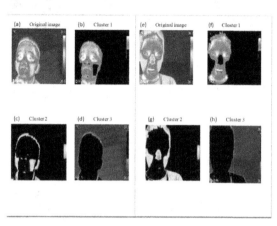

Fig. 3. Illustrates the clusters obtained by performing K – Means segmentation over the obtained thermal images

Figure 3 (a) original image -autistic child, (b) cluster depicting the hot spot regions in the segmented image, (c) cluster regions other than the hot spot (d) represents the cluster depicting the background regions. similarly (e) - (h) represents different clusters of normal (Figs. 4 and 5).

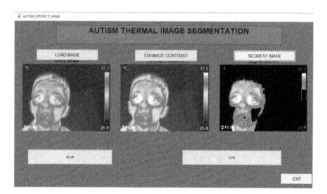

Fig. 4. Depicts the CAD tool which gives a display of the stages involved in the segmentation of the image of an autistic child

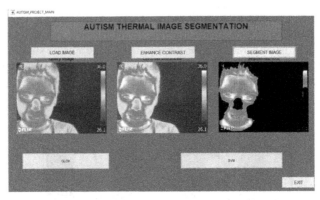

Fig. 5. Depicts the CAD tool which gives a display of the stages involved in the segmentation of the image of a normal child

Table 3 gives an illustration the features extracted from the thermal images of the autistic subjects in comparison with that of non-autistic subjects, which showcased a significant increase in values ($p < 0.05$) for the features namely mean, standard deviation, RMS, variance, kurtosis, energy, contrast, skewness, correlation, cluster shade, cluster prominence, entropy, sum average, sum variance and difference entropy.

Table 3. The GLCM features extracted from the segmented facial regions

Features	Normal	Autism	Significance
Mean	29.64 ± 8.89	23.4 ± 9.04	0.025
S.D	66.9 ± 11.55	60.52 ± 10.56	0.03
RMS	5.63 ± 1.37	4.63 ± 1.38	0.05
Variance	3157.86 ± 1155.79	2607.6 ± 813.66	0.03
Kurtosis	7.28 ± 3.4	10.66 ± 4.49	0.007
Skewness	2.29 ± 0.63	2.87 ± 0.75	0.01
Energy	0.61 ± 0.14	0.71 ± 0.100	0.03
Contrast	13.41 ± 18.83	8.69 ± 15.50	0.009
Correlation	0.84 ± 0.16	0.89 ± 0.05	0.002
Cluster prominence	336.19 ± 294.05	788.82 ± 108.51	0.05
Cluster shade	26.28 ± 23.22	136.08 ± 176.87	0.002
Entropy	7.21 ± 9.13	3.9 ± 6.14	0.01
Sum of average	259.75 ± 1311.0	10.98 ± 16.4	0.00
Sum of variance	33.58 ± 19.66	29.9 ± 9.294	0.00
Difference entropy	12.57 ± 22.64	5.78 ± 16.21	0.00

Table 4 represents the performance comparison of various machine learning classifier and deep learning classifier like dense net 121.Among the machine learning classifiers, SVM outperformed with an accuracy of 88% comparison to other classifiers.

As an overall performance, Dense net 121 achieved 89.47% accuracy compared to all other classifiers.

Table 4. Performance Comparison of various classifiers

Classifier	Precision	Recall	F1-score	Acc
ORB + SVM	89	86	88	88
ORB + Random forest	72	79	74	73
ORB + Naive Bayes	68	74	69	66
Dense net 121	90	89	89	47

5 Conclusion

Thermography is an effective diagnostic approach which provides a high resolution to acquire temperature changes. It is a potential modality used in a broad range of applications to achieve clinical and experimental solutions. This approach has therefore been used in this analysis to examine the fluctuations in temperature for various emotions between autistic and normal children. The mean facial skin temperature of the autistic children was observed to be significantly higher in comparison with normal children. Among the machine learning classifier implemented, SVM classifier outperformed well and attained the accuracy of 88% compared to random forest (73%) and Naïve bayes classifier (66%). The Dense-net 121provided better accuracy of 89.47% compared to the machine learning classifiers. The computer-aided diagnostic tool can be a predictable, reliable and a steadfast adjunct method in the diagnosis of the autistic children.

References

1. Research in Childbirth and Health Unit, School of Community Health and Midwifery, Faculty of Health and Wellbeing, University of Central Lancashire, UK, A. Topalidou, and N. Ali, "Infrared Emotions and Behaviors: Thermal Imaging in Psychology. Int. J. Prenat. Life Sci. **01**(01), 65–70 (2017). https://doi.org/10.24946/IJPLS.20.17.0101.110704
2. Kosonogov, V., et al.: Facial thermal variations: a new marker of emotional arousal. PLoS ONE **12**(9), e0183592 (2017). https://doi.org/10.1371/journal.pone.0183592
3. Engert, V., Merla, A., Grant, J.A., Cardone, D., Tusche, A., Singer, T.: Exploring the use of thermal infrared imaging in human stress research. PLoS ONE **9**(3) (2014). https://doi.org/10.1371/journal.pone.0090782
4. Zhou, N., Yang, T., Zhang, S.: An improved FCM medical image segmentation algorithm based on MMTD. Comput. Math. Methods Med. **2014**, 690349 (2014). https://doi.org/10.1155/2014/690349

5. Duarte, A., et al.: Segmentation algorithms for thermal images. Procedia Technol. **16**, 1560–1569 (2014). https://doi.org/10.1016/j.protcy.2014.10.178
6. Nanni, L., Brahnam, S., Ghidoni, S., Menegatti, E., Barrier, T.: Different approaches for extracting information from the co-occurrence matrix. PLoS ONE **8**(12), e83554 (2013). https://doi.org/10.1371/journal.pone.0083554
7. Huang, X., Zhang, L.: Road centreline extraction from high-resolution imagery based on multiscale structural features and support vector machines. Int. J. Remote Sens. **30**(8), 1977–1987 (2009). https://doi.org/10.1080/01431160802546837
8. Chaddad, A., Desrosiers, C., Hassan, L., Tanougast, C.: Hippocampus and amygdala radiomic biomarkers for the study of autism spectrum disorder. BMC Neurosci. **18**(1), 52 (2017). https://doi.org/10.1186/s12868-017-0373-0
9. Ingalhalikar, M., Parker, D., Bloy, L., Roberts, T.P.L., Verma, R.: Diffusion based abnormality markers of pathology: towards learned diagnostic prediction of ASD. Neuroimage **57**(3), 918–927 (2011). https://doi.org/10.1016/j.neuroimage.2011.05.023
10. Bosl, W., Tierney, A., Tager-Flusberg, H., Nelson, C.: EEG complexity as a biomarker for autism spectrum disorder risk. BMC Med. **9**(1), 18 (2011). https://doi.org/10.1186/1741-7015-9-18
11. Farhang, Y.: Face Extraction from Image based on K-Means Clustering Algorithms (2017). https://doi.org/10.14569/IJACSA.2017.080914
12. Park, H.-S., Jun, C.-H.: A simple and fast algorithm for K-medoids clustering. Expert Syst. Appl. **36**(2, Part 2), 3336–3341 (2009). https://doi.org/10.1016/j.eswa.2008.01.039
13. Rublee, E., Rabaud, V., Konolige, K., Bradski, G.: ORB: an efficient alternative to SIFT or SURF. In: Proceedings of the IEEE International Conference on Computer Vision, pp. 2564–2571. https://doi.org/10.1109/ICCV.2011.6126544
14. Chandra, M.A., Bedi, S.S.: Survey on SVM and their application in image classification. Int. J. Inf. Technol. **13**(5), 1–11 (2018). https://doi.org/10.1007/s41870-017-0080-1
15. Yekkehkhany, B., Safari, A., Homayouni, S., Hasanlou, M.: A comparison study of different kernel functions for SVM-based classification of multi-temporal polarimetry SAR data. ISPRS - Int. Arch. Photogramm. Remote Sens. Spat. Inf. Sci. **2**, 281–285 (2014). https://doi.org/10.5194/isprsarchives-XL-2-W3-281-2014
16. Latif, J., Xiao, C., Imran, A., Tu, S.: Medical imaging using machine learning and deep learning algorithms: a review. In: 2019 2nd International Conference on Computing, Mathematics and Engineering Technologies, ICoMET 2019, March 2019 (2019). https://doi.org/10.1109/ICOMET.2019.8673502

Efficient High-Resolution Image-to-Image Translation Using Multi-Scale Gradient U-Net

Kumarapu Laxman[1]([✉]), Shiv Ram Dubey[2], Baddam Kalyan[1], and Satya Raj Vineel Kojjarapu[1]

[1] Indian Institute of Information Technology, Sri City, Chittoor, India
{laxman.k17,kalyan.b17,satyarajvineel.k17}@iiits.in
[2] Indian Institute of Information Technology, Allahabad, Prayagraj, India
srdubey@iiita.ac.in

Abstract. Recently, Conditional Generative Adversarial Network (Conditional GAN) has shown very promising performance in several image-to-image translation applications. However, the uses of these conditional GANs are quite limited to low-resolution images, such as 256×256. The Pix2Pix-HD is a recent attempt to utilize the conditional GAN for high-resolution image synthesis. In this paper, we propose a Multi-Scale Gradient based U-Net (MSG U-Net) model for high-resolution image-to-image translation up to 2048×1024 resolution. The proposed model is trained by allowing the flow of gradients from multiple-discriminators to a single generator at multiple scales. The proposed MSG U-Net architecture leads to photo-realistic high-resolution image-to-image translation. Moreover, the proposed model is computationally efficient as compared to the Pix2Pix-HD with an improvement in the inference time nearly by 2.5 times. We provide the code of MSG U-Net model at https://github.com/laxmaniron/MSG-U-Net.

Keywords: Multi-Scale Gradient U-Net · Multiple scales · Conditional GANs · Pix2Pix-HD · Image-to-image translation

1 Introduction

Recently, image-to-image translation has gained huge popularity after the success of Generative Adversarial Networks (GANs) [7] in a wide range of image processing and computer vision applications [1,2,12,14]. In image-to-image translation, an image in a domain is generally transformed into the corresponding image in some other domain, such as translating semantically segmented label images into RGB images, aerial photos to maps, sketches to real faces, and indoor segmented images to real images.

In 2014, GAN was proposed by Goodfellow et al. [7] to synthesize photo-realistic images with the help of generator and discriminator networks. In 2017, the GAN was extended for image-to-image translation in form of conditional

B. Raman et al. (Eds.): CVIP 2021, CCIS 1567, pp. 33–44, 2022.
https://doi.org/10.1007/978-3-031-11346-8_4

GAN (i.e., Pix2Pix model) [8] which became very popular. Motivated from the conditional GAN, several variants of GANs have been developed for image-to-image translation [5,13,22]. However, these GAN models are generally not designed for the high-resolution image-to-image translations. Moreover, these models can only produce images of good quality up to 256×256 resolution.

To improve the quality of generated images, Perceptual Adversarial Networks (PAN) for Image-to-Image Transformation [18] were proposed which uses perceptual losses from pre-trained image classification networks such as VGG-19 [16]. However, its output resolution is also limited to 256×256. In an another attempt, a progressive GAN [10] is proposed to train the generator and discriminator networks with first low-resolution images then high-resolution images, which poses an additional burden on the training. In 2018, Ting-Chun Wang et al. [19] proposed the Pix2Pix-HD model for high-resolution image synthesis and semantic manipulation with the help of conditional GANs. The Pix2Pix-HD [19] performs well for high-resolution image-to-image translation (up to 2048×1024) as well. However, it is computational resource hungry (the complexity of Pix2Pix-HD is about 3.32 TeraFlops) and requires huge memory (at least 8GB of GPU VRAM) even during the inference time. Recently, multi-scale gradient for GAN (MSG-GAN) [9] is introduced for the high-resolution image generation by utilizing the gradient information at different scales. However, the power of multi-scale gradient is not yet utilized for the image-to-image translation. In this paper, we tackle these issues of high-resolution image-to-image translation with the help of the proposed efficient Multi-scale Gradient U-Net inspired from MSG-GAN [9] which requires significantly less computational resources and generates the high quality images.

Following are the main contributions of this paper:

- We propose a novel Multi-Scale Gradient U-Net (MSG U-Net) based GAN model for high-resolution image-to-image translation (up to 2048×1024) which is inspired from the MSG-GAN [9] architecture.
- The proposed MSG U-Net is very efficient as compared to the state-of-the-art GANs for high-resolution image-to-image translation. MSG U-Net requires half the memory (4GB of GPU VRAM) and computational resources (the complexity of MSG U-Net is about 1.28 TeraFlops) during inference time as compared to Pix2Pix-HD [19] while retaining the same level of details in the output images.

2   Proposed MSG U-Net GAN Model

In this section, we present the generator and discriminator architectures along with the objective function of the proposed MSG U-Net model.

2.1   Generator Architecture

MSG-GANs [9] generate high-resolution images up to 1024×1024 from latent vectors. It avoids the vanishing gradient problem faced by very deep networks

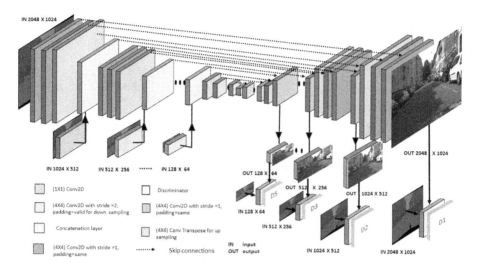

Fig. 1. The above figure shows the Network architecture of our proposed Multi-Scale Gradient U-Net (MSG U-Net) GAN model. The input from the source domain is provided to the network at various resolutions ranging from 128×64 to 2048×1024. Similarly, the generator network generates the output images in the target domain at various resolutions ranging from 128×64 to 2048×1024. The output image generated at a particular resolution is concatenated with the input image from the source domain at the same resolution and fed into the corresponding discriminator similar to Pix2Pix Conditional GAN [8]. The network uses multiple discriminators, i.e., one discriminator for each resolution.

by allowing the flow of gradients from the discriminator to the generator at multiple scales. Inspired by this work, we propose a new generator architecture multi-scale gradients for U-Net (MSG U-Net) for high-resolution image-to-image translation (upto 2048×1024 resolution) as shown in Fig. 1.

Encoder Part of MSG U-Net. Let the input image from the source domain be of resolution 2048×1024 fed to the encoder part of the network. The input image is passed through two convolutional blocks of kernel size 4×4 and stride 1. Each convolutional block consists of Convolution-BatchNorm-LeakyReLu layers. Then the resolution is reduced to 1024×512 by using a convolutional block of kernel size 4×4 with stride as 2. Then the output of the convolutional block is concatenated with the resized source image (1024×512), passed through a convolutional block having kernel size 1×1. In this way, we form the encoder part of the generator by providing input from the source domain at various scales from 2048×1024 to 128×64. After 128×64 input block, the encoder follows normal U-net architecture, and the resolution of convolutional block is reduced to 8×4. Providing input at different scales at different stages to the encoder leads to the learning of important features such as overall shape information from the low-resolution and detailed texture information from the high-resolution image.

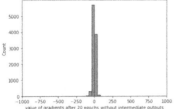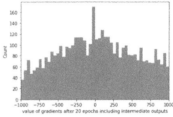

Fig. 2. The gradient distribution after 20 epochs of training when (left) the output at intermediate layers is not used, and (right) the output at intermediate layers is used.

Decoder Part of MSG U-Net. The output of the encoder from the 8×4 convolutional block is considered as the input to the decoder. First, the decoder up-samples to 8×16 using the transposed convolution block (TransposedConvolution-BatchNorm-LeakyRelu). The 8×16 output from the transposed convolutional block is added to the output from the corresponding 8×16 encoder block using skip connections followed by a convolutional block with stride 1. In this manner, the decoder upsamples upto 2048×1024 using transposed convolutional blocks. In addition to this, the decoder has branching at different layers to generate output images in the target domain from 128×64 to 2048×1024 resolutions simultaneously.

The process of generating outputs at intermediate layers in the generator network is inspired from MSG-GANs [9] and GoogLeNet [17]. It helps the network to alleviate the problem of vanishing gradients. As the discriminators not only take generator's final output as input but also the intermediate outputs, the gradients can flow from discriminators to the intermediate layers of the generator directly. This increases the stability during training and solves the problem of vanishing gradients when the U-Net architecture is very deep.

To illustrate the impact of having output of different resolutions at intermediate layers, we train the MSG U-Net with and without the intermediate output images for 20 epochs and show the gradient distribution in Fig. 2. It can be noticed that the gradients are very close to zero due to the gradient diminishing problem when output at intermediate layers are not used. Whereas the gradient is distributed better when the output at intermediate layers are used.

2.2 Discriminator Architecture

We use a modified version of multi-scale discriminators proposed in [19] while training. As our generator produces target images at different scales, we scale the source image to various scales and concatenate with generated output at corresponding scale and feed it to the discriminator as a fake sample(0). We also concatenate the source and actual target image at corresponding scale and feed it to discriminator as a real sample(1). Images at different resolutions are fed into different discriminators. However, the architecture of discriminator is same at all scales. We use the same patch discriminator as used in Pix2Pix [8]. We

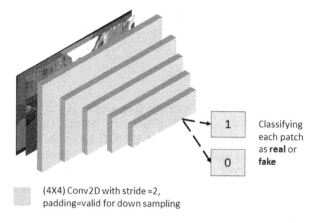

(4X4) Conv2D with stride =2,
padding=valid for down sampling

Classifying
each patch
as **real** or
fake

1

0

Fig. 3. Network architecture of discriminator, each discriminator handles image at one resolution/scale.

found that multiple discriminators lead to better stability during training than using single discriminator for all scales described in MSG-GAN [9] (Fig. 3).

2.3   Loss Function

We use the improved adversarial loss proposed in Pix2Pix-HD [19] along with perceptual loss using VGG-19 [16] as our loss function for generator and all discriminators. Let G be the generator and $D_1, D_2, ..., D_n$ be n discriminators. Let $D_k^{(i)}(X, Y)$ be the output of the ith layer of discriminator D_k when fed with input images $\{X, Y\}$. Let E_i be the total no. of elements in the ith layer of discriminator and P be total number of layers in discriminator. Consider x_k as the source image and y_k as the corresponding target image at resolution k with z_k as the corresponding generated output. For perceptual loss, assume F_k as the pre-trained VGG-19 [16] with frozen weights handling inputs at resolution k, U as the number of convolution layers in VGG-19 and $F_k^{(i)}(X)$ be the output of the ith layer of VGG-19 network F_k when fed with input image X. Consider V_i be the total no. of elements in i^{th} layer of VGG-19. The final objective/loss function L_{total} of the proposed MSG U-Net model can be written as:

$$L_{total} = \max_{G} \min_{D_1, D_2...D_n} \sum_{k=1}^{n} L_{GAN}(G, D_k)$$

$$+\alpha \sum_{k=1}^{n} \sum_{i=1}^{P} \frac{1}{E_i} [||D_k^{(i)}(x_k, y_k) - D_k^{(i)}(x_k, z_k)||_1] \qquad (1)$$

$$+\beta \sum_{k=1}^{n} \sum_{i=1}^{U} \frac{1}{V_i} [||F_k^{(i)}(y_k) - F_k^{(i)}(z_k)||_1]$$

where L_{GAN} denotes the adversarial loss and α and β are multiplication factor for feature loss [19] and perceptual loss [18], respectively.

3   Experiments and Results

We use five benchmark datasets, namely Cityscapes [4], NYU Indoor RGBD [11], Aerial Images to Maps [8], ADE20K dataset [20] and COCO-Stuff 10K [3]. Cityscapes dataset [4] consists of segmented RGB image of city streets in the source domain and corresponding photo-realistic image in the target domain at resolution 2048 × 1024. NYU Indoor RGBD dataset [11] consists of segmented indoor images in the source domain and corresponding real images in the target domain at resolution 512 × 512. Aerial Images to Maps dataset [3] consists of aerial photographs in the source domain and corresponding map of the image in the target domain at resolution 512 × 512. ADE20K dataset [20] consists of diverse segmentation annotations of scenes, objects, parts of objects, and in some cases even parts of parts in Source Domain and corresponding RGB images in target domain. COCO-Stuff 10K [3] is a mini-dataset of COCO-Stuff consisting of segmented images in source domain and corresponding RGB images in target domain. It is split into 9K training pairs and 1K test pairs.

For all the datasets, we split the dataset into official train and test splits as mentioned in the corresponding papers.

We provide a comprehensive quantitative comparison against state-of-the-art methods over five datasets. In all the experiments, we set the hyper-parameters α and β described in equation [1] to 10 and 0.25, respectively, based on the extensive hyper-parameter tuning. We use Peak Signal-to-Noise Ratio (PSNR), Structural Similarity Index (SSIM) [21], and Visual Information Fidelity (VIF) [15] as the evaluation metrics. We compare our method with the state-of-the-art image-to-image translation GANs, including Pix2Pix [8], Perceptual Adversarial networks (PAN) [18], Transformer models [6], and Pix2Pix-HD [19].

On the Segmentation datasets, namely Cityscapes [4], NYU Indoor RGBD [11], ADE20K dataset [20] and COCO-Stuff 10K [3], we use the additional metrics such as Pixel wise accuracy (Pixel acc) and mean intersection-over-union (Mean IoU) as used in Pix2Pix-HD [19] model. We follow the same evaluation protocol as Pix2Pix-HD [19] for these two metrics.

3.1   Quantitative Results

The experimental results in terms of the PSNR, SSIM and VIF are reported in Table 1 and 2 over Cityscapes, NYU Indoor RGBD, Aerial Images to Maps datasets, ADE20K dataset, and COCO-Stuff 10K datasets. Note that we remove the topmost input layer and the output layer of dimension 2048 × 1024 and resize the 1024 × 512 input and output resolution to 512 × 512 to facilitate the experiments on NYU Indoor RGBD, Aerial Images to Maps, ADE20K, and COCO-Stuff 10K datasets. From the results we can see that Transformer model [6] outperforms all other models. However, the output resolution is limited to

Table 1. The results show comparison of the proposed MSG U-net with state-of-the-art image-to-image translation GANs on Cityscapes [4], NYU Indoor RGBD [11] and Aerial Images to Maps [8] datasets.

Model	Cityscapes			NYU indoor RGBD			Aerial images to maps		
	PSNR	SSIM	VIF	PSNR	SSIM	VIF	PSNR	SSIM	VIF
Pix2Pix (256 × 256) [8]	15.74	0.42	0.05	18.08	0.45	0.07	26.20	0.64	0.02
PAN (256 × 256) [18]	16.06	0.48	0.06	19.23	0.54	0.11	28.32	0.75	0.16
Transformers **(256 × 256)** [6]	**24.12**	**0.70**	**0.16**	**25.87**	**0.81**	**0.29**	**32.79**	**0.88**	**0.25**
Pix2Pix-HD (512 × 512) [19]	–	–	–	25.01	**0.79**	**0.28**	32.32	0.87	0.24
Pix2Pix-HD (2048 × 1024) [19]	22.18	0.66	0.14	–	–	–	–	–	—
MSG U-Net(Ours) (512 × 512)	–	–	–	25.17	0.77	0.27	31.04	0.84	0.23
MSG U-Net(Ours) (2048 × 1024)	23.99	0.69	0.15	–	–	–	–	–	–

Table 2. The results show comparison of the MSG U-net with state-of-the-art image-to-image translation GANs on ADE20K dataset [20] and COCO-Stuff 10K dataset [3].

Model	ADE20K			COCO-Stuff 10K		
	PSNR	SSIM	VIF	PSNR	SSIM	VIF
Pix2Pix (256 × 256) [8]	20.97	0.53	0.04	22.14	0.54	0.05
PAN (256 × 256) [18]	22.19	0.62	0.11	23.66	0.64	0.134
Transformers **(256 × 256)** [6]	**28.78**	**0.83**	**0.21**	**29.53**	**0.85**	**0.29**
Pix2Pix-HD (512 × 512) [19]	27.25	0.76	0.18	**28.72**	**0.83**	**0.26**
MSG U-Net(Ours) (512 × 512)	**27.52**	**0.77**	**0.19**	28.2	0.81	0.25

Table 3. The results show comparison of the proposed MSG U-net with state-of-the-art image-to-image translation GANs with pixel wise accuracy (PAcc) and mean intersection over union (mIoU) on Cityscapes [4], NYU Indoor RGBD [11] and ADE20K [20] and COCO-Stuff 10K [3] datasets.

Model	Cityscapes		NYU RGBD		ADE20K		COCO-Stuff 10K	
	PAcc	mIoU	PAcc	mIoU	PAcc	mIoU	PAcc	mIoU
Pix2Pix (256 × 256) [8]	78.34	0.39	81.2	0.53	79.06	0.43	80.48	0.50
PAN (256 × 256) [18]	79.53	0.43	83.4	0.57	80.42	0.47	82.26	0.52
Transformer **(256 × 256)** [6]	**84.10**	**0.65**	**92.23**	**0.77**	**86.13**	**0.68**	**90.19**	**0.74**
Pix2Pix-HD (512 × 512) [19]	–	–	90.01	0.75	85.33	0.66	**88.52**	**0.73**
Pix2Pix-HD (2048 × 1024) [19]	83.78	0.64	–	–	–	–	–	–
MSG U-Net (512 × 512)	–	–	89.77	0.74	**85.79**	**0.67**	88.34	0.72
MSG U-Net (2048 × 1024)	84.02	0.64	–	–	–	–	–	–

256 × 256. Excluding Transformer model,it is noticed from the results that the proposed MSG U-Net outperforms the Pix2Pix, PAN, and Pix2Pix-HD models over Cityscapes [4] and ADE20K [20] datasets. However, the results of the MSG U-Net is very close to Pix2Pix-HD over NYU Indoor RGBD [11], Aerial Images to Maps [8], and COCO-Stuff 10K [3] datasets.

Table 4. Ablation study of MSG U-Net at 2048 × 1024 on Cityscapes dataset [4].

S.no	Model	CityScapes dataset results at 2048 × 1024				
–	–	PSNR	SSIM	VIF	Pixel acc	Mean IoU
1	U-Net **w/o multi-scale input and multi-scale output and w/o feature loss and w/o perceptual loss**	9.68	0.28	0.03	36.33	0.26
2	Multi scale gradient U-Net **w/o feature loss and w/o perceptual loss**	17.35	0.51	0.10	65.13	0.50
3	Multi scale gradient U-Net with feature loss **and w/o perceptual loss**	21.37	0.63	0.13	80.23	0.61
4	**Multi scale gradient U-Net with feature loss and perceptual loss (final)**	**23.99**	**0.69**	**0.15**	**84.02**	**0.64**

We observe a similar trend in Table 3 over pixel wise accuracy (Pixel acc, written as PAcc) and Mean IoU (mIoU) metrics, where our proposed MSG U-Net outperforms Pix2Pix-HD [19] over Cityscapes [4] and ADE20K [20] datasets. While the results are very close over NYU Indoor RGBD [11] and COCO-Stuff 10K [3] datasets.

Note that Pix2Pix-HD is 2.5 times computationally more expensive than our MSG U-Net at both 512 × 512 and 2048 × 1024 resolutions. Transformer network is 5 times computationally expensive even at 256 × 256 resolution. The detailed comparison of efficiency between the Pix2Pix-HD and our MSG U-Net is mentioned in Sect. 3.3. Thus, the proposed model is very efficient as compared to the Pix2Pix-HD and generates the output images with better or similar quality.

3.2 Ablation Study

To test the effectiveness of each component of the model, we perform a detailed ablation study by training and testing network by removing certain parts of the model as mentioned in Table 4. First, we use the baseline U-net architecture similar to Pix2Pix [8], but with increased input and output resolutions to 2048×1024 by adding convolutional and de-convolutional blocks with no inputs and outputs at multiple resolutions at intermediate layers. We observe very poor results and there is no multi scale input and output at intermediate layers. Thus, no multi-scale gradient results in very poor gradient signal while training as shown in Fig. 2 (1st graph). Then we add inputs and outputs at intermediate layers and separate discriminator for each output resolution. The addition of input image at multiple resolutions and separate discriminators dealing with corresponding assigned output resolution improves the results significantly as shown in Table 4 (2nd row). Results also have been improved noticeably by adding Feature loss [19] as shown in Table 4 (3rd row). Adding perceptual loss using VGG-19 [16] further improves the results by a small amount as sown in Table 4 (4th row).

Table 5. Computational efficiency comparison of Pix2Pix-HD and MSG U-Net architecture.

Network	No of parameters	Computational complexity	Inference time
Pix2Pix-HD (512 × 512) [19]	144.6 million	2.8 Tera-Flops	18 ms
Pix2Pix-HD (2048 × 1024) [19]	150.7 million	3.32 Tera-Flops	22 ms
MSG U-Net (ours) (512 × 512)	56.8 million	1.07 Tera-Flops	7 ms
MSG U-Net (ours) (2048 × 1024)	60.4 million	1.28 Tera-Flops	8 ms

3.3 Comparison of MSG U-Net and Pix2Pix Network Complexity and Inference Time

We compare the complexity of Pix2Pix-HD [19] with MSG U-net at both 512 × 512 and 2048 × 1024 resolutions as detailed in Table 5. All the inference times have been calculated using same GPU (Tesla V100). From the table we can see that Pix2Pix-HD at both resolutions, is 2.5 times slower than our MSG U-net model. This speed-up of our network can be attributed to the less no. of parameters (150 million in Pix2Pix-HD vs 60.4 million in MSG U-net). The efficiency is also due to the architecture choices of the network, Pix2Pix-HD [19] uses Resnet blocks for countering vanishing gradient effect and whereas we use U-net with inputs and outputs at intermediate layers to counter vanishing gradient effect. The choice of our architecture had resulted in less complexity and less parameters and therefore faster inference times. The Transformer model consists of many parameters and inefficient. It leads to 405 million parameters just to produce the output at 256 × 256 resolution over ADE20K dataset.

3.4 Qualitative Results

We present the images generated by the proposed MSG U-Net model and compare it with baseline Pix2Pix [8] and Pix2PixHD[19] methods in this section. To be precise Fig. 4 shows the source images, target images and generated images from Cityscapes dataset [4]. Fig. 5 shows results on NYU Indoor RGB-D dataset [11]. Figure 6 shows results on Aerial Images to Maps dataset [8]. The quality of the generated images can be easily observed for the high-resolution synthesis in these results.

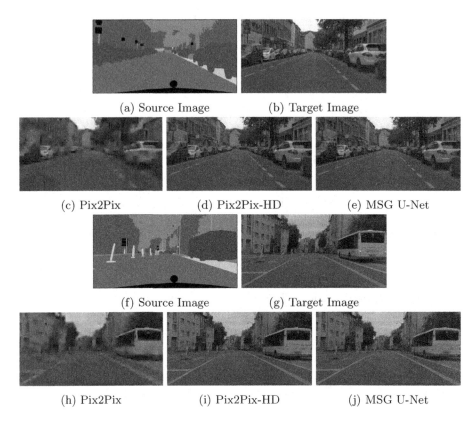

(a) Source Image   (b) Target Image

(c) Pix2Pix   (d) Pix2Pix-HD   (e) MSG U-Net

(f) Source Image   (g) Target Image

(h) Pix2Pix   (i) Pix2Pix-HD   (j) MSG U-Net

Fig. 4. Example results on Cityscapes dataset. Here, we convert segmented-RGB image to photo realistic image.

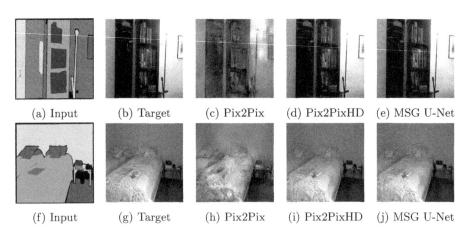

(a) Input   (b) Target   (c) Pix2Pix   (d) Pix2PixHD   (e) MSG U-Net

(f) Input   (g) Target   (h) Pix2Pix   (i) Pix2PixHD   (j) MSG U-Net

Fig. 5. Example results on NYU Indoor RGBD dataset images. Here, we convert segmented indoor images to photo realistic images.

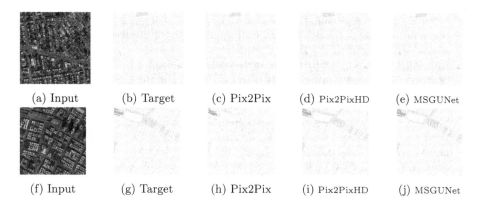

(a) Input   (b) Target   (c) Pix2Pix   (d) Pix2PixHD   (e) MSGUNet

(f) Input   (g) Target   (h) Pix2Pix   (i) Pix2PixHD   (j) MSGUNet

Fig. 6. Example results on Aerial Images to Maps dataset images. Here, we convert aerial photographs to maps.

4   Conclusion

In this paper, we proposed a Multi-scale gradient based U-Net (MSG U-Net) for high-resolution image-to-image translation. The proposed model shows better training due to the utilization of the gradients at different scales. The proposed MSG U-Net (1.28 Tera-Flops) is computationally efficient as compared to Pix2Pix-HD (3.32 Tera-Flops). In spite of being an efficient model, the MSG U-Net has shown either better or comparable performance over five benchmark datasets.

References

1. Babu, K.K., Dubey, S.R.: Csgan: cyclic-synthesized generative adversarial networks for image-to-image transformation. Expert Syst. Appl. **169**, 114431 (2020)
2. Babu, K.K., Dubey, S.R.: Pcsgan: perceptual cyclic-synthesized generative adversarial networks for thermal and nir to visible image transformation. Neurocomputing **413**, 41–50 (2020)
3. Caesar, H., Uijlings, J., Ferrari, V.: Coco-stuff: thing and stuff classes in context. In: Proceedings of the IEEE Conference on Computer Vision and Pattern Recognition, pp. 1209–1218 (2018)
4. Cordts, M., et al.: The cityscapes dataset for semantic urban scene understanding. In: Proceedings of the IEEE Conference on Computer Vision and Pattern Recognition (CVPR) (2016)
5. Emami, H., Aliabadi, M.M., Dong, M., Chinnam, R.B.: Spa-gan: spatial attention gan for image-to-image translation. IEEE Trans. Multimedia **23**, 391–401 (2020)
6. Esser, P., Rombach, R., Ommer, B.: Taming transformers for high-resolution image synthesis. In: Proceedings of the IEEE/CVF Conference on Computer Vision and Pattern Recognition, pp. 12873–12883 (2021)
7. Goodfellow, I., et al.: Generative adversarial nets. Adv. Neural Inf. Process. Syst. **27**, 2672–2680 (2014)

8. Isola, P., Zhu, J.Y., Zhou, T., Efros, A.A.: Image-to-image translation with conditional adversarial networks. In: Proceedings of the IEEE Conference on Computer Vision and Pattern Recognition (CVPR) (2017)
9. Karnewar, A., Wang, O.: Msg-gan: multi-scale gradients for generative adversarial networks. In: Proceedings of the IEEE/CVF Conference on Computer Vision and Pattern Recognition (CVPR) (2020)
10. Karras, T., Aila, T., Laine, S., Lehtinen, J.: Progressive growing of gans for improved quality, stability, and variation. arXiv preprint arXiv:1710.10196 (2017)
11. Silberman, N., Hoiem, D., Kohli, P., Fergus, R.: Indoor segmentation and support inference from RGBD images. In: Fitzgibbon, A., Lazebnik, S., Perona, P., Sato, Y., Schmid, C. (eds.) ECCV 2012. LNCS, vol. 7576, pp. 746–760. Springer, Heidelberg (2012). https://doi.org/10.1007/978-3-642-33715-4_54
12. Nema, S., Dudhane, A., Murala, S., Naidu, S.: Rescuenet: an unpaired gan for brain tumor segmentation. Biomed. Signal Process. Control **55**, 101641 (2020)
13. Park, T., Efros, A.A., Zhang, R., Zhu, J.-Y.: Contrastive learning for unpaired image-to-image translation. In: Vedaldi, A., Bischof, H., Brox, T., Frahm, J.-M. (eds.) ECCV 2020. LNCS, vol. 12354, pp. 319–345. Springer, Cham (2020). https://doi.org/10.1007/978-3-030-58545-7_19
14. Patil, P., Dudhane, A., Murala, S.: End-to-end recurrent generative adversarial network for traffic and surveillance applications. IEEE Trans. Veh. Technol. **69**, 14550–14562 (2020)
15. Sheikh, H.R., Bovik, A.C.: Image information and visual quality. IEEE Trans. Image Process. **15**(2), 430–444 (2006). https://doi.org/10.1109/TIP.2005.859378
16. Simonyan, K., Zisserman, A.: Very deep convolutional networks for large-scale image recognition. arXiv preprint arXiv:1409.1556 (2014)
17. Szegedy, C., et al.: Going deeper with convolutions. In: Proceedings of the IEEE Conference on Computer Vision and Pattern Recognition (CVPR) (2015)
18. Wang, C., Xu, C., Wang, C., Tao, D.: Perceptual adversarial networks for image-to-image transformation. IEEE Trans. Image Process. **27**(8), 4066–4079 (2018)
19. Wang, T.C., Liu, M.Y., Zhu, J.Y., Tao, A., Kautz, J., Catanzaro, B.: High-resolution image synthesis and semantic manipulation with conditional gans. In: Proceedings of the IEEE Conference on Computer Vision and Pattern Recognition (CVPR) (2018)
20. Zhou, B., Zhao, H., Puig, X., Fidler, S., Barriuso, A., Torralba, A.: Scene parsing through ade20k dataset. In: Proceedings of the IEEE Conference on Computer Vision and Pattern Recognition (CVPR) (2017)
21. Wang, Z., Bovik, A.C., Sheikh, H.R., Simoncelli, E.P.: Image quality assessment: from error visibility to structural similarity. IEEE Trans. Image Process. **13**(4), 600–612 (2004). https://doi.org/10.1109/TIP.2003.819861
22. Zhu, J.Y., Park, T., Isola, P., Efros, A.A.: Unpaired image-to-image translation using cycle-consistent adversarial networks. In: Proceedings of the IEEE International Conference on Computer Vision, pp. 2223–2232 (2017)

Generic Multispectral Image Demosaicking Algorithm and New Performance Evaluation Metric

Vishwas Rathi[✉][ID] and Puneet Goyal[ID]

Department of Computer Science and Engineering,
Indian Institute of Technology Ropar, Rupnagar, Punjab, India
{2018csz0009,puneet}@iitrpr.ac.in

Abstract. Color image demosaicking is key in developing low-cost digital cameras using a color filter array(CFA). Similarly, multispectral image demosaicking can be used to develop low-cost and portable multispectral cameras using a multispectral filter array (MSFA). In this work, we propose a generic multispectral image demosaicking algorithm based on spatial and spectral correlation. We also propose a new image quality metric Average-Normalized-Multispectral-PSNR (ANMPSNR), which helps in easily comparing the relative performance of different demosaicking algorithms. In experimental results, we prove the efficacy of the proposed algorithm using two publicly available datasets as per different image quality metrics.

Keywords: Demosaicking · Multispectral filter array · Spectral correlation · Interpolation

1 Introduction

Multispectral images (MSIs) capture more information about the scene as compared to standard color images. Therefore MSIs are widely used in different areas like medical imaging, food industry, remote sensing, or identifying materials [8–10]. In the past years, few single-sensor-based multispectral imaging systems [3,11,17,22] have been proposed based on MSFA, similar to the standard consumer digital camera, which is based on CFA. MSFA has more than three spectral bands compared to CFA and empowers us to develop low-cost and portable multispectral cameras. MSFA based multispectral camera captures only one spectral band information as each pixel location depending on the filter element in the MSFA covering the pixel location. This captured image where only one spectral band information is available at each pixel location is called a mosaicked image (raw image). The process of estimating missing spectral band information at each pixel location in the mosaicked images is called multispectral image demosaicking. The quality of the MSI generated depends on the efficiency of the multispectral demosaicking algorithm. However, multispectral image demosaicking is more challenging than color image demosaicking due to the highly sparse sampling of the spectral band in the MSFA.

B. Raman et al. (Eds.): CVIP 2021, CCIS 1567, pp. 45–57, 2022.
https://doi.org/10.1007/978-3-031-11346-8_5

As the applications of MSIs are diverse, different multispectral imaging systems [15, 17, 21] are introduced with varying numbers of spectral bands. So there is a need for an efficient generic multispectral image demosaicking method that can be used to generate varying band-size MSI depending on the applications. Many generic multispectral image demosaicking algorithms [1, 2, 13] are proposed, which fail to generate good quality MSIs. Here, we propose a generic multispectral image demosaicking algorithm based on simple non-redundant MSFAs. It uses both spatial and spectral correlation present in the mosaicked image to generate the complete multispectral image. First, we generate a pseudo panchromatic image (PPI) from the mosaicked image. Later, we use the PPI to generate a multispectral image by utilizing spectral correlation between PPI and each undersampled band in the mosaicked image. The PPI has a stronger correlation with each spectral band than bands considered pairwise [15].

The main contributions of our work are as follows: (1) We propose a generic multispectral image demosaicking based on the PPI as it is strongly correlated with each spectral band. (2) We develop a new metric, ANMPSNR, which facilitates one to quickly estimate how better a particular image can be reconstructed from a sparse image acquired using a single sensor camera and helps easily compare the relative performance of different demosaicking algorithms. (3) We also highlight the problem with simple non-redundant MSFAs when used for generic multispectral demosaicking algorithms.

The remaining paper is organized as follows. Section 2 reviews the existing multispectral image demosaicking algorithms. In Sect. 3 and Sect. 4, we describe our proposed algorithm and proposed metric, respectively. Section 5 presents our experimental results on two benchmark multispectral image datasets, and in Sect. 6, we present the conclusion and future work.

2   Related Work

In past years many demosaicking algorithms have been proposed for the different number of bands multispectral images. In this section, we discuss these different demosaicking algorithms [2, 4–6, 12, 14–16, 18, 19, 21] and their related MSFA patterns.

Miao and Qi proposed a first methodical generic MSFA formation method [12] based on a binary tree that can be used to create any number of band MSFA patterns. Miao et al. also proposed a binary tree based edge sensing (BTES) generic demosaicking algorithm [13]. BTES used edge correlation to estimate missing pixel values for each spectral band. BTES only considers spatial correlation to estimate missing pixel values. Therefore, BTES performs poorly, especially on the higher number of band images.

Brauers and Aach proposed a multispectral demosaicking image algorithm [2] which used 6-band simple non-redundant MSFA pattern arranged in 2×3 grid. [2] applied a low-pass filter to each spectral band to estimate the missing pixel values. Further, the quality of generated multispectral images is improved using the inter-band differences method. The simple non-redundant MSFA design patterns and corresponding low-pass filters were later generalized by [6]. Mizutani et al. [16] extended [2] to develop a scheme for a 16-band MSFA image by iterating the interpolation process multiple times. [2] algorithm can be generalized to varying band size multispectral images using filters designed by [6]. In [1], Aggarwal and Majumdar proposed a generic demosaicking algorithm based on learning interpolation parameters based on uniform MSFA patterns. This method requires original multispectral images for learning interpolation parameters, which are practically impossible to obtain in real-time.

Monno et al. [17] proposed a 5-band MSFA pattern based on [12] and a demosaicking algorithm. [17] used the concept of guide image (estimated from G-band), and later guide image is used as a reference image to interpolate remaining under-sampled bands. [17] is restrained to the MSFA patterns having probability of appearance (PoA) of G-band equals to 0.5 in the MSFA pattern, making other bands rigorously under sampled in higher band multispectral images.

Mihoubi et al. [14] proposed a multispectral demosaicking algorithm constrained to square-shaped simple MSFA patterns. Further, in [15], authors had improved their previous work by proposing a new estimation of intensity image. In [21], the authors proposed a 9-band multispectral imaging system based on binary tree based MSFA pattern having PoA of the middle band equals 0.5. The authors first estimate the middle band using image gradient in the demosaicking method and later used this estimated band as a guide image to interpolate other bands.

Rathi et al. [19] proposed a generic multispectral demosaicking approach based on spectral correlation present in the mosaicked image. The proposed approach first applied the bilinear interpolation and later used the spectral correlation differences progressively. However, Some deep learning-based image demosaicking algorithms [7,20] also have been recently suggested. But these algorithms, including [1] require the complete information of multispectral images (not just mosaicked images) for training their model parameters. But, these images will not be available in real practice for MSFA based multispectral camera devices intended to be developed.

3   Proposed Multispectral Demosaicking Algorithm

This paper proposes a generic multispectral image demosaicking algorithm based on spatial and spectral correlation present in the mosaicked image. Our proposed algorithm uses simple non-redundant MSFAs where each band has an equal probability of appearance. Here, we have used the concept of the PPI to estimate the missing pixel values of each spectral band. PPI has a stronger spectral correlation with each band compared to the band considered pair-wise. The PPI is defined at each pixel location as the average over all the spectral bands of a multispectral image.

$$I^{PPI} = \frac{1}{K} \sum_{k=1}^{K} I^k \tag{1}$$

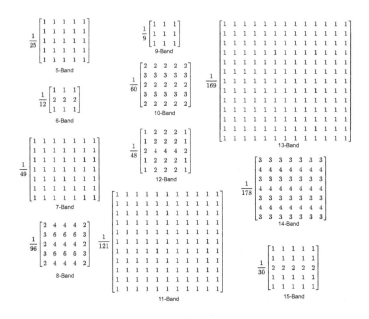

Fig. 1. Spatial filters used to generate the PPI from mosaicked image.

where, I^k is the kth spectral band of multispectral image **I** of size $M \times N \times K$. The size of the PPI is $M \times N$. However, to define the PPI from the mosaicked image, we use spatial filters H defined for each band-size mosaicked image as shown in Fig. 1. We calculate the PPI from mosaicked image for any k-band mosaicked image I_{MSFA} using corresponding filter H.

$$I^{PPI} = I_{MSFA} * H \qquad (2)$$

This spatial filter H is defined to consider at least one instance of each spectral band in the mosaicked image when centered at any pixel location. And the size of H should be the smallest and odd number size (e.g., 3×3, 5×5, 7×7, etc.). Each element of H (e.g., take pixel location (i, j) in H w.r.t. to its center) is set to $\frac{1}{x}$, where x is the number of times when the spectral band at the location (i, j) appears within the window of size of H. And finally, filter H is normalized to in order that all elements of H sum up to one.

The first part of our proposed algorithm estimates the PPI from the mosaicked image and uses it to generate the multispectral image. And in the second part, our algorithm estimates the PPI from the generated multispectral image and uses it to generate the improved version of demosaicked multispectral image. The second part of our proposed algorithm is iterated multiple times further to improve the quality of the generated multispectral image. Our proposed algorithm performs the following steps.

1. Generate the PPI I^{PPI} using Eq. 2.

2. For each band k, determine the sparse band difference $\tilde{\mathcal{D}}^k$ between PPI (I^{PPI}) and band k at the locations of band k in the mosaicked image.

$$\tilde{I}^k = I_{MSFA} \odot m^k \tag{3}$$

$$\tilde{\mathcal{D}}^k = \tilde{I}^k - I^{PPI} \odot m^k \tag{4}$$

where, The binary mask m^k has value 1 only at locations where k^{th} band's original values are present in the mosaicked image.

3. Now compute the fully-defined difference $\hat{\mathcal{D}}^k$ for each band k using Weighted Bilinear (WB) interpolation [6].

4. Now estimate each band k as follow:

$$\hat{I}^k = I^{PPI} + \hat{\mathcal{D}}^k \tag{5}$$

5. Repeat the following steps 6 and 7 a number of times $\mathcal{T}$ to further improve the quality of generated image in step 4.

6. Compute new estimate of the PPI using Eq. 1.

7. Generate multispectral images using steps 2, 3 and 4.

Now, all K bands are fully-defined and together form the complete multi-spectral image $\hat{\mathbf{I}}$.

4   New Proposed Metric: ANMPSNR

Peak signal-to-noise ratio (PSNR) and structure similarity (SSIM) metrics are the most often used performance metrics for comparing multispectral image demosaicking algorithms, and these are computed using the original images and the images reconstructed using the given algorithm(s). However, PSNR has a wide range and is image content dependent, and therefore the relative comparison of different methods becomes challenging. It lacks in giving quick estimation about how better can a particular image be reconstructed from a sparse image acquired using a single sensor camera and some demosaicking algorithm. Here, we propose a new metric ANMPSNR (Average Normalized Multispectral PSNR) which facilitates one to perform such estimation faster and also helps in easily comparing the relative performance of different demosaicking algorithms. For some particular K band n multispectral images and m different demosaicking algorithms considered for comparison, let P^K be a 2-D matrix of size $n \times m$ s.t. $P^K(i, algo)$ denotes the PSNR value obtained for the ith image using demosaicking algorithm $algo$ for the reconstruction. We define ANMPSNR as follows:

$$ANMPSNR^K_{algo} = \left(\frac{1}{n}\right) \sum_{i=1}^{n} \left(\frac{P^K(i, algo)}{max\left(P^K(i,:)\right)} \right) \tag{6}$$

For every image, it considers the relative performance, in terms of PSNR, in reference to the best performing algorithm for that image. It may also be noted that ANMPSNR is always positive, and its maximum value will be 1.

5   Experimental Results and Discussions

In this section, we evaluate the performance of the proposed algorithm and compare it with different generic multispectral image demosaicking algorithms on two benchmarks multispectral image datasets: TokyoTech [17], and Cave [23]. The TokyoTech dataset has 30 images of 31-band captured in the range from 420 nm to 720 nm at the equal spectral gap of 10 nm. The Cave dataset has 31 images of 31-band captured in the range of 400 nm to 700 nm at the equal spectral gap of 10 nm.

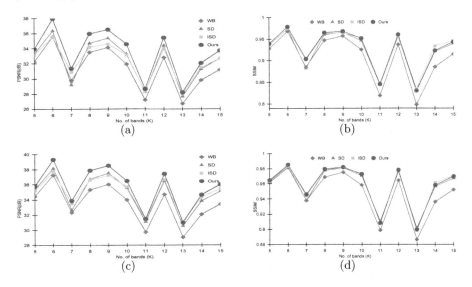

Fig. 2. Performance of different demosaicking algorithms based on simple non-redundant MSFAs. (a, b) Average PSNR and SSIM values, respectively on the TokyoTech dataset. (c, d) Average PSNR and SSIM values, respectively on the Cave dataset.

We evaluate different algorithms on 5-band to 15-band multispectral images. To generate the ground truth K-band multispectral image, we take K-bands at equal spectral gap starting from the first spectral band from the 31-band original image. Then we convert the K-band multispectral image to the mosaicked image based on the MSFA pattern corresponding to band K. We use the demosaicking algorithm to generate the multispectral image from the mosaicked image. To evaluate the efficacy of the demosaicking algorithm by comparing the demosaicked multispectral images with corresponding ground truth multispectral images on different image quality parameters. The value of $\mathcal{T}$ is chosen experimentally. We try different values of $\mathcal{T}$ in range 1 to 20 for different band size images and select the value of $\mathcal{T}$, which results in maximum PSNR value. We compare our proposed algorithm with the existing generic multispectral demosaicking algorithms like WB [6], SD [2], BTES [13], LMSD [1], ISD [16], PBSD [19], and PCBSD [18].

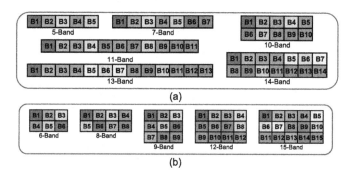

Fig. 3. Simple non-redundant MSFA patterns. (a) Non-compact shaped MSFA patterns. (b) Compact shaped MSFA patterns.

Table 1. Average PSNR values of different generic multispectral image demosaicking algorithms on both the datasets. Note: We consider only those bands where simple non-redundant MSFA patterns have compact shaped for a fair comparison.

K	TokyoTech								Cave							
	WB 2019 [6]	SD 2006 [2]	BTES 2006 [13]	LMSD 2014 [1]	ISD 2014 [16]	PBSD 2021 [19]	PCBSD 2021 [18]	Ours	WB 2019 [6]	SD 2006 [2]	BTES 2006 [13]	LMSD 2014 [1]	ISD 2014 [16]	PBSD 2021 [19]	PCBSD 2021 [18]	Ours
6	35.56	36.37	35.68	33.30	35.55	36.19	36.54	**37.95**	37.26	38.16	38.22	38.65	37.65	38.47	38.57	**39.32**
8	33.49	34.69	34.58	31.43	34.19	35.75	35.78	**35.96**	35.31	36.71	37.17	37.30	36.59	**38.30**	38.22	37.87
9	34.12	35.35	33.99	25.11	34.58	35.31	35.44	**36.50**	36.00	37.51	36.67	29.58	37.20	37.96	37.99	**38.50**
12	32.76	34.35	32.30	25.21	33.92	34.27	34.45	**35.41**	34.66	36.48	34.68	28.95	36.61	36.91	36.91	**37.41**
15	31.15	32.64	31.28	24.02	32.63	33.00	33.21	**33.67**	33.38	35.08	33.88	28.26	35.43	35.72	35.76	**35.98**
Avg.	33.42	34.68	33.57	27.81	34.17	34.90	35.08	**35.90**	35.32	36.79	36.12	32.55	36.70	37.47	37.49	**37.82**

In Fig. 2, we compare different generic demosaicking algorithms which use simple non-redundant MSFAs to capture the mosaicked image. Clearly, our proposed algorithm performs better than all other algorithms in terms of PSNR and SSIM values. Overall, our algorithm shows the improvement of 1.13 dB, and 0.7 dB in the PSNR values average over 5-band to 15-band multispectral images to the second-best performing algorithm on the TokyoTech and the Cave datasets, respectively. We notice the interesting behavior of demosaicking algorithms based on simple non-redundant MSFAs. They perform better on the 6, 8, 9, 12, and 15 bands size images than 5, 7, 10, 11, 13, and 14 bands size images. This is due to the compact nature of simple non-redundant MSFA patterns on the 6, 8, 9, 12, and 15 bands shown in Fig. 3. So for a fair comparison of the efficacy of our proposed algorithm, we compare it with all other generic multispectral demosaicking algorithms only on bands where simple non-redundant MSFA patterns have a compact shape. In Table 1, we show the comparison of our algorithm with all other generic multispectral image demosaicking algorithms in terms of PSNR value. Our algorithm performs better on these bands and shows an improvement of 0.83 dB and 0.33 dB on average over these bands in the PSNR value than PCBSD on the TokyoTech and the Cave datasets, respectively.

Table 2. Comparison of different multispectral image demosaicking algorithms based on ANMPSNR on the Tokyotech and the Cave dataset.

	TokyoTech								Cave							
K	WB 2019 [6]	SD 2006 [2]	BTES 2006 [13]	LMSD 2014 [1]	ISD 2014 [16]	PBSD 2021 [19]	PCBSD 2021 [18]	Ours	WB 2019 [6]	SD 2006 [2]	BTES 2006 [13]	LMSD 2014 [1]	ISD 2014 [16]	PBSD 2021 [19]	PCBSD 2021 [18]	Ours
6	0.931	0.954	0.935	0.881	0.934	0.951	0.960	**0.996**	0.938	0.960	0.962	0.973	0.948	0.968	0.971	**0.990**
8	0.914	0.949	0.944	0.869	0.937	0.979	0.980	**0.984**	0.914	0.951	0.962	0.966	0.948	**0.992**	0.990	0.981
9	0.928	0.963	0.924	0.689	0.943	0.962	0.965	**0.994**	0.931	0.970	0.948	0.766	0.962	0.982	0.983	**0.996**
12	0.919	0.966	0.907	0.713	0.956	0.964	0.968	**0.995**	0.923	0.972	0.924	0.772	0.976	0.984	0.983	**0.997**
15	0.914	0.960	0.918	0.712	0.962	0.972	0.978	**0.990**	0.922	0.969	0.936	0.782	0.979	0.988	0.989	**0.994**
Avg.	0.921	0.958	0.926	0.773	0.946	0.966	0.970	**0.992**	0.925	0.964	0.946	0.852	0.963	0.983	0.983	**0.991**

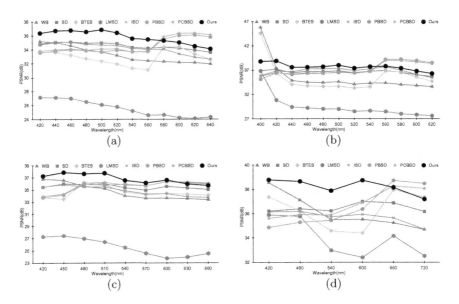

Fig. 4. Average PSNR values of each spectral band of different multispectral image demosaicking algorithms: (a, b) on 12-band multispectral images on the TokyoTech and Cave datasets, respectively. (c) on 9-band multispectral images. (d) on 6-band multispectral images.

In Table 2, we show the performance of these algorithms on the new metric ANMPSNR, and our algorithm shows better performance than other algorithms. Further, it can be noted that the ANMPSNR metric makes it easy and faster to compare different methods relatively. Tables 3 and 4 show the image-wise performance of different algorithms on the multispectral images of 6 and 12 bands from the TokyoTech and the Cave datasets, respectively. Figure 4 shows the PSNR value for each band on 6, 9, and 12-band multispectral images. Our proposed algorithm show almost consistent performance on all bands, whereas other algorithms like LMSD, BTES PBSD, and PCBSD show varying performance on different bands.

Figures 5 and 6 show the visual comparison of the sRGB images generated by the different multispectral image demosaicking algorithms for 6 and 12 bands

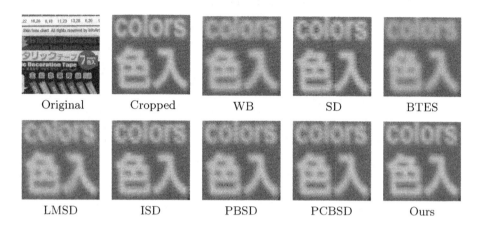

Original	Cropped	WB	SD	BTES
LMSD	ISD	PBSD	PCBSD	Ours

Fig. 5. Visual comparison of sRGB images generated from the 6 bands MSIs.

Table 3. Comparison of PSNR(dB) values for different multispectral image demosaicking methods on 30 images of the TokyoTech dataset.

	6-band								12-band							
Image	[6]	[2]	[13]	[1]	[16]	[19]	[18]	Ours	[6]	[2]	[13]	[1]	[16]	[19]	[18]	Ours
B.fly	36.8	37.6	36.6	37.4	35.7	37.1	37.6	**38.5**	33.9	35.4	33.4	25.3	34.0	35.2	35.5	**35.8**
B.fly2	32.0	31.2	30.6	30.9	30.8	30.6	31.0	**32.7**	27.9	28.6	26.8	21.0	28.4	28.0	28.4	**29.5**
B.fly3	39.4	40.8	38.9	39.3	40.6	40.4	40.8	**42.8**	35.5	37.7	34.5	27.2	37.6	37.0	37.5	**38.8**
B.fly4	38.7	40.8	38.1	39.6	40.2	40.5	40.5	**42.7**	35.0	37.6	34.1	27.9	37.5	37.6	37.6	**39.2**
B.fly5	38.2	40.4	37.6	37.1	40.4	39.9	40.0	**42.4**	34.7	37.4	33.7	25.2	37.7	37.1	37.3	**38.6**
B.fly6	35.1	36.4	34.7	34.9	36.4	36.4	36.7	**38.7**	31.6	33.5	30.8	24.4	34.1	33.5	33.7	**35.3**
B.fly7	39.7	41.6	39.0	40.4	41.5	41.2	41.3	**43.7**	36.1	39.1	34.9	27.8	39.6	38.9	38.9	**40.8**
B.fly8	37.6	40.4	37.2	38.7	39.5	40.1	40.3	**42.0**	34.4	37.5	33.9	26.7	37.3	37.5	37.5	**38.5**
CD	41.2	39.3	**41.3**	30.1	36.6	37.7	38.5	40.6	**37.8**	36.2	36.0	19.5	32.0	34.5	35.8	36.9
Charctr	32.3	35.9	31.9	34.6	36.9	36.0	35.5	**40.1**	27.7	32.3	27.0	20.4	34.0	32.3	32.1	**36.3**
Cloth	32.2	34.0	31.3	31.3	33.3	33.9	34.1	**36.1**	28.8	31.7	28.0	22.5	31.4	31.5	31.5	**33.2**
Cloth2	32.8	33.5	33.6	32.6	33.5	**34.5**	34.4	34.2	32.0	33.7	32.1	28.8	**34.3**	33.9	33.8	34.2
Cloth3	34.8	37.0	35.6	34.7	37.8	38.6	38.4	**38.7**	32.5	34.5	32.5	28.0	**35.4**	35.3	35.1	35.1
Cloth4	33.8	36.6	33.9	32.1	37.3	37.7	37.6	**39.1**	30.9	34.0	30.6	25.7	35.3	34.8	34.5	**35.4**
Cloth5	32.7	33.4	34.9	32.4	34.1	35.3	**35.4**	34.7	33.0	33.3	34.2	29.6	33.5	**34.8**	34.7	33.8
Cloth6	40.7	39.9	40.7	31.8	37.6	38.9	39.6	**41.0**	39.1	39.0	39.4	30.5	37.2	38.7	39.0	**39.5**
Color	**42.4**	40.4	41.4	38.6	38.8	38.2	39.0	40.6	**37.5**	37.3	35.3	24.9	35.5	35.6	36.2	36.4
C.chart	44.5	43.4	**46.1**	37.1	40.6	42.4	43.4	44.6	41.3	41.7	40.7	29.0	38.9	40.8	41.8	**42.2**
Doll	26.8	27.8	26.9	27.7	27.6	28.1	28.2	**28.5**	24.7	26.4	24.8	21.4	26.6	**26.7**	26.5	26.6
Fan	28.1	28.9	28.2	28.5	28.1	28.8	29.2	**30.1**	25.8	26.9	25.9	20.6	26.5	26.9	26.9	**27.6**
Fan2	30.7	31.5	31.3	31.0	30.1	31.2	31.9	**33.3**	27.8	29.3	28.0	21.9	28.3	29.2	29.4	**30.6**
Fan3	30.2	31.1	30.6	31.3	30.1	31.0	31.5	**32.7**	27.3	29.0	27.3	21.7	28.4	29.0	29.1	**30.1**
Flower	44.1	43.5	45.2	29.0	40.9	42.7	43.8	**45.4**	42.6	43.9	41.7	29.5	42.2	43.9	44.3	**45.6**
Flower2	44.5	43.4	**45.6**	31.5	40.9	42.6	43.6	45.3	43.8	43.8	42.6	30.6	41.2	43.5	44.0	**45.0**

(continued)

Table 3. (*continued*)

Image	6-band								12-band							
	[6]	[2]	[13]	[1]	[16]	[19]	[18]	Ours	[6]	[2]	[13]	[1]	[16]	[19]	[18]	Ours
Flower3	45.5	43.9	**45.8**	31.6	41.2	42.6	43.7	45.6	43.4	44.2	42.5	30.1	41.8	43.7	44.3	**45.9**
Party	31.8	31.8	33.4	32.1	30.5	31.8	32.4	**33.4**	28.9	29.9	29.4	24.7	28.8	29.8	30.2	**31.4**
Tape	32.0	32.5	32.2	31.3	32.3	32.7	32.7	**33.6**	28.8	29.5	28.9	24.3	29.7	29.7	29.6	**30.3**
Tape2	34.6	35.1	34.1	35.5	34.5	35.0	35.1	**36.8**	31.1	32.0	31.0	25.9	32.0	31.8	32.0	**32.9**
Tshirts	26.1	28.6	25.6	27.0	28.5	29.0	29.0	**29.7**	23.5	27.0	23.1	18.8	**28.3**	27.5	27.2	28.0
Tshirts2	27.7	30.1	28.2	29.0	30.2	30.9	30.9	**31.2**	25.6	28.4	26.0	22.7	**30.0**	29.4	29.1	29.3
Avg.	35.6	36.4	35.7	33.3	35.6	36.2	36.5	**38.0**	32.8	34.4	32.3	25.2	33.9	34.3	34.4	**35.4**

Table 4. Comparison of PSNR(dB) values for different multispectral image demosaicking methods on 31 images of the Cave dataset.

Image	6-band								12-band							
	[6]	[2]	[13]	[1]	[16]	[19]	[18]	Ours	[6]	[2]	[13]	[1]	[16]	[19]	[18]	Ours
balloon	42.8	43.9	43.6	44.3	43.3	44.1	44.2	**45.4**	39.7	41.4	39.7	31.9	41.1	41.2	41.8	**42.6**
beads	29.3	29.8	29.6	29.0	28.6	29.7	29.9	**30.8**	26.7	27.6	26.6	21.2	26.1	27.6	27.9	**28.3**
cd	38.9	38.6	**40.3**	37.4	37.6	38.4	38.7	39.5	37.3	37.6	37.5	27.9	35.6	37.4	37.7	**38.3**
chart&toy	31.9	33.3	32.6	**35.4**	33.3	33.9	33.7	34.3	29.1	31.1	29.2	24.4	31.9	31.8	31.5	**32.0**
clay	39.8	40.1	**42.9**	40.3	38.8	41.5	41.9	41.2	37.3	37.8	36.7	31.5	36.6	38.5	**39.2**	38.9
cloth	31.0	32.1	31.2	31.1	32.1	32.1	32.1	**33.4**	28.9	31.4	28.9	25.3	**32.5**	32.1	31.6	32.1
egy._stat	40.4	41.7	41.0	42.6	41.3	41.8	41.9	**42.9**	38.0	40.0	38.1	32.6	40.4	40.6	40.4	**40.9**
face	40.7	41.6	41.6	42.4	41.2	41.5	41.5	**42.9**	37.9	39.8	38.0	32.0	40.2	40.5	40.3	**40.6**
f&r_beers	41.4	41.5	41.6	41.2	40.7	40.9	41.1	**42.9**	38.1	39.2	37.8	29.6	39.1	39.1	39.2	**40.3**
f&r_food	40.0	40.3	40.0	39.4	39.3	39.7	40.0	**41.4**	37.2	38.9	36.6	29.6	38.5	38.9	38.9	**39.5**
f&r_lemnSlc	36.0	36.9	36.4	36.8	36.8	36.9	36.8	**37.7**	33.8	35.7	34.0	28.5	**36.4**	36.2	35.9	36.0
f&r_lemons	40.0	41.5	41.2	**42.8**	41.5	42.1	41.9	42.6	37.0	39.0	37.3	31.3	**40.0**	39.8	39.6	40.0
f&r_peppers	39.4	40.3	40.8	41.4	39.5	40.7	40.9	**41.7**	35.8	38.4	35.9	31.2	38.6	39.0	39.1	**40.0**
f&r_strawb	38.4	40.0	39.3	40.5	39.9	40.3	40.3	**41.1**	36.0	38.4	36.0	30.3	**39.3**	39.1	38.7	39.3
f&r_sushi	39.0	39.6	38.7	39.1	39.4	39.3	39.3	**40.8**	35.8	37.9	35.3	29.2	38.5	38.3	38.1	**38.6**
f&r_tomat	36.6	38.0	36.5	38.1	38.1	38.0	37.8	**38.6**	33.7	36.1	33.6	29.2	**37.3**	36.7	36.3	36.2
feathers	33.2	34.4	34.6	35.0	33.8	35.3	35.5	**35.9**	30.7	32.9	31.2	26.8	33.1	33.8	33.7	**34.2**
flowers	38.5	38.8	39.8	37.8	37.3	38.7	39.4	**40.3**	37.2	38.4	37.4	30.8	37.5	38.6	38.8	**39.5**
glass_tiles	28.7	29.7	30.5	**31.5**	29.7	30.8	30.9	30.7	26.6	28.4	27.3	25.1	29.1	29.1	29.0	**29.2**
hairs	40.1	41.8	41.3	**43.5**	41.9	42.7	42.5	42.6	38.1	40.6	38.2	32.9	**41.7**	41.3	40.9	41.3
jelly_bea.	30.7	32.4	31.6	32.2	32.0	32.9	33.1	**33.6**	28.3	31.0	28.7	23.6	31.5	31.8	31.6	**31.8**
oil_paint.	31.6	31.9	33.2	**34.6**	31.9	34.2	33.8	32.0	30.9	32.5	31.3	28.2	**33.6**	32.9	32.6	32.6
paints	32.5	33.2	33.2	34.3	32.6	33.1	33.3	**35.7**	28.1	30.4	28.5	22.1	31.2	31.1	31.1	**32.7**
photo&face	39.3	40.8	40.3	**42.5**	40.4	40.9	41.1	41.9	36.4	38.5	36.2	30.8	38.3	38.5	38.6	**39.5**
pompoms	40.2	40.2	40.7	38.7	39.0	40.0	40.4	**41.3**	38.1	38.7	37.7	29.4	37.0	38.2	38.9	**39.4**
r&f_apples	42.9	44.1	44.1	45.2	44.0	44.5	44.5	**45.3**	39.6	41.6	39.9	32.9	42.3	**42.6**	42.4	42.5
r&f_peppr	40.3	41.9	41.6	**43.5**	41.8	42.6	42.4	43.0	37.3	39.4	37.6	31.1	40.2	40.1	40.0	**40.4**
sponges	38.2	38.5	39.9	39.0	37.4	38.7	39.0	**40.1**	35.1	36.1	35.1	27.4	35.3	36.0	36.7	**36.9**
stuf._toys	40.2	40.5	41.0	38.9	38.8	39.9	40.5	**41.9**	37.2	39.0	36.4	27.6	37.9	38.6	38.9	**40.5**
superballs	39.5	40.0	40.2	40.0	39.4	40.1	40.1	**40.9**	37.8	39.7	36.6	31.7	39.2	39.8	40.0	**40.5**
thrd_spls	33.6	35.5	35.8	**39.7**	35.9	37.3	37.1	36.7	31.1	33.5	32.0	31.7	35.1	**35.2**	35.0	35.1
Avg.	37.3	38.2	38.2	38.6	37.7	38.5	38.6	**39.3**	34.7	36.5	34.7	29.0	36.6	36.9	36.9	**37.4**

multispectral images. Our proposed algorithm reproduces the sRGB images more accurately than the other MSID algorithms with fewer artifacts. PBSD and PCBSD produce zipper artifacts around the edges, whereas WB and BTES produce blurry images.

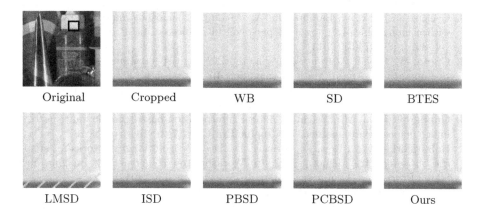

| Original | Cropped | WB | SD | BTES |

| LMSD | ISD | PBSD | PCBSD | Ours |

Fig. 6. Visual comparison of sRGB images generated from the 12 bands MSIs.

6   Conclusion and Future Work

We proposed a generic multispectral image demosaicking algorithm based on the PPI, which uses both spatial and spectral correlation present in the mosaicked image. The PPI is considered to have a stronger correlation with each band than bands are examined pair-wise. We show that compact-shaped simple non-redundant MSFA patterns achieve better demosaicking performance than non-compact-shaped simple non-redundant MSFA patterns. We also proposed a new performance evaluation metric for an easy and faster relative comparison of MSID methods. We evaluated the performance of the proposed MSID algorithm by comparing it with other existing generic MSID algorithms on multiple multi-spectral image datasets. Considering different performance metrics and also the visual assessment, the proposed algorithm's performance is consistently observed better than the existing generic multispectral image demosaicking algorithm on simple compact-shaped non-redundant MSFAs. In the future, we plan to extend it to binary tree based patterns [12] which are considered compact as compared to simple non-redundant MSFA patterns.

Acknowledgement. This work is sponsored by the DST Science and Engineering Research Board, India, under grant ECR/2017/003478.

References

1. Aggarwal, H.K., Majumdar, A.: Single-sensor multi-spectral image demosaicing algorithm using learned interpolation weights. In: Proceedings of the International Geoscience and Remote Sensing Symposium, pp. 2011–2014 (2014)
2. Brauers, J., Aach, T.: A color filter array based multispectral camera. In: 12 Workshop Farbbildverarbeitung, pp. 55–64 (2006)
3. Geelen, B., Tack, N., Lambrechts, A.: A compact snapshot multispectral imager with a monolithically integrated per-pixel filter mosaic. In: Proceeding of SPIE, vol. 8974, p. 89740L (2014)
4. Gupta, M., Goyal, P.: Demosaicing method for multispectral images using derivative operations. Am. J. Math. Manag. Sci. **40**(2), 163–176 (2021)
5. Gupta, M., Goyal, P., Ram, M.: Multispectral image demosaicking using limited MSFA sensors. Nonlinear Stud. **26**(3), 1–16 (2019)
6. Gupta, M., Ram, M.: Weighted bilinear interpolation based generic multispectral image demosaicking method. J. Graphic Era Univ. **7**(2), 108–118 (2019)
7. Habtegebrial, T.A., Reis, G., Stricker, D.: Deep convolutional networks for snapshot hypercpectral demosaicking. In: Workshop on Hyperspectral Imaging and Signal Processing: Evolution in Remote Sensing, pp. 1–5 (2019)
8. Jinju, J., Santhi, N., Ramar, K., Bama, B.S.: Spatial frequency discrete wavelet transform image fusion technique for remote sensing applications. Eng. Sci. Technol. Int. J. **2**(3), 715–726 (2019)
9. Liu, C., et al.: Application of multispectral imaging to determine quality attributes and ripeness stage in strawberry fruit. PLoS ONE **9**(2), 1–8 (2014)
10. Lu, G., Fei, B.: Medical hyperspectral imaging: a review. J. Biomed Optics **19**(1), 010901 (2014)
11. Martinez, M.A., Valero, E.M., Hernández-Andrés, J., Romero, J., Langfelder, G.: Combining transverse field detectors and color filter arrays to improve multispectral imaging systems. Appl. Optics **53**(13), C14–C24 (2014)
12. Miao, L., Qi, H.: The design and evaluation of a generic method for generating mosaicked multispectral filter arrays. IEEE Trans. Image Process. **15**(9), 2780–2791 (2006)
13. Miao, L., Ramanath, R., Snyder, W.E.: Binary tree-based generic demosaicking algorithm for multispectral filter arrays. IEEE Trans. Image Process. **15**(11), 3550–3558 (2006)
14. Mihoubi, S., Losson, O., Mathon, B., Macaire, L.: Multispectral demosaicking using intensity-based spectral correlation. In: Proceedings of the 5th International Conference on Image Processing, Theory, Tools and Applications, pp. 461–466 (2015)
15. Mihoubi, S., Losson, O., Mathon, B., Macaire, L.: Multispectral demosaicing using pseudo-panchromatic image. IEEE Trans. Comput. Imag. **3**(4), 982–995 (2017)
16. Mizutani, J., Ogawa, S., Shinoda, K., Hasegawa, M., Kato, S.: Multispectral demosaicking algorithm based on inter-channel correlation. In: Proceedings of the IEEE Visual Communications and Image Processing Conference, pp. 474–477 (2014)
17. Monno, Y., Kikuchi, S., Tanaka, M., Okutomi, M.: A practical one-shot multispectral imaging system using a single image sensor. IEEE Trans. Image Process. **24**(10), 3048–3059 (2015)
18. Rathi, V., Goyal, P.: Convolution filter based efficient multispectral image demosaicking for compact msfas. In: Proceedings of International Joint Conference on Computer Vision, Imaging and Computer Graphics, Theory and Application: VISAPP, pp. 112–121 (2021)

19. Rathi, V., Gupta, M., Goyal, P.: A new generic progressive approach based on spectral difference for single-sensor multispectral imaging system. In: Proceedings of International Joint Conference on Computer Vision, Imaging and Computer Graphics, Theory and Applications: VISAPP, pp. 329–336 (2021)
20. Shopovska, I., Jovanov, L., Philips, W.: RGB-NIR demosaicing using deep residual u-net. In: 26th Telecommunications Forum, pp. 1–4 (2018)
21. Sun, B., et al.: Sparse spectral signal reconstruction for one proposed nine-band multispectral imaging system. Mech. Syst. Signal Process. **141**, 106627 (2020)
22. Thomas, J.B., Lapray, P.J., Gouton, P., Clerc, C.: Spectral characterization of a prototype SFA camera for joint visible and NIR acquisition. Sensor **16**, 993 (2016)
23. Yasuma, F., Mitsunaga, T., Iso, D., Nayar, S.: Generalized assorted pixel camera: postcapture control of resolution, dynamic range, and spectrum. IEEE Trans. Image Process. **19**(9), 2241–2253 (2010)

A Platform for Large Scale Auto Annotation of Scanned Documents Featuring Real-Time Model Building and Model Pooling

Komuravelli Prashanth⬤, Boyalakuntla Kowndinya⬤, Chilaka Vijay⬤,
Dande Teja⬤, Vidya Rodge, Ramya Velaga, Reena Abasaheb Deshmukh,
and Yeturu Kalidas$^{(\boxtimes)}$⬤

Indian Institute of Technology Tirupati, Tirupati, India
ykalidas@iittp.ac.in

Abstract. Document digitization is an active area of research especially involving handwritten manuscripts. While the most common use cases involve digital libraries, there are other important applications in the area of electronic health records where handwritten text is predominant in developing worlds. The state-of-the-art approaches are domain-specific, and scaling across domains is still an open research problem. We report here a platform for real-time annotation and training of sub-region models in scanned documents using *model pools* and *plug-n-play of annotation services*. Given a document, sub-regions are annotated with textual labels. The textual regions themselves may correspond to characters or words or any other pattern of interest. For a given sub-region category, several sub-regions may be present in a given page or across pages. In the proposed system, a user needs to annotate only some of the sub-regions. A convolutional neural network (CNN) model is built for each of the sub-region categories, and *named sets or pools* of such models are prepared for application on any new document. We observe that a sub-region label may be provided by an existing optical character recognition system instead of a human annotator. In this regard, we have provisioned annotation as a service where any third-party system can be integrated into a plug-n-play mechanism. The state-of-the-art systems focused on having a pre-trained monolithic model which suffers from the problem of catastrophic forgetting when new sub-region classes are added over time. In our approach, due to sub-region specific models, the previous data models are not touched and hence providing a truly incremental learning solution. We have carried out the validation by choosing handwritten data sets belonging to different languages such as Devanagari, Kannada, Telugu, English that span diverse text patterns and the models produced by our sub-region detection algorithm were evaluated on documents containing hundreds of handwritten scripts by several authors. With respect to the performance of our models on the validation data sets, we found mAP scores for different data sets as follows: Devanagari words (96.18); Telugu words (93.20); Devanagari letters (100); Kannada letters (99.83); Tesseract English word-level annotations (90). We have

© The Author(s), under exclusive license to Springer Nature Switzerland AG 2022
B. Raman et al. (Eds.): CVIP 2021, CCIS 1567, pp. 58–70, 2022.
https://doi.org/10.1007/978-3-031-11346-8_6

also presented a single page annotation as proof of concept for annotation as a service for Kannada, Telugu, Malayalam, and English recognition to learn from Tesseract annotations.

Keywords: Annotation · Sub-region · Convolutional neural network · Model pool · Annotation as a service · Optical character recognition

1 Introduction

Document digitization involves annotation of sub-regions of scanned documents from across diverse domains and content categories. There are efforts worldwide on building state-of-the-art optical character recognition systems. However, they are specific to a given language, time period, and domain setting [14]. Some of the popular examples include Tesseract [19], E-aksharayan[1], OCRopus [11], and OCR Feeder[2]. For instance, Tesseract requires the following procedure: 1) pre processing of the image, 2) text localization 3) character segmentation 4) character recognition and 5) post processing. Similar procedures will follow in other OCR engines. A document with mixed text from two or more languages or patterns requires coordination between many disparate OCR engines. With this, the training time, ease of handling data, and combination of outputs become a challenge. Building one single system from scratch catering to diverse document content needs is extremely hard, if not impossible. However, we can have a system that unifies and leverages decades of effort into a single framework.

There are sub-region annotation data sets and platforms for general images [6, 18]. However, these applications do not make use of document-specific features of a sub-region. Also, the regions are comparatively larger than those of characters or words or textual regions peculiar to a document scenario.

Machine learning approaches involving a single monolithic model for multiple classes suffer from catastrophic forgetting when retrained on newer classes of data [16]. In the case of document sub-regions, the number of categories is expected to be several hundreds, and they arrive over time. Retraining the whole model would result in unwanted fluctuations in past predictions.

Some algorithms use ensemble or stack of models for a given task [10,15]. In an ensemble, each model is tightly related to the other model when their scores are combined to result in a single stronger model. However, the purpose of the ensemble is different from the concept of a model pool where individual sub-region models predict simultaneously on a given data point and especially a document in our scenario. We found tools such as *TagTog*[13], *Kconnect*[3] doing automatic text-based annotations using NLP models. In contrast, we did not find any tool in the field of image content retrieval that does auto-annotation of text in the scanned documents.

---

[1] http://ocr.tdil-dc.gov.in.

[2] https://wiki.gnome.org/Apps/OCRFeeder.

[3] http://kconnect.eu/semantic-annotation-for-medical-texts.

Annotation data set creation tools such as *Lionbridge AI* [7], *VIA Annotation Software* [3], *Microsoft VoTT*[4], and *Labelme* [2] only support manual annotation to create and export annotated data, thus limited to providing a tool kit to enable human annotations. There are tools such as CVAT[5] that provide automatic annotation support along with human annotation support by keeping the state-of-the-art object detection and text detection models at the back-end. However, this tool does not build models on the fly based on human annotations.

Table 1 elucidates whether the existing tools can support auto-annotation of text, building models based on user annotations, and whether the tools can extend support to documents from different languages. The column *Model building on the fly* implies whether the tool can create models for annotating text on the fly based on given user annotations. All the existing tools mentioned do not support automatic annotation of text for mixed language content.

Table 1. Feature check for existing tools for - (1) Manual annotation, (2) Auto-annotation, (3) Model building on the fly, (4) User-specific models, (5) Multi-lingual aspect, (6) Plug-n-play annotation services

Existing tools	(1)	(2)	(3)	(4)	(5)	(6)
TagTog	Yes	Yes	No	No	Yes	No
Kconnect and Lionbridge AI	Yes	Yes	No	No	No	No
VIA Annotation Software, Microsoft VoTT and Labelme	Yes	No	No	No	Yes	No
CVAT	Yes	No	No	No	No	No
Annotator (Our Platform)	**yes**	**yes**	**yes**	**yes**	**yes**	**yes**

The annotated sub-regions form data sets for each of the models. From a data set point of view, the annotators need not be restricted to the human users. A software program can provide the data set as well. In this regard, we have defined a web service API to provision annotation as a service. This mechanism allows plug-n-play addition of existing OCR systems thereby making the platform scalable across domains.

In this context, we report here a platform named *Annotator* for large-scale, crowd enabled, and domain agnostic document content annotation and retrieval. Our annotation platform supports 2D annotations by humans on document images and provides automatic annotation support by building AI models from human annotations. Our approach involves building sub-region specific data sets as part of the annotation interface. These data sets are then used to build light-weight single-class models. A number of such single-class models are actively applied when predicting a new input document. We leverage the fact that we are dealing with document content where many instances of the same sub-regions of a particular type have almost identical dimensions. Retraining models for one sub-region type without touching others would ensure plug-and-play capability to address newer classes of data over time and modifications. The annotation

---

[4] https://github.com/microsoft/VoTT.
[5] https://github.com/openvinotoolkit/cvat.

platform we developed provides a close-to-real-time interface to human users with respect to model training and the pattern learning algorithm was developed to remain domain and use-case agnostic for scanned documents.

The rest of the paper is organized as follows: In Sect. 2 we begin by introducing the platform by providing the definitions for key terms used to explain the platform and address the design of both the front-end and back-end of the platform. We explain the algorithm in the Sect. 3, and the data sets used for validation in Sect. 4. We describe the user scenario in Sect. 5. We present the results in Sect. 6, and conclude the paper with Sect. 7.

2   System Design

In this section, we describe the design of the *Annotator* platform by introducing the important terms that describe the platform. We present the details of the platform in Sect. 2.2.

2.1   Overview of the Platform

The platform *Annotator* features an annotation interface/area where users work on annotating the scanned documents and an auto-annotation engine that manages and builds CNN models [5] for the respective annotation classes. A desirable feature for our platform is to allow users an easy image annotation experience. We used LabelMe [2], a web-based tool to perform sub-region annotation for a given input document. Auto-annotation engine fetches semantic labels to the sub-regions marked by annotators. In this section, we provide the important terms to understand the platform in the Table 2. In the following section, we describe the design and development of *Annotator*.

Table 2. Important terms and definitions

Key terms	Definition
Annotation	Name/Label assigned by the user for a sub-region in the scanned document
Sub-region	An area selected in the image by the user that semantically represents text
Annotation class	A distinct sub-region/pattern in the image. Also called sub-region category
CNN models	Machine Learning models trained using CNN to predict(label) the sub-regions in the image
Anti-pattern	Salt and Peppered (Noised) sub-region or non-pattern context
Pattern	The sub-region given as positive instance of training data
Salt and Peppered sub-region	Noised version of the pattern created by the algorithm in the model training phase
Auto-annotations	Annotations made by the CNN models
Model pool	A model set ($>= 2$ models) created by the user to predict several annotation classes
AP (Average Precision)	Area under Precision-Recall curve of a CNN model
MAP (Mean AP)	AP averaged over several annotation classes (One CNN model works on one Annotation Class)

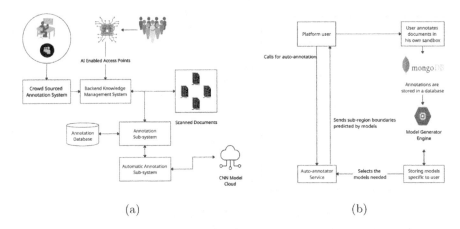

(a)   (b)

Fig. 1. Platform overview and user work flow - (a) Annotation platform overview and
(b) Sequence of steps involved in annotation, model building and prediction

2.2   Design Details of *Annotator*

We developed the *Annotator* as a web-based platform that enables users to log in
to their work-space and annotate documents entirely in an isolated environment.
Figure 1b details the process involved that an user would go through, while
using the application. The platform provides an interface to the end-users of
diverse categories serving a crowd annotation setting as depicted in Fig. 1a. This
section describes the design of the platform *Annotator* uncovering the front-end
and back-end of the platform. This section also details the work-flow of microservices [8] in the system and features the platform provides.

Web-Interface. The annotation area is provided to the user as a web-interface
and this constitutes the front-end of the platform. The following functionalities
describe the design of the front-end:

- All the annotated data is stored separately for each user, and so are the CNN
  models stored
- Users can work on different scanned documents, and the convolutional neural
  network(CNN) models users built can be used interchangeably across all the
  documents
- Users can also retrain the model for a sub-region
- All the models built by the user are shown in the model selection area on the
  same web page
- Users can pool a set of models (model pools) to auto-annotate several sub-
  region types (categories) at once

Auto-Annotation Engine. The creation and management of the CNN models
are handled by the auto-annotation engine. This constitutes the back-end of

the platform. The auto-annotation engine serves user requests from the web interface. Auto-annotation engine manages the machine learning models in a distributed fashion. Each CNN model is a single-class model. Auto-annotation engine builds single-class models for each sub-region category (annotation class). The design of the back-end describes the following functionalities:

- One CNN model will be built and stored for each annotation class
- Any number of CNN models can be activated to annotate the sub-regions for a document
- Input data to build the CNN model is the meta-data containing sub-region coordinates, annotation, and the document
- The annotated data predicted by models (auto-annotated data) broadly consists of sub-region coordinates and annotation class names along with other meta-data

3   Methodology

Traditional sub-region annotation algorithms use a single monolithic CNN model. However such an approach poses problems when newer classes are to be retrained. A retraining step disturbs the previous working behaviour of the CNN model on previous classes which is widely known as catastrophic forgetting problem. To address this, we have built one CNN model for each of the sub-region category. In general in a scanned document, multiple occurrences of a character or word would maintain the same shape and visual appearance. This is a critical observation to be leveraged upon. In case of general purpose images consistency of pixel content for a given category is not followed. For instance a person category will have rectangular sub-regions whose contents change drastically from one person to another person and its context. Based on this important peculiar characteristic we have built a class specific CNN of lower complexity have fewer layers than its monolithic counterpart.

The special cases such as correction of character label based on other characters falls into the domain aspect. Here again, we observe that the task of correction coming into picture, if at all a character is identified for a sub-region in a scanned document. Once an identification happens, then the correction can be addressed in the *post-processing* phase using models such as [12]

3.1   CNN Based Sub-region Specific Models

We used our CNN algorithm for the exclusion of non-patterns in a scanned document for learning individual patterns. In a convolutional neural network, filter learning depends not only on the abundance of patterns of interest but also on the presence of a non-pattern context. For training the model, an input image is a document, which is a combination of pattern of interest and non-pattern context. The non-pattern context can be other sub-region types or salt and pepper noised version of the pattern. Figure 2a is an example of synthetically generated train document with pepper noise as non-pattern and its corresponding label. We create n number of synthetic documents using manual annotations by following Algorithm 1.

Algorithm 1. Schematic for synthetic document generation

1: Select manually annotated sub-regions for a given sub-region class
2: Repeat the sub-regions on random locations in an empty canvas
3: Randomly select annotations for other sub-region classes or pepper noise as non-pattern
4: Implant non-pattern patches in the same document image in remaining empty locations

---

The steps of building a CNN model for a sub-region class are described below:

1. Creating synthetic documents by placing manual annotations for a sub-region class along with non-pattern context on empty canvases based on Algorithm 1
2. Creating a label for each synthetic document by creating another canvas having the same dimensions as document which corresponds to the presence or absence of pattern at the level of middle pixel
3. Build a per class simpler network as shown in Fig. 3 instead of deep monolithic model

Figure 2a shows sample synthetic train image created with the help of manual annotations and its corresponding label. The algorithm serves as a kernel in the automatic annotation of digital documents in diverse scenarios such as ancient manuscripts and handwritten health records.

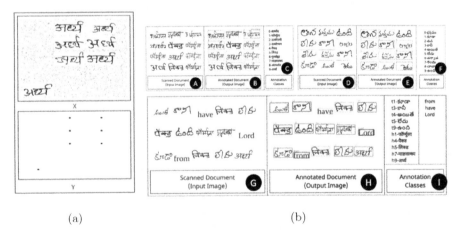

(a)   (b)

Fig. 2. Synthetic document and pattern generations - (a) sample train document image and its label and (b) pattern(sub-region) prediction by CNN algorithm for Devanagari and Telugu words.

3.2   Training Methodology

The loss function is formulated as a multi-layer convolutional pattern mapping problem from input tensor to output tensor. Input tensor corresponds to canvas tiled with optimal amount of pattern where as output tensor corresponds to another canvas of same size determines presence of pattern at middle pixel level. We have used Adam optimizer with learning rate of 0.001 for our experiments.

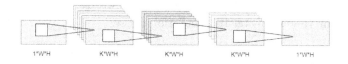

Fig. 3. Simple layer network architecture

3.3   Model Pooling

On a given document, a pool of models would be selected which simultaneously carry out annotation. The algorithm is novel in terms of employing a pool of multiple sub-region specific models. Each model itself is a very simpler network having just 3 to 4 layers apart from input layer (as shown in Fig. 3). As the users work with hundreds of models each day, helping users to pool models of their choice can help them deal with models efficiently. We have created two model pools namely *pool-devanagari*, and *pool-telugu*. They each contain 10 models for 10 annotation classes belonging to Devanagari and Telugu languages respectively. Figure 2b[A], Fig. 2b[B], Fig. 2c[C] collectively show the predictions made by the model pool *pool-devanagari*. Figure 2b[D], 2b[E], 2b[F] depict the pattern prediction for Telugu words, and Fig. 2b[G], 2b[H], 2b[I] depict the pattern prediction for document containing mixed language words.

4   Data Sets

The Devanagari script consists of 47 primary characters. This data set[6] contains only 36 character classes and 40 annotations for each class. We experimented on all the 36 character classes containing a total sum of 1.4K images. In the literature, Kannada language has 53 primary characters. This data set[7] is a collection of 25 image annotations for each of the 53 character classes. We experimented on 1.3K images belonging to all the 53 character classes. This data set [1] contains around 10K annotations for each of the 26 English capital alphabets. We experimented the entire data set. The Telugu script consists of 56 primary characters. This data set[8] contains 16 annotation classes and each annotation class contains

---

[6] http://www.iapr-tc11.org/mediawiki/index.php?title=Devanagari_Character_ Dataset.

[7] http://www.ee.surrey.ac.uk/CVSSP/demos/chars74k/.

[8] https://www.pseudoaj.com/2016/05/pseudoajdataset0-telugu-handwritten.html.

330 annotations. We have carried out our validations on all the 16 character classes containing a total sum of 5.3K images. Kannada handwritten digits data set [17] consists 6K annotations for each of the 10 Kannada digit classes. We have carried out our experiments on all the 60K present in this data set. MNIST handwritten digits data set[9] consists 6K annotations each for 10 digit classes. We have done our experiments on all the 60K annotations. The Devanagari words data set [4] consists of 90K annotations for different word classes, we have built models and carried out validations on 10 annotation classes. The Telugu words data set [9] contains 120K annotations for several words, we have built models and carried out validations on 10 annotation classes.

5   User Scenario

Consider a developer A who would like to add a feature that automatically analyzes medical prescription text in his startup application that sells medicines online. The application intends to ask users to upload medical prescriptions by the local doctors, and then it automatically recognizes the handwritten text to find appropriate medicines and adds them to the cart, thereby improving the overall user experience while purchasing medicines. Developer A manually collects the meaning for several handwriting patterns on prescriptions. Developer wishes to use the *Annotator* platform, so that it might help him reduce the workload to create the large data set.

Once A logins into the platform, it is displayed with the links to the documents to be annotated; once it selects a document, it is then navigated to the page to annotate a particular document (as shown in Fig. 4). It can use the drawing button (to the left of the page in Fig. 4[A]) to draw a bounding a box and the bounding box around the sub-region will be highlighted on the image as shown in Fig. 4[B], consequently it can see the annotations in a rectangular box at the right side of the page (Fig. 4[C]). The regions in the Fig. 4[A], [B], and [C] represent the annotation area. To build a model, A provides the name of the sub-region as shown in Fig. 4[E] and starts training the model with the button (in Fig. 4[F]). A receives the acknowledgement message after model building/failure (Fig. 4[D]). These two regions constitute the model-building area. Once the models are built by the model-generator engine in the back-end, A can select the sub-regions to be annotated by selecting models available (this is shown in Fig. 4[G]). The list of models pooled by him earlier and the list of individual pools are shown in Fig. 4[I] and [H] respectively. A checks one/more models (or model pools) to annotate one or more types of sub-region categories automatically. The button *Auto-Annotate* (as shown in Fig. 4[J]) triggers the models selected by the user to auto-annotate the document. To create new model pools specific to doctor or medicine type, it makes use of the model pooling feature (corresponds to Fig. 4[K]). developer A starts creating custom model pools for any of its new requirements. The button *pool fusion* takes the set union of models selected by the user and *pool intersection* takes the set intersection of models selected by the

---

[9] http://yann.lecun.com/exdb/mnist/.

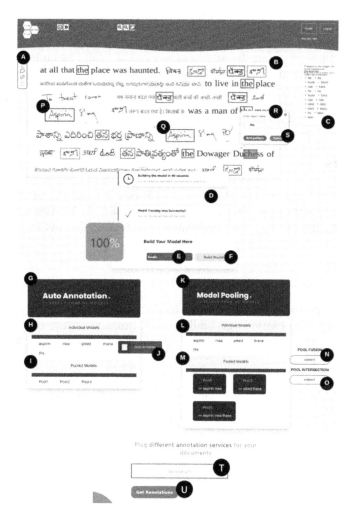

Fig. 4. Platform interface describing a user scenario *The circles [A-U] represent web elements relating to user actions

user. Figure 4[P] shows input annotation given by the user and Fig. 4[Q] shows the annotation done by the corresponding CNN model. The sub-regions shown in this image are taken from different data sets described in Sect. 6, for instance, Fig. 4[P], and Fig. 4[Q] are taken from the medical prescription[10] data set. In the case of false positives, *A* can report the falsely predicted sub-regions as an anti-patterns of interest. This can be observed in Fig. 4[R] (in a dialog box). *A* can click on the annotated sub-region and rename the falsely predicted sub-region on the dialog box or delete the annotation as shown in Fig. 4[R]. In the case,

---

[10] https://github.com/garain/Handwritten-and-Printed-Text-Classification-in-Doctors-Prescription.

A observes the models failing to recall some sub-regions, *A* can annotate them manually and retrain the model. *A* can make a program annotate a document, without *A* actually doing it, by adding a service that can respond to annotation requests in a specified data format. As shown in Fig. 4[T] *A* enters the URL of the annotation service that returns bounding box coordinates in a specified JSON format. After clicking on *Get Annotations* (Fig. 4[U]), the annotation area (Fig. 4[B]) renders the annotations obtained from the annotation service.

6 Results

A crowd enabled annotation platform is provided for annotation by users for diverse content categories (Fig. 1a). The platform allows for the annotation of documents of different language and category settings by providing annotation as a service.

6.1 Experimenting with Various Data Sets

We have presented the predictions obtained on the Kannada digits data set in the Fig. 5a. We have carried out similar evaluations on all the other data sets, and calculated *mAP* scores on each of the data set. We present the obtained scores in the Table 3.

Table 3. Average precision on each of the different data sets

Data set type	Data set	Classes	Mean	Min	Max
Words	Devanagari	10	96.18	91	100
	Telugu	10	93.20	90	95
Letters	Devanagari	36	100	100	100
	Kannada	53	99.83	95.27	100
	EMNIST capital	26	93.09	83	99
	Telugu	16	89.96	77.70	99.02
	EMNIST small	26	87.85	50	98
Digits	Kannada	10	99.90	99.56	100
	MNIST	10	95.72	90	99

6.2 Tesseract OCR Annotations

We trained models on annotations made by Tesseract to verify the extent of mimicking Tesseract OCR's behaviour. Figure 5b elucidates the behaviour of models in mimicking Tesseract OCR. The models were already trained on Tesseract annotations before the experiment. Figure 5b[A] is a sample test document used for the experiment and Fig. 5b[B], and [C] shows annotations made by models and that of by Tesseract. We observed an mAP score of 90 for the models trained on Tesseract annotations.

The platform *Annotator* can be accessed at https://services.iittp.ac.in/annotator. Training data sets, test images and predictions, class-wise average precision for all the data sets can be found at https://tinyurl.com/xk6hasmn.

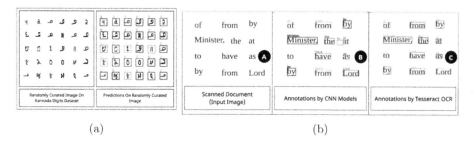

(a)   (b)

Fig. 5. Predictions and Tesseract mimicry (a) Predictions on Kannada digits and (b) Mimicking Tesseract OCR's behaviour

7   Conclusion

We report here a platform and a model building algorithm that does auto-annotation of documents by *building models in real-time*. The annotations can be provided by a human user as well as automatically by an annotation service program. Annotations can be performed *at scale* with the help of model-pools created. Our platform serves as a framework that features *domain adaptability*, multi and mixed language support all in one place. The method serves for personalized content annotation by any user with their own interpretation of content. Given a new document, a set of models apply region detection which the user is free to choose and customize. The documents themselves can have diverse sub-region level content even within the same document from different languages, usages, and settings. As a prototype, the model building algorithm has been successfully evaluated on diverse handwritten datasets from 4 languages on 197 classes of subregions on 388530 images where an aggregate mAP score of more than 95% is reported.

As future directions, we propose for the platform to have enhanced search interface, knowledge graph, shareable model pools and multimedia type annotation labels such as audio and video content.

References

1. Gregory, C., Saeed, A., Jonathan, T., André, V.S.: Emnist: extending mnist to handwritten letters. In: International Joint Conference on Neural Networks, pp. 2921–2926 (2017)

2. Bryan, C.R., Antonio, T., Kevin, P.M., William, T.F.: Labelme: a database and web-based tool for image annotation. Int. J. Comput. Vision **77**(1–3), 157–173 (2008)

3. Abhishek, D., Andrew, Z.: The VIA annotation software for images, audio and video. In: Proceedings of the 27th ACM International Conference on Multimedia, pp. 2276–2279 (2019)

4. Kartik, D., Praveen, K., Minesh, K., Jawahar, C.V.: Offline handwriting recognition on devanagari using a new benchmark dataset. In: International Workshop on Document Analysis Systems, pp. 25–30 (2018)

5. Aurelien, G.: Hands-on Machine Learning with Scikit-Learn and TensorFlow: Concepts, Tools, and Techniques to Build Intelligent Systems. O'Reilly Media, Newton (2017)

6. Ross, G.: Fast r-cnn. In: Proceedings of the IEEE International Conference on Computer Vision, pp. 1440–1448 (2015)

7. Réka, H., Ákos, D., Gábor, H., Nikita, M., Péter, H.: Annotatorj: an imagej plugin to ease hand annotation of cellular compartments. Molec. Biol. cell **31**(20), 2179–2186 (2020)

8. Vural, H., Koyuncu, H., Guney, S.: A systematic literature review on microservices. In: International Conference on Computational Science and its Applications, pp. 203–217 (2017)

9. Kartik, D., Praveen, K., Minesh, M., Jawahar, C.V.: Towards spotting and recognition of handwritten words in indic scripts. In: International Conference on Frontiers in Handwriting Recognition, pp. 32–37 (2018)

10. Li, H., Wang, X., Ding, S.: Research and development of neural network ensembles: a survey. Artif. Intell. Rev. **49**(4), 455–479 (2017). https://doi.org/10.1007/s10462-016-9535-1

11. Thomas, M.B.: The OCRopus open source ocr system. Doc. Recogn. Retrieval **6815**, 68150F (2008)

12. Thomas, M.B., Adnan, U.H., Mayce, A.A.,Faisal, S.: High-Performance OCR for Printed English and Fraktur using LSTM networks. In: 12th International Conference on Document Analysis and Recognition, vol. 1, pp. 683–687 (2013)

13. Juan, M.C., et al.: tagtog: interactive and text-mining-assisted annotation of gene mentions in PLOS full-text articles. In: Database, vol. 1 (2014)

14. Jamshed, M., Maira, S., Khan, R.A., Mueen, U.: Handwritten optical character recognition?: a comprehensive systematic literature review. IEEE Access **8**, 142642–142668 (2020)

15. Re, M., Valentini, G.: Ensemble methods: a review. In: Advances in Machine Learning and Data Mining for Astronomy, pp. 563–594 (2012)

16. Inyoung, P., Sangjun, O., Taeyeong, K., Injung, K.: Overcoming catastrophic forgetting by neuron-level plasticity control. In: Proceedings of the AAAI Conference on Artificial Intelligence, vol. 34, pp. 5339–5346 (2020)

17. Vinay, P.U.: Kannada-MNIST: a new handwritten digits dataset for the Kannada language. arXiv e-prints p. abs/1908.01242 (2019)

18. Joseph, R., Santhosh, D., Ross, G., Ali, F.: You only look once: unified, real-time object detection. In: IEEE Conference on Computer Vision and Pattern Recognition, vol. 1, pp. 779–788 (2016)

19. Ray, W.S.: History of the tesseract OCR engine: what worked and what didn't. In: Electronic Imaging Conference on Document Recognition and Retrieval, vol. 8658, p. 865802 (2013)

AC-CovidNet: Attention Guided Contrastive CNN for Recognition of Covid-19 in Chest X-Ray Images

Anirudh Ambati[1(✉)] and Shiv Ram Dubey[2]

[1] Indian Institute of Information Technology, Sri City, Chittoor, India
anirudh.ai7@iiits.in
[2] Indian Institute of Information Technology, Allahabad, India
srdubey@iiita.ac.in

Abstract. Covid-19 global pandemic continues to devastate health care systems across the world. At present, the Covid-19 testing is costly and time-consuming. Chest X-Ray (CXR) testing can be a fast, scalable, and non-invasive method. The existing methods suffer due to the limited CXR samples available from Covid-19. Thus, inspired by the limitations of the open-source work in this field, we propose attention guided contrastive CNN architecture (AC-CovidNet) for Covid-19 detection in CXR images. The proposed method learns the robust and discriminative features with the help of contrastive loss. Moreover, the proposed method gives more importance to the infected regions as guided by the attention mechanism. We compute the sensitivity of the proposed method over the publicly available Covid-19 dataset. It is observed that the proposed AC-CovidNet exhibits very promising performance as compared to the existing methods even with limited training data. It can tackle the bottleneck of CXR Covid-19 datasets being faced by the researchers. The code used in this paper is released publicly at https://github.com/shivram1987/AC-CovidNet/.

1 Introduction

Coronavirus disease 2019 (Covid-19) has emerged very fast as an emergent health risk disease affecting the whole world. It has been observed that this infection spreads through the surfaces which might be infected from the infected person. The spread of Covid-19 is categorized into different stages. The stage1 and stage2 refer to the small scale spread, whereas stage3 and beyond refer to the large scale spread due to chain reaction. Covid-19 pandemic is being witnessed as the toughest time of the century during April-May 2021 due to its 2nd wave which has already entered into stage3/stage4 (i.e., community spread) of Covid-19 infection spread. Thus, the pandemic has led to a huge burden on the healthcare systems across the world. Testing for Covid-19 is the most important part of the process and must be scaled as much as possible. CXR based testing can one of the fastest way using existing infrastructure and can be scaled very quickly and cost effectively. The radiograph image of the lungs can be captured using

---

Work done while at IIIT Sri City

© The Author(s), under exclusive license to Springer Nature Switzerland AG 2022
B. Raman et al. (Eds.): CVIP 2021, CCIS 1567, pp. 71–82, 2022.
https://doi.org/10.1007/978-3-031-11346-8_7

different imaging tools such as CT-Scan and X-Ray. Getting the CT-Scan is again a costly and time-consuming process. Moreover, only major hospitals have CT scanners. However, capturing an X-Ray is a very affordable as well as an efficient process. The covid-19 disease is caused by severe acute respiratory syndrome coronavirus-2 (SARS-COV-2) and the infected patients show distinct visual features in the Chest X-Ray (CXR) images. Hence, artificial intelligence based automated techniques can be utilized to detect the infection in CXR images. Such testing methods can be fast, scalable, economical, and affordable.

Researchers have tried to explore the artificial intelligence based deep learning techniques for Covid-19 detection, such as COVID-Net [36], CovidAID [22], COVID-CAPS [1], CovXNet [21], DarkCovidNet [26] and Convolutional Neural Network (CNN) Ensemble [6]. The lack of sufficient data to train and test the models is the main problem in the development of the deep learning based models for Covid-19 detection in CXR images. Hence, it is an urgent requirement to develop a deep learning model that would learn distinctive features from the limited data. In order to learn the discriminative and localized features, we propose an attention guided contrastive CNN (AC-CovidNet) for Covid-19 recognition from CXR images. Following are the commitments of this work:

- We propose a novel AC-CovidNet deep learning framework for Covid-19 recognition in CXR images.
- The use of the attention module enforces the learning of localized visual features corresponding to Covid-19 symptoms.
- The contrastive loss increases the discriminative ability and robustness of the model by learning the similarity between Covid-19 infected samples and dissimilarity between Covid-19 positive and negative samples.
- The impact of the proposed method is analyzed for different amount of training data w.r.t. the recent state-of-the-art models.

The remaining paper is organized as follows: Sect. 2 summarizes the related works; Sect. 3 illustrates the proposed AC-CovidNet model; Sect. 4 details the experimental settings; Sect. 5 presents the results and analysis; and finally Sect. 6 summarizes the findings with concluding remarks.

2   Related Works

It has been observed in the primary research conducted by Wang and Wong (2020) [36] that chest radiograph images can be used for the Covid-19 detection. It opened up the new urgent and demanding area of the possible usage of Artificial Intelligence for early, efficient and large-scale detection of viruses among people. Ng et al. released the imaging profile of the Covid-19 infection with radiologic findings [24]. Li et al. discovered the spectrum of CT findings and temporal progression of Covid-19 disease which reveals that this problem can be solved using imaging AI based tools [20]. Bai et al. performed a performance study of radiologists which can differentiate the Covid-19 from viral pneumonia on chest CT [4].

Deep learning is also utilized for Covid-19 detection from Chest X-Ray (CXR) images [23]. In one of the first attempts, CXR radiograph images are used for Covid-19 detection using a Deep Learning based convolutional neural network (CNN) model

COVID-Net [36]. A projection expansion projection extension module is used heavily in COVID-Net which is experimented on various configurations of the model. Authors used a human-machine collaborative design strategy to create COVID-Net architecture where human driven prototyping and machine based exploration is combined. A COVIDx dataset is also accumulated from various sources and being updated with new data. The dataset and models are publically released for further research [1]. Using COVID-Net model, 96% sensitivity is observed in [36] on a test set of 100 CXR images. A CovidAID model is proposed in [22] which is a pretrained CheXNet [29] - a 121 layer DenseNet [14] followed by a fully connected layer. Using the CovidAID model, 100% sensitivity is observed on a test set having 30 Covid-19 images. A capsule networks based deep learning model (COVID-CAPS) is investigated in [1]. Authors in [1] aim to prevent the loss of spatial information which is observed in CNN based methods. Using COVID-CAPS model, a sensitivity of 90% is reported on 100 test CXR images. CovXNet model [21] is proposed to use transferable multi-receptive feature optimisation. Basically, 4 different configurations of a network are utilized in CovXNet for training and prediction. Using CovXNet model, 91% sensitivity is reported on 100 test CXR images. The DarkNet architecture based DarkCovidNet model is introduced in [26] with You Only Look Once (YOLO) real time object detection system for Covid-19 detection. Using the DarkCovidNet model, a classification accuracy of 98.08% for binary classes and 87.02% for multi-class cases are observed. CNN ensemble of DenseNet201, Resnet50-v2 and Inception-v3 is utilized for Covid-19 recognition in [6]. Samples from only 2 classes (i.e., covid and non-covid) are used to train the CNN ensemble model. Using CNN ensemble model, a classification accuracy of 91.62% is reported. Researchers from [13] tried to develop an open source framework of algorithms to detect covid19 using CT scan images. Also, researchers at [15] developed Covid-CT using selftrans approach. We have tested these algorithms on our CXR dataset configurations.

From the above presented works, it is convincing that AI powered deep learning methods can play a vital role for the Covid-19 screening. The CT scans and CXR radiographs are used majorly for the imaging based techniques. Less attention has been given to CXR images so far due to the not so great generalization performance caused by the limited availability of data [2,7]. Given the need to conduct the mass screening at affordable cost, the further fast research over CXR images of lungs is very much needed using the limited data. Thus, in this paper, we utilize the capability of attention mechanism and contrastive learning to tackle the learning with limited data for Covid-19 recognition from CXR images.

3 Proposed AC-CovidNet CNN Model

In this section, first we provide a brief of deep learning, attention mechanism and contrastive learning. Then we present the proposed AC-CovidNet architecture.

---

[1] https://github.com/lindawangg/COVID-Net/.

3.1 Background

Deep learning has shown a great impact from last decade to solve many challenging problems [19]. Deep learning models consist of the deep neural networks which learn the important features from the data automatically. The training of the deep models is generally performed using stochastic gradient descent optimization [10, 17]. Convolutional neural network (CNN) based models have been used to deal with the image data, such as image classification [18], face recognition [32], image retrieval [9], hyperspectral image analysis [31], and biomedical image analysis [11].

Attention mechanism in deep learning facilitates to learn the localized features which is more important in the context of the problem of Covid-19 recognition from CXR images [3]. It is also discovered that the attention based model can outperform the plain neural network models [35]. The attention mechanism has been also utilized for different applications such as facial micro-expression recognition [12], breast tumor segmentation [34], and face recognition [30]. Thus, motivated from the success of attention mechanisms, we utilize it in the proposed model for Covid-19 recognition.

Contrastive learning is the recent trend to learn the similarity and dissimilarity between the similar and dissimilar samples in the abstract feature space for visual representations [5, 16]. Generally, contrastive learning is dependent upon the feature similarity between positive pairs and negative pairs [33]. The contrastive learning has shown very promising performance for different problems, such as face generation [8], image-to-image translation [27], medical visual representations [37], and video representation [28]. Thus, motivated from the discriminative and robust feature representation by contrastive learning, we utilize it in the proposed method.

3.2 Proposed Model

In this paper, we propose an attention guided contrastive CNN for Covid-19 recognition, named as AC-CovidNet. The architecture of the proposed AC-CovidNet model is illustrated in Fig. 1. The proposed model is based on the popular COVID-Net model [36]. It heavily uses light weight residual projection expansion projection extension (PEPX) mechanism. The PEPX component is shown in Fig. 1 (right side). This architecture also uses selective long range connectivity in model which improves the representational capacity. It also facilitates the training of the model easier. However, the extensive use of these long range connections may bring a lot of redundant low level features. In order to resolve this issue, the proposed model uses an attention mechanism. Attention helps the model to prioritize the regions of important w.r.t. the problem being solved. Attention is also useful to suppress the activations from the redundant features from the initial layers and helps to focus on the important features that are required to solve the given problem. We use the attention gates in the proposed architecture as suggested in [25], at various layers in the COVID-Net architecture where many long range connections are used. This improves the sensitivity as the model attends better to the important visual features of infected regions in CXR images due to Covid-19. As the difference between Covid-19 and Pneumonia features is very subtle, we propose to use the supervised contrastive loss. The contrastive loss facilitates the network to increase the distance between the learnt representation of the classes as much as possible.

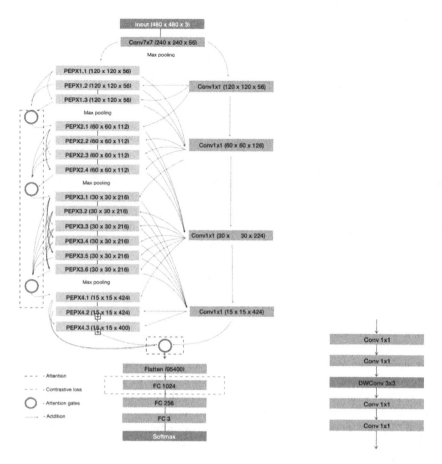

Fig. 1. Left: Architecture of the proposed AC-CovidNet. Right: Projection Expansion Projection Extension (PEPX) Module. Here, DWConv representsthe depth wise convolution operation.

Architecture. The proposed AC-CovidNet architecture is an extension of COVID-Net by utilizing the attention gates where multiple long range connections converge. The details of the architecture of the proposed model is illustrated Fig. 1. We use PEPX layers and attention gates heavily as a part of our architecture. We also use the contrastive loss function while training. The model is first trained using supervised contrastive learning before final fine tuning using supervised learning.

PEPX Layer. The architecture of a Projection-Expansion-Projection-Extension (PEPX) is shown in Fig. 1 (right side). The idea of this module is to project features into a lower dimension using the first two conv1x1 layers, then expand those features using a depthwise convolution layer (DWConv3x3) and project into lower dimension again using two conv1x1 layers. Thus, the PEPX layer leads to the efficient model by reducing the number of parameters and operations.

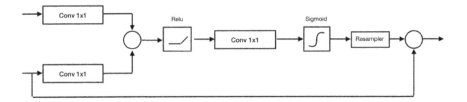

Fig. 2. The block diagram of an attention gate.

Attention Gate. We use attention gates in the proposed AC-CovidNet model at various layers as depicted in Fig. 1. The block diagram of the attention module is shown in Fig. 3. Features from multiple layers are passed through conv1x1 and are added together. Then, the aggregated features are passed through Relu activation function followed by conv1x1 and then sigmoid activation function. The feature map output of the sigmoid layer is then passed through a resampler (see Fig. 2). The output of the resampler is added to the features from the nearest input layer to the attention module in order to produce the output of the attention gate.

Network Details. The following are the main components of the proposed AC-CovidNet model. a) Encoder network, $E(.)$: It is the AC-CovidNet model as discussed above after removing the last three layers which form the classifier network. The encoder network maps the input image into a vector of size 1024. b) Projection network, $P(.)$: This network projects the output of the encoder network into a vector of size 128. This is a multilayer perceptron with input size of 1024, one hidden layer of length 512, and an output vector of size 128. This network is used while training the encoder and later discarded. c) Classifier network, $C(.)$: This is the last three layers of AC-CovidNet that take a 1024 length output of the encoder as the input and produces an output of size $c = 3$ (corresponding to the classes, Normal, Pneumonia, and Covid-19).

First we train the encoder network $E(.)$ with supervised contrastive loss (SupCon-Loss) using the projection network $P(.)$. Then we discard the projection network and add the classifier network $C(.)$ to the encoder network. Then we freeze the weights of the encoder model and train the classifier with categorical cross entropy loss. The training of the encoder of the proposed model is summarized in Algorithm 1.

3.3   Objective Function

We use the supervised contrastive learning method [16] to train the encoder network for feature extraction. We train the classifier network using the cross entropy loss function after freezing the encoder network.

Supervised Contrastive Loss. Contrastive loss is most commonly used in unsupervised and self-supervised learning. In order to adapt this method to supervised learning and take advantage of the labels available, the supervised contrastive learning has been

---

Algorithm 1: Training AC-CovidNet

E: Encoder Network, P: Projection Network
C: Classifier Network
$SupCon$: Supervised Contrastive Loss
$CrossEntropy$: Cross Entropy Loss
while $epochs - -$ **do**

> // Stage 1
> **for** batch X in $Data$ **do**
>> Initialize Z as null;
>> **for** x_i in X **do**
>>> $h_i = E(x_i)$;
>>> $z_i = P(h_i)$;
>>> $Z.append(z_i)$;
>>
>> **end**
>> $\mathcal{L}_{SC} = SupCon(Z_i)$;
>> Update E and P to minimise $\mathcal{L}_{SC}$;
>
> **end**

end
Discard $P(.)$ and freeze weights of $E(.)$;
Final model, $M(\boldsymbol{x}) = C(E(\boldsymbol{x}))$;
while $epochs - -$ **do**

> // Stage 2
> **for** batch X in $Data$ **do**
>> $\hat{Y} = M(X)$;
>> $\mathcal{L}_{CE} = CrossEntropy(Y, \hat{Y})$;
>> Update M to minimise $\mathcal{L}_{CE}$;
>
> **end**

end

---

investigated in [16]. This loss is used to train the encoder network of the proposed AC-CovidNet.

Consider $z_\ell = \mathrm{P}\left(\mathrm{E}\left(\boldsymbol{x}_\ell\right)\right)$ where $\boldsymbol{x}$ is the input and $A(i)$ is a set of all indices (I) except i. Then, the supervised contrastive loss is given as,

$$\mathcal{L}_{SC} = \sum_{i \in I} \frac{-1}{|P(i)|} \sum_{p \in P(i)} \log \frac{\exp\left(\boldsymbol{z}_i \cdot \boldsymbol{z}_p / \tau\right)}{\sum_{a \in A(i)} \exp\left(\boldsymbol{z}_i \cdot \boldsymbol{z}_a / \tau\right)}$$

where, $\tau \in \mathcal{R}^+$ is scalar temperature parameter, $P(i) \equiv \{p \in A(i) : \tilde{\boldsymbol{y}}_p = \tilde{\boldsymbol{y}}_i\}$ is the set of indices of all the positive samples other than i, and $|P(i)|$ is its cardinality. Note that $\tilde{\boldsymbol{y}}$ represents the class label.

Cross Entropy Loss. Cross entropy loss is used to train the classifier which takes input from the feature extractor. It produces the output probability corresponding to three class from the softmax activation function. The cross entropy loss is given as,

Table 1. Datasets configurations used for training and testing w.r.t. the number of samples in Covid-19, Pneumonia and Normal categories.

S. No	Configuration	Covid-19		Pneumonia		Normal	
		#Training Images	#Test Images	#Training Images	#Test Images	#Training Images	#Test Images
I	COVIDx-v1	517	100	7966	100	5475	100
II	COVIDx-v2	467	150	7916	150	5425	150
III	COVIDx-v3	417	200	7866	200	5375	200

Table 2. The results comparison in terms of the sensitivity.

Model	COVIDx-v1			COVIDx-v2			COVIDx-v3		
	Covid	Pneumonia	Normal	Covid	Pneumonia	Normal	Covid	Pneumonia	Normal
COVID-Net [36]	96	89	95	94.66	87.33	95.33	94	88.5	94
CovidAID [22]	93	95	73	91	92.66	70.66	88	92.5	74
Ensemble Learning CNNs [6]	89	91	87	87.33	92	86	83	91	89
DarkCovidNet [18]	86	88	92	84.66	84	89.33	84.5	89.5	90.5
Covid-Caps [1]	90	87	77	88	86	74	86.5	84.5	76
CovidCTNet [15]	83	76	89	79	74.33	87.66	79	74.5	88
Covid-CT [13]	87	82	86	85.66	79.33	85	85	77	85.5
CovXnet [21]	91	71	86	89.33	69.33	86.66	88	70	84
CovidNet + attention	95	86	95	95.33	82.66	95.33	94	87	94.5
CovidNet + contrastive loss	96	89	95	96	87.33	94	95	90	95
AC-CovidNet	**96**	**88**	**95**	**96.66**	**87.33**	**95.33**	**96.5**	**87.5**	**95**

$$\mathcal{L}_{CE} = -\frac{1}{N} \sum_{i=1}^{N} \sum_{j=1}^{3} y_i^j \cdot \log \hat{y}_i^j$$

where $\hat{y}_i^j$ and y_i^j are the output probability and ground truth value, respectively, for j^{th} class corresponding to i^{th} sample and N represents the number of samples in a batch.

4 Experimental Setup

4.1 Dataset Used

We use COVIDx dataset [36] in this work to experiment with the proposed AC-CovidNet model. It is the largest open-source dataset for Covid-19 Chest X-Ray (CXR) images currently available. This dataset is a combination of several other open datasets, including Covid-19 Image Data Collection, Covid-19 Chest X-ray Dataset Initiative, ActualMed Covid-19 Chest X-ray Dataset Initiative, RSNA Pneumonia Detection Challenge dataset, and Covid-19 radiography database. This dataset contains three classes of CXR images, i.e., Covid-19, Pneumonia and Normal. It has a total of 14,258 images from 14,042 patients. It has 7,966 Normal images, 5,475 Pneumonia images and 517 Covid-19 images in the training set and 100 images from each category in the test set. In our experiments we create three different sets of data by varying the distributions of samples in training and test sets. We name the original COVIDx dataset as COVIDx-v1 by following the above said distribution. COVIDx-v2 is the COVIDx dataset with

150 test images from each category and 7,916 Normal images, 5,425 Pneumonia images and 467 Covid-19 images in the training set. Similarly, COVIDx-v3 has 200 test images from each category and 7,866 Normal images, 5,375 Pneumonia images and 417 Covid-19 images in the training set. These configurations are summarized in Table 1 w.r.t. the number of samples in Covid-19, Pneumonia and Normal categories.

4.2 Training Settings

The proposed AC-COVIDNet model is pretrained on imagenet as suggested by [36]. Then the entire model is trained in two stages. In the first stage, the encoder network (i.e., feature extractor) is trained using contrastive loss function as suggested in [16] for feature extraction, so that the distance between the learnt features is optimized. In the second stage, the feature extractor is frozen and trained by adding a classifier on the top with cross entropy loss function. We train the proposed model as well as the state-of-the-art models on all three variations of COVIDx dataset, i.e., with 100, 150 and 200 test images of different categories. The models are trained using Adam optimiser [17]. The learning rate is set as 1.7e–4. The batch size of 64 is used. We use Relu activation function in every layer of the network and softmax in the last layer. Max-pooling is used after every batch of PEPX layers. The three versions of the COVIDx dataset are used for training and the sensitivity of the classes are compared. Covid-19 sensitivity is the percentage of instances with Covid-19 that are correctly identified. The model is trained using the computational resources provided by Google Colab. Keras deep learning library is used with tensorflow as a backend.

5 Experimental Results and Analysis

We test the proposed AC-CovidNet model on all three configurations of the COVIDx dataset and calculate the sensitivity for Covid-19 and other classes. In order to demonstrate the superiority of the proposed method, we also compute the results using state-of-the-art deep learning based Covid-19 recognition models, such as CovXNet [21], COVID-CAPS [1], CNN Ensemble [6], DarkCovidNet [26], COVID-Net [36], and CovidAID [22]. The results in terms of the sensitivity for the Covid-19 class are reported in Table 2. On configuration I (i.e., COVIDx-v1 dataset with 100 test images), configuration II (i.e., COVIDx-v2 dataset with 150 test images), and configuration III (i.e., COVIDx-v3 dataset with 200 test images), the observed Covid-19 sensitivity using the proposed AC-CovidNet model is 96%, 96.66%, and 96.5%, respectively. It can be observed in Table 2 that the proposed model outperforms the remaining models over all three settings of the COVIDx dataset.

Note that the proposed model is able to achieve better results than the other compared models because the proposed model learns the Covid-19 specific features using the attention module and increases the separation between different classes in feature space using the contrastive loss. In the configuration I of the dataset (with 100 test images), the performance of the proposed model is better than CovXNet, COVID-CAPS, CNN Ensemble, DarkCovidNet and CovidAID models and same as COVID-Net. Thus, in order to demonstrate the advantage of the proposed model, we compare the results with less number of training samples and more test samples. Basically, it depicts the generalization capability of the proposed model. On an expectation, a bigger test set can reflect the better generalization of the deep learning models. Thus, we experiment with configuration II having 467 training samples and 150 test samples of Covid-19 category. It can be seen in Table 2 that the proposed model is able to retain the similar performance by correctly classifying 145 Covid-19 images out of 150 in the dataset. However, the performance of other models dropped significantly. We also test the performance by further reducing the number of training samples and increasing the number of test samples in configuration III with 417 training images and 200 test images from Covid-19 category. It can be noticed that the performance of the proposed AC-CovidNet model is still similar. However, the other models drastically fail to generalize in case of limited training set. Thus, it clearly indicates that the proposed AC-CovidNet model is able to capture the robust and discriminative features pertaining to the Covid-19 infection and generalize well even with the limited training data. It also shows the positive impact of attention modules and contrastive learning for the Covid-19 recognition from CXR images.

The impact of the attention and contrastive mechanism is also investigated by considering the only attention and only contrastive mechanism with base network CovidNet (i.e., CovidNet + attention and CovidNet + contrastive loss, respectively). As shown in the results using these methods in Table 5, the performance of AC-CovidNet, which uses both attention and contrastive mechanisms, is improved than the models which use only attention and only contrastive mechanisms for Covid-19 recognition. We also report the results for other two classes in Table 5, i.e., Pneumonia and Normal. It is observed that the performance of the proposed model is comparable to the state-of-the-art for Pneumonia and Normal classes.

6   Conclusion

In this paper, an AC-CovidNet model is proposed for Covid-19 recognition from chest X-Ray images. The proposed model utilizes the attention module in order to learn the task specific features by better attending the infected regions in the images. The proposed model also utilizes contrastive learning in order to achieve the better separation in the feature space by increasing the discriminative ability and increasing robustness. The results are computed over three different configurations of Covid-19 dataset with varying number of training and test samples. The results are also compared with six recent state-of-the-art deep learning models. It is noticed that the proposed AC-CovidNet model outperforms the existing models in terms of the sensitivity for the Covid-19 category. Moreover, it is also observed that the performance of the proposed model is consistent with a limited training set. Whereas, the existing methods fail to do so. It shows the better generalization capability of the proposed method. The future work includes the utilization of recent development in deep learning to solve the Covid-19 recognition problem from chest X-Ray images with better performance.

References

1. Afshar, P., Heidarian, S., Naderkhani, F., Oikonomou, A., Plataniotis, K.N., Mohammadi, A.: COVID-CAPS: a capsule network-based framework for identification of COVID-19 cases from X-ray images. Pattern Recogn. Lett. **138**, 638–643 (2020)
2. Ahmed, K.B., Goldgof, G.M., Paul, R., Goldgof, D.B., Hall, L.O.: Discovery of a generalization gap of convolutional neural networks on COVID-19 X-rays classification. IEEE Access **9**, 72970–72979 (2021)
3. Bahdanau, D., Cho, K.H., Bengio, Y.: Neural machine translation by jointly learning to align and translate. In: 3rd International Conference on Learning Representations, ICLR 2015 (2015)
4. Bai, H.X., et al.: Performance of radiologists in differentiating COVID-19 from non-COVID-19 viral pneumonia at chest CT. Radiology **296**(2), E46–E54 (2020)
5. Chen, T., Kornblith, S., Norouzi, M., Hinton, G.: A simple framework for contrastive learning of visual representations. In: International Conference on Machine Learning, pp. 1597–1607. PMLR (2020)
6. Das, A.K., Ghosh, S., Thunder, S., Dutta, R., Agarwal, S., Chakrabarti, A.: Automatic COVID-19 detection from X-ray images using ensemble learning with convolutional neural network. Pattern Anal. Appl. **24**(3), 1111–1124 (2021). https://doi.org/10.1007/s10044-021-00970-4
7. DeGrave, A.J., Janizek, J.D., Lee, S.I.: AI for radiographic COVID-19 detection selects shortcuts over signal. Nat. Mach. Intell. **3**(7), 610–619 (2021)
8. Deng, Y., Yang, J., Chen, D., Wen, F., Tong, X.: Disentangled and controllable face image generation via 3D imitative-contrastive learning. In: Proceedings of the IEEE/CVF Conference on Computer Vision and Pattern Recognition, pp. 5154–5163 (2020)
9. Dubey, S.R.: A decade survey of content based image retrieval using deep learning (2020). arXiv preprint arXiv:2012.00641
10. Dubey, S.R., Chakraborty, S., Roy, S.K., Mukherjee, S., Singh, S.K., Chaudhuri, B.B.: diffGrad: an optimization method for convolutional neural networks. IEEE Trans. Neural Netw. Learn. Syst. **31**(11), 4500–4511 (2019)
11. Dubey, S.R., Roy, S.K., Chakraborty, S., Mukherjee, S., Chaudhuri, B.B.: Local bit-plane decoded convolutional neural network features for biomedical image retrieval. Neural Comput. Appl. **32**(11), 7539–7551 (2019). https://doi.org/10.1007/s00521-019-04279-6
12. Gajjala, V.R., Reddy, S.P.T., Mukherjee, S., Dubey, S.R.: MERANet: Facial microexpression recognition using 3D residual attention network (2020). arXiv preprint arXiv:2012.04581
13. He, X.: Sample-efficient deep learning for COVID-19 diagnosis based on CT scans. IEEE Transactions on Medical Imaging (2020)
14. Huang, G., Liu, Z., van der Maaten, L., Weinberger, K.Q.: Densely connected convolutional networks (2018)
15. Javaheri, T., et al.: CovidCTNet: An open-source deep learning approach to identify COVID-19 using CT image (2020)
16. Khosla, P., et al.: Supervised contrastive learning. Adv. Neural Inf. Process. Syst. **33**, 18661–18673 (2020)
17. Kingma, D.P., Ba, J.: Adam: a method for stochastic optimization (2014). arXiv preprint arXiv:1412.6980
18. Krizhevsky, A., Sutskever, I., Hinton, G.E.: ImageNet classification with deep convolutional neural networks. Adv. Neural Inf. Process. Syst. **25**, 1097–1105 (2012)
19. LeCun, Y., Bengio, Y., Hinton, G.: Deep learning. Nature **521**(7553), 436–444 (2015)

20. Li, M., et al.: Coronavirus disease (COVID-19): spectrum of CT findings and temporal progression of the disease. Acad. Radiol. **27**(5), 603–608 (2020)
21. Mahmud, T., Rahman, M.A., Fattah, S.A.: CovXNet: A multi-dilation convolutional neural network for automatic COVID-19 and other pneumonia detection from chest X-ray images with transferable multi-receptive feature optimization. Comput. Biol. Med. **122**, 103869 (2020)
22. Mangal, A., et al.: CovidAID: COVID-19 detection using chest X-ray (2020). arXiv 2004.09803, https://github.com/arpanmangal/CovidAID
23. Narin, A., Kaya, C., Pamuk, Z.: Automatic detection of coronavirus disease (COVID-19) using X-ray images and deep convolutional neural networks (2020). arXiv preprint arXiv:2003.10849
24. Ng, M.Y., et al.: Imaging profile of the COVID-19 infection: radiologic findings and literature review. Radiol. Cardiothorac. Imaging **2**(1), e200034 (2020)
25. Oktay, O., et al.: Attention U-Net: learning where to look for the pancreas (2018). arXiv preprint arXiv:1804.03999
26. Ozturk, T., Talo, M., Yildirim, E.A., Baloglu, U.B., Yildirim, O., Acharya, U.R.: Automated detection of COVID-19 cases using deep neural networks with X-ray images. Comput. Biol. Med. **121**, 103792 (2020)
27. Park, T., Efros, A.A., Zhang, R., Zhu, J.-Y.: Contrastive learning for unpaired image-to-image translation. In: Vedaldi, A., Bischof, H., Brox, T., Frahm, J.-M. (eds.) ECCV 2020. LNCS, vol. 12354, pp. 319–345. Springer, Cham (2020). https://doi.org/10.1007/978-3-030-58545-7_19
28. Qian, R., et al.: Spatiotemporal contrastive video representation learning (2020). arXiv preprint arXiv:2008.03800
29. Rajpurkar, P., et al.: CheXNet: Radiologist-level pneumonia detection on chest X-rays with deep learning (2017)
30. Rao, Y., Lu, J., Zhou, J.: Attention-aware deep reinforcement learning for video face recognition. In: Proceedings of the IEEE International Conference on Computer Vision, pp. 3931–3940 (2017)
31. Roy, S.K., Krishna, G., Dubey, S.R., Chaudhuri, B.B.: HybridSN: Exploring 3-D-2-D CNN feature hierarchy for hyperspectral image classification. IEEE Geosci. Remote Sens. Lett. **17**(2), 277–281 (2019)
32. Srivastava, Y., Murali, V., Dubey, S.R.: Hard-mining loss based convolutional neural network for face recognition. In: Fifth IAPR International Conference on Computer Vision and Image Processing (CVIP) (2020)
33. Tian, Y., Sun, C., Poole, B., Krishnan, D., Schmid, C., Isola, P.: What makes for good views for contrastive learning (2020). arXiv preprint arXiv:2005.10243
34. Vakanski, A., Xian, M., Freer, P.E.: Attention-enriched deep learning model for breast tumor segmentation in ultrasound images. Ultrasound Med. Biol. **46**(10), 2819–2833 (2020)
35. Vaswani, A., et al.: Attention is all you need (2017). arXiv preprint arXiv:1706.03762
36. Wang, L., Lin, Z.Q., Wong, A.: COVID-Net: a tailored deep convolutional neural network design for detection of COVID-19 cases from chest X-ray images. Sci. Rep. **10**(1), 19549 (2020). https://doi.org/10.1038/s41598-020-76550-z
37. Zhang, Y., Jiang, H., Miura, Y., Manning, C.D., Langlotz, C.P.: Contrastive learning of medical visual representations from paired images and text (2020). arXiv preprint arXiv:2010.00747

Application of Deep Learning Techniques for Prostate Cancer Grading Using Histopathological Images

Mahesh Gour$^{(\boxtimes)}$ ⓘ, Sweta Jain ⓘ, and Uma Shankar ⓘ

Maulana Azad National Institute of Technology, Bhopal 462003, India
maheshgour0704@gmail.com

Abstract. Prostate cancer is one of the most dangerous cancers that affect men around the world. Pathologists use a variety of approaches to grade prostate cancer. Among them, microscopic examination of biopsy tissue images is the most efficient method. A timely and accurate diagnosis plays a critical role in preventing cancer from progressing. The recent achievement of deep learning (DL), notably in the convolution neural networks (CNN), is exceptional in medicine. In this study, we have investigated and compared the performance of the state-of-the-art CNN models, namely MobileNet-V2, ResNet50, DenseNet121, DenseNet169, VGG16, VGG19, Xception, InceptionV3, InceptionResNet-V2, and EfficientNet-B7 for prostate cancer grading using histopathological images. The performance of pre-trained CNNs has been evaluated on the publicly available Prostate cancer grade assessment (PANDA) dataset. On this multiclass classification problem, the EfficientNet-B7 model has achieved the highest classification accuracy of 90.90%. With such a high rate of success, the EfficientNet-B7 model may be a useful method for pathologists in determining the stage of prostate cancer.

Keywords: Prostate cancer grading · Deep learning · Pre-trained convolutional neural networks · Histopathological image classification

1 Introduction

Prostate cancer (PCa) is the second most deadly cancer in men, with 1,276,106 new cases and 358,989 deaths reported in 2018 [1,2]. Prostate cancer is diagnosed using a PSA blood test, Multiparametric magnetic resonance imaging (MRI), and other imaging modalities. Among them, microscopic examination of biopsy tissue is the most efficient method [3]. The excised tissue is cut into very thin strips and dyed with hematoxylin and eosin (H&E) colors in this process. Using the Gleason grading system, an expert pathologist examines stained biopsy tissue parts under a microscope and looks for morphological patterns to grade the aggressiveness of prostate cancer.

Prostate cancer is traditionally classified using the Gleason grading system, which was established in the early 1960s and named after the expert pathologist

B. Raman et al. (Eds.): CVIP 2021, CCIS 1567, pp. 83–94, 2022.
https://doi.org/10.1007/978-3-031-11346-8_8

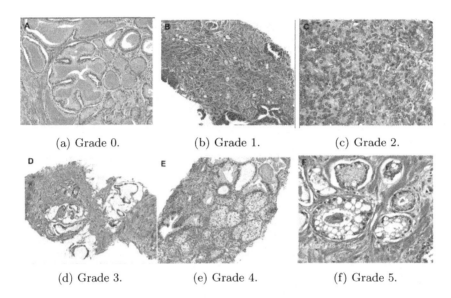

(a) Grade 0.   (b) Grade 1.   (c) Grade 2.

(d) Grade 3.   (e) Grade 4.   (f) Grade 5.

Fig. 1. Grades of prostate cancer

who created it [3]. In the cancerous cells, Dr. Donald Gleason noticed five distinct patterns [4,5]. On a scale of one to five, regular cells become tumor cells, as shown in Fig. 1, and Grade 0 means there was no cancer in the biopsy images. The primary well-separated tumor architecture is Gleason design 1. These glands are huge, oval-shaped, and nearly identical in size and shape to each other. Gleason 2 knobs are single, partitioned glands with a well-defined circumference. These glands are not as uniform as pattern1 and are arranged more loosely. Invasion is possible in pattern 2, but it is not possible in pattern1. The margins of Gleason pattern 3 are clearly infiltrative. The size and shape of these glands alternate. Gleason pattern 4 is characterized by irregular neoplastic gland masses. They seem to be mingled and difficult to discern. The development of a gland in Gleason pattern5 occurs on rare occasions. There are no glandular differences in the neoplasm. Based on the biopsy sample, pathologists allocate the first Gleason grade to the most predominant pattern and the second Gleason grade

Table 1. Gleason Grading System.

Grade group	Gleason score	Gleason pattern
1	≤ 6	$\leq 3+3$
2	7	3+4
3	7	4+3
4	8	4+4, 5+3, 3+5
5	9 or 10	4+5, 5+4, 5+5

to the second most predominant pattern. The Gleason score was calculated by adding the two patterns. For example, a score of 5+4 equals 9. The Gleason grade has been allocated based on the Gleason score, as shown in Table 1. This Gleason grading system is very time-consuming, laborious, and requires an expert.

Recently, deep learning-based approaches have shown great success in the field of medical image analysis [6–8]. In this study, we have developed a computer-aided diagnosis (CAD) system that can accurately predict prostate cancer grade from histopathological images. That can reduce pathologists' workload and improve their efficiency. In the proposed approach, we have systematically investigated the performances of the ten different state-of-the-art pre-trained CNN models for prostate cancer grading using transfer learning.

This paper is structured as follows. Section 2 presents the literature review for the task of Prostate cancer classification. Section 3 discusses the methods. Section 4 presents the experiments and results. And Sect. 5 concludes this study.

2 Literature Review

Computer-assisted grading is a useful tool for predicting the Gleason grades and improving the treatment options for prostate cancer. Recently, Deep neural networks has achieved state-of-the-art performance in prostate cancer diagnosis, as discussed in subsequent articles. Tabesh et al. [9] used distinct engineered features to classify benign vs. malignant cancer with 96.7% accuracy and low-grade vs. high-grade cancer with 81.0% accuracy in a report. Molin et al. [10] have proposed a method for classifying images into benign tissue vs. Gleason score 3–5 using a random forest and support vector machine classifier trained on CNN learned features. When classifying small patches of biopsy images, this approach had an accuracy of 81.1%, and when classifying whole images, it had an accuracy of 89.2%. Nguyen et al. [11] have proposed a method for training a logistic regression model on morphologically generated features and classifying Gleason grade 3 vs. grade 4 with an AUC of 82%. Adding shearlet magnitude and phase features to the features learned by CNNs increased the efficiency of a deep CNN, according to a survey[12]. In classifying the Gleason 3+4 pattern vs. Gleason 4+3 pattern, Zhou et al. [13] have proposed an algorithm that combined human-generated features with deep neural network learned features and achieved 75% accuracy. Tissue structural features derived from gland morphology are used to characterize a tissue pattern, according to Nguyen et al. [14]. In classifying benign vs. grade 3 vs. grade 4, this approach had an accuracy of 85.6%. Another study found that integrating morphological and texture characteristics improves the precision of classifying benign vs. malignant tissue by 79% [15]. Arvaniti et al. [16] had proposed a deep learning approach that correctly categorizes the patches into four classes: benign vs. Gleason grades 3–5 with 70% accuracy. A deep learning model for image classification was proposed by Liu et al. [17]. They have achieved an accuracy of 78.15% on diffusion-weighted magnetic resonance imaging (DWI) images.

Khani et al. [18] have used a Gleason 2019 challenge dataset to train a DeepLabV3+ model with MobileNetV2 as a backbone. With pathologists' annotations on the test subset, this model obtained a mean Cohen's quadratic kappa score of 0.56, which is higher than the inter-pathologists' kappa score of (0.55). Two convolutional DNN ensembles, each consisting of 30 Inception-V3 models pre-trained on ImageNet, were used in a recent method [19]. The first ensemble divides image patches into benign and malignant categories, while the second divides them into Gleason patterns 3–5. The area under the receiver operating characteristics curve for distinguishing between benign and malignant biopsy core AI was 0.997 on the independent test dataset and 0.986 on the external validation dataset. The AI achieved a mean pairwise kappa of 0.62 when assigning Gleason grades within the range of expert pathologists' corresponding values (0.60–0.73). Recently, in [20] feedback was taken from a large number of features for certain classifiers. The proposed approach has a 91.6% accuracy in classifying benign vs. malignant tumors and a 79.1% accuracy in classifying Grade 3 vs. Grades 4 & 5. Tsehay et al. [21] have developed a computer-aided detection (CAD) system for detecting Prostate cancer on mpMRI using biopsy points. They reported an area under the ROC curve (AUC) of 0.903. Karimi et al. [22] have used a logistic regression model to ensemble the predictions made by CNN's trained on three different image sizes. Their proposed approach classifies benign vs. malignant image patches with a 92% accuracy and Gleason grade 3 vs. Gleason grades 4 and 5 with an accuracy of 86%.

3   Methods

A Convolutional neural network (CNN) is generally used for image analysis tasks such as object detection, segmentation, and image classification. The fundamental architecture of CNN is depicted in Fig. 2. The input layer, convolutional layer, pooling layer, and dense layer and output layer are essential components of the CNN. The primary role of the initial layers of the CNN model is to extract the deep features from the input images, and the top layer plays the role of the classifier. This study has investigated ten pre-trained CNN models, which are discussed in the following section.

3.1   Pre-trained CNN Models

This section presents an overview of ten different pre-trained CNN architectures used in this study for prostate grading. Table 2 represents the details about the number of layers, number of learnable parameters, and input size of pre-trained models.

Inception-V3: Szegedy et al. [23] have introduced the Inception-V3 model. Inception-V3 is a convolutional neural network architecture from the Inception family that makes several improvements, including using Label Smoothing, Factorized 7 x 7 convolutions, and the use of an auxiliary classifier to propagate label

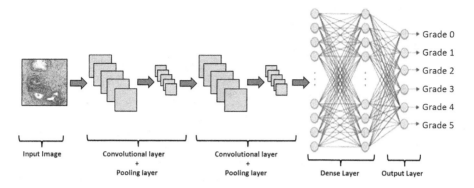

Fig. 2. A fundamental block diagram of convolutional neural network (CNN) architectures.

Table 2. Details of the pre-trained CNN architectures used in the study.

Models	Layers	Parameters (Millions)	Input size
Xception	126	22	299*299
VGG 16	23	138	224*224
MobileNet V3	88	13	224*224
DenseNet 121	121	8	224*224
DenseNet 169	169	14	224*224
VGG 19	26	143	224*224
Inception V3	159	23	299*299
ResNet 50	50	25	224*224
InceptionResNet-V2	780	55	224*224
EfficientNet B7	813	66	224*224

information lower down the network (along with the use of batch normalization for layers in the sidehead). Instead of choosing a kernel size between 1*1, 3*3, 5*5,... all the kernels are used at the same time in the Inception network, and instead of choosing between convolution and max pooling, we can use both as required. It is one of the advantages of the Inception network. However, there is a minor flaw with the Inception network in that using all of the kernels at once can result in an increase in the number of computations. A bottleneck layer was used at the start to reduce the number of computations. The 42 layers and 29.3 million parameters in the Inception-V3 network are impressive.

ResNet: The ResNet models were developed by He et al. [24]. ResNet won first prize in the ILSVRC and COCO classification challenge in 2015. For solving complex problems, stack some additional layers to the Deep Neural Networks so that performance was improved. Based on the number of layers ResNet models are distinctive i.e., ResNet 18, ResNet 34, ResNet 50, ResNet 101, ResNet 152. By increasing the additional layers or new layers to the network does not hurt the performance as regularization will skip over them. If the new layers are useful even in the presence of regularization, then the weights and kernels will become non-zero. So that by adding new layers, performance would not decrease; instead, it will increase slightly because of these skip connections.

VGGNet: VGGNet is proposed by Andrew Zisserman and his group named Visual Geometry Group at Oxford. VGGNet is a better version of AlexNet. AlexNet has many kernels, such as 11*11 kernels, 3*3 kernels, and 5*5 kernels. However, whereas VGGNet uses fixed 3*3 kernels with a stride of 1 and padding as same in convolutional layer and pooling layer, it uses fixed 2*2 kernels with a stride of 2 followed by 3 fully connected layers. There are mainly two models in VGGNet [25] one is VGG16, and the second one is VGG19. VGG16 has 16 layers, and VGG19 has 19 layers in depth. Both take the input image size of 224*224*3 (RGB image).

Xception: Chollet et al. [26] presented Xception in 2016. There are 36 layers in the Xception model, not including the completely connected layers at the top. The model includes depthwise separable layers, such as MobileNet, as well as "shortcuts," in which the output of some layers is combined with the output of previous layers. A 5-neuron completely linked layer was added on top of the convolutional layers, similar to MobileNet and VGG16.

DenseNet: DenseNet is a better version of ResNet. In ResNet, a layer only gets the output from the last second or third layer, and these outputs are added at the same depth. So it does not affect the depth by adding shortcuts. However, whereas in DenseNet, a layer in the dense gets all the outputs from the previous layers and adds in-depth. Compared to ResNet, Densenet [27] is more effective in computation and in terms of parameters. A 1*1 convolutional layer was added to decrease the computation so that the second convolutional layer has a settled input depth. In the Dense layer, it is easy to observe the feature maps, and it is easy to build a dense square by stacking the number of dense layers. Transition layers take this job in DenseNet.

MobileNet-V2: MobileNet-V2 '[28] is very similar to the ordinary CNN models, but there are three innovative structures used in it; the first one was depthwise separable convolution, and the operation here is divided into two parts. In depth-wise, it applies each filter per channel. It applies a 1*1 filter to all channels of the previous phase's output in terms of pointwise filtering. The second is the bottleneck, and the MobileNet-V2 combines pointwise convolution and bottleneck and uses pointwise to realize bottleneck. We lose much information if we use ReLU as an activation, so we use linear as an activation in the bottleneck to minimize information loss. The third is inverted residual, where we add an extension at the start of the block and use ReLU to add some non-linearity to the construct, and we shortcut here by adding the input and output together and then summarising them as the block's output to get better gradient propagation. These inverted residual blocks pile up and build up the whole model.

EfficientNet: The EfficientNet [29] model family consists of eight models ranging from B0 to B7, each successive model number denotes a variation with more parameters and greater accuracy. Depthwise Convolution + Pointwise Convolution: Reduces measurement costs while ensuring accuracy by splitting the first convolution into two steps. Inverse ResNet: A layer that squeezes the channels is followed by a layer that extends them in the first ResNet segment. In this way, it binds skip links to rich channel layers. Linear bottleneck: To prevent information loss from ReLU, linear activation is used in the final layer of each block. MBConv, an inverted bottleneck conv that was originally known as MobileNet-V2, is the most important building block for EfficientNet.

3.2   Pre-trained CNN Models Training

Most of the pre-trained CNN models are trained on the ImageNet dataset. In order to apply these model on the biopsy images of prostate cancer, transfer learning [30] has been used. The primary reason for using pre-trained CNN models is that it is quick to train and have higher performance on small datasets than CNNs that use randomly initialized weights. To fine-tune the pre-trained CNN models on the histopathological images of prostate cancer, the top layers of pre-trained CNNs have been replaced with the new top layers for fine-tuning. We have used Adam [31] optimizer for the training of the networks that minimize the loss and improves model performance. These models are trained with the learning rate of 0.0001, batch size of 32, and run for up to 50 epochs.

Table 3. Distribution of the biopsy images in the training, validation and test sets

Classes	Total	Training	Validation	Test
Grade 0	2892	2083	231	578
Grade 1	2666	1920	213	533
Grade 2	1343	967	108	268
Grade 3	1242	895	99	248
Grade 4	1249	899	100	250
Grade 5	1224	881	98	245

4   Experiments and Results

4.1   Dataset

The Prostate Cancer Grade Assessment (PANDA) Challenge - Dataset [32] is a publicly accessible repository containing 10,616 biopsy images divided into six classes. Karolinska Institute and Radboud University Medical Center collaborated with different pathologists to collect the biopsy images. Since each image is very large, so images were resized to 512*512 pixels and then cropped according to the network input sizes. The dataset has been split into a training set (80%) and a test set (the remaining 20%). Again the training set is further split into training (90%) and validation (10%) sets. Image distribution in different sets corresponding to each grade is shown in Table 3.

In order to evaluate the performance of the pre-trained models we have used performance metrics such as sensitivity, specificity, precision, F1-score and accuracy [8].

4.2   Results

The classification performance of the various pre-trained CNN models is represented in Table 4. It can be observed from Table 4, EfficientNet-B7 has achieved an accuracy of 90.90%, which is the highest among the pre-trained CNN models. The second highest performance is achieved by the InceptionResNet-V2 model. The EfficientNet-B7 has also outperformed the other pre-trained models in sensitivity, specificity, precision, and F1-score. It has shown an improvement of 1.93%, 1.96%, 0.42%, 1.67%, and 1.88% in accuracy, sensitivity, specificity, precision, and F1-score, respectively. On the other hand, the performance of the MobileNet-V2 model for prostate cancer grading is the poorest among the pre-trained CNN models.

Table 4. Performance of the pre-trained CNN Models.

Model	Accuracy (%)	Sensitivity (%)/recall	Specificity (%)	Precision (%)	F1-score (%)
MobileNet-V2	62.75	60.78	92.19	65.32	61.64
ResNet50	67.16	63.83	93.07	68.74	65.13
DenseNet121	72.86	70.00	94.24	75.91	71.81
DenseNet169	76.44	74.10	95.07	76.61	75.14
VGG16	81.57	80.00	94.04	84.76	81.41
VGG19	84.64	83.48	96.75	86.36	84.55
Xception	88.31	87.51	97.56	89.39	88.14
Inception-V3	88.46	86.90	96.20	91.05	89.05
InceptionResNet-V2	88.97	87.95	97.60	91.09	89.31
EfficientNet-B7	90.90	89.91	98.02	92.76	91.19

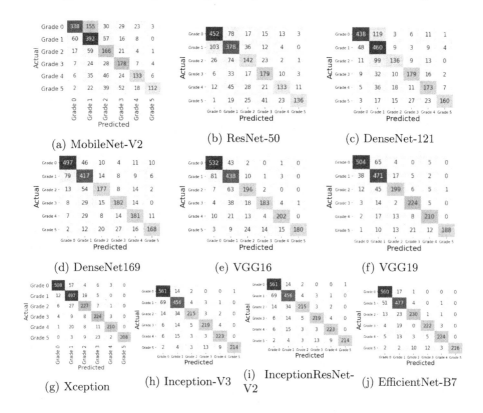

Fig. 3. Confusion matrix for the different Pre-trained CNN models.

Furthermore, the confusion matrix of the pre-trained CNNs is shown in Fig. 3. In the confusion matrix shows pre-trained models performances in terms of true positives, false positives, true negatives and false negatives. It can be seen in the Fig. 3, the EfficientNet-B7 has produces very few false positives and false negative compared to other pre-trained CNN models.

5   Conclusions

In this study, we have investigated state-of-the-art pre-trained models for prostate cancer grading from histopathological images. We have tested the performance of MobileNet-V2, ResNet50, DenseNet121, DenseNet169, VGG16, VGG19, Xception, Inception-V3, InceptionResNet-V2 and EfficientNet-B7 using different performance metrics. The performance of CNN models has been evaluated on the publicly available PANDA dataset. Our experimental results show that the EfficientNet-B7 model is best suited for the prostate cancer grading among the pre-trained networks. It achieved a classification accuracy of 90.90%. The performance of the computer-aided cancer grading system can be improved by deep model ensembling. Hence, in the future, we would like to explore ensemble techniques with pre-trained CNN models.

References

1. Bray, F., Ferlay, J., Soerjomataram, I., Siegel, R. L., Torre, L. A., Jemal, A. Global cancer statistics 2018: GLOBOCAN estimates of incidence and mortality worldwide for 36 cancers in 185 countries. CA: a cancer journal for clinicians, 68(6), 394–424 (2018). https://doi.org/10.3322/caac.21492
2. Rawla, P.: Epidemiology of prostate cancer. World J. Oncol. **10**(2), 63 (2019). https://doi.org/10.14740/wjon1191
3. Gleason, D.F.: Classification of prostatic carcinomas. Cancer Chemother. Rep. **50**, 125–128 (1966)
4. Epstein, J.I., Egevad, L., Amin, M.B., Delahunt, B., Srigley, J.R., Humphrey, P.A.: The 2014 international society of urological pathology (ISUP) consensus conference on Gleason grading of prostatic carcinoma. Am. J. Surg. pathol. **40**(2), 244–252 (2016). https://doi.org/10.1097/PAS.0000000000000530
5. Billis, A., Guimaraes, M.S., Freitas, L.L., Meirelles, L., Magna, L.A., Ferreira, U.: The impact of the 2005 international society of urological pathology consensus conference on standard Gleason grading of prostatic carcinoma in needle biopsies. J. Urol. **180**(2), 548–553 (2008). https://doi.org/10.1016/j.juro.2008.04.018
6. Gour, M., Jain, S., Agrawal, R.: DeepRNNetSeg: deep residual neural network for nuclei segmentation on breast cancer histopathological images. In: Nain, N., Vipparthi, S.K., Raman, B. (eds.) CVIP 2019. CCIS, vol. 1148, pp. 243–253. Springer, Singapore (2020). https://doi.org/10.1007/978-981-15-4018-9_23
7. Gour, M., Jain, S., Sunil Kumar, T.: Residual learning based CNN for breast cancer histopathological image classification. Int. J. Imaging Syst. Technol. **30**(3), 621–635 (2020). https://doi.org/10.1002/ima.22403
8. Gour, M., Jain, S.: Stacked convolutional neural network for diagnosis of COVID-19 disease from X-ray images (2020). arXiv preprint arXiv:2006.13817
9. Tabesh, A., et al.: Multifeature prostate cancer diagnosis and Gleason grading of histological images. IEEE Trans. Med. Imaging **26**(10), 1366–1378 (2007). https://doi.org/10.1109/TMI.2007.898536
10. Källén, H., Molin, J., Heyden, A., Lundström, C., Åström, K.: Towards grading Gleason score using generically trained deep convolutional neural networks. In: 2016 IEEE 13th International Symposium on Biomedical Imaging (ISBI), pp. 1163–1167. IEEE (2016, April). https://doi.org/10.1109/ISBI.2016.7493473
11. Nguyen, K., Jain, A.K., Sabata, B.: Prostate cancer detection: fusion of cytological and textural features. J. Pathol. Inf. **2**, 3 (2011). https://doi.org/10.4103/2153-3539.92030
12. Rezaeilouyeh, H., Mollahosseini, A., Mahoor, M.H.: Microscopic medical image classification framework via deep learning and shearlet transform. J. Med. Imaging **3**(4), 044501 (2016). https://doi.org/10.1117/1.JMI.3.4.044501
13. Zhou, N., Fedorov, A., Fennessy, F., Kikinis, R., Gao, Y.: Large scale digital prostate pathology image analysis combining feature extraction and deep neural network (2017). arXiv preprint arXiv:1705.02678
14. Nguyen, K., Sabata, B., Jain, A.K.: Prostate cancer grading: gland segmentation and structural features. Pattern Recogn. Lett. **33**(7), 951–961 (2012). https://doi.org/10.1016/j.patrec.2011.10.001

15. Diamond, J., Anderson, N.H., Bartels, P.H., Montironi, R., Hamilton, P.W.: The use of morphological characteristics and texture analysis in the identification of tissue composition in prostatic neoplasia. Hum. Pathol. **35**(9), 1121–1131 (2004)
16. Arvaniti, E., Fricker, K.S., Moret, M., Rupp, N., Hermanns, T., Fankhauser, C., Claassen, M.: Automated Gleason grading of prostate cancer tissue microarrays via deep learning. Sci. Rep. **8**(1), 1–11 (2018)
17. Huang, J., Tang, X.: A fast video inpainting algorithm based on state matching. In: 2016 9th International Congress on Image and Signal Processing, BioMedical Engineering and Informatics (CISP-BMEI), pp. 114–118. IEEE (October 2016). https://doi.org/10.1109/CISP-BMEI.2016.7852692
18. Khani, A.A., Jahromi, S.A.F., Shahreza, H.O., Behroozi, H., Baghshah, M.S.: Towards automatic prostate Gleason grading via deep convolutional neural networks. In: 2019 5th Iranian Conference on Signal Processing and Intelligent Systems (ICSPIS), pp. 1–6. IEEE (December 2019). https://doi.org/10.1109/ICSPIS48872.2019.9066019
19. Kelly, H., Chikandiwa, A., Vilches, L.A., Palefsky, J.M., de Sanjose, S., Mayaud, P.: Association of antiretroviral therapy with anal high-risk human papillomavirus, anal intraepithelial neoplasia, and anal cancer in people living with HIV: a systematic review and meta-analysis. Lancet HIV, **7**(4), e262–e278 (2020). https://doi.org/10.1016/S2352-3018(19)30434-5
20. Nir, G., et al.: Automatic grading of prostate cancer in digitized histopathology images: learning from multiple experts. Med. Image Anal. **50**, 167–180 (2018). https://doi.org/10.1016/j.media.2018.09.005
21. Tsehay, Y., et al.: Biopsy-guided learning with deep convolutional neural networks for prostate Cancer detection on multiparametric MRI. In: 2017 IEEE 14th International Symposium on Biomedical Imaging (ISBI 2017), pp. 642–645. IEEE (April 2017). https://doi.org/10.1109/ISBI.2017.7950602
22. Karimi, D., Nir, G., Fazli, L., Black, P.C., Goldenberg, L., Salcudean, S.E.: Deep learning-based Gleason grading of prostate cancer from histopathology images-role of multiscale decision aggregation and data augmentation. IEEE J. Biomed. Health Inf. **24**(5), 1413–1426 (2019). https://doi.org/10.1109/JBHI.2019.2944643
23. Szegedy, C., Vanhoucke, V., Ioffe, S., Shlens, J., Wojna, Z.: Rethinking the inception architecture for computer vision. In: Proceedings of the IEEE Conference on Computer Vision and Pattern Recognition, pp. 2818–2826 (2016)
24. He, K., Zhang, X., Ren, S., Sun, J.: Deep residual learning for image recognition. In: Proceedings of the IEEE Conference on Computer Vision and Pattern Recognition, pp. 770–778 (2016)
25. Liu, S., Deng, W.: Very deep convolutional neural network based image classification using small training sample size. In: 2015 3rd IAPR Asian Conference on Pattern Recognition (ACPR), pp. 730–734. IEEE (November 2015). https://doi.org/10.1109/ACPR.2015.7486599
26. Chollet, F. Xception: Deep learning with depthwise separable convolutions. In: Proceedings of the IEEE Conference on Computer Vision and Pattern Recognition, pp. 1251–1258 (2017)
27. Huang, G., Liu, Z., Van Der Maaten, L., Weinberger, K.Q.: Densely connected convolutional networks. In: Proceedings of the IEEE Conference on Computer Vision and Pattern Recognition, pp. 4700–4708 (2017)
28. Sae-Lim, W., Wettayaprasit, W., Aiyarak, P.: Convolutional neural networks using mobilenet for skin lesion classification. In: 2019 16th International Joint Conference on Computer Science and Software Engineering (JCSSE), pp. 242–247. IEEE (July 2019). https://doi.org/10.1109/JCSSE.2019.8864155

29. Tan, M., Le QV, E.: (1905) Rethinking Model Scaling for Convolutional Neural Networks (2019)
30. Pan, S.J., Yang, Q.: A survey on transfer learning. IEEE Trans. Knowl. Data Eng. **22**(10), 1345–1359 (2010)
31. Kingma, D.P., Ba, J.A.: A method for stochastic optimization (2014). arXiv preprint arXiv:1412.6980
32. Prostate cANcer graDe Assessment (PANDA) Challenge. https://www.kaggle.com/c/prostate-cancer-grade-assessment/data/ (2021). Accessed 20 April 2021

Dyadic Interaction Recognition Using Dynamic Representation and Convolutional Neural Network

R. Newlin Shebiah$^{(\boxtimes)}$ (iD) and S. Arivazhagan (iD)

Centre for Image Processing and Pattern Recognition, Department of Electronics and Communication Engineering, Mepco Schlenk Engineering College, Sivakasi, Tamilnadu 626005, India
{newlinshebiah,sarivu}@mepcoeng.ac.in

Abstract. Human interaction recognition can be used in video surveillance to recognise human behaviour. The goal of this research is to classify human interaction by converting video snippets into dynamic images and deep CNN architecture for classification. The human interaction input video is snipped into a certain number of smaller segments. For each segment, dynamic Image is constructed that efficiently encodes a video segment into an image with an action silhouette, which plays an important role in interaction recognition. The discriminative features are learned and classified from dynamic image using Convolutional Neural Network. The efficacy of the proposed architecture for interaction recognition is demonstrated by the obtained results on the SBU Kinect Interaction dataset, IXMAS, and TV Human Interaction datasets.

Keywords: Human interaction recognition · Dynamic image · Convolutional neural network

1 Introduction

Automated Video surveillance applications aims at detecting the anomalous activities portrayed by the person. The accomplishment of the complex activities in a strange environment is by relating the atomic actions performed by each individual present in the scene. For defining human interactions, along with atomic actions understanding collective behavior between people and the context in which the interaction happens is essential.

Changes in viewpoint results in changes in appearance and have a significant impact in framing an automated human interaction recognition system. Further, while interaction with other individuals' partial occlusion is common factor that hinders the performance of human interaction recognition system. With single view point typical movements or poses of action performing parts are not apparent it is difficult to discern between subtle diverse interaction types. This paper aims at classifying human interaction types by representing the human interaction from the video sequence to dynamic image based on their spatiotemporal characteristics and classify in to the predefined interaction categories.

B. Raman et al. (Eds.): CVIP 2021, CCIS 1567, pp. 95–106, 2022.
https://doi.org/10.1007/978-3-031-11346-8_9

The main contribution of this paper includes:

Representation of interaction with Dynamic image that effectively encodes motion and the appearance in a single image.

Further, the proposed deep learning based network is effective in learning discriminative features and categorize actions with improved computational efficiency.

2 Literature Survey

This section focusses on the literatures related to dyadic interactions considering the postures, movements, and coordination of both individual. Video interaction recognition includes the submodules like effective representation of the scenario with discriminative features followed by the classification of these characteristics into an interaction class. Traditionally human interaction recognition with handcrafted features like extracting motion salient points [1] in the video and template-based approaches [2]. Also, the premier features like Local Binary Pattern and Histogram of Oriented Gradients were used to identify the interactions [3]. With the successful landmark adventures by deep learning-based methods, 3D CNN [4], two-stream CNN [5], and multi-stream CNN [6], have demonstrated their usefulness in video representation by overcoming the problem-dependent limitation of hand-crafted features.

The complex problem of interaction recognition is solved by Ye et al. [7] with multi-feature fusion network. The features are learned parallelly by Inception and ResNet and the features are fused to obtain higher recognition accuracy. With this scheme maximum network performance is attained with minimal network parameters. Ibrahim et al. [8] learned the group behavior by capturing the temporal dynamics of the individual people with LSTM network. The aggregate information is obtained by the designed LSTM model for entire activity understanding. By learning the dynamic inter-related representation over time, Shu et al. [9] suggested a hierarchical long short-term concurrent memory to effectively resolve the challenge of human interaction recognition with numerous participants. Individual inter-related memory was aggregated by capturing concurrently long-term inter-related dynamics among numerous people rather than the dynamics of a single person. To learn the dis-criminative representation of a group activity, Tang et al. [10] presented a coherence limited graph LSTM. The CCG-LSTM modelled individual motions that were significant to the entire activity while suppressing motions that were not. To describe the long-term inter-related dynamics between two interacting people, Shu et al. [11] presented concurrence-aware long short-term sub-memories. With the use of a pre-trained CNN, Lee et al. [12] suggested a human activity representation approach based on the co-occurrence of individual action to anticipate partially seen interaction. To extract features with specific characteristics, Mahmood et al. [13] segmented full-body silhouettes and identified critical body parts that contributes to interaction recognition. Deng et al. [14] used Convolutional Neural Network to acquire action category of individual person and the group activity label is identified by investigating the relationship between individuals. Based on the co-occurrence of human behaviours and their activations, the image-based full-body feature describes the interaction. Each of the three components works in tandem with the LSTM to model individual level behaviour and video level interaction [15].

3   Proposed Methodology

Human Interaction Recognition is by capturing spatial and temporal information across video frames. The person executing the interaction will exhibits distinct characteristics in the commencement and offset of events. A dynamic image represents a change in appearance over time by compressing motion in a video clip into a single frame. The human interaction recognition architecture from dynamic image is shown in Fig. 1.

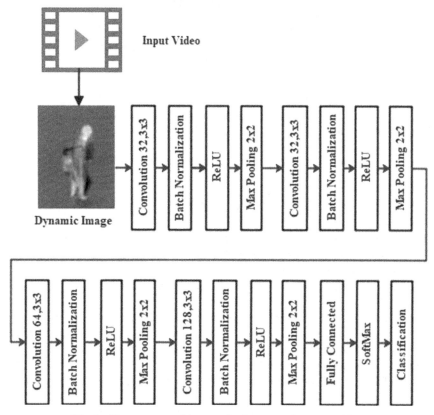

Fig. 1. Two stream architecture for human action recognition

3.1   Construction of Dynamic Image

The inputs videos are segments and each individual snippets are used for constructing dynamic image. Dynamic images are created by applying rank pooling directly to the image pixels of a video snippet, resulting in a single image for each video snippet. Dynamic imaging outperforms the well-known motion estimating technique, optical flow, in terms of efficiency and compactness. The dynamic picture is formed using a rank pooling classifier that sorts the frames of video snippets across time. Instead of processing with effective features, this classifier works directly on the image pixels.

Consider the human interaction video sequence composed of n frames represented as $f_1, f_2, \ldots\ldots, f_n$. Frame at time t represented as f_t is characterized by feature vector $\psi(f_t) \in \mathbb{R}^w$. If f_{t+1} succeeds f_t, the ordering is denoted by $f_{t+1} \succ f_t$. The frame transitivity characteristics are used to organize frames of video sequence pieces. The video frames are ordered using Rank SVM [16], uses a ranking function to get a score for each frame given as $S(t|w) = \langle w, f_t \rangle$, where $w \in \mathbb{R}^w$ is a vector of parameters or termed in general as weights for each frame. The weight vector w reflects the rank of the frames in the video. Therefore, the association of frames is by,

$$\text{i.e. } \forall\{f_1, f_2\} \ s.t. f_1 \succ f_2 \Rightarrow S(f_1|w) > S(f_2|w) \tag{1}$$

$$S(f_1|w) > S(f_2|w) = w.f_1 > w.f_2 \tag{2}$$

Using the RankSVM [30] framework, learning w is stated as a convex optimization problem as given below:

$$w^* = \rho(f_1, f_2, \ldots\ldots, f_n; \psi) = arg \min_d E(W) \tag{3}$$

$$E(w) = \frac{\lambda}{2}||w||^2 + \frac{2}{t(t-1)} \times \sum_{q>t} \max\{0, 1 - S(f_1|w) + S(f_2|w)\} \tag{4}$$

The first term in Eq. (4) is a quadratic regularizer, which is employed in SVMs, and the second term is a hinge-loss soft-counting the number of pairings $f_1 \succ f_2$ that the scoring function erroneously ranks.

The steps involved in dynamic image representation includes:

• Represent a video as a ranking function for its frames: $f_1, f_2, \ldots\ldots, f_n$.
• Represent the frames with its feature vector extracted from each individual frame f_t in the video: $\psi(f_t) \in \mathbb{R}^w$.
• Features are averages up to time t.
• Ranking function assigns a score to each frame in the video, which reflects the order of the frames in the video.
• Rank pooling: the process of constructing w* from a sequence of video frames.

3.2 Deep Learning Architecture for Action Recognition

The proposed architecture for human interaction recognition consists of 4 convolutional layers, 4 Max pooling layers, one fully connected layer and the output layer with Softmax classifier. The architecture accepts the input frame of size 128×128 and the first convolution layer uses 32 initial convolution filters with a kernel size of 3×3 and rectified linear unit (ReLU) activation function is applied to activate neurons of the next layers to make an effective action classification model. The second convolution layer applies 32 convolution filters with 3×3 kernel size. Further, the number of convolutional kernels is increased for Convolution 3 and Convolution 4 as 64, and 128 with 3×3

kernel size (Fig. 1). Batch normalization between convolutional layers and ReLU layer are used to increase the speed of learning and the overall classification accuracy. The last fully connected layer has 'n' neurons, where 'n' represents the number of classes of interactions and the classification results are fed as input to the Softmax classifier. Table 1 presents architecture summary and learnable parameters of the proposed architecture for the proposed Interaction Recognition model.

4   Experimental Results and Discussion – Human Interaction Recognition

The robustness of the suggested Action recognition algorithms is assessed using the SBU Kinect Interaction Dataset, IXMAS, and TV Human Interaction datasets and the results are reported here.

4.1   Dataset Details

SBU-Kinect-Interaction dataset [17] consists of RGB-D video sequences captured in a laboratory environment with 21 sets of people performing eight interactions. Approaching, departing, pushing, kicking, hitting, sharing an object, kissing, and shaking hands are the eight different human-human interactions categories reported in the database. Figure 2 shows sample frames from the SBU Kinect Interaction Dataset.

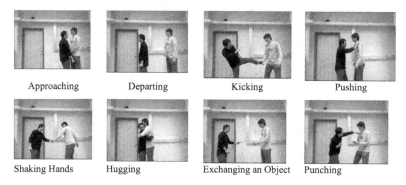

Approaching   Departing   Kicking   Pushing

Shaking Hands   Hugging   Exchanging an Object   Punching

Fig. 2. Sample frames from SBU Kinect Interaction Dataset

IXMAS action dataset [18] comprises of 1148 interaction sequences performed by 5 male & 5 female participants. It is a multi-view dataset with five different view angles. The eleven actions include: (i) Walking (ii) Waving (iii) Punching (iv) Kicking (v) Picking up (vi) Sitting down (vii) Checking Watch (viii) Crossing arms (ix) Scratching head (x) Getting up (xi) Turning around. Figure 3 shows sample frames from the IXMAS action dataset.

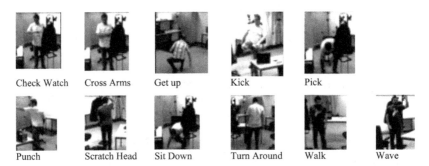

Check Watch   Cross Arms   Get up   Kick   Pick

Punch   Scratch Head   Sit Down   Turn Around   Walk   Wave

Fig. 3. Sample frames from IXMAS action dataset

The TV Human Interaction dataset [19, 20] is made up of brief video segments from popular TV shows that include handshakes, hugs, kisses, and high-fives, as well as negatives. As seen in Fig. 4, all interactions are acted upon, and the recording setting is tightly regulated.

Handshake   High-Five   Hug   Kiss   Negative

Fig. 4. Sample frames from TV Human Interaction dataset

4.2 Dynamic Image Generation

Dynamic images are effective and emotive in summarizing video content and are used to recognize human actions. Per-frame features can help with this. It captures the dynamics of the action as characterized by temporal fluctuations by encapsulating the action attributes and these features over the sequence. A video's temporal order is determined by training a linear ranking machine on the frames of the film. A given frame is converted into a d dimensional gray-scaled vector that encodes the appearance evolution using the rank pooling approach.

Figures 5, 6, and 7 show dynamic images of 8 actions from the SBU Kinect Interaction Dataset, 11 actions from the IXMAS action dataset, and 5 activity categories from the TV Human Interaction dataset, respectively. Furthermore, it is fascinating to note that in the case of dynamic image, the interacting objects are accentuated while the background fades away.

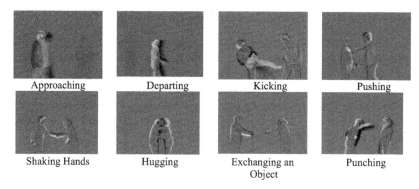

Approaching	Departing	Kicking	Pushing

Shaking Hands	Hugging	Exchanging an Object	Punching

Fig. 5. Dynamic images from SBU Kinect Interaction Dataset

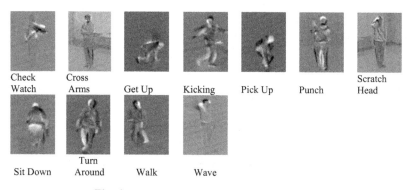

Check Watch	Cross Arms	Get Up	Kicking	Pick Up	Punch	Scratch Head

Sit Down	Turn Around	Walk	Wave

Fig. 6. Dynamic images from IXMAS Dataset

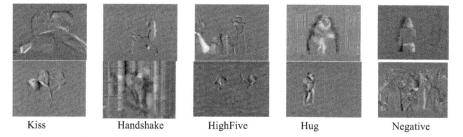

Kiss	Handshake	HighFive	Hug	Negative

Fig. 7. Dynamic images from TV Human Interaction dataset

4.3 Recognition Rate with Convolutional Neural Network

Table 1, Table 2, Table 3 and Table 4 displays the recognition rates for SBU Kinect Interaction Dataset, NIXMAS, OIXMAS and TV Human Interaction dataset, respectively. After each Convolution layer, ReLU is employed as the activation function to train the proposed CNN architecture. The learning rate is first set to 1×10^{-4}.

The developed models are trained for 30 epochs using stochastic gradient descent optimizer. The 75% of entire data is used to train the CNN model and remaining data is utilised to test the performance of the model.

Table 1. Recognition Accuracy Results using the Proposed Algorithm for SBU Kinect Interaction Dataset

	Approaching	Departing	Kicking	Pushing	Shaking hands	Hugging	Exchanging an object	Punching
Approaching	**98.21**	1.79	0	0	0	0	0	0
Departing	1.65	**98.35**	0	0	0	0	0	0
Kicking	0	0	**100**	0	0	0	0	0
Pushing	0.48	0	0	**99.52**	0	0	0	0
Shaking Hands	0	0	1.20	0	**98.80**	0	0	0
Hugging	0	0	0	0	0	**100**	0	0
Exchanging an Object	0	0	0	0	0	0	**100**	0
Punching	0	0	0	0	0	0	0	**100**
Average								**99.36**

Table 2. Recognition accuracy results using the proposed algorithm for NIXMAS dataset

	Check watch	Cross arms	Get up	Kicking	Pick up	Punch	Scratch head	Sit down	Turn around	Walk	Wave
Check watch	**97.16**	0	0	0	0.95	0	0	0	0.95	0	0.95
Cross arms	0	**98.89**	0	0	0	0	1.11	0	0	0	0
Get up	0	0	**98.93**	0	1.07	0	0	0	0	0	0
Kicking	0	0	0	**100**	0	0	0	0	0	0	0
Pick up	0	0	1.20	0	**97.61**	0	0	0	0	1.20	0
Punch	0	0	1.07	1.07	0	**96.80**	0	0	0	1.07	0
Scratch head	0	2.14	0	0	0	0	**97.86**	0	0	0	0
Sit down	0	0	0	0	0	0	0	**100**	0	0	0

(continued)

From Table 2, Table 3 and Table 4 it is observed that some misclassification occurs between the interactions sharing common movements.

Table 2. (*continued*)

	Check watch	Cross arms	Get up	Kicking	Pick up	Punch	Scratch head	Sit down	Turn around	Walk	Wave
Turn around	0	0	0	0	0	0	0	0	**100**	0	0
Walk	0.79	0	0	0	0	1.18	0	0	0	**96.85**	1.18
Wave	1.52	0	0	0	0.91	0	0	0	0	0	**97.58**
Average											**98.33**

Table 3. Recognition accuracy results using the proposed algorithm for OIXMAS dataset

	Check watch	Cross arms	Get up	Kicking	Pick up	Punch	Scratch head	Sit down	Turn around	Walk	Wave
Check watch	**97.60**	0	0	0.68	0	0	0	0	0	1.71	0
Cross arms	0	**99.05**	0	0.95	0	0	0	0	0	0	0
Get up	0	0	**100**	0	0	0	0	0	0	0	0
Kicking	1.03	0.68	0	**95.55**	0	1.03	0	0	1.71	0	0
Pick up	0	1.27	0	0	**98.73**	0	0	0	0	0	0
Punch	0	1.59	0	0	1.27	**95.56**	0	0	1.59	0	0
Scratch head	0	0	0	0	0	0	**98.41**	0	0	0	1.59
Sit down	0	0	1.04	0	0	0	1.38	**96.54**	0	0	0
Turn around	0	0	0	1.37	2.05	0	0	0	**95.21**	1.03	0
Walk	3.25	1.81	0	0	0	0.36	0	0	0.72	**93.86**	0
Wave	0	0	0	0	0.63	0	1.59	0	0	0	**97.78**
Average											**97.22**

Table 4. Recognition accuracy results using the proposed algorithm for TV interaction dataset

	Kiss	Handshake	High five	Hug	Negative
Kiss	**100**	0	0	0	0
Handshake	0.48	**95.69**	1.44	0	2.39
High Five	0.44	0	**99.11**	0.44	0
Hug	0.45	0	0	**99.55**	0
Negative	0.22	0.67	0.89	0.22	**97.99**
Average					**98.46**

Ablation study:
By deleting the initial convolution, batch normalisation, ReLu, and maxpooling layers, an ablation study was conducted to test the effectiveness of the deep architecture. Second, rather than using maximum pooling, average pooling is used. Experiments were conducted to evaluate the performance and justify the first layer's inclusion in the proposed deep architecture. The results obtained are shown in Table 5.

Table 5. Ablation study of human interaction recognition using proposed architecture.

	SBU Kinect interaction dataset	NIXMAS dataset	OIXMAS dataset	TV interaction dataset
Proposed architecture	**99.36**	**98.33**	**97.22**	**98.46**
Initial layers Removed	99.27	97.68	96.34	97.18
Average Pooling	98.84	97.32	96.34	98.46

State of art work on SBU Kinect Interaction dataset concentrated with skeleton points and Song et al. [21] used end-to-end spatial and temporal attention model with RNN and LSTM and achieved 91.51% accuracy. Liu et al. [22] used RGB and optical flow frames, training on the time sequences of 3D body skeleton joints and achieved 94.90% accuracy. Yun et al. [23] mapped 2D keypoints into 3D poses using a two-stream deep neural network and with Efficient Neural Architecture Search (ENAS) algorithm for modeling 3D poses and obtained 96.30% accuracy.

5   Conclusion

The dynamic representation from videos for human interaction recognition was investigated and analyzed in this paper. Furthermore, the dynamic image is compact, condensed, and effectively represents the video sequence's long-term dynamics. The deep framework that was created learns the discriminative features well and produces good recognition results. It has been claimed that the system performs well with minimal computing complexity and is resistant to action changes. On the SBU Kinect Interaction dataset, IXMAS, and TV Human Interaction datasets, the proposed system outperformed state-of-the-art methods for recognition of interactions.

References

1. Gao, C., Yang, L., Du, Y., Feng, Z., Liu, J.: From constrained to unconstrained datasets: an evaluation of local action descriptors and fusion strategies for interaction recognition. World Wide Web **19**, 265–276 (2016)
2. Tian, Y., Sukthankar, R., Shah, M.: Spatiotemporal deformable part models for action detection. In: Computer Vision and Pattern Recognition, (CVPR), pp. 2642–2649 (2013)
3. Bibi, S., Anjum, N., Sher, M.: Automated multi-feature human interaction recognition in complex environment. Comput. Ind. **99**, 282–293 (2018). ISSN 0166-3615, https://doi.org/10.1016/j.compind.2018.03.015
4. Ji, S., Xu, W., Yang, M., Yu, K.: 3d convolutional neural networks for human action recognition. IEEE Trans. Pattern Anal. Mach. Intell. **35**(1), 221–231 (2013)
5. Simonyan, A.Z.: Two-stream convolutional networks for action recognition in videos. In: Advances in Neural Information Processing Systems, pp. 568–576 (2014)
6. Tu, Z., et al.: Multistream CNN: learning representations based on human-related regions for action recognition. Pattern Recogn. **79**, 32–43 (2018)
7. Ye, Q., Zhong, H., Qu, C., Zhang, Y.: Human interaction recognition based on whole-individual detection. Sensors **20**(8), 2346 (2020). https://doi.org/10.3390/s20082346
8. Ibrahim, M.S., Muralidharan, S., Deng, Z., Vahdat, A., Mori, G.: A hierarchical deep temporal model for group activity recognition. In: Proceedings of the IEEE Conference on Computer Vision and Pattern Recognition, pp. 1971–1980 (2016)
9. Shu, X., Tang, J., Qi, G., Liu, W., Yang, J.: Hierarchical long short-term concurrent memory for human interaction recognition. IEEE Trans. Pattern Anal. Mach. Intell. (2019)
10. Tang, J., Shu, X., Yan, R., Zhang, L.: Coherence constrained graph lstm for group activity recognition. IEEE Trans. Pattern Anal. Mach. Intell. (2019)
11. Shu, X., Tang, J., Qi, G.-J., Song, Y., Li, Z., Zhang, L.: Concurrence-aware long short-term sub-memories for person-person action recognition. In: Proceedings of the IEEE Conference on Computer Vision and Pattern Recognition Workshops, pp. 1–8 (2017)
12. Lee, D.-G., Lee, S.-W.: Prediction of partially observed human activity based on pre-trained deep representation. Pattern Recogn. **85**, 198–206 (2019)
13. Mahmood, M., Jalal, A., Sidduqi, M.: Robust spatio-temporal features for human interaction recognition via artificial neural network. In: International Conference on Frontiers of Information Technology, pp. 218–223. IEEE (2018)
14. Deng, Z., Vahdat, A., Hu, H., Mori, G.: Structure inference machines: recurrent neural networks for analyzing relations in group activity recognition. In: Proceedings of the IEEE Conference on Computer Vision and Pattern Recognition, pp. 4772–4781 (2016)
15. Lee, D.-G., & Lee, S.-W.: Human Interaction Recognition Framework based on Interacting Body Part Attention (2021). http://arxiv.org/abs/2101.08967
16. Fernando, B., Gavves, E., JoseOramas, M., Ghodrati, A., Tuytelaars, T.: Rank pooling for action recognition. IEEE Trans. Pattern Anal. Mach. Intell. **39**(4), 773–787 (2017). https://doi.org/10.1109/TPAMI.2016.2558148
17. Yun, K., Honorio, J., Chattopadhyay, D., Berg, T.L., Samaras, D.: The 2nd International Workshop on Human Activity Understanding from 3D Data at Conference on Computer Vision and Pattern Recognition, CVPR 2012 (2012)
18. Weinland, D., Ronfard, R., Boyer, E.: Free viewpoint action recognition using motion history volumes. Computer Vision and Image Understanding (CVIU), vol. 104, no. 2–3 (2006)
19. Patron-Perez, A., Marszalek, M., Reid, I., Zisserman, A.: Struc-tured learning of human interactions in TV shows. Trans. Pattern Anal. Mach. Intell. **34**, 2441–2453 (2012)
20. Patron-Perez, A., Marszalek, M., Zisserman, A., Reid, I.D.: Highfive: Recognising human interactions in TV shows, in: British MachineVision Conference (BMVC) (2010)

21. Song, S.; Lan, C.; Xing, J.; Zeng, W., Liu, J.: An End-to-End Spatio-Temporal Attention Model for Human Action Recognition from Skeleton Data. In Proceedings of the AAAI Conference on Artificial Intelligence (AAAI), San Francisco, CA, USA, 4–9 February 2017

22. Liu, J., Wang, G., Duan, L., Abdiyeva, K., Kot, A.C.: Skeleton-based human action recognition with global context-aware attention LSTM networks. IEEE Trans. Image Process. (TIP) **27**, 1586–1599 (2018)

23. Pham, H.H., Salmane, H., Khoudour, L., Crouzil, A., Velastin, S.A., Zegers, P.: A unified deep framework for joint 3D pose estimation and action recognition from a single RGB camera. Sensors (Switzerland), **20**(7) (2020). https://doi.org/10.3390/s20071825

Segmentation of Unstructured Scanned Devanagari Newspaper Documents

Rupinder Pal Kaur[1]([✉]), Munish Kumar[2], and M. K. Jindal[3]

[1] Department of Computer Applications, Guru Nanak College, Muktsar, Punjab, India
chatharupinder@yahoo.com
[2] Department of Computational Sciences, Maharaja Ranjit Singh Punjab Technical University, Bathinda, Punjab, India
[3] Department of Computer Science and Applications, Panjab University Regional Centre, Muktsar, Punjab, India

Abstract. Newspapers are a great source of information. Very large projects are running worldwide to preserve the repository of this pile of data. One way is to digitize the pages and store them on a disk. But digitization preserves only the image, no searchable option can be made available on an image to search a particular headline or event. So, the appropriate way is to develop an OCR that could convert data into the process-able form. In this paper, a very novel technique is presented to completely segment the Devanagari news article. News documents may consist of images related to the event along with the text. So, images or graphics need to be separated first for further segmentation of blocks. If the newspaper article is only textual then the segmentation process will start by segmenting the body text (columns etc.) from the headline section. There could be many hurdles in the development of OCR for the newspaper due to the complex layout. Generally, the biggest problem is caused to poor paper and printing quality. Many problems have also been discussed in this article. This paper presents a complete segmentation of text/graphics, headlines, columns, lines, and characters. Proposed algorithms have achieved good accuracies on both textual as well non-textual document images.

Keywords: Text/graphics · Columns · Line segmentation · Devanagari

1 Introduction

Newspaper information needs to be preserved for future use that's why many organizations worldwide are running projects (web1, web2, web3, web4). From the digitized image, data cannot be searched if anyone needs to search a headline related to any event. Optical character recognition is the solution to make data searchable. In this digital day and age, it's become obligatory to possess all the available information during a digital form recognized by machines. within a country like India, where there's an abundance of data within the sort of manuscripts, ancient texts, books, etc. that are traditionally available in printed/handwritten form, such printed material is inadequate when it involves

B. Raman et al. (Eds.): CVIP 2021, CCIS 1567, pp. 107–117, 2022.
https://doi.org/10.1007/978-3-031-11346-8_10

searching information among thousands of pages. It's to be digitized and converted to a textual form in order to be recognized by machines doing searches of many thousand pages/second. Then only, true knowledge of Indian history, tradition, and culture would be available to the masses and therefore the digital revolution would be said to possess reached the knowledge age.

But there are many hurdles on the way to make OCR of newspaper articles. These problems can be:

- Presence of graphics/images in news documents related to the event.
- The variable font size of the text in body columns and headlines.
- Text is organized into columns that need to be segmented before line segmentation.
- Overlapping of lines due to heavily printed ink.
- Shorter lines generally in starting and ending of paragraph in a column.
- Mostly pixel density is taken into account to segment the text lines, but sometimes pixel density of text lines is very low.
- Degradations of text due to poor paper and printing quality.
- Lower character recognition due to bleed through characters.
- Mixing of numerals to describe date-time etc.
- Watermarks, marks of folding, marks of binding cause problems in the segmentation of blocks.
- Environmental factors like acidic reactions may degrade the quality of paper.

These are few hurdles discussed by various authors like Kaur and Jindal (2016) and found ourselves also that makes the development of OCR for a newspaper difficult task. Almost all Indian scripts are cursive in nature making them hard to recognize by machines. Scripts like Devanagari, Gujarati, Bengali, and many others have conjuncts or joint-characters increasing segmentation difficulties. To add to that, various fonts of various sizes used for printing texts over the years, the quality of paper, scanning resolution, images in texts, etc. asks for challenging image processing jobs in newspaper digitization. There are different entities in the newspaper document that need to be addressed or segmented before recognition. These entities are:

- Text region: text region is the main body of any news that describes the event that occurred. The font of text varies from newspaper to newspaper but generally, body text font is a smaller amount than title lines. Style and font remain the same for the whole-body text.
- Title: The title of the news article gives an introduction to the news. The font of the title is large than the body text. Many lines may be in the title region. Subtitles may also be present in the article. Titles run through columns, don't break in columns like body text.
- Horizontal and vertical lines: horizontal and vertical continuous or broken lines that separate articles on newspaper pages.
- Images: Digital photos present in the article associated with the event described in the article.
- Drawings: graphics present in the article like several maps etc.

Fig. 1. A sample newspaper article image

Figure 1 is representing a Devanagari newspaper article image with text and image. As mentioned above newspaper articles printed in any script may have above-said difficulties. Devanagari script itself poses many problems like:

- All the individual characters in the Devanagari script are joined by a headline called "Shiro Rekha" like in alike scripts for e.g., Gurumukhi. This poses difficulty to segment individual characters from the words. E.g.

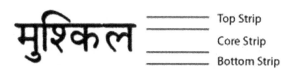

- There are many isolated dots, that are vowel modifiers, namely, "Anuswar" that sound from the nose, "Visarga", is a symbol that is put up in front of a character, and "Chandra Bindu" is a dot in the lower half-circle. These modifiers add up to the difficulty.
- Ascenders and Descender classification is also difficult, contribute to the complex nature of the script.
- Many complex 'Varan' (characters) can be formed like:

म्र   ज्ज   व्य   द्द

2 Related Work

Newspaper documents consist of images, headlines, columns, text lines, captions, etc. so all these blocks need to be segmented. Research papers have been reviewed keeping in view the entire segmentation requirement. A lot of papers are available that segment images/graphics at the international level. But in Indian script very few papers are present. Kaur et al. (2020) have presented a novel technique to segment images in a news article from the text. A combination of run-length smearing algorithm and projection profile has been implemented to segment the article image and text. Moreno-García et al. (2017) have proposed a method to segment images/drawing from engineering maps. The technique presented in the paper is based on heuristics-based that focus on localization and detection of symbols of the drawing. This technique shows the improved results as compared to the other three techniques proposed by Fletcher and Kasturi (1988), Lu (1998), and Tombre et al. (2002). Rege and Chandrakar (2012) have used a Run-length smearing algorithm (RLSA) and boundary parameters detection methods to segment a digitized document image into text and non-text document. In the pre-processing phase thresholding of document and noise removal are performed on the document image. For block extraction constrained RLSA is used. AND operator is further applied on resultant images. Using 4 connectivity boundaries are extracted and connected component analysis is done to separate the blocks as text and non-text blocks. Kumar et al. (2016) have used text area to label headlines, sub-headlines, paragraphs, etc. using an automatic layout analysis system. Morphological operations have been used to segment text/graphics regions.

The headline and column segmentation is an important phase in the proper development of OCR. A good technique to segment images of newspaper articles printed in English newspaper articles is proposed by Bansal (2014). Each node (block) is labeled based on the features of block-like appearance and some contextual features. Appearance features associate each node to label using the features of that block. This way all blocks of the image are segmented. Omee et al. (2013) proposed a technique to segment headlines and columns in news articles printed in Bangla script. The accuracy achieved by this technique is about 70.2%. To the best of our knowledge, none of these techniques have been tried to implement on the Devanagari script to segment headlines and columns. After segmenting the columns, lines need to be segmented to extract the character image. Kaur and Jindal (2019) have proposed a method to segment headlines from columns in Gurumukhi script newspaper article images. A good accuracy has been reported in the paper. Garg and Garg (2014) have proposed a piece-wise histogram projection to segment lines in the Devanagari script. The document was divided into 8 equal size vertical strips. Each strip was divided into horizontal stripes based on the white space in between the lines. In the end, segmented text lines were combined to form a text line. Many limitations were found in this method like overlapped or touched lines were not accurately segmented. Maximum accuracy is reported 93.9% when the document was divided into six vertical stripes. To segment characters printed in the Bangla script, Mahmud et al. (2003) proposed a method based on headline detections. First lines were segmented based on headline detection and word were separated by histogram projection. For character segmentation white space in between the characters was used. As Devanagari consist of half characters or sometimes a character was segmented into two different parts, then a depth-first search algorithm was applied to combine the characters. Estimating the height of text lines around 20 to 40 pixels, a method for segmentation of skewed text lines was proposed by Malgi and Gayakwad (2014). It was assumed in this paper that; the height of a text line can be up to 25 pixels. By extracting these values, headlines and baselines were detected. Accuracy reported in segmentation of headline was 78% and for baseline detection was 89%.

3   Experimental Work

Around 50 news articles from different newspapers like "Danik Bhaskar", "Dainik Jagran", and "Amar Ujala" were scanned on 300 dpi resolution. The newspaper page image was manually cropped to extract newspaper articles for experimentation. The cropped image was converted to binary or bitmap form using Otsu's method. The articles under experimentation were only text documents as well as documents that consist of both text and graphics mix regions. So, first text and graphics were needed to be segmented for further text segmentation.

a. **Text/graphic segmentation:** we experimented on many techniques before reaching the proposed method. The first experiment was done on the idea of detection of the boundary line of the image. It was observed from the scanned documents that the image has a black boundary line almost in every article. Its worked good on the images that had clear black boundary but failed in segmenting the image where pixels of boundary line were degraded due to poor printing or paper quality.

The proposed method is based on a hybrid of two techniques namely RLSA and projection profile. The process is divided into two phases. In the first phase, the image area is located using RLSA. To get accurate results both horizontal, as well as vertical run-length smearing algorithms, have been implemented. And in the second phase, the located image area is segmented from text using the projection profile method. Following are the steps in algorithm to segment an image call *text_image*.

Algorithm 1.1: text and image segmentation		
Phase 1:	RLSA	
	Step1.1	Load the scanned image *text_image*.
	Step 1.2	Fix the *threshold values for horizontal as well as vertical RLSA.
	Step 1.3	Apply horizontal RLSA on *text_image* to produce the resultant image hr_image.
	Step 1.4	Apply vertical RLSA on *text_image* to produce a resultant image *vr_image*.
	Step 1.5	Implement *AND* operator on hr_image and vr_image to produce a final RLSA image *rs_image* in which image area will be located.
Phase 2:	Projection Profile	
	Step 1.6	Apply horizontal projection profile on image *rs-image* to find out the largest strip (this strip consists of image).
	Step 1.7	Note the dimensions of largest strip.
	Step 1.8	Implement vertical horizontal projection profile to cut the image area
	Step 1.9	Save the segmented image with only text regions.

Following are the results of the above-proposed algorithm. Images in Fig. 2 are presenting the results of the implementation of phase 1 and phase 2 on a document shown in Fig. 1.

b. **Headline and column segmentation:** After the segmentation of the image, only text regions left in the document image that consists of different blocks like headlines, columns, etc. Headline needs to be segmented first because the headline is generally spanned over whole document that poses difficulty in segmentation of columns. Once headline is segmented it will easy to segment the text columns. For this purpose, white space pitch method is used. Following are the steps in segmentation of headline and columns:

(a)   (b)

(c)   (d)

पंचायत ने हैंडबाल खिलाड़ियों को बांटी किटें

फरीदकोट, 4
जुलाई (जसबीर
कौर/बांसल): गांव
कम्मेआना में गांव की
पंचायत की तरफ से
बाबा शैदू शाह स्पोर्ट्स
सैंटर के छोटे-छोटे
खिलाड़ियों को
स्पोट्स किट्स बांटी
गई। खेल विभाग के
की तरफ से बच्चों

खेल क्षेत्र के साथ जोड़ने के लिए निरंतर ही
प्रयास किया जा रहा है।
कोच श्री शर्मा की तरफ से गांववासियों
के सहयोग से बच्चों को हैंडबाल का खेल
खिलाने के लिए बाबा शैदू शाह स्पोर्ट्स सैंटर
चलाया जा रहा है। इस सैंटर में तैयार हुए बच्चे

जसपाल सिंह राजा संधू प्रधान कम्मेआना, डा.
मनजीत सिंह बिट्टू, गुरमीत सिंह संधू, रुपिन्द्र
सिंह आस्ट्रेलिया, नैब्ब सिंह खालसा, लखबीर
सिंह गिल व लवप्रीत सिंह ने किट बांटने की
रस्म अदा की और बच्चों को पूरा जीवन नशों
से दूर रहने के लिए प्रेरित किया।

(e)

Fig. 2. Text/graphic segmentation (a) Bitmap image of document in Fig. 1 (b) Horizontal RLSA (c) Vertical RLSA (d) Implementation of *AND* operator (e) image segmented from the text

Figure 3 is presenting the results of headline and column segmentation on the document presented in Fig. 2(e).

Fig. 3. Headline and column segmentation

c. **Text line segmentation:** The main objective of segmentation is to extract the character image. But to extract characters individual text lines need to be segmented. Devanagari is a script that consists of a headline that joins the characters to form a word. In most of the scripts headline detection method or white space, the pitch method is used to segment the text lines. In our method, we have used a hybrid technique to segment text lines. Few experiments were performed on existing techniques like projection profile, RLSA, median calculation but none of these techniques fully segmented the text lines. Limitations like over-segmentation, under segmentation, were faced in the projection profile method. The median calculation is the technique used to pose a headline for the text lines whose headline is not detected due to low pixel density. When line segmentation was tried by using median calculation, it segmented the text lines in the document where lines were few in number. But as in newspaper articles, there can be a large number of lines in a column. So, the median calculation also fails to segment text lines accurately. RLSA also combines two text lines as a one-line where overlapping was occurring.

So, we proposed a method based on two techniques that are median calculation and projection profile. Using projection profile headlines were detected and for the text lines whose headline was not detected due to low pixel density, we posed a false headline using median calculation. This method worked very well even on documents with a large number of text lines. Figure 4 is presenting the results of text line segmentation in the document presented in Fig. 2(e).

Fig. 4. Text line segmentation results in the columns

d. **Word and character segmentation:** Individual text line was segregated successfully to segment the words and further characters. As the characteristic of the Devanagari script word is formed by the conjunction of characters through the headline. Once lines were segmented it is easy to segment the words using the white space pitch method. Next to individual characters image was fetched by using the feature of headlines. The headline above the word was located used projection profile and was

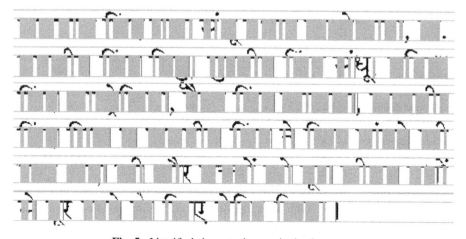

Fig. 5. Identified character images in the document

removed. This made way out clear to segment the characters. Then character image was segmented using a continuous run of white pixels. Figure 5 is presenting the results of identified images of characters and was individually segmented.

4 Discussion on Experimental Results

Experiments were carried out on a database of 50 documents that consist of both textual and non-textual document images. Text/graphics segmentation algorithm produced very good accuracy. Limitation in the algorithm was found when we implemented the technique on skewed documents. In these documents, text blocks were overlapped when the RLSA technique was implemented. Once RLSA failed to locate an accurate image area, the projection profile produced wrong segmentation results. The headline and column segmentation worked very well on all the documents. Text lines were segmentation algorithm produced very results even on the textual documents where the document was little skewed but was unable to segment the text line where skewness angle was large.

5 Conclusion

A complete segmentation of Devanagari newspaper article image has been presented in this paper. These algorithms can also be implemented where page layout is Manhattan. In non-Manhattan page layout pixels are place unevenly so the RLSA and projection profile techniques do not work properly on non-Manhattan page layout. Also, these algorithms can be implemented on the newspaper's articles from different Indian script like Gurumukhi, Bangla etc. that share common properties with Devanagari. Accuracy of different algorithm is given in Table 1. These accuracies have been calculated during complete segmentation of document images.

Table 1. Percentage accuracies of different techniques

Technique	No. of images	Correctly segmented	Accuracy
Text/graphic Segmentation	50	49	98%
Headline and column segmentation	50	49	98%
Text line segmentation	1235 text lines	1185	95.9%
character segmentation	9,880 characters images	9730	98.48%

We have experimented with these algorithms on documents from books and magazines also because these pages have a Manhattan layout generally.

References

[Web1] http://www.loc.gov/ndnp/

[Web2] http://www.neh.gov/us-ne://wspaper-program

[Web3] http://www.nla.gov.au/content/newspaper-digitisation-program

[Web4] https://www.kb.nl/en/organisation/research-expertise/digitization-projects-in-the-kb/dat abank-of-digital-daily-newspapers/the-ddd-project

Bansal, A.: Newspaper article extraction using hierarchical fixed point model. Document Analysis Systems (DAS). In: 11th IAPR International Workshop on IEEE, pp. 257–261 (2014)

Fletcher, L.A., Kasturi, R.: Robust algorithm for text string separation from mixed text/graphics images (1988). IEEE Trans. Pattern Anal. Mach. Intell. **10**(6), 910–918 (1988)

Garg, R., Garg, N.K.: An algorithm for text line segmentation in handwritten skewed and overlapped Devanagari script. Int. J. Emerging Trends Eng. Dev. **4**(5), 114–118 (2014)

Kaur, R.P., Jindal, M.K.: Headline and column segmentation in printed Gurumukhi Script Newspapers. In: Panigrahi, B.K., Trivedi, M.C., Mishra, K.K., Tiwari, S., Singh, P.K. (eds.) Smart Innovations in Communication and Computational Sciences. AISC, vol. 670, pp. 59–67. Springer, Singapore (2019). https://doi.org/10.1007/978-981-10-8971-8_6

Kaur, R.P., Jindal, M.K., Kumar, M.: Text and graphics segmentation of newspapers printed in Gurmukhi script: a hybrid approach. Vis. Comput. **37**(7), 1637–1659 (2020). https://doi.org/10.1007/s00371-020-01927-0

Kaur, R., Jindal, M.K.: Problems in making OCR of Gurumukhi script newspapers. Int. J. Adv. Res. Comput. Sci. **7**(6), 16–22 (2016)

Kumar, S.S., Rajendran, P., Prabaharan, P., Soman, K.P.: Text/Image region separation for document layout detection of old document images using non-linear diffusion and level set. Procedia Comput. Sci. **93**, 469–477 (2016)

Lu, Z.: Detection of text regions from digital engineering drawings. IEEE Trans. Pattern Anal. Mach. Intell. **20**(4), 431–439 (1998)

Mahmud, S.M., Shahrier, N., Hossain, A.D., Chowdhury, M.T.M., Sattar, M.A.: An efficient segmentation scheme for the recognition of printed Bangla characters. In: Proceedings of ICCIT, pp. 283–286 (2003)

Malgi, S.P., Gayakwad, S.: Line segmentation of devnagri handwritten documents. Int. J. Electron. Commun. Instrument. Eng. Res. Dev. (IJECIERD), **4**(2), 25–32 (2014)

Moreno-García, C.F., Elyan, E., Jayne, C.: Heuristics-based detection to improve text/graphics segmentation in complex engineering drawings. In: Boracchi, G., Iliadis, L., Jayne, C., Likas, A. (eds.) EANN 2017. CCIS, vol. 744, pp. 87–98. Springer, Cham (2017). https://doi.org/10.1007/978-3-319-65172-9_8

Omee, F.Y., Himel, MdS.S., Bikas, Md.A.N.: An Algorithm for headline and column separation in bangla documents. In: Abraham, A., Thampi, S. (eds.) Intelligent Informatics. ASCI, vol. 182, pp. 307–315. Springer, Heidelberg (2013). https://doi.org/10.1007/978-3-642-32063-7_32

Rege, P.P., Chandrakar, C.A.: Text-image separation in document images using boundary/perimeter detection. ACEEE Int. J. Signal Image Process. **3**(1), 10–14 (2012)

Tombre, K., Tabbone, S., Pélissier, L., Lamiroy, B., Dosch, P.: Text/graphics separation revisited. In: Lopresti, D., Hu, J., Kashi, R. (eds.) DAS 2002. LNCS, vol. 2423, pp. 200–211. Springer, Heidelberg (2002). https://doi.org/10.1007/3-540-45869-7_24

Automatic Classification of Sedimentary Rocks Towards Oil Reservoirs Detection

Anu Singha[1]($\boxtimes$), Priya Saha[2], and Mrinal Kanti Bhowmik[3]

[1] Sri Ramachandra Faculty of Engineering and Technology, Sri Ramachandra Institute of Higher Education and Research, Chennai, India
anusingh5012@gmail.com

[2] Department of Computer Science and Engineering, Lovely Professional University, Phagwara, Punjab, India

[3] Department of Computer Science and Engineering, Tripura University (A Central University), Agartala, India
mrinalkantibhowmik@tripurauniv.in

Abstract. In technological advancement, there are several techniques have discovered for exact identification of hydrocarbons which is being used by oil industries to detect the oil reservoirs. In this study, we have investigated and proposed system of detection and prediction of hydrocarbons under earth subsurface through microscopic rock image modality. This system presents a robust watershed segmentation approach for determining porosity where convolutional neural networks are used for classification of sandstone and carbonate rock samples. The system is tested on microscopic images of sandstone and carbonate rock samples, and detection observed in rocks is based upon estimation of total porosity. Experimental comparison of proposed system shows outperform over state-of-the-art methods.

Keywords: Oil reservoir · Microscopic rock samples · Convolutional neural network · Watershed · Porosity

1 Introduction

The hydrocarbon detection is to detect the amount of hydrocarbons (i.e. oil and gas) present in earth subsurface. Hydrocarbon deposits are not found in the underground lakes or pools since they are actually located in pore spaces of the porous sedimentary rocks [1, 2]. In this paper, a machine learning based on image processing method has used to analyze the porosity of sedimentary rocks. Edwin drake was the first American person drilled for oil and get a success in 1859 [3]. As time passes, various industries showed interests in drilling and get their success ratio less. Later on, studied on rocks came into a picture for oil observation, and pore size, volume, porosity, permeability are all the key properties associated with the characterization of any hydrocarbon reservoir [1]. Reservoir rock looks solid to the naked eyes but examining the rock through microscope reveals existence the tiny spaces in the rock [4]. By studying porosity of thin section from sedimentary rock samples under the microscopic image is one of the most favorable techniques for prediction and detection of oil reservoir in a rock.

B. Raman et al. (Eds.): CVIP 2021, CCIS 1567, pp. 118–129, 2022.
https://doi.org/10.1007/978-3-031-11346-8_11

Sedimentary rocks are basically categorized into three classes, namely, clastic, carbonate, and evaporitic [5]. The hydrocarbon deposits are found in clastic as well as in carbonate sedimentary rocks such as sandstone, limestone, dolomite, breccia, shale, etc. There are several earlier methods to detect oil reservoir such as physical examination, aerial photos, satellite images, and gravitational studies. Among them in gravitational studies, geologist used magnetometers to mark the changes location for finding new sources of oil. Recently, the methods like remote sensing, wildcatting, and geophysical surveys are useful where geophysical surveys have been used around the world for greater than five decades for oil and natural gas exploration. These surveys decide feature of the earth's subsurface by computing the physical divergence between rock types without seeing them directly by digging. The process of oil digging for hydrocarbon can be categorized into two main classes, namely, offshore and onshore [6]. The offshore digging linked with drilling below the seabed, where about 30% of the world fuel production comes from this drilling process. As offshore drilling relates to drilling in the ocean, the seismic imaging plays an important role in creating 3D image of the subsurface rocks. The main problem is that obtaining of the images, because the waves travel faster through salt than in rock. As a result, the final image cannot be accomplished. On the other hand, the onshore digging linked with drilling deep holes under the earth's surface, where about 70% of the global oil production comes from this drilling process. Herewith, it cannot precisely tell what types of rocks are below the surface and it can only predict the presence of hydrocarbons. Oil industries face challenges during drilling are pipe sticking, loss of circulation, pipe failures, mud contamination, hole cleaning, hole deviation, and so on.

To increase the possibility in search of a productive well, oil industries gather more information about the site or field before and after drilling. As a consequence, gathering information about the site or field before and after drilling is very helpful for industries which avoids drilling in unproductive wells. For geologists, it is a quiet challenging to determine the rock categories and the exact percentage of porosity (i.e., hydrocarbon deposits) in each type of rock through their eyes and subjective evaluation. In this paper, we have provided a combination of deep learning and machine learning based technique for classification and detection of oil reservoir by using scanning electron microscopic (SEM) imaging. Therefore, automating the process for detection of oil reservoir is highly needed to reduce the negative influence of subjective evaluation.

The contributions of this paper are summarized below:

I.   The paper provides the research community with annotated ground truth (GT) images of microscopic sandstone and carbonate samples from the DRSDR1 [7] dataset for pore space analysis which is previously not done.
II. The paper provides a proposed schematic system flow for estimating porosity of microscopic samples of hydrocarbon stones. The system flow is covering two portions as follows:

II.1. First portion analyses the classification performances of reservoir stones using state-of-the-art deep convolutional neural networks (CNN).
II.2. Second portion provides the segmentation output of pore spaces of reservoir stones using a robust watershed algorithm for pore space analysis.

III. The segmented microscopic reservoir stone images are then compared with ground truth via several performance evaluation metrics.

IV. Finally, estimated the porosity values and evaluated comparison of our proposed system with most widely used state-of-the-art hydrocarbon detection methods.

Rest of the paper is organized as follows: Sect. 2 discusses the review on oil reservoirs using multimodal imaging and in Sect. 3 discusses the methodology and the workflow of the proposed system. Section 4 is about experimental results and discussions. Finally, Sect. 5 consists of conclusion and future work.

2   Related Work

Image processing has been used in the field of geoscience for a long time. The scientists have been tried to use image processing in study of rock properties for prediction of porosity and permeability that are essential for petroleum industry. Image is a key feature due to its higher resolution where pores are visible more helps for correct determination of porosity. Image analysis by scientists all over the world have been brought revolution for oil industries in order to take out more important information from geological images [1]. Microscopic and Computer Tomography (CT) rock images are mostly used to analyze the samples for porosity and permeability calculations in computer vision for automate process. The seismic hyperspectral infrared spectroscopy images are also used. At the present time, computer vision is a revolution for oil industries as using new advance techniques help them to reduce cost and gives an accurate value. In order to conduct a systematic review, we have taxonomized the survey over three categories: conventional machine learning, deep learning approaches, and well-known rock datasets.

Timur et al. [8] had utilized scanning electron microscope (SEM) for studying pore spaces in rocks like sandstone, limestone, dolomite, shale, etc. The main advantage of using SEM that it works with a large depth of focus and magnification to show the detail structure of pore spaces. H. Taud et al. [9] presented a segmentation approach studying the hydrocarbon properties of pore spaces for porosity calculation over X-ray CT imaging. To classify carbonate rocks from thin sections, Marmo et al. [10] introduced a technique based on principle component analysis (PCA) over microscopic image analysis and multi-layer perceptron. In 2011, Grove et al. [3] developed a software, namely, ImageJ for calculating total optical porosity of blue resin saturated thin sections. The porosity of rock samples can also be measured directly as explained by Yusuf et al. [11] where they have examined 20 samples of rocks porosity ranging from 14.29% to 51.92%. The limitation of their study is that it cannot differentiate between different types of rocks. Zhang et al. [12] proved that the sandstone CT image analysis with Ostu thresholding gives better results for the oil reservoir detection. In 2012, Ghiasi-Freez et al. [2] proposed a semi-automated method for recognized and categorized five unalike types of porosity in microscopic samples i.e. interparticle, intraparticle, oomoldic, biomoldic, and vuggy using discriminant classifier such as linear discriminant analysis (LDA) and quadratic discriminant analysis (QDA). For estimating porosity automatically in carbonate and terrigenous rock samples of CCD camera, Mazurkiewicz et al. [13] also proposed an image analysis-based algorithm. The Ostu thresholding also used by Datta et al. [1]

for estimating porosity of different types of rocks like limestone, sandstone. Recently in 2017, Nurgalieva et al. [14] presented an approach called ISODATA algorithm which was preferred because it is iterative and correct to process microscopic images of carbonate rock.

Nowadays, petroleum industries are using deep learning-based models to rapidly predict porous media properties from images in a supervised learning process. Recently, Wu et al. [15] presented a convolutional based neural network (CNN) method for porosity calculation from microscopic images which achieved significant success. The main objective was to teach a deep learning framework for fast prediction of permeability. M. Abedini et al. [16] introduced two intelligent frameworks, namely, back-propagation network (BPN) and stacked autoencoder (SAE) that for detection types of porosity. The feature extracted from the rock sample of 682 pores were used for training. N. Alquahtani et al. [17] also utilized a CNN model to rapidly predict several porous media properties from micro-CT images of different sandstones. The deep CNN model trained and validated in an end-to-end regression scheme with input greyscale micro-CT images and output of several computed porous properties. O. Sudakov et al. [18] introduced a deep learning-based descriptors pore network approach on 3D scans of Berea sandstone subsamples images with X-ray micro-CT, and analyzed the predictive power of various descriptors where deep descriptor outperforms. In 2020, Y. Niu et al. [19] used a CNN to segment digital sandstone data based on high-resolution micro-CT and corresponding SEM. The results are evaluated in terms of porosity, permeability and pore size distribution from segmented data.

There are few related datasets of rock stones available.

DRSRD1 [20]: Digital Rocks Super Resolution Dataset 1 (DRSRD1) dataset which is consists of organized 2D slices and 3D samples of Bentheimer Sandstone and Estaillades Carbonate. 800 samples are accessible for training, 100 for validation and 100 for testing.

GIAS [21]: Geological Image Analysis Software (GIAS) is an image processing package written in MATLAB which facilitates the analysis of vesicle images. Nikon LS-2000 digital film was used to directly collected an sample of 320x256 petrographic thin sections.

LANDMASS 2 [22]: Large North-Sea Dataset of Migrated Aggregated Seismic Structures (LANDMASS) is a high quality seismic data used for oil and gas exploration which consists of total 4000 samples (1000 horizon, 1000 samples, 1000 samples and 1000 salt dome) of dimensions 150x300 pixels.

OMS [23]: Offshore Miocene Sandstone (OMS) thin section with resolution for all samples and all magnifications is 0.24 μm per pixel.

LS X-RAY [24]: A Large Scale X-RAY (LS X-RAY) micro-tomography dataset (LS X-RAY) dataset comprises of raw samples and segmented X-ray micro-tomography samples.

Oil reservoir detection one of the most fundamental and challenging problems in computer vision. Machine learning techniques have emerged as a powerful strategy for learning and classification rock feature representations but lack in accuracy. Whereas deep CNN remarkable break through recently and unexplored in the field of oil reservoir detection.

3   Methodology

Figure 1 shows a schematic diagram of our proposed workflow for oil reservoir detection. A dataset of 2D microscopic images of sandstone and carbonate samples are inputted for the training of CNN models. The stone sample images are then segmented using a modified robust watershed segmentation algorithm which is a required further phase to distinguish pores from the pores space. Then the pores are evaluated through performance metrics and porosity from the processed images.

3.1   Deep Nets for Classification of Different Rocks

In this study, we have used different CNN architectures for classification of rocks before segmentation to analyze rock samples.

The accomplishment of deep convolutional neural networks is accredited to their capability to learn rich image depictions, but they rely on assessing millions of parameters as well as necessitate a very bulk number of images. In our case, we have very less volume of rock samples data as compared to the requirements of CNN. An alternative which has been extensively used is to fine-tune and transfer learning the CNNs, that are pre-trained using large amount of image datasets such as ImageNet. The renowned CNN models in literature are VGG, ResNet, AlexNet and so on. The rock samples cannot be explored in a concrete way by small networks such as AlexNet sometimes. On the other-hand, the VGG16, VGG19, and ResNet50 makes improvement over AlexNet by substituting large number of filters, convolutional layers with multiple tiny 3 × 3 size kernels. These multiple stacked tiny size kernels along multiple non-linear layers increases depth of the architecture, which enables it to learn more concrete and complex features of rock samples. However, our trail experiments demonstration that only the usage of pre-trained networks with fine-tuning cannot deliver pleasing performance in a small rock dataset. Furthermore, the custom VGG16, VGG19, and ResNet50 based rock features progresses

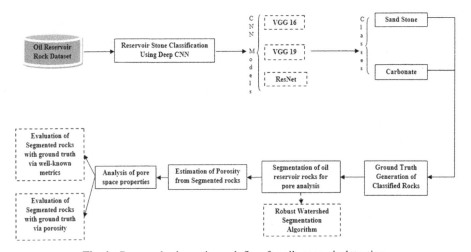

Fig. 1. Proposed schematic work flow for oil reservoir detection.

to a very great degree the performance of classification of microscopic rock samples. In custom models, the last Dense classification Softmax layer has been changed according to the number of rock types (classes) as presents in our rock dataset, and modified the fully connected layers according to our problem domain, and used the rest of pre-trained model as a fixed feature extractor.

3.2 Robust Rock Segmentation Approach for Pore Space Analysis

In watershed transform, we correspond to catchment basins as 'pore space' and ridgelines as 'grain' in sedimentary rocks, as shown in Fig. 2. The steps of our modified robust watershed algorithm as follow:

(i)   Add neighbors to priority queue, sorted by value.
(ii)   Choose local minima as region seeds.
(iii) Take top priority pixel from queue.
(a)   If all labeled neighbors have same label, assign to pixel. If we think pixel as center pixel, and calculate distance between all labeled neighbors with center and assigned to nearest one. At a time, a center and a labeled neighbor is considered while other neighbors compete as candidate neighbors.
(b)   Add all non-marked neighbors.
(iv)   Repeat step (iii) until finished.

For better visualization, few segmented output samples are shown in Fig. 3.

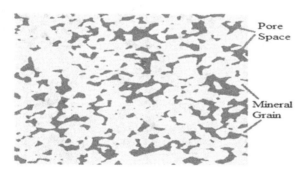

Fig. 2. A sedimentary microscopic rock sample [20].

4 Performance Evaluation

In this study, we have used the DRSRD1 [20] which is a dataset of total 2000 2D images with high resolution of 800×800 pixels of 1000 from sandstone and 1000 from carbonate samples. Those were cropped samples from the centre of the original cylindrical lens images of.PNG files. For experimental purpose, a total of 1600 images (i.e. 800 from sandstone and 800 from carbonate) are used for training, and rest of 200 images from each type of samples used for validation/testing during training of CNN models.

4.1 Ground Truth (GT) Generation

To exam the effectiveness of oil reservoir detection methods, the creation of annotation of region of interests in a microscopic rock sample is very crucial. Here we have implemented pixel level binary mask-based annotation to evaluate oil reservoir detection approaches. However, manual annotation of an accurate ground truth data often results in ambiguity and solid subjective bias. All the 2000 images of sandstone and carbonate samples are created binary mask using ImageJ software [25]. It can reliably classify pixels belongings to either pore space or grain: Pore Space - assigned binary value of 0, Grain assigned binary value of 1. Few samples and corresponding generated ground truth have shown in Fig. 3

4.2 Analysis of the Rock Samples Classification Using CNN Models

In this study, CNN models are used for classification to determine the labels: sandstone and carbonate from DRSRD1 dataset microscopic images. We empirically analyze the training and testing loss of CNN models, as shown in Table 1, with the tuning of hyper parameters for training the models are - optimizer: RMSProp, classification loss: weighted sigmoid cross entropy.

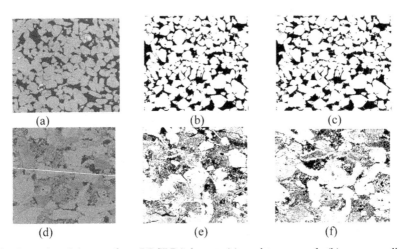

Fig. 3. Ground-truth images from DRSRD1 dataset. (a) sandstone sample (b) corresponding GT (c) segmented output (d) carbonate sample (e) corresponding GT (f) segmented output

We kept pre-trained option true when training the CNN networks to take weights value from the ImageNet multiclass competition dataset. During training, the input convolutional layers reduces the large dimensional original images to a small dimension (224 × 224) for learning speedup and less memory consumption. We trained the CNN network models for about 100 epochs on the training and validation dataset DRSRD1. Throughout training, a batch size of 32 have used, and the schedule learning rate slowly raises from $1e^{-5} = 0.004$ to $1e^{-2} = 0.135$ in the following order: $1e^{-5}$ for first 25

Table 1. Performance of rock samples classification.

CNN model	No. of epochs	Batch size	Training phase		Testing phase	
			Acc	Loss	Acc	Loss
VGG16	100	32	0.999	0.005	0.983	0.003
VGG19	100	32	0.998	0.027	0.979	0.015
ResNet50	100	32	0.987	0.006	0.972	0.001

epochs, $1e^{-4} = 0.018$ for next 25 epochs, $1e^{-3} = 0.049$ for next 25 epochs, and finally $1e^{-2}$ for last 25 epochs. If we start at a high learning rate our network models often diverges due to unstable gradients.

To overcome the overfitting and data pre-processing issues, first we have turned our data into pytorch dataset where images are randomly shuffled and split into train and validation sets through pytorch DataLoader. Here the training data samples are augmented to improve performance and reduce overfitting issues during training-validation. The data augmentation we have charted here are rotation, zooming, vertical and horizontal flipping.

We have observed that the training accuracy is 0.999 with 0.005 loss rate whereas the testing accuracy is 0.983 for VGG16 with 0.003 loss rate. As compare to VGG16, the training accuracy is slight lower in VGG19 and the testing accuracy correspondingly remains lower but testing loss rate is lesser with 0.015 than training loss 0.027. As compare to VGG16 and VGG19, Resnet50 performs well on training and testing loss whereas accuracy is slightly lower compared to both the architectures.

4.3 Performance Evaluation of the Segmented Pore Spaces

The analysis of segmented pore spaces via our proposed system has done in two ways.

First, we have estimated the correctness of modified robust watershed method for segmentation as compare to ground-truth. For this purpose, the well-known performance metrics such as F_1-score, recall, precision, accuracy, MCC, and sensitivity has been utilized, as shown in Fig. 4. From the Fig. 4, it seems that all the six metrics values for sandstone sample varies from 0.9822 to 1.00. Whereas the performances of segmentation for the carbonate samples are underperform than sandstone samples. The textural microscopic images of sandstone are sharper than carbonate images, which lead to easy segmentation of sandstone and correspondingly outperform in metric values than carbonate.

Second, we have analyzed the porosity values between ground truth and our proposed system via similarity index through Euclidean distance. The porosity is estimated as follows:

$$\text{Porosity}(P_t) = \text{Pore Volume}(V_p)/\text{Total Volume}(V_t) \times 100\% \tag{1}$$

From the graph in Fig. 5, we have seen that our proposed system producing nearest porosities against ground truth porosities. And the similarity index also showing analogous

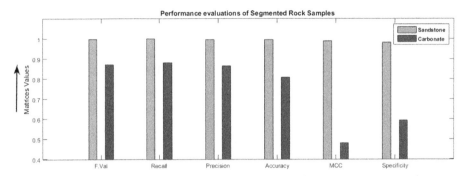

Fig. 4. Segmentation performance correctness measurement.

consequences where value of 0.0264 for carbonate samples and 0.0589 for sandstone samples.

4.4 Comparative Analysis with State-of-the-Arts

Pore spaces segmentation under microscopic medium rock samples has been one of the major research topics to detect the oil reservoirs. Numerous computer aided detection techniques have been proposed in the literature for porosity analysis. In our work, we have used selected most popular methods for comparative study. To provide a better assessment of overall performance and compare the performances among state-of-art methods, we used metrics like porosity. From the comparative analysis in Table 2, we have analyzed our proposed system performances outperform in case of sandstone samples. In case of carbonate samples, M. Abedini et al. [16] approach shows maximum 96.04%.

4.5 Discussion of Results Significance

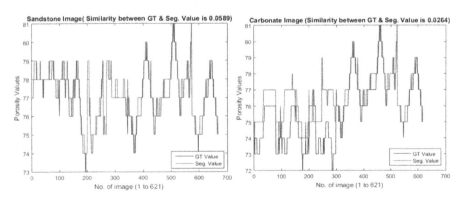

Fig. 5. Segmentation performance via porosity measurement.

Table 2. Comparative performance analysis of state-of-the-art techniques.

State-of-the-art approach	Sample	Max. porosity value
R. Marmo et al. [10]	Carbonate	93.5%
A.D. Yusuf et al. [11]	Sandstone	51.92%
D. Datta et al. [1]	Limestone	30%
	Sandstone	56%
B.S. Nabawy [26]	Sandstone	44.5%
L. Mazurkiewcz et al. [27]	Carbonate (Koscian)	20.1%
	Sandstone (Solec)	24.9%
R. Song et al. [28]	Sandstone	31.8%
	Carbonate	25%
M. Kashif et al. [29]	Sandstone	21.1%
M. Abedini et al. [16]	Carbonate	**96.04%**
Our Proposed System	Sandstone	**98.22%**
	Carbonate	89.02%

One of the factors remarkably influence the accuracy and loss of CNN based classification models is quantity of training microscopic images data. According to objective pursued in any deep learning study, suitable enough amount of input data must be provided. In this research, the collection of data was lesser in amount which creating over-fitting issues during model preparation. Although we have managed these issues via adjustment of hyper-parameters like dropout, batch normalization and most importantly data augmentation. Next influencing factor is convolutional operation through deeper layers investigation and differentiation of several types of attributes such as minerals, colors of minerals, and geometrical characteristics of sample stones. These attributes are utilized as a tool to differentiate and categorize pore spaces. Finally, the intension of this part of classification task is to assess the applicability of CNNs to make accurate predictions of sample labels as carbonate and sandstone.

The second experiment has been identified segmented pore spaces by robust watershed method. The images used in this study are microscopic blue-stain of thin section of sandstone and carbonate rock types with their different pore structures as shown in Fig. 3. Here, we have noticed the micritization, small size, and densely packed unclear boundary grains in some carbonate stones that are complex characteristics than sandstones. As a consequence, the contrast between grains and pore spaces not always result clearly which effects in performance measurement as shown in Fig. 4. Grains must have a well-defined internal structure and a clear boundary.

To assess the correctness of the proposed results in this research work, we need to be compared with the result presented in other publications which present the results of investigations of the same materials with different methods. Table 2 presents the results obtained on samples investigated by sandstone and carbonate analysis. From the comparative analysis in Table 2, we have observed our proposed system performances outperform in case of sandstone rocks. In case of carbonate rocks, M. Abedini et al. [16] approach shows maximum 96.04%.

5 Conclusion and Future Work

This study presents an easy and efficient technique which calculates rocks porosity from images for hydrocarbons for betterment of oil industries. We have used 2D microscopic images dataset for classification and analysis of image samples. For CNN model based classification, the features like minerals, colors of minerals, geometrical characteristics of microscopic samples are utilized to categorize pore spaces of sandstone and carbonate. To segment the pore spaces, a robust watershed method is presented. We have observed, the contrast between carbonate grains and pore spaces not always result clearly than sandstones. To assess the validation of the proposed results, we compared the result presented with other state-of-the-arts. We have observed that our proposed system performances are competitive.

In future, 3D samples from datasets can be used for determining more petro-physical properties.

Acknowledgement. The work presented here is being conducted in the Computer Vision Laboratory of Computer Science and Engineering Department of Tripura University (A Central University), Tripura, Suryamaninagar-799022, and Faculty of Engineering and Technology, Sri Ramachandra Institute of Higher Education and Research, Porur, Chennai-600116.

References

1. Datta, D., et al.: Determination of porosity of rock samples from photomicrographs using image analysis. In: Proceedings of IEEE 6th International Conference on Advanced Computing (IACC) (2016)
2. Ghiasi-Freez, J., et al.: Semi-automated porosity identification from thin section images using image analysis and intelligent discriminant classifiers. Comput. Geosci. **45**, 36–45 (2012)
3. Grove, C., et al.: jPOR: an ImageJ macro to quantify total optical porosity from blue-stained thin sections. Comput. Geosci. **37**(11), 1850–1859 (2011)
4. Pores in Rocks "Reservoir rock properties-slideshare.net/Christian akhilomel/". Accessed 15 Oct 2019
5. Sedimentary rocks classification: "RocksforKids.com/sedimentary-rocks". Accessed 10 Nov 2019
6. Offshore vs Onshore Oil Drilling. www.oilscams.org. Accessed10 Dec 2019
7. Jackson, S., et al.: A large scale X-Ray micro-tomography dataset of steady-state multiphase flow. Digital Rocks Portal (2019). http://www.digitalrocksportal.org. Assessed 20 Nov 2020
8. Timur, A., et al.: Scanning electron microscope study of pore systems in rocks. J. Geophys. Res. **76**(20), 4932–4948 (1971)
9. Taud, H., et al.: Porosity estimation method by X-ray computed tomography. J. Petrol. Sci. Eng. **47**, 209–217 (2005)

10. Marmo, R., et al.: Textural identification of carbonate rocks by image processing and neural network: methodology proposal and examples. Comput. Geosci. **31**, 649–659 (2005)
11. Yusuf, A., et al.: Determination of porosity in rocks over some parts of Gwagwalada area, Nigeria. New York Sci. J. **4**(11), 5–9 (2011)
12. Zhang, Y., et al.: Porosity analysis based on the CT images processing for the oil reservoir sandstone. In: International Conference on Automatic Control and Artificial Intelligence (ACAI 2012) (2012)
13. Mazurkiewicz, Ł., et al.: Determining rock pore space using image processing methods. Geol. Geophys. Environ. **39**(1), 45 (2013)
14. Nurgalieva, N.D., et al.: Thin sections images processing technique for the porosity estimation in carbonate rocks. In: Singh, D., Galaa, A. (eds.) GeoMEast 2017. SUCI, pp. 8–13. Springer, Cham (2017). https://doi.org/10.1007/978-3-319-61612-4_2
15. Wu, J., et al.: Seeing permeability from images: fast prediction with convolutional neural networks. Sci. Bull. **63**(18), 1215–1222 (2018)
16. Abedini, M., et al.: Porosity classification from thin sections using image analysis and neural networks including shallow and deep learning in Jahrum formation. J. Min. Environ. **9**, 513–25 (2018)
17. Alqahtani, N., et al.: Deep learning convolutional neural networks to predict porous media properties. Society of Petroleum Engineers (2018)
18. Sudakov, O., et al.: Driving digital rock towards machine learning: predicting permeability with gradient boosting and deep neural networks. Comput. Geosci. **127**, 91–98 (2019)
19. Niu, Y., et al.: Digital rock segmentation for petrophysical analysis with reduced user bias using convolutional neural networks. Water Resour. Res. **56**(2), e2019WR026597 (2020)
20. A Super Resolution Dataset of Digital Rocks (DRSRD1). https://www.digitalrocksportal.org/projects/211/publications. Accessed 25 Oct 2019
21. Geological Image Analysis Software. http://www.geoanalysis.org/jPOR.html. Accessed 28 Nov 2019
22. Datasets. https://github.com/olivesgatech/LANDMASS
23. Datasets. https://www.digitalrocksportal.org/projects/244/origin_data/978/
24. Datasets. https://www.digitalrocksportal.org/projects/229
25. Collins, T.J.: ImageJ for microscopy. Biotechniques **43**(1S), 25–30 (2007)
26. Nabawy, B.S.: Estimating porosity and permeability using Digital Image Analysis (DIA) technique for highly porous sandstones. Arab. J. Geosci. **7**(3), 889–898 (2013). https://doi.org/10.1007/s12517-012-0823-z
27. Mazurkiewicz, L., et al.: Determining rock pore space using image processing methods. Geol. Geophys. Environ. **39**, 45–54 (2013)
28. Song, R., et al.: Comparative analysis on pore-scale permeability prediction on micro-CT images of rock using numerical and empirical approaches. Energy Sci. Eng. **7**, 2842–2854 (2019)
29. Kashif, M., et al.: Pore size distribution, their geometry and connectivity in deeply buried Paleogene Es1 sandstone reservoir, Nanpu Sag, East China. Pet. Sci. **16**(5), 981–1000 (2019). https://doi.org/10.1007/s12182-019-00375-3

Signature2Vec - An Algorithm for Reference Frame Agnostic Vectorization of Handwritten Signatures

Manish Kumar Srivastava⬭, Dileep Reddy, Bhargav Kurma, and Kalidas Yeturu$^{(\boxtimes)}$⬭

Indian Institute Of Technology Tirupati, Tirupati, Andhra Pradesh, India
ykalidas@iittp.ac.in
https://iittp.ac.in/

Abstract. Online signature verification is an open research problem. The research in this field has widely evolved in the last decade, starting from the traditional approaches such as *dynamic time warping, hidden markov models, support vector machines* during the early part of the decade to modern approaches involving deep learning methodologies in the last few years. Online signature verification using deep neural networks is the state of the art. However training and retraining a deep learning model is computationally expensive.

We report here *Signature2Vec* algorithm that has 3 main features - (i) coordinate reference frame agnosticism for translation and rotation, (ii) horizontal and vertical scale invariance and (iii) high quality and lightweight forgery detection classifier. The *Signature2Vec* algorithm generates a vector embedding for a handwritten signature purely based on the time series of coordinates sampled while the signature is written. Our algorithm has performed at par with much better computational cost reductions over time aligned recurrent neural networks (TA-RNN) based approaches. We also propose an method of generating synthetic forgery data based on random strokes as subsequences of time series data of coordinate trace of a given signature. The synthetic forgery data assists in building personalized signature verification models only based on normal signatures which is usually the case. The *Signature2Vec* algorithm has yielded an average accuracy of 86% on the SVC-2004 dataset. Moreover the vector embedding generated by *Signature2Vec* when used for TA-RNN, the performance has improved compared to usage of raw features.

Keywords: Vectorization · Principal component analysis · Recurrent neural network · Online signature verification

1 Introduction

A signature is a bio-metric attribute used to verify the identity of an individual. It belongs to the behavioural bio-metric attributes related to the pattern of

---

The original version of this chapter was revised: The author's name "Bhargav Kurma" has been added to the list of authors. The correction to this chapter is available at https://doi.org/10.1007/978-3-031-11346-8_50

behaviour of a person. Verification based on these attributes is more difficult than verification based on physiological ones, but this process is less invasive than verification with physiological attributes like fingerprints, face. Moreover, the signature is an interesting behavioural attribute commonly accepted in society and in financial institutions. Thus, if the effectiveness of signature verification systems is very high, it may be of a great commercial use.

The signature verification problem can be viewed in two ways. The first is *online signature verification*, and the second is *offline signature verification*. The *online signature verification* uses dynamic information of a signature captured at the time signature is made. In comparison, the *offline signature verification* work on the scanned image of the signature. Our work is focused on the online signature verification problem.

There are mainly two categories of methods for signature verification - (i) vector encoding of a single signature and (ii) pairwise comparison of two signatures. The first approach is also called **global feature based method** [12]. In [2] Fourier coefficients of sequence of X coordinates and Y coordinates are determined as features, In [9] wavelet transformation of coordinate sequences are determined as features. In [10] the approach determines physics properties such as velocity of strokes, absolute displacement and 6 other properties. In [4] a subset of important features were determined from physics based approach of [10]. In [3,7] a *hidden markov model*(HMM) based approach is used for determining optimal states for X and Y coordinate sequences. In conjunction with a dynamic time warping (DTW) [1] based alignment of a set of sequences of variable length, a reference sequence is input to the HMM model to generate state sequence which is used in generation of the feature vector. However these approaches are *not rotation tolerant*. Rotation invariance has to be obtained either through construction of features that are based on previous subsequence of coordinates. There is a need for developing algorithms that simplify the state of the art and bring in rotational invariance.

The other class of approaches take a pair of signatures as input and determines their equivalence. One of the signature corresponds to normal case and the other signature corresponds to forgery case. In [1] DTW is used for alignment of two coordinate sequences. The aligned sequences are used in further steps such as determining a matching score for similarity or creation of vector representation of the pair for input to a forgery classifier. In [2] a bidirectional recurrent neural network (RNN) is used for computing similarity score. In [6] a time aligned RNN (TA-RNN) a siamese network [14] based RNN approach is used for classification of a pair of signatures as equivalent or different. In these methods, the machine learning model is complex involving thousands of parameters with a risk of overfitting to the given data. In addition a DTW based sequence alignment is sensitive to reference frame and leads to bias in the data set. Thus, present state-of-the-art deep learning approaches are not easily deployable in low-end devices such as smartphones, tablets, edge devices. Furthermore, it is practically difficult to ensure quality of the models as retraining the deep network suffers from the problem of *catastrophic forgetting* [15]. The problem is more pronounced in case of large organization when a large number of employees change jobs over time thereby changing datasets for deep learning based models. There is a need for simplifying algorithms that alleviate the need for alignment, reduce the number of parameters and enable individual specific models.

Another major challenge in the online signature verification problem is fewer signatures are available of a writer. Deep learning approaches get to bypass this challenge by treating the problem as writer-independent. Due to this change, they have now a large amount of data to train their model. However, this not only destroys the essence of behavioural attributes of the signature, which varies from person to person, but also make the problem computationally expensive, starting from initial training to any retraining in the future.

We present here *Signature2Vec* algorithm that only requires $(x_1, y_1) \ldots (x_n, y_n)$ coordinate sequence of variable length n, the coordinates ordered by time and generates a simple vector embedding. We use a principal component (PCA) based centering and reorientation of the data points to make the vector rotational and translational invariant. Our formulation also addresses horizontal and vertical scale invariance through division by appropriate scaling factors based on input. We demonstrated the performance of our approach on SVC-2004 [5] against TA-RNN based approach [10] and report equivalent or superior accuracies. Also presented here an approach similar to [8] to synthetically generate forgery data purely from normal data by defining variable length strokes and randomizing.

2   Datasets

This section discusses the dataset that is used for benchmarking and comparison of our proposed algorithms. SVC-2004 [5] is the dataset that has been used for the online signatures. This dataset contains the original online signatures as well as the forged online signatures of 40 users. For every user, the dataset provides 20 original and 20 forged online signatures. So in total, there are 1600 online signatures. Each online signature list of 7-dimensional feature-vector containing x-coordinate, y-coordinate, pen position, pen pressure, azimuth angle, altitude angle, and time at which other features were recorded. Here, x-coordinate and y-coordinate tells the position of the pen. Pen position tells whether the pen is up or down. If the pen is up, it will be 0 and 1 if it is down. Pen pressure is the pressure at the tip of the pen while signing on the screen. Altitude and azimuth angle record the angle of pen tilt. Low-end devices do not support complex features such as pen pressure and pen tilt. Thus only x-coordinate and y-coordinate are used in this work.

3   Proposed Algorithms

3.1   Signature Vectorization Algorithm

The *Signature2Vec* algorithm is for reference frame agnostic representation of an online signature that involves processing time-series data. The algorithm for vectorization of the online signatures is given in Algorithm 1. In the algorithm, *PCA()* function denotes principal component analysis [13] to determine the first component, *e* which denotes the eigenvector along which there is maximal spread of the data [13]. Here, we have used *PCA()* for two reasons. First, it reduces the dimensionality of the online signature and second, it outputs a vector which is rotational agnostic.

Algorithm 1. *Signature2Vec* (): Algorithm to vectorize the online signature

---
Require: M number of segments
Require: $S = [(x_i, y_i)]_{i=1}^{i=N}$ denotes online signature of a person ordered by time
   Here N denotes the number of coordinates sampled.
   Let M denote the number of segments.
 1: $s = \lfloor \frac{N}{M} \rfloor$
   Let mean of the segment be:
 2: $(\forall i \in [1 \ldots M]) \mu_i = mean(S[i : i + s])$
 3: $D = [\mu_1, \ldots, \mu_M]$
   Perform Principal Component Analysis(PCA) on D and determine first component.
 4: $e = PCA(D)$
   Determine projection of each point on to e,
 5: $D' = [d \in D : d \cdot e]$
   Make this vector horizontal and vertical scale invariant,
 6: $D^* = \frac{D'}{D'[-1]}$
 7: RETURN D^*

3.2   Synthetic Forged Online Signature Generation

Every time a person puts a signature will more or less maintain the coordinates' sequence. However, in the case of a forged signature, although the final set of coordinates may look almost identical to the original signature, there will be a substantial stroke sequence difference [8]. We developed an algorithm to generate synthetic forged variations of a given online signature. First, a random segment is chosen in a given coordinate sequence and is swapped with the first position. Then, the process is repeated several times as specified in an adjustable control parameter. The algorithm is given in (Algorithm 2).

Algorithm 2. SyntheticForgeryGeneration(): Algorithm for generation of synthetic forged online signatures

---

Require: K : K is percentage of signature taken as a stroke (a hyperparameter parameter)
Require: $S = [(x_i, y_i)]_{i=1}^{i=N}$ denote signature of a person
Require: C : Number of attempts for segment swap
   Here N denotes the number of coordinates sampled
1: $K = (N * K)/100$
2: $count = 0$
3: **while** $count < C$ **do**
4:    Randomly select an index ($\exists i \in [1, \ldots, N - K]$)
5:    $S[0 : K] \longleftrightarrow S[i : i + K]$
6:    $count = count + 1$
7: **end while**
8: RETURN S

3.3 Online Signature Verification Algorithm

We have posed the signature verification problem as a personalized (writer-dependent) binary classification problem. We have chosen random forest [11] for this, as random forest based methods are quite fast and have been used to solve many complex problems. We have posted the problem to preserve the behavioural attributes of the signature by using a personalized random forest classifier for each user. Given that number of forged online signatures will be synthetically generated. Thus, the number of forged signatures will be higher, and we used class balancing to keep the verification fair. The algorithm is given in Algorithm 3.

Algorithm 3. SignatureVerification():Algorithm for classification

---

Require: $O = \{O_i\}(i = 1 \ldots N_O)$ denote original online signatures of a person.
Require: $F = \{F_i\}(i = 1 \ldots N_F)$ denote forged/fake online signature
   Here, N_O denotes the number of original signature of the person.
1: $O[i] = S_i$ denotes i^{th} signature
   For each original signature, generate a set of forged variations and update F
2: **while** $i = 1 \ldots N_O$ **do**
3:    $F = F \cup SyntheticForgeryGeneration(O[i])$
4: **end while**
   Creating a data set of labeled vectors for all the signatures.
   Original is positive data, (x,1) x is the vector representation.
5: $D = (\forall i \in [1 \ldots N_O]) \{(Signature2Vec(O[i]), 1)\}$
   Forgery is negative data, (x,0) x is the vector representation
6: $D = (\forall i \in [1 \ldots |F|]) \{(Signature2Vec(F[i]), 0)\}$
7: $\Gamma = $ RandomForestClassifier()
8: $\Gamma.train(D)$
9: RETURN Γ

4 Results and Discussions

In this section, several experiments are described, and their results recorded on state-of-the-art deep learning approach(writer-dependent) and our proposed algorithms. The state-of-the-art deep learning approach used for the experiments is Time-Aligned Recurrent Neural Network (TA-RNN) [6] and dataset that is used is SVC-2004 discussed in Sect. 2. We take two different scenarios to keep the comparison fair. Also, the TA-RNN's architecture is modified to make it a writer-dependent RNN approach that takes a single input online signature. It predicts whether the signature is original or a forgery. This new RNN model is also used included in our experiments as a writer-dependent based approach.

4.1 Scenario I - Assessment of *Signature2Vec* Embeddings

For this scenario, we use RNN based deep learning model similar to TA-RNN but takes a single input. In this scenario, the RNN based deep learning model is analysed on two types of input. The first is the online signature, and the second is the vectorized online signature generated by Signature2Vec($M = 10$) algorithm. The results are provided in (Table 1). We observe that for vectorized online signature, the RNN model performed better than the RNN model on the online signature. The results show that our proposed Signature2Vec($M = 10$) algorithm improved the performance of the RNN model across all columns.

Table 1. The results when the online signature is used as input to RNN and when vectorized online signature is used as input to RNN. The columns indicate scores for Average AUC(*area under curve*), Average Precision, Average Accuracy and Average Recall scores.

	AUC	Precision	Accuracy	Recall
RNN using raw coordinate sequences	0.87	0.79	0.80	0.80
RNN using *Signature2Vec* vector embeddings	**0.90**	**0.85**	**0.83**	**0.85**

4.2 Scenario II - Effectiveness of *Signature2Vec* in Conjunction with Random Forest

We used two deep learning models TA-RNN and RNN, in this scenario and our proposed online signature verification algorithm. The input to RNN is an online signature. The input to TA-RNN is two online signatures(one original and one test). The input to our proposed online signature verification algorithm (SignatureVerification) is a vectorized online signature generated by our Signature2Vec ($M = 10$). The results are provided in (Table 2). The results show that our proposed signature vectorization algorithm followed by signature verification algorithm yields better results than RNN and TA-RNN across all parameters.

Table 2. The results when online signature verification is done on RNN, TA-RNN, and our proposed Signature Verification algorithm. The columns indicate scores for Average AUC (*area under curve*), Average Precision, Average Accuracy and Average Recall scores.

	AUC	Precision	Accuracy	Recall
RNN	0.87	0.79	0.80	0.80
TA-RNN	0.87	0.77	0.79	0.85
Our (Algorithm 3)	**0.91**	**0.86**	**0.86**	**0.87**

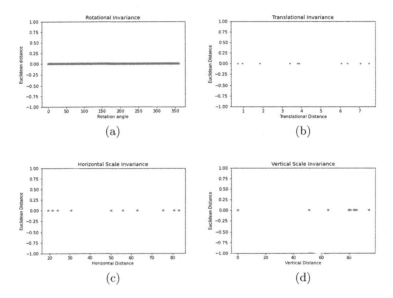

(a)   (b)

(c)   (d)

Fig. 1. Here Y axis is the euclidean distance between the vector representation generated by *Signature2Vec* algorithm of original online signature and its changed variation a) Rotation invariance of the algorithm. b) Translation invariance of the algorithm. c) Horizontal scale invariance of the algorithm. d) Vertical scale invariance of the algorithm.

4.3 *Signature2Vec* Embeddings - Rotational, Translational and Scale Invariance

Our Signature vectorization is computationally very simple in terms of time and space complexities and handles translation, rotation and scale variations. An online signature depends upon many factors such as behavioural attributes of the user, orientation of the device given to the user for signing and size of the box in which the user has put their signature. The orientation of the device and the size of the device is subject to change. So, the algorithm should be rotational, translational and scale-invariant. We have evaluated the ability of our algorithm to derive exact vector representations for coordinate sequences before, after rotation (Fig. 1(a)) for various translated version (Fig. 1(b)). We have also evaluated scaled variations along X and Y axes (Fig. 1(c), 1(d)).

5   Conclusions and Future Directions

We present here *Signature2Vec* algorithm for generation of vector embeddings for time series data of coordinate sequences. The process of generating the embeddings is computationally efficient and ensures rotational and translational invariance. The embeddings are also horizontal and vertical scale invariant, enabling the signature to be captured on devices of divers form factors. The *Signature2Vec* embeddings combined with a traditional random forest classifier has outperformed the state of the art computationally heavy deep neural network based approach. The algorithm can be extended to include multiple features and hence handle time series data of multivariate data points due to centering and reorientation based formulation. The method is ultra high speed and lightweight making it suitable for direct deployment on low end devices such as smart phone or edge computer.

References

1. Jeong, Y.S., Jeong, M.K., Omitaomu, O.A.: Weighted dynamic time warping for time series classification. Pattern Recogn. **44**(9), 2231–2240 (2011)
2. Nathwani, C.: Online signature verification using bidirectional recurrent neural network. In: 2020 4th International Conference on Intelligent Computing and Control Systems (ICICCS), pp. 1076–1078. IEEE (2020)
3. Van, B.L., Garcia-Salicetti, S., Dorizzi, B.: On using the viterbi path along with hmm likelihood information for online signature verification. IEEE Trans. Syst. Man Cybernet. Part B (Cybern.) **37**(5), 1237–1247 (2007)
4. Fierrez-Aguilar, J., Nanni, L., Lopez-Peñalba, J., Ortega-Garcia, J., Maltoni, D.: An on-line signature verification system based on fusion of local and global information. In: Kanade, T., Jain, A., Ratha, N.K. (eds.) AVBPA 2005. LNCS, vol. 3546, pp. 523–532. Springer, Heidelberg (2005). https://doi.org/10.1007/11527923_54
5. Yeung, D.-Y., et al.: SVC2004: first international signature verification competition. In: Zhang, D., Jain, A.K. (eds.) ICBA 2004. LNCS, vol. 3072, pp. 16–22. Springer, Heidelberg (2004). https://doi.org/10.1007/978-3-540-25948-0_3
6. Tolosana, R., Vera-Rodriguez, R., Fierrez, J., Ortega-Garcia, J.: Deepsign: deep on-line signature verification. IEEE Trans. Biomet. Behav. Ident. Sci. **3**(2), 229–239 (2021)
7. Fierrez, J., Ortega-Garcia, J., Ramos, D., Gonzalez-Rodriguez, J.: Hmm-based on-line signature verification: feature extraction and signature modeling. Pattern Recogn. Lett. **28**(16), 2325–2334 (2007)
8. Mathyer, J.: The expert examination of signatures. J. Crim. L. Criminol. Pol. Sci. **52**, 122 (1961)
9. L. Basavaraj, M.: Signature verification system based on wavelets. In: 2017 International Conference on Recent Advances in Electronics and Communication Technology (ICRAECT), pp. 149–153. IEEE (2017)

10. Luan, X.X.F.: Online signature verification based on stable features extracted dynamically. IEEE Trans. Syst. Man Cybern. Syst. **47**(10), 2663–2676 (2016)
11. Liaw, A., Wiener, M.: Classification and regression by random forest. R News **2**(3), 18–22 (2002)
12. Cpałka, K., Zalasiński, M.: On-line signature verification using vertical signature partitioning. Expert Syst. Appl. **41**(9), 4170–4180 (2014)
13. Wold, S., Esbensen, K., Geladi, P.: Principal component analysis. Chemometr. Intell. Lab. Syst. **2**(1–3), 37–52 (1987)
14. Bertinetto, L., Valmadre, J., Henriques, J.F., Vedaldi, A., Torr, P.H.S.: Fully-convolutional Siamese networks for object tracking. In: Hua, G., Jégou, H. (eds.) ECCV 2016. LNCS, vol. 9914, pp. 850–865. Springer, Cham (2016). https://doi.org/10.1007/978-3-319-48881-3_56
15. French, R.M.: Catastrophic forgetting in connectionist networks. Trends Cogn. Sci. **3**(4), 128–135 (1999)

Leaf Segmentation and Counting for Phenotyping of Rosette Plants Using Xception-style U-Net and Watershed Algorithm

Shrikrishna Kolhar[1,2] and Jayant Jagtap[3(✉)]

[1] Symbiosis International (Deemed University) (SIU),
Lavale, Pune, Maharashtra, India
[2] VPKBIET, Baramati, Maharashtra, India
shrikrishna.kolhar@vpkbiet.org
[3] Symbiosis Institute of Technology (SIT), Symbiosis International
(Deemed University) (SIU), Lavale, Pune, Maharashtra, India
jayant.jagtap@sitpune.edu.in
https://siu.edu.in/

Abstract. Leaf count is an important plant trait that helps for the analysis of plant growth in various plant phenotyping tasks. Overlapping leaves and nastic leaf movements are the major challenges in the recognition and counting of plant leaves. In this paper, we present a two-stage framework for the segmentation, counting and localization of plant leaves. In the first stage, we have designed an encoder-decoder-based deep neural network, namely Xception-style U-Net to segment plant leaves from the background. In the second stage for counting plant leaves, we use distance transform and watershed algorithm. The performance of the proposed method was tested on a publicly available leaf counting challenge (LCC) 2017 dataset that includes images of rosette plants, namely Arabidopsis thaliana and tobacco. In this work, Xception-style U-Net achieves improved segmentation accuracy on the test dataset with the dice coefficient of 0.9685. Xception-style U-Net, along with the watershed algorithm, achieves an average difference in leaf count (DiC) of 0.26 and absolute difference in leaf count ($|DiC|$) of 1.93, better than existing methods in the literature.

Keywords: Leaf segmentation · Leaf counting · Xception-style U-Net · SegNet · Watershed algorithm · Plant phenotyping

1 Introduction

In recent years, there is a huge rise in the demand for food and plant-derived products. Therefore, to obtain higher yields and to enhance the nutritional value of crops, plant phenotyping methods are designed to quantify and predict the effects of different management and environment-related factors. In the early

B. Raman et al. (Eds.): CVIP 2021, CCIS 1567, pp. 139–150, 2022.
https://doi.org/10.1007/978-3-031-11346-8_13

days, plant phenotyping was done manually, and hence it was slow, costly, and invasive. With advancements in imaging sensors, vision-based plant phenotyping methods play an important role in analyzing different stresses on plants [14]. Plant phenotyping involves various tasks such as plant trait estimation, accession classification, plant stress analysis, plant growth estimation, and modelling. Plant traits are used for crop variety selection, plant disease classification and prediction tasks. Therefore, plant trait estimation and analysis of plant traits is one of the emerging areas of research [23].

Automatic leaf segmentation and counting are one such complex problem due to plants' self-changing and dynamic nature. The first and most important task is to separate the plant from the background for counting plant leaves. Major challenges in automatic leaf segmentation and counting are rapid plant growth, varying shape and size of leaves, movement of leaves, variations in illuminations in outdoor environments and occlusion of leaves. It is evident that due to the nastic movement of leaves, the angular position of leaves changes periodically, which makes leaf tracking difficult. Further, overlapping leaves and water droplets on leaves make the task of leaf segmentation and counting even more difficult for machine vision systems [9,21].

This manuscript introduces a two-stage method for automatic leaf segmentation and counting for sample rosette plants, namely Arabidopsis thaliana and tobacco. In the first stage, we perform semantic segmentation of plant leaves using a deep neural network followed by a watershed algorithm in the second stage for leaf counting. We evaluate the performance of our approach on the leaf counting challenge 2017 (LCC) dataset [16]. The contributions of the proposed method are: (i) Deep learning-based leaf segmentation and counting algorithm for automatic plant phenotyping (ii) Semantic segmentation of plants using deep learning-based encoder-decoder architectures resulting in improved segmentation accuracy (iii) Watershed algorithm for leaf counting with improved leaf count estimates. (iv) The proposed method presents positional information about each leaf, unlike state-of-the-art methods used only for leaf count prediction.

2 Related Work

Recently, plant phenotyping is evolved as a key research area for many researchers working in the field of image processing and computer vision. Colour index-based segmentation and threshold-based segmentation methods are commonly used to segment plants from the background [5,12]. In one of the studies, k-means clustering, expectation minimization algorithm, distance transform and watershed algorithm were applied for extraction of plant leaves from background [3]. In one of the studies, hues with high green levels were used along with the Sobel operator to extract plants [24]. Thresholds on lab colour space components *a and *b were used to segment plant leaves [25]. Deep learning-based SegNet was used for the segmentation of fig plants from the background in open fig fields [11].

Plant phenotype estimation problems include segmentation and counting of leaves, detecting spikes and spikelets, estimating plant height and volume, plant growth estimation and modelling, etc. In one of the studies, a 3-D histogram was used along with a region growing algorithm for leaf segmentation and counting [17]. Aksoy et al. [2] used super-paramagnetic clustering along with a leaf shape model to determine plant growth signatures, leaf size and leaf count. Aich and Stavness [1] introduced a framework consisting of a deconvolutional network for leaf segmentation and a convolutional network for leaf counting. Pound et al. [18] used a convolutional neural network (CNN) with four stacked hourglass networks for localization and counting of wheat spikes and spikelets. Salvador et al. [20] used recurrent neural network (RNN) and Dobrescu et al. [10] used ResNet50 for estimation leaf size and count. In another work, first statistical image enhancement technique was used, and then graph-based method along with circular Hough transform (CHT) were applied to count leaves [15]. Buzzy et al. [7] used Tiny you only look once version 3 (YOLOv3) network for detection, localization and leaf counting.

After going through available literature, we think there is a scope for improvement in leaf segmentation and counting. Therefore, in this paper, we have attempted to design a deep learning-based automatic leaf segmentation and counting algorithm to improve leaf segmentation and leaf counting accuracy.

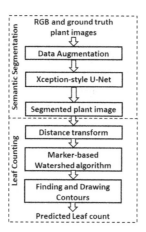

Fig. 1. Proposed leaf segmentation and counting algorithm using modified Xception-style U-Net and marker-based watershed algorithm

3   Methods

In this paper, we propose a two-stage approach for leaf counting as shown in Fig. 1. LCC dataset is the benchmark dataset used for testing our method. First, data augmentation is used to introduce variations in the plant image dataset. Then, encoder-decoder based architecture, namely Xception-style U-Net, is used to segment plant leaves from the background. RGB plant images along with corresponding ground-truth images are used to train the network. Segmentation helps in the localization of plant leaves. In the leaf counting phase, a watershed algorithm is applied on segmented plant images to mark the leaf region, separate each leaf, and draw contours to obtain the skeletons of plant leaves. The advantage of using a marker-based watershed is to reduce over-segmentation and noise. Apart from Xception-style U-Net, we have also tested SegNet [4], and U-Net [13,19,26] architectures and compared the results of all the three networks.

3.1 Proposed Xception-style U-Net Architecture

For the design of Xception-style U-Net, we use modified depth-wise separable convolutional layers with residual connections in the encoder part of the network [8,22]. As shown in Fig. 2, the modified Xception-style U-Net architecture consists of a total of 29 convolutional layers, out of which 8 are separable convolutional layers. Input encoder layer consists of 3×3 convolutional layer along with batch normalization and ReLU activation. The input layer is followed by four modules, each of which comprises two repeated implementations of ReLU activation, 3×3 separable convolutions and batch normalization layers. At the end of each module, 3×3 max-pooling is performed with a stride of 2×2. The encoder has linear residual connections with 1×1 convolutions. At each encoder stage, the number of filters is doubled, and feature maps are down-sampled by 2. The decoder comprises four modules, each with repeated implementations of ReLU activation, 3×3 transposed convolution and batch normalization. Residual connections on decoder side consist of up-sampling and 1×1 convolutions. At each step, encoder feature maps are combined with decoder feature maps to retain localization information along with complex features. At the output layer, sigmoid function is used to classify between plant and non-plant pixels.

3.2 Marker-Based Watershed Algorithm

The marker-based watershed algorithm is used in this paper for leaf counting purposes. First, distance transform or distance map is evaluated from segmented binary images outputted by the encoder-decoder architectures. Distance map is the Euclidean distance from foreground points (plant) to the nearest background points. In distance transform, the intensities of foreground pixels are replaced with their closest distance from the background pixel. Next, a maximum filter is applied, and the original image is dilated to obtain the coordinates of local peaks in the image. Connected component analysis using eight connectivity is performed on the calculated local peaks to obtain markers. The watershed function is applied with a negative distance map and markers as the parameters. Watershed transform gives an array of labels. The objects of interest that are plant leaves in the original image are obtained by iterating through the unique labels. Then, the contours are obtained and drawn around the leaves to locate them.

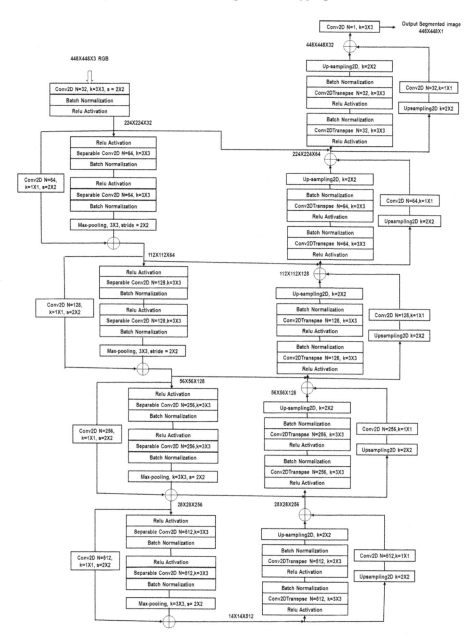

Fig. 2. Proposed Xception-style U-Net architecture. N indicates number of filters, k indicates size of filter kernel, s indicates stride and ⊕ represents adder layer

3.3   Dataset

LCC dataset is shared as part of computer vision problems in plant phenotyping (CVPPP) 2017 challenge. The dataset has four sub-parts, out of which A1, A2 and A4 consist of Arabidopsis thaliana plant images, whereas A3 contains tobacco plant images. The datasets consist of RGB images, ground-truth labels and corresponding leaf counts. Dataset A1 contains 128 images of size 500×530 pixels, A2 consists of 31 images of size 530×565 pixels, and A3 contains 27 RGB images of size 2448×2048 pixels. Dataset A4 shared by [6] contains 624 images of size 441×441 pixels. Each part of the dataset has different sets of problems. Dataset A1 images have changing and complex background with yellowish-green coloured mosses in the background. Whereas images in A2 and A4 have a comparatively uniform background with varying leaf shape and size, leaf movement around the centre of the plant, and occlusion of leaves. Dataset A3 contains high-resolution images with variations in leaf colours, varying light conditions and shadow effects.

3.4   Training and Testing of Networks for Leaf Segmentation

For the training of the networks, LCC dataset was divided into training, validation and test sets with 567 (70%), 162 (20%) and 81 (10%) images, respectively. As the size of images is not fixed, all images are resized to 448×448×3. Data augmentation techniques used are image rotation, zoom, shear, shift in width and height, horizontal and vertical flip. RGB images along with corresponding ground-truth images are fed to the network in batches of a size of 8. Adam optimizer with a learning rate of 0.00001 and dice loss is used for training of the network. The networks are trained for 80 epochs. Dice coefficient, F1-score, and mean absolute error (MAE) are used are used as evaluation metrics for testing segmentation performance. As shown in Table 1, the total number of trainable parameters is considered as an evaluation metric for the complexity of the segmentation network.

3.5   Leaf Counting Using Watershed Algorithm

The performance of the watershed algorithm is first tested on a test set with images included from A1, A2, A3, and A4 datasets. Then, leaf counts for individual datasets are also estimated. Predicted leaf counts are compared with ground truth leaf counts. To test the performance of the algorithm, we have used the mean difference in leaf count (DiC), the mean absolute difference in leaf count ($|DiC|$) and frequency of relative DiC as evaluation metrics. DiC gives a bias towards over-estimate or under-estimate, $|DiC|$ gives an average difference in the count.

4   Results and Discussion

The proposed algorithm for leaf segmentation and counting is evaluated on all the datasets A1, A2, A3 and A4. Figure 3 shows the results of segmentation for

Table 1. Segmentation performance analysis of SegNet, U-Net and proposed Xception-style U-Net.

Evaluation metric	SegNet	U-Net	Xception-style U-Net
Dice coefficient	0.9224	0.9638	0.9685
F1-score	0.9387	0.9652	0.9700
Mean absolute error	0.0128	0.0062	0.0050
Trainable parameters	33,377,795	31,032,837	3,316,993

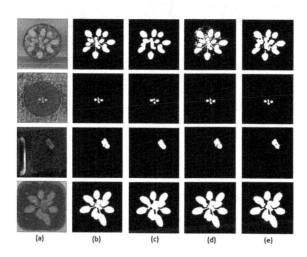

Fig. 3. Segmentation results for SegNet, U-Net and Xception-style U-Net. (a) Sample RGB images (b) Corresponding groundtruth images. (c) SegNet segmentation results. (d) U-Net segmentation results. (e) Proposed Xception-style U-Net segmentation results.

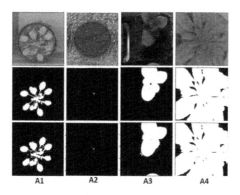

Fig. 4. Segmentation results for proposed Xception-style U-Net on challenging images from A1, A2, A3 and A4 datasets, respectively. Row 1 presents sample RGB images, row 2 gives corresponding ground truths and row 3 presents output segmented images (Color figure online)

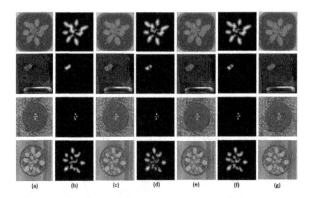

Fig. 5. Leaf counting using watershed algorithm on segmented images from SegNet, U-Net and proposed Xception-style U-Net. (a) RGB images. (b, d and f) distance transformed images. (c, e, and g) are RGB images with red-coloured contours for SegNet, U-Net and Modified Xception-style U-Net (Color figure online)

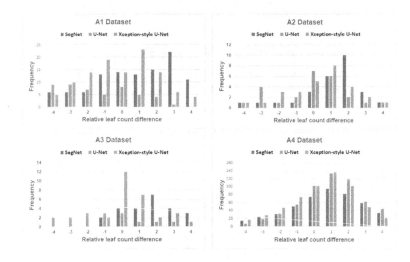

Fig. 6. Relative leaf count difference versus frequency graphs for A1, A2, A3 and A4

Table 2. Leaf segmentation performance comparison of SegNet, U-Net, and proposed Xception-style U-Net with state-of-the-art methods

Method	Dice coefficient
3-D histogram [17]	0.953
Seeded region growing algorithm [21]	0.916
Distance transform and watershed [3]	0.948
Graph-based method and CHT [15]	0.954
SegNet	0.925
U-Net	0.963
Proposed Xception-style U-Net	0.968

Table 3. Leaf count comparison between SegNet, U-Net, Xception-style U-Net combined with watershed.

Datasets	SegNet		U-Net		Xception U-Net	
	DiC	$|DiC|$	DiC	$|DiC|$	DiC	$|DiC|$
A1	1.32	2.76	−8.54	8.87	−0.68	2.34
A2	1.93	2.58	−1.12	2.22	0.48	1.90
A3	2.07	2.22	−4.33	5.07	0.85	1.01
A4	3.23	4.34	1.25	2.18	−0.16	2.31
Testset	2.53	3.07	−2.98	2.98	0.81	2.09
Average	2.22	2.99	−3.14	4.26	0.26	1.93

Table 4. Leaf count comparison of Xception-style U-Net plus watershed with state-of-the-art methods (In table NA indicates method not applied on A4)

Methods	DiC				$|DiC|$			
	A1	A2	A3	A4	A1	A2	A3	A4
3-D histogram [17]	−1.8	−1.0	−2.0	NA	2.2	1.2	2.8	NA
Region growing [21]	−3.5	−1.9	−1.9	NA	3.8	1.9	2.5	NA
Graph and CHT [15]	−0.9	1.2	−1.8	NA	2.0	3.8	1.8	NA
DCNN and CNN [1]	−0.33	−0.22	2.71	0.23	1.0	1.56	3.46	1.08
Proposed method	−0.68	0.48	0.85	−0.16	2.34	1.90	1.01	2.09

SegNet, U-Net and modified Xception-style U-Net. RGB images and corresponding ground truth are taken from the test set. It can be seen that SegNet cannot separate overlapping leaves and estimate the exact shape of leaves, whereas U-Net was found to be very good at the segmentation of overlapping leaves with precise shapes. But, in some cases, U-Net suffers from over-segmentation and noise in the background of the image as seen in Fig. 3(d). Xception-style U-Net performs better than U-Net in extraction of overlapped leaves with precise shapes and also less affected by over-segmentation and noise. Figure 4 presents segmentation results for Xception-style U-Net on challenging RGB images. We can see that the A1 RGB image has a greenish background similar to leaves, the A2 RGB image has a very tiny leaflet, A3 and A4 RGB images have significantly overlapped leaves. Irrespective of these challenging conditions, the segmented output images using Xception-style U-Net match significantly with corresponding ground truths. Also, as shown in Table 1, Xception-style U-Net requires around 3 million trainable parameters, significantly less than U-Net and SegNet, which need about 31 and 33 million trainable parameters, respectively. Table 1 presents the segmentation performance of SegNet, U-Net and Xception-style U-Net. Xception-style U-Net achieves dice coefficient of 0.9685, F1-score of 0.9700 and MAE of 0.005, which are better than SegNet and U-Net. Also, we can observe from Table 2 that Xception-style U-Net achieved better segmentation performance as compared to the existing methods in the literature.

In the leaf counting task, images segmented in the first stage are applied with distance transform, dilation, connected component analysis and marker-based watershed transform. Figure 5 shows the results of leaf counting in terms of distance transformed images and RGB images with leaves marked by red coloured contour lines. Contour lines help in the localization of each leaf. It is evident that distance transformed images obtained for U-Net and Xception-style U-Net segmented images are more precise in extracting overlap and shape of leaves than SegNet. It is also observed that in the case of green coloured background noise, simple U-Net shows poor results whereas Xception-style U-Net is affected less as seen in Fig. 5 (e)). Table 3 presents values of DiC and $|DiC|$ obtained for the test dataset as well as for all four subsets in LCC dataset. It can be seen that Xception-style U-Net achieves DiC of 0.26 and $|DiC|$ of 1.93, indicating better leaf counting accuracy than U-Net and SegNet. Therefore, it is evident that Xception-style U-Net along with watershed algorithm achieves better leaf count estimates. Figure 6 shows relative leaf count difference versus frequency graphs for datasets A1, A2, A3 and A4. The frequency of leaf count difference is high within the range -2 to $+2$, indicating better leaf count estimates for the proposed method. Table 4 presents comparative results of our proposed method with existing methods in the literature. Most existing methods are tested on datasets A1, A2 and A3 only. Lower values of DiC for the proposed method indicate that method is less biased towards under and over-estimates. The proposed method performs better than existing methods in terms of both bias (DiC) as well as average performance ($|DiC|$) for the A3 dataset and achieves comparable performance for A1, A2 and A4 datasets. Also, the proposed method performs well on a mixed test dataset with DiC of 0.81 and $|DiC|$ of 2.09, respectively.

5   Conclusion and Future Research Direction

This paper divides the leaf counting task into two phases, namely leaf segmentation and leaf counting. We have tested and analysed the performance of deep learning networks, namely SegNet, U-Net and Xception-style U-Net for leaf segmentation tasks. Xception-style U-Net and simple U-Net achieve better performance than SegNet and other state-of-the-art methods available in the literature. Xception-style U-Net and U-Net are better than SegNet in the segmentation of overlapping leaves. In the second phase, the marker-based watershed algorithm is used for leaf counting and to reduce the effect of over-segmentation and noise. Though U-Net is very good at the segmentation of overlapping leaves, it suffers from over-segmentation and background noise in some cases. Relative DiC frequency for the proposed method is high between -2 to $+2$, indicating improved accuracy in leaf count estimates. Therefore, Xception-style U-Net combined with watershed algorithm achieves better leaf count estimates than U-Net, SegNet and state-of-the-art methods. In the future, we can use this method to estimate the fresh weight of plants, which will help predict crop yield in advance.

References

1. Aich, S., Stavness, I.: Leaf counting with deep convolutional and deconvolutional networks. In: 2017 IEEE International Conference on Computer Vision Workshops (ICCVW), pp. 2080–2089. IEEE, October 2017. https://doi.org/10.1109/iccvw.2017.244
2. Aksoy, E.E., Abramov, A., Wörgötter, F., Scharr, H., Fischbach, A., Dellen, B.: Modeling leaf growth of rosette plants using infrared stereo image sequences. Comput. Electron. Agric. **110**, 78–90 (2015)
3. Al-Shakarji, N.M., Kassim, Y.M., Palaniappan, K.: Unsupervised learning method for plant and leaf segmentation. In: 2017 IEEE Applied Imagery Pattern Recognition Workshop (AIPR), pp. 1–4. IEEE, October 2017. https://doi.org/10.1109/aipr.2017.8457935
4. Badrinarayanan, V., Kendall, A., Cipolla, R.: SegNet: a deep convolutional encoder-decoder architecture for image segmentation. IEEE Trans. Pattern Anal. Mach. Intell. **39**(12), 2481–2495 (2017). https://doi.org/10.1109/tpami.2016.2644615
5. Bai, G., Ge, Y., Hussain, W., Baenziger, P.S., Graef, G.: A multi-sensor system for high throughput field phenotyping in soybean and wheat breeding. Comput. Electron. Agric. **128**, 181–192 (2016). https://doi.org/10.1016/j.compag.2016.08.021
6. Bell, J., Dee, H.M.: Aberystwyth leaf evaluation dataset (2016). https://doi.org/10.5281/ZENODO.168158, https://zenodo.org/record/168158
7. Buzzy, M., Thesma, V., Davoodi, M., Mohammadpour Velni, J.: Real-time plant leaf counting using deep object detection networks. Sensors **20**(23), 6896 (2020)
8. Chollet, F.: Xception: deep learning with depthwise separable convolutions. In: Proceedings of the IEEE Conference on Computer Vision and Pattern Recognition, pp. 1251–1258 (2017)
9. Dellen, B., Scharr, H., Torras, C.: Growth signatures of rosette plants from time-lapse video. IEEE/ACM Trans. Comput. Biol. Bioinf. **12**(6), 1470–1478 (2015)
10. Dobrescu, A., Giuffrida, M.V., Tsaftaris, S.A.: Leveraging multiple datasets for deep leaf counting. In: Proceedings of the IEEE International Conference on Computer Vision Workshops, pp. 2072–2079 (2017)
11. Fuentes-Pacheco, J., et al.: Fig plant segmentation from aerial images using a deep convolutional encoder-decoder network. Remote Sens. **11**(10), 1157 (2019)

12. Hamuda, E., Glavin, M., Jones, E.: A survey of image processing techniques for plant extraction and segmentation in the field. Comput. Electron. Agric. **125**, 184–199 (2016). https://doi.org/10.1016/j.compag.2016.04.024
13. Huang, H., et al.: UNet 3+: a full-scale connected UNet for medical image segmentation. In: ICASSP 2020–2020 IEEE International Conference on Acoustics, Speech and Signal Processing (ICASSP), pp. 1055–1059. IEEE, May 2020. https://doi.org/10.1109/icassp40776.2020.9053405
14. Humplík, J.F., Lazár, D., Husičková, A., Spíchal, L.: Automated phenotyping of plant shoots using imaging methods for analysis of plant stress responses – a review. Plant Methods **11**(1), 29 (2015). https://doi.org/10.1186/s13007-015-0072-8
15. Kumar, J.P., Domnic, S.: Image based leaf segmentation and counting in rosette plants. Inf. Process. Agric. **6**(2), 233–246 (2019). https://doi.org/10.1016/j.inpa.2018.09.005
16. Minervini, M., Fischbach, A., Scharr, H., Tsaftaris, S.A.: Finely-grained annotated datasets for image-based plant phenotyping. Pattern Recogn. Lett. **81**, 80–89 (2016). https://doi.org/10.1016/j.patrec.2015.10.013 https://doi.org/10.1016/j.patrec.2015.10.013 https://doi.org/10.1016/j.patrec.2015.10.013 https://doi.org/10.1016/j.patrec.2015.10.013
17. Pape, J.-M., Klukas, C.: 3-D histogram-based segmentation and leaf detection for rosette plants. In: Agapito, L., Bronstein, M.M., Rother, C. (eds.) ECCV 2014. LNCS, vol. 8928, pp. 61–74. Springer, Cham (2015). https://doi.org/10.1007/978-3-319-16220-1_5
18. Pound, M.P., et al.: Deep machine learning provides state-of-the-art performance in image-based plant phenotyping. Gigascience **6**(10), gix083 (2017)
19. Ronneberger, O., Fischer, P., Brox, T.: U-Net: convolutional networks for biomedical image segmentation. In: Navab, N., Hornegger, J., Wells, W.M., Frangi, A.F. (eds.) MICCAI 2015. LNCS, vol. 9351, pp. 234–241. Springer, Cham (2015). https://doi.org/10.1007/978-3-319-24574-4_28
20. Salvador, A., et al.: Recurrent neural networks for semantic instance segmentation. arXiv preprint arXiv:1712.00617 (2017)
21. Scharr, H., et al.: Leaf segmentation in plant phenotyping: a collation study. Mach. Vis. Appl. **27**(4), 585–606 (2015). https://doi.org/10.1007/s00138-015-0737-3
22. Sifre, L., Mallat, S.: Rigid-motion scattering for image classification. arXiv preprint arXiv:1403.1687 (2014)
23. Singh, A.K., Ganapathysubramanian, B., Sarkar, S., Singh, A.: Deep learning for plant stress phenotyping: trends and future perspectives. Trends Plant Sci. **23**(10), 883–898 (2018). https://doi.org/10.1016/j.tplants.2018.07.004
24. Wang, Z., Wang, K., Yang, F., Pan, S., Han, Y.: Image segmentation of overlapping leaves based on Chan–Vese model and Sobel operator. Inf. Process. Agric. **5**(1), 1–10 (2018). https://doi.org/10.1016/j.inpa.2017.09.005
25. Yin, X., Liu, X., Chen, J., Kramer, D.M.: Joint multi-leaf segmentation, alignment, and tracking for fluorescence plant videos. IEEE Trans. Pattern Anal. Mach. Intell. **40**(6), 1411–1423 (2018). https://doi.org/10.1109/tpami.2017.2728065
26. Zhou, Z., Rahman Siddiquee, M.M., Tajbakhsh, N., Liang, J.: UNet++: a nested U-Net architecture for medical image segmentation. In: Stoyanov, D., et al. (eds.) DLMIA/ML-CDS -2018. LNCS, vol. 11045, pp. 3–11. Springer, Cham (2018). https://doi.org/10.1007/978-3-030-00889-5_1

Fast and Secure Video Encryption Using Divide-and-Conquer and Logistic Tent Infinite Collapse Chaotic Map

Jagannath Sethi[✉], Jaydeb Bhaumik, and Ananda S. Chowdhury

Department of Electronics and Telecommunication Engineering, Jadavpur University,
Kolkata 700032, India
jagannathsethi@gmail.com,
{jaydeb.bhaumik,as.chowdhury}@jadavpuruniversity.in

Abstract. In this paper, we propose a fast and secure method for compression independent video encryption. A divide-and-conquer type approach is taken where frames in a video are processed at shot level. Temporal redundancy among the frames in a shot are exploited next to derive the difference frames, where some of the pixel values are already zero. A further sparse representation of the pixels are obtained by thresholding the non-zero values. We also propose a new chaotic map, namely, Logistic Tent Infinite Collapse map (LT-ICM) which has better chaotic range, complex behaviour, unpredictability, ergodicity, and sensitivity towards initial values and controlling parameters. We permute the pixels of each shot (left after thresholding) with reference to the indices of sorted chaotic sequence generated by LT-ICM. Substitution operation is applied next to change the pixel values. The substituted pixels are arranged into frames and pixels are further substituted at frame level with another chaotic sequence generated by LT-ICM. Experimental results establish that our proposed method is efficient in terms of encryption time, correlation coefficients and entropy values compared to some of the existing methods.

Keywords: Video encryption · Divide-and-conquer · Logistic Tent Infinite Collapse Map

1 Introduction

Video encryption using chaotic map has evolved as an important research topic in secure video data storage and transmission. In [1], authors discussed about video encryption with and without compression. Chaotic maps are popular for generating pseudorandom sequences as they are highly unpredictable, sensitive to initial states and control parameters and are ergodic in nature. Many chaotic maps like Sine, Logistic, Tent that have been used for encrypting the images and video suffer from lower chaotic ranges. So, a better chaotic map is necessary for ensuring more secure video encryption. Further, existing chaos based

B. Raman et al. (Eds.): CVIP 2021, CCIS 1567, pp. 151–163, 2022.
https://doi.org/10.1007/978-3-031-11346-8_14

uncompressed video encryption schemes do not necessarily exploit the temporal redundancy in a video [6,7]. Rather, they simply treat each frame as an
image for encryption. As a video deals with huge amount of data, it needs to be
processed efficiently while preventing illegitimate access and preserving infringe-
ment confidentiality. Clearly, direct encryption of all the frames of a video taken
together could be computationally very expensive. So, some efficient algorithmic
approach and use of temporal redundancy are required.

In this paper, we propose a fast and secure compression independent video
encryption scheme. Our solution is computationally efficient as we use a divide-
and-conquer type approach and exploit temporal redundancy. Better security
is achieved through a new chaotic map termed as Logistic, Tent and Infinite
Collapse Map (LT-ICM) with a higher chaotic range and more complex behavior.
We employ a divide-and-conquer type approach by dividing a video into shots
and then process the frames within each shot separately. Shots are obtained
by finding the changes between two consecutive frames using the sum squared
difference (SSD) measure [4]. Note that the frames within each shot are highly
correlated. So, we exploit temporal redundancy by obtaining difference frames
within a shot. Next, we threshold non-zero pixels in the difference frames to
further reduce the computational load for processing. The resulting set of sparse
pixels are represented using a 4-tuple with row position, column position, frame
number and intensity values. We use sorting based random permutation and
substitution in the first level of encryption. For the second level of encryption,
we use only XOR operation which makes encryption process fast. These steps are
repeated for each shot. The main contributions of our video encryption scheme
are now highlighted below:

1. We generate a new pseudorandom chaotic sequence using our LT-ICM chaotic
   map. The proposed map has better chaotic range, complex behaviour, unpredictability, ergodicity, and sensitivity towards initial values and controlling
   parameters.
2. We apply a divide-and-conquer type of approach where instead of processing
   all the frames of a video together, we process frames in a shot-wise manner.
   Further, a sparse representation of pixels within the frames in a shot are
   adopted by exploiting temporal redundancy. These steps make the proposed
   encryption scheme fast.

The remainder of the paper is structured as follows: In Sect. 2, we discuss the
related work. In Sect. 3, we describe our proposed video encryption architecture,
chaotic sequence generation and its performance analysis. Section 4 presents the
experimental result with analysis. The paper is concluded in Sect. 5.

2   Related Work

Video encryption without compression has many advantages over that of encryption with compression. While encrypting video with codec video data need to
satisfy different requirement like format complaint, codec complaint, quality of

video to be perceivable, minimum time for encryption and fixed bitrates. Authors in [6], used four chaotic maps for encrypting video in frame level. In [7] authors have presented their video encryption scheme by using substitution box operating on cipher block chaning mode where they have used 8, 12 dimensional chaotic map and Ikeda delay differential system for chaotic sequence generation. Scan based permutation is addressed in [3] for encrypting images and videos. Sethi et al. [15] presented a frame level encryption for uncompressed video using Logistic Sine Coupling Map. But they have not considered temporal redundancy and their method takes more time than that of our proposed method. Authors in [11] implemented a video encryption scheme employing combined Logistic and Tent map. In [12], authors presented video encryption using Logistic and Lorenz chaotic map.

In [5], authors generated quantum walks based substitution box for video encryption. Song et al. [8] proposed a quantum video encryption scheme employing improved Logistic map. A lightweight probabilistic keyframe encryption is addressed in [9] which woks in IoT system. Compressive sensing based efficient cryptosystem has been addressed in [10] which supports IoT environment. Chaotic system based on infinite collapse map are presented in [2]. There are some periodic windows and discontinuity in chaotic range. We generate a new chaotic map LT-ICM which overcomes these limitations. Most of the video encryption techniques addressed above are not that fast and also they have not considered the temporal redundancy. Our proposed divide-and-conquer compression independent video encryption method is fast as we deal with less number of non-zero pixel values in difference frames within shots. Also, our encryption scheme is secure as LT-ICM map is highly unpredictable in the chaotic range.

3   Proposed Architectures

In this section, we describe the details of our proposed method. This section consists of three parts. The first part consists of generation of the chaotic sequence using LT-ICM map and its performance analysis. The second part, deals with video to shot conversion, de-correlation of frames present within each shot and conversion of shot into sparse form. The third part deals with conversion of chaotic sequence based permuted and substituted sparse data into frame level data for each shot. After that update frames present in each shot are XOR-ed with a chaotic sequence which depends on initial state, controlling parameter and previous encrypted frame. The complete block diagram of video encryption scheme is presented in Fig. 1.

3.1   Pseudo-random Sequence Generation(PRSG)

Logistic map, Tent map and Iterative chaotic map with infinite collapse are common 1D chaotic maps. Mathematically, Logistic, Tent and ICM maps are defined in Eq. 1, 2 and 3 respectively.

$$x_{i+1} = r_1 x_i (1 - x_i) \tag{1}$$

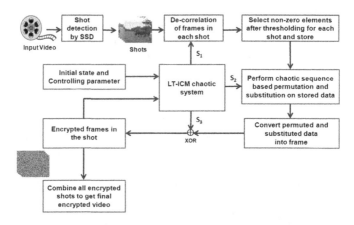

Fig. 1. Proposed block diagram of video encryption scheme

$$x_{i+1} = \begin{cases} 2r_2 x_i & \text{if } x_i < 0.5 \\ 2r_2(1 - x_i) & \text{if } x_i \geq 0.5 \end{cases} \qquad (2)$$

$$x_{i+1} = \sin(r_3/x_i) \qquad (3)$$

where r_1, r_2, r_3 are the controlling parameters for Logistic, Tent and ICM map respectively and $r_1 \in [0, 4]$, $r_2 \in [0, 1]$, $r_3 > 0$.

The chaotic range of former two chaotic maps is narrow. The Logistic and Tent map have chaotic behaviour when $r_1 \in [3.57, 4]$ and $r_2 \in [0.5, 1]$. A chaotic map is proposed using Logistic, Tent and ICM map(LT-ICM). Mathematically, the LT-ICM can be represented as:

$$x_{i+1} = \sin(r_3/(P(r_1, x_i) + Q(r_2, x_i) + 0.5)) \qquad (4)$$

As indicated in Eq. 4, the LT-ICM first adds the two base maps $P(r_1, x_i)$ and $Q(r_2, x_i)$ then shift the result by 0.5 and finally apply to the ICM map to generate the LT-ICM chaotic map output. The combination operation can effectively shuffle the chaos dynamics of the two base maps, and the ICM map produce very complex nonlinearity. Thus, the new chaotic map produced by the LT-ICM has complex behavior. We have considered $P(r_1, x(i))$ as Logistic map, $Q(r_2, x(i))$ as Tent map. For simplification, we consider $r_2 = 1 - r_1$ and $r_3 = r_1$. The generated LT-ICM chaotic map has better chaotic range, unpredictability and ergodicity than base maps. After modification, the LT-ICM can be represented as:

$$x_{i+1} = \begin{cases} \sin(r_1/(2x_i r_1 + (1 - r_1)x_i(1 - x_i) + 0.5)) & \text{if } x_i < 0.5 \\ \sin(r_1/(2(1 - x_i)r_1 + (1 - r_1)x_i(1 - x_i) + 0.5)) & \text{if } x_i \geq 0.5 \end{cases} \qquad (5)$$

3.2   Performance Analysis of Chaotic Sequence

For evaluating LT-ICM, we select different measures like bifurcation diagram, lyapunov exponent. We have also tested the sensitivity to initial condition and

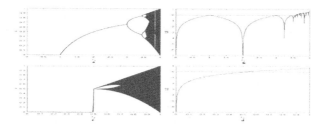

Fig. 2. Bifurcation diagram and LE of (a, b) Logistic map, (c, d) Tent map

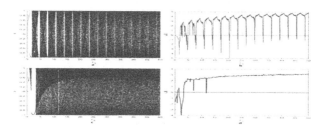

Fig. 3. Bifurcation diagram and LE of (a, b) ICM map, (c, d) LT-ICM map

controlling parameter for the proposed map by applying a minor change in both parameters. The correlation coefficient value for two sequences using LT-ICM map with minor change in controlling parameter and initial condition is nearer to zero. So the two sequences are different with any minor change in parameter and initial state. The entropy of proposed map is high for the chaotic range where lyapunov exponent is non-zero which indicate the generated sequence is unpredictable.

3.2.1 Bifurcation Diagram
For good chaotic performance, the attractor has to occupy the maximum regions in phase space. We consider 0.3 as initial state and iterate 20000 times for every map. Next we plot the all points in Phase space. We compare the result with base maps. Figure 2 shows the bifurcation diagram and Lyapunov exponent of Logistic and Tent map. In Fig. 3, the bifurcation diagram and Lyapunov exponent has shown for ICM map and proposesd LT-ICM map. From Fig. 3, we can see that the generated map is distributed in maximum regions of phase space within $(0, r_3)$ which indicate the LT-ICM is highly unpredictable and has good ergodicity.

3.2.2 Lyapunov Exponent (LE)
For a system to be chaotic it must have positive Lyapunov exponents. The value for proposed map is positive which tells the generated sequence is chaotic. The Logistic and Tent map have better chaotic behaviour in limited range. The ICM map has better chaotic range, but it has periodic behaviour for some range of controlling parameter. The proposed chaotic map covers maximum range of control-

ling parameter over which lyapunov exponent is non-zero. Figure 3 shows the distribution of LE with respect to the controlling parameter(r_3) within range(0,50). The Lyapunov Exponent for equation $x_{i+1} = G(x_i)$ is mathematically defined as follows:

$$\lambda_{G(x)} = \lim_{n \to \infty} (1/n) \ln | (G^n(x_0 + \epsilon) - G^n(x_0))/\epsilon | \tag{6}$$

where value of ϵ is very small. For higher control parameter, the ICM chaotic map behaves choatic in nature for entire range. In our prosed method, at lower value of control parameter there is no periodic window and it behaves more chaotic throughout the range of control parameter.

3.3   Proposed Encryption Scheme

3.3.1   Shot Boundary Detection
The first step for encrypting the video is to find the shots in a video. Prior to shot detection all the frames in video is reshaped to 2-D form by concatenating R,G,B components. Shot detection is performed by Sum Squared Difference(SSD) approach used in [4]. We, first find the sum squared difference between two consecutive frames. If the total change is more than 75% then a shot boundary is detected at that frame.

3.3.2   Frame De-correlation Within Shot
The frames present in a shot contain temporal redundancy and it is removed by taking XOR difference between a frame and its previous frame. First a chaotic sequence of same size as each frame is generated using Algorithm 1. For the first frame of each shot, XOR difference is computed between itself and the chaotic sequence. For all other frames, XOR differences are computed from the current frame and its previous frame so that all the processed frames in each shot contain less numbers of non-zero values. Thresholding is applied on non-zero elements to eliminate non-significant difference values hence to reduce encryption time and memory usages.

3.3.3   Encryption of Video
The sparse data obtained from the de-correlation stage are undergone chaotic sequence based permutation and substitution. Substituted, permuted and de-correlated data are converted into frame format, where unfilled positions in a frame are substituted with zero value. A new chaotic sequence is generated for every frame in each shot. The size of chaotic sequence is same as the dimension of each frame. The chaotic sequence generation process depends on initial state, controlling parameter and previous encrypted frame. Now XOR operation is performed between generated chaotic sequence and pixel values of current frame. All the encrypted frames in each shot are arranged to get color video frames in RGB form and encrypted shots are obtained after combining them. Finally all the encrypted shots are combined to get encrypted video. All the steps of video encryption is presented in Algorithm 2. The decryption is the inverse

Algorithm 1: Pseudorandom sequence generation(PRSG) using LT-ICM

Input: $(D, x_0, a_0,$ where D is frame of size [M,3N]

Output: Chaoticseq

1: Size of each frame $\leftarrow [M, 3N]$
2: Length of PRSG$\leftarrow [1, 3MN]$
3: $S = \sum_{i=1}^{3MN} D(i)$
4: if $S = 0$
5: $t \leftarrow 0$
6: else
7: $t = \frac{\sqrt{S}+5}{(S+255)}$
8: end
9: $x_1 = x_0 + t, a_1 = a_0 + t,$;
10: **for** $i = 1$ to $3MN$ **do**
11:    **if** $x_i < 0.5$ **then**
12:        $x_{i+1} = sin(a/(2ax_i + (1-a)x_i(1-x_i) + 0.5))$;
13:    **else**
14:        $x_{i+1} = sin(a/(2a(1-x_i) + (1-a)x_i(1-x_i) + 0.5))$;
15:    **end if**
16: $X(i) = floor(10^{10} \times (x_{i+1})) \mod 256$
17: **end for**
18: Chaoticseq=X;

---

of encryption process. Decryption is done by inverse substitution operation at frame level of each shot followed by inverse substitution and inverse permutation in sparse level and then inverse of de-correlation operation.

4   Experimental Results

We have tested our proposed method considering three standard videos used in [7] including Rhinos, Train, Flamingo. We also used six different videos of 150 frames of various sizes including Akiyo, Silent, Waterfall, Suzie, Salesman and Highway used in [5]. All experiments are done on a desktop PC with Intel(R) Core (TM) i5-9300H CPU having 2.40 GHz clock speed and 8 GB RAM. We used MATLAB 2020a for our implementation. We experimentally set $(x_0, a_0, x_1, a_1) = (0.65135, 30, 0.71835, 30.26180)$ as secret key. We compare our experimental results with different existing video encryption methods for different videos.

A) **Correlation Coefficient(CC) Analysis:** Ideally, the correlation coefficient of the original frame and the encrypted frame has to be 1 and 0 respectively. We perform experiment by considering 10000 randomly selected pixels with its adjacent pixels in all directions to find mean correlation coefficient. The mean CC for encrypted frame is nearer to zero for our method. Figure 4 shows the distribution of adjacent pixels for frame number 1 of Akiyo video in all directions for each channel component.

Algorithm 2: Encryption of video by divide-and-conquer approach

---

Input: (x_0, a_0, V), where V is input video
Output: Encrypted video
1: $[r, c, d, N_1]$=size(V)   ▷ N_1 is the number of frames
2: Reshape all the frames of video(V) by concatenating R,G,B components and get new video V_1
3: Find the shot boundaries of V_1 using SSD
4: **for** $i = 1 : N_2$ **do**   ▷ N_2 is the number of frames in the shot
5:    **if** $i = 1$ **then**   ▷ De-correlating the frames in the shot
6:        $S_1 = PRSG(\mathbf{0}, x_0, a_0)$ ▷ Reshape S_1 of size same as of V_1
7:        $V_2(:, :, i) = V_1(:, :, i) \oplus S_1$
8:    **else**
9:        $V_2(:, :, i) = V_1(:, :, i - 1) \oplus V_1(:, :, i)$
10:   **end if**
11: **end for**
12: Convert shot to sparse data by selecting only non-zero elements
13: $[R,C,F,Val]$=Shottosparse(shot)
14: Do thresholding by eliminating the pixel values within certain range e.g less than 5, 10, 15 and 20
15: **for** i=1 to L **do**   ▷ L is the length of non-zero elements in shot
16:   $S_2 = PRSG(\mathbf{0}, x_0, a_0)$
17:   $I_1 = sort(S_2)$ ▷ I_1 is the index of sorted S_2
18:   $Val_1(i) = Val(I_1(i))$
19:   **if** $i = 1$ **then**
20:       $Val_2(i) = Val_1(i) \oplus Val_1(L) \oplus S_2(i)$
21:   **else**
22:       $Val_2(i) = Val_2(i - 1) \oplus Val_1(i) \oplus S_2(i)$
23:   **end if**
24: **end for**
25: Convert encrypted sparse data to dense form data from its indices and values
26: **for** $i = 1 : N_2$ **do**
27:   **if** $i = 1$ **then**
28:       $S_3 = PRSG(\mathbf{0}, x_1, a_1)$ ▷ Reshape S_3 of size same as of Val_2
29:       $Val_3(:, :, i) = Val_2(:, :, i) \oplus S_3$
30:   **else**
31:       $S_3 = PRSG(Val_3(:, :, i - 1), x_1, a_1)$
32:       $Val_3(:, :, i) = Val_2(:, :, i) \oplus S_3$
33:   **end if**
34: **end for**
35: Reshape Val_3 to get color encrypted video frames and combine all encrypted frames to get encrypted shot
36: Repeat above steps for all the shots and combine all encrypted shots to get final encrypted video

---

B) **Histogram Analysis:** Histogram of encrypted video frames needs to have an uniform distribution for better security. Histogram of original frame number 1 of Akiyo video and its corresponding encrypted version for the R,G,B components are shown in Fig. 5. From Fig. 5, it is clear that our proposed

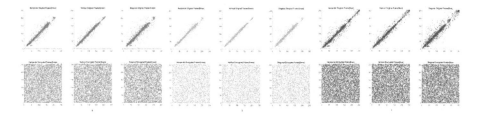

Fig. 4. Distribution of adjacent pixels for frame no.1 of Akiyo video and its encrypted frame (a) Red, (b) Green, (c) Blue (Color figure online)

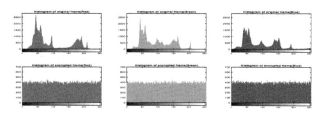

Fig. 5. Histogram of Akiyo video for its Red, Green, Blue components of original frame no.1 and its encrypted frame (Color figure online)

method will be able to defend statistical attacks as encrypted frame has uniform histogram.

C) **Video Quality Analysis**: Quality of an encrypted and a decrypted video are measured by the peak signal to noise ratio (PSNR) [13] and structural similarity index (SSIM) [14]. For higher security, the encrypted video should have low PSNR and low SSIM. The PSNR of encrypted video is less than 9 for all cases which indicates our proposed method is more secure. The SSIM values are nearer to zero for all encrypted videos which makes the videos secure. The PSNR and SSIM of decrypted video should be nearer to that of input video for better perception. We have also tested all the video for our cryptosystem by thresholding certain range of values in all the frames in shots. As the range of thresholding increases the mean encryption time decreases. However, the PSNR and SSIM of decrypted video decreases. So there is a trade-off between quality of the decrypted video and the mean encryption time. In Fig. 6 we have shown mean PSNR and mean SSIM of both encrypted and decrypted videos for different threshold values. For no tresholding, the mean PSNR and SSIM for decrypted videos are infinite and one respectively.

D) **Comparison with External Approaches**: We compare results obtained by our proposed method with other video/image encryption methods in terms of key space, mean encryption time, entropy and mean correlation coefficient. Entropy is used to measure the randomness of encrypted frames and mean correlation coefficient is used to measure correlation between adjacent pixels.

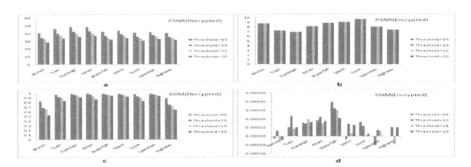

Fig. 6. Mean PSNR of decrypted and encrypted videos(a, b), mean SSIM of decrypted and encrypted videos

Table 1. Comparison of mean encryption time in seconds

Video names	Proposed method with thresholding					Valli et al. (2017) [7]			Ranjithkumar et al. (2019) [11]	Sethi et al. (2021) [15]
	No	5	10	15	20	Ikeda DDE	12D	8D		
Rhinos	0.6533	0.5421	0.4883	0.3911	0.4043	1.2147	1.7964	0.9124	0.5403	0.7946
Train	0.4485	0.3770	0.3313	0.2963	0.2857	0.9908	1.6493	0.8631	0.5178	0.8548
Flamingo	0.4228	0.3635	0.3030	0.2717	0.2555	1.1124	0.8402	0.8062	0.5982	0.8538

We now provide a comparison of **mean execution times**. We consider different cases for encrypting the video like taking all non-zero pixel values in processed frames in each shot and eliminating the pixels having values less than 5,10,15 and 20. It take less time as compare to other method for all cases. However it take very less time if we eliminate the processed pixel values less than 5,10,15 and 20 with the loss of some quality in the video. So the proposed method for encrypting the video is very efficient with respect to memory usage and real time security application. Table 1 shows the comparison of mean encryption time for different methods.

We now present a **key space analysis**. For any encryption technique 2^{128} is a reasonable key space such that it can resist brute force attack. Our method consists of four parameters in secret key (x_0, a_0, x_1, a_1). The precision for each parameter is considered as 10^{-14}, so the total key space is $10^{14\times4} = 10^{56} = 2^{186}$. So our method can defend against exhaustive brute force attack. Table 2 shows the comparison of key space with some recent methods. Decryption is not possible if there is very minor change in secret key which makes our system more robust against differential attacks. A minor change in secret key will produce different decrypted frame than that of original one which has been shown in Fig. 7. The attacker has knowledge of both plaintext and its ciphertext in case of known plaintext attack. In case of chosen plaintext attack, the attacker can get encrypted frames if some portion of input frames are imparted. As the chaotic sequence generation depends on substituted previous frames in the shot, so any minor change in secret key can make decryption impossible. Hence, our proposed method can defend both known and chosen plaintext attacks.

Table 2. Comparison of key space

Methods	El-Latif et al. (2020) [5]	Valli et al. (2017) [7]			Ranjithkumar et al. (2019) [11]	Kezia et al. (2008) [12]	Sethi et al. (2021) [15]	Proposed method
		8D	12D	Ikeda DDE				
Keyspace	2^{305}	8×2^{128}	3072×2^{128}	49152×2^{128}	2^{212}	2^{128}	256×2^{256}	2^{186}

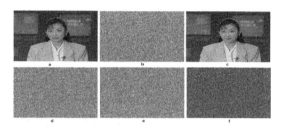

Fig. 7. (a) Original first frame of Akiyo video (b) encryption with key 0.65135, 30, 0.71835, 30.26180 (c) decryption with key 0.65135, 30, 0.71835, 30.26180 (d) decryption with key $0.65135+10^{-14}$, 30, 0.71835, 30.26180 (e) decryption with key $0.65135,30+10^{-14}$, 0.71835, 30.26180 (f) result of d - e

Finally, Table 3 shows the comparison of mean correlation coefficient and entropy of encrypted videos for different schemes.

Table 3. Comparison of average CC and entropy

Methods	CC after encryption			Entropy
	Horizontal	Vertical	Diagonal	
El-Latif et al. (2020) [5]	−0.0012	0.0004	0.0003	7.9984
Song et al. (2020) [8]	−0.0245	−0.0135	−0.0143	7.8708
Muhammad et al. (2018) [9]	0.0015	−0.0007	0.0006	**7.9998**
Unde et al. (2020) [10]	0.0030	0.0027	0.0014	7.9900
Sethi et al. (2021) [15]	0.0020	0.0048	0.0114	7.9993
Our proposed method	**−0.0002**	**−0.0002**	**−0.0002**	7.9989

From the above comparisons, it becomes evident that our method achieves good performance in terms of mean execution time, keyspace analysis, mean correlation coefficient and entropy values.

5   Conclusion

In this paper, we proposed a fast and secure video encryption method. A divide-and-conquer approach is employed to make the encryption fast by processing frames at shot level. Each shot is de-correlated and only pixels above a certain threshold within the difference frames are further processed. Secure sort based random permutation is used for shuffling and resulting shuffled data in each shot is substituted by frame independent chaotic sequence. The processed pixel values are converted into frame level. Once again the frames in each shot are substituted by a frame dependent unique sequence generated by the proposed LT-ICM chaotic map. Experimental results demonstrate that the proposed method has good result over existing approaches in terms of mean encryption time, mean correlation coefficient, key sensitivity, entropy, mean PSNR and SSIM.

References

1. Liu, F., Koenig, H.: A survey of video encryption algorithms. Comput. Secur. **29**(1), 3–15 (2010)
2. He, D., He, C., Jiang, L.G., Zhu, H.W., Hu, G.R.: Chaotic characteristics of a one-dimensional iterative map with infinite collapses. IEEE Trans. Circ. Syst. I Fundam. Theor. Appl. **48**(7), 900–906 (2001)
3. Maniccam, S.S., Bourbakis, N.G.: Image and video encryption using SCAN patterns. Pattern Recogn. **37**(1), 725–737 (2004)
4. Chu, W.S., Song, Y., Jaimes, A.: Video co-summarization: video summarization by visual co-occurrence. In: CVPR, pp. 3584–3592 (2015)
5. El-Latif, A.A.A., Abd-El-Atty, B., Mazurczyk, W., Fung, C., Venegas-Andraca, S.E.: Secure data encryption based on quantum walks for 5G internet of things scenario. IEEE Trans. Netw. Serv. Manage. **17**(1), 118–131 (2020)
6. Elkamchouchi, H., Salama, W.M., Abouelseoud, Y.: New video encryption schemes based on chaotic maps. IET Image Process. **14**(2), 397–406 (2020)
7. Valli, D., Ganesan, K.: Chaos based video encryption using maps and Ikeda time delay system. Eur. Phys. J. Plus **132**(12), 1–18 (2017). https://doi.org/10.1140/epjp/i2017-11819-7
8. Song, X.H., Wang, H.Q., Venegas-Andraca, S.E., El-Latif, A.A.A.: Quantum video encryption based on qubit-planes controlled-XOR operations and improved logistic map. Physica Stat. Mech. Appl. **537**, 122660 (2020)
9. Muhammad, K., Hamza, R., Ahmad, J., Lloret, J., Wang, H., Baik, S.W.: Secure surveillance framework for IoT systems using probabilistic image encryption. IEEE Trans. Ind. Inf. **14**(8), 3679–3689 (2018)
10. Unde, A.S., Deepthi, P.P.: Design and analysis of compressive sensing based lightweight encryption scheme for multimedia IoT. IEEE Trans. Circ. Syst. II Exp. Briefs **67**(1), 167–171 (2020)
11. Ranjithkumar, R., Ganeshkumar, D., Suresh, A., Manigandan, K.: A New one round video encryption scheme based on 1D chaotic maps. In: ICACCS, pp. 439–444 (2019)
12. Kezia, H., Sudha, G.F.: Encryption of digital video based on Lorenz chaotic system. In: Proceedings of the 16th International Conference on Advanced Computing and Communications, pp. 40–45 (2008)

13. Huynh-Thu, Q., Ghanbari, M.: The accuracy of PSNR in predicting video quality for different video scenes and frame rates. Telecommun. Syst. **49**, 35–48 (2012). https://doi.org/10.1007/s11235-010-9351-x
14. Wang, Z., Bovik, A.C., Sheikh, H.R., Simoncelli, E.P.: Image quality assessment: from error visibility to structural similarity. IEEE Trans. Image Process. **13**(4), 600–612 (2004)
15. Sethi, J., Bhaumik, J., Chowdhury, A.S.: Chaos-based uncompressed frame level video encryption. In: Giri, D., Raymond Choo, KK., Ponnusamy, S., Meng, W., Akleylek, S., Prasad Maity, S. (eds.) Proceedings of the Seventh International Conference on Mathematics and Computing . Advances in Intelligent Systems and Computing, vol. 1412. Springer, Singapore (2022). https://doi.org/10.1007/978-981-16-6890-6_15

Visual Localization Using Capsule Networks

Omkar Patil[(⊠)] [ID]

Indian Institute of Technology Madras, Chennai 600036, India
omkardpatil18@gmail.com

Abstract. Visual localization is the task of camera pose estimation, and is crucial for many technologies which involve localization such as mobile robots and augmented reality. Several convolutional neural network models have been proposed for the task against the more accurate geometry based computer vision techniques. However, they have several shortcomings and to our knowledge, this was the first effort that explored the use of an alternative architecture based on capsule-networks for the task. We achieved better results with capsules than with baseline-CNN PoseNet on small NORB dataset, modified for the task of camera pose estimation. Feature visualizations for both the networks produced more insights on their performance and behaviour. We found that there is a scope for improvement and hence propose few directions for future efforts.

Keywords: Capsules · Camera pose estimation · Visual localization

1 Introduction

1.1 Camera Pose Estimation

Camera pose prediction plays a crucial role in navigation and augmented reality systems. This task involves predicting the 6 degrees of freedom pose of the camera which has captured the given image from a known environment. From a modelling perspective, this translates to building a model on a dataset of images and their corresponding camera pose label (position and orientation) relative to a reference frame. Camera pose prediction has received widespread attention from the computer vision community in the form of SFM[1] [14]. SFM techniques which use descriptor matching have been fairly successful. Of late, the deep learning community has tried to tackle this problem with the introduction of end-to-end pose prediction algorithms using CNNs[2] [7]. The task of predicting the pose of camera that clicked a given image from a known scene requires the model to understand the geometry of the scene better than that would be necessary for an object detection model. Moreover, the features generated from CNNs are intentionally made invariant of the object's position through pooling operations, to improve object detection capabilities. Naturally, we can expect better results if our model is not invariant to affine degrees of freedom of objects in the image. This made us look for a fundamentally different way in which neural networks are organized - capsules.

---

[1] Structure from Motion.

[2] Convolutional neural networks.

© The Author(s), under exclusive license to Springer Nature Switzerland AG 2022
B. Raman et al. (Eds.): CVIP 2021, CCIS 1567, pp. 164–174, 2022.
https://doi.org/10.1007/978-3-031-11346-8_15

To the best of our knowledge, this is the first effort to explore and analyze the efficacy of capsule networks on this geometrical task. We also repurposed an existing image database for the task of partial-pose prediction of a camera. The rest of the paper is structured as follows. First we reviewed the relevant literature on visual localization and capsule networks, then in Sect. 2, illustrated the methods and architecture of the proposed capsule based network. After that we looked at the results achieved in Sect. 3 followed by conclusion and future work in Sect. 4.

1.2 Literature Review

Absolute Pose Regression Approach. Absolute camera Pose Regression (APR) train CNN to regress the camera pose for an input image. Kendall et al. (2015) first proposed PoseNet, to directly regress 6 degrees of freedom camera pose from an input image with GoogLeNet [7]. Walch et al. (2016) argued that high-dimensionality of the image encoding resulted in overfitting, and used LSTM for dimensionality reduction [18]. Consequent research in this field has tried to fuse more geometrical information about the scene into the network. Kendall and Cipolla (2017) extended PoseNet by adding geometrical constraints through reprojection loss [6]. Brahmbhatt et al. (2018) attempted to make the learning 'geometry-aware' by using visual odometry, translation and rotation constraints [1]. Research has shown that APR methods do not learn the geometry of the scene [16] and are significantly less accurate than structure-based methods [15].

Capsules Networks. A capsule is a group of neurons that try to represent the 'instantiation parameters' of a 'part' in the input image, possibly such as hue, texture, color or orientation. A layer in the capsule network is composed of such capsules, and different approaches have been proposed to transfer information from one layer to the next, with the understanding that capsules in successive layers represent the instantiation parameters of larger parts- which in turn are composed of conforming parts from the previous layer. We will encourage the reader to go through [4] and [5] for a solid understanding of capsule networks. Sabour et al. (2017) proposed a multi-layer capsule network in 2017 (DRCapsNet), which produced state of the art performance on MNIST [13]. DRCapsNet utilized dynamic routing for solving the problem of assigning parts to wholes (implying an assembly of conforming parts). Sabour et al. (2018) described a version of capsules (EMCapsNet) in which each capsule is represented by a 4×4 matrix and has a logistic activation unit [3]. Expectation-Maximization was used for assigning parts to wholes. DRCapsNet with dynamic routing achieved 2.7% test error rate on small NORB, which was on-par with the state-of-the-art. EMCapsNet with expectation maximization routing was successful in reducing the test error rate to 1.8%.

2 Method

2.1 Model Architecture

We created a capsule-network called 'PoseCap' based on dynamic routing capsules [13] that could be trained on a dataset of images and their corresponding camera-pose labels.

During inference, the network was designed to predict the pose of camera which clicked a given input image from the same scene. The output pose is expressed as $p = [x, q]$, x being the position and q quaternion of the camera orientation. A 2D³ convolutional layer (with 256 filters, 9 kernel size and stride 1) was used to extract the basic features from the image. Then a stack of 7 2D convolutional filters (with kernel size 9 and stride 2) act on the features to generate 8192 7D capsules. The 8192 -7D capsule outputs are then multiplied with a weight matrix W_{ij} representing part-whole transformations. Here, we have a fully connected layer with dynamic routing to produce a single 7D capsule.

For dynamic routing between capsule layers i and j, each capsule u_i is multiplied with a weight matrix W_{ij} which is intended to learn the geometry of the scene, and is independent of the input image. A capsule v_j in layer j is evaluated as-

$$v_j = \frac{\|s_j\|^2}{1 + \|s_j\|^2} \frac{s_j}{\|s_j\|} \tag{1}$$

Here $s_j = \sum_i c_{ij}\hat{u}_{j|i}$ and $\hat{u}_{j|i} = W_{ij}u_i$. The value c_{ij} is called the coupling coefficient and is to be tuned for each input image. The coupling coefficient is tasked with finding parts that conform with each other and creating a representation of a larger structure composed of those parts, also called as a 'whole'. The coupling coefficient is calculated as -

$$c_{ij} = \frac{\exp b_{ij}}{\sum_k \exp b_{ik}} \tag{2}$$

Here b_{ij} is initialized with 0 and updated iteratively

$$b_{ij|t} = b_{ij|t-1} + \hat{u}_{j|i} \cdot v_j \tag{3}$$

Experimentally it has been found that change in routing after 5 iterations is negligible [13]. Based on our tests, best results were achieved when 3 iterations of dynamic routing were performed on these capsule outputs for every input image to produce the camera pose estimation. This 7D capsule in the last layer represents the pose of the camera- the first 3 values being the location and last 4 the orientation in quaternion form. Choice of quaternion over rotation matrix comes from [7], as it is easier to map them to rotations by normalization to unit length. The implementation is in PyTorch [12] and can be found here[4] (Fig. 1).

Loss Function. To train the model, we used the loss function from Kendall et al. [7], Euclidean loss with stochastic gradient descent: $loss(I) = \|\hat{x} - x\| + \beta \left\| \hat{q} - \frac{q}{\|q\|} \right\|$, where the predicted pose p is $p = [x, q]$, x being the position and q quaternion of the camera orientation. Here β is a hyperparameter, used to keep the expected value of position and orientation errors approximately equal. We tested extensively to find the optimal value of β for our model.

---

[3] 2 dimensional.

[4] https://github.com/omkarpatil18/capsnet_dr_cvip.

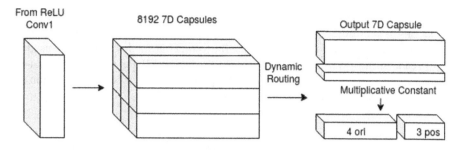

Fig. 1. Posecap network architecture

2.2 Model Hypothesis

Let us consider that an object such as a car will appear differently when looked at from different positions and orientations. When the appearance of a car changes due to change in observational pose; the set of lines, shapes, curves and colours of the car seen, also change. This set of attributes (lines and colours) together confined to a small patch in an image (whose size is decided by the filter dimensions) is what is referred to as a 'part'. When an image is fed into this network, the convolutional layer begins to extract the elementary features from it. Part instantiation parameters are then learnt from these features in the primary capsule layer, in over 8192 capsules. Instantiation parameters could be pose (position and orientation), deformation, hue and texture among others, describing that patch. Depending upon appearance of the car, only some features, and consequently only some capsules will get activated. Subsequently, all the instantiation parameters are multiplied by weights representing part-whole transformations. These weights are learnt while training, but are fixed irrespective of the camera position. A 'whole' is considered to be a larger patch of texture, colour and shapes. A 'whole' is composed of many parts in specific poses. Thus the part-whole relationship is dependent on the scene, rather than the camera pose. Every part makes prediction for a whole, but all the wholes don't align. Dynamic routing is used to get clusters of parts whose wholes align, and the corresponding wholes as the output. The deeper we go with the network, larger the capsule representations in size. We use the fact that the camera pose will be a function of how objects appear in its image, given the scene and constant camera focal length. Hence, we dynamically route the primary capsule outputs to produce a camera pose estimate.

2.3 Experimentation

Datasets. As a pilot, we experimented our network on the small-NORB dataset [11]. As we were interested in camera pose estimation, rather than predicting the class of the object given an image, we modelled the prediction of elevation and azimuth of the camera. The output of the model then becomes a 2D array representing elevation and azimuth, and Euclidean loss is used between the real and predicted values for backpropagation. This served as a good initiation point to explore, if capsules can outperform CNN based networks in a relatively simple setting. There are a total of 50 objects in the small-NORB dataset, and each object has over 972 images taken from different camera orientations, with 2 different cameras. We considered all images from a single camera of the first object instance- a hippopotamus, for testing our model. Finally, we used the Shop Facade scene from Cambridge Landmarks dataset [7] for testing on a real-life dataset. Here the output of the model is the full pose $p = [x, q]$, x being the position and q quaternion of the camera orientation.

Hyperparameters. We tested extensively to find the optimal hyperparameters for PoseCap and PoseNet on both the datasets- small NORB and Shop Facade. The hyperparameters are mentioned alongside the results. Adam optimizer [8] was primarily used to train both the models. The possible settings for hyperparameters were as follows (Table 1):

Table 1. Hyperparameter settings

Hyperparameter	Explanation	Standard values
beta 1 and beta 2	Coefficients used for computing running averages of gradient and its square	0.9 and 0.999
batchSize	Number of training images used in a batch	54 for small NORB and 77 for Shop Facade
loadSize	Resize image to this size	256 for PoseNet and 56 for PoseCap
fineSize	Crop image to this size	224 for PoseNet and 48 for PoseCap
lr	Learning rate	0.01/0.001/0.0001
beta	Factor with which error in orientation is multiplied	1/100/500/1000

Baseline. We used PoseNet [7] as our baseline. PoseNet uses a modified version of GoogLeNet [17], a 22 layer convolutional network with six inception modules. The major modifications are addition of a fully connected layer before the final regressor of feature size 2048, and replacement of the 3 softmax classifiers with affine regressors. The input image was rescaled so that the smallest dimension is 256 pixels before cropping to 224×224 pixel input to the GoogLeNet convnet.

3   Results and Discussions

We tested the models on two datasets - small NORB and Shop Facade. We used PoseNet as our baseline for comparison. The required output for small NORB dataset is elevation and azimuth of the camera which clicked the input image. The required output for Shop Facade dataset is the position and orientation of the camera. The results for small NORB are showcased first, followed by results for Shop Facade. Graphs are shown only for the best parameter setting found.

3.1 Small NORB

Baseline CNN - PoseNet. The network was modified to output elevation and azimuth of the camera which clicked the given image. Posenet was trained for 3 values of learning rate- 0.0001, 0.0005 and 0.001 with Adam optimization. 0.0001 learning rate achieved the lowest mean squared error loss of 44.67.

PoseCap. As is evident from Eq. 1, dynamic routing squashes the capsule output, restraining the network learning. Squashing is a non-linear function which maps the output from 0 to 1 to turn capsule outputs into probability estimates. To overcome this, we multiplied the capsule output by 360 and 90 for azimuth and elevation, respectively for the network to learn values between 0 and 1. The best result was obtained for a learning rate of 0.001 at 1490 epochs and mean squared error loss of 5.45 (Fig. 2).

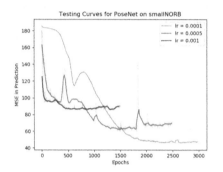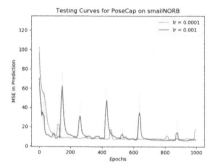

Fig. 2. Testing curve for PoseNet(L) and PoseCap(R) on small NORB

3.2 Shop Facade

Baseline CNN - PoseNet. Posenet was trained for 3 values of learning rate with Adam optimization. The best result was obtained for a beta of 100, with learning rate of 0.0005 at epoch number 425. The minimum position and orientation error was 1.25 m and 7.33 °C respectively.

PoseCap. Initially, we tested the PoseCap model without multiplying the outputs by a constant. We noticed that the position error did not decrease as the training progressed. We then trained for both position and orientation with the position outputs being multiplied by a constant - 100. The best result was achieved for a learning rate of 0.001, beta as 1000 and at epoch number 1110. The position and orientation error was 6.49 m and 12.91 °C, respectively.

Thereafter, we also trained for position (Cap-Pos-Net) and orientation (Cap-Ori-Net) separately. The output size of the network was adjusted accordingly in each case. For Cap-Pos-Net, the minimum error of 4.77 was obtained at learning rate of 0.001 at epoch number 320. The minimum error for Cap-Ori-Net was 5.45 at learning rate of 0.001, beta of 500 at epoch number 860.

3.3 Comparison Between PoseCap and PoseNet

PoseCap outperformed PoseNet on small NORB by achieving a far lower test error rate of 5.45 as compared to 44.67 (Table 2).

Table 2. Results on small NORB

Model	Error
PoseNet	44.67
PoseCap	**5.45**

PoseCap fell short in accuracy which was achieved by PoseNet on Shop Facade. Cap-Ori-Net gave better accuracy for orientation than PoseNet. These results look promising, given the fact that the PoseCap model performed better on small NORB. Therefore, improved capsule-based networks may perform better than CNN-based networks on the task of camera pose prediction (Table 3).

Table 3. Results on shop facade

Model	Position error	Orientation error
PoseNet	**1.25**	7.33
PoseCap	6.49	12.91
Caps-Ori-Net and Caps-Pos-Net	4.77	**5.45**

The results although below-par on Shop Facade, are not very surprising as capsule networks have previously reached state of the art on a simple dataset like MNIST [10] but underperformed on complex, real-life datasets like CIFAR-10 [9]. Sabour et al. (2017) discussed that capsules suffer from a drawback of generative models that tend to account for everything in the image [13]. They attributed their model's poor performance to varied backgrounds in CIFAR-10 [9], among other reasons. Similarly, we can expect the same for all the visual localization datasets, since they contain a heavy amount of noise such as pedestrians, vehicles and day-night changes.

3.4 Feature Visualizations

Feature visualizations were generated by optimizing the input image which resulted in the maximum activation of the selected filter in a layer [2]. We used the fact that neural networks are differentiable with respect to the input, and iteratively tuned the input in order to minimize the loss function- which is the negative of the norm of feature activations. We performed a comparative analysis between visualizations obtained from both the networks for two different datasets (Figs. 3 and 4).

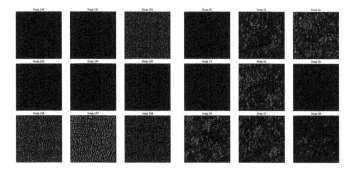

Fig. 3. Visualization of features for PoseNet trained on small NORB; left: before inception layer; right: Inception 5b, branch 3x

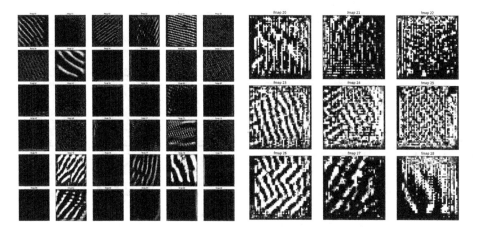

Fig. 4. Visualization of features for PoseCap trained on small NORB; left: Conv1 layer, filters 50–86; right: Primary capsules- filters 20–56, 1st convolutional layer

Small NORB. Feature visualizations produced by convolutional filters in the 'before inception' part of the network were not geometrically intuitive and seemed to detect textures at various scales. Further layers seemed to focus on specific patches in an image, rather than on definite lines or shapes. PoseCap successfully extracted lines of different thicknesses and directions as preliminary features for the network. Feature visualizations of primary capsules increased in complexity over the visualizations of previous layer, and also tried to detect certain patterns in an image. These patterns could have been formed from a combination of features detected in the previous layers. PoseCap produced more intuitive and geometrically relevant feature visualizations, which can be stated as the reason for its better performance (Figs. 5 and 6).

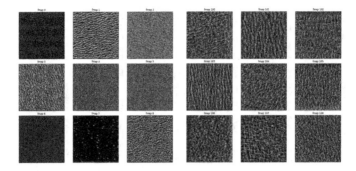

Fig. 5. Visualization of features for PoseNet trained on Shop Facade; left: before Inception; right: Inception 3a, branch 3x

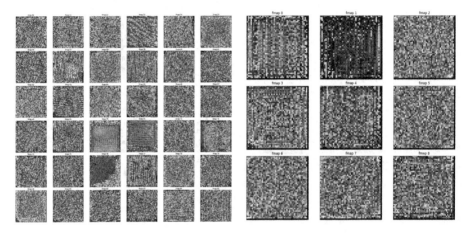

Fig. 6. Visualization of features for PoseCap trained on Shop Facade; left: Conv1 layer: filters 50–86; right: Primary Capsules: Filters20-56. 1st convolutional layer

Shop Facade. Feature visualizations produced by PoseNet are picturesque. Each filter in the convolutional layers in the 'before inception' part of the network is dominated by a distinctive colour and a specific pattern. The image turns kaleidoscopic and the patterns become complex as we go up the layers. In contrast, the filters in the convolutional layer of PoseCap did not seem to be dominated by a specific colour, but rather by a mix of colours, with concentrations in patches. Most filter visualizations also showed distinctive patterns. As we visualized activations in the primary capsule layer of the network, we observed an increase in the complexity of patterns, with no definite consistency in colour of the image. In view of the feature visualizations obtained above, the following conclusions can be drawn.

- CNN-based networks, specifically PoseNet are over-dependent on colour and textures to infer pose of the camera, rather than the shape and size of objects in the images. This can be inferred from dismal performance of the network on small

NORB, which consists of grey images, and better performance on multi-coloured and textured Shop Facade.

- PoseCap tried to extract edges and patterns from the image to infer pose of the camera, however did not use the colour and texture of the image effectively.
- Patterns in feature visualization for PoseNet were replicated throughout the image, indicating translational invariance, which was not the case with PoseCap.

4   Future Work and Conclusion

4.1   Future Work

Our model PoseCap performed sub-par to PoseNet on the Shop Facade dataset. A likely reason could be that we downsized the original image to suit the same capsule network for both the datasets. In future, modifying the network to accept larger image sizes could lead to better performance. Capsule networks, much like generative models tend to account for everything in the image [13]. The Shop Facade dataset has a high amount of noise including pedestrians in its images, which could explain PoseCap's unsatisfactory performance on it. Increasing the network size may consequently yield a rise in its pose prediction performance, making the model more robust to noise in images. Additional improvements like incorporating geometrical constraints through the loss function such as reprojection error [6], could be made.

4.2   Conclusion

We found that PoseCap (our proposed model based on Capsules) outperformed the chosen baseline- PoseNet, on small NORB dataset modified for the task of camera pose estimation. This paper concludes that Capsule based networks present a bright opportunity to overcome the deficiencies posed by CNNs, warranting further research in this direction. Capsule-based networks lend themselves to better geometrical interpretation, and also detect lines and subsequently shapes and patterns in images, as exemplified by the feature visualizations. Camera pose prediction is the ideal platform to test the core hypothesis of capsules, that they extract part instantiation parameters from image pixel intensities and form 'wholes' from 'parts' based on the likenesses of parts to each other. We thus establish that Capsules perform well on the problem of camera pose estimation and can produce competitive results in future.

Acknowledgements. This work was done as a part of the dual degree project requirement in Indian Institute of Technology Madras. I would like to acknowledge the informed guidance of Prof. Anurag Mittal for the same.

References

1. Brahmbhatt, S., Gu, J., Kim, K., Hays, J., Kautz, J.: Geometry-aware learning of maps for camera localization. In: 2018 IEEE Conference on Computer Vision and Pattern Recognition, CVPR 2018, Salt Lake City, UT, USA, 18–22 June 2018, pp. 2616–2625. IEEE Computer Society (2018). https://doi.org/10.1109/CVPR. 2018.00277. http://openaccess.thecvf.com/content_cvpr_2018/html/Brahmbhatt_Geometry-Aware_Learning_of_CVPR_2018_paper.html

2. Graetz, F.M.: How to visualize convolutional features in 40 lines of code, July 2019. https://towardsdatascience.com/how-to-visualize-convolutional-features-in-40-lines-of-code-70b7d87b0030

3. Hinton, G.E., Sabour, S., Frosst, N.: Matrix capsules with EM routing. In: 6th International Conference on Learning Representations, ICLR 2018, Vancouver, BC, Canada, April 30–May 3 2018, Conference Track Proceedings. OpenReview.net (2018). https://openreview.net/forum?id=HJWLfGWRb

4. Hui, J.: Understanding dynamic routing between capsules (capsule networks), November 2017. https://jhui.github.io/2017/11/03/Dynamic-Routing-Between-Capsules/

5. Hui, J.: Understanding matrix capsules with EM routing (based on Hinton's capsule networks), November 2017. https://jhui.github.io/2017/11/14/Matrix-Capsules-with-EM-routing-Capsule-Network/

6. Kendall, A., Cipolla, R.: Geometric loss functions for camera pose regression with deep learning. CoRR abs/1704.00390 (2017). http://arxiv.org/abs/1704.00390

7. Kendall, A., Grimes, M., Cipolla, R.: PoseNet: a convolutional network for real-time 6-DOF camera relocalization. In: 2015 IEEE International Conference on Computer Vision, ICCV 2015, Santiago, Chile, 7–13 December 2015, pp. 2938–2946. IEEE Computer Society (2015). https://doi.org/10.1109/ICCV.2015.336

8. Kingma, D.P., Ba, J.: Adam: a method for stochastic optimization (2017)

9. Krizhevsky, A.: Learning multiple layers of features from tiny images. Technical report (2009)

10. LeCun, Y., Cortes, C.: MNIST handwritten digit database (2010). http://yann.lecun.com/exdb/mnist/

11. LeCun, Y., Huang, F.J., Bottou, L.: Learning methods for generic object recognition with invariance to pose and lighting. In: 2004 IEEE Computer Society Conference on Computer Vision and Pattern Recognition (CVPR 2004), with CD-ROM, Washington, DC, USA, 27 June–2 July 2004, pp. 97–104. IEEE Computer Society (2004). https://doi.org/10.1109/CVPR.2004.144. http://doi.ieeecomputersociety.org/10.1109/CVPR.2004.144

12. Paszke, A., et al.: Automatic differentiation in PyTorch (2017)

13. Sabour, S., Frosst, N., Hinton, G.E.: Dynamic routing between capsules. In: Guyon, I., et al. (eds.) Advances in Neural Information Processing Systems 30: Annual Conference on Neural Information Processing Systems 2017, Long Beach, CA, USA, 4–9 December 2017, pp. 3856–3866 (2017). http://papers.nips.cc/paper/6975-dynamic-routing-between-capsules

14. Sattler, T., Leibe, B., Kobbelt, L.: Improving image-based localization by active correspondence search. In: Fitzgibbon, A., Lazebnik, S., Perona, P., Sato, Y., Schmid, C. (eds.) ECCV 2012. LNCS, vol. 7572, pp. 752–765. Springer, Heidelberg (2012). https://doi.org/10.1007/978-3-642-33718-5_54

15. Sattler, T., et al.: Benchmarking 6DOF outdoor visual localization in changing conditions (2018)

16. Sattler, T., Zhou, Q., Pollefeys, M., Leal-Taixé, L.: Understanding the limitations of CNN-based absolute camera pose regression. In: IEEE Conference on Computer Vision and Pattern Recognition, CVPR 2019, Long Beach, CA, USA, 16–20 June 2019, pp. 3302–3312. Computer Vision Foundation/IEEE (2019). https://doi.org/10.1109/CVPR.2019.00342. http://openaccess.thecvf.com/content_CVPR_2019/html/Sattler_Understanding_the_Limitations_of_CNN-Based_Absolute_Camera_Pose_Regression_CVPR_2019_paper.html

17. Szegedy, C., et al.: Going deeper with convolutions (2014)

18. Walch, F., Hazirbas, C., Leal-Taixé, L., Sattler, T., Hilsenbeck, S., Cremers, D.: Image-based localization with spatial LSTMs. CoRR abs/1611.07890 (2016). http://arxiv.org/abs/1611.07890

Detection of Cataract from Fundus Images Using Deep Transfer Learning

Subin Sahayam$^{(\boxtimes)}$ [ID], J. Silambarasan, and Umarani Jayaraman

Indian Institute of Information Technology Design and Manufacturing,
Kancheepuram, Chennai 600127, India
{coe18d001,coe17b022,umarani}@iiitdm.ac.in

Abstract. Damaged protein structures on the lens form a cloudy layer
called a cataract. It causes difficulty in viewing the objects. Cataracts
can lead to loss of vision if it is unnoticed. The cataract-affected lens
can be surgically removed and replaced with an artificial lens. Fundus
images, captured by the ophthalmologist, provide information about the
clouding in the lens. The level of haziness in the image conveys the severity of the cataract. Interpretation of the images also plays a major role in
the diagnosis. Automating the diagnosis process can reduce human error,
aid in mass screening, and early detection of cataracts. An EfficientNet
based convolution neural network approach is proposed to automatically
detect the presence of cataracts using the fundus images. EfficientNet is
a convolutional neural network model that uses a scaling technique to
compound factor to adjust all dimensional parameters evenly. Its scaling approach consistently scales network breadth, depth, and resolution
with a set of predefined scaling coefficients. Experiments have been conducted on the publicly available ODIR dataset (Ocular Disease Intelligent Recognition) and the proposed method is validated using K - fold
cross-validation. EfficientNetB0 achieved better performance than other
transfer learning methods with a sensitivity, specificity, dice score, and
accuracy of 0.9921 on the validation dataset.

Keywords: Cataract · Fundus images · ODIR dataset · Data
augmentation · EfficientNet · K-Cross validation

1 Introduction

A cataract is a condition when a cloudy, thick layer is developed in the eye's
lens. The proteins which are present in the lens break down to form clumps
which in turn result in degraded quality of images sent to the retina. The aging
of the eye is a major cause of cataract formation. Other contributing factors
to the formation of cataracts are diabetes, usage of drugs, ultraviolet radia-
tion, smoking, consumption of alcohol, nutritional deficiency, and family history
[3]. According to the World Health Organization (WHO), the leading cause of
impairment of vision is cataracts. The cataract is approximately responsible for

B. Raman et al. (Eds.): CVIP 2021, CCIS 1567, pp. 175–186, 2022.
https://doi.org/10.1007/978-3-031-11346-8_16

51% of the world's cases of loss in vision [6]. The symptoms of having cataracts include blurred vision, the reduced perception of colors, having difficulty driving at night due to the effect of glare and fogginess, difficulty in seeing in low light environments. It can disturb the daily activities of the individual and can lead to loss of vision if it is not treated on time [14]. The retinal blood vessels are clearly visible in a regular fundus image, while the images belonging to the cataract are cloudy, blurry, and lacks details such as well-defined blood vessels and optic disc [20].

The diagnosis of the presence of a cataract requires a qualified specialist. The ophthalmologist performs a slit-lamp exam, refraction, and visual acuity test to diagnose the presence of a cataract. The infrastructure in many rural and semi-urban aren't developed yet to make the testing accessible to common people. It contributes to a large portion of people not receiving adequate treatment on time or surgery to remove the cataract-affected lens. An effective way to identify the presence of a cataract is through fundus images. Fundus images convey plenty of information about the interior surface of the eye. Rather than observing the eye directly, stereoscopic fundus images make it easier to see the details of the retina (the interior surface of the eye). The main advantage of fundus photography is its a non-invasive procedure and relatively takes a lesser amount of time. It also involves a relatively less sophisticated instrument to capture the fundus image, hence increasing the accessibility [13].

There has been significant improvement in employing machine learning models to solve problems in the medical field. It has a great potential in making the testing of cataracts much more accessible to people [13]. The objective of the work is to study transfer deep learning models to classify the fundus image obtained by the ophthalmologist into two classes namely, cataract and normal. The contributions of the work are highlighted here:

- Data Augmentation: The number of images from the dataset is increased in size by altering the brightness of the images. Cataract images have features similar to poorly illuminated fundus images.
- A study on EfficientNetB0, AlexNet, AlexNet + Support Vector Machines, and GoogleNet transfer learning models for the binary classification of cataract and normal fundus images.
- Sensitivity, specificity, dice score, and accuracy metrics are used to analyze and evaluate the performance of the models.
- The best performing model among these transfer learning models is then k-fold cross-validated (k = 5) to show its robustness.

2   Related Works

In [16], the authors have discussed an automated cataract classification system that can classify different levels of the cataract from the fundus images, namely: Normal, Mild, Moderate, Severe. The automated cataract classification learning makes use of a pre-trained neural network (CNN). The model is utilized for the extraction of the features and the resultant output is taken as input for the support vector machine. The research work makes use of a combination of several public datasets. High-Resolution fundus dataset [2] consists of 15 images belonging to each class of normal, diabetic retinopathy, and glaucoma. STARE [8] dataset consists of 400 raw images and DIARETDB0 [10] dataset consists of 130 fundus images in which 20 belong to normal class and 110 belong to diabetic retinopathy class. Some other datasets with fundus images are E-optha [4], DRIVE dataset [17], FIRE dataset [7].

In [16], the authors have discussed the extraction of Green-channel as part of preprocessing. The advantages of using G-channels are: It provides a greater balance of luminance compared to the other two channels. The distinction between background and blood vessel is enhanced. The Green channel has less noise than the red or blue channel. Alexnet [12], a pre-trained transfer learning model is for feature extraction. The extracted features are given to an SVM model to perform classification. The two-class accuracy is 100% and the four-class accuracy is 92.91%.

In [1], the authors have proposed 3 methods for classification to differentiate four classes (3 disease classes and 1 normal class). The method discussed uses three distinct classifier types: Artificial Neural Network, Fuzzy, and Adaptive Neuro-Fuzzy Classifier. For the work, they have considered a dataset consisting of 135 persons. It consists of normal, cataract, and glaucoma images. The dataset has been obtained by the Eye Center, Kasturba hospital, Manipal. Different types of preprocessing employed include Histogram Equalization, followed by Binarization. To binarize the image, a hard threshold is selected. The resultant image is trained on an artificial neural network, fuzzy classifier, and adaptive neuro-fuzzy classifier. The artificial neural network achieved an accuracy of 86.67%, the fuzzy classifier achieved 93.33% and the adaptive neuro-fuzzy classifier achieved an accuracy of 92.94%.

In [20], the authors have proposed a fundus image-based approach for classifying images using linear discriminant analysis. They conducted classification experiments through a linear discrimination analysis assisted by AdaBoost. The data used for the detection process is collected by an ophthalmologist [5]. The dataset consists of 460 fundus images with varying cataract severity. Linear discriminant analysis is an approach aimed at identifying a space that distinguishes data with minimum square distance for the extracted features. The classifier achieved 95.22% for the two-class problem and 81.52% for the four-class problem.

3   Proposed Method

In the proposed method, four different models namely, AlexNet [12], AlexNet + SVM [16], GoogleNet [18] and EfficientNetB0 [19] have been considered for the study. These models are pre-trained on the ImageNet dataset. The model architecture and weights learned are then transferred, fine-tuned for binary classification (cataract vs normal) of fundus images. Hence, such models are called transfer learning models. Alexnet is the first deep learning model that introduced

ReLU as an activation function. GoogleNet utilizes inception blocks that allow the usage of filters of different sizes that aids in learning features of varying scale. Since these models are the most popularly used transfer learning models, they have been considered for the study.

The Efficientnet [19] is a recent deep learning model that uses a scaling technique to compound factor to adjust all dimensional parameters evenly. It has 8 variants with each variant containing more number of parameters and depth, starting from EfficientNetB0 to EfficientNetB7. The AlexNet [12] architecture contains 61 million parameters, while the EfficientNetB0 consists of approximately 5.3 million parameters. AlexNet approximately has 12 times the number of parameters when compared with EfficientNetB0. Despite the lower number of parameters, EfficicentNetB0 outperforms AlexNet in the ImageNet dataset [19]. The reasons for the better performance of the EfficientNetB0 architecture could be attributed to Pointwise convolution and Depthwise convolution, Inverse ResNet block, and Linear bottleneck. Explicit normalization is not necessary as it is incorporated within the model itself. The architecture scales more effectively by managing network depth, width, and quality, resulting in improved efficiency [19].

The block diagram of the proposed method is shown in Fig. 1. The size of the input image for the proposed method is $(224 \times 224 \times 3)$ and the pixel intensity ranges between [0,255]. Before training, augmented data is generated by creating two copies of both cataract and normal images. In the first copy, the intensity values are increased by a factor of 1 fold and in the second copy, the intensity values are decreased by a factor of 1 fold. The newly augmented set of images have been split in a 70:30 ratio for training: validation.

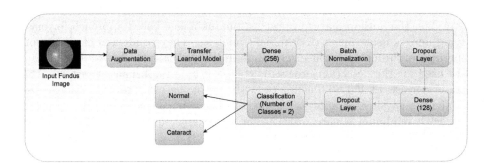

Fig. 1. Block diagram of the proposed method

In the proposed method, the architecture and the pre-trained weights obtained on the Imagenet dataset have been used for training. The model makes use of binary cross-entropy as the loss and ADAM [11] as the optimizer. The loss function is useful in increasing the ability to tune the parameters of the model. Every predicted class probability is compared to the ground truth, which is either 0 or 1. The resulting log loss or binary cross-entropy loss is calculated as given in Eq. 1. It produces a high value for significant differences as it approaches 1 and the lower score as it approaches 0.

$$H_p(q) = -\frac{1}{N} \sum_{i=1}^{N} y_i \cdot log(p(y_i)) + (1 - y_i) \cdot log(1 - p(y_i)) \tag{1}$$

4 Experimental Results

4.1 Dataset

ODIR (Ocular Disease Intelligent Recognition) [9] has been used to conduct experiments on the proposed method. The database is a collection of patient data obtained from Shanggong Medical Technology Co., Ltd. via various healthcare facilities centers throughout China. Classes are labeled by a specialist under the supervision of quality control professionals. Figure 2 shows a normal image and a cataract image from the ODIR dataset.

a) Normal image   b) Cataract image

Fig. 2. The sample images belonging to the ODIR dataset

The dataset consists of the eye images that are affected with 12 different diseases such as Diabetic Retinopathy, Glaucoma, Age-related Macular Degeneration, Hypertension, Pathological Myopia, Cataracts. Among all possible diseases, the images affected with cataracts are extracted for experimental study. The data after segregation consists of 300 Normal fundus images and 303 Cataract affected images. The summary of the dataset considered for the experiments is given in Table 1.

Table 1. Statistics of dataset - before augmentation

Total number of images	6392
Number of normal fundus images	300
Number of cataract fundus images	303

4.2   Data Augmentation

One of the strategies to increase the size of the dataset is to perform data augmentation. Some data augmentation methods are Translation, Addition of noise, Rotation, Flipping, and Random erasing. Brightness factor has been considered for data augmentation as low-intensity fundus images can get misclassified as a cataract. The brightness of the images can be affected by different configurations used by the fundus camera and varying procedures for capturing fundus images among different hospitals. The model needs to know the difference between a low-intensity fundus image and a cloudy cataract image. The images are augmented with an increase as well as a decrease of brightness by 1 fold.

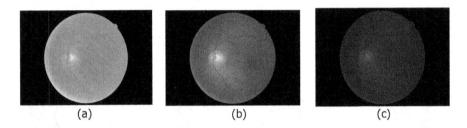

Fig. 3. Brightness altered images a) Increased b) Normal c) Reduced

Figure 3 represents the different images as a result of augmenting the original image. The detailed statistics about the dataset after augmentation are given in Table 2.

Table 2. Statistics of dataset - after augmentation

Type of images		Number of images	Total number of images
Normal	Captured	300	900
	Brightness increased	300	
	Brightness reduced	300	
Cataract	Captured	303	909
	Brightness increased	303	
	Brightness decreased	303	

4.3   Evaluation Metrics

The performance of the various transfer learning models has been analyzed using accuracy, sensitivity, specificity, and dice score metrics. They are defined as follows,

$$Accuracy = \frac{TP + TN}{TP + FP + FN + FP} \tag{2}$$

$$Sensitivity = \frac{TP}{TP + FN} \tag{3}$$

$$Specificity = \frac{TN}{TN + FP} \tag{4}$$

$$Dice\ Score = \frac{2TP}{2TP + FP + FN} \tag{5}$$

where,

TP - the number of True Positives (the number of images correctly classified as a cataract)

TN - the number of True Negatives (the number of images correctly classified as normal)

FP - the number of False Positives (the number of images incorrectly classified as a cataract)

FN - the number of False Negatives (the number of images incorrectly classified as normal)

Sensitivity quantifies the correct classification of the cataract images and specificity quantifies the correct classification of the normal images. The dice score quantifies the amount of correctly classified cataracts taking into consideration the number of misclassified cataracts as normal and normal images as cataracts.

4.4   Results and Comparison

Different images that are present in the dataset accommodate variation in the brightness of the images captured. The augmented dataset is used by the proposed model for training, validation, and testing. The overall dataset is split in the ratio 70:30 for training: validation. It is shown in Table 3. The initial setting and hyperparameters used for training are summarized in Table 4. The proposed model is executed using Google Colab. The transfer learning models are trained for 25 epochs on 1265 fundus images and have been validated on 544 images.

Table 3. Split of dataset used for training, validation and testing

Split	Number of images
Training dataset	1265
Validation dataset	544
Total	1809

Table 4. Pre-training settings for all models

Initialization	Weights	ImageNet
	Bias	0
Optimizer	Adam [11]	
Training	Epoch	25
	Batch size	32
	Learning rate (α)	0.0001

Figure 4 depicts the accuracy vs epoch plot and loss vs epoch plot. The graphs imply that the models converge around 10 epochs. It can be observed that as the number of epochs increases, the validation accuracy and loss approaches the training accuracy and loss curve. It can be inferred that the model does not overfit.

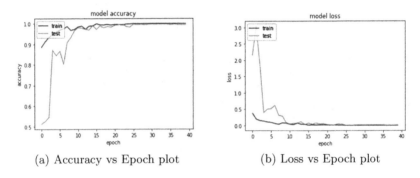

(a) Accuracy vs Epoch plot   (b) Loss vs Epoch plot

Fig. 4. Shows the a) accuracy vs epoch plot and b) loss vs epoch plot for EfficientNetB0

The sensitivity, specificity, dice score, and accuracy of EfficientNetB0 [19], Alexnet [12], Alexnet+SVM [16], and GoogleNet [18] on the validation dataset with 544 images has been tabulated in Table 5. It can be observed that Efficient-NetB0 outperforms all the other transfer learning models in every other metric. From the results, the blocks in EfficientnetB0 namely, Pointwise convolution + Depthwise convolution, Inverse ResNet block, and Linear bottleneck play a vital role in achieving significantly better results. The model is further studied to evaluate its robustness.

4.5   EfficientNetB0

Table 6 shows the confusion matrix obtained by the predictions using Efficient-NetB0 on the 544 validation dataset images. It can be observed that the Effi-cientNetB0 model has correctly classified all cataract images (270 images) while it classified 271 normal images correctly out of 274 normal images.

Table 5. Comparison of validation results with other existing models with ODIR dataset

Framework	Sensitivity	Specificity	Dice score	Accuracy
GoogleNet [18]	0.9048	0.9407	0.9216	0.9227
Alexnet [12]	0.9011	0.9481	0.9231	0.9245
Alexnet+SVM [16]	0.9084	0.9481	0.9271	0.9282
EfficientNetB0 [19]	0.9921	0.9921	0.9921	0.9921
EfficientNet-B3 [15]	0.9949	0.9786	–	0.9902
FL-EfficientNet-B3 [15]	0.9898	0.9872	–	0.9890
BCL-EfficientNet-B3 [15]	0.9974	0.9872	–	0.9945
FCL-EfficientNet-B3 [15]	0.9949	0.9914	–	0.9938

Table 6. The confusion matrix for the classification results obtained using EfficientNetB0

		Ground truth	
		Cataract	Normal
Prediction	Cataract	270	3
	Normal	0	271

Figure 5 shows three sample false positives when using EfficientNetB0 for prediction. It can be observed that both the false-positive images have poor contrast and thereby having high similarity to mildly affected cataract images. This poor contrast could have resulted in misclassification.

The receiver operating characteristic (ROC) curve obtained between the false positive rate and the true positive rate is shown in Fig. 6. It can be observed that the sharp increase in the ROC curve demonstrates the performance of the EfficientNetB0 model.

K-Fold cross-validation has been performed by considering with K value as 5. It demonstrates the consistency and the robustness of the trained model. A mean with low standard deviation are ideal for a robust and consistent model. From the results of the 5-fold cross-validation tabulated in Table 7, it can be observed that the trained EfficientB0 model is robust and consistent with its results.

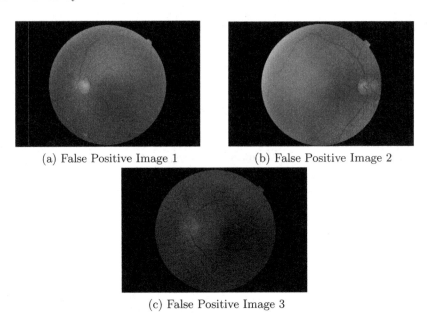

(a) False Positive Image 1   (b) False Positive Image 2

(c) False Positive Image 3

Fig. 5. Shows two example false positives when predicting using EfficientNetB0

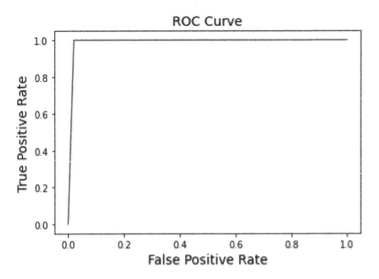

Fig. 6. The receiver operating characteristic (ROC) curve for the EfficientNetB0 transfer learning model

Table 7. Results of 5-fold cross validation using EfficientNetB0

	Dice score	Sensitivity	Specificity	Accuracy
1st fold	0.9802	0.9763	0.9841	0.9802
2nd fold	0.9921	1.0000	0.9844	0.9921
3rd fold	0.9921	0.9921	0.9921	0.9921
4th fold	0.9880	1.0000	0.9767	0.9881
5th fold	0.9883	0.9769	1.0000	0.9881
Mean	**0.9881**	**0.9881**	**0.9890**	**0.9875**
Standard deviation	**0.0049**	**0.0049**	**0.0118**	**0.0089**

5 Conclusion

Deep transfer learning models namely, AlexNet, AlexNet + Support vector machines, GoogleNet, and EfficientNetB0 have been studied to automatically classify the presence of a cataract in fundus images. The EfficientNetB0 outperformed all the other transfer learning models. The performance of the model can be attributed to Pointwise convolution + Depthwise convolution, Inverse ResNet block, and Linear bottleneck. The experiments have been conducted on the ODIR dataset. Data augmentation involving increasing and decreasing the brightness of the images has been performed. The low contrast images would have aided in the good performance of the EfficientNetB0 model. EfficientNetB0 achieved a sensitivity, specificity, dice score, and accuracy of 0.9921 on the validation dataset of 544 images. The robustness and the consistent performance of the model have been established by 5 - fold cross-validation.

As a part of future work, the authors aim to study the multi-class classification of eye diseases. The authors also aim to explore cascade, knowledge-distillation and ensemble-based methods for multi-class classification. Recent advances in deep learning, like capsule nets, can also be explored.

References

1. Acharya, U.R., Kannathal, N., Ng, E., Min, L.C., Suri, J.S.: Computer-based classification of eye diseases. In: 2006 International Conference of the IEEE Engineering in Medicine and Biology Society, pp. 6121–6124. IEEE (2006)
2. Budai, A., Bock, R., Maier, A., Hornegger, J., Michelson, G.: Robust vessel segmentation in fundus images. Int. J. Biomed. Imaging **2013**, 154860–154860 (2013)
3. Cheng, H.: Causes of cataract. BMJ Brit. Med. J. **298**(6686), 1470 (1989)
4. Decencière, E., et al.: Teleophta: machine learning and image processing methods for teleophthalmology. Innov. Res. BioMed. Eng. **34**(2), 196–203 (2013)
5. Foster, P., Wong, T., Machin, D., Johnson, G., Seah, S.: Risk factors for nuclear, cortical and posterior subcapsular cataracts in the Chinese population of Singapore: the Tanjong Pagar survey. Br. J. Ophthalmol. **87**(9), 1112–1120 (2003)

6. Hayashi, R.: Gene expression and the impact of an antioxidant supplement in the cataractous lens. In: Handbook of Nutrition, Diet, and the Eye, pp. 551–568. Elsevier (2019)
7. Hernandez-Matas, C., Zabulis, X., Triantafyllou, A., Anyfanti, P., Douma, S., Argyros, A.A.: Fire: fundus image registration dataset. J. Model. Ophthalmol. 1(4), 16–28 (2017)
8. Hoover, A., Kouznetsova, V., Goldbaum, M.: Locating blood vessels in retinal images by piecewise threshold probing of a matched filter response. IEEE Trans. Med. Imaging 19(3), 203–210 (2000)
9. International Ocular Disease Intelligent Recognition, P.U.: dataset - grand challenge (2019). https://odir2019.grand-challenge.org/dataset/
10. Kauppi, T., et al.: DIARETDB0: evaluation database and methodology for diabetic retinopathy algorithms. Mach. Vis. Pattern Recognit. Res. Group Lappeenranta Univ. Technol. Finland 73, 1–17 (2006)
11. Kingma, D.P., Ba, J.: Adam: a method for stochastic optimization. In: Bengio, Y., LeCun, Y. (eds.) 3rd International Conference on Learning Representations, ICLR 2015, San Diego, CA, USA, 7–9 May 2015, Conference Track Proceedings (2015). http://arxiv.org/abs/1412.6980
12. Krizhevsky, A., Sutskever, I., Hinton, G.E.: ImageNet classification with deep convolutional neural networks. Commun. ACM 60(6), 84–90 (2017)
13. Li, J., et al.: Automatic cataract diagnosis by image-based interpretability. In: 2018 IEEE International Conference on Systems, Man, and Cybernetics (SMC), pp. 3964–3969. IEEE (2018)
14. Liu, Y.C., Wilkins, M., Kim, T., Malyugin, B., Mehta, J.S.: Cataracts. Lancet 390(10094), 600–612 (2017)
15. Luo, X., Li, J., Chen, M., Yang, X., Li, X.: Ophthalmic disease detection via deep learning with a novel mixture loss function. IEEE J. Biomed. Health Inform. (2021)
16. Pratap, T., Kokil, P.: Computer-aided diagnosis of cataract using deep transfer learning. Biomed. Signal Process. Control 53, 101533 (2019)
17. Staal, J., Abràmoff, M.D., Niemeijer, M., Viergever, M.A., Van Ginneken, B.: Ridge-based vessel segmentation in color images of the retina. IEEE Trans. Med. Imaging 23(4), 501–509 (2004)
18. Szegedy, C., et al.: Going deeper with convolutions. In: Proceedings of the IEEE Conference on Computer Vision and Pattern Recognition, pp. 1–9 (2015)
19. Tan, M., Le, Q.: EfficientNet: rethinking model scaling for convolutional neural networks. In: International Conference on Machine Learning, pp. 6105–6114. PMLR (2019)
20. Zheng, J., Guo, L., Peng, L., Li, J., Yang, J., Liang, Q.: Fundus image based cataract classification. In: 2014 IEEE International Conference on Imaging Systems and Techniques (IST) Proceedings, pp. 90–94. IEEE (2014)

Brain Tumour Segmentation Using Convolution Neural Network

Karuna Bhalerao[1], Shital Patil[1,2], and Surendra Bhosale[1(✉)]

[1] Department of Electrical Engineering, VJTI, Mumbai, India
krbhalerao_m19@el.vjti.ac.in, snpatil_p17@ee.vjti.ac.in,
sjbhosale@vjti.org.in
[2] Department of Instrumentation Engineering, RAIT, Navi Mumbai, India

Abstract. Automatic brain tumor segmentation is an ill-posed problem. In this paper, we propose convolution neural network based approach for brain tumor segmentation. The proposed network made up of encoder-decoder modules. The encoder modules are designed to encode the input brain MRI slice into set of features while the decoder modules for the generation of the brain tumor segmentation map from the encoded features. To maintain the structural consistency, feature maps obtained on the encoder side are shared with the respective decoder modules using skip connections. We have used training set of the BraTS-15 dataset to train the proposed network for brain tumor segmentation. While, its testing set is used to validate the proposed network for brain tumor segmentation. The experimental analysis consists the comparison of the proposed and existing methods for brain tumor segmentation with the help of Dice similarity coefficient and Jaccard index. Comparison with the existing methods show that the proposed method outperforms other existing methods for brain tumor segmentation.

Keywords: Tumour segmentation · CNN · cGAN

1 Introduction

The most aggressive brain tumors in adults are gliomas, which arise from glial cells and the surrounding infiltrative tissues [41]. Low-grade gliomas (LGG) and high-grade gliomas (HGG) are the two types, with HGG being the most aggressive. Currently, approximately 130 distinct forms of high-grade and low-grade brain tumors are recognized, with average survival times ranging from 12 to 15 months. Because of their diverse behavior in terms of shape and feature, brain tumor segmentation is a difficult task [22]. Furthermore, the depth of a tumor varies greatly from one person to the next. Because of its non-invasive properties and advanced image assessment in soft tissues, magnetic resonance imaging (MRI) is preferred over other imaging modalities for the diagnosis and treatment of brain malignancies. Different types of tissue comparison images have been created using MRI modalities, which allow for the extraction of valuable structural records, enabling for the identification and treatment of tumors in their sub-regions. T1 weighted scans, which identify normal tissues from tumorous ones, are obtained by using unusual pulse sequences. 2) T2 weighted scans to demarcate the

B. Raman et al. (Eds.): CVIP 2021, CCIS 1567, pp. 187–197, 2022.
https://doi.org/10.1007/978-3-031-11346-8_17

edema area, which results in a bright picture area. 3) T1-Gd scans employ comparison agents that, as a result of their buildup, produce a vivid sign near tumor borders. 4) FLAIR scans use water molecule suppression signals to identify Cerebrospinal fluid (CSF) from the edema zone. These scans are helpful to a radiologist in annotating specific regions of brain tumors. Slice-by-slice labeling of brain tumors using MRI scans, on the other hand, is a time-consuming and tiring task. This burden can be alleviated by using computer vision techniques to automate segmentation [44].

For the automatic segmentation of brain tumors, computer vision techniques and computer device development are developing as study areas. Any of these ways has yielded promising results, but there is no clear winner because these ideas have yet to be implemented in hospitals. Convolution neural networks (CNNs) have recently emerged as the approach of choice for implementing state-of-the-art picture segmentation problems [25]. BraTS [27], in collaboration with MICCAI, was the first to use CNN to segment brain tumors. Convolution layers measure the output image using raw image intensities as inputs. It enables deep learning to be independent of the brain MRI scan tumor segment's handcrafted properties. Using non-linear algorithms and many qubits, high levels of complexity in investigating complicated structures can be addressed.

2   Literature Survey

Support vector machine [2] and random forest [23] have become popular for automatic brain tumor segmentation thanks to developments in machine learning techniques. However, such approaches enable the collection of hand-crafted characteristics for the development of the matching machine learning model. Ronneberger et al. [39] originally introduced a completely complex U-Net system in 2015, inspired by deep learning technology. A contractor path and a symmetrical expansion route are integrated into U-Net, with skip connections in between. For boundary pixel prediction, mirror approaches were used. Dong et al. [5] proposed a totally convoluted network for brain tumor diagnosis and segmentation, influenced by the U-Net concept. The network was less successful in segmenting the LGG cohort's enhanced area. In addition, Kong et al. [21] presents the composite Pyramid U-Net brain tumor segmentation model. They also improved the U-Net model, which displays global context knowledge in a variety of regional settings. Alex et al. [1] proposed utilizing a totally convoluted neural network to cluster brain cancers from multimodal MR images (FCNN). They employed a 23-layer voxel-based classification with a single forward pass preceded by a linked component analysis to reduce false positives. On the BraTS dataset, Havaei et al. [15] increased brain tumor segmentation results. In their system, they used two-way and cascaded architectures. For both local and global features, the two-way structure is used to identify two receptive fields. The visual properties of the marker and the position of the patch in the brain MRI image are used to estimate the pixel mark. Wang et al. [43] employed CNN for automated brain tumor segmentation and modified cascaded structure. Hussain et al. [17], on the other hand, proposed a patch-based technique for brain tumor segmentation and employed cascaded deep CNN.

The proposed encoder-decoder architecture by Noh et al. [30] in the field of semantic segmentation of real sceneries comprises of particular convolution and pooling layers and reveals high-resolution characteristics in low-level noticeable edges. Badri-narayanan *et al.* [3] proposed SegNet, a redesigned encoder-decoder architecture that overcomes the problems of [30]. The max-pooling indexes successfully store all information without remembering the float-precision image features, and the following decoder uses particular indices to display the input feature map(s). SegNet was extended by Drozdzal *et al.* [6] for the brain tumor segmentation tumors. Authors in [39] took advantage of the advantages of identity mappings (*ie*: small skip connections) rather than the extensive skip links employed in U-Net. These identity mappings enable for the development of a deeper CNN without the gradient fading, as well as quick network learning with correct recovery of spatial information lost during down sampling. Small kernel sizes have been employed by researchers to develop a deeper network architecture [16, 36, 40]. Deep CNN 3×3 kernels were added by Pereira *et al.* [36]. To produce feature maps, this model employed less weights, resulting in less over-fitting. Different architectures are utilized for LGG and HGG. Using a limited volumetric constraint in the post-processing step, the error caused by inaccurate cluster categorization was minimized. For exact brain lesion segmentation, Kamnitsas *et al.* [19] includes a fully-connected, conditional random field (CRF) 3D CNN. The 11-layer 3D CNN design covers nearby picture patches in a single pass while allowing for the inherent class mismatch. For multi-scale feature extraction, they employed a dual route design. For brain tumor segmentation, Cui *et al.* [4] employs a deep cascaded NN, which combines a tumor detection network and an intra-tumoral classification network. Lin *et al.* [24] also employs dense CRF-learning in conjunction with CNNs for segmentation refinement. Zhao *et al.* [47] employed FCNN in conjunction with CRF to improve tumor segmentation performance. All of the previous methods relied on a patch-based methodology, in which medical scans were divided into patches for training and testing. As a result, a model that takes the entire medical scan as an input and uses both local and global characteristics to handle the data imbalance class is required.

3 Related Work

Convolution neural network (CNN)-based techniques have been investigated for most computer vision applications in recent years like image-to-image style transfer [18], image super-resolution [26, 42], image depth-estimation [12–14], image de-hazing [7–9, 9–11], moving object segmentation [31–35], image inpainting [37] (especially for image-to-image translation tasks). The CNN's image-to-image translation strength has also been applied to medical picture segmentation. In medical image processing, CNN-based approaches are extensively utilized and have the potential to generate high-quality findings [29, 45]. Xue *et al.* [45] proposed an end-to-end adversarial network for segmenting brain tumors from MRI scan findings. The fundamental idea for this segmentor (*i.e.* generator) network as an FCNN for producing segmentation label maps and a problematic network (*i.e. discriminator*) for multi-scale L1 failure is based on the standard generative adversarial network (GAN) architecture. The vital network was given two inputs: ground truth label maps masked the real brain MRI pictures, and anticipated segmentor label maps obscured the actual brain MRI images. In a min-max training scheme, segmentor and critical networks are alternately trained: segmentor learning

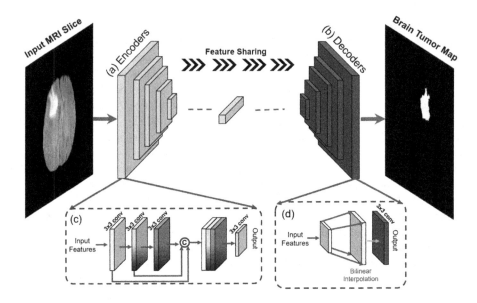

Fig. 1. The proposed approach for brain tumor segmentation. (a) Trail of encoder modules (b) trail of decoder modules (c) layer architecture of encoder and (d) decoder module.

seeks to minimize multi-scale loss of L1, while critical learning aims to maximize the same loss function. The author suggested an unpaired conditional adversarial training strategy for brain tumor segmentation in [28]. Rezaei *et al.* [38] extended conditional GAN [18] for brain tumor segmentation in MRI images. For BraTS 2017, a semantic CNN and an adversarial network were suggested.

In this research, we suggest a convolution neural network-based technique for brain tumor segmentation, which is based on previous approaches. The following are the highlights of the planned project.

- A novel CNN architecture is proposed for brain tumor segmentation.
- The proposed network is built upon the principles of residual and dense feature sharing.
- The proposed network is validated on BraTS-2015 and compared with the state-of-the-art existing approaches.

Rest of the paper is organized as follows:

Sections 1 and 2 illustrate the introduction and literature survey on brain tumor segmentation respectively. Section 3 discusses the related work to the proposed approach. The proposed approach for brain tumour segmentation is discussed in the Sect. 4. The proposed network training details are explored in Sect. 5. The experimental analysis has been carried out in Sect. 6. The conclusion about the proposed approach for brain tumour segmentation has been drawn in Sect. 7.

4   Convolution Neural Network for Brain Tumor Segmentation

The proposed network comprises encoder-decoder architecture. The encoder network encodes the input brain MRI slice into set of features while the decoder network generates the brain tumour segmentation map from the encoded features. The proposed network is divided into two parts *viz.* 1) Encoder 2) Decoder as shown in the Fig. 1 (a). In the following sub-sections, the proposed encoder and decoder networks are discussed in detail.

Encoder: The proposed encoder network comprises eight encoder modules. Each encoder module consist of trail of convolution layers followed by the batch normalization and leaky rectified linear unit (leaky ReLU). Here, convolution layer learns the deep features relevant to the brain tumor. Whereas, the leaky ReLU with leaky factor $= 0.2$ designed to generate the non-linearity in the network features. Batch normalization is employed to normalize the learned feature maps. As shown in the Fig. 1, the feature response of each convolution layer is concatenated along channel direction and processed through the bottleneck convolution layer with stride $= 2$. Here, purpose of the bottleneck layer with stride $= 2$ is to extract more deep features at different scale.

The trail of the encoder modules follow a simple process *i.e.* feature extraction through convolution layers followed by the bottleneck down-sampling convolution layer. Thus, eight encoder modules process the input brain MRI slice of 256×256 size and finally reach a feature vector of size $1 \times 1 \times 512$. The proposed encoder module is shown in the Fig. 1 (c) and its use is shown in Fig. 1 (a).

Decoder: Task of the decoder module is to decode the encoder feature maps and up-sample them to the next scale. To maintain the network symmetry, we have designed eight decoder modules. Each decoder module comprises bilinear interpolation followed by a convolution layer, batch-normalization and leaky ReLU with leaky factor $= 0.2$. We make use of bilinear interpolation operation to up-sample the encoder feature maps by a factor of 2. Thus, with trail of the eight decoder modules, the proposed generator network finally generates the brain tumour segmentation map. The proposed decoder module is shown in the Fig. 1 (b) and (d).

Parameter Details of the Proposed Generator Network: Let a series of 3×3 Convolution-BatchNormalization-LeakyReLu layer (Encoder module) having n filters and stride '2' denoted as `cnv3sd2_LR-n`. Similarly, a Bilinear interpolation-3×3 Convolution-BatchNormalization-LeakyReLu layer (Decoder module) with n filters and up-sampling factor '2' denoted as `Up2cnv3_LR−n`. Skip connections between the encoder and respective decoder are as per shown in Fig. 1 (a). With this setting, proposed generator network is represented as,

`cnv3sd2_LR−32` $\rightarrow$ `cnv3sd2_LR−64` $\rightarrow$ `(cnv3sd2_LR−128)` $\times$ 5 $\rightarrow$
`(Up2cnv3_LR−128)` $\times$ 4 $\rightarrow$ `Up2cnv3_LR−64` $\rightarrow$ `Up2cnv3_LR−32` $\rightarrow$
`Up2cnv3_LR−16` $\rightarrow$ `cnv3sd1_Tanh−3`.

Table 1. Performance comparison between the proposed method and existing state-of-the-art methods for the whole tumor segmentation on BraTS 2015 database. Note: DSC stands for Dice Similarity Coefficient

Method	Publication year	DSC
Pereira *et al.* [36]	2016	0.78
Yi *et al.* [46]	2016	0.89
Dong *et al.* [5]	2017	0.86
Zhao *et al.* [47]	2018	0.8
Kamnitsas *et al.* [19]	2017	0.85
Cui *et al.* [4]	2018	0.89
Xue *et al.* [45]	2018	0.85
Kong *et al.* [21]	2018	0.8993
Kolekar *et al.* [20]	2021	0.9225
Proposed method		0.9425

5   Network Training Details

The proposed networks training aspects are explained in this section. The proposed system is trained to encode an input brain MRI image into a collection of features, then generate a brain tumor segmentation map using those features. The presented network for brain tumor segmentation is trained using the BraTS-2015 database [27]. There are 220 HGG and 54 LGG patient scans in total. BraTS-2015 includes FLAIR scans having resolution of $1 \times 1 \times 1 mm^3$ with an scan size of $240 \times 240 \times 155$. Each of these consists of 155 brain MRI slices. Each scan yielded two-dimensional slices. We used 70% of the 14415 MRI slices to train the proposed network for brain tumor segmentation. The proposed network is built on the GoogleColab platform.

6   Experimental Results

In this Section, we have analysed the performance of the proposed and existing methods for brain tumor segmentation. We have considered Dice similarity coefficient (DSC) and sensitivity to evaluate the performance of the proposed and existing methods for brain tumor segmentation. Mathematical formulation of the DSC and J is as follows:

$$DSC = \frac{2\,|A \cap B|}{|A| + |B|} \qquad J = \frac{DSC}{2 - DSC} \qquad (1)$$

where, A and B are the brain tumor segmentation map generated by the proposed method and the ground truth brain tumor segmentation map respectively.

The experimental results are divided into quantitative and qualitative analysis discussed as follows.

Table 2. Performance comparison between the proposed method and existing state-of-the-art methods for the whole tumor segmentation on BraTS 2015 database.

Method	Publication year	Sensitivity
Pereira *et al.* [36]	2016	0.87
Zhao *et al.* [47]	2018	0.81
Kamnitsas *et al.* [19]	2017	0.88
Cui *et al.* [4]	2018	0.87
Xue *et al.* [45]	2018	0.8
Kong *et al.* [21]	2018	0.9581
Kolekar *et al.* [20]	2021	0.9553
Proposed method		0.9653

6.1 Quantitative Evaluation

We have considered 30% brain MRI slices from BraTS-2015 dataset for quantitative analysis. There is no overlap of these 30% brain MRI slices with the training data. The quantitative evaluation of the proposed and existing methods is given in Tables 1 and 2. Method [20] has the second best *i.e.* 0.9225 DICE similarity coefficient. Whereas the proposed method achieves highest *i.e.* 0.9425 DICE similarity coefficient. The increment in the performance supports the robustness of the proposed network for brain tumor segmentation task. Similar is the case with sensitivity. Method [21] achieves highest 0.9553 sensitivity value. While, the proposed network achieves the 0.9653 sensitivity value.

It is observed from the Tables 1 and 2 that the proposed method outperforms the other existing methods for brain tumour segmentation in terms of the evaluation parameters.

6.2 Qualitative Analysis

Along with quantitative analysis, we have also carried out the qualitative/visual analysis. We have considered sample brain MRI images for the analysis. For comparative analysis, we have considered [20] approach. Figure 2 shows the results of the proposed and existing method for brain tumor segmentation. The binary maps generated from the network are mapped on the input brain MRI slice for better understanding. Green, red and blue color indicates the accurate segmentation, under-segmentation and over-segmentation respectively. It is clearly observed from 2 that the brain tumor segmentation maps generated by the proposed method approaches towards the ground truth segmentation maps. Also, the proposed approach does less under and over segmentation when compared with the [20] approach. We give this credit to the proposed network which is made up of encoder-decoder architecture with the proposed dense feature sharing within the encoder block. To show the effectiveness of the proposed dense feature sharing approach against the recent brain tumor segmentation approach, we have carried a visual comparison between them and shown in the Fig. 2. It is clearly observed that the proposed network outperforms the recent brain tumor segmentation approach.

(a) Input MRI slice   (b) cGAN   (c) Proposed Method   (d) Ground Truth Map

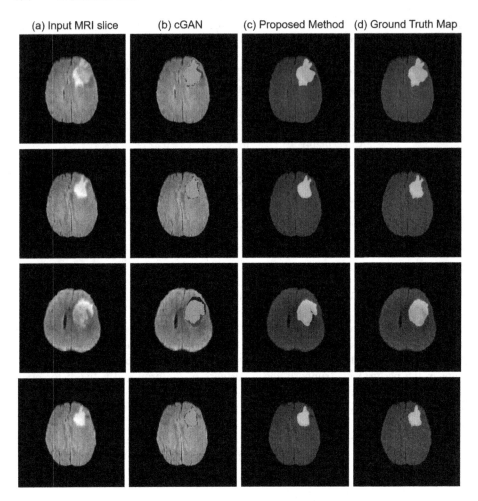

Fig. 2. Visual results of the proposed approach for brain tumour segmentation. Brain tumour segmentation map obtained using proposed approach are mapped on the original brain MRI image. (a) Input brain MRI image (b) cGAN [20] (c) proposed approach (d) ground truth. *Green, red and blue color indicates the accurate segmentation, under-segmentation and over-segmentation respectively.* (Color figure online)

7   Conclusion

In this paper, we have proposed a brain tumor segmentation approach based on the convolution neural network. We have designed a encoder-decoder based network architecture to generate the brain tumor segmentation map for given input brain MRI slice. Unlike traditional approach, we propose a dense feature sharing approach within each encoder block. Also, the features learned at each encoder are shared with the respective decoder which helps to get the more accurate brain tumor segmentation map. We have utilized the 70% and 30% brain MRI slices of BraTS-2015 dataset to train and test the proposed network for brain tumor segmentation respectively. Both qualitative and quantitative analysis has been carried out to validate the proposed network for the brain tumor segmentation. The experimental analysis shows that the proposed method outperforms the other existing methods for brain tumor segmentation.

References

1. Alex, V., Safwan, M., Krishnamurthi, G.: Brain tumor segmentation from multi modal MR images using fully convolutional neural network. In: Medical Image Computing and Computer Assisted Intervention-MICCAI, pp. 1–8 (2017)
2. Ayachi, R., Ben Amor, N.: Brain tumor segmentation using support vector machines. In: Sossai, C., Chemello, G. (eds.) ECSQARU 2009. LNCS (LNAI), vol. 5590, pp. 736–747. Springer, Heidelberg (2009). https://doi.org/10.1007/978-3-642-02906-6_63
3. Badrinarayanan, V., Kendall, A., Cipolla, R.: SegNet: a deep convolutional encoder-decoder architecture for image segmentation. IEEE Trans. Pattern Anal. Mach. Intell. 39(12), 2481–2495 (2017)
4. Cui, S., Mao, L., Jiang, J., Liu, C., Xiong, S.: Automatic semantic segmentation of brain gliomas from MRI images using a deep cascaded neural network. J. Healthc. Eng. **2018** (2018)
5. Dong, H., Yang, G., Liu, F., Mo, Y., Guo, Y.: Automatic brain tumor detection and segmentation using U-net based fully convolutional networks. In: Valdés Hernández, M., González-Castro, V. (eds.) MIUA 2017. CCIS, vol. 723, pp. 506–517. Springer, Cham (2017). https://doi.org/10.1007/978-3-319-60964-5_44
6. Drozdzal, M., Vorontsov, E., Chartrand, G., Kadoury, S., Pal, C.: The importance of skip connections in biomedical image segmentation. In: Carneiro, G., et al. (eds.) LABELS/DLMIA -2016. LNCS, vol. 10008, pp. 179–187. Springer, Cham (2016). https://doi.org/10.1007/978-3-319-46976-8_19
7. Dudhane, A., Biradar, K.M., Patil, P.W., Hambarde, P., Murala, S.: Varicolored image dehazing. In: Proceedings of the IEEE/CVF Conference on Computer Vision and Pattern Recognition, pp. 4564–4573 (2020)
8. Dudhane, A., Hambarde, P., Patil, P., Murala, S.: Deep underwater image restoration and beyond. IEEE Sig. Process. Lett. **27**, 675–679 (2020)
9. Dudhane, A., Murala, S.: Cˆ2msnet: a novel approach for single image haze removal. In: 2018 IEEE Winter Conference on Applications of Computer Vision (WACV), pp. 1397–1404. IEEE (2018)
10. Dudhane, A., Murala, S.: CDNet: single image de-hazing using unpaired adversarial training. In: 2019 IEEE Winter Conference on Applications of Computer Vision (WACV), pp. 1147–1155. IEEE (2019)
11. Dudhane, A., Singh Aulakh, H., Murala, S.: Ri-GAN: an end-to-end network for single image haze removal. In: Proceedings of the IEEE Conference on Computer Vision and Pattern Recognition Workshops (2019)
12. Hambarde, P., Dudhane, A., Murala, S.: Single image depth estimation using deep adversarial training. In: 2019 IEEE International Conference on Image Processing (ICIP), pp. 989–993. IEEE (2019)
13. Hambarde, P., Dudhane, A., Patil, P.W., Murala, S., Dhall, A.: Depth estimation from single image and semantic prior. In: 2020 IEEE International Conference on Image Processing (ICIP), pp. 1441–1445. IEEE (2020)
14. Hambarde, P., Murala, S.: S2DNet: depth estimation from single image and sparse samples. IEEE Trans. Comput. Imaging **6**, 806–817 (2020)

15. Havaei, M., et al.: Brain tumor segmentation with deep neural networks. Med. Image Anal. **35**, 18–31 (2017)
16. He, K., Zhang, X., Ren, S., Sun, J.: Deep residual learning for image recognition. In: Proceedings of the IEEE Conference on Computer Vision and Pattern Recognition, pp. 770–778 (2016)
17. Hussain, S., Anwar, S.M., Majid, M.: Brain tumor segmentation using cascaded deep convolutional neural network. In: 2017 39th Annual International Conference of the IEEE Engineering in Medicine and Biology Society (EMBC), pp. 1998–2001. IEEE (2017)
18. Isola, P., Zhu, J.Y., Zhou, T., Efros, A.A.: Image-to-image translation with conditional adversarial networks. In: 2017 IEEE Conference on Computer Vision and Pattern Recognition (CVPR), pp. 5967–5976. IEEE (2017)
19. Kamnitsas, K., et al.: Efficient multi-scale 3D CNN with fully connected CRF for accurate brain lesion segmentation. Med. Image Anal. **36**, 61–78 (2017)
20. Kolekar, P., Kendule, J.: Brain tumour segmentation using convolution neural network. J. Xian Univ. Arch. Technol. (2018)
21. Kong, X., Sun, G., Wu, Q., Liu, J., Lin, F.: Hybrid pyramid U-net model for brain tumor segmentation. In: Shi, Z., Mercier-Laurent, E., Li, J. (eds.) IIP 2018. IAICT, vol. 538, pp. 346–355. Springer, Cham (2018). https://doi.org/10.1007/978-3-030-00828-4_35
22. Li, Z., Wang, Y., Yu, J., Guo, Y., Cao, W.: Deep learning based radiomics (DLR) and its usage in noninvasive IDH1 prediction for low grade glioma. Sci. Rep. **7**(1), 5467 (2017)
23. Liaw, A., Wiener, M., et al.: Classification and regression by randomforest. R News **2**(3), 18–22 (2002)
24. Lin, G.C., Wang, W.J., Wang, C.M., Sun, S.Y.: Automated classification of multi-spectral MR images using linear discriminant analysis. Comput. Med. Imaging Graph. **34**(4), 251–268 (2010)
25. Liu, J., et al.: A cascaded deep convolutional neural network for joint segmentation and genotype prediction of brainstem gliomas. IEEE Trans. Biomed. Eng. (2018)
26. Mehta, N., Murala, S.: MSAR-Net: multi-scale attention based light-weight image super-resolution. Pattern Recogn. Lett. **151**, 215–221 (2021)
27. Menze, B.H., et al.: The multimodal brain tumor image segmentation benchmark (BraTs). IEEE Trans. Med. Imaging **34**(10), 1993 (2015)
28. Nema, S., Dudhane, A., Murala, S., Naidu, S.: RescueNet: an unpaired GAN for brain tumor segmentation. Biomed. Sig. Process. Control **55**, 101641 (2020)
29. Nie, D., et al.: Medical image synthesis with deep convolutional adversarial networks. IEEE Trans. Biomed. Eng. (2018)
30. Noh, H., Hong, S., Han, B.: Learning deconvolution network for semantic segmentation. In: Proceedings of the IEEE International Conference on Computer Vision, pp. 1520–1528 (2015)
31. Patil, P., Murala, S.: FGGAN: a cascaded unpaired learning for background estimation and foreground segmentation. In: 2019 IEEE Winter Conference on Applications of Computer Vision (WACV), pp. 1770–1778. IEEE (2019)
32. Patil, P.W., Biradar, K.M., Dudhane, A., Murala, S.: An end-to-end edge aggregation network for moving object segmentation. In: Proceedings of the IEEE/CVF Conference on Computer Vision and Pattern Recognition, pp. 8149–8158 (2020)
33. Patil, P.W., Dudhane, A., Chaudhary, S., Murala, S.: Multi-frame based adversarial learning approach for video surveillance. Pattern Recogn. **122**, 108350 (2022)
34. Patil, P.W., Dudhane, A., Kulkarni, A., Murala, S., Gonde, A.B., Gupta, S.: An unified recurrent video object segmentation framework for various surveillance environments. IEEE Trans. Image Process. **30**, 7889–7902 (2021)

35. Patil, P.W., Thawakar, O., Dudhane, A., Murala, S.: Motion saliency based generative adversarial network for underwater moving object segmentation. In: 2019 IEEE International Conference on Image Processing (ICIP), pp. 1565–1569. IEEE (2019)
36. Pereira, S., Pinto, A., Alves, V., Silva, C.A.: Brain tumor segmentation using convolutional neural networks in MRI images. IEEE Trans. Med. Imaging **35**(5), 1240–1251 (2016)
37. Phutke, S.S., Murala, S.: Diverse receptive field based adversarial concurrent encoder network for image inpainting. IEEE Sig. Process. Lett. **28**, 1873–1877 (2021)
38. Rezaei, M., et al.: A conditional adversarial network for semantic segmentation of brain tumor. In: Crimi, A., Bakas, S., Kuijf, H., Menze, B., Reyes, M. (eds.) BrainLes 2017. LNCS, vol. 10670, pp. 241–252. Springer, Cham (2018). https://doi.org/10.1007/978-3-319-75238-9_21
39. Ronneberger, O., Fischer, P., Brox, T.: U-net: convolutional networks for biomedical image segmentation. In: Navab, N., Hornegger, J., Wells, W.M., Frangi, A.F. (eds.) MICCAI 2015. LNCS, vol. 9351, pp. 234–241. Springer, Cham (2015). https://doi.org/10.1007/978-3-319-24574-4_28
40. Simonyan, K., Zisserman, A.: Very deep convolutional networks for large-scale image recognition. arXiv preprint arXiv:1409.1556 (2014)
41. Smoll, N.R., Schaller, K., Gautschi, O.P.: Long-term survival of patients with glioblastoma multiforme (GBM). J. Clin. Neurosci. **20**(5), 670–675 (2013)
42. Thawakar, O., Patil, P.W., Dudhane, A., Murala, S., Kulkarni, U.: Image and video super resolution using recurrent generative adversarial network. In: 2019 16th IEEE International Conference on Advanced Video and Signal Based Surveillance (AVSS), pp. 1–8. IEEE (2019)
43. Wang, G., Li, W., Ourselin, S., Vercauteren, T.: Automatic brain tumor segmentation using cascaded anisotropic convolutional neural networks. In: Crimi, A., Bakas, S., Kuijf, H., Menze, B., Reyes, M. (eds.) BrainLes 2017. LNCS, vol. 10670, pp. 178–190. Springer, Cham (2018). https://doi.org/10.1007/978-3-319-75238-9_16
44. Wu, Z., Paulsen, K.D., Sullivan, J.M.: Adaptive model initialization and deformation for automatic segmentation of t1-weighted brain MRI data. IEEE Trans. Biomed. Eng. **52**(6), 1128–1131 (2005)
45. Xue, Y., Xu, T., Zhang, H., Long, L.R., Huang, X.: SeGAN: adversarial network with multiscale l 1 loss for medical image segmentation. Neuroinformatics, 1–10 (2018)
46. Yi, D., Zhou, M., Chen, Z., Gevaert, O.: 3-D convolutional neural networks for glioblastoma segmentation. arXiv preprint arXiv:1611.04534 (2016)
47. Zhao, X., Wu, Y., Song, G., Li, Z., Zhang, Y., Fan, Y.: A deep learning model integrating FCNNs and CRFs for brain tumor segmentation. Med. Image Anal. **43**, 98–111 (2018)

Signature Based Authentication: A Multi-label Classification Approach to Detect the Language and Forged Sample in Signature

Anamika Jain[1,2(✉)], Satish Kumar Singh[2], and Krishna Pratap Singh[2]

[1] Centre for Advanced Studies, AKTU, Lucknow, India
[2] Indian Institute of Information Technology, Allahabad, India
anamika06jain@gmail.com, {sk.singh,kpsingh}@iiita.ac.in

Abstract. In this work, we have proposed a multi-label classification algorithm for signature images that can be used to solve multiple objectives: i) It can tell the identity of the image. ii) Can interpret the language of the content written in the image. iii) It can also identify whether the given image is the genuine signature of the person or the forged one. This paper has used the pretrained model GoogLeNet, that has been finetuned on the largest signature dataset present (GPDS). GoogLeNet is used to extract the features from the signature images, and these features are fed to the three-layer neural network. The neural network has been used for the classification of the features of the image. The model has been trained or tested against two regional datasets Hindi and Bengali datasets.

Keywords: Signature · Behavioral · Neural network · Classification

1 Introduction

Biometric has been used as a tool to provide security in different real-life applications to identify that the user is genuine or a forged user. Previously, the human body's measurement has been considered as the biometric of the person. Later, with the advancement of technology and necessity, different forms of biometric (Fingerprint, Face, Iris, Signature, etc.) came into the existence. Based on the properties of the different biometric traits, it has been divided into two parts, physiological (Fingerprint, Face, etc.) and behavioral (Signature, Gait, etc.) [9].

The handwritten signature is the most widely used biometric because of its low-cost and straightforward acquisition process, and also it has been used in most applications like finance, education, administration, etc. Signature biometric has been divided into two types based on its acquisition process, i.e., online and offline signatures. In the online acquisition process, signatures have been collected on the electronic pad, and in this mode, along with the signature images, other information of the signature(like pressure, coordinates, angle, etc.) has also been recorded. On the other hand, in the offline acquisition process, signatures

B. Raman et al. (Eds.): CVIP 2021, CCIS 1567, pp. 198–208, 2022.
https://doi.org/10.1007/978-3-031-11346-8_18

are being collected on the paper with the help of the writing tool, later these sheets are digitized, and signatures are cropped accordingly [14]. In offline mode, only signature images are collected no other information is present along with the signature. The absence of the additional information makes the offline mode of the signature the challenging problem, and most of the work in the signature domain has been performed over the offline mode of the signature images [13].

Being the cost-friendly and straightforward biometric, signature prone to forgery. Three main types of forgery have been reported in the literature, i.e., simple, random, and skilled. The other person's genuine signature has been considered as the genuine signature for the different users in random forgery. In simple forgery, the forger has the information about the user's name and tries to bluff the genuine signature of the user. Finally, in the case of skilled forgery, the forger has the genuine signature of the user and practices for the signature.

There can be two approaches to solve the offline signature problem i.e. static, and dynamic. In the static method, the geometrical details of a signature have been considered and in the dynamic method, the information from the static image has been extracted dynamically [9].

The rest of the paper is divided into four sections. Section 2 describes the state of the art related to the manuscript and the motivation behind the proposed work. In Sect. 3 proposed method is discussed. Experimental setup and results have been discussed in Sect. 4. Section 5 summarizes the conclusion of the proposed work.

2   Related Work

There are many methods [2, 4–6, 12, 15, 16, 18, 20] that have been described in the literature for authentication of the signature. Most of the methods that are presented in the literature are based on hand-featured engineering. However, signature images do not have much textural information in the image, and these hand-engineered features do not contribute more to the feature set [10]. Many deep learning methods have recently been presented for classification and object detection and achieved great success. Also, many methods have been presented in the literature for the authentication of the signature [2, 4, 5, 20].

In [5], authors have used siamese network for verification of the signature. Siamese network is the twin and weight shared network. Distance-based loss function has been used in the siamese network. In [5], authors have created a genuine-genuine and genuine- forged pair of the signature images. In their work, they have utilized the contrastive loss function. The contrastive loss function used euclidean distance. They have reduced the distance between genuine - genuine pairs and increased the distance between genuine-forged pairs at the time of the network training. To overcome the limitation of the Neural network i.e., it accepts the same size input images because of the fixed number of neurons in the fully connected layer, authors [11] have presented a method that used Spatial Pyramid Pooling (SPP). SPP provides the fixed-length feature set that has been generated from the different size images.

In signature biometrics, data is a major concern. Unfortunately, we do not have an ample amount of data to train CNN. To address this issue, authors in [4] used only one genuine signature of the person. They found the sequence of connected pixels in four directions, and a feature set has been formed with these four sequences. For classification of the feature set, one-class SVM has been used. In [2], the author has presented a method for verification of the signature that uses both writer-dependent and independent methods. In this method, they have also used two-channel CNN, however, this network has not shared the weights among them. Moreover, unlike the siamese network, this network does not focus on the distance metric.

In [20], authors have used four-stream CNN with attention block. Two streams of the network used discriminative samples from the four streams of the network, and the other two took inverse samples. With the help of the attention block, information of the inverse stream transfers to the discriminative stream, and this block also forces the network to extract the necessary features from the signature image. With these four streams, three pairs have been formed by merging alternative streams. Before the fully connected layer, global average pooling (GAP) has been applied. Finally, with the help of majority voting, the decision has been taken.

Signature is a simple and mostly used biometric in most of the fields, however, forgery of signatures is very easy. Therefore, it is necessary to identify that the genuine person or the impostor attempts to access the system. Therefore, it is required to build a system that will identify the forged signature. To address this problem, we have proposed a multilabel system for the authentication of the signature images. In the proposed work we have identified the forged signature, class of the signer, and language in which the user has signed. In the proposed work, we have not introduced any forged signatures at the time of training, only genuine signatures are considered.

3 Proposed Work

The objective of the proposed method is to provide a method that can identify the forged samples provided to the system without being trained on the forged samples. The proposed method can perform three tasks simultaneously, i) Identify the language of the signature, ii) Identify the class of a person, iii) Differentiate between genuine and forged signature. Figure 1 shows the full overview of the proposed method. The Signature dataset has been divided into two parts one is for training and the other is reserved for testing purposes. The training set of the images undergone pre-processing. From the pre-processed images, the features extracted have been extracted from the pre-trained GoogLeNet. The extracted features have been further divided into two sets training and validation. With the extracted features Artificial Neural Network has been trained.

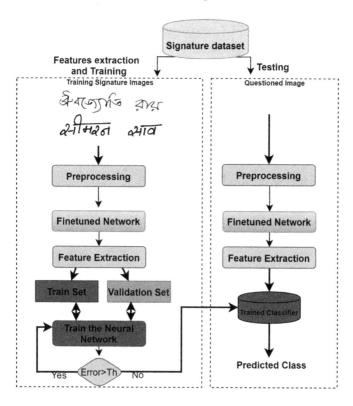

Fig. 1. Brief diagram of the proposed method

Figure 2 shows the detailed block diagram of the proposed method that has been shown in Fig. 1. The detailed block diagram of the proposed method has been divided into five parts i) Finetuning of the pretrained model, ii) Preprocessing of the signature images, iii) feature Extraction of the images, iv) Training of the ANN, v) Testing of the method. These parts are described in the later sections.

3.1 Finetuning

In this work, we have utilized the pretrained GoogLeNet model for feature extraction. The GoogLeNet has been pretrained with the IMAGENET dataset. Detailed information about GoogLeNet has been presented in [19]. We have used GoogLeNet because of its architecture and less number of parameters [17]. The pretrained GoogLeNet has been finetuned over the largest signature dataset available(GPDS Synthetic). At the time of fine-tuning we have used SGDM (Stochastic Gradient Descent Optimizer) and cross-entropy loss function. Cross entropy loss function has been described in Eq. 1

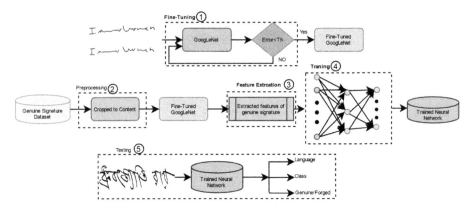

Fig. 2. Block diagram of proposed method

$$L = -\sum_{c=1}^{M} y_{o,c} log(p_{o,c}) \qquad (1)$$

where M is the number of classes, p is the probability of event, y is the predictor.

3.2   Dataset Preparation

In the proposed work, we have presented a method that can solve three problems, and it can simultaneously tell the class, language of the image, and predict that the given image is genuine or a forged image. We have mixed the Bengali and Hindi dataset in one dataset, which signifies that 260 individuals are present in this dataset.

3.3   Preprocessing

As we know, the signature images do not have much textural information, mostly white portions in the image. Before performing feature extraction, we have cropped the signature image to the content present in the image. The maximum white background of the image has been subtracted. Figure 3a shows the original image and 3b shows the cropped image.

In the proposed work, we have utilized a pretrained model (GoogLeNet) that requires specific images in the input layer. This restriction is because of the fixed number of neurons in the fully connected layer. To use the pretrained model in our network, we have to resize the input images to the size of 224×224. The detailed discussion about pre-processing has been presented in [17].

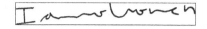

(b) Cropped Signature Image

(a) Original Signature Image

Fig. 3. Sample signature images

3.4 Feature Extraction

Features play a vital role in performing discrimination between the images. To achieve high performance, it is required that the feature set should be robust. We have extracted the features from the finetuned GoogLeNet network before the fully connected layer in this work.

3.5 Training of the Artificial Neural Network

The extracted features of the signature images have been fed to the ANN. ANN has three layers, one input layer, one hidden layer, and one output layer. The input layer has 1024 neurons with a ReLU activation function. With the ReLU activation function, the negative value of the feature set has been removed. Function of ReLU can be defined as $R(z) = max(0, z)$. The hidden layer contains 512 neurons with a ReLU activation function. The output layer has 264 neurons with a softmax activation function. The softmax function generates the probabilistic score for each feature set corresponding to each class. Based on the higher probabilistic score, the class of the feature has been decided. The details of the hyperparameters have been shown in Table 1.

Table 1. Parameters used for training of the ANN

Parameter name	Parameter value
Batch size	64
Optimizer	ADAM
Input layer neurons	1024
Activation function	ReLU
Hidden layer neurons	512
Activation function	ReLU
Output layer neurons	264
Activation function	Softmax
Epoch	100

The model accepts three loss functions for each of the tasks (Language, Class, Genuine/Forgery). For Language and class classification we have used cross-entropy loss function and for genuine/forgery detection we have used binary cross-entropy (refer Eq. 1). For the final decision binary cross entropy has been considered. Hence the complete loss will

$$L_{Lang} = -\sum_{c=1}^{M} yL_{o,c} log(pL_{o,c})$$

$$L_{Cls} = -\sum_{c=1}^{M} yC_{o,c} log(pC_{o,c}) \quad (2)$$

$$L_{Gen-Forg} = -(ylog(p) + (1-y)log(1-p))$$

$$L_{Total} = L_{Lang} + L_{Cls} + L_{Gen-Forg}$$

Here $L_{Lang}, L_{Cls}, and L_{Gen-Forg}$ is the loss for language, class, and genuine and forgery detection respectively. For genuine and forgery detection M will be 2 because for genuine and forgery detection there are only two classes. Here M is the number of classes, p is the probability of the event, o is the observation and c is class of the observation.

4   Experiment and Results

In this section we have described the training strategy, experimental setup, and results of the proposed method.

4.1   Training Strategy

In deep learning models, the initials layers are used to detect the edges, and the other high-frequency details from the images, while the deeper layers are responsible for the generalized features. We have utilized the finetuned model that was used in [17], more details regarding the network have been discussed in [17].

We have used the genuine signature of the images in the training process in this work, and testing has been performed using the forged and genuine signature. The genuine signature of the dataset has been divided into two sets, one for training (18 images) and the second for validation (2 images).

While training the network, we have used five-fold cross-validation. Each fold gets 14 images for training and four images for validation of the fold.

4.2   Experimental Setup

This experiment has been performed over a personal computer having the configuration intel(R) Core(TM) i7-7700 CPU @ 3.60 GHz, having 16 GB RAM. To perform this experiment we have utilized MATLAB along with python. Finetuning and feature extraction has been done in MATLAB and for the training of the Neural Network, we have used python.

4.3   Dataset

To check the robustness of the proposed method, we have performed this experiment on a different dataset. These datasets have different languages like Hindi, English, Bengali.

GPDS. This dataset has samples of 4000 individuals [7,8]. Each individual has 24 genuine and 30 forged signatures. The pretrained model GoogLeNet has been finetuned over this dataset.

BHSig260. BHSig260 dataset involves samples of two regional languages, i.e. Hindi and Bengali [16]. 100 individuals have participated to produce the Bengali dataset, and 160 individuals have been contributed to collect the Hindi dataset. In both the dataset, each signer has 24 genuine and 30 forged samples.

4.4   Performance Measures

To evaluate the proposed method, we have used accuracy and loss, EER (Equal Error Rate), and AER as the performance measure. EER is defined where the False Positive and False rejection curve coincides. AER (Average Error Rate) is defined as the average of False Positive Rate and False Rejection Rate.

$$ACC = \frac{TP + TN}{TP + TR + FP + FR} \tag{3}$$

$$AER = \frac{FPR + FRR}{2} \tag{4}$$

4.5   Results and Discussion

In Table 3 the results with the proposed method have been shown. The overall accuracy consists of the three tasks, i.e., identification of the class, forgery, and language. With the proposed method, we have achieved an accuracy of 98.85%, EER of 3.61%, and 16.65% AER on the BHSig260 dataset. In the literature, authors have used AER and accuracy as the comparative measure and for a fair comparison, we have also extracted similar measures.

From Table 3, it is clear that proposed system performed better as compared to the methods [1,3,16].

We have also experimented with the different optimizers, and the results with the different optimizers are shown in Table 2. It has been seen from the Table 2 that with ADAM we have achieved higher performance.

The proposed method is ablated, the different module in the pipeline does not affect the performance of the other module.

Figure 4 shows the relation between False Positive Rate and False Rejection Rate. The figure shows that our proposed method has very less EER (Equal Error Rate).

Table 2. Performance of the proposed method on different optimizer

Optimizer	Accuracy (%)
ADAM	98.85
SGD	98.85
rmsprop	98.7

It is clear from Table 3 that the proposed method gives better results as compared to the [1,3,16]. [16] has reported a 32.72% Average error rate and 87.28% accuracy in their method over the BHSig260 dataset. They have used Uniform local patterns in their method. While [1,3] has reported 23.15% and 20.11% AER respectively. They have not included accuracy measures in their work.

Table 3. Accuracy over BHSig260 dataset using proposed method

Method	$Acc_{overall}$ (%)	AER (%)
ULBP [16]	87.28	32.72
Fuzzy similarity measure [1]	-	23.15
Fusion of hybrid texture features [3]	-	20.11
Proposed	**98.85**	**16.65**

- means authors have not reported

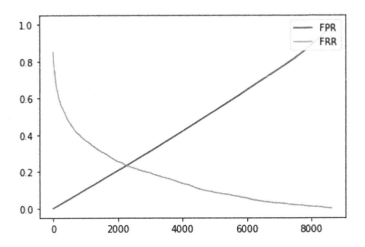

Fig. 4. False positive rate vs false rejection rate

5   Conclusion

Signature verification is considered as the most challenging field in computer vision because of its high inter-class similarity. Also, it becomes quite difficult when skilled forgery has been introduced in the system. Building a system that can distinguish between the genuine and skilled forged signature is required to solve this problem. This paper developed a model that can distinguish between the forged and genuine samples without seeing the forged sample. We have extracted features of the signature images using the fine-tuned GoogLeNet, and these features are fed to the Artificial Neural Network. With the proposed method, we have increased the system's accuracy to 98.85%, and the AER is lower than the state-of-the-art methods on the BHSig260 dataset.

References

1. Alaei, A., Pal, S., Pal, U., Blumenstein, M.: An efficient signature verification method based on an interval symbolic representation and a fuzzy similarity measure. IEEE Trans. Inf. Forensics Secur. **12**(10), 2360–2372 (2017)
2. Berkay Yilmaz, M., Ozturk, K.: Hybrid user-independent and user-dependent offline signature verification with a two-channel CNN. In: Proceedings of the IEEE Conference on Computer Vision and Pattern Recognition Workshops, pp. 526–534 (2018)
3. Bhunia, A.K., Alaei, A., Roy, P.P.: Signature verification approach using fusion of hybrid texture features. Neural Comput. Appl. **31**(12), 8737–8748 (2019). https://doi.org/10.1007/s00521-019-04220-x
4. Bouamra, W., Djeddi, C., Nini, B., Diaz, M., Siddiqi, I.: Towards the design of an offline signature verifier based on a small number of genuine samples for training. Expert Syst. Appl. **107**, 182–195 (2018)
5. Dey, S., Dutta, A., Toledo, J.I., Ghosh, S.K., Lladós, J., Pal, U.: SigNet: convolutional Siamese network for writer independent offline signature verification. CoRR abs/1707.02131 (2017). http://arxiv.org/abs/1707.02131
6. Dutta, A., Pal, U., Lladós, J.: Compact correlated features for writer independent signature verification. In: 2016 23rd International Conference on Pattern Recognition (ICPR), pp. 3422–3427, December 2016. https://doi.org/10.1109/ICPR.2016.7900163
7. Ferrer, M.A., Diaz-Cabrera, M., Morales, A.: Synthetic off-line signature image generation. In: 2013 International Conference on Biometrics (ICB), pp. 1–7. IEEE (2013)
8. Ferrer, M.A., Diaz-Cabrera, M., Morales, A.: Static signature synthesis: a neuromotor inspired approach for biometrics. IEEE Trans. Pattern Anal. Mach. Intell. **37**(3), 667–680 (2014)
9. Ferrer, M.A., Vargas, J.F., Morales, A., Ordonez, A.: Robustness of offline signature verification based on gray level features. IEEE Trans. Inf. Forensics Secur. **7**(3), 966–977 (2012)
10. Hafemann, L.G., Sabourin, R., Oliveira, L.S.: Writer-independent feature learning for offline signature verification using deep convolutional neural networks. In: 2016 International Joint Conference on Neural Networks (IJCNN), pp. 2576–2583. IEEE (2016)

11. He, K., Zhang, X., Ren, S., Sun, J.: Spatial pyramid pooling in deep convolutional networks for visual recognition. IEEE Trans. Pattern Anal. Mach. Intell. **37**(9), 1904–1916 (2015). https://doi.org/10.1109/TPAMI.2015.2389824
12. Jagtap, A.B., Sawat, D.D., Hegadi, R.S., Hegadi, R.S.: Verification of genuine and forged offline signatures using Siamese neural network (SNN). Multimed. Tools Appl. **79**, 35109–35123 (2020)
13. Jain, A., Singh, S.K., Singh, K.P.: Handwritten signature verification using shallow convolutional neural network. Multimed. Tools Appl. **79**, 1–26 (2020)
14. Jain, A.K., Nandakumar, K., Ross, A.: 50 years of biometric research: accomplishments, challenges, and opportunities. Pattern Recogn. Lette. **79**, 80 – 105 (2016). https://doi.org/10.1016/j.patrec.2015.12.013, http://www.sciencedirect.com/science/article/pii/S0167865515004365
15. Okawa, M.: Synergy of foreground–background images for feature extraction: offline signature verification using fisher vector with fused kaze features. Pattern Recogn. **79**, 480 – 489 (2018). https://doi.org/10.1016/j.patcog.2018.02.027, http://www.sciencedirect.com/science/article/pii/S0031320318300803
16. Pal, S., Alaei, A., Pal, U., Blumenstein, M.: Performance of an off-line signature verification method based on texture features on a large indic-script signature dataset. In: 2016 12th IAPR Workshop on Document Analysis Systems (DAS), pp. 72–77. IEEE (2016)
17. Singh, S.K., Pratap Singh, K., Janin, A.: Multitask learning using GNet features and SVM classifier for signature identification. IET Biometrics **10**, 117–126 (2020)
18. Sharif, M., Khan, M.A., Faisal, M., Yasmin, M., Fernandes, S.L.: A framework for offline signature verification system: best features selection approach. Pattern Recogn. Lett. (2018). https://doi.org/10.1016/j.patrec.2018.01.021, http://www.sciencedirect.com/science/article/pii/S016786551830028X
19. Szegedy, C., et al.: Going deeper with convolutions. In: Proceedings of the IEEE Conference on Computer Vision and Pattern Recognition, pp. 1–9 (2015)
20. Wei, P., Li, H., Hu, P.: Inverse discriminative networks for handwritten signature verification. In: Proceedings of the IEEE Conference on Computer Vision and Pattern Recognition, pp. 5764–5772 (2019)

A Data-Set and a Real-Time Method for Detection of Pointing Gesture from Depth Images

Shome S. Das$^{(\boxtimes)}$ (iD)

Indian Institute of Science, Bangalore, India
shomedas@iisc.ac.in

Abstract. Nowadays, the trend is to use hand gestures to interact with digital devices such as computers, robots, drones, VR interfaces, etc. While interacting with digital devices, selection, pick and place, and navigation are important tasks which can be performed using pointing gestures. Thus, detection of pointing gestures is an important step for pointing gesture based interaction. In computer vision-based analysis of gestures, depth images of the hand region have been predominantly used. Currently, the only existing method to detect pointing gesture from depth images of the hand region has sub optimal performance as shown in our experiments. This can be attributed to the lack of a large data-set that could be used to detect pointing gestures. To overcome this limitation, we create a new large data-set (1,00,395 samples) for pointing gesture detection using depth images of the hand region. The data-set has a large variation in the hand poses and in the depth of the hand with respect to the depth sensor. The data-set will be made publicly available. We also propose a 3D convolutional neural network based real-time technique for pointing gesture detection from depth images of the hand region. The proposed technique performs much better than the existing technique with respect to various evaluation measures.

Keywords: Pointing gesture · Depth image · Natural interaction

1 Introduction

Nowadays the trend is to use hand gestures to interact with computers, robots, drones, VR interfaces, etc. For e.g. a drone (refer Fig. 1a) could be directed to move in a particular direction using a pointing gesture. In another scenario, a robot (refer Fig. 1b) could be instructed using pointing gesture to pick up an object from a location and place it in a different location. In a home automation scenario, a pointing gesture could be used to control household devices (refer Fig. 1c). Pointing gestures could also be used to interact with virtual reality interfaces such as a keyboard (refer Fig. 1d). A device that is expected to act on pointing gestures should be able to distinguish pointing gestures from other

B. Raman et al. (Eds.): CVIP 2021, CCIS 1567, pp. 209–220, 2022.
https://doi.org/10.1007/978-3-031-11346-8_19

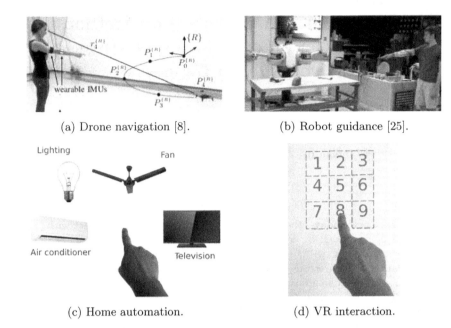

(a) Drone navigation [8].   (b) Robot guidance [25].

(c) Home automation.   (d) VR interaction.

Fig. 1. Pointing gestures used in interactions with various setups.

frequently used random gestures. Detection of pointing gestures (PGD) is thus an important step for pointing gesture-based interaction.

In computer vision based analysis of gestures, depth images have been often used to avoid the limitations imposed by use of RGB data (such as lack of robustness to variation in illumination and skin color). There exist techniques that detect pointing gestures from depth images by using cues from multiple body parts like head, shoulder, elbow, and wrist (Fig. 2a). However, these techniques suffer from issues related to occlusion (due to one body part overlapping with another), limited operational area (due to need for viewing multiple joint location simultaneously), etc. This can be avoided if only the hand region is used instead of the entire body for the detection of pointing gestures (Fig. 2b).

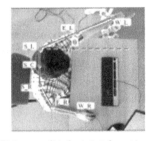   

(a) Using multiple joint locations [3].   (b) Using only hand region [5]

Fig. 2. Different ways to detect pointing gestures using computer vision.

Currently, the only existing method [6] for PGD from depth images of the hand region has sub optimal performance (refer Table 2). The existence of a limited number of techniques for PGD from depth images may be attributed to lack of suitable data-set. The data-set should have a large number of samples, have a large variation within the data-set and have comparable number of pointing and non-pointing samples.

We create a new large data-set (1,00,395 samples) for pointing gesture detection in depth images. The data-set has a large variation in the poses of pointing and random gestures (Fig. 7a and 7b). It also has adequate variation in the depth of the hand with respect to the depth sensor. It is a balanced data-set with comparable number of pointing and random gesture samples. The proposed data-set could be used to create pointing gesture detection techniques which could be used to activate pointing gesture based interaction with robots, computers, drones, VR setups etc.[1] We also propose a real time technique for detecting pointing gestures from depth images of the hand. We assume that the hand region has already been detected in the depth image using currently available techniques [11–13,15,18,27]. As shown in Table 2, the proposed method performs better than the only existing technique [6] that performs hand region based pointing gesture detection using depth images.

2   Related Work

Table 1. Comparison of the proposed data-set with existing ones. Abbreviations-N_p, N_r: No. of pointing gesture and non pointing gesture samples respectively.

Data-set	N_p	N_r	Data type	View point	Hand region based
HANDS [20]	0	12,000	RGB-D	Non ego-centric	Yes
IPN [2]	2,21,190	8,00,000	RGB	Non ego-centric	No
HGM-4 [9]	0	4000	RGB	Non ego-centric	Yes
DVS gesture [1]	0	1342	Event camera frames	Non ego-centric	No
Egofinger [10]	93,729	0	RGB	Ego-centric	Yes
Egogesture [26]	0	29,53,224	RGB-D	Ego-centric	Yes
NVgesture [17]	0	1532	RGB-D	Non ego-centric	Yes
IMHG [23]	704	132	RGB-D	Non ego-centric	No
Proposed data-set	46,918	53,477	Depth	Non ego-centric	Yes

As stated in Sect. 1, a data-set for PGD should preferably have depth data, large number of samples, a comparable number of pointing and non-pointing gestures and be hand region based. The data-set needs to be in non ego-centric view point for interactions with robots, computers, drones, home automation systems etc. We review the recent gesture data-sets in Table 1 which shows that none of the existing data-sets satisfy these conditions. So we create a new data-set that satisfies all the above conditions (refer Table 1). The data-set has large

---

[1] The link to the data-set is at https://github.com/shomedas/PGD.

variation in the orientation and depth of the hand w.r.t. the RGB-D sensor similar to real world scenarios.

Currently, there exists only a single technique [6] for detection of pointing gestures from depth images of the hand. However, multiple techniques exist which detect pointing gestures using cues from multiple body parts like head, shoulder, elbow, and wrist. These techniques are not comparable to our technique, since our method uses only the hand region. However, for the sake of completeness, we review all the related techniques in the literature.

HMMs have been used in some methods to detect pointing gestures. Park and Lee [22] use a stereo RGB camera setup for detecting pointing gestures. They track the hand using a particle filter. Pointing gestures are detected using a two-stage hidden Markov model (HMM), where the first stage maps the hand position to the surface of a hemisphere around the subject and the second HMM stage consisting of the motion stages of pointing gesture is used to detect the pointing gesture. Nickel et al. [19] use a stereo calibrated RGB cameras to detect pointing gestures. They use the hand's motion during a pointing gesture to train a hidden Markov model. The HMM is used to recognize pointing gestures. The use of RGB data for detection of pointing gestures has various limitations such as lack of robustness to variation in illumination and skin color, false detections due to overlap of skin color with other body parts etc. In [7], a time of flight (TOF) camera is used to detect and process pointing gestures. HMMs are used to model the individual motion phases of the pointing gesture. This technique requires the user's hand and head to be simultaneously visible to the TOF camera which constrains the location of the subject with respect to the camera.

In [14], a pointing gesture is detected whenever a subject raises his hand up to the shoulder level. This assumption is not always true, since some subjects may not be capable of raising the arm to the shoulder level or the direction of pointing may be below shoulder level (like pointing to an object on the floor). Similarly, Obo et al. [21] use constraints on the shoulder and elbow angles in a genetic algorithm framework to detect pointing gestures. However, the same joint angles may be true for other gestures as well. They use a Kinect2 based setup.

Huang et al. [10] have created a training data-set of pointing gestures of RGB images captured using cell phone cameras. The bounding box of the pointing gestures are marked, which are used to train a fast region-based CNN (FRCNN)framework to detect pointing gestures in RGB images.

Matikainen et al. [16] use a stereo RGB camera to detect pointing gestures and process the same. They model the pointing gesture as a circular movement (around the shoulder joint) of the hand from the neutral position to a raised pointing position. The pointing gesture is detected by fitting a circle/ellipse on the optic flow resulting from the movement of the hand. The weakness of this method is that some pointing gestures may not involve a rotation around the shoulder joint. Conversely, there are other gestures (like stop gesture) which involve a similar circular motion around the shoulder joint.

Cordo et al. [6] detect pointing gestures from segmented hand depth images. Their technique works without the use of information about other joint locations and without the use of RGB data. This is the only method that can be directly compared to our proposed technique. They convert the depth image to a point-cloud. They use classification trees with second and third order moments of the point-cloud as features. This method performs poorly on various evaluation metrics for classification, as revealed with the experiments conducted on the data-set captured by us. Our method performs significantly better than the method of [6] on all the evaluation metrics as shown in Table 2.

3   Proposed Method

The task that we pursue here is to detect pointing gestures from segmented images of the hand region in depth images. We assume that segmentation of the hand region from depth images is a solved problem as there exist algorithms [11–13,15,18,27] which do the same. So we acquire a data-set of segmented depth images of the hand. The data-set consist of images from two types of gestures, namely pointing and non-pointing. We also design a 3D convolutional Neural Network (CNN) which acts as a binary classifier to detect pointing gestures from the data-set consisting of pointing and non-pointing gestures. The process of data collection and the design of the 3D CNN are described below.

3.1   Creation of a Large Data-Set for Detecting Pointing Gestures

For creating a data-set of images of hand region for pointing and non-pointing gestures, we need to accurately segment the hand from the rest of the depth image. [4] has compared recent works on hand region detection from depth images with the method proposed by them using mIOU (mean intersection over union). None of the methods (including he one by [4]) had an mIOU of 1 i.e. none of them could accurately segment hand region in depth images for all test cases. So, we do not use the existing hand segmentation methods to detect the hand, since they have limited accuracy. Instead, we devise a new and accurate method (refer Fig. 5 for segmentation results) to capture the hand region from the RGB and depth images from an RGB-D sensor. This method needs the subject to wear a blue wristband as shown in Fig. 3 during the capture of the data-set.

The subjects are made to stand in front of the RGB-D sensor (refer Fig. 3) to execute the gestures. The distance of the hand from the RGB-D sensor is varied from 35 cm to 125 cm. The data-set consists of pointing as well as non-pointing gestures. The pointing gestures have been performed at various distances from the RGB-D sensor and at various orientations with respect to the sensor coordinate frame.

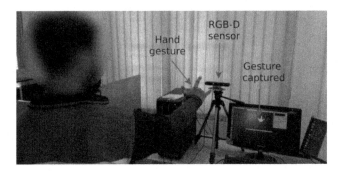

Fig. 3. Setup for capturing the data-set. (Color figure online)

The non-pointing gestures are random postures created by keeping the finger in many positions without creating finger contortions. For the capture of random gestures, the subject is asked to vary the wrist joint angle in all possible orientations in front of the RGB-D sensor. We have collected the data-set from ten subjects with a total of 53,477 negative samples and 46,918 positive samples (total number of samples equals 1,00,395). The subjects are asked to put on a blue colored forearm band during the data capture.

The hand is segmented from rest of the body using the following constraints.

- The hand is the object that is nearest to the RGB-D sensor. The rest of the body is farther away.
- Forearm band has blue hue that is distinguishable from the human skin hue.

Fig. 4. A sample input image captured by the RGB-D sensor.

First, the depth and the RGB image are captured using the RGB-D sensor. An example RGB image corresponding to the depth image is shown in Fig. 4. The depth image is smoothened using a median filter to remove any stray noise. Then the depth (D_{min}) of the point (P) nearest to the RGB-D sensor is detected. This point is on the hand region, since the hand is nearer to the RGB-D sensor than the rest of the body. Then a thresholding of the depth image is performed

(a) Hand region with fore- (b) Hand region with spu- (c) Hand region only.
arm.   rious edges.

Fig. 5. Sequential segmentation of the hand region from the depth image. (Color figure online)

to retain the points which are within a distance range of D_{min} and $D_{min} + L$ where L is the length of the hand. The entire hand along with some region of the blue forearm band remain after the depth thresholding (refer Fig. 5a).

To remove the forearm band region, we use a two-step process:

- The blue hue of the arm band is used to detect the forearm region and remove the same from the depth and the RGB images (refer Fig. 5b).
- Some pixels from the forearm region remain. The mean depth of the hand (D_{mean}) is computed from the depth image. The max depth is calculated as $D_{max} = 2 * D_{mean} - D_{min}$. The depth image is thresholded to capture points lying between D_{min} and D_{max} (refer Fig. 5c).

The RGB image corresponding to the output of a sample depth image is shown in Fig. 5c. The final data-set consists of the depth images of the hand region only. The flowchart for the data-set capture method is given by Fig. 6.

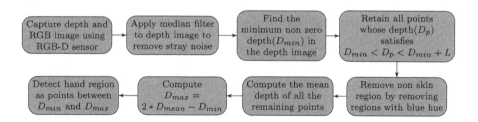

Fig. 6. Flowchart to build the data-set for the detection of pointing gestures.

Pointing and random gesture samples from the data-set are shown in Figs. 7b and a, respectively. The pointing pose was also varied as shown in Fig. 8. The data-set was collected from ten right-handed male subjects. The subjects were asked to point at random directions for the collection of positive samples. The indicated directions are however not a part of the data-set. They were asked to perform random gestures for the negative samples. We use a PrimeSense Carmine 1.09 RGB-D sensor to capture the hand images.

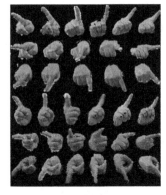

(a) Sample images of non-pointing ges-   (b) Sample images of pointing gestures
tures from the data-set.   from the data-set.

Fig. 7. Sample images from the data-set.

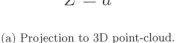

Fig. 8. Variation of pointing pose in the data-set.

3.2 Deep Learning Based Detection of Pointing Gesture

The depth image of the hand region is projected to 3D using RGB-D sensor parameters (Fig. 9a). Then the point-cloud of the hand region is voxelized (Fig. 9b). Voxel occupancy is computed as the ratio of the number of points in the voxel to the maximum number of points in any voxel in the voxel grid.

$$X = (x - c_x) * d/f_x$$
$$Y = (y - c_y) * d/f_y$$
$$Z = d$$

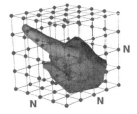

(a) Projection to 3D point-cloud.   (b) Voxelization of point-cloud.

Fig. 9. Projection of the depth data to 3D and voxelization of the resultant pointcloud. Here f_x and f_y denote the focal length in pixels, c_x, c_y location of the center of the image. (x,y) denotes location in depth image while d is the depth at that location. (X,Y,Z) denotes the corresponding location in 3D.

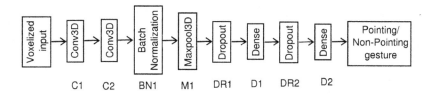

Fig. 10. 3D CNN used to distinguish a pointing from a non-pointing gesture.

The resultant voxel occupancy map is fed as input to the proposed 3D CNN (Fig. 10). The 3D CNN consists of two 3D convolutional layers C1 (kernel size = (3,3,3), number of filters = 8) and C2 (kernel size = (3,3,3), number of filters = 16), a batch normalization layer BN1, a max pool layer, M1 (pool size = (2,2,2)), two drop-out layers, DR1 (rate = 0.25) and DR2 (rate = 0.5) and two dense layers, D1 (number of units = 4096) and D2 (number of units = 1) as shown in Fig. 10. An Adam optimizer is used for training the 3D CNN. The parameters of the adam optimizer are learning rate, beta1, beta2 and epsilon are set at 0.001, 0.9, 0.999 and 1e-07 respectively. The learning rate is set to 0.001. The training is performed for 25 epochs. The batch size is set to 64.

4   Results and Comparison

The metrics used for comparing the proposed technique and the only other existing technique [6] that uses depth image of the hand region for pointing gesture recognition are accuracy, precision, recall (or true positive rate), true negative rate, false positive rate and false negative rate (refer [24] for definitions).

The proposed and the existing methods [6] are both evaluated using the captured data-set using leave-one-subject-out strategy. The average of all the permutations of the subjects gives the mean value for each of the metric used. The experiments were conducted in three depth ranges viz. 35 cm to 65 cm, 65 cm to 95 cm and 95 cm to 125 cm. In Table 2 we represent the mean of the evaluation metric within each range vs the mean depth of the range.

As shown in Table 2, the proposed method has high values (>0.9) for accuracy, precision, recall and true negative ratio. It has low values (<0.1) for false positive and false negative ratios. The mean time taken by the proposed method for conversion of a depth image to point-cloud, voxelization (using GPU) and the classification by the 3D-CNN are 6.7 ms, 6.1 ms and 1 ms, respectively (total <14 ms). Thus, the proposed method is suitable for real time operation. The proposed method performs much better than Cordo's method [6] w.r.t. all the relevant metrics as shown in Table 2. The proposed method cannot be fairly compared to techniques other than [6] for pointing gesture detection, as they use multiple body parts/joints to detect the pointing gesture, while the proposed method uses only the hand region for the same. The deterioration in the performance of the proposed method with increasing distance is likely due to the reduction in the accuracy of the RGB-D sensor with increasing distance.

Table 2. Comparison of the proposed method with the only technique available in the literature for depth and hand region based pointing gesture detection, Cordo et al., 2015 [6] using relevant metrics. The evaluation metrics are computed at various depth ranges using the leave-one-subject-out method, and then averaged over all the permutations.

Depth	35 cm to 65 cm		65 cm to 95 cm		95 cm to 125 cm	
	Proposed	[6]	Proposed	[6]	Proposed	[6]
Accuracy	0.9559	0.7384	0.9477	0.7341	0.9350	0.7278
Precision	0.9507	0.7754	0.9487	0.7731	0.9289	0.6774
Recall	0.9552	0.6039	0.9464	0.6651	0.9144	0.7163
TNR	0.9519	0.8551	0.9469	0.8007	0.9432	0.7359
FPR	0.0481	0.1448	0.0530	0.1992	0.0576	0.2640
FNR	0.0447	0.3960	0.0535	0.3349	0.0855	0.2836

Table 3, analyzes the number of samples correctly classified by the proposed method but not by [6] and vice-versa. The notations in Table 3 are defined below:

- T1 and T2: the two techniques which are being compared (proposed & [6]).
- N1: number of samples in the entire depth range incorrectly classified by T1.
- N21: number of samples in the entire depth range incorrectly classified by T1 but correctly classified by T2.

Table 3. Analysis of samples correctly classified by the proposed method but incorrectly classified by [6] and vice-versa. The number of samples is collated from the leave-one-out experiments for all the subjects.

Gesture class	Technique T1	Technique T2	N1	N21	Ratio = N21/N1
Pointing	Proposed	[6]	2514	1023	0.4069
Pointing	[6]	Proposed	15496	14028	0.9053
Non-pointing	Proposed	[6]	3456	1955	0.5657
Non-pointing	[6]	Proposed	11581	10080	0.8704

Table 3 shows that the number of samples misclassified by the proposed method is much less than that of the existing method [6] for both pointing and non-pointing gestures. Also, the proposed method correctly classifies a large fraction of the samples incorrectly classified by [6]. A smaller fraction of the samples misclassified by the proposed method are classified correctly by the existing method [6]. This shows the superiority of the proposed method over [6].

5   Conclusion

We have created a new data-set for the detection of pointing gestures from depth images of the hand. The data-set is more suitable than existing data-sets for creating techniques for detection of pointing gestures for pointing gesture based interaction with robots, computers, VR interface, home automation setups etc.

We have also proposed a real-time 3D convolutional neural network based method for detection of pointing gestures using depth images of the hand region. The proposed method overcomes the limitations of the existing depth and RGB based techniques for pointing gesture detection. Our method has significantly better performance than the only existing method [6] that uses depth image of the hand region to distinguish between pointing and non-pointing gestures.

References

1. Amir, A., et al.: A low power, fully event-based gesture recognition system. In: Proceedings of the IEEE Conference on Computer Vision and Pattern Recognition, pp. 7243–7252 (2017)
2. Benitez-Garcia, G., Olivares-Mercado, J., Sanchez-Perez, G., Yanai, K.: IPN hand: a video dataset and benchmark for real-time continuous hand gesture recognition. In: 2020 25th International Conference on Pattern Recognition (ICPR), pp. 4340–4347. IEEE (2021)
3. Boboc, R.G., Dumitru, A.I., Antonya, C.: Point-and-command paradigm for interaction with assistive robots. Int. J. Adv. Rob. Syst. **12**(6), 75 (2015)
4. Bojja, A.K., et al.: HandSeg: an automatically labeled dataset for hand segmentation from depth images. In: 2019 16th Conference on Computer and Robot Vision (CRV), pp. 151–158. IEEE (2019)
5. Boulabiar, M.-I., Burger, T., Poirier, F., Coppin, G.: A low-cost natural user interaction based on a camera hand-gestures recognizer. In: Jacko, J.A. (ed.) HCI 2011. LNCS, vol. 6762, pp. 214–221. Springer, Heidelberg (2011). https://doi.org/10.1007/978-3-642-21605-3_24
6. Cordo, S., Bernardino, A., Gomes, R.: Fingerpointer-pointing gestures for collaborative robots (2015)
7. Droeschel, D., Stückler, J., Behnke, S.: Learning to interpret pointing gestures with a time-of-flight camera. In: Proceedings of the 6th International Conference on Human-Robot Interaction, pp. 481–488 (2011)
8. Gromov, B., Gambardella, L.M., Giusti, A.: Robot identification and localization with pointing gestures. In: 2018 IEEE/RSJ International Conference on Intelligent Robots and Systems (IROS), pp. 3921–3928. IEEE (2018)
9. Hoang, V.T.: Hgm-4: a new multi-cameras dataset for hand gesture recognition. Data Brief **30**, 105676 (2020)
10. Huang, Y., Liu, X., Zhang, X., Jin, L.: A pointing gesture based egocentric interaction system: dataset, approach and application. In: Proceedings of the IEEE Conference on Computer Vision and Pattern Recognition Workshops, pp. 16–23 (2016)
11. Joo, S.I., Weon, S.H., Choi, H.I.: Real-time depth-based hand detection and tracking. Sci. World J. **2014** (2014)
12. Joo, S.I., Weon, S.H., Hong, J.M., Choi, H.I.: Hand detection in depth images using features of depth difference. In: Proceedings of the International Conference on Image Processing, Computer Vision, and Pattern Recognition (IPCV), p. 1. The Steering Committee of The World Congress in Computer Science, Computer (2013)

13. Karbasi, M., Bhatti, Z., Nooralishahi, P., Shah, A., Mazloomnezhad, S.M.R.: Real-time hands detection in depth image by using distance with kinect camera. Int. J. Internet Things **4**(1A), 1–6 (2015)
14. Lai, Y., Wang, C., Li, Y., Ge, S.S., Huang, D.: 3D pointing gesture recognition for human-robot interaction. In: Control and Decision Conference (CCDC), 2016 Chinese, pp. 4959–4964. IEEE (2016)
15. Marin, G., Fraccaro, M., Donadeo, M., Dominio, F., Zanuttigh, P.: Palm area detection for reliable hand gesture recognition. In: Proceedings of MMSP, vol. 2013, p. 120 (2013)
16. Matikainen, P., Pillai, P., Mummert, L., Sukthankar, R., Hebert, M.: Prop-free pointing detection in dynamic cluttered environments. In: 2011 IEEE International Conference on Automatic Face and Gesture Recognition and Workshops (FG 2011), pp. 374–381. IEEE (2011)
17. Molchanov, P., Yang, X., Gupta, S., Kim, K., Tyree, S., Kautz, J.: Online detection and classification of dynamic hand gestures with recurrent 3D convolutional neural network. In: Proceedings of the IEEE Conference on Computer Vision and Pattern Recognition, pp. 4207–4215 (2016)
18. Nguyen, H.D., Na, I.S., Kim, S.H.: Hand segmentation and fingertip tracking from depth camera images using deep convolutional neural network and multi-task SegNet. arXiv preprint arXiv:1901.03465 (2019)
19. Nickel, K., Scemann, E., Stiefelhagen, R.: 3D-tracking of head and hands for pointing gesture recognition in a human-robot interaction scenario. In: Sixth IEEE International Conference on Automatic Face and Gesture Recognition, Proceedings. pp. 565–570. IEEE (2004)
20. Nuzzi, C., Pasinetti, S., Pagani, R., Coffetti, G., Sansoni, G.: Hands: an RGB-D dataset of static hand-gestures for human-robot interaction. Data Brief **35**, 106791 (2021)
21. Obo, T., Kawabata, R., Kubota, N.: Pointing gesture detection for human-robot communication in informationally structured space. In: 2017 IEEE Symposium Series on Computational Intelligence (SSCI), pp. 1–5. IEEE (2017)
22. Park, C.B., Lee, S.W.: Real-time 3D pointing gesture recognition for mobile robots with cascade HMM and particle filter. Image Vis. Comput. **29**(1), 51–63 (2011)
23. Shukla, D., Erkent, Ö., Piater, J.: A multi-view hand gesture RGB-D dataset for human-robot interaction scenarios. In: 2016 25th IEEE International Symposium on Robot and Human Interactive Communication (RO-MAN), pp. 1084–1091. IEEE (2016)
24. Wikipedia Contributors: Precision and recall – Wikipedia, the free encyclopedia (2022). https://en.wikipedia.org/w/index.php?title=Precision_and_recall&oldid=1086319787. Accessed 6 May 2022
25. Wolf, M.T., Assad, C., Vernacchia, M.T., Fromm, J., Jethani, H.L.: Gesture-based robot control with variable autonomy from the JPL BioSleeve. In: 2013 IEEE International Conference on Robotics and Automation, pp. 1160–1165. IEEE (2013)
26. Zhang, Y., Cao, C., Cheng, J., Lu, H.: EgoGesture: a new dataset and benchmark for egocentric hand gesture recognition. IEEE Trans. Multimedia **20**(5), 1038–1050 (2018)
27. Zhang, Z., Zhang, Z., Zhang, H., Zeng, D.: Accurate per-pixel hand detection from a single depth image. Opt. Eng. **56**(3), 033107 (2017)

VISION HELPER: CNN Based Real Time Navigator for the Visually Impaired

Chetan Maheshwari, Pawan Kumar, Ajeet Gupta,
and Oishila Bandyopadhyay$^{(\boxtimes)}$ (iD)

Indian Institute of Information Technology Kalyani, Kalyani, West Bengal, India
oishila@iiitkalyani.ac.in

Abstract. Visually impaired persons often face difficulty to move around in new environment, especially on road. Information about the presence of different objects in his/her surroundings can help the person to move independently. This work focuses on development of a Convolution Neural Network (CNN) based portable assistive system for visually impaired people. The system will provide real-time auditory description of the object appearing in the visually challenged person's way along with its relative location. This assists the person to move independently inside house and workplace or on streets. The proposed system will capture real-time video through the camera of the android mobile set of the user (visually challenged person). The video input will be processed by trained CNN model and the object classification result will be used to compute the relative location of the object and to generate the warning for collision in form of auditory description for the user.

Keywords: Convolutional Neural Network (CNN) · Common Objects in Context (COCO) · YOLOv3 (You Only Look Once version-3) · Assistive system · Auditory description

1 Introduction

Visual impairment and vision loss caused by various diseases makes the life more challenging for many people. Visual information about the nearby objects can help such persons to continue their normal indoor and outdoor movements independently. With the advent of technology, researchers have come up with assistive technologies such as 'Smart Cane' for obstacle detection[4], non-visual desktop access for making computer access easy for visually challenged people, 'TechRead' - a reading assistance for visually impaired [7]. With recent advancements in deep neural network, real-time object detection for visually challenged people can be achieved with high accuracy [13]. This work proposes a Convolutional Neural Network (CNN) based system that compute the location of the objects present in real-time video captured by a mobile camera and generate collision warning in form of auditory alert. This android app based portable assistive system for visually challenged person will help the person to move independently.

© The Author(s), under exclusive license to Springer Nature Switzerland AG 2022
B. Raman et al. (Eds.): CVIP 2021, CCIS 1567, pp. 221–231, 2022.
https://doi.org/10.1007/978-3-031-11346-8_20

2   Related Work

In recent years different research groups have developed assistive technologies to reduce the difficulties of visually challenged people. IoT, AI and GPS based technologies have been used by researchers to develop different wearable assistive systems. Wearable smart goggles [12], sensor based smart walking stick [4], GPS based video calling apps [1] are few such systems. For visually impaired person, information about the surrounding objects (human, animal, vehicle etc.) can help him/her to move independently. In recent times, researchers have explored different deep neural network based models to develop efficient systems that could be used by visually impaired persons to detect objects in their surroundings [13]. Felzenszwalb et al. have proposed Deformable Part Model (DPM) to detect the location of the object in the image [6]. They have used root filter to detect the object location. A cell phone based portable blind aid device has been proposed by Evanitsky [5]. In this device, the images captured by cell phone camera have been analysed to detect the moving objects in the navigation path of the blind person. That information has been provided to the person in form of audio. Camera and sensor mounted intelligent glasses were used by H. O. Cervantes to design blind aid system [3]. The images captured by the camera and sensors were used by the server for object detection and analysis. The result of the analysis was sent back to the user's audio output device.

The essential features of any assistive system for visually challenged person includes the following:

- system should be portable and lightweight
- system should be user friendly and easy to operate
- location of the objects present in user's path and their direction of motion should be detected accurately
- system should not be an additional gadget that may draw other's attention and create uncomfortable situation for the user
- cost of the system should be within the range of common people

In view of this scenario, the present work proposes a CNN based mobile app that will use camera of an android mobile phone to capture the real time video of the navigation path of the user, perform object detection using CNN, compute the location and direction of movement of the objects present in the video, and generate the collision warning in form of auditory description for the visually impaired person (user). The audio will be available to the user through the speaker of the mobile phone.

3   Proposed Model

Proposed model consists of three main components.

- Object detection using YOLOv3 based CNN architecture
- Object location analysis
- Auditory description generation

Figure 1 shows different phases of the proposed system.

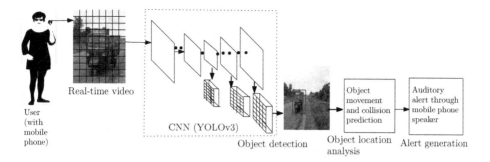

Fig. 1. Block diagram of the proposed system

3.1   Object Detection

The system processes the real-time video captured by the mobile camera to detect the objects present in the video. The object detection is performed using pre-trained CNN based model. Object detection from real time video can be performed using different CNN models such as Single Shot MultiBox Detector (SSD) [9], ResNet-101, and YOLOv3 [10]. In order to select suitable CNN model to perform real time object detection for the proposed assistive system, speed, accuracy and energy efficiency of different models are considered [2,11]. As YOLOv3 uses batch normalization, it works faster compared to other one-shot models. It also shows better average precision for small (320×320 pixels) and medium (416×416 pixels) size objects. The proposed model is designed for small and medium size objects. Hence YOLOv3 model is selected for object detection. The model is trained with the common objects of COCO dataset that appear near the surroundings of any person at home and on roads. YOLOv3 is capable of classifying several objects belong to different classes. The images of the objects such as human, domestic animals (cat, dog, cow etc.), furniture (chair, table, bed), vehicles (car, bike, bicycle, truck, bus) with appropriate label are used to train the model.

3.2   Object Location Analysis

YOLOv3 localizes the classified object by generating a bounding box enclosing the object. It also computes the object confidence score. The model provides the center coordinates (px, py) and the height (fh) and width (fw) of each bounding box. In order to compute the object location and direction of movement of the object from input video with set of frames (F), each of size $m \times n$, Algorithm 1 is proposed.

Algorithm 1: Object location and direction of movement detection

---

Input: (F_j, F_{j-1})
Result: alert
[m,n]=size of (F_j);
$\{ dleft, dright \} \in \{ (0 \ldots m/2, 0 \ldots n), (m/2 \ldots m, 0 \ldots n) \}$;
thr_dleft=$\{m/4, n/2\}$;
thr_dright=$\{3m/4, n/2\}$;
foreach $(\{px_i, py_i\} \in F_j)$ **do**
  | alert[i]='N';
  | $\Delta d = (|(px_{i-1} - px_i)^2 + (py_{i-1} - py_i)^2|)^{1/2}$;
  | area1=$fh_{i-1} \times fw_{i-1}$;
  | area2=$fh_i \times fw_i$;
  | %Check box center for location% ;
  | **if** $((px_i, py_i \in dleft)$ AND $(\Delta d \leq thr\_dleft))$ **then**
  | | alert[i]='LEFT'
  | **end**
  | **if** $((px_i, py_i \in dright)$ $AND(\Delta d \leq thr\_dright)$ **then**
  | | alert[i]='RIGHT'
  | **end**
  | **if** $((px_i, py_i > thr\_dleft)$ AND $((px_i, py_i < thr\_dright)$ **then**
  | | alert[i]='CL'
  | **end**
  | %Check box size for direction of movement% ;
  | **if** $area1 < area2$ **then**
  | | alert[i]=alert[i] + 'TOWARDS'
  | **end**
  | **if** $area1 > area2$ **then**
  | | alert[i]=alert[i] + 'AWAY'
  | **end**
end

As the assistive system captures real time video, the input video stream flows to the CNN model (YOLOv3) and objects present in each frame are identified by the model with bounding boxes (location of center, height, width) along with object confidence scores. The proposed Algorithm 1 uses this bounding box information associated with each identified object to detect the location and direction of motion of the objects in each frame (F_j). It compares the bounding box center locations (px, py) of each pair of consecutive frames and determine the location of the object by comparing it with the threshold value. To compute the threshold value, each frame $(m \times n)$ is partitioned into left and right section. The center position of the left section is considered as the left threshold $(m/4, n/2)$ and center of the right section is used as right side threshold $(3m/4, n/2)$. If the center position of the bounding box remains within the range of $(m/4, n/2) < px_i, py_i < (3m/4, n/2)$, it is treated as a probable case of head-on collision (alert='CL'). Direction of movement is detected by comparing the size of the bounding boxes in consecutive frames. The size increases if the object moves towards the camera (alert='*TOWARDS*'). When the object moves away from the camera, the bounding box size reduces in each consecutive frame (alert='*AWAY*'). The algorithm compares the size of each bounding box in consecutive frames. No change in bounding box size and location of the center indicates that both the camera (user position) and object become stationary. The information about the object location and direction of movement are stored and return by the algorithm for future use (alert). The '*LEFT*' and '*RIGHT*' value indicate the position of the object in left and right direction with respect to camera (user). Alert '*CL*' indicates the position of the object on the path of the camera. This may be a case of possible collision if the object moves towards the camera without changing it's position in subsequent frames. The algorithm generates the alert message for all objects detected in each frame. These information are used later to generate the final message and audio warning for collision cases.

3.3   Auditory Description Generation

The alert message returned by the Algorithm 1 is used to generate the suitable text for auditory description. Each bounding box generated by the CNN model appears with a classname. The proposed Algorithm 1 uses the bounding box information to generate the alert message. The final message and the respective auditory description are generated based on both object class name and alert message. The formation of the final message can be represented as follows -

- case I: alert = $RIGHT\ TOWARDS$, object class = X,
  final message= 'Warning for collision'+'as'+$\langle X \rangle$ + 'is coming from right'
- case II: alert = $LEFT\ TOWARDS$, object class = X,
  final message: 'Warning for collision'+'as'+$\langle X \rangle$ + 'is coming from left'
- case III: alert = $CL\ TOWARDS$, object class = X,
  final message: 'Warning for collision'+'as'+$\langle X \rangle$ + 'is moving towards you'
- case IV: alert = $N\ TOWARDS$, object class = X,
  final message: $\langle X \rangle$ + 'is at safe distance.'
- case V: alert = $LEFT\ AWAY$, object class = X,
  final message: $\langle X \rangle$+ 'is going away.'

The final message for each object detected in a frame is displayed on the screen. The system generates auditory description for all final messages with 'Warning for collision'. The TexttoSpeech class available in android environment is used to generate the auditory description of the collision warning.

4   Experimental Results

The model was initially implemented in python using a Laptop with Intel core i5 5th Generation 2.2GHz x64 based processor, $8GB$ RAM and 2MP web cam. Later it is ported to Android using an android app building environment.

4.1   Dataset and Training

COCO dataset [8] is used to train the model. The images of common objects such as all domestic animals, vehicles, human, outdoor objects, and indoor objects are the set of objects detected by the model. 37 classes under 9 super-category classes of the COCO dataset are used for training, validation, and testing. A total of 244532 images are taken from COCO dataset and 80% of these images are used for training and 10% for validation. Remaining 10% images along with few videos with the above mentioned objects are used for testing of the model. The input videos (outdoor) are taken in daylight and in sunny weather. The super-category classes along with their detail categories considered for this work include - person, vehicle (bicycle, car, motorcycle, bus, train, truck), outdoor (traffic light, fire hydrant, stop, parking meter, bench), animal (bird, cat, dog, horse, sheep, cow, elephant), furniture (chair, couch, potted plant, bed, dining table, toilet), indoor (sink, book, clock), accessories (umbrella, suitcase, handbag), appliances (refrigerator, cellphone, sink, microwave), electric (TV, laptop). Later the weights and configuration file of the re-trained model are used to develop the android application. Android mobile device with Octa-core 1.6GHz Cortex-A53 CPU, Mali-T830 MP1 GPU with Exynos 7870 Octa processor, ARM microarchitecture with 2GB RAM and a 13MP rear camera is used for app development.

4.2   Testing

The system is tested with real time videos captured by the camera of the android mobile. The ground truth of each of these videos are marked by individual present during capture of the video. The response of the proposed vision helper for 9000 frames of a real-time video of 5 minutes with a frame processing rate of 30 frames/second has been shown in Fig. 2. It has been observed that on an average 6 objects are present in every frame. Figure 2 shows the accuracy of collision prediction in each of these 9000 frames. The true positive (TP), true negative (TN), false positive (FP) and false negative (FN) cases for the system are defined as follows.

– True positive (TP) - ground truth: collision, predicted: collision (collision alert) and direction of object movement is also detected correctly.
– True negative (TN) - ground truth: no collision, predicted: no collision ('safe to move' for user) and direction of object movement is also detected correctly.
– False positive (FP) - ground truth: no collision, predicted: collision, direction of object movement is detected correctly.
– False negative (FN) - ground truth: collision, predicted: no collision, direction of object movement is detected wrongly.

TP, TN, FP and FN values are used to compute precision, recall, accuracy and F1 score metrics to evaluate the performance and reliability of the proposed system (Eq. 1). Precision (Pr) represents the number of correct positive predictions done and recall (Rc) measures count of the available correct instances that are detected by the Algorithm (1).

$$Pr = \frac{TP}{TP+FP}, \quad Rc = \frac{TP}{TP+FN}$$

$$F1Score = 2 \times \frac{Pr \times Rc}{Pr+Rc}, \quad Accuracy = \frac{TP+TN}{TP+FP+TN+FN}$$

(1)

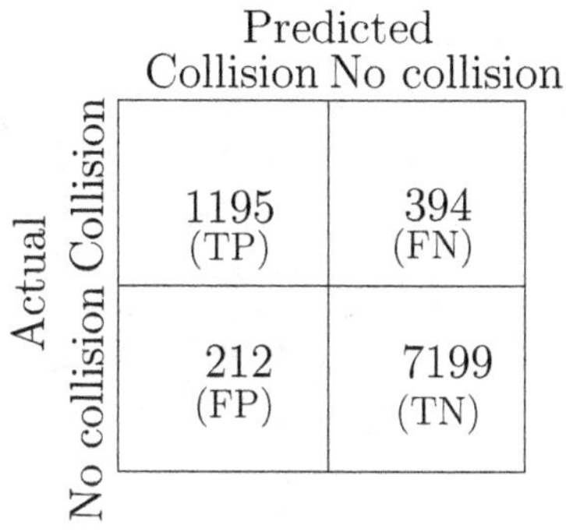

Predicted
Collision No collision

	Collision	No collision
Actual Collision	1195 (TP)	394 (FN)
Actual No collision	212 (FP)	7199 (TN)

Fig. 2. Confusion matrix

The proposed system shows a precision of 0.85, recall value 0.75, accuracy 93.3%, and F1 score 0.8. It has been observed that few false positive cases are reported in a situation where user narrowly escape the collision due to small gap between user and object. In those cases, the system has detected the direction of movement of the object correctly. It has been observed that the response time of the system with present setup is 1.5 to 2 s. Figure 4 shows the different positions of the object and the respective alert messages generated by the system.

4.3   Test Scenarios and Observations

The behaviour of the proposed system is also studied under few special scenarios mentioned below.

– Multiple objects: If multiple objects appear in the path of the user, the system will generate alert message for each collision warning detected. In case of multiple alerts of collision, the user will apply his consciousness to prioritize the alert and react accordingly. Figure 3 shows a scenario where user is moving towards a car which is on back gear. The system generates collision warning and auditory description of the warning message for the car (shown in red text). The other objects present in the same frame such as person, bicycle, motorbike are also detected by the system and respective final messages are generated (shown in white text). Similar collision warning will also be generated if the object remains stationary and the user moves towards the object.

Fig. 3. Multiple object detection and message generation

- Both the object and the user are moving: In the proposed system, the object detection is performed frame-wise and collision alert is generated based on the position of the bounding box (surrounding the object) and direction of motion of the object with respect to the user. Hence, movement of the object towards or away from the user will be detected and final message will be generated accordingly.
- Object and user cross each other: In all such cases the system generates warning for collision as the center of object bounding box appear within collision threshold range.
- Speed of the object: The system calculates the speed of the object as rate of change of center position of the bounding box of an object in two consecutive frames.

$speed = \Delta d / \Delta t$

where $\Delta d = F_{j+1}(px_i, py_i)$ - $F_j(px_i, py_i)$ and Δt represents the frame processing time. The speed is displayed along with the bounding box of the object (Fig. 3). But it is not included in the final message and audio description as it might confused the visually impaired user reacting to the message.

5   Realtime Application

The app based system developed in this work can be used by a visually impaired person (user) in the following manner.

- User will start the app with the help of voice command to Google Assistant which will use Google Assistant AI to open the app.
- User will carry the mobile in the chest pocket with the back side camera of the mobile facing the front side. In that way the mobile camera will be able to capture the front side view of the user's pathway. Mobile may also be carried in the mobile case vertically fixed with the belt of the user.

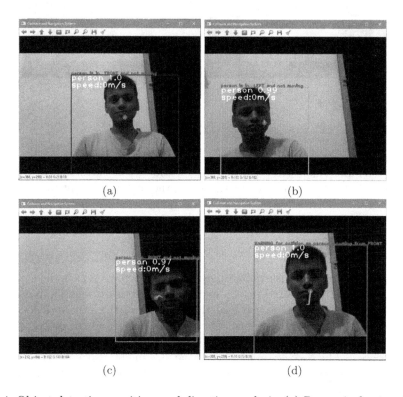

(a)   (b)

(c)   (d)

Fig. 4. Object detection, position, and direction analysis: (a) Person in front and not moving, (b) Person in left and not moving, (c) Person in right and not moving, (d) Collision warning:Person coming towards you, (e) Collision warning:Person coming from left, (g) Person moving away from you, (h) Person moving away in left, (i) Person moving away in right

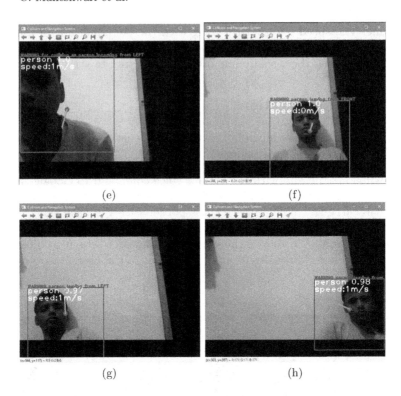

(e)   (f)

(g)   (h)

Fig. 4. (*continued*)

– Earphone and caller mike connected with the mobile can be used to run the
  app and listen the auditory description of the objects present in front of the
  user.

6 Conclusion

The proposed application is capable of detecting objects present in the navigation
path of the visually impaired person and inform him/her about the possibilities
of collision. It has been observed that the accuracy of the system depends on a
few conditions such as the distance between the camera and the object, position
of the camera, presence of light, and weather condition (rain, fog, mist etc. for
outdoor cases). The speed of movement of the user might also affect the accuracy,
if the user moves very fast. One of the main issues involving object detection is
the processing speed and the frame rate dropping. Use of retrained deep neural
network has helped in addressing those issues during app development. The
proposed system for real time object detection using mobile phone would be
particularly helpful for the visually challenged people.

References

1. Bai, J., Lian, S., Liu, Z., Wang, K., Liu, D.: Smart guiding glasses for visually impaired people in indoor environment. IEEE Trans. Consum. Electron. **63**(3), 258–266 (2017). https://doi.org/10.1109/TCE.2017.014980
2. Bochkovskiy, A., Wang, C., Liao, H.M.: Yolov4: optimal speed and accuracy of object detection. ArXiv:2004.10934v1, pp. 1–14 (2020)
3. Cervantes, H.O.: Intelligent glasses for the visually impaired. U.S. Patent No. 9 488, 833, 8 November 2016
4. Chanana, P., Paul, R., Balakrishna, M., Rao, P.: Assistive technology solutions for aiding travel of pedestrians with visual impairment. J. Rehab. Assis. Technol. Eng. (2017). https://doi.org/10.1177/2055668317725993
5. Evanitsky, E.: Portable blind aid device. U.S. Patent No. 8 606, 316, 10 December 2013
6. Felzenszwalb, P.F., Girshick, R.B., McAllester, D., Ramanan, D.: Object detection with discriminatively trained part-based models. IEEE Trans. Pattern Anal. Mach. Intell. **32**(9), 1627–1645 (2010)
7. Kala, J., Kwatra, K., Kumar, R., Chanana, P., PVM Rao, M.B.: Tactile diagrams for science and mathematics: Design, production and experiences of students with blindness. ICT Assistive Technology and Assistive Devices for facilitating curriculum transactions (2017)
8. Lin, T., et al.: Microsoft COCO: common objects in context. CoRR (2014). abs/1405.0312
9. Liu, W., Anguelov, D., Erhan, D., Szegedy, C., Reed, S., Fu, C.-Y., Berg, A.C.: SSD: Single Shot MultiBox Detector. In: Leibe, B., Matas, J., Sebe, N., Welling, M. (eds.) ECCV 2016. LNCS, vol. 9905, pp. 21–37. Springer, Cham (2016). https://doi.org/10.1007/978-3-319-46448-0_2
10. Redmon, J., Farhadi, A.: Yolo9000: better, faster, stronger. In: IEEE Conference on Computer Vision and Pattern Recognition, pp. 7263–7271 (2017)
11. Redmon, J., Farhadi, A.: Yolov3: an incremental improvement. ArXiv:abs/1804.02767 pp. 1–14 (2018)
12. Tanveer, M.S.R., Hashem, M.M.A., Hossain, M.K.: Android assistant eyemate for blind and blind tracker. In: International Conference on Computer and Information Technology (ICCIT), pp. 266–271 (2015). https://doi.org/10.1109/ICCITechn.2015.7488080
13. Wong, Y., Lai, J., Ranjit, S., Syafeeza, A., Hamid, N.A.: Convolutional neural network for object detection system for blind people. J. Telecommun. Electron. Compu Eng. **11**(2), 1–6 (2019)

Structure-Texture Decomposition-Based Enhancement Framework for Weakly Illuminated Images

K. M. Haritha[✉][iD], K. G. Sreeni[iD], Joseph Zacharias[iD], and R. S. Jeena[iD]

Department of Electronics and Communication Engineering, College of Engineering Trivandrum, Thiruvananthapuram, India
harithakm97@gmail.com, joseph.zacharias@cet.ac.in

Abstract. Images acquired in poor illumination conditions are characterized by low brightness and considerable noise which constrain the performance of computer vision systems. Image enhancement thus remains crucial for improving the efficiency of such systems. To improve the visibility of low-light images, a novel image enhancement framework based on the structure-texture decomposition is proposed in this paper. Firstly, the low-light image is split into structure and texture layers using the total-variation (TV) based image decomposition approach. The structure layer is initially diffused using Perona-Malik (PM) diffusion model and the local and global luminance enhancement is incorporated in the structure-pathway using an expanded model of biological normalization for visual adaptation. In the texture pathway, the suppression of local noise and the enhancement of image details are attained with the estimation of the local energy of the texture layer and the strategy of energy weighting. Eventually, the final enhanced image of improved quality is obtained by merging the modified structure and texture layers. The effectiveness of the proposed framework is validated using no-reference image quality metrics including IL-NIQE, BRISQUE, PIQE, and BLIINDS-II. The experimental results show that the proposed method outperforms the state-of-the-art approaches.

Keywords: Image enhancement · Low-light images · Nighttime images · Perona-Malik diffusion · Luminance correction · Image decomposition

1 Introduction

Natural image is a relevant source of information that helps people understand the connotation of information. Computer vision has witnessed a faster growth in recent times which resulted in the increased use of digital image processing systems in various areas such as intelligent transportation, object detection, and tracking. Some irresistible factors existing in the course of image acquisition lead to the degradation of overall image quality. Especially, in weak illumination

B. Raman et al. (Eds.): CVIP 2021, CCIS 1567, pp. 232–243, 2022.
https://doi.org/10.1007/978-3-031-11346-8_21

situations like nighttime, and rainy days, the reflection of light from the target might be frail resulting in image defects such as color distortions and noise. The performance of computer vision-based techniques is highly restricted due to such images with degraded quality. Low-light image enhancement primarily aims at enhancing the visual quality of low-light images by refining their overall contrast and suppressing the noise, for better processing by humans and machines and to attain efficient real-time performance.

To serve the purpose of image enhancement several methods have been proposed in the literature. The majority of the conventional enhancement techniques concentrate on altering the image histogram to reveal additional pictorial information. Histogram equalization (HE) upgrade the global contrast of the image by expanding its overall intensity range [16]. The classic HE technique has spawned plenty of other algorithms. For instance, contrast limited adaptive histogram equalization (CLAHE) [15] applies various regularization terms to the histogram to achieve better results. The context information and two-dimensional histogram of an image are utilized in the contextual and variational contrast algorithm [2], to accomplish nonlinear data mapping for low-light image enhancement. This algorithm was further refined by incorporating the layered difference representation of a two-dimensional histogram (LDR) [11].

Edwin Land proposed the Retinex theory based on visual information processing in the human visual system and the property of color constancy [10]. Based on Retinex theory several image enhancement methods have been presented by various researchers. Jobson et al. presented the fundamental Retinex method named single-scale Retinex (SSR) [9] which was then accompanied by multi-scale Retinex (MSR) [18] and multi-scale Retinex with color restoration (MSRCR) [8]. The majority of the conventional Retinex methods eliminate the illumination component and perceive the reflectance as the ultimate enhanced image which results in the loss of image naturalness. To overcome this constraint, Wang et al. introduced the naturalness preserved enhancement algorithm (NPE) by jointly processing the reflectance and illumination component using bi-log transformation and bright pass filter [23]. Moreover, a weighted variational model was introduced in [5] for the better preservation of image details. Recently, Guo et al. introduced a fast enhancement algorithm centered on the effective estimation of illumination map [6]. Li et al. introduced the robust Retinex model by further considering a noise map to upgrade the features of weakly illuminated images affected by rigorous noise [12]. Moreover, a fractional-order fusion model was formulated in [4] to retrieve more hidden details from the darker portions of the image.

The review of the literature depicts that most of the prevailing algorithms for the enhancement of low-light images suffer from either noise amplification or over-enhancement issues thereby resulting in poor subjective interpretation. To address each of these issues and to improve the visibility of the images captured in weak illumination conditions, we propose a structure-texture decomposition-based enhancement framework in this paper. Firstly, the structure-texture components are separated from the image using the TV-based image decomposition

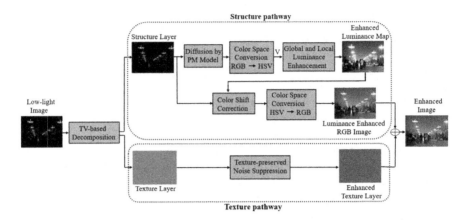

Fig. 1. The framework of the proposed image enhancement model.

method and are processed in parallel in the structure and texture pathways before being integrated to generate the final enhanced image. The strategy of parallel pathways aims at the up-gradation of image visibility while attaining a balance between luminance enhancement and detail-preserved noise suppression. The rest of the sections in this paper are structured as follows. The proposed image enhancement methodology is detailed in Sect. 2. In Sect. 3 the experimental results and their comparative analysis are presented. The paper is concluded in Sect. 4 with a summary of the findings and the future works.

2   Proposed Methodology

The proposed image enhancement framework is depicted in Fig. 1. This framework is inspired by [24] and mainly includes four stages. The structure and texture layers are initially separated from the image and transferred into parallel pathways. The structure layer generally extracts the low-frequency information present in the image i.e. luminance, which is then processed and adapted to an acceptable level in the structure-pathway. On the other hand, the high-frequency information i.e. details and noise present in the texture layer will be refined in the texture pathway by achieving a detail preserved noise suppression. In the last stage, the final enhanced image can be obtained by merging the processed layers from the parallel pathways. The following subsections will discuss each of these four stages in detail.

2.1   TV-based Structure-Texture Image Decomposition

Enhancing the brightness of the image directly will increase the noise levels, making noise suppression or removal more difficult. With the strategy of parallel pathways, we can accomplish luminance enhancement and noise suppression in the structure and texture pathways respectively. We use the total-variation-based

(a) Low-light image (b) Structure layer (c) Texture layer

Fig. 2. Example of structure-texture decomposition of the image. The global noise estimated in the red, green, and blue channels of the image is marked in the texture layer. (Color figure online)

image decomposition approach to split the input image into two pathways [1]. The input image $I^c(x,y)$ is assumed to be the superimposition of structure layer $I_s^c(x,y)$ and texture layer $I_t^c(x,y)$ i.e.:

$$I^c(x,y) = I_s^c(x,y) + I_t^c(x,y) \tag{1}$$

The structure layer is then extracted from the image using the TV regularisation approach given in [20]. Along with the structure-texture decomposition, the global noise estimation (σ^c) is determined using the fast noise variance estimation method in [7]. After extracting the structure layer, the corresponding texture layer is obtained by subtracting the structure layer $I_s^c(x,y)$ from the original image $I^c(x,y)$.

An example of structure-texture image decomposition with noise estimation is demonstrated in Fig. 2. As shown, the luminance component is primarily transferred into the structure layer, whereas minute details and noise exist in the texture layer. Hence the luminance can be modified in the structure-pathway without amplifying the noise components.

2.2 Adaptive Luminance Enhancement

In structure-pathway, the luminance of the image is enhanced to a reasonable level using an expanded biological normalization model. We incorporate the Perona-Malik diffusion model [14] into the method in [24] to further enhance the contrast of edges. Initially, the structure layer of the image is smoothed using the PM diffusion model and the diffused structure layer is then transformed from RGB color space to HSV space, and the V component is taken as the luminance data. Then the uneven illumination is corrected by integrating the local and global luminance enhancement using the visual adaptation model based on the Naka-Rushton(NR) equation [17].

Diffusion Using PM Model: Perona-Malik diffusion is an anisotropic diffusion approach that aims to reduce the image noise without eliminating the details, edges, and other significant features of the image. PM model is used for smoothing the images while enhancing the contrast of the edges. Choosing the diffusion coefficient as a function of the image gradient avoids the smoothing of edges and enables the isotropic diffusion in the inner regions of the image. The anisotropic diffusion is achieved iteratively using the four-adjacent neighbor discretization approach [14]. In this work, the number of iterations used is 50 since increasing the number of iterations further will lead to the diffusion of edges resulting in the loss of desired image features.

Luminance Correction with Visual Adaptation: The visual adaptation and the correction of image luminance are accomplished in the structure-pathway using an expanded biological normalization model. After diffusion using the PM model, the diffused structure layer is then transformed from RGB color space to HSV space, and the V component is taken as the luminance data. To enhance the luminance information of the image, we use a revised form of the Naka-Rushton equation which defines the responsive behavior of the human visual system [17]. Since the conventional Naka-Rushton equation neglect the local features present in the image, a modified NR equation that robustly integrate the global and local image features is used, which is formulated as

$$L_O(x,y) = \frac{[L_I(x,y)]^n}{[L_I(x,y)]^n + \omega_L(x,y) \cdot [\varepsilon_L(x,y)]^n + \omega_G(x,y) \cdot \varepsilon_G{}^n} \tag{2}$$

where $L_I(x,y)$ and $L_O(x,y)$ represent the luminance component of the structure layer and the enhanced luminance map respectively. n is the contrast adaptation factor that controls the global contrast of the image, which is computed as a function of global enhancement factor ε_G i.e. $n = \exp(\varepsilon_G)$. The extent of luminance adaptation depends on the global and local luminance enhancement factors ε_G and $\varepsilon_L(x,y)$. The weights $\omega_L(x,y)$ and $\omega_G(x,y)$ optimize the impact of $\varepsilon_L(x,y)$ and ε_G. The global enhancement level ε_G is determined as

$$\varepsilon_G = \frac{M_G}{1 + w_S \cdot S_G} \tag{3}$$

where M_G and S_G represent the mean and standard deviation of $L_I(x,y)$ respectively. The impact of standard deviation is controlled by the factor w_S. In this work, we set $w_S = 5$ since a lower value cannot provide the required brightness and a higher value over enhance the images. Even though the global enhancement factor modifies the overall brightness of the image, it is not sufficient, particularly when both dark and bright areas are present in the image. Hence to further alter the local brightness of the image, the local enhancement factor $\varepsilon_L(x,y)$ is formulated as

$$\varepsilon_L(x,y) = \varepsilon_G \cdot \frac{L_I(x,y)}{1 + w_S \cdot S_L(x,y)} \tag{4}$$

(a) Low-light image   (b) r=0   (c) r=0.1   (d) $r = 0.3$

Fig. 3. The impact of the value of parameter r on the luminance enhancement.

where $S_L(x, y)$ represents the standard deviation determined over a 21×21 window of the luminance map $L_I(x, y)$. The contribution of global and local enhancement factors in the NR equation is controlled by the weights $\omega_G(x, y)$ and $\omega_L(x, y)$, which is formulated as

$$\omega_G(x, y) = [L_I(x, y)]^r \tag{5}$$

$$\omega_L(x, y) = 1 - \omega_G(x, y) \tag{6}$$

where r is the factor that regulates the impact of local and global enhancement levels in the NR equation. r regulate the extent of dynamic range compression in the enhanced luminance map. For $r = 0$, Eq. (2) reduces to conventional NR equation [17] and hence it cannot retain the local features of the image. The impact of parameter r on the luminance enhancement is shown in Fig. 3 which clearly shows the improved benefit of the revised Naka-Rushton equation over the conventional NR equation ($r = 0$). At $r = 0.3$ the dynamic range of the image is excessively compressed. Therefore, for visually better results, we set $r = 0.1$ in this work. Adjusting the dynamic range may weaken the contrast in certain areas of the image. So, an additional difference of gaussian (DoG) filter is further incorporated to improve the contrast and sharpen the image details. In addition to this, the enhanced structure layer is subjected to typical post-processing that involves the clipping of pixels exceeding [0, 1] and normalization. Retrieving the output RGB image directly from the HSV space can result in over-saturation in certain images with light sources. For this reason, a color shift correction is further performed as mentioned in [24].

2.3 Texture-Preserved Noise Suppression

To limit the effect of noise while preserving the image details, we use an approach of noise suppression instead of noise removal. The local energy of the texture layer gives an appropriate estimate of the local noise, with the assumption that the level of noise is uniform over the entire image. The areas of the image with low energy are assumed to be noise, whereas the areas with high energy are considered to be essential details that should be restored. Hence, the weights of texture preservation $\lambda^c(x, y)$ are evaluated by convolving the detail layer with a gaussian filter of standard deviation 21. Based on this, the texture preserved noise suppression is achieved as

$$O_t^c(x, y) = I_t^c(x, y) \cdot \lambda^c(x, y) \tag{7}$$

A low value of $\lambda^c(x, y)$ represents the smooth areas of images, which will be treated as noise and will be suppressed. On the other hand, a high value of $\lambda^c(x, y)$ indicates a detail-rich region, which will be restored eventually.

2.4 Reconstruction of Enhanced Image

The enhanced luminance component from the structure-pathway is fused with the processed texture layer from the texture-pathway to generate the final enhanced image of improved visibility, which is given as

$$O^c(x, y) = O_s^c(x, y) + w_t \cdot O_t^c(x, y) \tag{8}$$

where w_t stabilize the suppression of noise and enhancement of details. Choosing a higher value for w_t (0.6 and above) will over-enhance the image details and hence to avoid this constraint we set $w_t = 0.3$ in this work.

3 Experimental Results and Discussion

The experimental results of the proposed image enhancement framework, as well as its subjective and objective assessment, are discussed in this section. The reliability of the proposed method is validated by comparing it with the existing enhancement approaches such as NPE [23], Simultaneous Reflection and Illumination Estimation (SRIE) [5], LDR [11], low-light illumination map estimation (LIME) [6], Robust Retinex model (RRM) [12] and Fractional-Order fusion model for Low-Light image enhancement (FFM) [4]. The methods were tested on two datasets, PKUnight and LDRpoor. PKUnight consists of 43 nighttime images of size 400 × 300, collected from the PKU-EAQA dataset [3]. LDRpoor includes a collection of 70 low-light images from the datasets provided by LDR [11], LIME [6], and Division channel [19]. Experiments were carried out in MATLAB R2019b on a Windows 10 PC with 8 GB of RAM and a 1.8 GHz processor.

The comparison of the results of our framework with the existing enhancement algorithms is depicted in Fig. 4 and Fig. 5. The proposed framework enhances the contrast and the luminance of dark scenes to an acceptable level, whereas the LDR method exhibit substantial color degradation (Fig. 4 (c)). The enhancement results of SRIE are generally dark, particularly for backlight scenes, and hence the results lack adequate details (Fig. 4 (b)). Although the NPE algorithm can provide rich texture and details, the lightness can be retained only in well-revealed areas. When compared to the conventional methods, RRM shows excellent noise suppression performance, but the results have a low global contrast as seen in Fig. 5 (f). Similarly, the enhancement results of FFM are generally dark and possess the chance of inadequate enhancement.

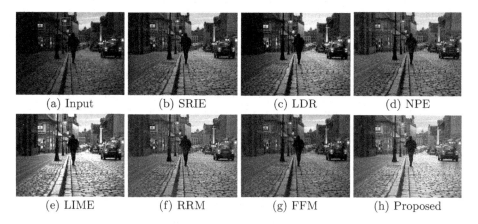

Fig. 4. Comparison of the results of the proposed method with existing enhancement methods on the PKUnight dataset.

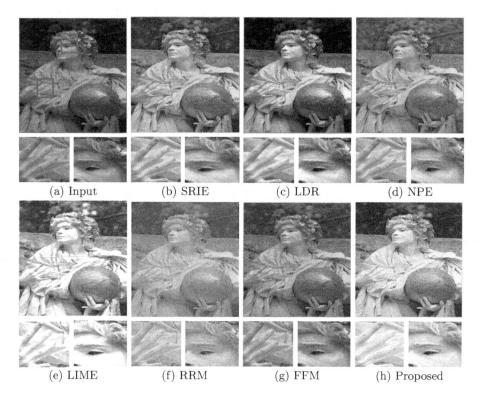

Fig. 5. Comparison of the results of the proposed method with existing enhancement methods on the LDRpoor dataset.

Table 1. Average quantitative results of various enhancement methods on the PKU-night dataset in terms of four quality metrics: IL-NIQE, BISQUE, PIQE, and BLINDS-II.

Metric	SRIE	LDR	NPE	LIME	RRM	FFM	Proposed
IL-NIQE($\downarrow$)	23.275	22.817	23.200	25.409	21.916	22.630	**21.315**
BRISQUE($\downarrow$)	22.834	22.988	25.177	25.983	29.365	23.553	**21.920**
PIQE($\downarrow$)	29.107	31.216	32.298	34.063	42.786	28.364	**27.380**
BLIINDS-II($\downarrow$)	10.593	10.372	10.581	13.523	20.418	11.104	**9.081**

Table 2. Average quantitative results of various enhancement methods on the LDR-poor dataset in terms of four quality metrics: IL-NIQE, BISQUE, PIQE, and BLINDS-II.

Metric	SRIE	LDR	NPE	LIME	RRM	FFM	Proposed
IL-NIQE($\downarrow$)	23.115	22.811	23.594	24.013	22.824	23.866	**22.105**
BRISQUE($\downarrow$)	19.375	19.812	**17.496**	20.305	22.178	18.896	18.463
PIQE($\downarrow$)	33.432	32.486	32.629	33.687	37.381	**30.182**	31.528
BLIINDS-II($\downarrow$)	11.878	11.657	11.007	14.507	14.321	13.378	**10.578**

Even though LIME brightens dark areas and exhibits exceptional performance regarding texture and details, the method results in the over-enhancement of the areas with comparatively high intensity (zoomed areas in Fig. 5 (e)). The proposed method, on the other hand, reveals more details and thereby achieves a better balance of luminance, contrast, and details.

3.1 Quantitative Evaluation

In addition to the subjective assessment, the enhancement results are quantitatively assessed using four blind image quality metrics, including an integrated local natural image quality evaluator (IL-NIQE) [25], blind/referenceless image spatial quality evaluator (BRISQUE) [13], perception-based image quality evaluator (PIQE) [22], and blind image integrity notator using DCT statistics (BLIINDS-II) [21]. IL-NIQE is an opinion unaware and feature-enriched no-reference image quality evaluator.

On the other hand, BRISQUE and BLIINDS-II evaluates the performance of detail enhancement by quantifying the naturalness of the image. PIQE measures the degree of distortion existing in images, inspired by the human-perception-based strategy [22]. For each of these four metrics, a lower value indicates better quality of images. The quantitative comparison results of the enhancement algorithms on the PKUnight and LDRpoor datasets are given in Table 1 and 2 respectively. As observed, our method acquires the best score in the PKUnight dataset, for all image quality metrics, which indicates the superior performance of our framework. In the LDRpoor dataset, our method attains the best value for

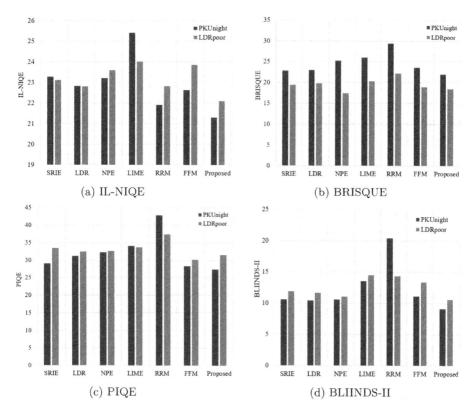

Fig. 6. Comparison of the average scores of image quality metrics IL-NIQE, BRISQUE, PIQE, and BLIINDS-II.

IL-NIQE and BLIINDS-II and the second-best value for BRISQUE and PIQE. Although NPE has a high BRISQUE score, the method magnifies the noise in the darker portions. Similarly, FFM risk the problem of under-enhancement. Figure 6 compares the average score of the four image quality metrics for the PKUnight and LDRpoor datasets respectively. Thus the results of the qualitative evaluation are consistent with the results of quantitative evaluation using the blind evaluation metrics, which validate the robustness of our approach. Thus our method effectively balances image luminance and details and can produce decent enhancement results.

4   Conclusion and Future Work

In this paper, we have presented a novel structure-texture decomposition-based image enhancement framework. The structure and texture components are initially decomposed from the image, which is then processed in parallel in the structure and texture pathway and are finally integrated to generate the enhanced image. The two-pathway processing and global-to-local luminance brightening strategy employed in our work can effectively upgrade the visibility of low-light images, and thereby attain a balance between luminance enhancement and detail-preserved noise suppression. Experimental results on PKUnight and LDRpoor dataset show that our method is quantitatively and qualitatively robust when compared to state-of-the-art methods. The effectiveness of the enhancement results was evaluated using blind image quality metrics that include IL-NIQE, BRISQUE, PIQE, and BLINDS-II. The proposed method acquires the best scores in the PKUnight dataset, for all the metrics, which indicates the superior performance of the method. In the LDRpoor dataset, the method attains the best value for IL-NIQE and BLIINDS-II and the second-best value for BRISQUE and PIQE. The proposed framework mainly concentrates on enhancing detail-visibility, particularly in dark portions of the image, which may reduce the overall dynamic range of the image, causing a loss of visual naturalness. Hence the future works will concentrate on integrating more efficient and versatile visual adaptation techniques to enhance the visual naturalness and perceptual quality of images.

Acknowledgment. Portions of the research in this paper use the PKU-EAQA dataset collected under the sponsorship of the National Natural Science Foundation of China.

References

1. Aujol, J.F., Gilboa, G., Chan, T., Osher, S.: Structure-texture image decomposition-modeling, algorithms, and parameter selection. Int. J. Comput. Vision **67**(1), 111–136 (2006)
2. Celik, T., Tjahjadi, T.: Contextual and variational contrast enhancement. IEEE Trans. Image Process. **20**(12), 3431–3441 (2011)
3. Chen, Z., Jiang, T., Tian, Y.: Quality assessment for comparing image enhancement algorithms. In: Proceedings of the IEEE Conference on Computer Vision and Pattern Recognition, pp. 3003–3010 (2014)
4. Dai, Q., Pu, Y.F., Rahman, Z., Aamir, M.: Fractional-order fusion model for low-light image enhancement. Symmetry **11**(4), 574 (2019)
5. Fu, X., Zeng, D., Huang, Y., Zhang, X.P., Ding, X.: A weighted variational model for simultaneous reflectance and illumination estimation. In: Proceedings of the IEEE Conference on Computer Vision and Pattern Recognition, pp. 2782–2790 (2016)
6. Guo, X., Li, Y., Ling, H.: Lime: low-light image enhancement via illumination map estimation. IEEE Trans. Image Process. **26**(2), 982–993 (2016)
7. Immerkaer, J.: Fast noise variance estimation. Comput. Vis. Image Underst. **64**(2), 300–302 (1996)
8. Jobson, D.J., Rahman, Z.U., Woodell, G.A.: A multiscale retinex for bridging the gap between color images and the human observation of scenes. IEEE Trans. Image Process. **6**(7), 965–976 (1997)
9. Jobson, D.J., Rahman, Z.U., Woodell, G.A.: Properties and performance of a center/surround retinex. IEEE Trans. Image Process. **6**(3), 451–462 (1997)
10. Land, E.H., McCann, J.J.: Lightness and retinex theory. Josa **61**(1), 1–11 (1971)

11. Lee, C., Lee, C., Kim, C.S.: Contrast enhancement based on layered difference representation of 2D histograms. IEEE Trans. Image Process. **22**(12), 5372–5384 (2013)
12. Li, M., Liu, J., Yang, W., Sun, X., Guo, Z.: Structure-revealing low-light image enhancement via robust retinex model. IEEE Trans. Image Process. **27**(6), 2828–2841 (2018)
13. Mittal, A., Moorthy, A.K., Bovik, A.C.: No-reference image quality assessment in the spatial domain. IEEE Trans. Image Process. **21**(12), 4695–4708 (2012)
14. Perona, P., Malik, J.: Scale-space and edge detection using anisotropic diffusion. IEEE Trans. Pattern Anal. Mach. Intell. **12**(7), 629–639 (1990)
15. Pisano, E.D., Zong, S., Hemminger, B.M., DeLuca, M., Johnston, R.E., Muller, K., Braeuning, M.P., Pizer, S.M.: Contrast limited adaptive histogram equalization image processing to improve the detection of simulated spiculations in dense mammograms. J. Digit. Imaging **11**(4), 193 (1998)
16. Pizer, S.M., et al.: Adaptive histogram equalization and its variations. Comput. Vis. Graphics Image Process. **39**(3), 355–368 (1987)
17. Pu, X., Yang, K., Li, Y.: A retinal adaptation model for HDR image compression. In: Yang, J., et al. (eds.) CCCV 2017. CCIS, vol. 771, pp. 37–47. Springer, Singapore (2017). https://doi.org/10.1007/978-981-10-7299-4_4
18. Rahman, Z.U., Jobson, D.J., Woodell, G.A.: Multi-scale retinex for color image enhancement. In: Proceedings of 3rd IEEE International Conference on Image Processing, vol. 3, pp. 1003–1006. IEEE (1996)
19. Rivera, A.R., Ryu, B., Chae, O.: Content-aware dark image enhancement through channel division. IEEE Trans. Image Process. **21**(9), 3967–3980 (2012)
20. Rudin, L.I., Osher, S., Fatemi, E.: Nonlinear total variation based noise removal algorithms. Physica D **60**(1–4), 259–268 (1992)
21. Saad, M.A., Bovik, A.C., Charrier, C.: Blind image quality assessment: a natural scene statistics approach in the DCT domain. IEEE Trans. Image Process. **21**(8), 3339–3352 (2012)
22. Venkatanath, N., Praneeth, D., Bh, M.C., Channappayya, S.S., Medasani, S.S.: Blind image quality evaluation using perception based features. In: 2015 Twenty First National Conference on Communications (NCC), pp. 1–6. IEEE (2015)
23. Wang, S., Zheng, J., Hu, H.M., Li, B.: Naturalness preserved enhancement algorithm for non-uniform illumination images. IEEE Trans. Image Process. **22**(9), 3538–3548 (2013)
24. Yang, K.F., Zhang, X.S., Li, Y.J.: A biological vision inspired framework for image enhancement in poor visibility conditions. IEEE Trans. Image Process. **29**, 1493–1506 (2019)
25. Zhang, L., Zhang, L., Bovik, A.C.: A feature-enriched completely blind image quality evaluator. IEEE Trans. Image Process. **24**(8), 2579–2591 (2015)

Low Cost Embedded Vision System for Location and Tracking of a Color Object

Diego Ayala[1,2(✉)], Danilo Chavez[2], and Leopoldo Altamirano Robles[1]

[1] Instituto Nacional de Astrofísica, Óptica y Electrónica (INAOE), Puebla, Mexico
ayala.diego@inaoe.edu.mx, robles@inaoep.mx
[2] Escuela Politécnica Nacional, Quito, Ecuador
danilo.chavez@epn.edu.ec

Abstract. This paper describes the development of an embedded vision system for detection, location, and tracking of a color object; it makes use of a single 32-bit microprocessor to acquire image data, process, and perform actions according to the interpreted data. The system is intended for applications that need to make use of artificial vision for detection, location and tracking of a color object and its objective is to have achieve at reduced terms of size, power consumption, and cost.

Keywords: Image processing · Color tracking · Low-cost vision system

1 Introduction

Several fields such as industrial, military, scientific and civil have chosen to make use of computer vision in order to recognize the existence of objects and their location, among other features; most of these systems need a personal computer and the execution of the software that processes the image data. Applications such as unmanned vehicle systems, autonomous robots, among others, have limitations of space, consumption, robustness and weight, making the use of a personal computer to be impractical, or requiring complex and expensive methods to transmit the image to a fixed station that processes the image and re-transmit the data interpretation. Reduced size systems have been implemented on commercial boards such as the so called Cognachrome Vision System but it requires an external camera connected to a RCA protocol adapter [1], yet another similar work was made by a team at Carnegie Mellon University [2] but it lacks of an embedded user interface and costs more than the development proposed in this document, which is a compact embedded vision system, lightweight, with a low power consumption, and written in widely used C/C++ language it handles: the image acquisition, processing, and a user interface altogether on a board and camera that are roughly USD 90 in price. The proposed system intends to be a cheaper, easy to replicate, and yet a viable and modern alternative to the ones researched by A. Rowe et al. [2], R. Sargent et al. [1]; its further development could contribute to applications that require to detect, locate and/or track a color object and have strong limitations in: size, power consumption and cost.

B. Raman et al. (Eds.): CVIP 2021, CCIS 1567, pp. 244–255, 2022.
https://doi.org/10.1007/978-3-031-11346-8_22

2   Capturing and Display of the Image

This project uses a HY-Smart STM32 development board, it includes a STM32F103 microcontroller to process data, it gets the image from an OV7725 camera that is configured in RGB565 format, with a QVGA (320 × 240) resolution. It also includes a touch screen in which the target object can be selected, its color defines the threshold that is used to create a binary image in the process of artificial vision known as segmentation. After the segmentation is done, an algorithm recognizes the contour of the image and its center, once located, a PID algorithm commands 2 servos (pan, tilt) in order to track the objective.

2.1   Image Acquisition

The project make use of the OV7725 camera in a RGB565 format, which employs 2 bytes per pixel, allocating 5 bits for red, 6 for green, and 5 for blue as seen on Fig. 1. An individual frame has 320 × 240 pixels of information which are constantly been sent to a FIFO memory named AL422B; the microcontroller accesses this data when required, instead of receiving periodic interruptions from the camera.

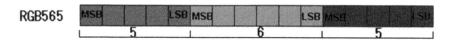

Fig. 1. RGB565 format contains 16 bits of information per pixel. (Color figure online)

2.2   Displaying the Image

A TFT-LCD screen of 320 × 240 pixels displays the image, it is operated by the SSD1289 integrated circuit that communicates with the microcontroller through 8080 parallel protocol. A resistive film above the screen, in conjunction to the XPT2046 integrated circuit, locates the position of a single pressure point on the screen and sends the data via SPI interface. The microcontroller has a peripheral block called FSMC (Flexible Static Memory Controller) which allows it to communicate with external memories meeting the timing requirements, previously some parameters must be set: the type of memory to be read (SRAM, ROM, NOR Flash, PSRAM), data bus width (8 or 16 bits), the memory bank to be used, waiting times, among other features. The use of the above-mentioned integrated circuits allows the microcontroller to seamlessly read and write the camera and display respectively, and allows a user interface as depicted on Fig. 2, although the display could be discarded in order to increase frames per second, and decrease cost, and weight.

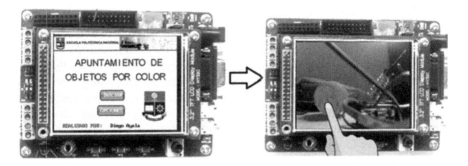

Fig. 2. Image of the interface and user interaction with the screen.

3 Image Processing

The 76800 pixels contained in each frame need to be processed in order to detect and locate the color object, this task is described as segmentation of the image. Once located a PID controller centers the field of view of the camera on the center of the region of interest.

3.1 Image Segmentation

The segmentation consists on separating the region of interest in the image based on the chosen color. As each pixel is obtained from the camera, it is compared with a threshold value for each channel, and the result is stored into a binary image. The binary image is allocated in memory as an array of $2400 \times 32bit$ numbers where each bit is a pixel of the binary image (see Fig. 3), the color boundaries can be selected via the interface, two approaches are being considered: RGB color space and normalized RGB.

Fig. 3. On the left the original image, on the right the binary image. (Color figure online)

RGB Color Space. Maximum, and minimum boundaries are set for each of the three color components (red, green and blue), if the scanned pixel is within the 3 ranges, then it is stored as "one" in the binary image, otherwise is a "zero". This computing is fairly fast, achieving 10,2 fps; but a disadvantage arise in the event of a change of illumination, for instance if light intensity is decreased the red, blue and green components vary in proportion to this change, and can get out of the threshold, the same occurs with an increase in light intensity.

Normalized RGB. In this color space, instead of using directly each RGB component, the proportion *rgb* is calculated by dividing the luminance I of every single pixel [3].

$$I = R + G + B \tag{1}$$

$$r = R/I, g = G/I, b = B/I \tag{2}$$

As the name suggests, in the normalized RGB the summation of rgb components equals to one, due to this only r and g values are calculated to attain the hue information, this results in the rg chromaticity space seen on Fig. 4, which is bi-dimensional and theoretically invariant to changes of illumination. The invariance mentioned can be noted in the example given on Fig. 5 where three pixels o an orange sphere are evaluated, the R component varies along this points in nearly half of its value, selecting a threshold in RGB color space would neglect a considerable part of the sphere due to the large of R. However, while the RGB values vary, their proportions with respect of the intensity (I) keep the same, thus the values of rgb are invariant to the distinct illumination levels. An experimental result is documented on Fig. 9.

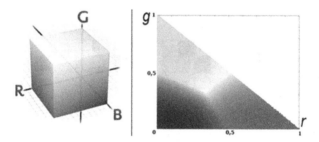

Fig. 4. On the left RGB color space, on the rg chromaticity space. (Color figure online)

3.2 Description of the Region of Interest

To analyze the data incoming from the image segmentation, an algorithm demarks the contour of the group of contiguous pixels in the binary image, once this is done it establish the upper, lower, rightmost, and leftmost limits, and also both horizontal and vertical location of the center of the object. The algorithm starts by scanning the binary image from the top left corner, to the right and downwards until it find a line of contiguous pixels, if it exceeds a preset width then it finds the rightmost pixel of the grouping and proceeds to find the pixels of the contour. Figure 6 shows how the algorithm runs along the contour of a sector of detected pixels, the process find the initial line (in this case the first line is a single pixel width, and is shown in red color), from here the

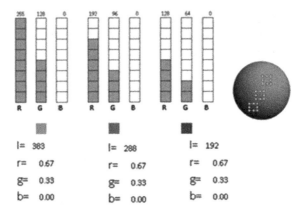

Fig. 5. Three different color pixels are chosen from an orange sphere, rgb components are computed on each case. (Color figure online)

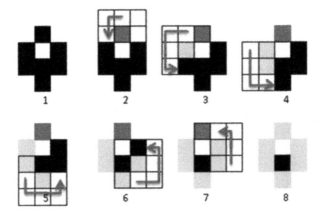

Fig. 6. Example of contour recognition for a group of pixels. (Color figure online)

contour path begins, as a rule the algorithm begins to search for the next valid counter-clockwise pixel in a 3 × 3 matrix, initiating the inspection from the next position to the last sensed pixel. To continue the contour detection, the center of the next matrix is at the position of pixel detected earlier. Whenever a contour pixel is detected it is evaluated to update the upper, lower, rightmost, and leftmost limits of the grouping of pixels. The contour inspection stops once the initial pixel is reached.

3.3 Tracking

The camera is located in the top of a Pan-Tilt platform represented on Fig. 7, in order to perform the tracking movements two servo motors are installed: HS-785HB servo motor (located at the bottom of the platform) and the HS-645MG (located on top).

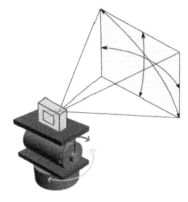

Fig. 7. Representation of the Pan-Tilt platform holding the camera.

The control algorithm that governs the movements of both servos is a proportional-integral (PI) controller. Although the system is composed of servomotors, a modeling of the dynamic response was made in order to represent the platform with the camera installed, the result is a first-order transfer function (Gp) whose parameters: gain (K) and time constant (τ) are experimentally acquired.

Closed-loop Analysis. The PI controller was chosen to eliminate the offset error, a block representation of the system in continuous time domain is depicted on Fig. 8.

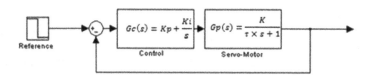

Fig. 8. Simplified block diagram of the closed loop system.

The vision system gets feedback through the position of the detected object relative to the camera, the controller will govern the PWM that moves the servomotors in order to move the camera so its center is aligned with the object's center, both variables are relative to the angular location of the camera, so the error signal is invariant to the absolute angular location of the platform, in other words the error is just measured as the difference between the detected position and the center of the camera's field of view. The block diagram of Fig. 8 can be simplified into a single block to obtain the following transfer function representing the whole system:

$$Tf(s) = \frac{Gp(s) \times Gc(s)}{Gp(s) \times Gc(s) + 1} \tag{3}$$

Further calculation leads to the following second order transfer function:

$$Tf(s) = \frac{s \times (Kp \times K) + Ki \times K}{s^2 \times \tau + s \times (1 + Kp \times K) + Ki \times K} \tag{4}$$

The poles of the closed loop system are given by the roots of the polynomial on the denominator [4]:

$$p(s) = s^2 + s \times (2\xi\omega_n) + \omega_n^2 \tag{5}$$

$$ts = \frac{4}{\xi \times \omega_n} \tag{6}$$

The damping factor (ξ) and natural frequency (ω_n) determine the percentage overshoot (PO) and settling time (ts) present in the transient response of a step input [4]:

$$PO = 100\% \times e^{\frac{-\xi \times \pi}{\sqrt{1-\xi^2}}} \tag{7}$$

The controller's constants (Kp and Ki) can be solved performing the replacements required in Eqs. (4), (5), (6) and (7).

$$Kp = \frac{1}{K} \times (\frac{8 \times \tau}{t_s - 1}) \tag{8}$$

$$Ki = \frac{1}{K} \times \frac{16 \times \tau}{(t_s)^2 \times \frac{ln(\frac{PO}{100\%})^2}{\pi^2 + ln(\frac{PO}{100\%})^2}} \tag{9}$$

Discretization of the Controller. The described PI controller (Gc) is expressed in continuous time-domain. To make an algorithm executable by the microcontroller the PI controller must be discretized. This is achieved by the bilinear transformation function Eq. (10) which transforms the transfer function from continuous time domain to the discrete time domain [5]:

$$G(z) = G(s)\big|_{s=\frac{2(z-1)}{T(z+1)}} \tag{10}$$

where T is the sampling time. Applying the transformation to the PI controller we obtain the following transfer function:

$$Gc(z) = Kp + \frac{Ki \times T(z+1)}{2(z-1)} = \frac{U(z)}{E(z)} \tag{11}$$

The discrete time domain controller can be expressed in a single line mathematical operation, thus finally obtaining the control law:

$$U_{[k]} = U_{[k-1]} + E_{[k-1]} \times (Ki \times \frac{T}{2} - Kp) + E_{[k]} \times (Ki \times \frac{T}{2} + Kp) \tag{12}$$

where U[k] is the instantaneous value of the control action (value servomotor PWM pulse), U[k-1] the previous value, the error E[k] is the difference between the center of the camera and the center of the object; the controller updates this values every time a frame is acquired which occurs at sampling a time T, on the other hand Kp and Ki are constants determined by the Eqs. (8) and (9) respectively.

4   Tests and Results

4.1   Image Segmentation

The transformation to the rg chromaticity space gives better segmentation results as can be seen on Fig. 9, nevertheless the calculation of each pixel takes more time than RGB color space, resulting in a relatively slower frame rate of 10fps. For the rest of this tests rg chromaticity segmentation is chosen, as it is more reliable.

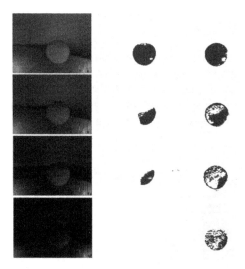

Fig. 9. (Left) An orange sphere is illuminated at 4 poor intensity scenarios. (Center) Results of RGB565 segmentation. (Right) Results of the rg chromaticity segmentation. (the color to detect was chosen during the highest level of illumination for both types of segmentation) (Color figure online)

4.2   Detection of Distinct Color Objects

Figure 10 shows distinct objects whose color is not much different from each other. The image has: a red cloth, a small yellow sphere, a large orange sphere, and an envelope of pale yellow. In each of the 4 experiments the respective color is selected, and the location of the objects is performed appropriately.

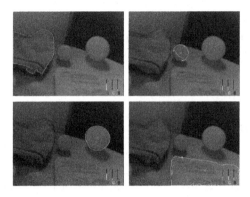

Fig. 10. Different objects of similar color are being recognized. (Color figure online)

4.3 Location and Tracking

An orange object was attached to a coupled shaft which a circular motion, similar to a clock (Fig. 11). Tracking is disabled and the object's position is measured as pixels, which returns a circle with a mean radius of $R = 87.57$ pixels and a standard deviation $\sigma = 8.69$, this along with the observed plot suggests that location data incorporates some glitches that can be addressed to partial unrecognized regions thus computing a different centroid.

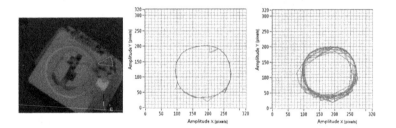

Fig. 11. (Left) An Orange triangle making a clockwise motion. (Center) Location at 3820 ms per revolution, (Right). Location at 1108 ms per revolution. (Color figure online)

However this doesn't cause an instability when the servos are activated for tracking, as demonstrated in a test where a color object was chosen, brought to a corner of the camera's range of vision and then tacking was activated enabling the servomotors to move the center of the camera to the object's location, the behavior can be observed on Fig. 12. Position of the object settles to the center after roughly 1,6 s after tracking activation, similar results were obtained on latter tests. The whole system is displayed on Fig. 13.

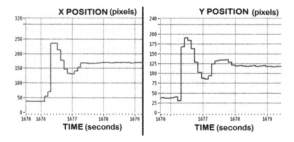

Fig. 12. Tracking an object from a corner to the center of the field of view.

Fig. 13. Physical implementation the system.

4.4 Cost and Power Consumption

The data presented on Table 1 and 2, include the system operating with both the LCD screen, and the pan and tilt platform; even though it is totally functional without them.

Table 1. Price of components for the proposed Low-Cost embedded vision system

Product	Price [USD]
HY-Smart STM32 (STM32F103VCT+TFT LCD+Board)	59.00
OV7725 camera + AL422B FIFO Module	30.00
SPT200 Direct Drive Pan & Tilt System	45.99
Total	**134.99**

With the listed price of 134.99 USD the system is cheaper than the one proposed in the work of A. Rowe (199 USD) [2], unfortunately a comparison with the Cognachrome Vision System [1] is not possible as the price-tag of their system is not publicly available, on the latter a clear strength arises from the fact that the proposed system is made from already available and cheap components in the consumer market. Also it is worth noting that the system can be greatly reduced on its components being STM32F103VCT the main component at a price of 9.07 USD, which is capable enough to process image data when compared to newer architectures and solutions such as the well-known Raspberry PI, which costs 35 USD.

Table 2. Electrical characteristics of the proposed Low-Cost embedded vision system

Item	Average	Max	Unit
Supply voltage	5	5	V
Operating current	200	1100	mA
Frequency	72	–	MHz
Start-up time	500	–	mS
RS-232 bit-rate	9600	921600	bps
Refresh rate	10.9	–	fps

The power consumption is 1 W on average, therefore it can be operated in the scope most autonomous systems; with a refreshing rate of 10.9 fps and standard RS-232 output of data, it could be easily implemented on industry processes such as: fruit classification, object location, and others. Much of the weight, power usage, and overall dimensions can be further lowered without the servomotors and LCD depending on the application.

5   Conclusions

The deterring effects of uncontrolled illumination are greatly diminished by the use of the rg chromaticity space enabling this system to detect, locate, and track a colored object satisfactorily, while being low-cost (under 200USD), compact ($30 \times 13 \times 19$ cm including the platform), and energy-saving (200 mA on average at 5 V).

The ability of this system to recognize chromaticity along with location data can be greatly improved in a controlled environment making it a suitable and economic option for industrial applications; according to the requirements additional work is needed for the system to locate multiple objects at the same time, and more tasks that other systems achieve running operating systems, nonetheless, this system present a significant reduction in cost, size and power consumption, which makes it viable to be fitted on small unmanned vehicles.

Further development of this work can be done to increase the frames per second rate, both the camera and microcontroller have newer versions in the market by the date, all the algorithms used in this work are written in C++ so they can be implemented in other systems as well and become adaptable to variety of requirements.

References

1. Sargent, R., Wright, A.: The Cognachrome Color Vision System
2. Rowe, A., Rosenberg, C., Nourbakhsh, I.: A Low Cost Embedded Color Vision System. Carnegie Mellon University, Pittsburgh (2002)
3. Balkenius, C., Johansson, B.: Finding Colored Objects in a Scene. Lund University (2007)
4. Ogata, K.: Modern Control Engineering. University of Minnesota, Minneapolis (2002)
5. Massachusetts Institute of Technology Department of Mechanical Engineering. Signal Processing: Continuous and Discrete. MIT OpenCourseWare, (2008)

Towards Label-Free Few-Shot Learning: How Far Can We Go?

Aditya Bharti[1(✉)], N. B. Vineeth[2], and C. V. Jawahar[1]

[1] International Institute of Information Technology Hyderabad, Hyderabad, India
`aditya.bharti@research.iiit.ac.in`
[2] Indian Institute of Technology Hyderabad, Hyderabad, India

Abstract. Few-shot learners aim to recognize new categories given only a small number of training samples. The core challenge is to avoid overfitting to the limited data while ensuring good generalization to novel classes. Existing literature makes use of vast amounts of annotated data by simply shifting the label requirement from novel classes to base classes. Since data annotation is time-consuming and costly, reducing the label requirement even further is an important goal. To that end, our paper presents a more challenging few-shot setting with almost no class label access. By leveraging self-supervision to learn image representations and similarity for classification at test time, we achieve competitive baselines while using **almost zero** (0–5) class labels. Compared to existing state-of-the-art approaches which use 60,000 labels, this is a **four orders of magnitude (10,000 times) difference**. This work is a step towards developing few-shot learning methods that do not depend on annotated data. Our code is publicly released at https://github.com/adbugger/FewShot. (This work was supported by the IMPRINT program.)

Keywords: Few shot · Self-supervised · Deep learning

1 Introduction

Few-shot learners [10,33,39] aim to learn novel categories from a small number of examples. Since getting annotated data is extremely difficult for many natural and man-made visual classes [20], such systems are of immense importance as they alleviate the need for labelled data.

Few-shot learning literature is extremely diverse [41] with multiple classes of approaches. Meta-learning [10,29,30] is a popular class of methods which use experience from multiple base tasks to learn a base learner which can quickly adapt to novel classes from few examples. There has been immense progress using the meta-learning frameworks [1,11,16,27,43]. While extremely popular, such approaches are computationally expensive, require that the base tasks be related to the final task, and need many training class labels for the base tasks. Other approaches focus on combining supervised and unsupervised pipelines [4,12,34]

B. Raman et al. (Eds.): CVIP 2021, CCIS 1567, pp. 256–268, 2022.
https://doi.org/10.1007/978-3-031-11346-8_23

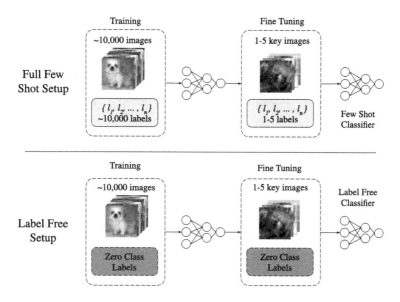

Fig. 1. Label-free Few-shot Classification: Proposed setting *(Best viewed in color)* (Color figure online)

and others alleviate the data requirement by generating new labelled data using hallucinations [17]. Recent methods [5,40] have also established strong baselines with computationally extremely simple training pipelines and classifiers. However, these methods either do not address the label requirement, or cannot be easily extended to new network architectures. This work is a step towards developing few-shot learning methods that do not depend on annotated data.

Recent work in contrastive learning [5,19,21] has shown that it is possible to learn useful visual representations without class labels by learning image similarity over multiple augmented views of the same data, paired with a suitable training strategy and a loss function. We leverage SimCLR [5] and MoCo [19] to develop training methods with restricted label access. Since image similarity is an effective pre-training task for few-shot [22], we perform image classification using image similarity as shown in Fig. 1. We perform test time classification by choosing the key image most similar to the input to be classified. The network is thus completely unaware of any class label information.

Our key contributions are as follows:

- A new challenging label-free few-shot learning setup.
- An easy to adapt, computationally and conceptually simple, end to end label free pipeline.
- Competitive performance using **almost zero** class labels. Compared to the approximately 60,000 class labels used by existing state-of-the-art, this is a **four orders of magnitude** improvement.
- We examine classification quality and the impact of limited label information in our ablations.

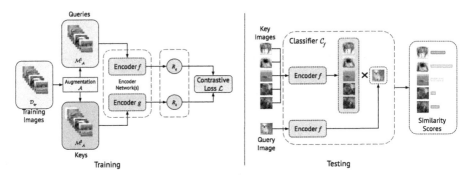

Fig. 2. General overview of our pipeline. **Left**: Self-supervised training to learn contrastive representations without labels. See Algorithm 1 for further details. **Right**: Image classification using image similarity for few-shot classification without using labels. Images are encoded using the model learned in the training phase. Further details in Algorithm 2. *(Best viewed in color)* (Color figure online)

2   Related Work

There is a great diversity of few-shot learning literature [41]. In this section we discuss motivating works from related fields.

2.1   Related Perspectives

Metric learning methods "learn to compare". By learning image similarity, a model can use similarity to label instances of novel classes by comparing with known examples. It is also an effective pre-text task for few-shot learning [22]. These models learn by conditioning predictions on distance metrics such as cosine similarity [39], Euclidean distances [33], network based [36], ridge regression [3], convex optimization based [25], or graph neural networks [32]. Regularization techniques such as manifold mixup [26], combined with supervised pipelines, also improve accuracies.

Self supervised methods remove the need for annotated data by using a supervisory signal from the data itself. A number of pretext tasks such as predicting image coloration [24,44], predicting image patch positions [9,28], and predicting image rotations [15] are used in the literature. Combining self-supervision with supervised approaches [4,12,34] has also resulted in improved accuracies over few-shot tasks. Finally, [5,19,21,37] learn contrastive representations by applying simple transforms on input images and predicting image similarity. By learning to predict image similarity in the presence of distortions, the network can effectively distill information, making it suitable for quick adaptation on novel classes. We leverage two recent contrastive approaches in our work: SimCLR [5] and MoCo [19].

3 Approach: Few-Shot Learning with Almost No Labels

Since learning image similarity is useful for few-shot tasks [22], we focus on learning contrastive representations during our training phase. This allows us to ignore the labels completely, unlike [22]. Following a contrastive learning approach, we first apply two different data augmentations to an input image, generating two augmented images. The task for our neural network $f(\cdot)$ is to learn image representations such that the encoding of two augmented images generated from the same input are as similar as possible. Algorithm 1 presents a detailed description of one training epoch, and Fig. 2 presents a visual overview.

Given an input minibatch $\mathcal{M}$ a stochastic augmentation module $\mathcal{A}$ generates two minibatches, one of the query images $\mathcal{M}_{\mathcal{A}}^q$, and the other of the key images $\mathcal{M}_{\mathcal{A}}^k$ by performing two different image transforms. For a given query image, q the key image generated from the same input is denoted k_+, and k_- otherwise. Pairs of query and key generated from the same input (q, k_+) are denoted positive and negative (q, k_-) otherwise.

Encoder networks $f(\cdot)$ and $g(\cdot)$ are used to learn representations of key and query images respectively. Note that depending on the setting, these networks may be the same. Network $f(\cdot)$ is used for downstream test time tasks. After computing the encoded representations R_k of the key, and R_q of the query, the networks are trained to maximize the representation similarity for positive pairs, and minimize for negative pairs. This is achieved by minimizing the following contrastive loss in Eq. 1

Algorithm 1: Overall Training Methodology

Input: Augmentation Module $\mathcal{A}(\cdot)$
Input: Encoders $f(\cdot)$ $g(\cdot)$
Input: Constrastive Loss Module $\mathcal{L}(q, k^+, \{k^-\})$
Data: Training dataset $\mathcal{D}_{tr}$
Result: Trained network $f(\cdot)$

for *minibatch $\mathcal{M}$ in $\mathcal{D}_{tr}$* **do**

    $\mathcal{M}_{\mathcal{A}}^q, \mathcal{M}_{\mathcal{A}}^k = \mathcal{A}(\mathcal{M})$;   // get augmented minibatches

    $\{R_q\} = f(\mathcal{M}_{\mathcal{A}}^q)$;   // encode query representations

    $\{R_k\} = g(\mathcal{M}_{\mathcal{A}}^k)$;   // encode key representations

    for *query R_q in $\{R_q\}$* **do**

        $R_{k+} = $ ChoosePositive$(R_q, \{R_k\})$;   // positive key image

        $\{R_{k-}\} = $ ChooseNegative$(R_q, \{R_k\})$;   // negative key images

        $\mathcal{L}(R_q, R_{k+}, \{R_{k-}\})$;   // minimize contrastive loss

        UpdateParams(f, g) ;   // update network parameters

    end

end

return f

$$\mathcal{L}(R_q, R_{k^+}, \{R_{k^-}\}) = -\log \frac{\exp s(R_q, R_{k^+})/\tau}{\exp s(R_q, R_{k^+})/\tau + \sum_{R_{k^-}} \exp s(R_q, R_{k^-})/\tau} \qquad (1)$$

where τ is a temperature hyperparameter, and $s(\cdot, \cdot)$ is a similarity function.

SimCLR Base. In this setting, we treat augmented minibatches of key and query images on an equal footing with no distinction. Starting from an input minibatch of N images, there are $2N$ positive pairs and $2N(2N-2)$ negative pairs. The same network $f(\cdot)$ is used to embed both keys and queries. A cosine similarity function is used in the contrastive loss (Eq. 1), $s(\mathbf{x}, \mathbf{y}) = \mathbf{x}^T\mathbf{y}/|\mathbf{x}||\mathbf{y}|$. This setup is referred to as OURS_S in our results.

MoCo Base. This setting decouples the number of negative samples from the batch size. Once the key and query images have been generated from the input, the few-shot task is formulated as a dictionary lookup problem. The dictionary consists of *key* images, and the unknown image to be looked up is the *query*. The keys are encoded using a momentum encoder, which maintains the set of positive and negative samples per query. The query (non-momentum) encoder is used for downstream few-shot tasks. This setting uses a dot product as the similarity function for contrastive loss $s(\mathbf{x}, \mathbf{y}) = \mathbf{x}^T\mathbf{y}$ and is referred to as OURS_M in our results.

3.1   Testing Framework

We present our general testing framework and provide details of the specific test time classifiers used for our experiments. The testing phase consists of multiple few-shot tasks, following accepted practice [40]. Each C-way K-shot task consists

---

Algorithm 2: Test Phase: N-way, K-shot Task

Input: Trained Encoder f
Input: Classifier $\mathcal{C}_f$
Input: Similarity Function $s(\mathbf{x}, \mathbf{y})$
Data: $N \times Q$ query images: $\{(q_i, y_{q_i})\}$
Data: $N \times K$ test images: $\{(k_i, y_{k_i})\}$
Result: Accuracy on task
correct $\leftarrow 0$;
foreach *query image* q_i **do**
    // return index of most similar key since classifier has no label
      access
    $l = \mathcal{C}_f(q_i, \{k_j\})$;
    if $y_{q_i} == y_{k_l}$ **then** correct = correct + 1;
end
return correct$/(N \times Q)$

---

of K key images, and Q query images from C novel classes each. Using the $C * K$ key images, the trained network must classify the $C * Q$ query images.

Given the set of key images $\{k\}$, a query image q to be classified, and the trained network $f(\cdot)$ from the training phase, a classifier $\mathcal{C}_f$ matches q with its most similar key image k_j. The classification is deemed correct if q and k_j have the same label, as determined by a separate verifier since the classifier does not have access to labels. See Algorithm 2 for a concise representation of our testing framework.

Inspired by [6,40], we study the use of two different test time classifiers: the 1-Nearest Neighbor classifier (1NN) from SimpleShot [40] and a soft cosine attention kernel (ATTN) adapted from Matching Networks [39].

The 1NN classifier chooses the key image which minimizes the Euclidean distance between the key and the query image under consideration.

$$\mathcal{C}_f(q, \{k\}) = \arg \min_j |f(q) - f(k_j)|^2 \qquad (2)$$

The ATTN classifier chooses the key image corresponding to each query using an attention mechanism that provides a softmax over the cosine similarities. Unlike Matching Networks [39], we take an *argmax* instead of a weighted average over the labels of the key image set since the classifier has no access to the probability distribution over the labels, or the number of labels.

$$\mathcal{C}_f(q, \{k\}) = \arg \max_j a_{\{k\}}(q, k_j)$$

$$a_{\{k\}}(q, k_j) = \frac{\exp c(f(q), f(k_j))}{\sum_i \exp c(f(q), f(k_i))} \qquad (3)$$

$$c(\mathbf{x}, \mathbf{y}) = \frac{\mathbf{x} \cdot \mathbf{y}}{|\mathbf{x}| \cdot |\mathbf{y}|}$$

We introduce the effect of limited label information in the multi-shot setting as part of our ablation studies. Inspired by ProtoNets [33] and MatchNets [39], we compute class centroids as representatives for classification. Since computing class centroids requires label information, we present those experiments as part of our ablation studies separately in Sect. 4.3.

4   Experiments

4.1   Experimental Setup

We describe the experimental setup in this section, including datasets, evaluation strategy, and hyperparameters for reproducibility.

Datasets. We use experiments on three popular few-shot image classification benchmarks.

The *miniImageNet* dataset [39] is a subset of ImageNet [8] and is a common few-shot learning benchmark. The dataset contains 100 classes and 600 examples per class. Following [30], we split the dataset into 64 base classes, 16 validation classes, and 20 novel classes. Following [39], we resize the images to 84 × 84 pixels via rescaling and center cropping.

We also perform experiments on a subset of the CIFAR-100 [23] dataset, as in [29]. This dataset consists of 100 image classes in total with each class having 600 images of size 32 × 32 pixels. Following the setup in [29], we split the classes into 60 base, 20 validation, and 20 novel classes for few-shot learning. This dataset is referred to as **CIFAR-100FS** in our experiments.

We also use the **FC100** [29] (FewShot CIFAR100) dataset for our experiments. The 100 classes of the CIFAR-100 [23] dataset are grouped into 20 superclasses to minimize information overlap. The train split contains 60 classes belonging to 12 superclasses, the validation and test splits contain 20 classes belonging to 5 superclasses each. Q (as in Sect. 3.1) is chosen to be 15 across all datasets.

Evaluation Protocol. We follow a standard evaluation protocol following earlier literature in the field [31, 40]. The classifier is presented with 10,000 tasks and average accuracy is reported. Given a test set consisting of C novel classes, we generate an N-way K-shot task as follows. N classes are uniformly sampled from the set of C classes without replacement. From each class, K key and $Q = 15$ query images are uniformly sampled without replacement. The classifier is presented with the key images and then used to classify the query images. Following prior work [40], we focus on 5-way 1-shot and 5-way 5-shot benchmarks.

Models and Implementation Details. All experiments use a ResNet-50 [18] backbone. SimCLR [5] pre-training is done for 500 epochs with a learning rate of 0.1, Nesterov momentum of 0.9, and weight decay of 0.0001 on the respective datasets. Data augmentations of RandomResizedCrop and ColorDistortion were found to achieve the best results. The augmentations use default hyperparameters from [5].

MoCo [19] pre-training is done for 800 epochs over the respective training sets using the default parameters from MoCo-v2 [7]. Downstream tasks use the query (non-momentum) encoder network.

Table 1. Average accuracy (in %) on the miniImageNet dataset. [1]Results from [2], which did not report confidence intervals. [2]AmDimNet [4] used extra data from the ImageNet dataset for training the network used to report mini-Imagenet numbers. [3]Results from our experiments adapting the published training code from [42]. OURS was implemented here using OURS_S pipeline and ATTN classifier. See Table 4 for more pipeline and classifier variants.

	Approach	Setting		Labels used
		1-shot	5-shot	
Fully supervised	MAML [10]	49.6 ± 0.9	65.7 ± 0.7	50,400
	CloserLook [6]	51.8 ± 0.7	75.6 ± 0.6	50,400
	RelationNet [36]	52.4 ± 0.8	69.8 ± 0.6	50,400
	MatchingNet [39]	52.9 ± 0.8	68.8 ± 0.6	50,400
	ProtoNet [33]	54.1 ± 0.8	73.6 ± 0.6	50,400
	Gidaris et al. [13]	55.4 ± 0.8	70.1 ± 0.6	50,400
	TADAM [29]	58.5 ± 0.3	76.7 ± 0.3	50,400
	SimpleShot [40]	62.8 ± 0.2	80.0 ± 0.1	38,400
	Tian et al. [38]	64.8 ± 0.6	82.1 ± 0.4	50,400
	S2M2 [26]	**64.9 ± 0.2**	**83.2 ± 0.1**	50,400
	Gidaris et al. [12]	63.77 ± 0.45	80.70 ± 0.33	50,400
Semi supervised	Antoniou et al. [2][1]	33.30	49.18	21,600
With finetuning	AmDimNet [4][2]	**77.09 ± 0.21**	**89.18 ± 0.13**	21,600
Semi supervised	Wu et al. [42][3]	32.4 ± 0.1	39.7 ± 0.1	0
And label free	BoWNet [14]	**51.8**	**70.7**	0
	Ours	50.1 ± 0.2	60.1 ± 0.2	0

Table 2. Average accuracy (in %) on the CIFAR100FS dataset. [1]Results from [25]. [2]Results from our experiments adapting the published training code from [42]. OURS was implemented here using OURS_S pipeline and ATTN classifier. See Table 4 for more pipeline and classifier variants.

	Approach	Setting		Labels used
		1-shot	5-shot	
Fully supervised	MAML [10][1]	58.9 ± 1.9	71.5 ± 1.0	48,000
	RelationNet [36][1]	55.0 ± 1.0	69.3 ± 0.8	48,000
	ProtoNet [33][1]	55.5 ± 0.7	72.0 ± 0.6	48,000
	R2D2 [3][1]	65.3 ± 0.2	79.4 ± 0.1	48,000
	MetaOptNet [25]	72.8 ± 0.7	85.0 ± 0.5	60,000
	Tian et al. [38]	73.9 ± 0.8	86.9 ± 0.5	48,000
	S2M2 [26]	**74.8 ± 0.2**	**87.5 ± 0.1**	48,000
	Gidaris et al. [12]	73.62 ± 0.31	86.05 ± 0.22	48,000
Semi supervised	Wu et al. [42][2]	27.1 ± 0.1	31.3 ± 0.1	0
And label free	Ours	**53.0 ± 0.2**	**62.5 ± 0.2**	0

Table 3. Avg accuracy (in %) on FC100 dataset. [1]Results from [25]. [2]Results from our experiments adapting published training code from [42]. OURS was implemented here using OURS_S pipeline and ATTN classifier. See Table 4 for more pipeline and classifier variants.

	Approach	Setting		Labels used
		1-shot	5-shot	
Fully supervised	ProtoNet [33][1]	35.3 ± 0.6	48.6 ± 0.6	48,000
	TADAM [29][1]	40.1 ± 0.4	56.1 ± 0.4	48,000
	MTL [35]	45.1 ± 1.8	57.6 ± 0.9	60,000
	MetaOptNet [25]	**47.2 ± 0.6**	**62.5 ± 0.6**	60,000
	Tian et al. [38]	44.6 ± 0.7	60.9 ± 0.6	48,000
Semi supervised	Wu et al. [42][2]	27.4 ± 0.1	32.4 ± 0.1	0
And label free	Ours	**37.1 ± 0.2**	**43.4 ± 0.2**	0

Table 4. An ablation study of multiple classifiers on various backbones. Average accuracy and 95% confidence intervals are reported over 10,000 rounds. The '-C' classifiers use class labels to compute the centroids per class. Best results per dataset and few-shot task are in **bold**.

Train	Test	miniImagenet		CIFAR100		FC100	
		1-shot	5-shot	1-shot	5-shot	1-shot	5-shot
Ours_S	1NN	48.7 ± 0.2	59.0 ± 0.2	52.0 ± 0.2	61.7 ± 0.2	36.0 ± 0.2	42.6 ± 0.2
	Attn	**50.1±0.2**	60.1 ± 0.2	**53.0±0.2**	62.5 ± 0.2	**37.1±0.2**	43.4 ± 0.2
	1NN-C	-	**64.6±0.2**	-	**65.8±0.2**	-	**47.2±0.2**
	Attn-C	-	63.6 ± 0.2	-	63.8 ± 0.2	-	46.0 ± 0.1
Ours_M	1NN	29.7 ± 0.1	39.0 ± 0.1	26.7 ± 0.1	31.1 ± 0.2	28.1 ± 0.1	33.2 ± 0.2
	Attn	36.0 ± 0.2	45.2 ± 0.1	27.9 ± 0.1	32.3 ± 0.2	30.4 ± 0.1	35.2 ± 0.2
	1NN-C	-	45.1 ± 0.2	-	32.4 ± 0.2	-	34.9 ± 0.2
	Attn-C	-	48.4 ± 0.2	-	32.4 ± 0.1	-	35.6 ± 0.2

4.2   Results

Tables 1, 2 and 3 present our results on the miniImageNet, CIFAR100FS and FC100 datasets respectively. For a more comprehensive comparison, we also adapt the work presented in Wu et al. [42] to include another unsupervised method in these results. Accuracies are averaged over 10,000 tasks and reported with 95% confidence intervals. Note that we report the number of labels used by each method in each of the above tables. The number of labels used by the methods are computed as follows: if the network trains by performing gradient updates over the training labels, we count the labels in the training set; if the network fine-tunes over the test labels or uses test labels to compute class representations, we count the labels in the test set; if the network uses training and validation data to report results, we count training and validation labels. Unless otherwise specified in the respective works, we assume that the validation set is not used to publish results, and that the train and test pipelines are the same.

Our method achieves strong baselines on the benchmarks while using extremely limited label information, as can be seen in the comparison with Wu *et al.* [42] which operates in the same setting. These are the only two methods across all benchmark datasets that use **almost no** label information. BowNet [14] operates in a similar setting and performs well on the mini-Imagenet benchmark by computing cluster centres in the representation space as a visual vocabulary. Other methods are provided for comparison and the label count is calculated accordingly. The supervised methods use tens of thousands of labels, which can be very expensive depending on a particular domain. Our methodology seeks to provide a pathway to solving problems in such settings with no annotation cost whatsoever.

A higher number of input images increases the classification accuracy, as seen in our 5-way-5-shot tasks. The best results are achieved over the challenging miniImageNet dataset, followed by CIFAR100FS and FC100 datasets. This is expected as FC100 is a coarse-grained classification task and is specifically constructed to have dissimilar classes.

In Sect. 3.1, we proposed the use of two test-time classifiers: 1NN and ATTN. We report ablation studies on their performances in Table 4. While the 1NN classifier achieves strong baselines (in line with previous work [5]), the ATTN classifier consistently improves accuracies by 2–10%, with more impressive gains in the multi-shot setting. This suggests that using different distance measures in the representation space is a valid area for future inquiry.

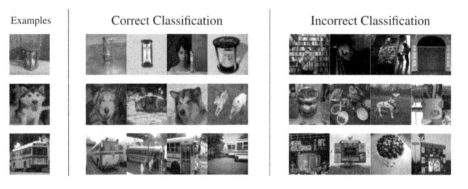

Fig. 3. Visualizing a few examples from the miniImagenet test set using the OURS_S pipeline. **Far Left:** One labelled example visualized per class. **Middle:** Few correctly classified examples from the test set. **Right:** Mis-classified examples. Similarity in texture and coarse object category are contributing factors for mis-classification.

4.3 Ablation Studies

In this section, we explore different variations of our pipeline and investigate the effect on performance across datasets. Table 4 presents the results.

What if we had labels? To investigate the effect of introducing labels at test time, we introduce CENTROID versions of our classifiers: 1 Nearest Neighbours Centroid (1NN_CENTROID), and Soft Cosine Attention Centroid (ATTN_CENTROID), in the multi-shot setting. Following [33,39,40], the CENTROID versions of these classifiers compute class representatives as the centroids of the key images provided at test time. Few-shot classification is then done by comparing each query image against each class centroid, essentially treating the class representative (or exemplar) as the new key image for that class. Using label information to compute class centroids increases performance by 2–4%.

Qualitative Analysis: Figure 3 presents a few qualitative examples from our results on the *mini*ImageNet dataset using our OURS_S pipeline. In the second row, we observe that the network fails on a fine-grained classification task. It classifies a DALMATIAN image (black and white polka-dotted dog) as a HUSKY. Since both categories are dog breeds, they are closely related and pose a difficult few-shot problem. However, when the classes are coarse-grained and fairly well-separated, our method shows that one can achieve reasonable performance with limited label information.

5   Conclusion

We present a new framework for few-shot classification extremely limited label information using computationally simple pipelines. This is more challenging than existing work which uses label information at various points during training or inference. By learning contrastive representations using self supervision, we achieve competitive baselines while using **almost no** labels, which is orders of magnitude fewer labels than existing work. In our ablation studies, we present a qualitative analysis of our classifier and investigate the effect of limited label information. Our results indicate that the choice of self-supervised training task and distance function in the representation space are interesting lines of future inquiry. We also show that using limited label information to compute class representatives at test time is beneficial. This suggests that clustering quality has a direct impact on performance. The objective was to achieve a reasonable performance using few-shot classification with limited label information. We believe this work is an important first step towards label-free few-shot learning methods.

References

1. Antoniou, A., Edwards, H., Storkey, A.: How to train your MAML. In: ICLR (2019)
2. Antoniou, A., Storkey, A.: Assume, augment and learn: unsupervised few-shot meta-learning via random labels and data augmentation. In: ICML (2019)
3. Bertinetto, L., Henriques, J.F., Torr, P., Vedaldi, A.: Meta-learning with differentiable closed-form solvers. In: ICLR (2019)
4. Chen, D., Chen, Y., Li, Y., Mao, F., He, Y., Xue, H.: Self-supervised learning for few-shot image classification (2019)

5. Chen, T., Kornblith, S., Norouzi, M., Hinton, G.: A simple framework for contrastive learning of visual representations. In: ICML (2020)
6. Chen, W.Y., Liu, Y.C., Kira, Z., Wang, Y.C., Huang, J.B.: A closer look at few-shot classification. In: ICLR (2019)
7. Chen, X., Fan, H., Girshick, R., He, K.: Improved baselines with momentum contrastive learning (2020). arXiv preprint arXiv:2003.04297
8. Deng, J., Dong, W., Socher, R., Li, L.J., Li, K., Fei-Fei, L.: ImageNet: a large-scale hierarchical image database. In: CVPR (2009)
9. Doersch, C., Gupta, A., Efros, A.A.: Unsupervised visual representation learning by context prediction. In: ICCV (2015)
10. Finn, C., Abbeel, P., Levine, S.: Model-agnostic meta-learning for fast adaptation of deep networks. In: ICML (2017)
11. Finn, C., Xu, K., Levine, S.: Probabilistic model-agnostic meta-learning. In: NeurIPS (2018)
12. Gidaris, S., Bursuc, A., Komodakis, N., Pérez, P.P., Cord, M.: Boosting few-shot visual learning with self-supervision. In: ICCV (2019)
13. Gidaris, S., Komodakis, N.: Dynamic few-shot visual learning without forgetting. In: CVPR (2018)
14. Gidaris, S., Bursuc, A., Komodakis, N., Pérez, P., Cord, M.: Learning representations by predicting bags of visual words. In: Proceedings of the IEEE/CVF Conference on Computer Vision and Pattern Recognition, pp. 6928–6938 (2020)
15. Gidaris, S., Singh, P., Komodakis, N.: Unsupervised representation learning by predicting image rotations. In: ICLR (2018)
16. Grant, E., Finn, C., Levine, S., Darrell, T., Griffiths, T.: Recasting gradient-based meta-learning as hierarchical bayes (2018). arXiv preprint arXiv:1801.08930
17. Hariharan, B., Girshick, R.: Low-shot visual recognition by shrinking and hallucinating features. In: ICCV (2017)
18. He, K., Zhang, X., Ren, S., Sun, J.: Deep residual learning for image recognition. In: CVPR (2016)
19. He, K., Fan, H., Wu, Y., Xie, S., Girshick, R.: Momentum contrast for unsupervised visual representation learning. In: CVPR (2020)
20. Horn, G.V., Perona, P.: The devil is in the tails: fine-grained classification in the wild (2017). CoRR abs/1709.01450, http://arxiv.org/abs/1709.01450
21. Ji, X., Henriques, J.F., Vedaldi, A.: Invariant information clustering for unsupervised image classification and segmentation. In: ICCV (2019)
22. Koch, G., Zemel, R., Salakhutdinov, R.: Siamese neural networks for one-shot image recognition. In: ICML-W (2015)
23. Krizhevsky, A.: Learning multiple layers of features from tiny images. University of Toronto (2009)
24. Larsson, G., Maire, M., Shakhnarovich, G.: Learning representations for automatic colorization. In: ECCV (2016)
25. Lee, K., Maji, S., Ravichandran, A., Soatto, S.: Meta-learning with differentiable convex optimization. In: CVPR (2019)
26. Mangla, P., Kumari, N., Sinha, A., Singh, M., Krishnamurthy, B., Balasubramanian, V.N.: Charting the right manifold: manifold mixup for few-shot learning. In: WACV (2020)
27. Nguyen, C., Do, T.T., Carneiro, G.: Uncertainty in model-agnostic meta-learning using variational inference. In: WACV (2020)
28. Noroozi, M., Favaro, P.: Unsupervised learning of visual representations by solving jigsaw puzzles. In: ECCV (2016)

29. Oreshkin, B., Rodríguez López, P., Lacoste, A.: Tadam: Task dependent adaptive metric for improved few-shot learning. In: NeurIPS (2018)
30. Ravi, S., Larochelle, H.: Optimization as a model for few-shot learning. In: ICLR (2017)
31. Rusu, A.A., et al.: Meta-learning with latent embedding optimization. In: ICLR (2019)
32. Satorras, V.G., Estrach, J.B.: Few-shot learning with graph neural networks. In: ICLR (2018)
33. Snell, J., Swersky, K., Zemel, R.: Prototypical networks for few-shot learning. In: NeurIPS (2017)
34. Su, J.C., Maji, S., Hariharan, B.: Boosting supervision with self-supervision for few-shot learning (2019). ArXiv abs/1906.07079
35. Sun, Q., Liu, Y., Chua, T.S., Schiele, B.: Meta-transfer learning for few-shot learning. In: CVPR (2019)
36. Sung, F., Yang, Y., Zhang, L., Xiang, T., Torr, P.H., Hospedales, T.M.: Learning to compare: relation network for few-shot learning. In: CVPR (2018)
37. Tian, Y., Krishnan, D., Isola, P.: Contrastive multiview coding (2019). arXiv preprint arXiv:1906.05849
38. Tian, Y., Wang, Y., Krishnan, D., Tenenbaum, J.B., Isola, P.: Rethinking few-shot image classification: a good embedding is all you need? In: Vedaldi, A., Bischof, H., Brox, T., Frahm, J.-M. (eds.) ECCV 2020. LNCS, vol. 12359, pp. 266–282. Springer, Cham (2020). https://doi.org/10.1007/978-3-030-58568-6_16
39. Vinyals, O., Blundell, C., Lillicrap, T., kavukcuoglu, k., Wierstra, D.: Matching networks for one shot learning. In: NeurIPS (2016)
40. Wang, Y., Chao, W.L., Weinberger, K.Q., van der Maaten, L.: Simpleshot: Revisiting nearest-neighbor classification for few-shot learning (2019)
41. Wang, Y., Yao, Q., Kwok, J.T., Ni, L.M.: Generalizing from a few examples: a survey on few-shot learning. ACM Comput. Surv. (CSUR) **53**(3), 1–34 (2019)
42. Wu, Z., Xiong, Y., Yu, S.X., Lin, D.: Unsupervised feature learning via nonparametric instance discrimination. In: CVPR, pp. 3733–3742 (2018)
43. Yoon, J., Kim, T., Dia, O., Kim, S., Bengio, Y., Ahn, S.: Bayesian model-agnostic meta-learning. In: NeurIPS (2018)
44. Zhang, R., Isola, P., Efros, A.A.: Colorful image colorization. In: ECCV (2016)

AB-net: Adult- Baby Net

Sahil Salim Makandar, Ashish Tiwari, Sahil Munaf Bandar[(⊠)], and Allen Joshey

Global Edge Software Limited, Bangalore 560059, India
{sm.sahil,t.ashish,bm.sahil,j.allen}@globaledgesoft.com

Abstract. The problem of estimating and classifying age from a given input image is age old. With the advancement of modern technology and recent progress in the field of deep learning it has been made possible to gain success for this particular application. We present a novel algorithm inspired by the Multi-Task Cascaded Convolutional Neural Networks architecture and a subsequent pipeline to a Prediction architecture thus defining an end - to - end pipeline, which can predict with great certainty the age group, from a given input image. We introduce approaches in data preparation techniques such as Complex Negatives and IOU based segregation which proves beneficial to the reduction of false-positive classification of samples. Thus significantly proving on benchmarks to achieve robust performance with regard to the age classification problem. The proposed method is able to accurately predict and has been benchmarked on the FDDB dataset [7].

Keywords: Face detection · Face classification · Adult-Baby detection

1 Introduction

The applications of deep learning have grown popular thanks to its robustness with which it can achieve results with great certainty. Attempts to solve problems relating to face alignment, detection and recognition have only benefited from the rise of deep learning applied to computer vision.

Earlier work includes approaches from classical computer vision that try to extract unique features that demarcate a human face. The ideas brought in by Dalal et al. and Triggs et al. based on [4] Histogram of Oriented Gradients (HOG) feature descriptors have attempted to capture essential features in order to localize known structures like persons in natural settings. Such methods have also been applied to the face detection task where the authors make use of such features to try and extract unique representations aiding in the process of localizing similar patterns in given images. However, such methods, fall prey to the issues that would exist due to lighting, scale and pose changes of the face itself. The Viola-Jones [5] algorithm thus proved to be a turning point as a face detection algorithm, also being one of the first as such that made use of a cascaded setup which led to its success. Additionally, utilization of selective Haar-Like features and ultimately subjecting it to a trained classifier gave it a significant boost in its accuracy of detecting faces in real world scenarios with close to real-time results. Unfortunately, varied poses and expressions of the face itself, combined with unexpected lighting can prove to be degrading to the algorithm's performance.

B. Raman et al. (Eds.): CVIP 2021, CCIS 1567, pp. 269–280, 2022.
https://doi.org/10.1007/978-3-031-11346-8_24

The emergence of Convolutional Neural networks has proven to be the de facto standard for Deep Learning based approaches towards visual processing. CNN's combine the power of hand crafted features along with the ability to learn from data, thus being able to pick up subtle patterns. Seminal work like VGG-16 [11], ResNet [12] and its subsequent architectures have proven to be good candidates in the field of detection and classification. However due to the size and depth of the model and complexity in terms of computation the robustness of this approach comes at the price of computational speed. Our papers proposes a method by which one can discriminate between an Adult and Baby's face from a given input image. Owing to this particular application, works such as DEX [3] have proven to gain great accuracy by employing the use of an ensemble of CNN's in order to first detect and subsequently predict the age owing its success to the VGG16 [11] backbone that is used. Another approach to face detection was introduced by cascading CNNs in the early works of [2] and subsequently gave rise to Multitask Cascaded Convolutional Networks. [2] Introduced the idea of calibrating and making use of face alignment which would aid in the detection process, and also proposed the idea of refining the quality of the output at each stage of the cascade.[1] took this idea further and modified the cascade to have a "Proposal", "Refinement" and "Output" stage. Also the concept of an image pyramid was used to have scale invariance and thus the following algorithms proved to be robust to scale too.

Inspired by the works mentioned before, we propose a 4 stage pipelined approach which, given an input image would produce a classification that classifies into either a Baby or Adult face.

Our contributions from this paper are as follows:

- Provide an end to end pipeline to accurately classify between Adult and baby faces.
- Data preparation techniques that provide good candidates of positive, partial, negative and "complex negative" samples which help in the learning process, leading to more discriminative features and ultimately reducing the amount of False Positives.

2   Approach

Our Approach features a multistage cascade of CNNs Networks whose end goal is to be able to predict from a given image the classification value, key points of face landmarks and its bounding box values. In order to do so our preprocessing step involves the resizing and scaling of the image at different required scales to construct an image pyramid. This forms the set of inputs that is required by our pipeline.

Cascade 1:
Our implementation is thus inspired by [1] and [2] which proposes resizing our input image to size 12×12.This cascade consists of only Convolutional Networks thus drawing inspiration from FCN [10]. The results obtained thus provide us with face classification information and its corresponding Bounding box values and Facial landmark values. The architecture is shown in Fig. 1.

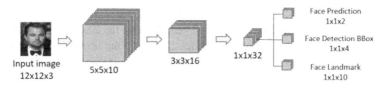

Fig. 1. The first filter stage is composed of Fully Convolutional Neural networks.

Cascade 2:

The architecture for this is visualized in Fig. 2. Next from the previous cascade the samples that have been classified as candidates would thus serve as the input to this stage. The candidate input now rescaled to 24×24 is now filtered through 3 convolutional filters and later a fully connected layer. This stage helps weed out any misclassification that had happened from the previous stage and also helps to align and correct the bounding box values with respect to the current frame of reference.

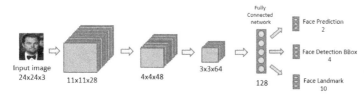

Fig. 2. The second filter stage consists of a fully connected network (Dense).

Cascade 3:

The third cascade serves as another filter stage building on the input from our previous stage. Here our input image is resized to 48x48 and in addition we have a network that selectively refines the input image and produces the best estimate of the face classification, bounding box prediction and the face landmarks. This can be visualized in Fig. 3.

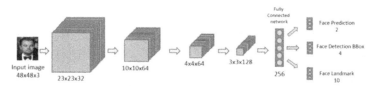

Fig. 3. The third filter stage that acts as the final stage of filtering.

Cascade 4:

The final cascade serves as the stage which proves to be the best bet at clearly distinguishing between a face that belongs to a said class. Here the Image is resized to have a dimension of 227 × 227.The final layer is a "Softmax" layer that produces probabilities of the required classes. The architecture for the same is given in Table 1.

Table 1. Final classifier architecture

Block	Operator	Kernel Size	#Channels	Stride (h, w)
1	Conv	7 × 7	96	4,4
	Batch Normalization	–	–	–
	Max Pool	3 × 3	96	2,2
	Dropout(0.25)	–	–	–
2	Zero Pad (2,2)	–	–	–
	Conv	5 × 5	256	1,1
	Batch Normalization	–	–	–
	Max Pool	3 × 3	256	2,2
	Dropout(0.25)	–	–	–
3	Zero Pad (1,1)	–	–	–
	Conv	3 × 3	384	1,1
	Batch Normalization	–	–	–
	Max Pool	3 × 3	384	2,2
	Dropout(0.25)	–	–	–
4	Dense	–	512	–
	Batch Normalization	–	–	–
	Dropout(0.5)	–	–	–
5	Dense	–	512	–
	Batch Normalization	–	–	–
	Dropout(0.5)	–	–	–
Output	Dense	–	2(No. of Classes)	–

We leverage the advantages in presented by Batch Normalization [13] .Secondly, we introduce a small amount of dropout after every pooling layer to help reduce over fitting.

The network consist of only three convolutional layers and two dense layers. Our smaller network thus reduces the risk of over fitting in order to achieve the face classification task. We pass RGB images to our network which are resized to 256 × 256 and cropped to 227 × 227. Finally, the output of the dense layer is fed to a softmax layer that will give the probability for each class. The prediction itself is made by taking the class with the maximal probability for the given test image.

2.1 Data Preparation Methodology

The data preparation becomes key in the success of our proposed algorithm. Our Data can be segregated into 4 parts. The data is split by measuring IOU overlaps and taking this as a key metric, we go ahead to segregate the data into one of 3 types: **Positive, Negative** and **Partial** ground truths. An additional label forms as part of landmarks and this is used to make 5 key landmarks that form the part of the face, namely both the eyes, the nose, and the two extremities of the mouth.

Our methodology of creating the data for training is based on the IOU overlap and can be created as follows. We have used and trained our networks on the WIDER FACE Dataset [8].

Negative and Complex Images:
The negative Images are created keeping in mind the features the network must learn in order to classify as "non-face". Particularly in order to achieve a highly accurate differentiation we introduce a set of "**Complex Negative**" images which prove to be best candidates of a negative sample thus aiding in making a better classification.

Creation of Negative data

For each training sample we first create 50 randomly selected crops of size rl where $rl \in$ Rand $(12, min (H, W)/2)$.

Next, in order to compute the respective Bounding Boxes of 50 such crops we take the top left corner to be nx, a random value between $(0,W\text{-}rl)$ and similarly ny to be a value between $(0,H\text{-}rl)$.

We then crop a box whose dimensions are given by nx, ny and have a width and height of rl

We now resize this cropped region to $Nwidth$ as required by the network

We thus have 50 such samples from a single Training Image.

Only those samples qualify as negative samples whose IOU with the ground truth is less than 30% (0.3).

The motivation for a Complex negative is to present a good candidate input that maximizes the discrimination power of the network. In doing so for each training sample we select 5 randomly selected bounding boxes that are in the vicinity of the Ground Truth.

Creation of Complex negative data

---

rl forms the size of the intended "Complex negative" image. *rl* ϵ Rand (*12, min (H, W)/2)*.

Next, in order to create the top left edge of the Bounding Boxes, we take dx and dy as the offset from the respective Ground truth's top left corner. Where $x1, y1, h, w$ are the Ground Truth BBox's values.

dx ϵ Rand (*max (-size, -x1), w)*.

dy ϵ Rand (*max (-size, -y1), h)*.

Values that go beyond the scope of the image are ignored.

The criterion to qualify as Complex negative remains the same as it was for a negative image, i.e. the IOU with the ground truth would be less than 30% (0.3)

In total the number of Negative samples from a single training image thus leads to a maximum of 55.

Creation of Positive and Partial Face:
Much like how we create augmented negative data from each training example we proceed with the creation of positive samples which prove to be best candidates for the "face" classification and partial examples that become good candidates of partially occluded or visible faces in order to facilitate learning.

Creation of Positive and Partial data

Thus we consider the size of the crop to be 80% of *max (h, w)* and the offset to be ± 20% of *max (h, w)*.

In doing so we produce crops with bounding box coordinates at $x1, y1$ at the top left corner and subsequently $x2, y2$.

The given region is considered to be a positive Sample if it's IOU w.r.t Ground Truth is above 65%(0.65) and if it has an overlap between 40-65%(0.4 - 0.65),then it would be considered to be a partial Sample.

The two key factors to keep in mind for best results are as follows:

1. The size of the cropped region must be large enough and have a big receptive field such that the network would be able to learn key features.
2. The offset chosen from the Ground Truth must be relatively small so as to have a good overlap between the generated Bounding Box and Ground Truth's Bounding Box.

In total the number of Positive and Partial samples from a single training image thus leads to a maximum of 20.

Landmarks:
The samples used for training the landmarks is the LFW (Labelled Faces in the Wild)

[6] dataset which provides annotations of 2 eyes, the nose, and the extremities of the mouth that makeup a total of 5 such landmarks.

2.2 Training

The segregated 4 types of data are fed into the First Filter stage along with their corresponding labels. The Landmark dataset used is the LFW dataset [6]. The weights in all layers are initialized with random values from a zero mean Gaussian with standard deviation of 0.01. The network is trained, from scratch without initializing weights of other pretrained model. Training itself is performed using stochastic gradient decent with image batch size of 32 images. The initial learning rate is 0.001, reduced to 0.0001 after 10K iterations. Our best experiment on classifying adult and baby was obtained using the Adam optimizer with an initial learning rate of 0.0001. An L2 weight decay of 0.0005 was also applied. The loss for the training and validation set is visualized in Fig. 4.

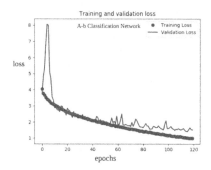

Fig. 4. Shows the loss over the training and validation set

The Activation function used is PReLu for the first 3 cascades and ReLu for the Final one. Each network is trained separately and in the order of its occurrence, thus constructing an end-to-end pipeline for a given image. Non-Max suppression is then applied to arrive at the best given detection box from the given output. The network is trained in batches of size 64 which would sample 64 samples from the Landmark annotation data, 64 samples each from the Positive and Partial data and 64 * 3 samples from the Negative data. This is done in order to balance out the distribution of the data in a uniform manner. Table 2 provides an insight into the computational speeds at each stage of the cascade. This had been carried out on an Intel Core i5-6200 CPU at 2.30 GHz (quad core)

2.3 Cascade 1:

The primary purpose of the first cascade is to act as a simple preliminary discriminator, in doing so the inputs to this network are the previously created dataset .The focus was to be able to discriminate at a preliminary level between a face and non-face input. In

Table 2. Computational speeds

Filter stage	300 times Forward (s)	Average per Inference (s)
1st	0.12179756164550781	0.0004059918721516927
2nd	0.35630321502685547	0.0011876773834228515
3rd	0.4085566997528076	0.001361855665842692

order to reinforce this a weighting factor ω_{face} is used as part of the total loss and is set to 1. 10 filters of size $3 \times 3 \times 3$ are used, followed by 16 filters of size $3 \times 3 \times 10$, which feeds into 32 filters of size $3 \times 3 \times 16$, from which we can gather the outputs as needed in Figure 1.

Cascade 2:
Much like the first cascade, the purpose of the second cascade is to further filter the candidate samples from the previous stage. The candidate samples produced by the previous stage form the set of inputs, and the same procedure is followed but this time with setting *Nwidth* as 24 and this network is thus trained. Importance is given to the face prediction task and the weighting factor ω_{face} is 1. 28 filters of size $3 \times 3 \times 3$ are used, followed by 48 filters of size $3 \times 3 \times 28$, which feeds into 64 filters of size $3 \times 3 \times 48$, which is later flattened and fed to dense layers as per Fig. 2.

Cascade 3:
The Final stage of refinement happens at this network and will produce the best results for all the desired outputs. The weighting factor ω_{face} here remains to be 1 for the prediction task, meanwhile the weighting factor $\omega_{Landmark}$ for the 'landmark' loss is also set to 1. The weighting factor for BBox detection loss ω_{BBox} remains the same at 0.5. 32 filters of size $3 \times 3 \times 3$ are used, followed by 64 filters of size $3 \times 3 \times 32$, which feeds into 64 filters of size $3 \times 3 \times 64$, and is later subject to a final Convolutional layer of 128 filters of size $2 \times 2 \times 64$. Following this a set of Dense layers are employed as per Fig. 3.

Cascade 4:
The Final stage in our 4 stage cascade is adept at classifying the given face, Given that the previous stages take care of the detection problem. This stage forms the discriminator stage that ultimately classifies a faces into the Adult or Baby class. The training set for the same was derived from a mixture of standard datasets and custom images. The entire pipeline of our approach is visualized in Figure 5.

Fig. 5. The entire pipeline of our approach

Face Prediction Loss:
The face prediction problem can be thought of as a two class classification problem.

Thus we proceed with the binary cross entropy loss L_i^{Fbb} for the face prediction's loss calculation as given below. Where L_i^{pred} is the predicted value and L_i^{GT} is the Ground Truth Label for each sample i.

$$L_i^{FP} = -(y_i^{GT} \log(y_i^{pred})) + (1 - y_i^{pread})(1 - \log(y_i^{GT})) \tag{1}$$

Face Bounding Box Detection Loss:
The aim here is to produce a bounding box for a given face that the network has identified in order to localize the face within the image. The network is expected to produce the top left corner and its corresponding width and Height. Here the objective function to minimize is the discrepancy between the Ground Truth Value and the predicted value.

A simple Euclidean loss L_i^{Fbb} is used in order to compute the loss. Where L_i^{GT} is the Ground Truth and L_i^{pred} is the predicted value.

$$L_i^{Fbb} = ||y_i^{GT} - y_i^{pred}||_2^2 \tag{2}$$

Landmark Detection Loss:
Similar to how the Face Bounding Box detection task is formulated, here we consider the points to be the 5 landmarks i.e. 2 eyes, 1 nose, 2 extremities of the mouth. A Euclidean loss L_i^{Land} is thus applied to compute the landmark detection loss. Here y^{LandGT} are the annotated set of landmark points and $L_i^{Landpred}$ are the predicted values.

$$L_i^{Land} = y_i^{LandGT} - y_i^{Landpred}||_2^2 \tag{3}$$

Total Loss:
The total loss at each of the first 3 stages is a weighted summation of the individual losses from each task. Thus, in order to facilitate the learning we also introduce a multiplication factor (Gateval) that allows us to selectively consider the landmark loss while back-propagating. This is key when we are training only for the landmarks in each of the first 3 Cascades. Training can be carried out in 2 phases for the initial 3 Cascades.

The 1st phase takes the Positive, Negative and Part samples to produce the Classification and its respective bounding boxes. The 2nd phase Includes setting the multiplication factor *Gateval* to 0 for the Classification and bounding box detection losses. By setting *Gateval* to 1 we selectively consider only the Landmark detection loss and the network therefore learns to predict the landmark's location. Thus the overall target to minimize becomes:

$$Total\ Loss = \text{Gateval} \cdot \omega_{face} \cdot L_i^{FP} + \text{Gateval} \cdot \omega_{BBox} \cdot L_i^{Fbb} + \text{Gateval} \cdot \omega_{Landmark} \cdot L_i^{Land} \tag{4}$$

| (a) | (b) | (c) |

Fig. 6. a) Cascade 1 results with large number of false positives of face bounding boxes. b) Cascade 2 results with lesser false positives. c) Cascade 3 with the best results of detected faces.

Classification Loss (Cross-Entropy Loss):
Each predicted class probability is compared to the actual class desired output (GT_i). The score calculated penalizes the model based on its deviation from the actual value. The logarithmic nature yields a larger score for large differences close to 1 and smaller score for small differences tending to 0. P_i is the predicted value.

$$L_{class} = -\sum_{i=0}^{n} GT_i \, \log(P_i) \tag{5}$$

3 Conclusion

In our work we have leveraged the learning ability of multiple cascades of Convolutional filters. The key contribution comes in adding the final output stage that manages to accurately learn to discriminate between adult and baby faces, even with instances where fabrics that seem similar to baby's clothing could prove adversarial.

Table 3. Presents the Report of our results Benchmarked on the FDDB dataset [7]

	Precision	Recall	F1-Score
Face	0.97	0.90	0.94
Accuracy	–	–	0.89
Weighted Avg	0.95	0.88	0.91

Table 4. Presents the Report of our results as compared to other methods

Model	True Positive Rate
Ours	0.9048
MTCNN [1]	0.9504
Cascade CNN [2]	0.8567

Table 5. Our Results on the OUI-Adience Dataset [9] for classification

Classification	Precision	Recall	F1-score
Child	0.97	0.77	0.86
Adult	0.86	0.98	0.92

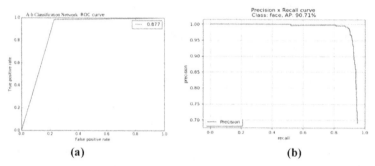

(a)   (b)

Fig. 7. a) The ROC Curve for classification **b)** The Precision –Recall curve of our approach on face classification.

The given approach has achieved state-of-the-art performance in terms of metrics such as Accuracy, Precision and recall on challenging datasets like the FDDB dataset [7]. Figure 7 shows the results obtained. We have been successful at reducing the amount of false positive triggers with our approach aiding us in achieving the results. As showcased in Table 5 we can see the classification results for adult and baby classification on the OUI-Adience dataset [9] and combination of the our custom dataset. The future scope of this work would be to improve upon its inference speed, making it suitable to run seamlessly on mobile and edge devices. Table 3 shows the results that we have managed to achieve testing on the FDDB dataset [7]. Table 4 showcases our Performance on the FDDB dataset [7] against other methods [1, 2].

Acknowledgments. This work was carried at Global Edge Software Limited and we wish to acknowledge its support and resources made available in order to achieve this. The content is the sole responsibility of the authors, it does not necessarily represent the official views of Global Edge Software Limited and we would like to thank the members of the AI team from the cloud practice for their help.

References

1. Xiang, J., Zhu, G.: Joint face detection and facial expression recognition with MTCNN. In: 2017 4th International Conference on Information Science and Control Engineering (ICISCE), pp. 424–427 (2017). https://doi.org/10.1109/ICISCE.2017.95
2. Li, H., Lin, Z., Shen, X., Brandt, J., Hua, G.: A convolutional neural network cascade for face detection. In: 2015 IEEE Conference on Computer Vision and Pattern Recognition (CVPR), pp. 5325–5334 (2015). https://doi.org/10.1109/CVPR.2015.7299170
3. Rothe, R., Timofte, R., Van Gool, L.: DEX: deep EXpectation of apparent age from a single image. In: 2015 IEEE International Conference on Computer Vision Workshop (ICCVW), pp. 252–257 (2015). https://doi.org/10.1109/ICCVW.2015.41, Author F.: Contribution title. In: 9th International Proceedings on Proceedings, pp. 1–2. Publisher, Location (2010)
4. Dalal, N., Triggs, B.: Histograms of oriented gradients for human detection. In: 2005 IEEE Computer Society Conference on Computer Vision and Pattern Recognition (CVPR'05), vol. 1, pp. 886–893 (2005). https://doi.org/10.1109/CVPR.2005.177
5. Viola, P., Jones, M.: Rapid object detection using a boosted cascade of simple features. In: Pro ceedings of the 2001 IEEE Computer Society Conference on Computer Vision and Pattern Recognition. CVPR 2001, pp. I-I (2001). https://doi.org/10.1109/CVPR.2001.990517
6. Huang, G.B., Ramesh, M., Berg, T., Learned-Miller, E.: Labeled Faces in the Wild: A Database for Studying Face Recognition in Unconstrained Environments. University of Massachusetts, Amherst, Technical Report 07–49, October 2007
7. Jain, V., Learned-Miller, E.: FDDB: A Benchmark for Face Detection in Unconstrained Settings. Technical Report UM-CS-2010-009, Dept. of Computer Science, University of Massachusetts, Amherst (2010)
8. Yang, S., Luo, P., Loy, C., Tang, X.: WIDER FACE: A Face Detection Benchmark. In IEEE Conference on Computer Vision and Pattern Recognition (CVPR) (2016)
9. Eidinger, E., Enbar, R., Hassner, T.: Age and gender estimation of unfiltered faces. In: Transactions on Information Forensics and Security (IEEE-TIFS), special issue on Facial Biometrics in the Wild, 9(12), 2170–2179 (2014)
10. Long, J., Shelhamer, E., Darrell, T.: Fully convolutional networks for semantic segmentation. In: 2015 IEEE Conference on Computer Vision and Pattern Recognition (CVPR), pp. 3431–3440 (2015). https://doi.org/10.1109/CVPR.2015.7298965
11. Simonyan, K., Zisserman, A.: Very deep convolutional networks for large-scale image recognition. In: ICLR (2015)
12. He, K., Zhang, X., Ren, S., Sun, J.: Deep residual learning for image recognition. In: 2016 IEEE Conference on Computer Vision and Pattern Recognition (CVPR), pp. 770–778 (2016). https://doi.org/10.1109/CVPR.2016.90
13. Ioffe, S., Szegedy, C.:. Batch normalization: accelerating deep network training by reducing internal covariate shift. In: Proceedings of the 32nd International Conference on In ternational Conference on Machine Learning – vol. 37, pp. 448–456. JMLR.org (2015)

Polarimetric SAR Classification: Fast Learning with k-Maximum Likelihood Estimator

Nilam Chaudhari[1]([✉])[ID], Suman K. Mitra[1][ID], Srimanta Mandal[1][ID],
Sanid Chirakkal[2][ID], Deepak Putrevu[2], and Arundhati Misra[2]

[1] Dhirubhai Ambani Institute of Information and Communication Technology,
Gandhinagar, Gujarat, India
{nilam_chaudhari,suman_mitra,srimanta_mandal}@daiict.ac.in
[2] Advanced Microwave and Hyperspectral Techniques Development Group
(AMHTDG), Space Applications Center, ISRO, Ahmedabad, Gujarat, India
{sanid,dputrevu,arundhati}@sac.isro.gov.in

Abstract. Classification of polarimetric synthetic aperture radar (SAR) images into different ground covers becomes challenging when the terrain under consideration is heterogeneous in nature. A finite mixture model-based Wishart mixture model (WMM) classifier can efficiently incorporate heterogeneity of terrain using multiple Wishart components. The expectation-maximization (EM) is the most widely used algorithm for learning parameters of such statistical models. However, the convergence of the EM algorithm is very slow. Moreover, the information contained in the polarimetric SAR images is in complex numbers and the size of the data is often very large. Therefore, they incur a large amount of computational overhead. The training of the classifier becomes very slow due to these reasons. In this paper, a k-maximum likelihood estimator (k-MLE) algorithm is employed for learning of the parameters in WMM classifier. As k-MLE is an iterative process, different algorithm initialization approaches such as random, global K-means, and k-MLE++ are analyzed. The algorithm is compared with the traditional EM algorithm in terms of classification accuracy and computational time. The experiments are performed on six different full polarimetric SAR datasets. The results show that the classification accuracy using k-MLE is comparable to the traditional EM algorithm while being more computationally efficient. The initialization using k-MLE++ results in better modeling compared to random and global K-means.

Keywords: Polarimetric SAR · k-Maximum likelihood estimator ·
Classification · Expectation-maximization · Wishart mixture model

1 Introduction

Polarimetric synthetic aperture radar (SAR) remote sensing has expanded new research areas in the field of advanced earth observation. The optical remote sensing depends on sunlight illumination. Henceforth, it works only during the daytime and requires clear weather. The polarimetric SAR efficiently addresses the limitations of optical remote sensing. It uses radar technology to illuminate the target. The SAR transmits the microwave signals and receives its backscatters to characterize the target image. The microwave signals can surpass the cloud, rain, and mist due to their longer wavelength. Therefore, it can work in all weather conditions and even during nighttime.

Classification of polarimetric SAR image is a frontier research topic in remote sensing. It is useful in many applications such as land mapping, urbanization, and crop estimation. Many statistical [7,10] and neural network [1,8,14] approaches have been applied till now. The Wishart classifier proposed by Lee et al. [10] is one of the well-known and most widely used classifiers using complex Wishart distribution. However, it works well only for the homogeneous terrain. Then, for heterogeneous terrain a K-distribution [12] and G-distribution [5] based models are proposed. They both are product based models which assume the received signal is a product of texture component and speckle component. Later, Gao et al. [7] proposed Wishart mixture model (WMM) classifier for heterogeneous terrain along with expectation-maximization (EM) [4] algorithm for parameter estimation. The WMM have shown outstanding improvements compared to Wishart. However, one of the major drawbacks of the EM algorithm is slow convergence [3,4]. Therefore, the training of the classifier becomes slow. In addition to that, the information contained in polarimetric SAR image is in complex numbers and often contains a large amount of data. It incurs more computational costs. Therefore, it makes the training of the classifier even slower.

Nielsen [16] proposed k-maximum likelihood estimator (k-MLE) for parameter estimation which is faster and more efficient than traditional EM algorithm. The k-MLE and its variants are being used in the literature. Schwander et al. [19] employed k-MLE to estimate the parameters of generalized Gaussian distribution. In another work by Schwander and Nielsen [18], k-MLE is employed for the mixture of gamma distributions. Yang et al. [22] used k-MLE for the change detection application of polarimetric SAR images. Saint-Jean and Nielsen [17] proposed variant of k-MLE and applied it for the motion retrieval application. To our knowledge, no other work has used k-MLE for the classification problem of polarimetric SAR images. In this paper, we employ k-MLE to estimate the parameters of WMM for polarimetric SAR image classification. As k-MLE is an iterative algorithm, its convergence depends on the choice of the initial points. Therefore, we analyze different initialization approaches such as random, global K-means [13] and k-MLE++ [16].

The contributions of the paper are summarized as follows:

- The k-MLE algorithm is employed to estimate the parameters of WMM, which is further used to perform the classification of polarimetric SAR images.
- Different initialization approaches are analyzed for k-MLE such as random, global K-means and k-MLE++.
- The k-MLE is compared with traditional EM algorithm in terms of classification accuracy and computational time for full polarimetric SAR images.

2 Polarimetric SAR Data Representation

Polarimetric SAR sensor captures both amplitude and phase information of microwave signals. The data can be represented using Sinclair matrix as [11]

$$\mathbf{S} = \begin{bmatrix} S_{HH} & S_{HV} \\ S_{VH} & S_{VV} \end{bmatrix}. \tag{1}$$

Here, each S_{RT} is a complex number, where R is receiving polarization and T is transmitting polarization. From Sinclair matrix, a covariance matrix ($\mathbf{C}_3$) is derived as [11]

$$\mathbf{C}_3 = \begin{bmatrix} \langle S_{HH}S_{HH}^* \rangle & \langle S_{HH}S_{HV}^* \rangle & \langle S_{HH}S_{VV}^* \rangle \\ \langle S_{HV}S_{HH}^* \rangle & \langle S_{HV}S_{HV}^* \rangle & \langle S_{HV}S_{VV}^* \rangle \\ \langle S_{VV}S_{HH}^* \rangle & \langle S_{VV}S_{HV}^* \rangle & \langle S_{VV}S_{VV}^* \rangle \end{bmatrix}. \tag{2}$$

The covariance matrix follows a Wishart mixture model [7]. The probability density function for covariance matrix $\mathbf{X}$ and K mixture components is [7],

$$p(\mathbf{X}|\mathbf{V}_1,\ldots,\mathbf{V}_K,\sigma_1,\ldots,\sigma_K) = \sum_{k=1}^{K} \sigma_k \mathcal{W}_d(\mathbf{X}|n,\mathbf{V}_k), \tag{3}$$

where $\mathbf{V}_1,\ldots,\mathbf{V}_K$ represent centers and $\sigma_1,\ldots,\sigma_K$ represent weights of mixture distributions. $\mathcal{W}_d$ is a Wishart distribution which can be represented as

$$\mathcal{W}_d(\mathbf{X}|n,\mathbf{C}) = \frac{n^{nd}|\mathbf{X}|^{n-d}e^{-n\,\mathrm{tr}(\mathbf{V}_k^{-1}\mathbf{X})}}{\Gamma_d(n)|\mathbf{V}_k|^n}, \tag{4}$$

where $\Gamma_d(\cdot)$ is a d-variate gamma function, $\mathrm{tr}(\cdot)$ is a trace function. d is a dimension of the matrix $\mathbf{X}$ and n is a degrees of freedom.

3 Methodology

The traditional EM algorithm uses a soft-clustering technique to estimate the parameters. It has a slow convergence rate and maximizes the expected log-likelihood instead of the complete log-likelihood. Whereas, the k-MLE [16] uses a hard-clustering technique while assigning the data points to the mixture component. Therefore, it has a fast convergence rate. Moreover, the k-MLE maximizes the complete log-likelihood.

Exponential family distributions are very convenient and most commonly used in many applications. Many widely used statistical distributions such as Gaussian, Bernoulli, Poission, Binomial, Gamma, Beta, and Wishart belong to exponential family. If x follows the exponential distribution then its probability density or mass function can be represented in the canonical decomposition as

$$p(x;\theta) = \exp(\langle t(x),\theta \rangle - F(\theta) + k(x)). \tag{5}$$

where θ represents natural parameters, $\langle \cdot \rangle$ represents inner product, $t(x)$ represents sufficient statistics, $F(\theta)$ represents log-normalizer, and $k(x)$ represents carrier measure.

For samples $x_1, \ldots, x_n$ following exponential distribution, mixture weights $w_1 \ldots w_k$ and latent variables $z_1, \ldots, z_n$, the complete log-likelihood of mixture of exponential family can be written as

$$\bar{l}'(x_1, z_1, \ldots, x_n, z_n) = \frac{1}{n} \sum_i \sum_j \delta(z_i)(\log p(x_i; \theta_j) + \log \omega_j), \qquad (6)$$

where $\delta(z_i)$ denotes indicator function which returns 1 if x_i belongs to component j, otherwise 0. The parameter θ is estimated by differentiating Eq. 6 with respect to θ such that maximum complete log-likelihood is achieved. The differentiation results into [16]:

$$\nabla F(\hat{\theta}_j) = \frac{1}{|C_j|} \sum_{x \in C_j} t(x). \qquad (7)$$

Now, the function F is differentiable and strictly convex. Therefore, its convex conjugate F^* using Legendre transform can be expressed as [16],

$$F^\star(\eta) = \sup_\theta \{\langle \theta, \eta \rangle - F(\theta)\}, \qquad (8)$$

where the maximum can be obtained by taking differentiation with respect to θ. That gives expression of $\eta = \nabla F(\theta)$. η represents expectation parameter [16].

The strictly convex and differentiable function F obeys Legendre duality. The Legendre duality states that first derivatives of function F and its convex conjugate F^* are inverse of each other i.e., $\nabla F = (\nabla F^*)^{-1}$ and $\nabla F^* = (\nabla F)^{-1}$. That gives the expression of $\theta = \nabla F^*(\theta)$. The Legendre duality can be used to convert between θ and η parameterization.

A Bregman divergence is a generic distance measure that works for any statistical distributions. There exist a bijection between Bregman divergence and exponential families given as [16]

$$\log p(x \mid \theta_j) = -B_{F^*}(t(x) : \eta_j) + k(x) + F^*(t(x)), \qquad (9)$$

where B_{F^*} is the Bregman divergence which can be expressed as

$$B_{F^*}(t(x_i) : \eta_j) = F^*(t(x_i)) - F^*(\eta_j) - \langle t(x_i) - \eta_j, (\nabla F^*)(\eta_j) \rangle. \qquad (10)$$

The complete log-likelihood function from Eq. 6 and Eq. 10 becomes [16]

$$\bar{l}' = \frac{1}{n} \sum_{i=1}^n \min_{j=1}^k (B_{F^*}(t(x_i) : \eta_j) - \log w_j). \qquad (11)$$

The Wishart distribution mentioned in Eq. 4 is also a member of exponential family. By converting it into canonical decomposition using Eq. 5 and using Legendre transform given in Eq. 8, the following parameters are derived:

- Sufficient statistics: $t(\mathbf{Z}) = -\mathbf{Z}$
- Natural parameter: $\Theta = n\mathbf{V}^{-1}$
- Carrier measure: $k(\mathbf{Z}) = (n-d)\log|\mathbf{Z}|$
- Log-normalizer: $F(\Theta) = -dn\log n + n\log\left|\frac{n}{\Theta}\right| + \log\Gamma_p(n)$
- Legendre dual log-normalizer: $F^*(\eta) = -n + dn\log n - n\log(-\eta) + \log\Gamma_p(n)$
- Gradient of log-normalizer: $\nabla F(\Theta) = -\frac{n}{\Theta}$
- Gradient of Legendre dual log-normalizer: $\nabla F^*(\eta) = -\frac{n}{\eta}$

Now, the unknown parameters component centers (i.e., $\mathbf{V}_1, \ldots, \mathbf{V}_K$) and weights (i.e., $\sigma_1, \ldots, \sigma_K$) for each class of WMM can be estimated using k-MLE algorithm [16]. Different initialization approaches can be embedded to k-MLE such as random, global K-means, and k-MLE++. The important steps of the proposed method are described as follows:

Step 1: Take training samples for each class based on ground truth labels.
Step 2: Choose number of mixture components K using elbow method [21].
Step 3: Initialize component centers for each class to initiate k-MLE as each class is following WMM. The centers are initialized using random, global K-means or k-MLE++. The weights are initialized as $1/K$ for random, or proportion of samples in resultant clusters for global K-means and k-MLE++ initialization.
Step 4: Execute k-MLE for each class to estimate the centers and weights.
Step 5: Perform classification of polarimetric SAR image with estimated parameters of WMM using the maximum a posteriori (MAP) criterion.

4   Experimental Results

In this section, the experimental results and analysis of the k-MLE algorithm along with different initialization approaches are discussed. The experiments are conducted on six full polarimetric SAR L-band datasets. The details of the datasets are mentioned in Table 1. The first five are benchmark datasets available publicly. Figure 1, 2, 3, 4 and 5 show their Pauli RGB and ground truth images. The Mysore dataset is obtained from SAC-ISRO. Its ground truth is generated manually. For that, the locations of places of interest are marked using a handheld GPS receiver by conducting a field visit in the same duration when the SAR image was obtained. A cloud-free Sentinel-2 optical image of the same duration is also obtained as shown in Fig. 6. Then, the ground truth is generated by constructing polygon masks over fields using the optical image and GPS placemark points.

The datasets are converted in $\mathbf{C}_3$ matrix format and processed with Lee Refined speckle filter using PolSARPro v6.0 (Biomass Edition) [20] software. Using ground truth, 10% randomly chosen samples from each class are selected as training set and the rest are selected as testing set. The WMM classifier is trained using k-MLE. Then it performs classification with estimated parameters using MAP criterion. The classification results and algorithm convergence are

Table 1. Details of the full polarimetric SAR datasets used in experiments

Name	Region	Sensor	Acquired on	Size	Classes
Flevoland15 [20]	Flevoland, Netherlands	AIRSAR	16 August, 1989	750 × 1024	15
Flevoland7 [2]	Flevoland, Netherlands	AIRSAR	16 June, 1991	750 × 700	7
SFRS2 [9]	San Francisco Bay, USA	RADARSAT-2	August, 1989	1800 × 1380	5
SFAIRSAR [9,20]	San Francisco Bay, USA	AIRSAR	9 April, 2008	900 × 1024	5
Landes [2]	Landes, France	AIRSAR	19 June, 1991	1050 × 1000	6
Mysore	Mysore, India	RADARSAT-2	29 August, 2017	3489 × 3352	11

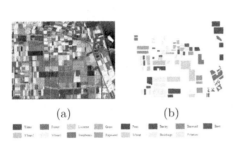

(a)   (b)

Fig. 1. Flevoland15: (a) Pauli RGB (b) Ground truth [6]

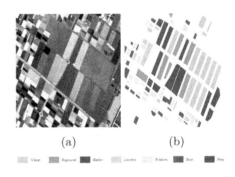

(a)   (b)

Fig. 2. Flevoland7: (a) Pauli RGB (b) Ground truth [6]

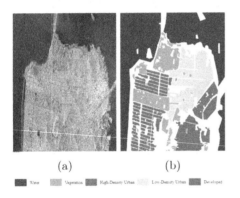

(a)   (b)

Fig. 3. SFRS2: (a) Pauli RGB (b) Ground truth [15]

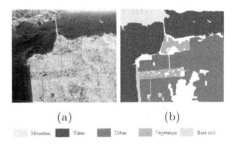

(a)   (b)

Fig. 4. SFAIRSAR: (a) Pauli RGB (b) Ground truth [15]

compared with the traditional EM algorithm. In the experiments, a fast version of global K-means proposed by Gadhiya et al. [6] is used. The experiments are conducted using a system having Microsoft Windows 10 Pro operating system (64-bit) with Intel Core i5-6200U CPU processor, and 8 GB RAM. All the algorithms are implemented using the Python programming language.

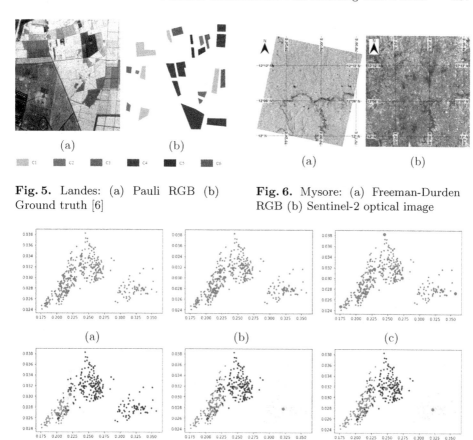

| | C1 | | C2 | | C3 | | C4 | | C5 | | C6 |

(a)   (b)

Fig. 5. Landes: (a) Pauli RGB (b) Ground truth [6]

Fig. 6. Mysore: (a) Freeman-Durden RGB (b) Sentinel-2 optical image

(a)   (b)   (c)

(d)   (e)   (f)

Fig. 7. Scatter plot (C_{11} vs. C_{22}) of Landes dataset ($C3$ class) with (a)–(c) depicts initialization of k-MLE using random, global K-means, and k-MLE++ respectively (blue dots are data points and red dots are initial points for k-MLE), and (d)–(f) are resultant clusters generated after executing k-MLE. (Color figure online)

Figure 7 shows initialization in k-MLE using random, global K-means, and k-MLE++, and its resultant clusters on $C3$ class of Landes dataset. The k-MLE uses hard membership assignment so the clusters are generated after execution of the algorithm. The random initialization selects points randomly considering uniformly distributed data. It may cause poor initialization as shown in Fig. 7(a) which further results into poor clusters using k-MLE as shown in Fig. 7(d). On the other hand, the global K-means tries to minimize the Wishart distance of all the data points to their cluster centers using global search. Then, the cluster centers are selected as initial points. Figure 7(b) shows the initialization using global K-means. The initial points are very close to the resultant cluster centers shown in Fig. 7(e). They are better than random initialization. The k-MLE++

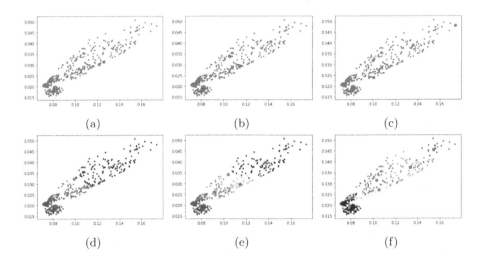

Fig. 8. Scatter plot ($\mathbf{C}_{11}$ vs. $\mathbf{C}_{22}$) of Landes dataset ($C5$ class) with (a)–(c) depicts initialization of k-MLE using random, global K-means, and k-MLE++ respectively (blue dots are data points and red dots are initial points for k-MLE), and (d)–(f) are resultant clusters generated after executing k-MLE. (Color figure online)

follows a different strategy. It chooses the first seed randomly. Then, for each data point, it computes the Bregman divergence from the nearest previously chosen seed. The probability of selecting the next seed from the data points is directly proportional to the Bregman divergence from its nearest previously chosen seed as described in [16]. Thus, it selects the farthest points with high probability. The same idea is depicted in Fig. 7(c). The resultant clusters are similar to the global K-means approach.

Figure 8 shows for the $C5$ class of the Landes dataset. The global K-means has better initialization approach than random. Hence, it generates better clusters than random. The k-MLE++ follows a farthest point selection strategy. It generates even better clusters than global K-means. The clusters are generated using k-MLE++ are in such a way that the data points are closer to their cluster centers than in global K-means as shown in Fig. 8. A similar thing has been observed for the $C6$ class as shown in Fig. 9. Here also the k-MLE++ gives better results than random and global K-means.

The WMM class-wise f1-score in percentage and overall accuracy (OA) comparing EM and k-MLE algorithm for each dataset are shown in Table 2, 3, 4 and 5. The comparison includes initialization using global K-means (GK-means) and k-MLE++ for k-MLE algorithm, and global K-means for EM algorithm. For the datasets except Flevoland15 and Mysore, the k-MLE with k-MLE++ performs slightly better than EM algorithm and global K-means initialization.

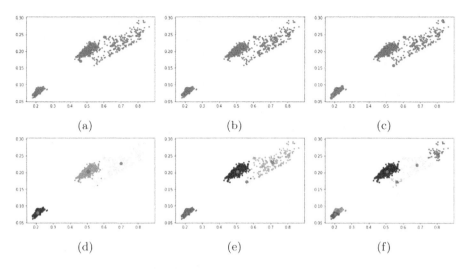

Fig. 9. Scatter plot ($\mathbf{C}_{11}$ vs. $\mathbf{C}_{22}$) of Landes dataset *C6* class with (a)–(c) depicts initialization of k-MLE using random, global K-means, and k-MLE++ respectively (blue dots are data points and red dots are initial points for k-MLE), and (d)–(f) are resultant clusters generated after executing k-MLE. (Color figure online)

Figure 10 shows the log-likelihood of EM and k-MLE algorithm up to 50 iterations for *Bare soil*, *Barley* and *Buildings* classes of Flevoland15 dataset. Here, the algorithm is said to be converged if there is not much change between the log-likelihood of consecutive iterations. In the experiments, if the change in log-likelihood is less than 0.001% of the initial log-likelihood then the algorithm is considered to be converged. Even though the classification accuracy of EM and k-MLE are almost equivalent, the k-MLE converges much faster than the EM algorithm. In the *Bare soil* case where the EM algorithm takes 25 iterations to converge, the k-MLE algorithm converges in 14 iterations. For *Barley* class, the EM algorithm takes 46 iterations, whereas k-MLE takes only 12 iterations. And for the *Buildings*, EM takes 14, whereas k-MLE takes 9 iterations. The log-likelihood of k-MLE is also better compared to the EM algorithm.

Table 8 shows the computational time required for training and testing of the Flevoland15 dataset using EM and k-MLE algorithms. The training time includes the time required to run EM or k-MLE algorithm and the time required to run the initialization algorithm. Testing time includes the time required to predict class labels of testing samples. The training time of k-MLE is much less compared to the EM algorithm for all the initialization approaches. The testing time remains the same (Table 8).

Table 2. Classification results (f1-score and overall accuracy) of Flevoland7 using EM and k-MLE algorithm with different initialization methods

Class label	EM	k-MLE	
	GK-means	GK-means	k-MLE++
Wheat	98.98	99.00	**99.14**
Rapeseed	**99.91**	**99.91**	99.90
Barley	99.39	99.41	**99.45**
Lucerne	94.97	94.77	**96.21**
Potatoes	**99.15**	**99.15**	99.14
Beat	96.99	96.94	**97.05**
Peas	92.87	**92.89**	92.68
OA	98.88	98.88	**98.98**

Table 3. Classification results (f1-score and overall accuracy) of Landes using EM and k-MLE algorithm with different initialization methods

Class label	EM	k-MLE	
	GK-means	GK-means	k-MLE++
C1	**84.41**	84.21	84.21
C2	79.98	79.81	**80.36**
C3	**97.62**	97.52	97.56
C4	97.31	97.43	**97.51**
C5	95.41	**95.54**	95.36
C6	**78.17**	77.78	77.60
OA	90.73	90.68	**90.74**

Table 4. Classification results (f1-score and overall accuracy) of Flevoland15 using EM and k-MLE algorithm with different initialization methods

Class label	EM	k-MLE	
	GK-means	GK-means	k-MLE++
Water	**99.21**	99.17	98.85
Forest	**91.95**	91.71	90.60
Lucerne	96.82	96.66	**97.14**
Grasses	**92.50**	92.44	92.11
Peas	**97.61**	97.60	97.54
Barley	**97.18**	**97.18**	96.93
BareSoil	**96.66**	96.49	95.48
Beat	94.73	94.85	**95.45**
Wheat2	**87.20**	86.96	86.75
Wheat3	**95.45**	95.42	95.21
Stembeans	97.19	97.10	**97.48**
Rapeseed	**87.46**	87.31	86.26
Wheat	**93.58**	93.40	93.27
Buildings	**80.80**	79.69	74.60
Potatoes	**90.61**	90.43	90.13
OA	**93.72**	93.61	93.32

Table 5. Classification results (f1-score and overall accuracy) of Mysore using EM and k-MLE algorithm with different initialization methods

Class label	EM	k-MLE	
	GK-means	GK-means	k-MLE++
Ragi	85.99	85.58	**87.68**
Ginger	**69.35**	68.69	67.02
Rice	96.50	**96.68**	95.61
Urban	96.53	96.45	**96.69**
Water	96.34	**96.68**	94.54
Arecanut	75.07	73.90	**77.44**
Banana	**61.25**	59.39	57.89
Sugarcane	76.70	76.56	**78.73**
Coconut	**84.13**	83.33	72.08
Fallow	51.61	53.44	**55.11**
Mgs. Mine	82.75	82.87	**85.06**
OA	92.63	**92.73**	91.75

Table 6. Classification results (f1-score and overall accuracy) of SFRS2 using EM and k-MLE algorithm with different initialization methods

Class label	EM	k-MLE	
	GK-means	GK-means	k-MLE++
Water	**99.85**	**99.85**	99.84
Vegetation	71.90	71.51	**72.98**
H.D. Urban	70.98	**71.25**	70.83
L.D. Urban	68.19	**68.40**	67.25
Developed	77.68	77.83	**78.03**
OA	85.54	85.54	**85.73**

Table 7. Classification results (f1-score and overall accuracy) of SFAIRSAR using EM and k-MLE algorithm with different initialization methods

Class label	EM	k-MLE	
	GK-means	GK-means	k-MLE++
Mountain	46.25	46.43	**60.47**
Water	96.01	96.00	**98.04**
Urban	92.53	92.57	**92.85**
Vegetation	61.39	61.67	**63.10**
Bare soil	82.21	**82.26**	80.97
OA	88.69	88.75	**90.58**

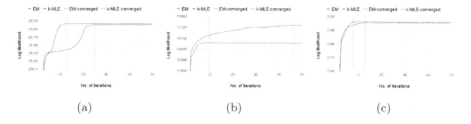

(a)   (b)   (c)

Fig. 10. Comparison of convergence rate using EM and k-MLE algorithms on Flevoland15 dataset of (a) Bare soil (b) Barley (c) Buildings

Table 8. Timing analysis of EM and k-MLE algorithm using Flevoland15 dataset

Algorithm	Initialization	Training (s)	Testing (s)
EM	Radom	38.34	1.18
	Global K-means	17.86	1.18
k-MLE	Random	1.96	1.18
	Global K-means	10.09	1.18
	k-MLE++	12.75	1.18

5 Conclusion

The classification of polarimetric SAR images having heterogeneous regions was performed using WMM. The k-MLE algorithm was employed for parameter learning in WMM and compared with the traditional EM algorithm. The k-MLE was found to converge computationally much faster than the EM algorithm. In the case of classification results, the overall accuracy of k-MLE was comparable to the EM algorithm. Among different initialization approaches, the k-MLE++ was found to generate better clusters and results in better classification accuracy for most of the datasets used in experiments.

References

1. Ahishali, M., Kiranyaz, S., Ince, T., Gabbouj, M.: Classification of polarimetric SAR images using compact convolutional neural networks. GISci. Remote Sens. **58**(1), 28–47 (2021). https://doi.org/10.1080/15481603.2020.1853948
2. ASF: Dataset: AIRSAR, NASA 1991. https://search.asf.alaska.edu/. Accessed ASF DAAC 09 April 2021
3. Couvreur, C.: The EM Algorithm: A Guided Tour, pp. 209–222. Birkhäuser Boston, Boston (1997). https://doi.org/10.1007/978-1-4612-1996-5_12
4. Dempster, A.P., Laird, N.M., Rubin, D.B.: Maximum likelihood from incomplete data via the EM algorithm. J. Roy. Stat. Soc. Ser. B (Methodol.) **39**(1), 1–22 (1977)
5. Freitas, C.C., Frery, A.C., Correia, A.H.: The polarimetric G distribution for SAR data analysis. Environmetrics Official J. Int. Environmetrics Soc. **16**(1), 13–31 (2005)
6. Gadhiya, T., Roy, A.K.: Superpixel-driven optimized Wishart network for fast polsar image classification using global k-means algorithm. IEEE Trans. Geosci. Remote Sens. **58**(1), 97–109 (2020). https://doi.org/10.1109/TGRS.2019.2933483
7. Gao, W., Yang, J., Ma, W.: Land cover classification for polarimetric SAR images based on mixture models. Remote Sens. **6**(5), 3770–3790 (2014). https://doi.org/10.3390/rs6053770
8. Hua, W., Xie, W., Jin, X.: Three-channel convolutional neural network for polarimetric SAR images classification. IEEE J. Sel. Top. Appl. Earth Observ. Remote Sens. **13**, 4895–4907 (2020). https://doi.org/10.1109/JSTARS.2020.3018161
9. IETR: San Francisco polarimetric SAR datasets (2019). https://ietr-lab.univ-rennes1.fr/polsarpro-bio/san-francisco/
10. Lee, J.S., Grunes, M.R., Kwok, R.: Classification of multi-look polarimetric SAR imagery based on complex Wishart distribution. Int. J. Remote Sens. **15**(11), 2299–2311 (1994). https://doi.org/10.1080/01431169408954244
11. Lee, J.S., Pottier, E.: Polarimetric Radar Imaging: From Basics to Applications. CRC Press, Boca Raton (2009)
12. Lee, J.S., Schuler, D.L., Lang, R.H., Ranson, K.J.: K-distribution for multi-look processed polarimetric SAR imagery. In: Proceedings of IGARSS 1994 - 1994 IEEE International Geoscience and Remote Sensing Symposium, vol. 4, pp. 2179–2181 (1994). https://doi.org/10.1109/IGARSS.1994.399685
13. Likas, A., Vlassis, N., Verbeek, J.J.: The global k-means clustering algorithm. Pattern Recogn. **36**(2), 451–461 (2003)
14. Liu, H., Luo, R., Shang, F., Meng, X., Gou, S., Hou, B.: Semi-supervised deep metric learning networks for classification of polarimetric SAR data. Remote Sens. **12**(10) (2020). https://www.mdpi.com/2072-4292/12/10/1593
15. Liu, X., Jiao, L., Liu, F.: PoLSF: PoLSAR image dataset on San Francisco. arXiv preprint arXiv:1912.07259 (2019)
16. Nielsen, F.: k-MLE: a fast algorithm for learning statistical mixture models. In: 2012 IEEE International Conference on Acoustics, Speech and Signal Processing (ICASSP), pp. 869–872 (2012). https://doi.org/10.1109/ICASSP.2012.6288022
17. Saint-Jean, C., Nielsen, F.: Hartigan's method for k-MLE: mixture modeling with Wishart distributions and its application to motion retrieval. In: Nielsen, F. (ed.) Geometric Theory of Information. SCT, pp. 301–330. Springer, Cham (2014). https://doi.org/10.1007/978-3-319-05317-2_11

18. Schwander, O., Nielsen, F.: Fast learning of gamma mixture models with k-MLE. In: Hancock, E., Pelillo, M. (eds.) Similarity-Based Pattern Recognition, pp. 235–249. Springer, Heidelberg (2013)
19. Schwander, O., Schutz, A.J., Nielsen, F., Berthoumieu, Y.: k-MLE for mixtures of generalized gaussians. In: Proceedings of the 21st International Conference on Pattern Recognition (ICPR2012), pp. 2825–2828 (2012)
20. STEP-ESA: Polsarpro v6.0 (biomass edition) toolbox. https://step.esa.int/main/toolboxes/polsarpro-v6-0-biomass-edition-toolbox/
21. The Scikit-YB developers: Elbow method - yellowbrick v1.2.1 documentation. https://www.scikit-yb.org/en/latest/api/cluster/elbow.html
22. Yang, W., Yang, X., Yan, T., Song, H., Xia, G.S.: Region-based change detection for polarimetric SAR images using Wishart mixture models. IEEE Trans. Geosci. Remote Sens. **54**(11), 6746–6756 (2016). https://doi.org/10.1109/TGRS.2016.2590145

Leveraging Discriminative Cues for Masked Face Recognition in Post COVID World

Hiren Pokar(✉), Nilay Patel, Himansh Mulchandani🆔, Ajitesh Singh, Rinkal Singh, and Chirag Paunwala🆔

Electronics and Communication Engineering Department, Sarvajanik College of Engineering and Technology, Surat, India
hirenpokar31072@gmail.com

Abstract. The post COVID world has completely disrupted our lifestyle, where wearing a mask is necessary to protect ourselves and others from contracting the virus. However, face masks have proved to be challenging for facial biometric systems, in the sense that these systems do not work as expected when wearing masks as nearly half of the face is covered, thus reducing discriminative features that the model can leverage. Most of the existing frameworks rely on the entire face as the input, but as the face is covered, these frameworks do not perform up to the mark. Moreover, training another facial recognition system with mask images is challenging as the availability of datasets is limited, both qualitatively and quantitatively. In this paper, we propose a framework that shows better results without significant training. In the proposed work, firstly we extracted the face using SSD, then by obtaining Facial Landmarks for utilizing the cues from other dis-criminative parts for facial recognition. The proposed framework is able to out-perform other frameworks on facial mask images and also found ~4.5% increment in accuracy.

Keywords: Single Shot Detector (SSD) · Multi-task learning · MTCNN · Mask removal · FaceNet

1 Introduction

The post COVID world has presented many challenges to our lives, especially with our routine tasks, where it's mandatory to wear masks before going to any public place among many others. Wearing a mask is necessary as it's the only way to protect us from contracting this deadly virus. However, wearing a mask is not very convenient, and it also challenges the biometric systems where facial recognition is utilized. Face recognition is one of the most reliable and efficient biometric authentication systems, as it is contactless and also works without any other manual input. Moreover; recent face recognition models have achieved real-time performance on smartphones, and hence it is one of the most widely used biometric authentication systems on smartphones, tablets, computers, and attendance systems of many institutions. However, these systems have been challenged in the post COVID world, as wearing a mask hides a lot of the discriminative information which is leveraged by such systems.

© The Author(s), under exclusive license to Springer Nature Switzerland AG 2022
B. Raman et al. (Eds.): CVIP 2021, CCIS 1567, pp. 294–305, 2022.
https://doi.org/10.1007/978-3-031-11346-8_26

Existing frameworks such as A Rai [11] is not accurate in the case of masked images as their model has been trained on images of full face, and hence masks hide the discriminative information. Face recognition is especially tough to train, as it not only requires huge datasets, but also lots of computing power like heavy performance GPUs. Hence, training the existing frameworks for mask faced images would pose the following challenges.

1. Availability of datasets. Most of the facial recognition datasets that are available do not have mask images MTFL (Multi-Task Facial Landmark) [5] (or any standard dataset like LFW (Labelled Faces in the Wild) or YTF (YouTube Faces dataset), and the datasets that have mask images either have overlaid the mask artificially using some image processing algorithm or have a limited number of mask images. This wouldn't reflect the real-world distribution, and hence even after training, the performance of the model may not be up to the mask.
2. Availability of computing power. Most of the architectures and datasets of face recognition algorithms are gigantic, and hence require a lot of computing power. Not only compute power, but also it requires days and months of training and testing.

Hence, in this paper, a method is proposed which overcomes the above limitations and utilizes the existing frameworks and information to effectively recognize masked face images. For most of the framework, the existing models have been used, hence effectively proving the aforementioned claim. The entire framework works in three stages:

1. Masked face detection.
2. Landmark localization.
3. Masked face recognition (using the discriminative parts only).

2 Related Work

We have divided related work in to mainly two subparts based on study: Face Detection and Face Recognition.

Face Detection: To make a robust face recognition system, the problem of face detection should be addressed first. DLib frontal face detector [21] uses the Histogram of Oriented Gradients (HOG) to extract features, which are then processed through a Support Vector Machine (SVM). Here, the distribution of gradient directions is used as a feature. Furthermore, DLib offers a more sophisticated CNN-based face detector, which does not operate in real-time when run on CPUs, which is one of our primary goals [22]. Haar Cascades based algorithm was proposed by Viola-Jones [15] in 2001 and it extracts features from images. The best features are then selected via Adaboost. This reduces the original features approximately three times. But applying all these features in a sliding window will consume a lot of time and the accuracy of this detector in occluded environments is not appreciable. In addition to detecting the face, MTCNN based technique proposed by Zhang [3] also detects five key points, i.e., facial landmarks. It utilizes a cascade structure with three stages of CNN. Single Shot Detector (SSD) [8] is a Caffe model which uses ResNet-10 as its backbone for face detection. It is faster than all mentioned above but it has more false-positive rates. Multitask cascaded neural network (MTCNN) face detection is widely adopted because of its robustness and fast detection rate. It has also been used in FaceNet [1].

Face Recognition: From an early age, face recognition has always been one of the most researched topic in computer vision. Since the past two decades, face recognition has evolved from early Geometric and Holistic based approaches [9, 14, 15] to the current Deep learning methods such as [1, 6]. FaceNet [1] has shown remarkable improvement and performance compared to other existing algorithms and has achieved state-of-the-art results in the many benchmark face recognition datasets such as Labelled Faces in the Wild [18] and YouTube Face Database [19]. Its architecture is adopted by many proposed methods such as [10, 11] for embedding generation. As in the method proposed by Aashish et al. [11], faces were extracted by MTCNN [3] and are fed to the FaceNet model for generating embedding, and then these generated embeddings are compared with embeddings of images stored in the database. They have boosted the accuracy by increasing the dataset by little data augmentation and extra padding. But this kind of approach does not work well on a person wearing a mask. To increase the recognition rate on mask images method such as MaskTheFace [10] is a tool proposed to mask faces effectively to create large datasets of masked faces, which can be utilized to train an effective facial recognition system with accurate masked face recognition. For the FaceNet system, they saw a 38 percent increase in true positive rate.

3   Proposed Work

This section introduces proposed model which includes Single-shot face detector, Facial Landmark Localization, Mask Removal and Embedding generation. The Block diagram is shown in Fig. 2.

3.1   Single Shot Detection

Images captured from cameras most likely have background along with the face, which is unnecessary and non-discriminative. Most of the face recognition algorithms eliminate the background in order to enhance the performance of face recognition algorithms, and hence, in the proposed framework, we use SSD [8] which has been trained for detecting faces. This is essential so that after face detection, landmarks can be detected, and finally face recognition can be performed. Out of the many existing face detectors, SSD stood out for giving the best performance based on speed and occlusions (i.e., face covered by the mask). As MTCNN delivers state of art performance and it is being widely adopted for face detection, we tried to compare its performance with SSD. SSD has a similar architecture as YOLO which makes it much faster, for which it is able to deliver real-time performance [8]. Based on the inference time, SSD processes on average 22 Frames Per Second (FPS) on Intel i5 10th Gen processor, and for the same hardware specification

MTCNN processes over 15 FPS. However, MTCNN isn't as accurate as SSD when the face is covered with mask. From randomly picked 200 images of faces with masks, MTCNN was able to detect faces with accuracy of ~95.5% whereas SSD detected faces with an accuracy of ~99.5%. Figure 1 shows some examples of face images covered with mask.

Fig. 1. Masked face Images where MTCNN didn't detect the faces

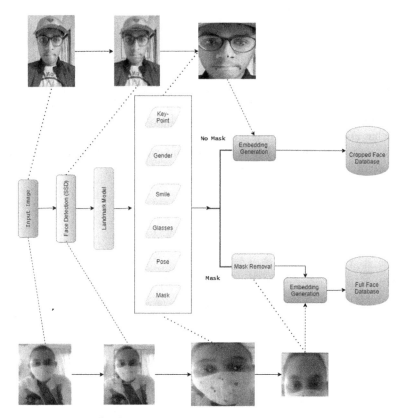

Fig. 2. Block diagram of proposed framework

3.2 Facial Landmark Localization with Mask Recognition

As the SSD detector only predicts the bounding box of the face, rather than the facial landmarks, in proposed algorithm lightweight model is used to detect the landmarks of the face. This landmark model is an essential part of this framework because, in order to extract the discriminative part of the face, that is, eyes along with the forehead, it is important to detect landmarks. The algorithm needs to take the discriminative parts into account only when facial features are covered with some non-facial objects such as masks which can lead to false predictions. Therefore, it is also necessary to detect the mask beforehand.

As shown in [5], facial landmark detection is not a standalone problem, when it is trained along with some related auxiliary tasks such as smile, gender, glasses, and pose then it performs reasonably well compared to training it with a single task. The intuition behind multi-task learning is that the neural net learns complex correlation between the auxiliary task and main task which lets the model develop a more general intuition of the main task (e.g., a smiling face obviously will have wider lips than not a smiling face). Thus, by using the same idea of multi-task learning, we can fulfill two tasks using a single network: the first is landmark detection and the second is mask detection. In complex scenarios, such as where the subject may be smiling, the difference between the eye key points and mouth landmark may vary, and hence, it is important to determine if the subject is smiling, and hence, smiling is used as an auxiliary task. Moreover, it is also important to find the pose of the subject, as based on the pose, the position of landmarks may change significantly. Hence by using auxiliary tasks such as smile, pose detection, the performance on primary task, that is, landmark detection is improved. Lastly, mask detection has also been added to this framework, as it can help in determining the parts of face to use for recognition, that is forehead and eyes in case of masked face or full face in case of non-masked face (Fig. 3).

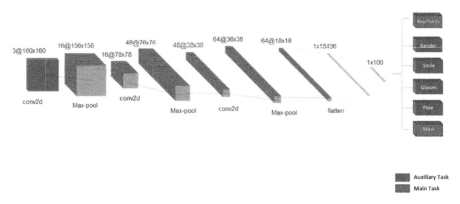

Fig. 3. Architecture of multi task face landmark model

The proposed work is extension of the model [5] with a separate output layer for Mask detection. Primary tasks are localization of 5-landmark (left eye, right eye, left lip, right lip and nose) and mask detection & auxiliary tasks are smile, gender, glasses and pose so in total the model has six output layers for each task. Each task has a different loss function and specified weightage which simply is the amount of contribution in learning the parameters. The weightage of each loss is decided based on the importance of task with respect to the primary task, and hence smile and pose have a higher weightage compared to other tasks. Moreover, multiple experiments were conducted to determine the best suitable weights, and the weights presented in the table were the best outcome. Model takes a 160×160 RGB image as an input and predicts all 6 tasks based on the input. The first output layer is a landmark localization task, it outputs 10 values where the first 5 values are x-coordinate and the rest are y-coordinate. It's a regression problem so the Mean Square Error (MSE) Eq. (1) is used for calculating loss. Last output layer which holds mask detection task, as it is a binary classification problem (mask/no mask), loss would be better written in binary cross-entropy Eq. (6). All auxiliary tasks are briefed in Table 1 and all the parameters related to them are kept the same as in [5]. Final objective loss Eq. (7) formed by combining losses from each task multiplied with its weightage, for computing gradients to update learning parameters.

Table 1. Loss function used for various tasks and their respective weightage.

Task	Loss function	Loss equation	Weightage
Landmark detection	Mean square error	$L_l(y) = \frac{1}{N}\sum_{i=1}^{N}\sum_{j=1}^{10}\|x_j^{[i]} - \hat{x}_j^{[i]}\|^2$ (1)	7
Smiling/or not	Binary cross-entropy	$L_s(y) = -\frac{1}{N}\sum_{i=1}^{N}x^{[i]}.\log\left(\hat{x}^{[i]}\right) + \left(1 - x^{[i]}\right).\log\left(1 - \hat{x}^{[i]}\right)$ (2)	3
Gender (M/F)	Binary cross-entropy	$L_g(y) = -\frac{1}{N}\sum_{i=1}^{N}x^{[i]}.\log\left(\hat{x}^{[i]}\right) + \left(1 - x^{[i]}\right).\log\left(1 - \hat{x}^{[i]}\right)$ (3)	2
Wearing Glasses	Binary cross-entropy	$L_{gl}(y) = -\frac{1}{N}\sum_{i=1}^{N}x^{[i]}.\log\left(\hat{x}^{[i]}\right) + \left(1 - x^{[i]}\right).\log\left(1 - \hat{x}^{[i]}\right)$ (4)	1
Pose ($-60°$ to $+60°$)	Categorical cross-entropy	$L_p(y) = -\frac{1}{N}\sum_{i=1}^{N}\sum_{c=1}^{5}x_c^{[i]}.\log(\hat{x}_c^{[i]})$ (5)	3
Wearing Mask/or not	Binary cross-entropy	$L_m(y) = -\frac{1}{N}\sum_{i=1}^{N}x^{[i]}.\log\left(\hat{x}^{[i]}\right) + \left(1 - x^{[i]}\right).\log\left(1 - \hat{x}^{[i]}\right)$ (6)	5

$$L(y) = 7L_l(y) + 3L_s(y) + 2L_g(y) + 1L_{gl}(y) + 3L_p(y) + 5L_m(y) \qquad (7)$$

For training we used Adam (Adaptive Moment Estimation) as the optimizer because its adaptive moment feature converges model faster to local minima [20]. The method is efficient when working with large problems involving a lot of data or parameters as it requires less memory. We kept batch size as 64 and number of epochs to 40 to prevent model to be over fitted. The model is trained with the dataset size of 10,000 with 9000 training images and 1000 validation images on a NVIDIA GPU GeForce GTX 1660Ti. After the training, obtained mask detection accuracy is 99.87% on training data and 93.23% on validation data. The proposed model becomes better with mask detection as well as helped to decrease loss of landmark detection tasks. The MSE loss for landmark detection task was found to be less than 3.19 units when it is trained with mask detection. Figure 4 shows training and validation losses.

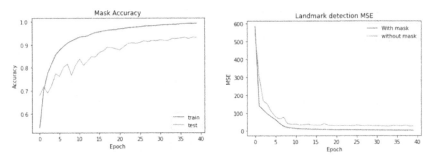

Fig. 4. Training and validation graphs of Mask classification accuracy and Face Landmark Detection MSE respectively.

3.3   Mask the Dataset

To train the multi-task facial landmark detection model for mask recognition, we need to synthetically "mask" the images, as the provided dataset does not have masked faces. 68 facial coordinates using dlib landmark detector [21] are extracted for this task. Once 68 landmarks are detected, masks to the corresponding points of interest are added. For this, the mask images need to be annotated such that the key points on the mask match the key points of the mouth and region beyond that. Hence, in the proposed work 27 out of 68 facial landmarks from the face are extracted. This is because, the keypoints of eyes are irrelevant. Now, the key points on the mask and face image are matched, and mask image is appended to face image using transformation matrix. Here, the 3×3 transformation matrix is computed by finding the homographic relation between facial key points and mask keypoint. Then using this transformation matrix, mask image is transformed as per the face alignment and the transformed-mask image is then stitched onto the face image over the face. This process has been illustrated in Fig. 5.

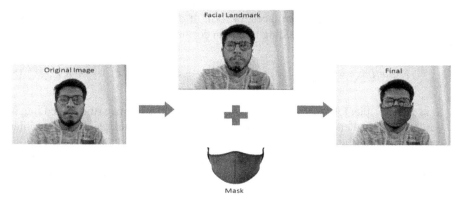

Fig. 5. Adding mask to the original image without mask.

3.4 Mask Removal

Decision of mask removal through cropping is based on whether the person is wearing a mask. This is to ensure fewer false recognition rates for e.g., if a person wears a particular-colored mask, and if a different person happens to wear that same type of mask, the model will predict both as the same person. So, to avoid such behavior in the model, we have cropped the image below the nose which eliminates most of the mask. Using the nose coordinate obtained from the facial landmark model, mask region can be cropped. However, in case of person not wearing mask, the features of entire face has been extracted as it can lead to more accurate predictions. Therefore, a person wearing a mask follows the normal flow without face cropping. Figure 6 illustrates the mask removal in case of a person wearing mask.

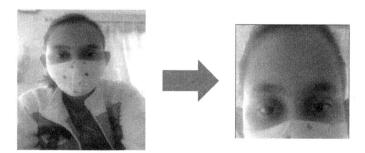

Fig. 6. Mask removal in the input image.

3.5 Embedding Generation

FaceNet [1] is a face recognition system developed by researchers at Google that achieved state-of-the-art results on a wide range of face recognition datasets. It can be used to extract high-quality features from faces, in form of embedding, which can be used to identify faces with similar embedding based on cosine distance.

$$TripletLoss = \sum_{i}^{N} \left[\left\| f\left(x_i^{\alpha}\right) - f\left(x_i^{P}\right) \right\|_2^2 - \left\| f\left(x_i^{\alpha}\right) - f\left(x_i^{P}\right) \right\|_2^2 + \alpha \right] \qquad (8)$$

It uses the Triplet loss function consisting of aspects like Positive (the embedding of the same faces is called positives), Negative (the embedding of different faces is called negatives), Anchor (the face being analysed is called the anchor). The learning objective is to minimize the distance between an anchor and positive and maximize the distance between the anchor and negative of the person with the other embedding. In proposed work, 128-dimensional embedding for both cropped face database as well as full face database is generated. The newly generated embedding are used as feature vectors, then they are fed to the FaceNet model for recognition and verification based on defined threshold value. After storing the embedding, we implement the full code. When any person faces the camera with or without mask, the proposed algorithm starts generating the final embedding and comparing it with other embedding from the dataset. The person with the lowest cosine distance is then recognized.

4   Results

For a thorough evaluation of our recognition algorithm on out-of-distribution and real-world data, a dataset known as ECE 2017 (As there are not many open source dataset containing faces covered with mask of individual person, and for these we have formed our own ECE 2017 dataset) is created of 13 people with 15 images of each person. Out of them, 10 images are without mask faces and the rest 5 images are with mask. In proposed work, the Masked Face Recognition Dataset [2] is also used in which three types of masked face datasets are involved: (i) Masked Face Detection Dataset (MFDD), (ii) Real-world Masked Face Recognition Dataset (RMFRD) and (iii) Simulated Masked Face Recognition Dataset (SMFRD).

The proposed model is evaluated on the Masked Face Recognition dataset [2] and ECE 2017 dataset and recorded the recognition accuracy of 96.01% and 99.23% respectively. The proposed algorithm is compared with the existing face-recognition algorithm Ashish et al. [11] and found ~4.5% increment in accuracy with proposed approach as shown in Table 2.

Table 2. Model accuracy on Face Recognition

Dataset	Existing framework [11]	Proposed framework
Masked Face Recognition dataset [2]	92.55%	96.012%
ECE 2017 dataset	96.23%	99.23%

Cases where Aashish et al. [11] approach fails to obtain correct output are highlighted in Table 3. Main reason of failure is due to MTCNN used for face detection which is not able to detect faces in case of occlusion or masked faces. While in proposed model, SSD is used as a face detection model which is faster and more accurate in detecting masked face images. As shown, in the first and third images from the Table 3, Aashish et al. approach fails due to the occlusion by mask while using discriminative approach we tend to compare only useful features which leads to increase the recognition performance.

Table 3. Comparison of proposed framework with framework proposed by Aashish et al.

Person Image	Person identity	Ashish et al [11] predictions	Our model predictions
	X	Y	X
	A	Face not detected	A
	B	C	B
	A	Face not detected	A

Figure 7 illustrates the working of framework throughout all stages, i.e. Face Detection (Red Bounding Box), Landmark Localization (Green dots) and Face Recognition (Name written in Blue).

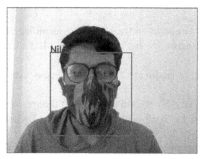 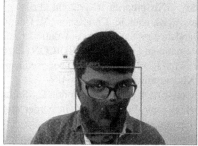

Fig. 7. Output of all stages. (Color figure online)

## 5	Conclusion

Considering the limitations of existing methods, we proposed a framework which overcomes the limitations of existing frameworks, without retraining the model extensively. Based on the results, the proposed framework is objectively better than the other frameworks, and hence it can be concluded that removing the non-discriminative parts and retaining the few discriminatory parts can still be leveraged for face recognition. In proposed work, dataset is synthetically generated, it could not reflect the real-world distribution and hence the performance, although good, could have still been better on real world images. A future direction of this work could be to aggregate more naturally generated images and train the model, which may lead to better results.

References

1. Schroff, F., Kalenichenko, D., Philbin, J.: Facenet: a unified embedding for face recognition and clustering. In: Proceedings of the IEEE Conference on Computer Vision and Pattern Recognition, pp. 815–823 (2015)
2. Wang, Z., Wang, G., Huang, B., Xiong, Z.: Masked face recognition dataset and application. arXiv preprintarXiv:2003.09093
3. Xiang, J., Zhu, G.: Joint face detection and facial expression recognition with MTCNN. In: 2017 4th International Conference on Information Science and Control Engineering (ICISCE), Changsha, pp. 424–427 (2017)
4. Daniel, S.T., Li, M., Margaret, H.: Face recognition: from traditional to deep learning methods. arXiv preprint arXiv:1811.00116
5. Zhang, Z., Luo, P., Loy, C.C., Tang, X.: Facial landmark detection by deep multi-task learning. In: Fleet, D., Pajdla, T., Schiele, B., Tuytelaars, T. (eds.) ECCV 2014. LNCS, vol. 8694, pp. 94–108. Springer, Cham (2014). https://doi.org/10.1007/978-3-319-10599-4_7
6. Elmahmudi, A., Ugail, H.: Deep face recognition using imperfect facial data. Future Gener. Comput. Syst. **99**, 213–225 (2019). ISSN 0167-739X
7. Li, F.-F., Fergus, R., Perona, P.: One-shot learning of object categories. IEEE Trans. Pattern Anal. Mach. Intell. **28**(4), 594–611 (2006)
8. Liu, W., Anguelov, D.: SSD: Single Shot MultiBox Detector. UNC-Chapel Hill, Zoox Inc., Google Inc, University of Michigan, Ann-Arbor. arXiv preprint arXiv:1512.02325
9. Singh, S., Singh, D., Yadav, V.: Face recognition using HOG feature extraction and SVM classifier. **8**, 6437–6440 (2020). https://doi.org/10.30534/ijeter/2020/244892020
10. Anwar, A.: Raychowdhury, A.: Masked Face Recognition for Secure Authentication. Department of Electrical and Computer Engineering, Georgia Institute of Technology, Atlanta, GA, USA. arXiv preprint arXiv:2008.11104
11. Rai, A., Karnani, R., Chudasama, V., Upla, K.: An end-to-end real-time face identification and attendance system using convolutional neural networks. In: 2019 IEEE 16th India Council International Conference (INDICON) (2019)
12. Thewlis, J., Albanie, S.: Unsupervised learning of landmarks by descriptor vector exchange. arXiv preprint arXiv:1908.06427
13. Thenuwara, S.S., Premachandra, C., Sumathipala, S.: Hybrid approach to face recognition system using PCA & LDA in border control. In: 2019 National Information Technology Conference (NITC) (2019)
14. Kanade, T.: Picture processing by computer complex and recognition of human faces. Ph.D. thesis, Kyoto University (1973)

15. Tikoo, S., Malik, N.: Detection of Face using Viola-Jones and Recognition Using Back Propagation Neural Network. Department of Electrical and Electronics and Communication Engineering, The NorthCap University, Gurgaon. arXiv Preprint arXiv:1701.08257
16. Szegedy, C., et al.: Going deeper with convolutions. In: Proceedings of the IEEE Conference on Computer Vision and Pattern Recognition, pp.1–9 (2015)
17. Yang, W., Jiachun, Z.: Real-time face detection based on YOLO. In: 2018 1st IEEE International Conference on Knowledge Innovation and Invention (ICKII), pp. 221–224 (2018)
18. Balaban, S.: Deep learning and face recognition: the state of the art. arXiv preprint arXiv: 1902.03524
19. Ferrari, C., Berretti, S., Del Bimbo, A.: Extended YouTube faces: a dataset for heterogeneous open-set face identification. IN: 2018 24th International Conference on Pattern Recognition (ICPR), pp. 3408–3413 (2018)
20. Kingma, D.P., Ba, J.L.: Adam: a method for stochastic optimization. arXiv preprint arXiv: 1412.6980
21. Hearst, M.A., Dumais, S.T., Osuna, E., Platt, J., Scholkopf, B.: Support vector machines. In: IEEE Intelligent Systems and Their Applications, vol. 13, no. 4, pp. 18–28 July–August 1998. https://doi.org/10.1109/5254.708428
22. King, D.E.: Max-margin object detection. arXiv abs/1502.00046 (2015)

Pretreatment Identification of Oral Leukoplakia and Oral Erythroplakia Metastasis Using Deep Learning Neural Networks

Rinkal Shah[✉] and Jyoti Pareek

Department of Computer Science, Gujarat University, Ahmedabad, Gujarat 380009, India
{rinkalshah,jspareek}@gujaratuniversity.ac.in

Abstract. Without a doubt, Oral cancer is one of the malignancies worldwide which need to be diagnosed as early as possible because if not detected at early stage, the prognosis remains ineffective and can cause irreversible damage when diagnosed at advanced stages. Researchers have worked many years with Biopsy, Computerized Tomography (CT), and Magnetic Resonance Imaging (MRI) images for the precise identification. With the advancement of Medical Imaging, Machine Learning, and Deep Learning, early detection and stratification of oral cancer is possible. In this research, we have designed a Convolution Neural Network (CNN) model to classify oral cancer types: Leukoplakia and Erythroplakia on 550 oral images taken by the camera. We have trained our network with a Training-Validation ratio of 50–50%, 75–25%, and 80–20% on 20, 50, and 80 epochs. The comparative analysis has been performed using the precision, recall, f1-score, and confusion matrix. The highest accuracy achieved is of 83.54% with 0.87 f1-score for Leukoplakia and 0.78 f1-score for Erythroplakia. The proposed model accuracies were then compared with five different pre-defined architectures of CNN (VGG16, ResNet-50, Xception, EfficientNetB4, InceptionResNetV2).

Keywords: Oral cancer · Leukoplakia · Erythroplakia · Convolution Neural Network (CNN) · VGG16 · Residual Network (ResNet) · Xception · EfficientNet · InceptionRestNet

1 Introduction

Cancers related to Oral Cavity are increasing at an alarming rate all over the globe. It is one of the leading origins of death in India. Oral cancer is a disease that causes the complex process of uncontrolled and abnormal growth of cells in the mouth, initially a painless swollen white patch, then gradually transforms into a red patch. To avoid its conversion into head and neck cancer sub-type, it should be diagnosed and treated early. It spreads not only in the surrounding tissue with the potential to invade other parts of the body and proliferation through the blood vessels but also leads to non-healing ulceration. It causes lump formation over the lips, tongue, or floor of the mouth and on the surface of the hard and soft palate, cheeks, sinuses, and pharynx (throat). Several factors affect this type of pathology, including lack of self-care, unhealthy eating habits,

B. Raman et al. (Eds.): CVIP 2021, CCIS 1567, pp. 306–315, 2022.
https://doi.org/10.1007/978-3-031-11346-8_27

delayed professional assistance, ignorance or unnoticed lesions, history or hereditary incidence of oral cancer, tobacco use, snuff, and regular drinking of alcohol. Even direct access to the sun for a longer duration may increase the chances of lip cancer [1]. In men, the risk of developing oral cancer is twice more than in women, especially men over 50, who face the highest risk. As per recent estimates, nearly 3.50 billion people are affected by oral diseases worldwide. Over 530 million children face dental caries of primary teeth [2]. Around 657,000 new cases of oral cavity and pharynx cancers are found each year, and more than 330,000 deaths globally based on WHO records [3]. Oral cancer accounts for around 30% of all cancers in India. As per Global Cancer Statistics (2018) estimates, 1,19,992 new cases and 72,616 deaths in India are reported each year due to these types of cancers [4]. Benign growths are the primary phase of cancer that neither affect other tissues nor spread to other parts of the body. Pre-cancerous conditions called dysplasia are harmless growths that can turn into cancer over the period where Cancer tumors are abnormal growths that can spread into nearby tissues and to other body parts [5].

1.1 Oral Cancer Types

Oral Squamous Cell Carcinoma (OSCC) forms almost 90% of the total oral cancers, where the throat and mouth are lined with squamous cells, and this cancer can develop when squamous cells mutate and become abnormal. The sign of such abnormality can be seen as a white and red patch inside the mouth and lips. 5% of tumors are Verrucous Carcinoma (VC) which grows slowly and rarely spreads but may invade nearby tissues. While Minor salivary gland carcinomas may develop on minor salivary glands located throughout the lining of the throat and mouth, Lymphoma may develop in lymph tissue. Benign oral cavity tumors include different types of tumors like Fibroma, Leiomyoma, Papilloma, Rhabdomyoma, and many more may develop in the oropharynx and oral cavity. Leukoplakia and Erythroplakia cancers are abnormal cells that may develop in the mouth and throat. 25% of Leukoplakia become pre-cancerous while 70% of Erythroplakia are cancerous. Erythroleukoplakia is a patch with both red and white areas [6]. The chronic disease of the oral cavity that may arise by inflammation and progressive fibrosis of the submucosal tissues is known as Oral Submucous Fibrosis (OSF). This cancer leads to rigidity and eventually the inability to open the mouth [7].

With the remarkable advancement in computer-aided techniques, Deep Learning (DL) plays a vital role in Medical Science. Upgrading from the traditional methods, quick analysis, and diagnosis of cancers could be possible using DL. It can learn from the data which are used as an input. Convolution Neural Network is the most successful method of DL for analysis in the medical field. CNN extracts the features from the input dataset and trains the model that can be used to classify oral cancers [8]. The vision of this research is to classify oral cancer into Leukoplakia or Erythroplakia subtypes. We have used an approach of Deep Learning to classify pre-cancerous images into either Leukoplakia or Erythroplakia. The model has been developed, and the performance is measured in terms of accuracy, precision, recall, f1-score, and confusion matrix.

2 Literature Review

Over the past many years, various researches have been conducted the study, to detect oral cancers based on different inputs such as clinical information of patients, biopsy images, pap-spear microscopic images, CT, and MRI images. Most of the explorations using various Deep Neural Networks get through Oral Squamous Cell Carcinoma (OSCC), Oral Potentially Malignant Disease (OPMD), and early detection of oral cancers with the help of medical images. Decision Support System (DSS) for detecting Oral Squamous Cell Carcinoma (OSCC) has been developed by N. Kripa et al. with an accuracy of 90% using Feedforward Neural Network (FNN) in MATLAB on histopathology images [9]. Qiuyun Fu et al. have taken into consideration the Biopsy-proven and clinical photographic images and calculated Receiver Operating Characteristic (ROC) curve to evaluate deep learning algorithm results from which they differentiated Oral Cavity Squamous Cell Carcinoma (OCSCC) lesions from around five thousand different photographs of oral cancer patients collected from various hospitals and reported 95% of Area under the curve (AUC) [10]. Taking samples of biopsy is a painful process and needs high-definition tools to take images. The study of differentiating healthy cells and tumor cells using an oral dataset is taken place by Hakan Wieslander et al. from pap-smear microscopic images. By applying different CNN layers with the VGG network and ResNet, the accuracy range received between 84% to 86% with 5-fold evaluation [11]. Research in the latest time, Bibek Goswami et al. have implemented CNN to detect the normal and different stages of oral submucous fibrosis from microscopic images of stained biopsy samples collected from the oral department and pictures taken by a microscope, he got an overall accuracy of 99.4%. The dataset consisted of 100 images [12].

Evolving modality of Deep Learning, Three-dimensional Convolutional Neural networks (3DCNN), has been applied on CT images to detect oral cancer at the early stage [13]. Multi-class classification of Oral Squamous Cell Carcinoma (OSCC) also has been performed by Navarun Das et al. on an oral biopsy image and applied CNN model followed by transfer learning. They have used pre-trained networks such as Alexnet, VGG-16, VGG-19, and Resnet-50 with multiple layers and compared with the proposed CNN model having an accuracy of 96.6% for 50 epochs [14].

Bofan Song et al. have used auto-fluorescence, white light imaging, and hybrid dual-model imaging techniques to detect oral cancer. Firstly, they have collected images with the help of an external peripheral intraoral attachment LED with the android phone, and MatConNet (an open-source toolbox) is utilized with a small number of images (191 patients). They even applied transfer learning and data augmentation of the VGG-CNN-M module with 4-fold cross-validation and achieved 86.9% accuracy to detect "Normal" or "Oral Potentially Malignant Lesions (OPML)" [15].

Rajaram Anantharaman et al. limited their scope to cold sore and canker sore, which are types of oral implications caused by Herpes Simplex Virus Type 1 (HSV-1). The images they have collected are from the public domain and are also limited to 40 only. They applied the Mask-RCNN model developed in 2017, extended the Faster-RCNN model for semantic segmentation, and achieved pixel accuracy of 74% [16].

The data utilized by most of the researchers here are medical images. Still, Haron et al. [17] initiated reviewing of mobile phone images. They compared it with the clinical diagnosis made by specialists, which was then further extended by Roshan Alex and his co-mates by using the Bounding Box Method on a combination of annotation from multiple clinicians by generating composite annotation, additionally applied transfer learning on various images to detect Oral Cancer and Oral Potentially Malignant Disease (OPMD) and got promising results of F1-score with ResNet-101 as 87.07% and object detection with Recurrent CNN (R-CNN) with 41.18% [18].

From the research, we can conclude that most researchers have focused on the primary identification of type Oral Squamous Cell Carcinoma (OSCC), Oral Potentially Malignant Disease (OPMD) and Oral Submucous Fibrosis (OSF). In the proposed work, we have focused mainly on Leukoplakia and Erythroplakia. These are oral cancers where abnormal cells develop in the mouth and throat. 25% of Leukoplakia become precancerous, which may develop white patches inside the significant areas of the mouth, while Erythroplakia is more serious, having red patches.

3 Proposed Work

We have collected the images of Leukoplakia (See Fig. 1(A))) and Erythroplakia (See Fig. 1(B)), distributed them into two sets (Training and Testing), trained using the CNN model, and subsequently described the data into 1. Data preparation 2. Model Training and 3. Results and Discussion.

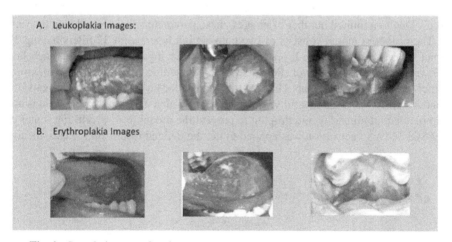

Fig. 1. Sample images of oral cancer types (A) Leukoplakia and (B) Erythroplakia

3.1 Data Preparation

The World Wide Web is the source for images of Leukoplakia and Erythroplakia. These two variants of pre-cancerous anomalies, white patches (Leukoplakia) and red patches (Erythroplakia), develop inside the oral cavity. (**Note:** The keywords used to find the related images were: "Leukoplakia", "White oral lesions", "Early Leukoplakia", "Oral Leukoplakia on the tongue", "Oral Leukoplakia on teeth", "Oral Leukoplakia on the jaw", "Erythroplakia", "Red oral lesions", "Early Erythroplakia" "Oral Erythroplakia on the tongue", "Oral Erythroplakia on teeth" and "Oral Erythroplakia on the jaw".) 1200 photographs were collected of both types, later discarded blurred and poor-quality images. Approximately 550 pictures were stream lined for the model. These photographs were further divided into 80% training and 20% testing sets. The training set comprises of 237 Leukoplakia and 234 Erythroplakia images, while the testing set contains 53 Leukoplakia and 26 Erythroplakia pictures. The validation set includes split values of 0.2, 0.3, and 0.4 splits.

3.2 Model Training

The proposed CNN architecture (See Fig. 2) training is explained as follows:

All experiments to create a CNN model from scratch were done using Python programming language on a Windows system using an ANACONDA platform with an intel core i5 processor and 8GB RAM. Open-source libraries like Keras with TensorFlow were used as a backend to implement a deep learning framework. The images have been scaled down to 1/255 using ImageDataGenerator, in view of time-consuming high-resolution image training. Data augmentation has been used to train the model with a better understanding of pixels and to overcome the problem of "overfitting". The parameters for Data Augmentation have been set to rotation range as 30°, shear and zoom range as 0.15, width and height shift range is 0.2 with horizontal and vertical flips as "true". Due to a limited number of images, these parameters were found conclusive.

The proposed model consists of two convolution layers with 32 filters having 3*3 kernel size, two convolution layers with 64 filters having 3*3 kernel size, each layer followed by max-pooling layer (Pool size 2*2 and padding zero), to take the maximum elements of filters' feature map. Then the fully connected layer was added. The activation function "RELU" is used in a fully connected layer with a 0.5 dropout rate. Relu is used to implement nonlinearity and dropout to prevent the model from overfitting. Later on, the "SOFTMAX" activation was applied to get the defined results on the classification

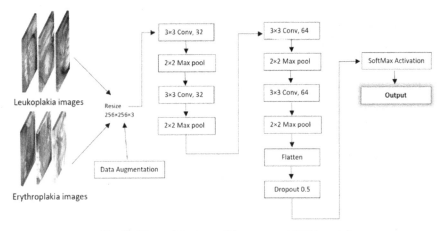

Fig. 2. The architecture of the proposed CNN model

problem. The model has been complied with the "Adam" optimizer to minimize the cost function. In the model, "RMSprop" and "Adam" were both used for all the experiments. Accuracy and reliable f1-score were promising with "Adam". The small batch size provides better training stability and performance. As per the availability of RAM, 64 batch size fits the model. The independent validation at 0.2, 0.3, and 0.4 splits on 20, 50, and 80 epochs.

3.3 Results and Discussion

Table 1 explains training, validation, and testing accuracies with resultant precision, recall, and f1-score.

The f1-score is reliable than the accuracy as the dataset we have used is imbalanced. By looking at the results, the f1-score here we received is 0.90 for detecting Leukoplakia and 0.81 for detecting Erythroplakia with 20 epochs on 80–20% Training ~ Validation ratio with an accuracy of 87.34% but with low training accuracy compared to others. Though the highest accuracy achieved by the model is 84.81% with 0.4 splits and 80 epochs which trains 100% accurately, the f1-score received by the model is 0.85 and 0.75 for Leukoplakia and Erythroplakia. The f1-score is important in terms of balancing precision and recall. Precision (True Positive/ (True Positive + False Positive)) is the total true positive class prediction that will measure if the patient is actually suffering from oral cancer disease and it is predicted correctly. If precision is not high, it may affect the patient if he is really suffering from any oral cancer and detected false. While recall (True Positive/(True Positive + False Negative)) states actual true positive value and important in measuring oral cancer patient is having Leukoplakia or Erythroplakia and needs treatment. The recall is important to minimize the false-negative results. The highest f1-score received with the model is 0.87 and 0.78 for Leukoplakia and Erythroplakia considering maximum training accuracy as 99.48% for 0.3 splits on 80 epochs.

Table 1. Results of the proposed network with different validation splits and epochs

Validation split	Epochs	Training accuracy	Validation Accuracy	Testing accuracy	Cancer type	Precision	Recall	F1-score
0.2	20	85.9	87.5	86.06	Leukoplakia	0.96	0.83	0.89
					Erythroplakia	0.73	0.92	0.81
0.2	50	89.58	89.06	83.54	Leukoplakia	0.93	0.81	0.87
					Erythroplakia	0.70	0.88	0.78
0.2	80	96.35	90.62	75.95	Leukoplakia	0.93	0.70	0.80
					Erythroplakia	0.59	0.88	0.71
0.3	20	84.62	85.94	86.07	Leukoplakia	0.96	0.83	0.89
					Erythroplakia	0.73	0.92	0.81

(continued)

Table 1. (*continued*)

Validation split	Epochs	Training accuracy	Validation Accuracy	Testing accuracy	Cancer type	Precision	Recall	F1-score
0.3	50	84.62	89.06	84.81	Leukoplakia	0.94	0.83	0.88
					Erythroplakia	0.72	0.88	0.79
0.3	**80**	**99.48**	**93.75**	**83.54**	**Leukoplakia**	**0.93**	**0.81**	**0.87**
					Erythroplakia	**0.70**	**0.88**	**0.78**
0.4	20	82.05	87.5	87.34	Leukoplakia	0.92	0.89	0.90
					Erythroplakia	0.79	0.85	0.81
0.4	50	88.54	90.62	86.07	Leukoplakia	0.96	0.83	0.89
					Erythroplakia	0.73	0.92	0.81
0.4	**80**	**100**	**96.88**	**81.01**	**Leukoplakia**	**0.91**	**0.79**	**0.85**
					Erythroplakia	**0.67**	**0.85**	**0.75**

The confusion matrix of high precision, high recall, and high f1-score is visualized in Fig. 3.

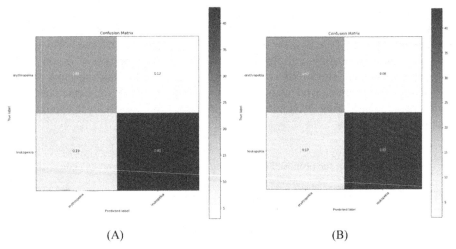

(A)   (B)

Fig. 3. (A) Confusion matrix of 0.3 splits with 80 epochs (B) Confusion matrix of 0.4 splits with 80 epochs

Both 0.3 and 0.4 splits training accuracy with 80 epochs results are high. If we look at f1-score and confusion matrix, 0.4 splits with 80 epochs have greater true positive values for Leukoplakia as 83% and Erythroplakia as 92% while 0.3 splits with 80 epochs values 81% and 88% respectively. Representing the model with an 80–20% training and validation sets ratio gives better results than the 75–25% ratio.

We have also compared the prepared architecture with VGG16, ResNet50, Xception, EfficientNetB4, and InceptionResNetV2. Each architecture has its innovative principles.

Despite various convolutional architectures, we have taken these five to cover different layers. VGG is built upon the principle of simple and homogenous topology. It extracts features having a low spatial resolution in the deep architecture [19]. VGG16 has 16 layers with five blocks and having a max-pooling layer in each block. VGG16 is chosen over VGG19 because of less memory utilization. The Deep Learning Group of google came with an idea of an inception block. It provides feature abstraction at different spatial scales with branching within one layer [20]. Xception by google is better than inception as it is modified depth-wise convolution with 36 layers. In 2015, the concept of skip connections was introduced by ResNet [21] to train deep CNNs, which was then utilized. Resnet50 has 50 layers, two layers more than ResNet. After it gained popularity, this concept was utilized by most of the succeeding networks, such as Inception-ResNet, Wide ResNet, ResNeXt, etc. [22–24]. EfficientNet was developed using a multi-objective architecture with accuracy and floating-point operations from B1 to B7 with different input shapes. EfficientNetB4 is used to take an increased input shape (380) than the proposed model input shape (256). InceptionResNetV2 architecture utilizes residual connections other than filter concatenation having 164 layers [25].

In our experiment, Oral Leukoplakia and Oral Erythroplakia images were trained on five different Convolutional Neural Network architectures VGG16, ResNet50, Xception, EfficientNetB4, and InceptionResNetV2. The training accuracy, validation accuracy, and testing accuracies are carried out on all the said networks. It can be noted that the maximum training accuracy achieved is from InceptionResNetV2 Network, which is 90.69%, validation accuracy is 62.71%, and the testing accuracy is 67.09% (See Table 2).

Table 2. Results of Different Networks accuracies

Network	Training Accuracy	Validation Accuracy	Testing Accuracy
Vgg16	55.91	52.54	67.09
Resnet50	72.56	68.06	67.09
Xception	85.77	52.54	67.09
EfficientNetB4	90.69	47.46	32.91
InceptionResNetV2	90.69	62.71	67.09
Proposed Model	**99.48**	**93.75**	**83.54**

The gained highest result is due to residual connections with a maximum of 164 layers from other architectures. It also helps to train faster with similar computational cost as Inception [21]. The dataset we have used is small; the results might get accurate and better with datasets in large numbers. We have achieved better results with the proposed model.

4   Conclusion

From the previous research, we can observe a limited number of images of biopsy, CT, and MRI are used by researchers, and their experiments were focused on primary oral cancers like OSCC, OSF and OPMD. In comparison, the proposed model has experimented with a larger images dataset of oral cancers like Leukoplakia and Erythroplakia taken from camera. We have presented a new architecture with different validation splits, experimented and compared the accuracy, precision, recall, and f1-scores values. We have also carried out the experiments with the same set of images on pre-defined CNN architectures and concluded that the proposed model gives better accuracy. Also, it shows better performance when time and computational cost complexities are measured. The pre-trained networks took much time to train because of the multiple layers in them. It may perform better with the huge dataset. It is to be seen that if the proposed model performs better with a very large data set as well. In future, we will perform the experiments with a much larger balanced image dataset. We will work on the multi-class classification of oral cancer types with bigger data set. The dataset can also be created from different real-time imaging techniques. We will also work on how to deal with unbalanced data.

References

1. Webmd. https://www.webmd.com/cancer/oral-cancer-screening#1. Accessed 12 Mar 2020
2. World Health Organization. https://www.who.int/news-room/fact-sheets/detail/oral-health. Accessed 12 Mar 2020
3. The Oral Cancer Foundation. https://oralcancerfoundation.org/. Accessed 12 Dec 2020
4. NICPR. (n.d.). Oral Cancer. India Against Cancer. http://cancerindia.org.in/oral-cancer/. Accessed 03 Jan 2021
5. Cancer.org. What Are Oral Cavity and Oropharyngeal Cancers. https://www.cancer.org/cancer/oral-cavity-and-oropharyngeal-cancer/about/what-is-oral-cavity-cancer.html. Accessed 11 Nov 2020
6. Cancercenter.com. Types Of Oral Cancer: Common, Rare and More Varieties, Cancer Treatment Centers of America. https://www.cancercenter.com/cancer-types/oral-cancer/types. Accessed 05 Oct 2020
7. Emedicine.medscape.com. Oral Submucous Fibrosis: Background, Pathophysiology, Etiology. https://emedicine.medscape.com/article/1077241. Accessed 05 Oct 2020
8. Xiao, Y., Wu, J., Lin, Z., Zhao, X.: A deep learning-based multi-model ensemble method for cancer prediction. Compute Methods Prog. Biomed. 153(C), 1–9 (2018)
9. Kripa, N., Vasuki, R., Surendhar, P.A.: Design of a decision support system for detection of oral cancer using matlab. Int. J. Eng. Adv. Technol. (IJEAT) ISSN: 2249-8958, Volume-8 Issue-5 (2019)
10. Fu, Q., et al.: A deep learning algorithm for detection of oral cavity squamous cell carcinoma from photographic images: a retrospective study. EClinical Med. 27, 100558 (2020)
11. Wieslander, H., Forslid, G., et al.: Deep Convolutional Neural Networks for Detecting Cellular Changes Due to Malignancy, IEEE International Conference on Computer Vision Workshops (ICCVW), Venice, 2017, pp. 82–89 (2017). https://doi.org/10.1109/ICCVW.2017.18
12. Goswami, B., Chatterjee, J., Paul, R.R., Pal, M., Patra.: Classification of oral submucous fibrosis using Convolutional neural network. In: 2020 National Conference on Emerging Trends on Sustainable Technology and Engineering Applications (NCETSTEA) (2020). https://doi.org/10.1109/ncetstea48365.2020.9119950 R
13. Xu, S., et al.: An early diagnosis of oral cancer based on three-dimensional convolutional neural networks. IEEE Access 7, 158603–158611 (2019)

14. Das, N., Hussain, E., Mahanta, L.B.: Automated classification of cells into multiple classes in epithelial tissue of oral squamous cell carcinoma using transfer learning and convolutional neural network. Neural Netw. **128**, 47–60 (2020). https://doi.org/10.1016/j.neunet.2020.05.003
15. Song, B., et al.: Automatic classification of dual-modality, smartphone-based oral dysplasia and malignancy images using deep learning. Biomed. Opt. Express **9**(11), 5318 (2018). https://doi.org/10.1364/boe.9.005318
16. Anantharaman, R., Velazquez, M., Lee, Y.: Utilizing mask R-CNN for detection and segmentation of oral diseases. In: IEEE International Conference on Bioinformatics and Biomedicine (BIBM), Madrid, Spain, pp. 2197–2204 (2018). https://doi.org/10.1109/BIBM.2018.8621112
17. Haron, N., et al.: Mobile phone imaging in low resource settings for early detection of oral cancer and concordance with a clinical oral examination. Telemed. e-Health **23**(3), 192–199 (2017)
18. Welikala, R., et al.: Automated detection and classification of oral lesions using deep learning for early detection of oral cancer. IEEE Access **8**, 132677–132693 (2020)
19. Simonyan K, Zisserma.: A very deep convolutional networks for large-scale image recognition. ICLR **75**:398–406 (2015). https://doi.org/10.2146/ajhp170251
20. Szegedy, C., Liu, W., Jia, Y., et al.: Going deeper with convolutions. In: 2015 IEEE Conference on Computer Vision and Pattern Recognition (CVPR), pp. 1–9. IEEE (2015)
21. Wu, S., Zhong, S., Liu, Y.: Deep residual learning for image steganalysis. Multimed. Tools Appl. **77**(9), 10437–10453 (2017). https://doi.org/10.1007/s11042-017-4440-4
22. Zagoruyko, S., Komodaki, N.: Wide residual networks. In: Proceedings Br Mach Vis Conf 2016 87.1–87.12 (2016). https://doi.org/10.5244/C.30.87
23. Szegedy, C., Ioffe, S., Vanhoucke, V.: Inception-v4, Inception-ResNet and the Impact of Residual Connections on Learning. arXiv Prepr arXiv160207261v2 **131**:262–263 (2016). https://doi.org/10.1007/s10236-015-0809-y
24. Xie, S., Girshick, R., Dollar, P., et al.: Aggregated residual transformations for deep neural networks. In: 2017 IEEE Conference on Computer Vision and Pattern Recognition (CVPR), pp. 5987–5995. IEEE (2017)
25. Khan, A., Sohail, A., Zahoora, U., Qureshi, A.S.: A survey of the recent architectures of deep convolutional neural networks. Artif. Intell. Rev. **53**(8), 5455–5516 (2020). https://doi.org/10.1007/s10462-020-09825-6

Soft Biometric Based Person Retrieval for Burglary Investigation

K. Iyshwarya Ratthi$^{(\boxtimes)}$ ⓘ, B. Yogameena ⓘ, and A. Jansi Rani

Thiagarajar College of Engineering, Madurai 625015, TamilNadu, India
iyshwaryakannan10@gmail.com, ymece@tce.edu

Abstract. Burglar investigations increase day by day and growing up as a never-ending issue in the world. Surveillance systems are deployed in the general public for security, and many urban communities and nations are currently equipped with such systems. However, this is hard to recognize the face from the surveillance footage for authentication because of the lower resolution and the distance present between the sensor and the person. In such situations, existing problems utilize many traits from the human being to distinguish the Person. Height, attire color, gender, attire type, and build usually describe a person. Such characteristics of a person are said to be soft biometrics traits; these attributes are trained in such a manner to recognize the robber. To resolve this issue, we build-up a Deep Learning-based approach, Soft Bio-metric based-Person Retrieval (SB-PR), which uses Mask Region-based Convolutional Neural Network (R-CNN) and You Only Look Once (YOLO V4) to recognize the suspect using height and attire color, and gender. A joint framework addressing various challenges namely low-resolution, view and pose-variance are proposed. On the typical person recovery dataset of the Jewelry Shop Theft Dataset (JSTD), we achieve an average Intersection of Union (IoU) of 0.506. Thus, We hope our proposed framework will reduce the burden of manual query search of person recovery in the closed-circuit television (CCTV) security system.

Keywords: Soft biometrics · Video surveillance · Semantic description · Person retrieval

1 Introduction

During the past few years, dozens of cameras are installed all around public places under the intelligence video monitoring programs. Such programs are being developed continuously that resulted to advances in video content analysis algorithms. International application and interest in CCTV for the public environment have succeeded in forensic responses committed to crime and terrorism. The best-case scenario can help find events, in real-time or near real-time, to minimize potential injuries. Recently, trait acknowledgment like age, gender orientation, stature, fabric tone, and type brings much attention to its

B. Raman et al. (Eds.): CVIP 2021, CCIS 1567, pp. 316–327, 2022.
https://doi.org/10.1007/978-3-031-11346-8_28

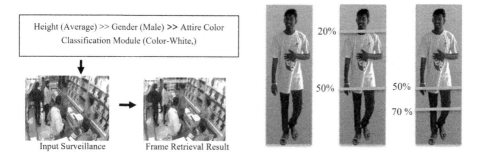

Fig. 1. (a) Sample person recovery using a semantic depiction. (b) Patch extraction of leg and torso segment obtained from the segmented person.

promising results in applications like person re-distinguishing proof, quality-based person pursuit, and person recovery in video surveillance. These days, urban areas are furnished with many observation cameras, which consistently store reconnaissance information. To recognize particular person physically from those recordings conceivably requires an ample amount of duration to finish. Utilizing computer vision procedures to completely robotize the above task shows an enormous interest inside the local examination area. The latest thing primarily settles this errand on picture questions, which have significant restrictions and probably aren't appropriate for helpful utilization. Hence, we examined this task involving person recovery with semantic depictions to confront these limits. Figure 1(a) outlines the process of recovering or recognizing a person utilizing a semantic portrayal. Person recovery with picture-based inquiries are used for searching a person. Given the picture question, it discovers the comparability between the investigation and that reconnaissance film. This issue needs, at any rate, one picture as a question, which has a significant constraint, practically speaking. We propose to utilize a semantic depiction of a person's recovery to resolve the impediment of picture-based person recovery. This process does not require any particular frame that contains the query person. Semantic displays can also offer details directly about the human appearance. We propose SB-PR - a deep learning based person recovery in video surveillance to utilize this semantic portrayal for person recovery. The SB-PR takes a semantic depiction and a reconnaissance outline as information and yields the right recovered person distinguishing them using a bounding box. We make use of Mask R-CNN for each person's exact discovery and occurrence division in the reconnaissance outline. It utilizes Height (Metric unit), Leg and Torso segment (Attire colour) and Gender (Male/Female) as course channel. The stature channel is planned to utilize camera adjustment boundaries, while any remaining channels depend totally upon the neural organizations of the networks (CNN): DenseNet-161. The comprehensive methodology is depicted in Fig. 2, and we will discuss more in Sect. 3. In synopsis, the primary commitments about our paper are as follow:

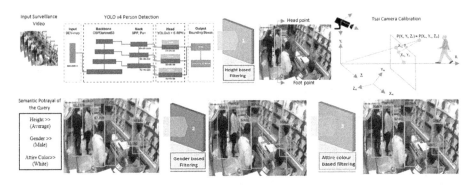

Fig. 2. Proposed framework-soft biometric based person retrieval (SB-PR).

- We study the issue of person recovery with the semantic portrayal in a security surveillance system.
- We utilize mask R-CNN that gives an exact sectioned limit of clear head and feet focus. A better assessment of true stature is derived. Acts as a good assists in extricating the exact fix for our Attire Color Classification.
- Tested height (metric units) is adopted as a feature in-order to detect the person's position (sedentary or upright). Hence, the volume limits the scanning space of a person who is in a upright position.
- A renewed person recovery approach has been proposed that uses person descriptors-based course filtering which limits the pursuit of recognized person.

The remainder of this paper is as per the following. Section 2 depicts related work for a suspect's follow-up and recovery in video surveillance that's momentarily referenced. Our method of dealing with SB-PR framework and its modules are detailed in Sect. 3. The trial, the execution, and the outcomes are depicted and appeared in Sect. 4. Segment 5 examines various experimental results carried out. Section 6 spotlights the conceivable future work. Section 7 acknowledges and finishes up the paper.

2   Related Work

2.1   Person Retrieval Methodologies

During recent times, several algorithm have boomed up to recognise a subject using a semantic query. From the detected subjects various features have been extracted and these features in later stages are used in searching the person of interest [5]. Zhou et al. [28] Wengert et al. [25] has presented a content-based image retrieval (CBIR), and has explained how algorithms use the color information for picture-based application. Wang et al. [24] depict the distribution of the pixels in the spatial domain. Fang et al. [3] and Chaisorn et al. [1] framed an Attention Networks for Person Retrieval (ANPR) framework that addressed the

Fig. 3. Sample of JSTD dataset created which addresses vast imaging properties.

relevance and importance of social signal integration. Schumann et al. [22] has explained the choice in classifier design. They have classified them into the single classifier for an attribute or a single classifier for all features. This is an important [13,15] aspect of obtaining good accuracy as each attribute is entirely exclusive. Zhao et al. [27] and Ryan et al. [6] have proposed a supervised person re-id called a salience matching algorithm. They have addressed selection and evaluation of intermediate and mid-semantic attributes to define people. Farenzena et al. [4] has presented an appearance-based algorithm that identifies a person classifying the method as the single-shot and multi-shot approaches. Bertillon et al. [3,11, 12] was the one who designed the very first person-detection system that detects the suspects. Ye et al. [26] framed a Homogeneous Augmented Tri Modal (HAT) technique for Visible InfraRed Person Re-Identification that addressed challenges faced in matching query between day-time and night-time imaging. Raval et al. [16,19,20] have addressed identifying subjects from video recordings utilizing the descriptions given. This follows the baseline of forensics. The preliminary stage is with primary biometrics, and the second stage is with soft biometrics. One will use these traits upon the fine-tuning of primary biometric characteristics. Denman et al. [2] and Dangwei et al. [17] have developed a new technology to create an avatar using the semantic query using particular-filter approach. This avatar helps in searching the person of interest from the vast footage present.

Table 1. Comparison study of the proposed methodology with various state-of-the-art algorithms.

Algorithm	Proposed SB-PR	Li et al. [18]	Tian et al. [26]	Galiyawala et al. [6]
Quantitative measure/Person Tag	Estimated height (in cm)	Estimated height (in cm)	Estimated height (in cm)	Estimated height (in cm)
Person A	172.60	172.74	174.25	174.90
Person B	168.64	168.78	169.29	169.94
Person C	174.89	175.03	175.54	176.19

2.2 Semantic Query Based Person Retrieval

As far as we know, the present state-of-the-art algorithm designed for gender prediction have been reported with 64% accuracy, respectively. Gender based algorithms [7,21] has been given as an in-depth learning solution for measuring gender using a single face image without using landmarks using the convolutional neural networks (CNNs) in ImageNet. However, as they move further into the CNN based methods, their approach has become more abstract and challenging to interpret. Gonzalez-Sosa et al. [8] has proposed continuous shape details extracted from body silhouettes and structural information stored in HOG definitions. But, the evaluation shows the dependency of performance on the visibility of the person's body in the particular frame considered instead of the resolution. Variations due to alignment, swapping are addressed using [14] the recent Layer-wise Relevance Propagation (LRP) algorithm. Halsten et al. [9] has proposed an algorithm to search and find the query person using the provided semantic description, which consists of various details regarding the query person like the attire color and type (especially clothes that are found down the waist), the height information and the build.

3   The Proposed Soft-Biomatric Based Person Retrieval Framework

This segment presents a deep learning-based course sifting, where the sequence-based person retrieval is proposed to detect the suspect from the numerous footages available. Here, course sifting means the sequence of person retrieval. It retrieves the person by Gender, attire, then by height. This approach for person recovery in closed circuit security monitoring called the SB-PR (see Fig. 2) represents the total flow graph of SB-PR.

3.1   Height Estimation

Individual tallness always tends to be an invariant parameter, which assists in recognizing a person's sedentary and upright stature. Tsai camera [23]

Fig. 4. Experimental result of JSTD dataset depicting person retrieval (Robber) using the semantic query (Height >> 175 cm, Gender >> Male, Attire color >> Blue) (Color figure online)

adjustment explains the appraise on recognizing people's tallness by coordinating bounding box directions to simple directions. Identified foot and head points of the person are processed on the example that's shown in the height estimation (see Fig. 1(b)). The steps involved in computing the individual's height assessment are as follows: Provided the camera adjustment boundaries, inherent boundaries network (I_m), a translation vector (t_v) and a rotation lattice (R_m) are registered. These are formulated into a matrix named $T = I_m[R_m|t_v]$. By utilizing spiral mutilation boundaries, head and foot focuses are undistorted. Using the converse change of T we set $F = 0$ which is used to determine the directions X and Y. The X and Y coordinates are those which likewise describe height. Determined height helps narrow down the inquiry space inside the test reconnaissance outline, dependening on the semantic depiction (for example, average stature (100–130 cm)). The normal tallness (H_{avg}) is registered over all the observation outlines in a given video arrangement. Ridiculous preparation of video grouping shows that the normal tallness assessed from computerized head and feet point is more noteworthy than was H_{avg} (Fig. 4).

3.2   Attire Colour Classification Module

Mask R-CNN creates a people mark with an occurrence division. Utilizing this, the middle and leg districts are extricated. From the recognized bounding box and occasion division, the upper half (20%)—torso, the reaming 50 to 70% addresses leg segment of the individual. These segmentation levels are shown in Fig. 1(b). Segregates division has been carried out for obtaining the middle and leg divide without the foundation to extract the attire tone grouping. The JSTD dataset contains 12 Torso essential and optional shading, four intermediate material sort, eight middle fabric designs, 12 Leg material essential tone and auxiliary tone, and eight leg material examples. Analysing various comparative matches, the methodology will refine the outcomes by utilizing each given sample. This component, of course, assists with narrowing down the inquiry space. Moreover, to overcome the aftereffect of the final module, gender module is been proposed. It is inferred from it that addition of gender module improves the presentation when the surveillance outline is packed.

3.3 Gender Classification

By using height and different semantic portrayals, the proposed approach recovers the query for maximum cases. However, whilst one-of-a-kind fits come after the last module, so the methodology makes use of Gender as the previous module for retrieving or checking the final retrieved query. Thus, complete self-perceptions of the gender classes were being used for fine-tuning.

4   Experiment

This segment examines various insights concerning the outline of the created dataset used in evaluation, various execution measures in order to assess the proposed methodology and execution procedure.

4.1   Dataset Overview and Performance Metric

Our work utilizes the Jewelry Shop Theft Dataset (JSTD) created (see Fig. 3), with 42 unconstrained video sections (9050 frames). 1280×780 is the frame height and width of the dataset. The dataset created is collected from a vast environment with under varied illumination conditions, and the performance was evaluated accordingly. Both continuous and categorical based performance metric has been utilized as three types of biometric traits are considered here. Means Square Error (MSE) Eq. 1 and Root mean square error (RMSE) Eq. 2 are used to measure the performance of height estimation. Where, y, and n represent the predicted value, actual value and total count of the data. Followed by performance measure of gender and attire color based on confusion matrix [10] and Receiver Operating Characteristic curve (ROC) as they are categorical variables (see Fig. 7). Further measurements utilize Intersection over Union (IoU) given by Eq. 3. An IoUavg is determined per video by averaging the value of overall video successions to acquire an accuracy measure.

$$MSE = \frac{1}{n} \sum_{l=1}^{n} (y_i - y_i^-) \tag{1}$$

$$RMSE = \sqrt{\frac{1}{n} \sum_{l=1}^{n} (y_i - y_i^-)} \tag{2}$$

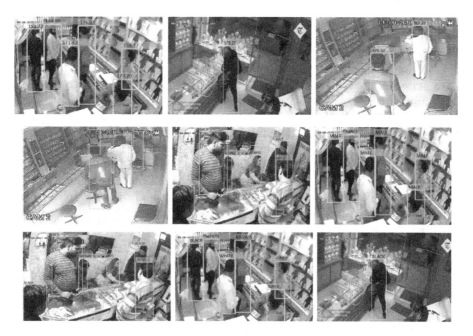

Fig. 5. TRUE POSITIVE AND TRUE NEGATIVE Experimental results of the state-of-the art algorithms depicting each attribute in order.

Fig. 6. FALSE POSITIVE AND FALSE NEGATIVE Experimental results of the state-of-the art algorithms depicting each attribute due to various conditions like illumination effects, resolution of the footage etc.,

$$IoU = \frac{D \cap GT}{D \cup GT} \tag{3}$$

where D is the bounding box output of the algorithm and GT is the Ground Truthbounding box.

4.2   Implementation Details

All analyses run in Tensorflow 1.8.

Data Augmentation and DenseNet Training. Once the frames with fractional impediments are eliminated and processed as a preparation set. There are about 8657 frames. In this manner, preparing DenseNet with just 8657 images incurs over-fitting, not utilizing an information increase. Each frame is on a level plane, where its brightness is expanded by a gamma value of 1.25 and further vertically flipped. Gender and attire Color models are calibrated utilizing DenseNet - 161, pre-prepared on the ImageNet dataset. The JSTD dataset comprises 1604 patches partitioned into 12 middle and leg essential and optional tones, eight middle and leg examples, and four middle sorts. Additional patches for preparing these characteristics are removed utilizing four human body markers (see Fig. 1(b)). To manipulate the change due to lighting, the patches were expanded with a gamma value of 1.25. From there on, nearly 17258 patches were created which were further partitioned as training (60%) and validation 40%) sets. As the calculation cost of the training procedure is very similar for every descriptor. The organizations were ready for 15 iterations. The learning rate was set as 0.001, dropout set as 0.30 and scaled down bunch estimate as 64. Table 1 shows the approval exactness of various height estimations. For the gender characterization, the underlying information increase created 106580 pictures for preparing gender descriptors, which is about multiple times more significant than the first preparing set (9050).

5   Experimental Evaluation and Discussion

This segment covers the qualitative and quantitative test results. In Fig. 5, pictures from left to right demonstrate the yield of the attribute modules that depicts a portion of true specific dependent on semantic depictions.

This info test outlines for 120 images in which the female faces were predicted correctly (true negative). For 42 image, there was no male but still, it was detected and the prediction was male found (false positive). For 43 image, the gender was detected but the predicted gender was not correct (false negative). We have addressed them as True Male (TM), True Female (TF), False Male (FM), False Female (FF) as in Igual et al. [10]. In Fig. 6, the method gives false results because of the following conditions: (a) Due to illumination conditions, wrong shading grouped which yields false attire colour (b) Multiple people with impediment (c) Same class seems when numerous people come into the reconnaissance edge and (d) False predictions of Height when part of the person is only present in the footage. The performance analysis is given in Table 2 and Fig. 7(a), where a comparison of the proposed algorithm with the state-of-the art methods are given, and the same for attire colour classification is evaluated and tabulated as shown in Table 3 and Fig 7(b). There is about 1.25% increase in the performance of the proposed algorithm which proves to be an efficient algorithm.

Table 2. Performance analysis of the gender classification with the-state-of-the-art algorithms.

Performance metric	Accuracy (%)	Precision (%)	Recall (%)	IoU (%)
Proposed SB-PR	80.08	84.72	81.66	93.29
Galiyawala et al. [6]	75.63	80.95	72.42	90.42
Igual et al. [10]	74.78	82.97	69.42	82.73

Table 3. Performance analysis of attire color classification with the-state-of-the-art algorithms.

Performance metric	Accuracy (%)	Precision (%)	Recall (%)	IoU (%)
Proposed SB-PR	93.25	91.38	81.23	86.40
Galiyawala et al. [6]	91.00	90.18	78.37	80.89
Sami et al. [11]	89.43	86.56	78.11	70.75

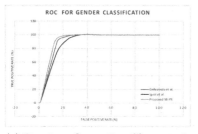 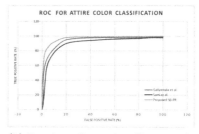

(a) Receiver Operating Characteristics (ROC) curve depicting the performance of gender classification

(b) Receiver Operating Characteristics (ROC) curve depicting the performance of attire color classification

Fig. 7. Qualitative performaance analysis of the proposed methodology.

6   Conclusion and Future Work

SB-PR's proposed methodology recovers the person in the surveillance footages dependent on the semantic depiction of Height, gender, and attire color. We built up a possible characteristic-based person recovery for security examination under different testing conditions, like occlusion, low resolution, bad image quality, various people, and posture. This methodology is evaluated on the JTDS dataset. We have utilized semantic division, which permits better height assessment and exact shading patch extraction from attire color and gender models functioned admirably. The experimental results show that the upside of our methodology for trait-based person recovery from the video is dependent on the question under various testing conditions. There is about 1.25% increase in the performance of the proposed algorithm, which proves to be an efficient algorithm. The conceivable future work will improve the outcomes by adding other delicate biometrics such as build and skin tone. Thus, it centers on the above circumstances, which are to be taken cautiously alongside hardly any unique testing conditions.

Acknowledgements. This paper has been supported under the Department of Science and Technology (DST), Fast Track Young Scientist Scheme for the project entitled, "Intelligent Surveillance System for Crowd Density Estimation and Human Action Analysis" with reference no. SR/FTP/ETA-49/2012.

References

1. Chaisorn, L., Wong, Y.: Video analytics for surveillance camera networks. In: 2013 19th IEEE International Conference on Networks (ICON), pp. 1–6. IEEE (2013)
2. Denman, S., Halstead, M., Fookes, C., Sridharan, S.: Searching for people using semantic soft biometric descriptions. Pattern Recogn. Lett. **68**, 306–315 (2015)
3. Fang, P., Zhou, J., Roy, S.K., Ji, P., Petersson, L., Harandi, M.T.: Attention in attention networks for person retrieval. IEEE Trans. Pattern Anal. Mach. Intell. (2021)
4. Farenzena, M., Bazzani, L., Perina, A., Murino, V., Cristani, M.: Person re-identification by symmetry-driven accumulation of local features. In: 2010 IEEE Computer Society Conference on Computer Vision and Pattern Recognition, pp. 2360–2367. IEEE (2010)
5. Feris, R., Siddiquie, B., Zhai, Y., Petterson, J., Brown, L., Pankanti, S.: Attribute-based vehicle search in crowded surveillance videos. In: Proceedings of the 1st ACM International Conference on Multimedia Retrieval, pp. 1–8 (2011)
6. Galiyawala, H., Shah, K., Gajjar, V., Raval, M.S.: Person retrieval in surveillance video using height, color and gender. In: 2018 15th IEEE International Conference on Advanced Video and Signal Based Surveillance (AVSS), pp. 1–6. IEEE (2018)
7. Ghosh, S., Bandyopadhyay, S.K.: Gender classification and age detection based on human facial features using multi-class SVM. Br. J. Appl. Sci. Technol. **10**(4), 1–15 (2015)
8. Gonzalez-Sosa, E., Dantcheva, A., Vera-Rodriguez, R., Dugelay, J.L., Brémond, F., Fierrez, J.: Image-based gender estimation from body and face across distances. In: 2016 23rd International Conference on Pattern Recognition (ICPR), pp. 3061–3066. IEEE (2016)
9. Halstead, M., Denman, S., Sridharan, S., Fookes, C.: Locating people in video from semantic descriptions: a new database and approach. In: 2014 22nd International Conference on Pattern Recognition, pp. 4501–4506. IEEE (2014)
10. Igual, L., Lapedriza, A., Borras, R.: Robust gait-based gender classification using depth cameras. EURASIP J. Image Video Process. **2013**(1), 1–11 (2013)
11. Jaha, E.S., Nixon, M.S.: From clothing to identity: manual and automatic soft biometrics. IEEE Trans. Inf. Forensics Secur. **11**(10), 2377–2390 (2016)
12. Jain, A., Bolle, R., Pankanti, S. (eds.): Biometrics: Personal Identification in Networked Security. Kluwer Academic Publishers, London (1999)
13. Kalayeh, M.M., Basaran, E., Gökmen, M., Kamasak, M.E., Shah, M.: Human semantic parsing for person re-identification. In: Proceedings of the IEEE Conference on Computer Vision and Pattern Recognition, pp. 1062–1071 (2018)

14. Lapuschkin, S., Binder, A., Muller, K.R., Samek, W.: Understanding and comparing deep neural networks for age and gender classification. In: Proceedings of the IEEE International Conference on Computer Vision Workshops, pp. 1629–1638 (2017)
15. Layne, R., Hospedales, T.M., Gong, S., Mary, Q.: Person re-identification by attributes. In: BMVC, vol. 2, p. 8 (2012)
16. Li, D., Chen, X., Huang, K.: Multi-attribute learning for pedestrian attribute recognition in surveillance scenarios. In: 2015 3rd IAPR Asian Conference on Pattern Recognition (ACPR), pp. 111–115. IEEE (2015)
17. Li, D., Zhang, Z., Chen, X., Huang, K.: A richly annotated pedestrian dataset for person retrieval in real surveillance scenarios. IEEE Trans. Image Process. 28(4), 1575–1590 (2018)
18. Li, S., Nguyen, V.H., Ma, M., Jin, C.-B., Do, T.D., Kim, H.: A simplified nonlinear regression method for human height estimation in video surveillance. EURASIP J. Image Video Process. 2015(1), 1–9 (2015). https://doi.org/10.1186/s13640-015-0086-1
19. Lin, T.-Y., et al.: Microsoft COCO: common objects in context. In: Fleet, D., Pajdla, T., Schiele, B., Tuytelaars, T. (eds.) ECCV 2014. LNCS, vol. 8693, pp. 740–755. Springer, Cham (2014). https://doi.org/10.1007/978-3-319-10602-1_48
20. Raval, M.S.: Digital video forensics: description based person identification. Cover Story, p. 9 (2012)
21. Rothe, R., Timofte, R., Van Gool, L.: Deep expectation of real and apparent age from a single image without facial landmarks. Int. J. Comput. Vision 126(2), 144–157 (2018)
22. Schumann, A., Specker, A., Beyerer, J.: Attribute-based person retrieval and search in video sequences. In: 2018 15th IEEE International Conference on Advanced Video and Signal Based Surveillance (AVSS), pp. 1–6. IEEE (2018)
23. Tsai, R.: A versatile camera calibration technique for high-accuracy 3d machine vision metrology using off-the-shelf TV cameras and lenses. IEEE J. Robot. Autom. 3(4), 323–344 (1987)
24. Wang, J., Hua, X.S.: Interactive image search by color map. ACM Trans. Intell. Syst. Technol. (TIST) 3(1), 1–23 (2011)
25. Wengert, C., Douze, M., Jégou, H.: Bag-of-colors for improved image search. In: Proceedings of the 19th ACM International Conference on Multimedia, pp. 1437–1440 (2011)
26. Ye, M., Shen, J., Shao, L.: Visible-infrared person re-identification via homogeneous augmented tri-modal learning. IEEE Trans. Inf. Forensics Secur. 16, 728–739 (2020)
27. Zhao, R., Ouyang, W., Wang, X.: Person re-identification by salience matching. In: Proceedings of the IEEE International Conference on Computer Vision, pp. 2528–2535 (2013)
28. Zhou, W., Li, H., Tian, Q.: Recent advance in content-based image retrieval: a literature survey. arXiv preprint arXiv:1706.06064 (2017)

A Deep Learning Framework for the Classification of Lung Diseases Using Chest X-Ray Images

M. Vyshnavi[1], Bejoy Abraham[2], and Sivakumar Ramachandran[1(✉)] (iD)

[1] Department of Electronics and Communication Engineering,
College of Engineering Trivandrum, Thiruvananthapuram, Kerala, India
sivan@cet.ac.in
[2] Department of Computer Science and Engineering,
College of Engineering Perumon, Kollam, Kerala, India

Abstract. Automated screening and classification of various lesions in medical images can assist clinicians in the treatment and management of many systemic and localized diseases. Manual inspection of medical images is often expensive and time-consuming. Automatic image-analysis employing computers can alleviate the difficulties of manual methods for screening a large amount of generated images. Inspired by the great success of deep learning, we propose a diagnostic system that can classify various lung diseases from chest X-ray images. In this work, chest X-ray images are applied to a deep-learning algorithm for classifying images into pneumothorax, viral pneumonia, COVID-19 pneumonia and healthy cases. The proposed system is trained with a set of 4731 chest X-ray images, and obtained an overall classification accuracy of 99% in images taken from two publicly available data sets. The promising results demonstrate the proposed system's effectiveness as a diagnostic tool to assist health care professionals for categorizing images in any of the four classes.

Keywords: CNN · Pneumothorax · Viral pneumonia · COVID-19

1 Introduction

The past decade has witnessed tremendous developments in the field of artificial intelligence (AI). It has made remarkable achievements in sensory information perception, allowing computers to represent complex data in a much better way. The major advancements include in the applications, namely self-driving vehicles, natural language processing (NLP), web-search, machine learning (ML) and computer vision. Deep learning (DL) is a neural network framework inspired by the human brain and is considered to be a subset of ML. Such frameworks automatically learn discerning features from a given data and can extract very complex nonlinear relationships. Recent developments in AI, together with high computational power of machines and the availability of a large amount of data for

B. Raman et al. (Eds.): CVIP 2021, CCIS 1567, pp. 328–339, 2022.
https://doi.org/10.1007/978-3-031-11346-8_29

training the networks, paved the way for DL algorithms that even surpass human performance in many task-specific applications. In this paper, a DL framework is tuned to classify a four-class problem that effectively predicts various disorders present in the human lungs. The proposed system effectively segregates a given image into viral pneumonia, COVID-19 pneumonia, pneumothorax or a healthy case. Figure 1 shows sample chest X-ray images of diseased and healthy subjects.

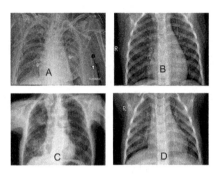

Fig. 1. Sample chest X-ray images used in the present study. Examples of (a) healthy, (b) viral pneumonia, (c) COVID-19, and (d) pneumothorax X-ray images.

Currently, many biomedical applications are using DL techniques to obtain image features, and thereby used for diagnosing various diseases [5–8]. Using transfer learning, deep neural networks can be trained with ease and require only fewer images for training a model. Several DL-based research works are published in the literature for the diagnosis of lung diseases. Vikash et al. used the concept of transfer learning for the detection of pneumonia using pre-trained ImageNet models [9]. For lung region identification and different types of pneumonia classification, Xianghong et al. [12] used a customized VGG-16 model. Wang et al. [24] used a large data set to classify and localize common thoracic diseases. Abraham et al. [3,4] explored an ensemble of pre-trained CNNs for the prediction of COVID-19 from X-ray images and CT scans. Mangal et al. presented [17] a novel deep neural network-based model called COVIDAID to decide treatment in COVID patients. Waheed et al. [23] developed an Auxiliary Classifier Generative Adversarial Network (ACGAN) to generate synthetic chest X-ray images. Rajpurkar et al. [20] developed a 121 layer CNN (CheXNet) to detect 14 different pathologies on chest X-ray images using an ensemble of different networks. Several research groups have reported the detection of COVID-19 using deep machine learning techniques applied on chest X-ray images.

This work proposed a system based on deep learning for accurate classification of chest X-ray images into normal, viral pneumonia, COVID-19 pneumonia, and pneumothorax. The proposed pipeline employs the underlying architecture of Resnet-18 [13], a CNN framework for this four-class classification problem. The method is devoid of any preprocessing steps and will be beneficial for clinicians to differentiate the four class of images considered in the study.

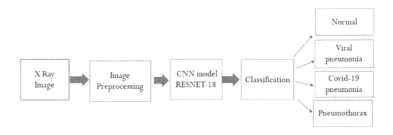

Fig. 2. Block schematic of the proposed pipeline. Input images are resized in the pre-processing stage and fed into the underlying architecture of Resnet model. The features obtained are classified for the prediction into one of the four classes of images. The proposed methodology consists of mainly three stages, namely (a) pre-processing stage, (b) feature extraction from the CNN model, and (c) classification into one of the category- COVID-19 pneumonia, viral pneumonia, pneumothorax or a normal chest X-ray image.

2   Materials and Methods

2.1   Data Set

The images used in the present study were obtained from two publicly available data sets, namely COVID-19 radiography data set [10] and Kaggle SIIM-ACR Pneumothorax segmentation competition data set [2]. Table 1 shows the overview of various classes of images present in the two data sets.

Table 1. Data set description of different images used in the study. Here, C, V, P and N denotes COVID-19 Pneumonia, Viral Pneumonia, Pneumothorax and Normal chest X-ray images, respectively. DS-1 represents the COVID-19 radiography dataset, and DS-2 include chest X-Ray Images for pneumothorax classification and segmentation.

Dataset used	Resolution	Type of data	Cases
DS-1 [10]	1024 × 1024	Private	V (1345)
			C (1200) N (1341)
DS-2 [2]	1024 × 1024	Private	P (12047)

COVID-19 Radiography Data Set. This data set is the winner of the COVID-19 data set award by Kaggle Community. The data set [10] contains chest X-ray images of 1345 viral pneumonia images, 1200 COVID-19 pneumonia images, and 1341 normal images. All images present in the data set have a resolution of 1024 × 1024 pixels.

Chest X-Ray Images for Pneumothorax Classification and Segmentation. This [2] data set contains pneumothorax images from Kaggle SIIM-ACR Pneumothorax segmentation competition. The data set contains 12,047 pneumothorax chest X-ray images. From this data set, we randomly selected 1230 images for our study. The resolution of all images are fixed to 1024×1024 pixels.

2.2 Methodology

The proposed methodology uses the underlying architecture of Resnet-18 for image class prediction as diseased or healthy. In a DL framework, a large number of images are required to train the neural network. In this work, the size of the data set available is limited. Hence, the concept of transfer learning is used to overcome this problem of limited data size. The models trained on a large massive data set of images are again used for a new problem at hand. This makes learning more faster with good results. Here, the output layer of the pre-trained ResNet18 model is modified and used for classifying a given image to one of the four classes. Figure 2 shows the block schematic of the proposed pipeline, and below, we elaborate on the various steps present in the methodology.

Pre-processing. The raw Chest X-Ray images obtained are converted to RGB scale during the preparation of data set. The input images of size 1024×1024 pixels are then resized to 224×224 pixels before applying as input to the network model.

Network Architecture. The ResNet-18 CNN model [13] is trained to classify images into 1000 different classes. The pre-trained network is trained on more than one million images from the ImageNet database [11]. We use this pre-trained version to classify chest X-ray images in hand.

The basic building block of Resnet architecture consists of modules called residual blocks, which is as shown in Fig. 3. The network employs residual blocks that assist in the generation of enhanced features by adding features from previous layers using skip connection to a learned residue. The network weights are normalized using batch normalization technique that reduces the variance between successive layers and speed-up the training process [25]. The features extracted from a layer is linearly transformed before it is applied to the succeeding layers. The image classification model is built without making use of dropouts. The activation function used is rectified linear activation function (ReLU). The output of the model is a fully connected layer appended by a Softmax function that classifies the given input to one of the four classes. Table 2 shows the architecture of the model used for the study.

Table 2. The model architecture used in the proposed study.

	Layer name	Type	Filter	Size/Stride	Output
1x	conv1	Convolutional	64	$7 \times 7/2$	$112 \times 112 \times 64$
1x	conv_2x	Convolutional	Maxpool	$3 \times 3/2$	$56 \times 56 \times 64$
2x	conv_2x	Convolutional	64	3×3	$56 \times 56 \times 64$
		Convolutional	64	3×3	$56 \times 56 \times 64$
2x	conv_3x	Convolutional	128	3×3	$28 \times 28 \times 128$
		Convolutional	128	3×3	$28 \times 28 \times 128$
2x	conv_4x	Convolutional	256	3×3	$14 \times 14 \times 256$
		Convolutional	256	3×3	$14 \times 14 \times 256$
2x	conv_5x	Convolutional	512	3×3	$7 \times 7 \times 512$
		Convolutional	512	3×3	$7 \times 7 \times 512$
1x	Average pool	Average pool		7×7	$1 \times 1 \times 512$
1x	Fully connected	Fully connections		512×4	4

During network training, the loss is computed using the cross-entropy loss function. The model error is calculated using this loss function, which is represented as L_{CE}:

$$L_{CE} = -\sum_{i=1}^{N} p_i log q_i \qquad (1)$$

where p_i and q_i denote the ground-truth, and softmax probabilities for the i-th class, respectively. If model prediction deviates much from ground truth label, cross-entropy loss increases. In order to reduce the losses, the network attributes such as weights and learning rate are changed using an optimizer functions. The optimizer used is Adam [16] that adjusts network weights to lower the loss slowly over time, based on the learning rate.

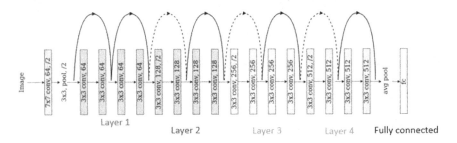

Fig. 3. The architecture showing skip connections in the Resnet framework [13]. These shortcut connections perform identity mapping, and their outputs are added to the outputs of the stacked layers.

3 Results and Discussion

The proposed study is intended to classify chest X-ray images into one of the four classes of lung diseases, namely pneumothorax, viral pneumonia, COVID-19 pneumonia or a healthy case. For evaluating the performance of the proposed system, we used two publicly available data sets. The images of each class present in the two data sets are combined and is randomly divided as the train (80% of total data) and test sets (20% of total data). The effectiveness of the proposed system is evaluated by finding performance parameters on the test images. Table 3 shows the number of images in each class used in the training and testing phase of our study.

After resizing to 224 × 224 pixels, the input images are fed into the CNN framework for feature extraction. The batch size is set to 8 and the model is trained for 20 epochs. The batch size and epochs are fixed empirically after performing rigorous experimentation with the employed data set. The optimizer used is ADAM and the learning rate is set to 0.0001. The hyperparameters are set empirically and all implementations are done in PyTorch.

3.1 Evaluation

Five performances metrics, namely accuracy (Acc.), precision (Prec.), sensitivity (Sens.), F1 score (F1), and specificity (Spec.) are evaluated for obtaining the system performance.

$$Acc._{classi} = \frac{TP_{classi} + TN_{classi}}{TP_{classi} + TN_{classi} + FP_{classi} + FN_{classi}} \tag{2}$$

$$Prec._{classi} = \frac{TP_{classi}}{TP_{classi} + FP_{classi}} \tag{3}$$

$$Sens._{classi} = \frac{TP_{classi}}{TP_{classi} + FN_{classi}} \tag{4}$$

$$F1_{class_i} = 2\frac{Prec._{classi} \times Sens._{classi}}{Prec._{classi} + Sens._{classi}} \tag{5}$$

$$Spec._{classi} = \frac{TN_{classi}}{TN_{classi} + FP_{classi}} \tag{6}$$

where TP, TN, FP and FN denotes true positive, true negative, false positive and false negative, respectively.

Table 3. Number of images used for training and testing the proposed methodology. The training set contains fairly equal number of images in the four classes.

Types	Total images	Train set	Test set
Normal	1231	1028	203
Viral pneumonia	1100	944	166
COVID-19 pneumonia	1200	1006	194
Pneumothorax	1230	1032	198

Table 4. Performance evaluation of the proposed method. The results obtained are based on the evaluation performed on 761 images from the two data sets.

Evaluation parameter	Value
Accuracy	99.00%
Precision	98.7%
Sensitivity	97.4%
F_1 Score	98.04%
Specificity	99.6%

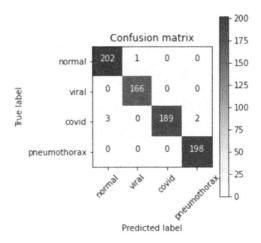

Fig. 4. Confusion matrix

3.2 Experiments

Table 4 summarizes the overall classification accuracy, precision, sensitivity, and specificity of the proposed system in the two data sets. The pre-trained network exhibits very good performance in terms of all these performance metrics. Figure 4 shows the confusion matrix obtained for the 761 test images. In the whole experiment, one normal image is misclassified as viral pneumonia and none of viral pneumonia or pneumothorax images is predicted incorrectly. The system wrongly predicted three COVID-19 pneumonia images as normal.

It is observed that the model is more confused between COVID-19 pneumonia and normal images. In this regard, the sensitivity of the proposed system in classifying COVID-19 pneumonia and normal images needs to be improved. In Table 5, we show the performance metrics obtained for various inter-class experiments conducted in our study. The high-performance measures obtained for the remaining classes show that the network performs well in discriminating various classes.

Table 5. Performance measures computed for various inter-class experiments.

Parameters	COVID-19 and viral	COVID-19 and pneumothorax	COVID-19 and normal	Normal and pneumothorax	Viral and pneumothorax	Normal and viral
Accuracy	100%	99.4%	99.2%	100%	100%	99.7%
Precision	100%	100%	100%	100%	100%	100%
Sensitivity	100%	98.9%	98.4%	100%	100%	99.5%
Specificity	100%	100%	100%	100%	100%	100%
F1_Score	100%	99.45	99.19%	100%	100%	99.75%

To show the effectiveness of the proposed study, experiments were conducted using various standard DL models, namely AlexNet, VGG-16, Densenet-161, and ResNext-50. In Table 6, we show the performance comparison of different deep learning models along with the proposed method, using the underlying architecture of Resnet-18. The architecture of Alexnet consists of eight layers-five convolutional layers and three fully-connected layers. This classification model obtained an accuracy of 95.3%. The VGG-16 makes an improvement over AlexNet by replacing large kernel-sized filters in the first and second convolutional layers and obtained an accuracy of 94.17%. The speciality of DenseNet is that each layer in DenseNet obtains additional inputs from all the preceding layers and transmits its own feature maps to all the subsequent layers. The DenseNet-161 obtained an accuracy of 96.67%. With the use of "cardinality", ResNext reduces the number of hyperparameters needed by the conventional ResNet models. Using ResNext-50 an accuracy of 94.17% is achieved. Table 6 shows that the ResNet-18 based model outperforms all the other networks in this four-level classification with an overall accuracy of 99.00%.

Table 6. Performance of proposed study in various deep learning models.

Model	Accuracy
Proposed method	99.0%
Alexnet	95.3%
Densenet161	96.67%
ResNext-50	94.17%
VGG-16	94.17%

3.3 Discussion

The use of DL networks has surpassed the performance of human in many classification tasks. The extensive use of DL networks in the past decade paved the way for opening a new era in machine vision. In the present study, we make use of Resnet-18 architecture to classify three types of lung diseases in chest X-ray images. Moreover, our study includes the prediction of pneumonia related to COVID-19 pandemic, which recently outbreaks worldwide.

Table 7. Comparison of the proposed method with state-of-art techniques present in the literature. Most of the studies use the same data set as present in the proposed study.

Study	Model	Data set	Performance
Chowdhury et al. [10]	Custom made pretrained models with transfer learning	COVID-19 Radiography database [10]	– Acc. 97.9% – Prec. 97.95% – Sens. 97.90% – Spec. 98.8%
Singh et al. [22]	Four CNN based-learners along with Naive Bayes as meta-learner.	COVID-19 chest radiography database[10]	– Acc. 98.67% – Kappa score 0.98 – F-1 scores of 100%, 98%, and 98%
Ohata et al. [19]	Combination of CNN and machine learning.	Private data set	Acc. and F1-score – MobileNet architecture with SVM classifier 98.5% – DenseNet201 with MLP(second dataset) 95.6%
Karhan et al. [15]	ResNet50	SIRM COVID-19 dataset [1]	– Acc. 99.5%
Abraham et al. [4]	Multiple pre-trained CNNs along with CFS and Bayesnet	COVID-19 chest radiography data base [10]	– Acc. 96.3%
Sethi et al. [21]	Convolutional Neural Networks (CNN): Inception V3, ResNet50, Xception, MobileNet	Publicly available data set on GitHub repository	Acc. – Inception-V3 98.1% – ResNet50 82.5% – MobileNet 98.6% – Xception 97.4%
Narin et al. [18]	Combination of ResNet-50 and support vector machines (SVM)	COVID-19 chest radiography database [10]	– Sens. 96.35% with the 5-fold cross-validation method.
Irmak et al. [14]	Convolutional Neural Network	COVID-19 Radiography data set[10]	– Acc. 99.20%
Proposed method	ResNet-18	– COVID-19 Radiography Database [10] – SIIM-ACR Pneumothorax Segmentation [2]	– Acc. 99.00% – Prec. 98.7% – Sens. 97.4% – F1-score 98.04% – Spec. 99.6%

A total of 4731 images are used for training and validation. The images are obtained from two different data sets and hence, there exists wide variability among images. The confusion matrix shows that the model performance obtained while classifying COVID-19 pneumonia and healthy images is not optimum when compared with other classification performed. The model predicts the presence of considered respiratory diseases based on features extracted from an entire X-ray image.

For comparison with existing state-of-the-art techniques in this field, in Table 7, we summarize the results obtained from recent research work employing deep learning models. For quantitative comparison, we have selected those research works that used the same data sets as those employed in our study. The promising results obtained in this study shows the effectiveness of the proposed approach in classifying images for lung disease diagnosis.

4 Conclusion

In this work, a CNN based transfer learning approach is presented for the automatic detection of four class of images. The pre-trained network is trained, validated and tested to classify normal, pneumonia, COVID-19 pneumonia, and pneumothorax chest X-ray images. The overall classification accuracy, precision, sensitivity, and specificity of the proposed system are obtained as 99.00%, 98.7%, 96.7%, and 99.6%, respectively.

The rapid screening of diseases maintaining high accuracy, helps clinicians in the mass-screening of images. Since there exist variations in the expertise of the radiologists and a large degree of variability in the input images from X-ray machines, the chances of prediction error in diagnosis are high. Hence, the need for an automated computer-aided system for screening various diseases attracts high demand. In this perspective, the proposed system can be used as a diagnostic tool in the preliminary screening of various lung disorders.

References

1. Italian society of medical radiology (SIRM) covid-19 dataset: https://www.sirm.org/category/senza-categoria/covid-19/. Accessed July 2020
2. SIIM-ACR pneumothorax segmentation. https://www.kaggle.com/c/siim-acr-pneumothorax-segmentation. Accessed Nov 2020
3. Abraham, B., Nair, M.S.: Computer-aided detection of COVID-19 from CT scans using an ensemble of CNNs and KSVM classifier. Signal Image Video Process. **40**(4), 1–8 (2021)
4. Abraham, B., Nair, M.S.: Computer-aided detection of COVID-19 from x-ray images using multi-CNN and Bayesnet classifier. Biocybern. Biomed. Eng. **40**(4), 1436–1445 (2020)
5. Munir, K., Elahi, H., Ayub, A., Frezza, F., Rizzi, A.: Cancer diagnosis using deep learning: a bibliographic review. Cancers **11**(9), 1235 (2019)
6. Lundervold, A.S., Lundervold, A.: An overview of deep learning in medical imaging focusing on MRI. Z. Med. Phys. **29**(2), 102–127 (2019)

7. Shen, L., Margolies, L.R., Rothstein, J.H., Fluder, E., McBride, R., Sieh, W.: Deep learning to improve breast cancer detection on screening mammography. Sci. Rep. **9**, 1–12 (2019)

8. Ramachandran, S., Niyas, P., Vinekar, A., John, R.: A deep learning framework for the detection of Plus disease in retinal fundus images of preterm infants. Biocybern. Biomed. Eng. **41**(2), 362–375 (2021)

9. Chouhan, V., et al.: A novel transfer learning based approach for pneumonia detection in chest X-ray images. Appl. Sci. **10**(2), 559 (2020)

10. Chowdhury, M.E.H., et al.: Can AI help in screening viral and Covid-19 pneumonia? IEEE Access **8**, 132665–132676 (2020)

11. Deng, J., Dong, W., Socher, R., Li, L.-J., Li, K., Fei-Fei, L.: ImageNet: a large-scale hierarchical image database. In: 2009 IEEE Conference on Computer Vision and Pattern Recognition, pp. 248–255. IEEE (2009)

12. Gu, X., Pan, L., Liang, H., Yang, R.: Classification of bacterial and viral childhood pneumonia using deep learning in chest radiography. In: Proceedings of the 3rd International Conference on Multimedia and Image Processing, pp. 88–93 (2018)

13. He, K., Zhang, X., Ren, S., Sun, J.: Deep residual learning for image recognition (2015). arXiv preprint arXiv:1512.03385 (2016)

14. Irmak, E.: A novel deep convolutional neural network model for Covid-19 disease detection. In: 2020 Medical Technologies Congress (TIPTEKNO), pp. 1–4. IEEE (2020)

15. Karhan, Z., Akal, F.: Covid-19 classification using deep learning in chest X-ray images. In: 2020 Medical Technologies Congress (TIPTEKNO), pp. 1–4. IEEE (2020)

16. Kingma, D.P., Ba, J.: Adam: a method for stochastic optimization. arXiv preprint arXiv:1412.6980 (2014)

17. Mangal, A., et al.: CovidAID: COVID-19 detection using chest X-ray. arXiv preprint arXiv:2004.09803 (2020)

18. Narin, A.: Detection of Covid-19 patients with convolutional neural network based features on multi-class X-ray chest images. In: 2020 Medical Technologies Congress (TIPTEKNO), pp. 1–4. IEEE (2020)

19. Ohata, E.F., et al.: Automatic detection of Covid-19 infection using chest X-ray images through transfer learning. IEEE/CAA J. Automatica Sinica **8**(1), 239–248 (2020)

20. Rajpurkar, P., et al.: CheXNet: radiologist-level pneumonia detection on chest X-rays with deep learning. arXiv preprint arXiv:1711.05225 (2017)

21. Sethi, R., Mehrotra, M., Sethi, D.: Deep learning based diagnosis recommendation for Covid-19 using chest X-rays images. In: 2020 Second International Conference on Inventive Research in Computing Applications (ICIRCA), pp. 1–4. IEEE (2020)

22. Singh, R.K., Pandey, R., Babu, R.N.: COVIDScreen: explainable deep learning framework for differential diagnosis of COVID-19 using chest X-rays. Neural Comput. Appl. **33**(14), 8871–8892 (2021). https://doi.org/10.1007/s00521-020-05636-6

23. Waheed, A., Goyal, M., Gupta, D., Khanna, A., Al-Turjman, F., Pinheiro, P.R.: CovidGAN: data augmentation using auxiliary classifier GAN for improved Covid-19 detection. IEEE Access **8**, 91916–91923 (2020)
24. Wang, X., Peng, Y., Lu, L., Lu, Z., Bagheri, M., Summers, R.M.: Chest X-ray8: hospital-scale chest X-ray database and benchmarks on weakly-supervised classification and localization of common thorax diseases. In: Proceedings of the IEEE Conference on Computer Vision and Pattern Recognition, pp. 2097–2106 (2017)
25. XIoffe, S., Szegedy, C.: Batch normalization: accelerating deep network training by reducing internal covariate shift. In: International Conference on Machine Learning, pp. 448–4566 (2015)

Scene Graph Generation with Geometric Context

Vishal Kumar$^{(\boxtimes)}$, Albert Mundu, and Satish Kumar Singh

Indian Institute of Information Technology Allahabad, Prayagraj, India
vishal.rishu26@gmail.com, {phc2016001,sk.singh}@iiita.ac.in

Abstract. Scene Graph Generation has gained much attention in computer vision research with the growing demand in image understanding projects like visual question answering, image captioning, self-driving cars, crowd behavior analysis, activity recognition, and more. Scene graph, a visually grounded graphical structure of an image, immensely helps to simplify the image understanding tasks. In this work, we introduced a post-processing algorithm called Geometric Context to understand the visual scenes better geometrically. We use this post-processing algorithm to add and refine the geometric relationships between object pairs to a prior model. We exploit this context by calculating the direction and distance between object pairs. We use Knowledge Embedded Routing Network (KERN) as our baseline model, extend the work with our algorithm, and show comparable results on the recent state-of-the-art algorithms.

Keywords: Visual relationship detection · Scene graph · Image understanding · Deep learning · Geometric context

1 Introduction

Image contains much information and understanding it has become a challenging task in computer vision. With recent breakthroughs [1,5,11,15] in object detection, there is a growing demand for scene graph generation as it helps in scene understanding tasks like visual question answering, image captioning, self-driving car and crowd-behavior analysis. Scene graphs are used to represent the visual image in a better and more organized manner that exhibits all the possible relationships between the object pairs. The graphical representation of the underlying objects in the image showing relationships between the object pairs is called a scene graph [6].

Object detection is important but detecting only the objects in an image is insufficient to understand the scene. For example, in an image of a woman with a motorcycle, the woman may be riding the motorcycle, standing beside it, or simply holding it. Here, the object pair is 'woman' and 'motorcycle'; the possible

---

V. Kumar and A. Mundu—Equal contributors.

B. Raman et al. (Eds.): CVIP 2021, CCIS 1567, pp. 340–350, 2022.
https://doi.org/10.1007/978-3-031-11346-8_30

relationships (predicates) are 'riding', 'standing', and 'holding'. Understanding these distinct relationships between the object pairs is important for adequate scene understanding. Relational reasoning between different objects or regions of random shape is crucial for most recent notable tasks such as image captioning, self-driving cars (cite recent projects) in the computer vision domain.

Visual Relationship Detection refers to detecting and localizing the objects present in the image and finding associated relationships $<predicate>$ between the object pairs $<object - subject>$. The object pairs $<object - subject>$ are related by $<predicate>$ and this relationship is represented as a triplet of $<object - predicate - subject>$ in the scene graph. In this work, we first detect and localize the object pairs and classify the interaction or the predicate between each of the object pairs. It is similar to object detection but with a large semantic space in which the possible relationships between each pair are much higher than the objects. Reasoning and analyzing such possible combinations of relationships and organizing them in a graph enhances the understanding of the scene broadly.

It is observed that in any image, the objects present in it are highly correlated, and the pattern is repeatedly occurring [17]. For example, "man" and "woman" both wear clothes, "car" tends to have "wheels"; such strong regularities can be found between the different objects. Thus, the distribution of real-world relations becomes highly skewed and unbalanced. The existing models perform better when the relationships are more frequent and poorly when the relationships are less frequent. [2] introduces a structured knowledge graph that includes the correlations among the existing objects and the relationships between the pairs to address this unbalanced distribution problem. However, the spatial geometric relationships, which are highly present in the real-world distribution, significantly contribute to understanding the scene and are less exploited in the existing works. The relationships such as near, far, top, down, beside, left, right are geometric relationships that frequently appear. Our work aims to add geometric relationships and refine the relations that the baseline model predicts.

2   Related Work

In recent computer vision researches, detection algorithms have made tremendous breakthroughs in detecting and localizing the objects in an image. With such achievements, the research has gained much attention to visual relationship detection. Detecting only the objects in the image does not help in understanding the underlying scene. However, detecting objects and the relationships between the object pairs can lead to proper understanding and improve detection based on the scene's context.

Initial works [2,8,16,17] have used the object detectors [5,11] to extract the region proposals of the objects and tried to improve scene graph generation task by incorporating 1) **language priors** [8] from semantic word embeddings, 2) **co-occurrence matrix** [2] of objects and their relationships and 3) **motifs** [17]. Due to sparse distribution of relationships in the existing datasets [7,8],

Chen et al. [3] tried to generate scene graphs from limited labels using few-shot learning. Also, Tang et al. [14] observed that the scene graph generation task performs poorly due the severe training bias and thus introduced scene graph generation (SGG) framework based on the casual inference.

2.1   Visual Relationship Detection

The main objective of this model was to detect the relationships between object pairs, i.e., visual relationships in an image. [8] proposed two modules: 1) **visual appearance module**, which learns the occurrence of predicate and object relationships. After learning the appearance, it merges them to anticipate the visual relationships between objects jointly. 2) **language module** helps to recognize the closer predicates with the help of pretrained word vectors. It converts visual connections into a vector space, from which the module optimizes them depending on their proximity to one another. It projected all the relationships into a feature space, allowing semantically related relationships to be closer together. [8] released a full-fledged dataset named VRD that is now standard for state-of-the-art comparisons. The dataset contains images with labeled objects and annotations from which the relationships between the object pairs are inferred. Following [8], the several works [2,4,14,16,17] have addressed unique problems in the SGG task and solved them by introducing their own techniques with major improvements.

2.2   Graph Inference

[16] proposed the first end-to-end model that generates scene graphs by inferring the visual relationships across every object pair of an image. The model uses standard RNNs to reason the visual relationships between object pairs and uses message passing iteratively to improve the predictions by passing contextual cues between the nodes and edges of the model architecture. [17] proposed a model that predicts the most frequent relations among the object pairs; uses alternating highway-LSTMs to address the graph inference problem to detect the objects' and predicates' labels using global context. [2] addresses the unbalanced distribution issues of the relationships in the existing datasets [7,8] and uses the statistical correlation knowledge graph to regularize the semantic space between object pairs and their relationships. [2] uses Graph Gated Neural Network to route the knowledge graph through the network iteratively and predicts the labels and relationships of the objects. [14] observed that the scene graph generation task could perform poorly due to training bias. Hence, based on the causal inference, they proposed SGG framework, which would draw counterfactual causality from the trained graph to infer the effect from bad bias, which should be removed. In this work, we use KERN's routing network [2] to infer the objects and their relationships.

2.3   Routing Network with Embedded Knowledge

Chen et al. [2] proposed a network that is based on knowledge routing, which learns the objects and relationships between them by embedding a statistical correlation knowledge graph. The network uses Faster RCNN [11] to detect a collection of region proposals in an image. A graph is created to connect the regions, and a graph neural network is utilized to generate contextually relevant descriptions to determine the class label for every region. For every object pair with the predicted label, we use a graph neural network to predict their predicates, and we create an additional graph to link the provided pair of objects, including all possible predicates. The scene graph is generated once the process is completed for all object pairs. We employ this routing network in our work and extend it with a geometric context post-processing algorithm.

3   Proposed Solution

To have more insights on the dataset [7], we categorized the relations based on higher relation types - **Geometric, Possessive, Semantic, Misc.**, similar to [17]. In Table 1, geometric and possessive types dominate the whole dataset. However, the geometric relations that are crucial to scene understanding in indoor and outdoor scenes are yet to be exploited. In this work, we estimate the geometric relationships of every object pairs using geometric parameters - **distance, direction** shown in Fig. 1, after the region proposals are regenerated and validate them on the model's output [2]. We append the geometric relationships if the reasoning module of the model fails to predict; also, we filter the geometric relations if the model's predicted relations become too ambiguous. As the dataset [7] has 15 geometric relations, we further categorized them based on the parameters. For example, if the **distance** between the pair of the objects is small, we categorize it as **near** and **far** on the other hand. Moreover, estimating the **direction**, we further categorize the geometric relations as top, bottom, under, left, right.

3.1   Geometric Context

Using the baseline model [2], we extract the model's predicted object labels (o_i), relations $(r_{i \rightarrow j})$, bounding boxes (B_i) and triplets $< o_i, r_{i \rightarrow j}, o_j >$ for post-processing. We take the bounding boxes (B_i) as input to the proposed algorithm, and calculate the two parameters - 1) **distance** L and 2) **direction** θ. For calculating L and θ, we first find the centroids of the boxes B_i and B_j as C_i, C_j respectively. Taking center coordinates, we use **L2 Distance** to calculate the distance L between the object pairs; trigonometric function to calculate the direction θ from o_i to o_j as illustrated in Fig. 1. We perform this operation for all possible object pairs detected by the baseline model.

Based on these parameters, how do we categorize the geometric relations defined in the dataset? We decide on categorizing the relations based on the following functions -

$$f(\theta) = \begin{cases} r_1, & \text{if } -45° < \theta \leq 45° \\ r_2, & \text{if } -135° < \theta \leq -45° \\ r_3, & \text{if } 45° < \theta \leq 135° \\ r_4, & \text{if } \theta > 135° \text{ or } \theta \leq -135° \end{cases} \qquad (1)$$

where r_i is the relation, $i \in [1, 4]$ and r_i represents 'right', 'top', 'left', and 'down' respectively.

$$f(L) = \begin{cases} l_1, & \text{if } L < \sqrt{(l_{box}^2 + h_{box}^2)}/2 \\ l_2, & \text{else} \end{cases} \qquad (2)$$

where l_1 and l_2 represents predicates 'near' and 'far' respectively; l_{box}, h_{box} denotes length and height of the bounding box. We concatenate the results of Eqs. 1 and 2 with the baseline's model [2] triplets to add and refine the geometric relations as shown in Fig. 3.

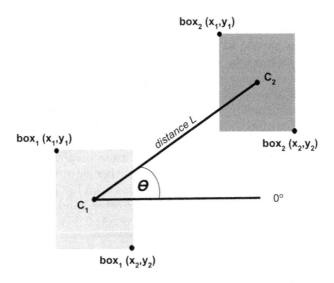

Fig. 1. Calculation of Geometric Parameters: *distance* L and *angle* θ. We use L to estimate the nearness of the objects. θ is used to estimate the direction of the objects with respect to every object. C_i where $i \in \{1, 2\}$ is the centroid of box_i; (x_i, y_i) is the coordinate of the box_i

In the result Sect. 6, we show how the relationships between objects are predicted accurately after the post-processing algorithm. In short, we extract the predicted bounding boxes of an image and the predicted classes using KERN model. After calculating the centroids of the bounding boxes and the distance between them. We then calculate the directions between each bounding boxes. Using the distance and direction, we infer geometric relationships between the objects. We also added 6 predicate classes to our visual genome dataset [7]. Two predicate classes - above and near was already present in the state-of-the art dataset.

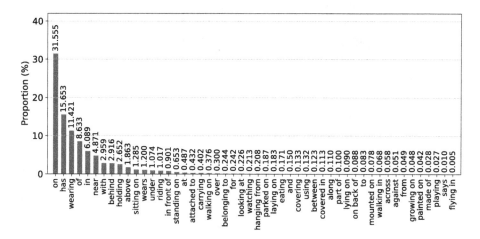

Fig. 2. Frequency distribution of relations (predicates) in Visual Genome dataset [7].

4 Dataset

4.1 Visual Genome

The visual genome dataset [7] contains 1,08,077 images, 5.4M region descriptions, 1.7M visual question answers, 3.8M object instances, 2.8M attributes and 2.3M relationships. It has 150 object classes and 50 unique relationships with the frequency histogram shown in Fig. 2. Table 1 shows higher relation types of the dataset. The dataset is used for scene graph generation, scene understanding, image retrieval, image captioning, and visual question answering.

Table 1. Types of relations in Visual Genome dataset [17]. 50% of the relations in the dataset are geometric relations, followed by 40% possessive relations.

Types	Examples	#Classes	#Instances
Geometric	Near, far, under	15	228k (50.0%)
Possessive	In, with	8	186k (40.9%)
Semantic	Eating, watching, riding	24	39k (8.7%)
Misc	Made of, from, for	3	2k (0.3%)

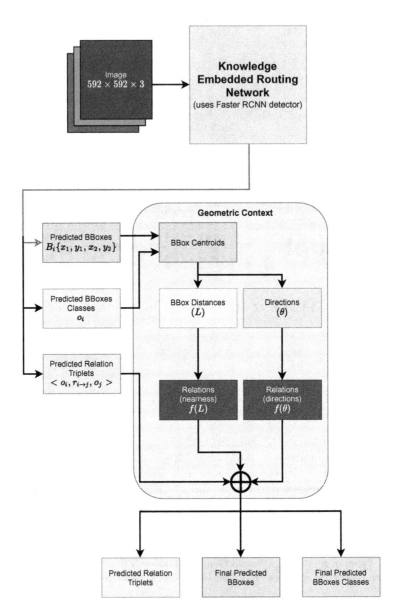

Fig. 3. Proposed architecture: **Geometric Context**. We feed an input image to the KERN [2] and extract the predicted bounding boxes (B_i), classes (o_i), and relation triplets $< o_i, r_{i \to j}, o_j >$ from the model. Using B_i and o_i, we calculate the centroids of the bounding boxes. We use the centroids to calculate L and θ as illustrated in Fig. 1. $(i, j) \in \{1, \ldots, N\}$, N is the number of predicted bounding boxes. $\oplus$ denotes concatenation of the predicted relations, addition of bounding boxes and classes (if any) into three categories similar to KERN's output.

5   Implementation

We use Faster RCNN [11] detector to construct the candidate region set, similar to previous efforts [16,17] for scene graph construction. As in [16,17], the detector uses VGG16-ConvNet [13] as its backbone network, which has been pretrained on ImageNet [12]. Both GGNN's iteration step is set at three. We employ anchor sizes and aspect ratios similar to YOLO-9000 [10] and initialize input image size to 592×592, as described in [17]. We then utilize the stochastic gradient descent(SGD) technique with the strength of a moving object as 0.9, the number of training examples utilized in one iteration equals 2 and 0.0001 weight loss to train the model that detects the regions on the target dataset. The learning rate for our model is initialized at 0.001 and then divided by ten whenever the validation set's mean average precision reaches a plateau. After that, we use the Adam method and set the number of training examples utilized in one iteration equals two and the strength of a moving object as 0.9, 0.999 to train our entirely-associated layers in addition to the neural network with layered graphs, freezing the parameters of all the present convolution layers in this activity. We set the initial tuning parameter as 0.00001, then split it by ten when the validation set fraction of the relevant sets that are successfully retrieved reaches a plateau.

5.1   Tasks

The goal of a scene graph creation is to predict the collection of triplets of $<object - predicate - subject>$. We are assessing our suggested technique with three tasks, previously seen in [16].

- **Predicate classification (PredCls)**: Given the box regions of the object pairs, the task is to predict the predicate.
- **Scene graph classification (SGCls)**: Given the box regions, the task is to predict the object categories of the boxes and the predicate between the pairs of the objects.
- **Scene graph generation (SGGen)**: This task is to detect the box regions, object categories, and the predicates between each detected object pair.

5.2   Evaluation Metrics

The recall@K (abbreviated as R@K) measure is used to evaluate all scene graph generation approaches. It measures the proportion of actual relationship triplets in an image's best K predictions of the triplet. The breakdown of various connections in the visual genome dataset is quite unequal, and the performance of the most common relationships easily dominates this statistic. Hence, we also use a new metric, mean recall@K (abbreviated as mR@K), to analyze every predicate effectively. This measure computes R@K for each relationship's samples separately, then mR@K is calculated by averaging R@K among all connections. R@K computed with the constraint setting [2] only extracts one relationship. In order to get multiple relationships, other studies ignore this limitation, resulting in higher recall values [9]. For comparisons, we evaluate the Recall@K and the mean Recall@K with constraints.

6   Results

Table 2. Comparison with state-of-the methods on mean Recall@K.

	Method	SGGen		SGCls		PredCls		Mean
		mR@50	mR@100	mR@50	mR@100	mR@50	mR@100	
Constraint	IMP [16]	0.6	0.9	3.1	3.8	6.1	8.0	3.8
	SMN [17]	5.3	6.1	7.1	7.6	13.3	14.4	9.0
	KERN [2]	6.4	7.3	9.4	10.0	17.7	19.2	11.7
	Ours	6.4	7.3	**9.5**	**10.1**	**17.9**	**19.4**	**11.8**

The scene graph generation task is evaluated using Visual Genome [7], which is the most significant benchmark for analyzing the problem of scene graph generation. In this section, we show and compare our proposed technique with existing works - visual relationship detection (VRD) [8], iterative message passing (IMP) [16], neural motif (SMN) [17] and knowledge embedded routing network (KERN) [2].

We show the results on these methods for the given three tasks in mR@K and R@K. As we can see in Table 2, our algorithm outperforms other methods in the constrained setting. However, it does not give any significant improvements over the other methods in the unconstrained setting since the predicates provided by our algorithm are less significant compared to previous predicates.

Table 3 shows the Recall@50 and Recall@100 values on the three major tasks on the Visual Genome dataset for a complete comparison with existing techniques. As we can see in the Table 2 and 3, our method gives good results for both the metrics mR@K and R@K in the constraint setting. We also compared our work on predicate classification recall values with KERN [2] results (Table 4). As we can see in the results, only two predicates - 'above' and 'near' has better results than the KERN model. Figure 4 shows the qualitative results produced by the model after the geometric context algorithm.

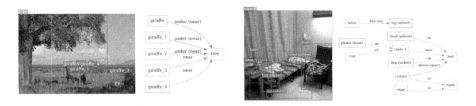

Fig. 4. Qualitative results from our model in the Scene Graph Generation (SGGen) setting. The green boxes are the correct predicted boxes and the red boxes are the boxes from the ground truth boxes which the model failed to predict. The green and red edges are the correct predicted relations(predicates) and ground truth relations (model failed to predict) respectively. (Color figure online)

Table 3. Comparison with state-of-the methods on Recall@K

	Method	SGGen		SGCls		PredCls		Mean
		R@50	R@100	R@50	R@100	R@50	R@100	
Constraint	VRD [8]	0.3	0.5	11.8	14.1	27.9	35.0	14.9
	IMP [16]	3.4	4.2	21.7	24.4	44.8	53.0	25.3
	SMN [17]	**27.2**	**30.3**	35.8	36.5	65.2	67.1	43.7
	KERN [2]	27.1	29.8	36.7	37.4	65.8	67.6	44.1
	Ours	27.1	29.8	**36.9**	**37.8**	**66.1**	**68.1**	**44.3**

Table 4. Compared our work with KERN model on predicate classification recall@50 and recall@100.

Predicate	KERN		Ours	
	R@50	R@100	R@50	R@100
Above	17.0	19.4	**20.4**	**25.6**
Near	38.8	45.5	**42.0**	**51.1**
At	32.2	37.3	32.2	37.3
Has	78.8	81.3	78.8	81.3
Wearing	95.8	97.1	95.8	97.1

7 Conclusion

Using only the object co-occurrence knowledge of an image is still insufficient to predict the relationship between object pairs effectively. If we provide geometric context with object co-occurrence knowledge, we can further improve the relationship predictions. In this work, we use geometric context with the object co-occurrence knowledge [2] and achieved relatively better results than existing methods. The future scope of this algorithm would be to evaluate its capability in different scene graph models and check its significance.

References

1. Carion, N., Massa, F., Synnaeve, G., Usunier, N., Kirillov, A., Zagoruyko, S.: End-to-end object detection with transformers. In: Vedaldi, A., Bischof, H., Brox, T., Frahm, J.-M. (eds.) ECCV 2020. LNCS, vol. 12346, pp. 213–229. Springer, Cham (2020). https://doi.org/10.1007/978-3-030-58452-8_13
2. Chen, T., Yu, W., Chen, R., Lin, L.: Knowledge-embedded routing network for scene graph generation. In: The IEEE Conference on Computer Vision and Pattern Recognition (CVPR), pp. 6156–6164, June 2019. https://doi.org/10.1109/CVPR.2019.00632

3. Chen, V.S., Varma, P., Krishna, R., Bernstein, M., Re, C., Fei-Fei, L.: Scene graph prediction with limited labels. In: Proceedings of the IEEE/CVF International Conference on Computer Vision, pp. 2580–2590 (2019)
4. Chen, Y., Rohrbach, M., Yan, Z., Shuicheng, Y., Feng, J., Kalantidis, Y.: Graph-based global reasoning networks. In: 2019 IEEE/CVF Conference on Computer Vision and Pattern Recognition (CVPR), pp. 433–442 (2019)
5. Girshick, R.: Fast R-CNN. In: 2015 IEEE International Conference on Computer Vision (ICCV), pp. 1440–1448 (2015). https://doi.org/10.1109/ICCV.2015.169
6. Johnson, J., et al.: Image retrieval using scene graphs. In: Proceedings of the IEEE Conference on Computer Vision and Pattern Recognition, pp. 3668–3678 (2015)
7. Krishna, R., et al.: Visual genome: connecting language and vision using crowd-sourced dense image annotations. In: The IEEE Conference on Computer Vision and Pattern Recognition (CVPR) (2016)
8. Lu, C., Krishna, R., Bernstein, M., Fei-Fei, L.: Visual relationship detection with language priors. In: Leibe, B., Matas, J., Sebe, N., Welling, M. (eds.) ECCV 2016. LNCS, vol. 9905, pp. 852–869. Springer, Cham (2016). https://doi.org/10.1007/978-3-319-46448-0_51
9. Newell, A., Deng, J.: Pixels to graphs by associative embedding (2018)
10. Redmon, J., Farhadi, A.: Yolo9000: Better, faster, stronger (2016)
11. Ren, S., He, K., Girshick, R., Sun, J.: Faster R-CNN: towards real-time object detection with region proposal networks. IEEE Trans. Pattern Anal. Mach. Intell. **39**, 1137–1149 (2017). https://doi.org/10.1109/TPAMI.2016.2577031
12. Russakovsky, O., et al.: ImageNet large scale visual recognition challenge. Int. J. Comput. Vis. **115**(3), 211–252 (2015). https://doi.org/10.1007/s11263-015-0816-y
13. Simonyan, K., Zisserman, A.: Very deep convolutional networks for large-scale image recognition (2015)
14. Tang, K., Niu, Y., Huang, J., Shi, J., Zhang, H.: Unbiased scene graph generation from biased training. In: Proceedings of the IEEE/CVF Conference on Computer Vision and Pattern Recognition (CVPR), June 2020
15. Wu, Y., Kirillov, A., Massa, F., Lo, W.Y., Girshick, R.: Detectron2 (2019). https://github.com/facebookresearch/detectron2
16. Xu, D., Zhu, Y., Choy, C.B., Fei-Fei, L.: Scene graph generation by iterative message passing. In: 2017 IEEE Conference on Computer Vision and Pattern Recognition (CVPR), pp. 3097–3106 (2017)
17. Zellers, R., Yatskar, M., Thomson, S., Choi, Y.: Neural motifs: scene graph parsing with global context. In: The IEEE Conference on Computer Vision and Pattern Recognition (CVPR), June 2018

Deep Color Spaces for Fingerphoto Presentation Attack Detection in Mobile Devices

Emanuela Marasco[1]([✉]), Anudeep Vurity[1], and Asem Otham[2]

[1] Center for Secure and Information Systems,
George Mason University, Fairfax, USA
{emarasco,avurity}@gmu.edu
[2] Acuant, Los Angeles, USA
aothman@acuant.com

Abstract. Fingerphotos are fingerprint images acquired using a basic smartphone camera. Although significant progress has been made in matching fingerphotos, the security of these authentication mechanisms is challenged by presentation attacks (PAs). A presentation attack can subvert a biometric system by using simple tools such as a printout or a photograph displayed on a device. The goal of this research is to improve the performance of fingerphoto presentation attack detection (PAD) algorithms by exploring the effectiveness of deep representations derived from various color spaces. For each color space, different convolutional neural networks (CNNs) are trained and the most accurate is selected. The individual scores output by the selected CNNs are combined to yield the final decision. Experiments were carried out on the IIITD Smartphone Fingerphoto Database, and results demonstrate that integrating various color spaces, including the commonly used RGB, outperforms the existing fingerphoto PAD algorithms.

Keywords: Colorspace · Presentation attack detection · FingerPhoto

1 Introduction

As government services become more dependent on mobile technology, these devices become more subject to attacks that aim to gain unauthorized access to sensitive information. To address this issue, fingerprint identification has been deployed in mobile systems. The sensors embedded in mobile devices are small, and the resulting images acquired with them are, therefore, of limited size. The integration of common smartphones in the sensing and authentication process would enable relevant applications such as device unlocking and mobile payments [2]. However, while capacitive fingerprint sensors can be embedded in newer smartphones, billions of existing smartphones are being excluded. Furthermore, fingerprints are currently proprietary and inaccessible in smartphones.

B. Raman et al. (Eds.): CVIP 2021, CCIS 1567, pp. 351–362, 2022.
https://doi.org/10.1007/978-3-031-11346-8_31

Fingerphoto-based technologies can enable the use of fingerprints in smartphones for authentication on a large-scale such as National ID programs where accurate, usable, and low-cost systems are required. A fingerphoto is an image of the frontal part of a finger captured by a smartphone camera. Fingerphotos to fingerphotos matching has recently achieved a True Acceptance Rate (TAR) of 99.66% at False Acceptance Rate (FAR) of 0.1% by fusing four fingers, and a TAR of 85.62% at FAR = 0.1% by using individual fingers [2]. Accurate comparison of fingerphotos against slap fingerprints has also been achieved, with a TAR of 95.79% at FAR of 0.1% when fusing four fingers, and a TAR of 76.63% using individual fingers [2]. Despite relevant advances in matching, this technology is vulnerable to presentation attacks (PAs) [23]. PAs refer to techniques that inhibit the intended operation of a biometric capture system and interfere with the acquisition of the true identity [15]. PAs can either conceal an individual's identity or impersonate someone else. Presentation attack detection (PAD) modules classify biometric samples as being live (non-spoof) or fake (spoof). In this paper, we focus on two types of replica: *i)* print attacks, realized using a color paper-printout placed in front of the phone camera, and *ii)* photo attacks, carried out by displaying the original image in front of the capturing device.

Existing fingerphoto PADs based on the extraction of textural descriptors such as Dense Scale Invariant Feature Transform (DSIFT), Locally Uniform Comparison Image Descriptor (LUCID), and Local Binary Patterns (LBP) from RGB images did not reach high accuracy. Processing only RGB images may limit the approach since a spoof can only be modeled in terms of percentages of the three primaries composing its color in such a color model. Choosing an appropriate color space can provide a more robust analysis. Differences between live human fingers and display attacks can be detected better when they are modeled using suitable color descriptors. RGB may be ideal for image color generation but less suited for color description. In color models such as HSI (hue, saturation, intensity), the intensity component is decoupled from the color-carrying information (hue, saturation); thus, they are better aligned to how humans perceive color attributes.

The contribution of this paper is to explore deep representations of different color spaces and effectively integrate them for enhancing the performance of fingerphoto PADs. The proposed analysis includes robustness to unconstrained acquisition including background variations. The rest of the paper is structured as follows: Sect. 2 reviews research conducted on fingerphoto PADs, Sect. 3 discusses the proposed approach, Sect. 4 presents the experimental results, while Sect. 5 draws our conclusions and discusses future work.

2   Related Work

In fingerprint scanners, PAs have been detected by either gathering further evidence of the vitality of the subject (e.g., sensing blood circulation, or fluids - perspiration patterns - secreted when touching surfaces) or by passive methods detecting the presence of known materials (e.g., material structure, lack of high-resolution detail) [15]. Several software-based methods, including Fourier Transform (FT), Local Binary Patterns (LBP), Binarized Statistical Image Features (BSIF), Local Phase Quantization (LPQ), Weber Local Image Descriptor or Histograms of Invariant Gradients (HIG), have been investigated for PAD [5,6]. Existing efforts in biometric liveness detection have been expanded by considering the assessment of activities, motivations, intent, and capabilities of attackers. However, these liveness detection approaches are not explicitly designed for mobiles and generally unsuited for portable devices [1].

At the same time, the possibility of spoofing fingerphoto-based systems is real, and despite the risk, only a few research efforts have been spent to mitigate the issue. In 2013, Stein et al. [22] discussed a technique for fingerphoto PAD that measures the light reflected from the finger exposed to the LED of the camera, as well as the position, distance, and sharpness properties of the finger. An overall Equal Error Rate (EER) of 3% was reported on video stream data collected from 37 subjects. In 2016, Taneja et al. evaluated LBP, DSIFT, and LUCID on a database of spoofs that they created by extending the previously published IIITD Smartphone Fingerphoto Database [23]. The lowest EER reported is 3.7% and was achieved by SVM trained with LBP features on the complete dataset. DSIFT and LUCID reported EER of 5.37 and 22.22%, respectively. Although the EER was not very high, the performance was poor when considering TAR at FAR $= 0.1\%$. In general, descriptors commonly used in spoofing literature yield very poor results for fingerphotos.

In 2018, Wasnik et al. discussed an approach in which input images are processed at multiple scales through a Frangi filter. From the generated maximum filter response (MFR) images, LBP, HOG, and BSIF features are extracted [24]. Bona Fide Presentation Classification Error Rate (BPCER) was 1.8% for print photo attacks, 0.0% for display attacks, and 0.66% for replay attacks at Attack Presentation Classification Error Rate (APCER) $= 10\%$ by a SVM. Results pertain to data collected from 50 subjects using iPhone and iPad Pro devices. Fujio et al. investigated fingerphoto spoof detection under noisy conditions (e.g., blurring). The original images were filtered to simulate distortions due to camera defocus and hand movements effects. An AlexNet was trained using the database created by Taneja et al., and a Half Total Error Rate (HTER) of 0.04% was reported [4,23]. This model showed robustness to blurred images.

3   The Proposed System

To date, fingerphotos have been processed only in the form of RGB images without modifying them for classification tasks including PAD. In this paper, we discuss a framework in which fingerphoto RGB images are converted into multiple color spaces before classification.

Color is a powerful descriptor that can simplify object identification. A color space is a specific organization of colors helping to produce a digital representation of colors [7]. In a color space, each color is represented by a single point which provides a three-dimensional object containing all realizable color combinations. Radiance, luminance, and brightness are the basic quantities used to describe the quality of a chromatic light source. Based on experimental evidence, 65% of the human cones are sensitive to human light, 33% to green light, and only 2% to blue. Brightness embodies the chromatic notion of intensity; luminance indicates the amount of energy from a light source perceived by an observer, while radiance indicates the total amount of energy that flows from the light source. In image processing, color models can be divided into three main categories: *i)* device-oriented, where color is specified in a way that is compatible with the hardware tools used; *ii)* user-oriented, utilized to link human operators to the hardware used (human perception of color); and *iii)* device-independent, where color signals do not depend on the characteristics of the given device which allows the connection of different hardware platforms.

In the proposed system, various architectures of Convolutional Neural Networks (CNNs) are trained to classify images in different color spaces [7]. Each network is fed with raw inputs (e.g., normalized images), which transform into gradually higher levels of representation (e.g., edges, local shapes, object parts), and the first few layers act as a feature extractor [13]. In convolutional networks, three architectural ideas ensure shift and distortion invariance: local receptive fields, shared or repeated weights and spatial (or temporal) sub-sampling [14]. The capacity of CNNs can be controlled by varying their depth and breadth; furthermore, valid assumptions about the nature of the images can be made (e.g., locality of pixel dependencies) [13]. Thus, CNNs have much fewer connections than the standard forward-feed neural networks with layers of similar size, resulting in easier training. As illustrated in Fig. 1, for a given color space, we first determine which CNN classifies it with the highest accuracy. Then, the individual confidence scores yielded by the most accurate networks are integrated at score-level to output the overall classification decision.

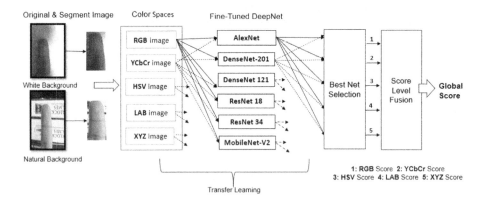

Fig. 1. The Proposed Architecture. The input RGB fingerphoto image is segmented and then converted into various color spaces. Each individual network learns to classify a single color model. For each color space, the most accurate deep net is selected. The contributions from the individual color spaces are then combined to obtain the final decision.

Information fusion in biometrics has been proven to be able to enhance recognition accuracy compared to a system that exploits only a single source. An effective fusion scheme must be implemented to integrate the evidence provided by multiple sources [11]. Biometric information can be combined at sensor or feature-level, or decision or score-level. While the amount of information to integrate progressively decreases from the sensor-level to the decision-level, the degree of noise also decreases [16]. Different integration schemes can be designed; the most effective are explained as follows:

- Feature-level Fusion. Features extracted from different color spaces are concatenated to create a single feature vector that can feed a classifier.
- Score-level Fusion. The combination of different color spaces occurs after obtaining a deep representation of each individual color space [18]. This scheme combined the confidence scores output by the individual CNNs. A threshold determined in training is then applied to the score produced by the fusion scheme.
- Decision-level Fusion. Individual classification decisions are fused. This approach is bandwidth efficient since only decisions requiring a single bit, are transmitted to the fusion engine.

In this work, we implement score-level fusion in which the scores output by the individual deep networks are fused via simple sum rule.

Before training the models, the images were segmented for background removal. The segmentation algorithm uses an adaptive skin color thresholding [20]. The procedure converts them into RGB image into the corresponding CMYK scale in which the magenta component is thresholded using the Otsu method to generate the binary mask representing the skin region of the fingerphoto [17]. A rectangular ROI is then determined and cropped. The segmented images are then transformed into different color spaces. Before training, the segmented images are resized by preserving the aspect ratio, see Table 1.

3.1 Architecture and Fine-Tuning of the DeepNets

Given the limited availability of fingerphoto spoof data, fine-tuning was applied for implementing transfer learning [10]. To adapt the pre-trained models to the PAD binary classification task, the last fully-connected layer was modified from 1000-way SoftMax to 2-way SoftMax. The parameters were estimated by using the Adaptive Moment Estimation (Adam) Optimization algorithm. Adam optimizer computes an adaptive learning rate for each parameter, while gradient descent uses a constant learning rate. Optimizers update the model in response to the output of the loss function, and thus they assist in minimizing it. Let $\mathbf{Y}$ be the vector of labels (i.e., the ground truth) and $\mathbf{Y'}$ be the vector of the predictions. The Softmax layer is combined with the Cross-Entropy (CE) Loss. The loss represents the distance between $\mathbf{Y}$ and $\mathbf{Y'}$, see Eq. (1). It increases as the predicted probability diverges from the actual label. The smaller the loss, the better is the model.

$$\text{CELoss}: \quad D(\mathbf{Y}, \mathbf{Y'}) = -\frac{1}{N}\sum Y_i log(Y_i') \tag{1}$$

where N is the number of training samples.

- **AlexNet**: The architecture is featured by five convolutional and three fully-connected layers, with ReLU activation function. The architecture is featured by Rectified Linear Units (ReLUs) with activation $f = max(x, 0)$ for their ability to be trained faster than *tanh* units, with a local response normalization applied. The model was pre-trained on ImageNet, and the last fully-connected layer was fed to a 1000-way Softmax [12].

- **ResNet**: The Deep Residual learning framework aims to address the problem of performance degradation in deeper networks. A residual network (ResNet) results from constructing a deeper counterpart of a shallower architecture in which the added layers are identity mapping while the other layers are copied from the learned shallower model. The stacked layers fit a residual mapping $F(x) = H(x) - x$ where $H(x)$ is the desired underlying mapping that can be recast into $F(x) + x$ [8]. The residual mapping is assumed to be easier to be optimized than the original one. Depending on the number of layers, there exist different variants of ResNet such as ResNet 18, ResNet 34, ResNet 121, and ResNet 201.

- **MobileNet-V2**: The architecture is based on an inverted residual structure in which the input and output of the residual block are thin bottleneck layers. The convolution is split into two separate layers: depthwise convolution that performs lightweight filtering by applying a single convolutional filter per input channel, and pointwise convolution that builds new features through computing linear combinations of the input channels [19]. Depthwise convolution reduces computation compared to traditional layers.

- **DenseNet**: In a DenseNet, each layer is connected to every other layer in a feed-forward fashion. This network utilizes dense connections between layers, through Dense Blocks, where we connect all layers (with matching feature-map sizes) directly with each other [9]. The deep layers can access all the feature-maps created by preceding levels, thus encouraging features reused. DenseNet variants include DenseNet 121, DenseNet 161, Dense 201.

3.2   Implementation of Mobile Deep Learning

Despite the relative efficiency of the CNNs local architecture, the training of large CNNs needs to be facilitated by powerful GPUs and highly-optimized implementation of 2D convolution applied in large-scale to high-resolution images.

Low-power consumption is one of the main factors driving the development of mobile processors. Snapdragon is a family of mobile systems on a chip (SoC) processor architecture provided by Qualcomm [21]. Qualcomm Snapdragon SoC is built around the Krait processor architecture. Adreno GPU in this architecture delivers improved advanced graphics performance. Specifically, Snapdragon 800 processor consists of the 28nm HPm quad-core Krait 400 CPU for high performance, Adreno 330 GPU for improved graphics performance, Hexagon DSP for low power operation, and Gobi True 4G LTE modem for connectivity. To support the next-generation data-centric mobile devices, processor architectures must be designed considering these approaches [3]. In Table 1, we report the memory and computational power required to execute the algorithms used in this work. The CNNs were trained using NVIDIA k80 GPU (12 GB RAM per GPU). The notation FLOPs indicates floating point operations per second.

Table 1. Memory and computational power requirements

	Input size	Parameter memory	Feature memory	FLOPs
AlexNet	227 × 227	233 MB	3 MB	727 MFLOPs
ResNet18	224 × 224	45 MB	23 MB	2 GFLOPs
ResNet34	224 × 224	83 MB	35 MB	4 GFLOPs
DenseNet 121	224 × 224	31 MB	126 MB	3 GFLOPs
DenseNet 201	224 × 224	77 MB	196 MB	4 GFLOPs
MobileNet	224 × 224	17 MB	38 MB	579 MFLOPs

4 Experimental Results

4.1 Dataset

For this study, we used the IIITD smartphone fingerphoto database of live images and the spoof fingerphotos created from it [20]. Samples pertain to 64 individuals in two different backgrounds, in controlled and uncontrolled illumination. Two subsets White-Indoor (WI) and White-Outdoor (WO), are created by capturing fingerphotos with white background in both indoor (controlled illumination) and outdoor (uncontrolled illuminations) conditions. Similarly, the capture with a natural background in both indoor and outdoor conditions generated two subsets Natural-Indoor (NI) and Natural-Outdoor (NO). Each subset NI, NO, WI, and WO contains 8 samples of the right index and right middle fingers per individual, therefore a total of 1024 images (64 subjects x 2 fingers x 8 instances).

The spoof fingerphotos were created from the IIITD smartphone fingerphoto database by randomly selecting 2 instances out of 8 per subject [23]. Three photo attacks using three different mobile devices (Apple iPad, Dell Inspiron laptop, and Nexus) as well as one printout attack (HP Color-LaserJet CP2020 Series PCL6 printer at 600 ppi) were created. OnePlusOne and Nokia devices were used during capture under spoof attacks. The display mechanisms were realized using: (a) Apple iPad with Retina display with 2048 × 1536 resolution, (b) Nexus 4 with 1280 × 760 resolution, and (c) Dell Inspiron N5110 Laptop with 1280 × 720 resolution. Spoof data pertains to 64 subjects and featured by 2 illumination types, 2 background variations, 2 finger instances, 2 capture mechanisms and 4 display mechanisms (1 printout + 3 photos) for a total of 8192 spoofs. The complete database used in this study consists of 12,288 fingerphoto images (4096 live and 8192 spoof).

4.2   Evaluation Procedure

To assess the proposed framework, we refer to the performance metrics defined in the ISO/IEC 30107-3 standard on biometric presentation attack detection part related to testing and reporting performance metrics for evaluating biometric presentation attacks. The assessment scheme is reported below:

- Attack Presentation Classification Error Rate (APCER): Proportion of attack presentations incorrectly classified as normal presentations, i.e., false acceptance of spoof samples.
- Normal Presentation Classification Error Rate (NPCER): Proportion of normal presentations incorrectly classified as attack presentations, i.e., false rejection of live samples.
- Equal Error Rate (EER): The intersection point of the percentage of normal presentation classification error rate and attack presentation classification error rate.
- Receiver Operating Characteristic (ROC) curves to assess the accuracy.

In this paper, we establish a baseline in the two scenarios white vs. white and natural vs. natural background; then, we study the effects of background changes without the influence of variations in lighting conditions (indoor vs. outdoor). We also analyze robustness versus both illumination and background changes by training the system on the complete database. In all the experiments, data was split into 50% training, and 50% testing and the subjects were mutually exclusive between training and testing.

4.3   Results

In this section, we discuss the performance of the proposed approach and compare it to existing algorithms used for fingerphoto spoof detection to date. From the histograms shown in Fig. 2, we can observe how good is the separation between live and spoof in the HSV model. In this color space, the characteristics hue (H), saturation (S), and brightness (B or V) are generally used to distinguish one color from another. The H attribute represents the dominant color, S is the level of purity or amount of white light mixed with a hue, and V indicates intensity. In the H channel, live distributions are concentrated below 50, which may be typical of actual live skin color. In the S channel, live samples can reach noticeable peaks in the ranges 100–130 and 50, which differs from spoof samples. In V, only live images are distributed above 150, which indicates high brightness.

Table 2 reports the results of AlexNet fine-tuned on individual color spaces under background variations. The experiments were conducted using different display and capture mechanisms. XYZ reached the lowest EER in the white vs. natural setting, which shows promising performance whether the training is carried out on images with white background and the authentication in more unconstrained conditions. XYZ is efficient on low-resolution capture mechanisms with natural background. When the complete dataset is used, HSV achieved

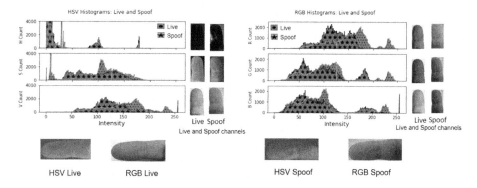

Fig. 2. Histograms of the RGB and HSV color spaces. The y-axis refers to the number of pixels for each component H, S, V, and R, G, B.

Table 2. EER % for robustness to background variations

Display	Capture	White vs. White					Natural vs. Natural				
		RGB	YCbCr	HSV	LAB	XYZ	RGB	YCbCr	HSV	LAB	XYZ
Print	Nokia	5.712	5.314	1.953	6.250	4.687	3.154	5.078	**1.954**	5.859	2.734
	OPO	2.734	7.421	3.320	5.957	3.320	4.351	6.641	3.515	4.687	3.955
iPad	Nokia	2.978	3.050	1.562	4.687	4.296	4.296	5.517	2.343	5.078	3.906
	OPO	3.467	5.851	2.734	4.882	3.906	5.371	6.641	3.515	4.785	4.248
Smart Phone	Nokia	4.541	3.185	2.246	4.394	2.343	3.955	4.687	2.734	4.687	3.166
	OPO	0.051	7.212	3.906	5.761	3.222	3.515	4.638	**1.953**	4.980	3.515
Laptop	Nokia	2.099	4.003	1.562	4.296	3.150	**1.953**	5.469	2.050	5.419	3.102
	OPO	**0.035**	4.296	1.367	4.199	3.906	3.417	3.516	**1.953**	5.859	4.736
Complete Dataset		3.112	4.980	1.953	4.199	4.492	3.710	3.516	3.417	5.273	4.002

Display	Capture	White vs. Natural					Natural vs. White				
		RGB	YCbCr	**HSV**	LAB	**XYZ**	RGB	YCbCr	HSV	LAB	XYZ
Print	Nokia	37.540	22.656	14.063	33.594	24.805	17.188	17.188	9.766	16.016	14.063
	OPO	35.938	16.058	19.141	37.109	28.418	10.938	12.012	5.859	11.523	12.500
vsiPad	Nokia	6.641	12.891	6.738	34.765	**4.004**	**3.516**	7.813	1.953	6.543	4.590
	OPO	8.789	14.844	14.746	14.746	9.082	5.859	8.789	4.297	11.328	10.547
Smart Phone	Nokia	10.156	**4.541**	8.398	14.063	12.109	**3.187**	7.031	4.688	7.227	6.641
	OPO	7.910	10.938	8.984	13.574	9.473	5.762	10.938	3.906	9.668	5.859
Laptop	Nokia	7.813	**4.102**	10.547	17.188	9.668	5.469	8.594	**3.129**	8.594	6.641
	OPO	12.891	9.375	**4.688**	15.430	8.203	5.762	8.984	5.176	8.887	5.957
Complete Dataset		34.668	20.215	17.871	36.645	27.246	10.156	13.184	5.176	7.813	9.473

the lowest EER. In this scenario, multiple PAs types are mixed and variations pertain to both illumination (outdoor/indoor) and background (white/natural). The model trained on RGB images performed well on attacks realized with laptop-opo and smartphone-opo. High-resolution capture mechanisms seem to have a positive impact on the RGB color model when the background is white. ROC curves pertaining to the analysis of the robustness of each color model to background variations are illustrated in Fig. 3. This specific case study refers to the use of AlexNet. In cross-background, while the performance of most color models including RGB significantly deteriorates, HSV exhibits robustness. This represents a promising performance when dealing with unconstrained acquisition.

For each color space, we selected the most accurate deep network. From Table 3, we can observe that on the complete dataset the lowest EER is provided by ResNet-34 for the color spaces RGB and XYZ, MobileNet for HSV and YCbCr; while ResNet-18 represents the best architecture for the LAB color space. Table 4 reports the fusion results of the proposed framework and compares it to existing fingerphoto PADs. Color spaces were combined by averaging the scores output by the individual best networks. The EER obtained by the fusion of the best three color scores is the lowest: 2.12%. RHY indicates the model fusing RGB, HSV, and YCbCr; RHYL fuses RGB, HSV, YCbCr and LAB; RHYLX fuses the five color spaces used in this work. RHY provides the best performance.

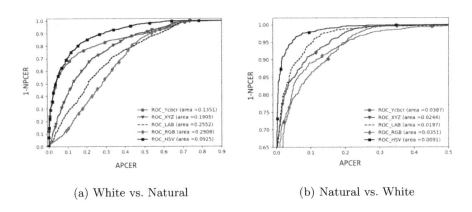

(a) White vs. Natural   (b) Natural vs. White

Fig. 3. ROC curves for the experiments on the robustness to background variations.

Table 3. Selection of the best networks on the complete dataset (EER%)

	Complete dataset				
	RGB	HSV	Ycbcr	LAB	XYZ
MobileNet- V2	3.541	**2.707**	**3.445**	**4.21**	4.871
DenseNet-201	14.258	15.36	15.258	15.266	17.587
ResNet-34	**3.174**	2.714	4.207	4.612	**4.772**
ResNet-18	3.242	3.112	4.052	4.124	4.854
DenseNet 121	9.981	8.127	12.211	11.948	14.571
AlexNet	3.361	2.811	4.505	5.571	4.829

Table 4. Comparison of the proposed system to the state-of-the-art (EER%)

	RHY	RHYL	RHYLX	LBP +SVM	DSIFT +SVM	LUCID+SVM
Complete	2.12%	2.71%	3.291%	3.71%	5.37%	2.22%

5 Conclusions

Fingerphotos acquired with common smartphone cameras could enable an effective approach for authentication. Since this technology is vulnerable to spoof attacks, the proposed efforts focus on enhancing its security. We discuss the first investigation that integrates multiple color models for accurate fingerphoto PADs. Our methodology transforms fingerphoto RGB images into various color spaces and trains a different deep network for each of them. For each color space, the best deep representation is determined and the corresponding individual outputs are combined at the score-level. Experiments were carried out using different display mechanisms on a publicly available database. Results demonstrate the superiority of the proposed framework compared to existing approaches that mainly operate and process only RGB images. We will extend the experiments by exploring additional integration strategies including deep fusion.

Acknowledgement. This work was supported by the National Science Foundation (NSF) under award CNS-1822094.

References

1. Akhtar, Z., Micheloni, C., Piciarelli, C., Foresti, G.L.: MoBio_LivDet: mobile biometric liveness detection. In: IEEE International Conference on Advanced Video and Signal Based Surveillance (AVSS), pp. 187–192 (2014)
2. Deb, D., Chugh, T., Engelsma, J., Cao, K., Nain, N., Kendall, J., Jain, A.: Matching fingerphotos to slap fingerprint images. arXiv preprint arXiv:1804.08122 (2018)
3. Deng, Y.: Deep learning on mobile devices: a review. In: Mobile Multimedia/Image Processing, Security, and Applications 2019, vol. 10993, pp. 52–66. SPIE, May 2019
4. Fujio, M., Kaga, Y., Murakami, T., Ohki, T., Takahashi, K.: Face/fingerphoto spoof detection under noisy conditions by using deep convolutional neural network. In: BIOSIGNALS, pp. 54–62 (2018)
5. Ghiani, L., Hadid, A., Marcialis, G.L., Roli, F.: Fingerprint liveness detection using binarized statistical image features. In: IEEE Biometrics: Theory, Applications and Systems (BTAS), pp. 1–6 (2013)
6. Gottschlich, C., Marasco, E., Yang, A., Cukic, B.: Fingerprint liveness detection based on histograms of invariant gradients. In: IEEE International Joint Conference on Biometrics, pp. 1–7 (2014)
7. Gowda, S.N., Yuan, C.: ColorNet: investigating the importance of color spaces for image classification. In: Jawahar, C.V., Li, H., Mori, G., Schindler, K. (eds.) ACCV 2018. LNCS, vol. 11364, pp. 581–596. Springer, Cham (2019). https://doi.org/10.1007/978-3-030-20870-7_36
8. He, K., Zhang, X., Ren, S., Sun, J.: Deep residual learning for image recognition, pp. 770–778 (2016)

9. Huang, G., Liu, Z., Van Der Maaten, L., Weinberger, K.Q.: Densely connected convolutional networks, pp. 4700–4708 (2017)
10. Yosinski, J., Clune, J., Bengio, Y., Lipson, H.: How transferable are features in deep neural networks? In: Advances in Neural Information Processing Systems (2014)
11. Kittler, J., Hatef, M., Duin, R.P., Matas, J.: On combining classifiers. IEEE Trans. Pattern Anal. Mach. Intell. **20**(3), 226–239 (1998)
12. Krizhevsky, A., Sutskever, I., Hinton, G.E.: Imagenet classification with deep convolutional neural networks. Adv. Neural. Inf. Process. Syst. **25**, 1097–1105 (2012)
13. LeCun, Y., Huang, F., Bottou, L.: Learning methods for generic object recognition with invariance to pose and lighting. In: IEEE Computer Society Conference on Computer Vision and Pattern Recognition (CVPR), vol. 2, p. II-104 (2004)
14. LeCun, Y., Bengio, Y.: Convolutional networks for images, speech, and time series. In: The Handbook of Brain Theory and Neural Networks, vol. 3361, no. 10 (1995)
15. Marasco, E., Ross, A.: A survey on antispoofing schemes for fingerprint recognition systems. ACM Comput. Surv. **47**(2), 28:1–28:36 (2014). https://doi.org/10.1145/2617756. http://doi.acm.org/10.1145/2617756
16. Marasco, E., Ross, A., Sansone, C.: Predicting identification errors in a multibiometric system based on ranks and scores. In: Fourth IEEE International Conference on Biometrics: Theory, Applications and Systems, September 2010
17. Otsu, N.: A threshold selection method from gray-level histograms. IEEE Trans. Syst. Man Cybern. **9**(1), 62–66 (1979)
18. Ross, A., Jain, A., Nandakumar, K.: Information fusion in biometrics. In: Handbook of Multibiometrics, pp. 37–58 (2006)
19. Sandler, M., Howard, A., Zhu, M., Zhmoginov, A., Chen, L.C.: MobileNetV2: Inverted residuals and linear bottlenecks, pp. 4510–4520 (2018)
20. Sankaran, A., Malhotra, A., Mittal, A., Vatsa, M., Singh, R.: On smartphone camera based fingerphoto authentication. In: IEEE 7th International Conference on Biometrics Theory, Applications and Systems (BTAS), pp. 1–7 (2015)
21. Singh, M.P., Jain, M.K.: Evolution of processor architecture in mobile phones. Int. J. Comput. Appl. **90**(4), 34–39 (2014)
22. Stein, C., Nickel, C., Busch, C.: Fingerphoto recognition with smartphone cameras, pp. 1–12 (2012)
23. Taneja, A., Tayal, A., Malhorta, A., Sankaran, A., Vatsa, M., Singh, R.: Fingerphoto spoofing in mobile devices: a preliminary study. In: IEEE Biometrics: Theory, Applications and Systems (BTAS), pp. 1–7 (2016)
24. Wasnik, P., Ramachandra, R., Raja, K., Busch, C.: Presentation attack detection for smartphone based fingerphoto recognition using second order local structures. In: 2018 14th International Conference on Signal-Image Technology & Internet-Based Systems (SITIS), pp. 241–246 (2018)

Cancelable Template Generation Using Convolutional Autoencoder and RandNet

Pankaj Bamoriya[1] , Gourav Siddhad[2] , Pritee Khanna[1]([envelope]) ,
and Aparajita Ojha[1]

[1] PDPM Indian Institute of Information Technology, Design and Manufacturing,
Jabalpur 482005, India
{1911009,pkhanna,aojha}@iiitdmj.ac.in
[2] Indian Institute of Technology, Roorkee 247667, India
g_siddhad@cs.iitr.ac.in

Abstract. The security of biometric systems has always been a challenging area of research to safeguard against the day-by-day introduction of new attacks with the advancement in technology. Cancelable biometric templates have proved to be an effective measure against these attacks while ensuring an individual's privacy. The proposed scheme uses a convolutional autoencoder (CAE) for feature extraction, a rank-based partition network, and a random network to construct secured cancelable biometric templates. Evaluation of the proposed secured template generation scheme has been done on the face and palmprint modalities.

Keywords: Cancelable biometric · Convolutional autoencoder · RandNet · Random permutation flip · Secure sketch · Seperable convolution

1 Introduction

Biometric refers to measuring the physical and behavioral human characteristics and performing calculations related to these characteristics. Biometric features are measurable and distinct characteristics that are obtained from the processing of raw biometric data. These features can be used for labeling and describing a person. A wide range of applications of biometric systems can be easily seen in various aspects of our daily lives. These systems are used for multiple purposes like identifying a person, unlocking devices, controlling access to a personal or any other security system. It is essential to safeguard personal biometric data since it is unique and can not be modified. Storing biometric data into the system can result in the exposure of the data during a breach in the system. Once the data is exposed, it can then be used for illegitimate access and unfortunately, biometric data cannot be recovered [1].

To secure an individual's biometric data, it can be distorted by using a user-specific token/key to creating a pseudo-identity (PI). The PI generated with different tokens will also be distinct [5]. During enrollment, the PI is stored in the database and used during authentication for similarity matching. In case of an attack, the PI can be lost, but the attacker will not be able to recreate the original biometric and hence the biometric is safe [19]. In such a scenario, another PI can be generated using a different token/key. For an individual, different PIs can be generated and stored for different biometric systems. This process is known as cancelable biometrics, which must satisfy the properties such as non-invertibility, cancelability, revocability, and diversity [11]. To address the privacy and security issues of biometric data, a scheme is presented in this work to generate secure biometric templates. The neural networks are proven to be excellent for feature extraction [4]. A convolutional autoencoder is trained in the proposed study to extract the features and then randnet and random permutation are used to generate cancelable biometric templates.

The rest of the paper is organized as follows. Section 2 discusses the related works. Section 3 explains the methodology and experimental setup. Results are discussed in Sect. 4, and finally, the work is concluded in Sect. 5.

2   Literature Review

The concept of cancelable biometrics was first proposed by Ratha et al. [22] in 2001. Since then, many methods have been proposed for generating cancelable biometric templates. Nandakumar and Jain [20] proposed construction of pseudonymous identifier (PI) and auxiliary data (AD). In these techniques, the template is processed at the time of enrollment, and PI and AD are constructed. Both of these are stored in the database for future use. At the time of authentication, the query template is processed, and a PI is generated. The stored PI is fetched from the database. Then the comparison of the generated and stored PI is made for authentication.

Talreja et al. [29] proposed a secure multi-biometric system that uses deep neural networks and forward error control codes for error-correction coding. Different convolutional neural networks (CNNs) were used for feature extraction from Face and Iris biometrics. Each CNN is a VGG-19 [25] pre-trained on ImageNet [2] as a starting point, followed by fine-tuning on different datasets. Two-fusion architectures, fully connected and bilinear, are implemented to develop a multi-biometric shared representation. The shared representation is used to generate a binary cancelable template by selecting a different set of reliable and discriminative features for each user. This binary template is passed through an error-correcting decoder to find the closest codeword. This codeword is hashed to generate the final cancelable template.

Hammad et al. [8] proposed a multimodal biometric system that uses CNN for feature extraction and Q-Gaussian multi-support vector machine as a classifier based on feature level and decision level fusion. The outputs from different layers of CNN were regarded as features for feature-level fusion. The biometric system is based on the fusion of electrocardiogram (ECG) and fingerprint. BioHashing [17] is applied to attain cancelability of biometric templates. Liu et al. [16] proposed Finger Vein Recognition (FVR-DLRP) algorithm based on DL and RP. Feature points are extracted from Finger Vein, and RP is performed using a user-specific key. Deep belief network is used to generate templates.

Phillips et al. [21] enhanced the BioCapsule method [28] by incorporating deep learning techniques for pre-processing and feature extraction. They also extended BioCapsule's domain from iris to face recognition. They used multi-task convolutional neural network (MTCNN) (cascaded CNN) method [32], which is a combination of three CNNs for alignment, segmentation, and facial landmark detection. After detection and segmentation, FaceNet was used to extract facial features as 512 dimensions Euclidean space. These features are classified using SVM. Jang and Cho [12] proposed a deep table-based hashing framework that generates binary code from CNN-based features by using the index of hashing table. Noise embedding and intra-normalization were used to distort the biometric data and to enhance non-invertibility. They proposed a new segment-clustering loss and pair-wise Hamming loss for training the network.

Sudhakar and Gavrivola [27] proposed a cancelable system for iris images. CNN is used to extract features from iris images, and RP is used to generate the cancelable biometric template. SVM is used for classification. They made use of both iris of an individual by fusing the projection matrix of both left and right iris to enhance the performance of the system. Mai et al. [18] proposed the use of ResNet [9] to extract the features from the biometric samples, splitting them into partitions and construct templates. The network architecture of this scheme is quite heavy in terms of the number of trainable parameters. The same technique has been updated in the proposed work to reduce the network complexity and number of trainable parameters.

Siddhad et al. [24] proposed a lightweight convolutional autoencoder (CAE) based feature extraction method. The CAE is trained on multiple datasets and used for feature extraction. Then random noise and random convolution are used for constructing cancelable biometric templates. Singh et al. [26] proposed a CNN-based feature extraction to generate cancelable biometric templates for knuckle prints. Then the CNN, called finger-dorsal feature extraction net (FDFNet), is trained and used to extract the features from knuckle prints. A representative image is created by taking the mean across all features corresponding to a single subject. This representative image is binarized by using the zero-crossing technique after taking the inner product with the orthonormal matrix, which acts as a key.

3   Methodology

The flowchart of the method can be seen in Fig. 1. The proposed method for cancelable biometric template generation is comprised of two steps, feature extraction and generating a secure template. Features are extracted from samples during the **enrollment phase**. A CAE is trained on the biometric dataset for feature extraction. A rank-based partition network is used for splitting the extracted features into two parts (b_a and b_b). These feature partitions are given to randnet network and encoder. The encoder encodes the feature partition with

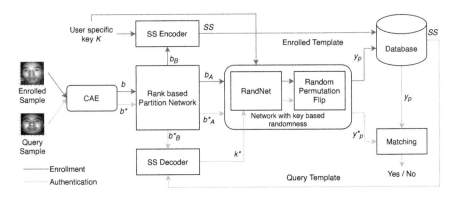

Fig. 1. Overview of the proposed cancelable biometric system

low rank (b_b) using a user-specific key (k). This encoded output is the secured sketch (SS) that is stored in the database instead of the key. The key k is given to the randnet module, which is a fully connected neural network with key-based randomness. The other feature partition with high rank (b_a) is presented to the randnet module for the generation of a template by inducing randomness using key k. The neurons in the randnet are randomly activated and deactivated based on the user-specific key. The output of the randnet is given to a random permutation flip network. Random flip mechanism permutates the input randomly. The output of random permutation flip network (y_p) is the final secured template, which is stored in the database for matching purposes at the time of authentication. Details of CAE, randnet module, and random permutation flip network are discussed below.

In the **authentication phase**, the query sample is given to the CAE for feature extraction. The features are ranked using the rank-based partition network. Again, these features are partitioned into two parts (b_a^* and b_b^*). Low rank feature partition (b_b^*) and the secure sketch (SS) fetched from the database are fed to the SS decoder. The decoder decodes the secure sketch in correspondence to the feature partition of the query sample to get the key (k^*). The key can be decoded successfully only if the feature partition of the enrolled and query sample are sufficiently similar. This key (k^*) and high rank feature partition (b_a^*) is given to the randnet network. The output of the randnet is given to a random flip mechanism which permutates the input randomly. The output is the generated query template (y_p). Now the query (y_p) and the enrolled (y_p^*) template stored in the database are matched. If the matching satisfies a certain threshold, it is a match; otherwise, it is not a match.

3.1 Proposed CAE

A convolutional autoencoder (CAE) is trained for extracting the features from the biometric samples. The same network can be used to extract features from multiple modalities like face and palmprint. The CAE consists of two networks, an encoder and a decoder. The architecture of the encoder and decoder can

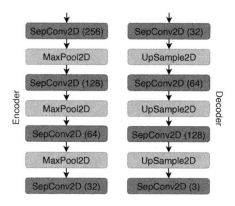

Fig. 2. Architecture of CAE

Table 1. Comparison of CAE models for different configuration

Coding variables	Layer type	# Param	MSE	MAE	PSNR
2048	**Conv2D**	800,491	0.01	0.06	50.81
	SepConv2D	98,862	0.01	0.07	58.58
4096	**Conv2D**	798,163	0.00	0.05	52.35
	SepConv2D	98,366	0.00	0.05	59.04
8192	**Conv2D**	499,523	0.00	0.03	59.17
	SepConv2D	62,494	0.00	0.04	66.47

be seen in Fig. 2. The encoder network consists of four 2-dimensional separable convolution layers. In these convolution layers, 256, 128, 64, and 32 filters are subsequently used. Each convolution layer has ReLU [10] activation. Three max-pooling layers are used between the four 2-dimensional separable convolution layers to decrease the feature map dimensions. The number of learnable parameters is reduced and increases the computational efficiency. Similarly, the decoder network consists of four 2-dimensional separable convolution layers with 32, 64, 128, and 3 filters and ReLU activation. Three upsampling layers are used between the four 2-dimensional separable convolution layers. The filter size of convolution and separable convolution layers is 3×3 in both encoder and decoder. The network is fed with images of size 128 × 128 and therefore the input images are resized to this size. Also, the datasets are supposed to be preprocessed in case the dataset is nonaligned. MTCNN [32] can be used for detecting landmarks and alignment based on these landmarks.

The CAE model architecture has been finalized after experimenting with various model configurations. Performance analysis of the CAE has been done with varying coding variables and replacing traditional convolutional layers with separable convolution layers to make the model lightweight in terms of trainable parameters. Experiments are performed with three CAEs with convolution layers

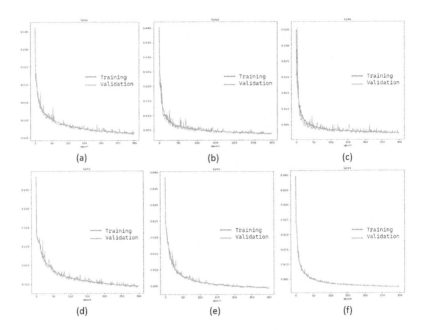

Fig. 3. Training and validation loss of CAE for CASIA Face NIR. Row 1: Models with convolution layers (a) 2048, (b) 4096, and (c) 8192 coding variables; Row 2: Models with separable convolution layers (d) 2048, (e) 4096, and (f) 8192 coding variables

having 2049, 4096, and 8192 coding variables. The same experiments are repeated with separable convolution layers. The experiments were performed with CASIA Face NIR, ORL Face, IITD Palmprint, and PolyU Palmprint.

The enrolled image is given as input to the encoder network of the CAE which does the feature extraction task. Figure 3 is showing the training and validation loss observed for CASIA Face NIR dataset. From Fig. 3, it can be seen that the CAE with separable convolution layers are showing better convergence as compared to the CAE with convolution layers. Also, the best performance was observed with the network trained with 8192 coding variables. Training these CAEs on different datasets showed similar patterns. The performance of the various CAE model configurations has also been analyzed on numerous parameters like the number of trainable parameters, mean square error (MSE), mean absolute error (MAE), and peak signal-to-noise ratio (PSNR). It can be seen from Table 1 that The CAEs with separable convolution layers are lightweight and perform better than the CAEs with convolution layers. The CAE with SeparableConv2D layers having 8192 coding variables shows a better performance as compared to the other configurations.

3.2   Rank Based Partition Network

The features extracted from the CAE are flattened and presented to the rank-based partition network. The extracted features are partitioned so that the template and secure sketch can not be linked together. This network uses the pearson correlation coefficient (PCC) [13] to rank the extracted features using Eq. 1.

$$r = \frac{\sum (x_i - \overline{x})(y_i - \overline{y})}{\sqrt{\sum (x_i - \overline{x})^2 \sum (y_i - \overline{y})^2}} \tag{1}$$

where, r is the correlation coefficient, x_i and $\overline{x}$ denote the samples and mean of x-variables, and y_i and $\overline{y}$ denote the samples and mean of the y-variables.

This network first ranks the extracted features and then partitions them based on their ranks. These two partitions are used for different purposes, i.e., construction of secure sketch and secure template. To generate a better template, it is desired to find out the key features from the extracted features. Therefore, high rank features are used to construct the template by passing those to rand-net and low rank features are given to SS encoder for secure sketch generation [18]. A user specific key is randomly generated having the same size as the split-ted feature partitions. The low rank features are summed with the generated user-specific key to construct the secure sketch. If the extracted features are partitioned randomly, then it might be possible that most of the key features are used for the construction of a secure sketch and not the template.

3.3 RandNet and Random Permutation Flip Mechanism

RandNet is a fully connected network used to introduce randomness in the generated templates. The high rank features are given to the randnet network. The randnet consists of two fully connected dense layers. Both of these layers have 512 hidden units. The first hidden layer has ReLU [6] activation function. The neurons in the randnet are activated and deactivated based on a user-specific key (k). The output of the randnet is given to the random permutation flip mechanism, which permutes these contents [3]. It also flips their sign. The output of this random permutation flip mechanism is the desired secure template (y_p) stored in the database.

3.4 Template Generation

Figure 4b shows the filter maps generated for a sample image given in Fig. 4a from CASIA Face NIR dataset by using the proposed CAE. Figure 4c shows the feature partition given to the randnet module, while Fig. 4d shows the feature partition given to the encoder module. The output of randnet module is the desired cancelable template generated using key k as shown in Fig. 4e. This template is stored in the database for authentication purposes. Second row depicts the filter maps, partitions, and template for the query image sample of the same user.

4   Results and Discussion

Experiments are performed on various datasets of the face and palmprint modalities. Table 2 shows the description of the datasets used for experimentation and

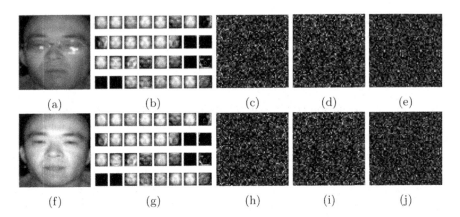

Fig. 4. Templates generated for a sample image from CASIA Face NIR. Row 1: (a) Enrolled Image, (b) CAE filter maps output, (c) Partition 1 (b_a), (d) Partition 2 (b_b), and (e) Enrolled template generated with key k; Row 2: (f) Query Image, (g) CAE filter maps output, (h) Partition 1 (b_a^*), (i) Partition 2 (b_b^*), and (j) Test template generated with key k

Table 2. Details of datasets used for experimentation

Dataset	Subjects	Samples	Resolution
CASIA Face NIR [15]	194	20	80×80
ORL Face [23]	40	10	92×118
IITD Palmprint [14]	216	6	150×150
PolyU Palmprint [31]	500	20	400×400

evaluation. The performance of the proposed method has been evaluated on two face datasets [15,23] and two palmprint datasets [14,31].

4.1   Performance Analysis

The performance of a biometric system is measured on the system's ability to distinguish between genuine and imposter subjects based on some threshold. False accept rate (FAR) is the rate of imposters classified as genuine by the system. If the system has high FAR, most imposters subjects can be accepted as genuine, degrading the biometric system performance. Hence, a low value of FAR is desired. False reject rate (FRR) is the rate of genuine subjects classified as an imposter by the system. If the system has high FRR, then it can reject genuine subjects. Hence, FRR should also be kept low. The point where FAR and FRR are equal is known as the Equal error rate (EER) [30]. For an ideal biometric system, the EER is 0. Table 3 summarizes EER values obtained with the proposed method on the face and palmprint datasets.

The performance is compared with three recent works here. Sudhakar and Gavrilova [27] proposed their method for template generation on iris images and

Table 3. Comparision of EER

Method	Face		Palmprint	
	CASIA NIR	ORL	IITD	PolyU
Sudhakar and Gavrilova (2019) [27]	0.45	0.41	0.13	0.11
Mai et al. (2021) [18]	0.00	0.01	0.03	0.01
Siddhad et al. (2021) [24]	0.02	0.03	0.00	0.00
Proposed Work	**0.00**	**0.00**	**0.00**	**0.00**

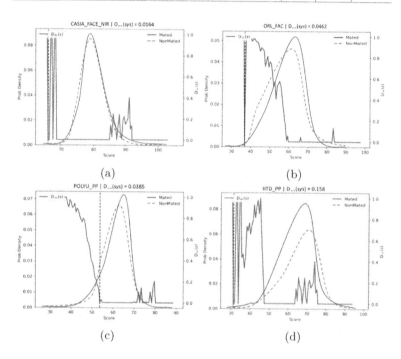

(a)   (b)

(c)   (d)

Fig. 5. Unlinkability analysis for the templates extracted by proposed method for (a) CASIA Face, (b) ORL Face, (c) PolyU Palmprint, and (d) IITD Palmprint

therefore it is not performing well for face and palmprint datasets. Mai et al. [18] performs well on face datasets, but its performance gets slightly lower on palmprint datasets. The results from Siddhad et al. [24] are good on palmprint datasets, but there is a slight drop in the performance on face datasets as their network was proposed for palmvein and palmprint datasets. EER from the proposed method are zero for both face and palmprint datasets. This shows the suitability of the proposed scheme for more than one biometric modality.

4.2 Unlinkability Analysis

Cancelable templates must be diverse. Unlinkability ensures that the transformed templates from the same subject using different keys are unlinkable. Evaluation of unlinkability has been done using the benchmark metrics $D_{\leftrightarrow}(s)$ and $D_{\leftrightarrow}^{sys}$ defined in [7]. $D_{\leftrightarrow}(s)$ is a local and $D_{\leftrightarrow}^{sys}$ is a global score-wise measure determined from the probability ratio of mated and non-mated scores. In the case of a fully unlinkable system, $D_{\leftrightarrow}^{sys}$ is 0. While in the case of a fully linkable system, $D_{\leftrightarrow}^{sys}$ is 1. The proposed method's unlinkability is dependent on the transformed template and secure sketch. The unlinkability graphs for the datasets used in experimentation are shown in Fig. 5, ensuring unlinkability to a more significant extent. CASIA Face, ORL Face, and PolyU Palmprint have unlinkability close to 0, whereas IITD Palmprint is a bit away.

4.3 Non-invertibility Analysis

Non-invertibility is a crucial characteristic that every cancelable biometric template transformation scheme must satisfy, as the security of the transformed templates depends upon it. It should be computationally impracticable to invert the transformed templates into original biometric data. The non-invertibility of the proposed work depends upon the difficulty in reconstructing the original input query sample from the transformed template and secure sketch. In the proposed method, the size of generated template is $1/4^{th}$ of the size of input biometric sample (here, 128×128). It is not possible to regenerate the input biometric sample from the generated template without using a trained CAE.

Reconstruction models are another threat to biometric system security as these systems try to reconstruct the original biometric data from the transformed templates and secure sketch [1,18]. The generation of a template and secure sketch from the proposed system are based on the user-specific key (k). The reconstruction model cannot reconstruct the original biometric data from the templates and secure sketch without the key. The key is neither given to user nor stored in the database. For estimation of key, there are two possibilities, either guess the key or estimate the intermediate feature partition. The key is a randomly generated subject specific token of size 4096. The intermediate feature partition also has a size of 4096, further encoded using the key. The estimation of both, the randomly generated key and intermediate feature partition is computationally infeasible. Hence, the proposed work satisfies the non-invertibility.

5 Conclusion

The proposed scheme uses a CAE to generate secure biometric templates that are cancelable, non-invertible, and privacy-preserving. The templates are generated using features extracted from the CAE and subject-specific keys. A secure sketch is constructed by encoding a feature partition using a key and stored in the system instead of storing the keys with users. The key can be decoded from the secure sketch only if the enrolled sample and query sample are adequately similar. The proposed method proves to be unlinkable to a reasonable extent for the datasets used. The generated template has a reduced size $(1/4^{th})$ as compared to the enrolled biometric sample. The proposed method is lightweight in terms of the number of trainable parameters and the verification performance is also good.

References

1. Cao, K., Jain, A.K.: Learning fingerprint reconstruction: From minutiae to image. IEEE Trans. Inf. Forensics Secur. **10**(1), 104–117 (2014)
2. Deng, J., Dong, W., Socher, R., Li, L.J., Li, K., Fei-Fei, L.: ImageNet: a large-scale hierarchical image database. In: 2009 IEEE Conference on Computer Vision and Pattern Recognition, pp. 248–255. IEEE (2009)
3. Durstenfeld, R.: Algorithm 235: random permutation. Commun. ACM **7**(7), 420 (1964)
4. Dusmanu, M., et al.: D2-Net: a trainable CNN for joint description and detection of local features. In: Proceedings of the IEEE/CVF Conference on Computer Vision and Pattern Recognition, pp. 8092–8101 (2019)
5. Feng, Y.C., Lim, M.H., Yuen, P.C.: Masquerade attack on transform-based binary-template protection based on perceptron learning. Pattern Recognit. **47**(9), 3019–3033 (2014)
6. Glorot, X., Bordes, A., Bengio, Y.: Deep sparse rectifier neural networks. In: Proceedings of the Fourteenth International Conference on Artificial Intelligence and Statistics, pp. 315–323. JMLR Workshop and Conference Proceedings (2011)
7. Gomez-Barrero, M., Galbally, J., Rathgeb, C., Busch, C.: General framework to evaluate unlinkability in biometric template protection systems. IEEE Trans. Inf. Forensics Secur. **13**(6), 1406–1420 (2018). https://doi.org/10.1109/TIFS.2017.2788000
8. Hammad, M., Liu, Y., Wang, K.: Multimodal biometric authentication systems using convolution neural network based on different level fusion of ECG and fingerprint. IEEE Access **7**, 26527–26542 (2018)
9. He, K., Zhang, X., Ren, S., Sun, J.: Deep residual learning for image recognition. In: Proceedings of the IEEE Conference on Computer Vision and Pattern Recognition, pp. 770–778 (2016)
10. Ide, H., Kurita, T.: Improvement of learning for CNN with ReLU activation by sparse regularization. In: Proceedings of the International Joint Conference on Neural Networks, vol. 2017-May, pp. 2684–2691 (2017)
11. Jain, A.K., Nandakumar, K., Nagar, A.: Biometric template security. EURASIP J. Adv. Signal Process. **2008**, 1–17 (2008)
12. Jang, Y.K., Cho, N.I.: Deep face image retrieval for cancelable biometric authentication. In: 2019 16th IEEE International Conference on Advanced Video and Signal Based Surveillance (AVSS), pp. 1–8. IEEE (2019)
13. Kirch, W. (ed.): Pearson's Correlation Coefficient, pp. 1090–1091. Springer, Netherlands, Dordrecht (2008). https://doi.org/10.1007/978-1-4020-5614-7_2569
14. Kumar, A.: Incorporating cohort information for reliable palmprint authentication. In: 2008 Sixth Indian Conference on Computer Vision, Graphics & Image Processing, pp. 583–590. IEEE (2008)

15. Li, S.Z., Chu, R., Liao, S., Zhang, L.: Illumination invariant face recognition using near-infrared images. IEEE Trans. Pattern Anal. Mach. Intell. **29**(4), 627–639 (2007)
16. Liu, Y., Ling, J., Liu, Z., Shen, J., Gao, C.: Finger vein secure biometric template generation based on deep learning. Soft. Comput. **22**(7), 2257–2265 (2017). https://doi.org/10.1007/s00500-017-2487-9
17. Lumini, A., Nanni, L.: An improved biohashing for human authentication. Pattern Recognit. **40**(3), 1057–1065 (2007)
18. Mai, G., Cao, K., Lan, X., Yuen, P.C.: Secureface: face template protection. IEEE Trans. Inf. Forensics Secur. **16**, 262–277 (2020)
19. Mai, G., Lim, M.H., Yuen, P.C.: Binary feature fusion for discriminative and secure multi-biometric cryptosystems. Image Vis. Comput. **58**, 254–265 (2017)
20. Nandakumar, K., Jain, A.K.: Biometric template protection: bridging the performance gap between theory and practice. IEEE Signal Process. Mag. **32**(5), 88–100 (2015)
21. Phillips, T., Zou, X., Li, F., Li, N.: Enhancing biometric-capsule-based authentication and facial recognition via deep learning. In: Proceedings of the 24th ACM Symposium on Access Control Models and Technologies, pp. 141–146 (2019)
22. Ratha, N.K., Connell, J.H., Bolle, R.M.: Enhancing security and privacy in biometrics-based authentication systems. IBM Syst. J. **40**(3), 614–634 (2001)
23. Samaria, F.S., Harter, A.C.: Parameterisation of a stochastic model for human face identification. In: Proceedings of 1994 IEEE Workshop on Applications of Computer Vision, pp. 138–142. IEEE (1994)
24. Siddhad, G., Khanna, P., Ojha, A.: Cancelable biometric template generation using convolutional autoencoder. In: Singh, S.K., Roy, P., Raman, B., Nagabhushan, P. (eds.) CVIP 2020. CCIS, vol. 1376, pp. 303–314. Springer, Singapore (2021). https://doi.org/10.1007/978-981-16-1086-8_27
25. Simonyan, K., Zisserman, A.: Very deep convolutional networks for large-scale image recognition. arXiv preprint arXiv:1409.1556 (2014)
26. Singh, A., Arora, A., Jaswal, G., Nigam, A.: Comprehensive survey on cancelable biometrics with novel case study on finger dorsal template protection. J. Bank. Financ. Technol. **4**(1), 37–52 (2020). https://doi.org/10.1007/s42786-020-00016-z
27. Sudhakar, T., Gavrilova, M.: Multi-instance cancelable biometric system using convolutional neural network. In: 2019 International Conference on Cyberworlds (CW), pp. 287–294. IEEE (2019)
28. Sui, Y., Zou, X., Du, E.Y., Li, F.: Design and analysis of a highly user-friendly, secure, privacy-preserving, and revocable authentication method. IEEE Trans. Comput. **63**(4), 902–916 (2013)
29. Talreja, V., Valenti, M.C., Nasrabadi, N.M.: Multibiometric secure system based on deep learning. In: 2017 IEEE Global Conference on Signal and Information Processing (globalSIP), pp. 298–302. IEEE (2017)
30. Wayman, J.L., Jain, A.K., Maltoni, D., Maio, D.: Biometric Systems: Technology, Design and Performance Evaluation. Springer Science & Business Media, Heidelberg (2005). https://doi.org/10.1007/b138151
31. Zhang, D.: Polyu palmprint database. Biometric Research Centre, Hong Kong Polytechnic University (2006). http://www.comp.polyu.edu.hk/biometrics/
32. Zhang, K., Zhang, Z., Li, Z., Qiao, Y.: Joint face detection and alignment using multitask cascaded convolutional networks. IEEE Signal Process. Lett. **23**(10), 1499–1503 (2016)

Homogeneous and Non-homogeneous Image Dehazing Using Deep Neural Network

Manan Gajjar and Srimanta Mandal[(⊠)]

DA-IICT, Gandhinagar, Gujarat, India
201911027@daiict.ac.in, in.srimanta.mandal@ieee.org

Abstract. Haze poses challenges in many vision-related applications. Thus, dehazing an image becomes popular among vision researchers. Available methods use various priors, deep learning models, or a combination of both to get plausible dehazing solutions. This paper reviews some recent advancements and their results on both homogeneous and non-homogeneous haze datasets. Intending to achieve haze removal for both types of haze, we propose a new architecture, developed on a convolutional neural network (CNN). The network is developed based on reformulating the atmospheric scattering phenomenon and estimating haze density to extract features for both types of haze. The haze-density estimation is supplemented by channel attention and pixel attention modules. The model is trained on perceptual loss. The quantitative and qualitative results demonstrate the efficacy of our approach on homogeneous as well as non-homogeneous haze as compared to the existing methods, developed for a particular type.

Keywords: Dehazing · CNN · Homogeneous haze · Non-homogeneous haze

1 Introduction

Haze is a natural phenomenon that occurs due to the atmospheric particles that cause scattering and deflection of light. These particles may consist of different molecules, aerosol, water droplet etc. [29]. Thus, when a scene is captured by a camera, a portion of the information gets lost due to the scattering and absorption of lights caused by the particles. Further, a portion of atmospheric light gets added in the capturing process due to the scattering effect [29]. As a result, captured image is obscured by haze effect, which becomes even more for long-range scenery. The contrast and the variance of the image get reduced and the colors of the scene contents also get dull. This results in a lack of visual vividness, appeal, and poor visibility of the objects along with a reduced range of effective surveillance. This degradation has proportionality with the depth of the object. As a result, haze appears to be denser at the farthest objects than the closer ones. This behavior makes the haze homogeneous in nature. This can be modelled mathematically using [24, 28, 29]

$$H(x) = C(x)\tau(x) + \lambda(1 - \tau(x)), \tag{1}$$

B. Raman et al. (Eds.): CVIP 2021, CCIS 1567, pp. 375–386, 2022.
https://doi.org/10.1007/978-3-031-11346-8_33

where $C(x)$ is the clear scene without the haze involvement, $H(x)$ is the degraded scene due to haze, $\tau(x)$ is the medium transmission that contains information about depth at each pixel, λ is the global illumination or atmospheric light and x is the pixel location in the image. The transmission coefficient $\tau(x)$ represents how much of the light reaches the camera without scattering. In term of depth, $\tau(x)$ is defined as $\tau(x) = e^{-\sigma\delta(x)}$. Here $\delta(x)$ is the depth or distance of the object at that pixel from the camera, and σ is the scattering coefficient of the atmosphere. This suggests that when $\delta(x)$ goes to infinity, $\tau(x)$ approaches to zero. Hence, the captured image will be $H(x) = \lambda$. This suggests that to reduce the haze effect, accurate estimation the medium transmission map is the key.

In some cases, the degradation phenomenon is not depth varying. For example, smog generally appears to be dense near factories. This kind of haze is non-homogeneous in nature. In this case, finding out haze density can play a significant role. Most of the existing works either deal with spatially varying homogeneous haze or address non-homogeneous haze. In this paper, we try to address both type of haze in a single framework based on convolutional neural network (CNN). Our proposed model try to estimate the significant parameters of both types of haze using atmospheric model and density map estimator, and combine them for dehazing any type of haze without any prior information. The channel attention and pixel attention modules in the haze density estimator improves the estimation accuracy as well as the results. Main contributions can be summarized as:

1. We propose a deep learning based dehazing model that can work for homogeneous as well as non-homogeneous haze without any prior information.
2. The combination of atmospheric model based parameter and haze density estimator plays the main role in our network.
3. The model can produce competitive results on any type of haze with out re-training the model.

2   Related Works

The word haze is generally used to denote visibility reducing aerosols. Depending on its characteristics, we can divide it into two types: Homogeneous and Non-Homogeneous haze (see Fig. 1). Homogeneous haze has a uniform density across the region. Mostly, hazes of natural origin are of this type. Long-range scenery photographs are highly affected by this type of haze. Non-Homogeneous Haze

Fig. 1. Haze Types: Homogeneous Haze (Left) & Non-Homogeneous Haze (Right)

has non-uniform haze density across the region and generally they consist in a small area. Photography consisting of this type of haze contains patches with varying density. Existing methods can be divided into two types: i) Traditional and ii) Deep learning based techniques.

2.1   Traditional Techniques

Image Dehazing is an ill-posed problem. Methods proposed in early 20's rely on multiple images or inputs from the user to remove haze. For example, a few works suggest polarization-based methods [26,34,35], where they use polarization property of the light to get the depth map information. This requires multiple images to be captured through a polarizer while changing its angles. A few other works [27,28] require one or more restrictions to achieve dehazing. For example, reference constraints are required to capture several scene images under different weathers. Some methods [20] gets depth mapping from a user or a 3D model.

However, in practice, depth information is not easily available neither are multiple images or other constraints. These solutions have limitations in online dehazing applications. This motivates researchers to propose dehazing methods that use a single image. These methods heavily rely on traits of haze-free or hazy images. For example, Tan [38] has proposed a method that uses contrast characteristics of a haze-free image. Haze reduces contrast, so by directly maximizing the local contrast in a patch, one can enhance the visibility. However, this very basic approach introduces blocky artifacts around the regions where the depth varies sharply. Fattal [14] has proposed a solution that generates the transmission map using the reflectance of a surface. This solution assumes that the scene depth and the albedo are independent of each other at the local patch level. However, in the case of dense haze where a vast diffused solar reflection is present at the scene, this hypothesis does not hold. He et al. [17] proposed a new prior by observing the property of clear outdoor images. This prior is known as Dark Channel Prior or DCP. This uses the fact that one of the color channels of RGB in the outdoor image has considerably low intensity. DCP fails in the sky regions, where the intensity of pixels are close to that of atmospheric light. Recently, patch similarity has also been studied to estimate transmission map like parameter for dehazing of atmospheric and underwater images [23]. Apart from these, some haze relevant features like maximum contrast, hue disparity, color attenuation [39] have also been explored for dehazing.

2.2   Deep Learning Models

Following the recent advancements in deep learning and bio-inspired neural networks, and their success in other high-level computer vision tasks of image detection and segmentation, a few deep learning based methods are also proposed for low-level vision tasks such as image dehazing and reconstructions. Here we discuss a few closely related deep learning architectures.

Dehaze-Net. Cai et al. [8] have proposed Dehazenet that produces results with good performance indices compared to statistical approaches. DehazeNet learns the function to map hazy image to the transmission map in an end-to-end manner [8]. After estimating transmission map $\tau(x)$, atmospheric light λ is estimated. Then, the haze-free image is achieved by

$$C(x) = \frac{1}{\tau(x)}H(x) - \lambda\frac{1}{\tau(x)} + \lambda \qquad (2)$$

AOD-Net. Li et al. [21] have proposed AOD-Net that gives better results as compared to existing networks. Most of the existing works estimate $\tau(x)$ and λ independently, which often amplifies the reconstruction error. AOD-Net estimates both key parameters together by combining them into one variable K

$$C(x) = K(x)H(x) - K(x) + m \qquad (3)$$

where K is

$$K(x) = \frac{\frac{1}{\tau(x)}(H(x) - \lambda) + (\lambda - m)}{H(x) - 1} \qquad (4)$$

The combined estimation of these two parameters not only reduces reconstruction error but also mutually refines each other and creates more realistic lightning conditions and structural details as compared to overexposure caused in other models [7]. More deep learning based dehazing methods have been proposed, and can be found in the following references [11,31].

Trident Dehazing Network. The atmospheric scattering model fails when haze is non-homogeneous. At NTIRE 2020 Non-Homogeneous Dehazing challenge [5], a novel Trident Dehazing Network (TDN) has been proposed to address this issue. TDN [22] learns the mapping function from a non-homogeneous hazy image to its haze-free counterpart. The architecture consists of three sub-networks: one reconstrcuts coarse-level features, another one adds up the details of haze-free image features and the third one generates the haze density of different regions of the hazy image. Finally the feature maps of these sub-nets are concatenated and fed to deformabale convolution block to produce the final result.

Apart from these methods, a few notable works are mentioned as follows. DenseNet based encoder and decoder have been used to jointly estimate transmission map and atmospheric light for dense haze scenario [16]. Haze color corrections and visibility improvement modules have been employed to address the issues of chromatic cast in bad weather condition [13]. A physical-model based disentanglement and reconstruction method has been introduced in dehazing an image with the help of multi-scale adversarial training [1]. Multi-scale features have also been utilized for image dehazing [10,40]. GAN-based architecture using residual inception has been utilized in image dehazing [12]. To reduce haze effect for autonomous driving, a fast and resource constraint network has been proposed [25].

3   Proposed Model

Both models AOD-net and TDN give good performance on homogeneous and non-homogeneous haze, respectively. However, both models fail to perform better on other haze type. We propose a novel architecture that can handle both types of haze quite well.

3.1   Base Model

Transmission map of the atmospheric model plays an important role in homogeneous dehazing and haze denisty map is quite significant in non-homogeneous dehazing. Proposed model estimates these both parameters in two different subnets: *K-estimation* subnet and *Density-estimation* subnet. We learn transmission map $\tau(x)$ and global atmospheric light λ jointly using K-estimation subnet. This targets homogeneous haze features of an image. The second subnet generates haze density map using an encoder-decoder architecture with skip connections, which is similar to *U-Net* [18] (see Fig. 2). We have six down-sampling and six up-sampling blocks with the connection between shallow and deeper layers. We also append an additional 3×3 convolution layer for output refinement. The combined output of both the subnets is fed into a convolution block, batch normalization and relu activation in a sequence. This is the base architecture of our proposed model and an example result is shown in Fig. 3. The image is taken from O-Haze dataset [4]. The base model can reduce the haze effect from the image up to some extent. However, the results have some distortion. To achieve visual vividness and sharpness we carried out some novel modifications, as discussed next.

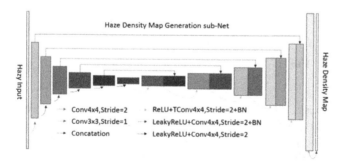

Fig. 2. UNet architecture used in Haze Density Map generation subnet [22]

3.2   Adapting Base Model for Visual Enhancement

For improvement, we use channel attention and pixel attention blocks.

Channel and Pixel Attention Blocks. To overcome loss in visual vividness, we use *Channel Attention* block from FFA-Net [30]. Our aim is to target color

Fig. 3. Base model output (Left-to-right): Hazy; Result of base model; Ground truth

attenuation and hue disparity properties by exploiting the relationship of features between color channels and generating a channel attention map. *Pixel Attention* block [30] is known to generate sharper results [41]. We connect both attention blocks (Fig. 4) to the Haze density map generation subnet. Two channel attention blocks followed by a pixel attention block are added between the last two decoder layers of the density map generation subnet. One more pair of blocks is added after the final convolution layer of the density map generation subnet. These attention modules not only reduce the color loss but also help generate better density maps.

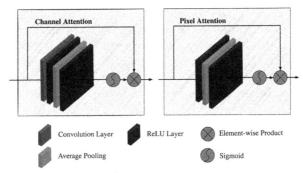

Fig. 4. Channel attention & Pixel atttention block

Perceptual Loss. To further increase the sharpness, we use perceptual loss[19], which performs quite well in image restoration tasks [15,32]. The output of both the subnet is concatenated and fed into a convolution block after batch normalization and activation layers. The output with 3 color channels is then fed into the loss model which is generated by selecting few bottom layers of pre-trained vgg16 [37]. Only selecting the output from VGG16 model does not do a good perceptual loss since the final output is made more of concepts than of features. We select the outputs from layers $1, 2, 9, 10, 17$ and 18 as loss-model outputs. These layers' weights are frozen during training. The aim is to sharpen the result by calculating the high-level difference. Lastly, we follow another 3×3 convolution layer which gives a clearer haze-free image. The layout of these final model architecture is shown in Fig. 5. The model is trained on a batch size of 8 for 20 epochs with a learning rate of $1e - 4$. The weight decay is $1e - 2$.

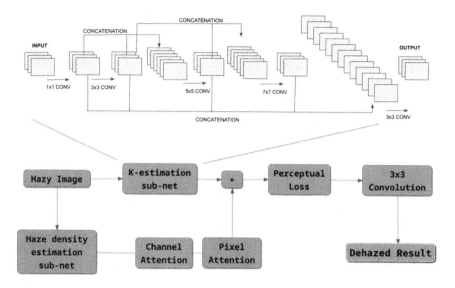

Fig. 5. Proposed model

4   Experimental Results

4.1   Datasets and Model Details

A major issue in learning based image dehazing is the requirement of hazy and clear ground truth images under identical conditions such as weather, light, and wind. Hence, most of the available training datasets are augmentations on ground truth images such as NYU-2-Hazy [36]. Recently NTIRE challenge has employed new realistic image dehazing datasets: I-Haze [6], O-Haze [4], and Dense-Haze [2]. However, most of these augmented datasets assume that haze is homogeneously distributed over the scene, which may not be the case in many real scenes where haze may be non-homogeneous in nature. To this end, a new dataset NH-Haze [3] has been introduced by manually generating the haze in some areas of haze-free image. For training the model we use the mixture of synthetic NYU-Haze and Dense-Haze datasets and 10 out of 55 images from the NH-Haze dataset. The evaluation is done on three separate datasets. I-Haze is a synthetic haze dataset generated using depth information of indoor images. O-Haze is also a synthetic haze dataset but for outdoor images. NH-Haze consists of outdoor images with non-homogeneous haze. Images used in training from the NH-Haze dataset are excluded from the evaluation. Our model has 55M parameters and it requires 338 MB of disk space.

4.2   Quantitative Evaluation

We evaluate our results in terms of PSNR and SSIM values in Table 1. The results of our method are compared with NLD [7], MSC [33] TensorFlow implementation of TDN [22], AOD-Net [21] and GCA [9]. Comparison shows that

Table 1. Evaluation on different datasets

		NLD [7]	MSC [33]	GCA [9]	AOD [21]	TDN [22]	BM	Proposed
I-Haze	PSNR	14.12	15.22	14.95	15.61	15.13	15.56	16.43
	SSIM	0.654	0.755	0.719	0.712	0.706	0.674	0.698
O-Haze	PSNR	15.98	17.56	16.28	16.64	15.43	16.23	17.65
	SSIM	0.585	0.650	0.645	0.725	0.708	0.710	0.720
NH-Haze	PSNR	–	–	–	14.54	19.31	15.38	16.93
	SSIM	–	–	–	0.621	0.712	0.684	0.695

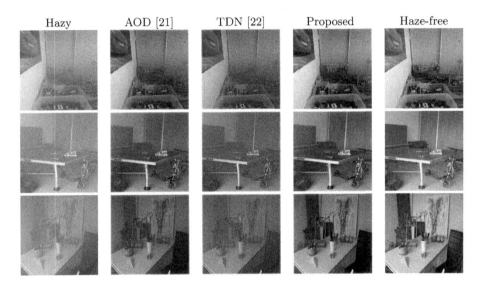

Hazy   AOD [21]   TDN [22]   Proposed   Haze-free

Fig. 6. Results on I-Haze dataset [6]

the proposed model has better PSNR and SSIM values for I-Haze and O-Haze datasets. However, for NH-Haze, TDN method still performs better than ours. The reason being that the TDN method is specifically tailored to reduce the NH-Haze, but it fails to reduce homogeneous haze, effectively. On the other hand, our method can reduce both types of haze quite well without retraining the network. The results can be further improved by appropriate weighting the two sub-nets (K-estimation and haze density estimation) in our network.

4.3   Qualitative Results

Figures 6, 7 and 8 show final dehazed output images of Proposed Model and other state-of-the-art dehazing models for I-Haze, O-Haze, and NH-Haze datasets, respectively. From left to right are Hazy images, outputs of AOD-Net [21], outputs of TDN [22], outputs of Proposed Model, and Haze-free(ground truth) images. One can observe that the proposed model is able to produce better results as compared to the existing approaches for homogeneous hazy images from the I-Haze and O-Haze datasets. For non-homogeneous haze, the proposed model is slightly lagging behind the TDN, which is developed for non-homogeneous haze only. However, the proposed model is able to reduce the haze effect better than the methods, developed for homogeneous haze. This is due to the combination of blocks that are responsible for estimating homogeneous and non-homogeneous haze properties.

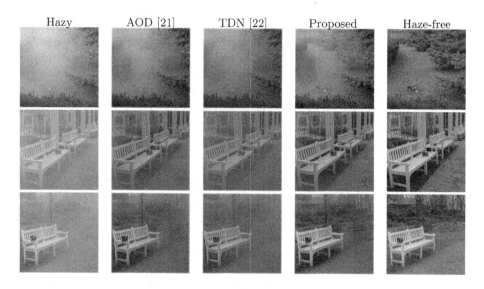

Fig. 7. Results on O-Haze dataset [4]

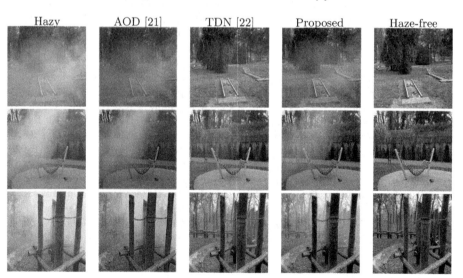

Fig. 8. Results on NH-Haze dataset [3]

5   Conclusion

In this paper, we have addressed the ill-posed problem of image dehazing in the presence of homogeneous and/or non-homogeneous haze. For homogeneous case, estimating transmission map is the key, whereas density map plays an important role for non-homogeneous haze. Our deep architecture aims to estimate these key parameters in a single framework to deal with both types of haze. We have experimented with homogeneous as well as non-homogeneous hazy images to demonstrate the efficacy of our model. The produced results are superior than the existing methods for homogeneous haze. This suggests that the K-estimation module works as intended in generating features for homogeneous haze. For non-homogeneous haze, the proposed model has produced competitive results, which can be further improved by assigning appropriate weights between the K-estimation and density map estimation. Our model performs quite well when the haze type is unknown or both types of haze are present.

References

1. Towards perceptual image dehazing by physics-based disentanglement and adversarial training 32. https://ojs.aaai.org/index.php/AAAI/article/view/12317
2. Ancuti, C.O., Ancuti, C., Sbert, M., Timofte, R.: Dense-haze: a benchmark for image dehazing with dense-haze and haze-free images. In: 2019 IEEE International Conference on Image Processing (ICIP), pp. 1014–1018. IEEE (2019)
3. Ancuti, C.O., Ancuti, C., Timofte, R.: NH-HAZE: an image dehazing benchmark with non-homogeneous hazy and haze-free images. In: Proceedings of the IEEE/CVF Conference on Computer Vision and Pattern Recognition Workshops, pp. 444–445 (2020)
4. Ancuti, C.O., Ancuti, C., Timofte, R., De Vleeschouwer, C.: O-HAZE: a dehazing benchmark with real hazy and haze-free outdoor images. In: Proceedings of the IEEE Conference on computer Vision and Pattern Recognition Workshops, pp. 754–762 (2018)
5. Ancuti, C.O., Ancuti, C., Vasluianu, F.A., Timofte, R.: Ntire 2020 challenge on nonhomogeneous dehazing. In: Proceedings of the IEEE/CVF Conference on Computer Vision and Pattern Recognition Workshops, pp. 490–491 (2020)
6. Ancuti, C., Ancuti, C.O., Timofte, R., De Vleeschouwer, C.: I-HAZE: a dehazing benchmark with real hazy and haze-free indoor images. In: Blanc-Talon, J., Helbert, D., Philips, W., Popescu, D., Scheunders, P. (eds.) ACIVS 2018. LNCS, vol. 11182, pp. 620–631. Springer, Cham (2018). https://doi.org/10.1007/978-3-030-01449-0_52
7. Berman, D., Avidan, S., et al.: Non-local image dehazing. In: Proceedings of the IEEE Conference on Computer Vision and Pattern Recognition, pp. 1674–1682 (2016)
8. Cai, B., Xu, X., Jia, K., Qing, C., Tao, D.: DehazeNet: an end-to-end system for single image haze removal. IEEE Trans. Image Process. **25**(11), 5187–5198 (2016)
9. Chen, D., et al.: Gated context aggregation network for image dehazing and deraining. In: 2019 IEEE Winter Conference on Applications of Computer Vision (WACV), pp. 1375–1383. IEEE (2019)

10. Chen, S., Chen, Y., Qu, Y., Huang, J., Hong, M.: Multi-scale adaptive dehazing network. In: IEEE/CVF Conference on Computer Vision and Pattern Recognition Workshops (CVPRW), pp. 2051–2059 (2019). https://doi.org/10.1109/CVPRW.2019.00257
11. Dong, H., et al.: Multi-scale boosted dehazing network with dense feature fusion. In: Proceedings of the IEEE/CVF Conference on Computer Vision and Pattern Recognition, pp. 2157–2167 (2020)
12. Dudhane, A., Aulakh, H.S., Murala, S.: RI-GAN: an end-to-end network for single image haze removal. In: IEEE/CVF Conference on Computer Vision and Pattern Recognition Workshops (CVPRW), pp. 2014–2023 (2019). https://doi.org/10.1109/CVPRW.2019.00253
13. Dudhane, A., Biradar, K.M., Patil, P.W., Hambarde, P., Murala, S.: Varicolored image de-hazing. In: 2020 IEEE/CVF Conference on Computer Vision and Pattern Recognition (CVPR), pp. 4563–4572 (2020). https://doi.org/10.1109/CVPR42600.2020.00462
14. Fattal, R.: Single image dehazing. ACM Trans. Graph. (TOG) 27(3), 1–9 (2008)
15. Gholizadeh-Ansari, M., Alirezaie, J., Babyn, P.: Deep learning for low-dose CT denoising using perceptual loss and edge detection layer. J. Digit. Imaging 33(2), 504–515 (2020)
16. Guo, T., Li, X., Cherukuri, V., Monga, V.: Dense scene information estimation network for dehazing. In: 2019 IEEE/CVF Conference on Computer Vision and Pattern Recognition Workshops (CVPRW), pp. 2122–2130 (2019). https://doi.org/10.1109/CVPRW.2019.00265
17. He, K., Sun, J., Tang, X.: Single image haze removal using dark channel prior. IEEE Trans. Pattern Anal. Mach. Intell. 33(12), 2341–2353 (2010)
18. Isola, P., Zhu, J.Y., Zhou, T., Efros, A.A.: Image-to-image translation with conditional adversarial networks. In: Proceedings of the IEEE Conference on Computer Vision and Pattern Recognition, pp. 1125–1134 (2017)
19. Johnson, J., Alahi, A., Fei-Fei, L.: Perceptual losses for real-time style transfer and super-resolution. In: Leibe, B., Matas, J., Sebe, N., Welling, M. (eds.) ECCV 2016. LNCS, vol. 9906, pp. 694–711. Springer, Cham (2016). https://doi.org/10.1007/978-3-319-46475-6_43
20. Kopf, J., et al.: Deep photo: Model-based photograph enhancement and viewing. ACM Trans. Graph. (TOG) 27(5), 1–10 (2008)
21. Li, B., Peng, X., Wang, Z., Xu, J., Feng, D.: AOD-Net: all-in-one dehazing network. In: Proceedings of the IEEE International Conference on Computer Vision, pp. 4770–4778 (2017)
22. Liu, J., Wu, H., Xie, Y., Qu, Y., Ma, L.: Trident dehazing network. In: Proceedings of the IEEE/CVF Conference on Computer Vision and Pattern Recognition Workshops, pp. 430–431 (2020)
23. Mandal, S., Rajagopalan, A.: Local proximity for enhanced visibility in haze. IEEE Trans. Image Process. 29, 2478–2491 (2019)
24. McCartney, E.J.: Optics of the atmosphere: scattering by molecules and particles. New York (1976)
25. Mehra, A., Mandal, M., Narang, P., Chamola, V.: ReviewNet: a fast and resource optimized network for enabling safe autonomous driving in hazy weather conditions. IEEE Trans. Intell. Transp. Syst. 22(7), 4256–4266 (2021). https://doi.org/10.1109/TITS.2020.3013099
26. Namer, E., Schechner, Y.Y.: Advanced visibility improvement based on polarization filtered images. In: Polarization Science and Remote Sensing II, vol. 5888, p. 588805. International Society for Optics and Photonics (2005)

27. Narasimhan, S.G., Nayar, S.K.: Removing weather effects from monochrome images. In: Proceedings of the 2001 IEEE Computer Society Conference on Computer Vision and Pattern Recognition, CVPR 2001, vol. 2, p. II. IEEE (2001)
28. Narasimhan, S.G., Nayar, S.K.: Contrast restoration of weather degraded images. IEEE Trans. Pattern Anal. Mach. Intell. **25**(6), 713–724 (2003)
29. Nayar, S.K., Narasimhan, S.G.: Vision in bad weather. In: Proceedings of the Seventh IEEE International Conference on Computer Vision, vol. 2, pp. 820–827. IEEE (1999)
30. Qin, X., Wang, Z., Bai, Y., Xie, X., Jia, H.: FFA-Net: feature fusion attention network for single image dehazing. In: Proceedings of the AAAI Conference on Artificial Intelligence, vol. 34, pp. 11908–11915 (2020)
31. Qu, Y., Chen, Y., Huang, J., Xie, Y.: Enhanced pix2pix dehazing network. In: Proceedings of the IEEE/CVF Conference on Computer Vision and Pattern Recognition, pp. 8160–8168 (2019)
32. Rad, M.S., Bozorgtabar, B., Marti, U.V., Basler, M., Ekenel, H.K., Thiran, J.P.: Srobb: targeted perceptual loss for single image super-resolution. In: Proceedings of the IEEE/CVF International Conference on Computer Vision, pp. 2710–2719 (2019)
33. Ren, W., Liu, S., Zhang, H., Pan, J., Cao, X., Yang, M.-H.: Single image dehazing via multi-scale convolutional neural networks. In: Leibe, B., Matas, J., Sebe, N., Welling, M. (eds.) ECCV 2016. LNCS, vol. 9906, pp. 154–169. Springer, Cham (2016). https://doi.org/10.1007/978-3-319-46475-6_10
34. Schechner, Y.Y., Narasimhan, S.G., Nayar, S.K.: Instant dehazing of images using polarization. In: Proceedings of the 2001 IEEE Computer Society Conference on Computer Vision and Pattern Recognition, CVPR 2001, vol. 1, p. I. IEEE (2001)
35. Schechner, Y.Y., Narasimhan, S.G., Nayar, S.K.: Polarization-based vision through haze. Appl. Opt. **42**(3), 511–525 (2003)
36. Silberman, N., Hoiem, D., Kohli, P., Fergus, R.: Indoor segmentation and support inference from RGBD images. In: Fitzgibbon, A., Lazebnik, S., Perona, P., Sato, Y., Schmid, C. (eds.) ECCV 2012. LNCS, vol. 7576, pp. 746–760. Springer, Heidelberg (2012). https://doi.org/10.1007/978-3-642-33715-4_54
37. Simonyan, K., Zisserman, A.: Very deep convolutional networks for large-scale image recognition. arXiv preprint arXiv:1409.1556 (2014)
38. Tan, R.T.: Visibility in bad weather from a single image. In: 2008 IEEE Conference on Computer Vision and Pattern Recognition, pp. 1–8. IEEE (2008)
39. Tang, K., Yang, J., Wang, J.: Investigating haze-relevant features in a learning framework for image dehazing, pp. 2995–3002, June 2014. https://doi.org/10.1109/CVPR.2014.383
40. Zhang, J., Tao, D.: FAMED-Net: a fast and accurate multi-scale end-to-end dehazing network. IEEE Trans. Image Process. **29**, 72–84 (2020). https://doi.org/10.1109/TIP.2019.2922837
41. Zhao, H., Kong, X., He, J., Qiao, Yu., Dong, C.: Efficient image super-resolution using pixel attention. In: Bartoli, A., Fusiello, A. (eds.) ECCV 2020. LNCS, vol. 12537, pp. 56–72. Springer, Cham (2020). https://doi.org/10.1007/978-3-030-67070-2_3

Improved Periocular Recognition Through Blend of Handcrafted and Deep Features

Aryan Lala[1], Kalagara Chaitanya Kumar[2], Ritesh Vyas[3(✉)],
and Manoj Sharma[1]

[1] Bennett University, Greater Noida, India
[2] Deepsight AI Labs, Bengaluru, India
[3] Lancaster University, Lancaster, UK
`ritesh.vyas157@gmail.com`

Abstract. Periocular region is the area surrounding human eye. It has emerged as an effective biometric trait due to its robust nature, requirement of less user cooperation and relative invariance to aging effects. Owing to these advantages, we intend to present a more secure and safe periocular recognition approach by fusing the matching scores of handcrafted and deep learning features. The handcrafted descriptor is made to analyze the periocular images at multiresolution level and understand the relationship within local pixel neighborhood. On the contrary, deep learning features are extracted using the strong potential of transfer learning. This research is completed on a publicly available standard periocular database to substantiate the performance of proposed method.

Keywords: Biometrics · Handcrafted features · Deep features · Periocular recognition

1 Introduction

With an increase in the usage of mobile devices, like smartphones and tablets, the need for biometric identification is growing [13]. To identify a person based on their physiological and behavioral traits biometrics is very important [15]. These attributes are unique for every individual and some of these traits consist of fingerprint, iris, face, palm print, signature, periocular, ear etc. [1]. Every trait is used in different applications for different purposes depending on their weaknesses and strengths. None of the trait is best and can neither be used for all applications [15].

Fingerprint and face recognition are the most commonly used traits in mobile devices, but they have some disadvantages. Fingerprint is vulnerable to theft or forgery, since it is unfeasible to remove fingerprint information after every use, and is delicate to unforeseen behaviours, which leads to decrease in recognition performance. Face recognition methods are better than fingerprint recognition

B. Raman et al. (Eds.): CVIP 2021, CCIS 1567, pp. 387–397, 2022.
https://doi.org/10.1007/978-3-031-11346-8_34

since they are researched and developed more however occlusion, due to masks worn to prevent coronavirus, surgical masks worn by healthcare professionals, clothing to prevent sun exposure or veils for religious reasons, is a major problem in face recognition [1]. Additionally, face trait requires conditions like right lighting and fully frontal face images [3]. For iris biometrics, the quality of the captured images, constrained nature of the user's environment and accurate segmentation of iris region from the whole eye image determines the accuracy of biometric recognition [1]. Also, iris trait requires great user cooperation since the distance between the sensor and the subject should be minimum [6].

In this article we work upon the periocular region, also known as the ocular region. It is the facial area surrounding the eye comprising the eyelids, eyelashes, eyebrows, and skin around the eye. This region provides vast information and texture valuable for a periocular biometric system. It also has advantage over iris region, when iris resolution is low, as periocular recognition can be implemented in low quality images [3]. Moreover, the periocular region is beneficial over the face biometric when the images captured contain occluded mouth and nose of the subject [6]. Furthermore, periocular traits can be obtained from either one of the face image or iris image, and can also be captured from any existing smartphone camera operating in visible spectrum with no additional hardware required [9].

The present work is an attempt to develop a score level fusion of handcrafted features and deep features for periocular recognition. The hand-crafted feature extractor performs multiresolution analysis through wavelet transforms, and local texture representation through an exclusive neighbourhood relationship. For extracting deep features, we use transfer learning from pre trained CNN models. We propose the fusion as it can improve the performance of hand-crafted features and bring improvement in the performance of periocular recognition. Extracting deep features through transfer learning would result in state-of-the-art results. This work is carried out on near infrared periocular images of a publicly available Cross-Eyed dataset.

2   Literature Survey

Shao et al. [13] proposed an eye-based recognition approach, which comprises of static and dynamic features as the eye features. The static feature was the periocular feature extracted using the deep neural networks whereas the dynamic feature was the saccadic feature obtained by the saccadic velocity. Hernandez-Diaz et al. [5] addressed the challenge of cross-spectral periocular recognition, which usually generates substantial decrease in performance as opposed to matching in the same spectrum. They proposed an image translation technique based on conditional generative adversarial networks (CGANs) to convert the periocular images amongst the spectra so that the matching could be performed in the same spectrum. The experiments were performed through a variety of handcrafted and CNN descriptors.

Umer et al. [15] proposed a novel technique for biometric recognition by fusing scores due to iris and periocular biometrics, through features extracted from renowned CNN architectures like VGG16, ResNet50 and InceptionV3. Boutros et al. [2] investigated the possibility of utilizing the internal camera of Head Mounted Displays (HMD) for biometric verification, using the captured ocular images, taking into consideration the low computation power of such devices. Behera et al. [1] proposed an attention-based twin deep CNN, called variance-guided attention-based cross-spectral network (VGACNet), having shared parameters to effectively match the periocular images in cross spectral environment.

Raja et al. [9] proposed two new feature extraction techniques, deep sparse features (DSF) and deep sparse time frequency features (DeSTiFF), in order to develop effective periocular recognition framework for images captured from smartphones. Zanlorensi et al. [17] performed an extensive experiments with several CNN architectures employed in state-of-the-art methods for ocular research. The authors evaluated the methods in the closed-world and open-world protocols, considering the identification and verification tasks and showed that the Multi-task model achieved the best results. In other work, Zanlorensi et al. [18] proposed an attribute normalization scheme based on generative deep learning frameworks, in order to reduce the within-class variability in unconstrained periocular recognition.

In view of the literature presented in this section, it could be inferred that the deep features have played prominent role in recognition of periocular images, irrespective of the underlying framework (smartphone/cross spectral). This motivated us to incorporate the deep features into consideration. However, deep architectures suffer from black box problem, limiting their explanability. Hence, we consider both the handcrafted and deep features for utilizing the potential of periocular recognition to its fullest strength.

3   Proposed Methodology

Feature extraction is a method where we obtain information from the algorithms. For a model to perform well, it is cardinal that we choose best information. Lot of research was done on periocular region and commendable results were obtained. Recently, Kumar et al. [6] proposed hand crafted feature extractor for periocular recognition using multiresolution analysis through wavelet transforms, followed by local texture representation by using an exclusive neighborhood relationship and it achieved state-of-the-art results. Many Deep learning approaches [8,10,19] have also been applied in periocular domain but could not perform well due to limited data and need for huge computational power. In this paper we propose an optimal strategy by fusion of individual performances of hand crafted and deep learning features. The overall proposed methodology is demonstrated through Fig. 1. More details are furnished in the subsequent subsections.

3.1   Handcrafted Feature Extraction

The handcrafted method aims to improve accuracy by applying multiresolution analysis with the help of wavelet transform, which helps in decomposing the

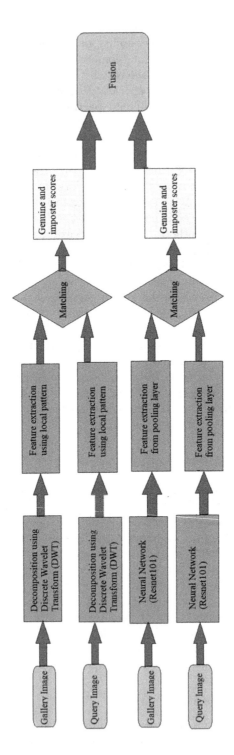

Fig. 1. The overall proposed methodology

information. After that, a texture representation algorithm called Directional Threshold Local Binary Pattern (DTLBP) [14] is used to extract information from local neighborhood. The methodologies employed are discussed below.

Discrete wavelet transform (DWT) [7] is a tool which helps in breaking up information into a number of sets and the information can be presented in either time series or as frequency bands. Of all the wavelets available, we employed Daubechies wavelets as they outperformed other wavelets according [6]. Further, directional threshold local binary pattern (DTLBP) [14] is a very popular tool due to its effortless implementation, usage and its novel thresholding methodology. In addition, it is also sturdy towards noise and considers information from all the 8 directions. The mathematical operation of DTLBP is, it takes center pixel as threshold and assigns '1' or zero by taking the mean of surrounding pixels in 8 directions and compares the mean with center pixel. If mean is greater than center pixel, DTLBP will label it as '1', else the binary number '0' will be assigned. The binary numbers will be changed to decimal numbers and the obtained decimal number will be assigned to the center pixel. Similar operation would be done for all the pixels of the digital image. DTLBP, as mentioned above, in addition to decreasing the noise, strengthens the disparateness as its thresholding technique leverages information from neighboring pixels. All these features aid in improving the accuracy of identifying the subjects.

3.2   Deep Feature Extraction

In order to extract features from deep learning models, the first task is choosing the architecture. Of all the deep learning architectures present, we chose to proceed with ResNet101 [4]. The ResNet model is chosen to leverage from its unique property of identity mapping from the exclusive shortcut connections, which can in turn help to mitigate the problem of vanishing gradient. Another reason for choosing ResNet101 is purely empirical and ResNet101 produces state-of-the-art results. As we aim to solve the problem using transfer learning and fine tuning, we used the publicly available model.

Transfer learning is process where a deep learning model trained for one problem can be used to improve the performance for other challenges. The reason for this improvement is because the weights learned by the initial layers of the deep learning models are generalizable across various domains. For the problem at hand we froze 10 layers and trained rest of the layers on cross eyed dataset. ResNet101 has operational layers like Convolutional layer, Pooling layer, Batch Normalization layer, and activation layer. ResNet101 has huge depth and with series of convolutional layers. The advantage of using ResNet101 is its skip connections that allows alternative path for the gradient while learning, making it easier for the model to learn.

In order to evaluate the proposed approach, dense layer with 120 nodes and activation sigmoid is added as cross eyed database has 120 subjects. The model is trained for 10 epochs using Stochastic Gradient Descent Classifier with learning rate $3e{-}4$. After training, we discard the output layers and extract the features from 'Global average pooling layer'. Regarding the data split, 60% of samples for each class are used for retraining the model. Whereas, 15% and 25% of samples are employed for the tasks of validation and testing, respectively.

3.3 Fusion

By utilizing the above mentioned methods, information like genuine and imposter scores are obtained from both the deep learning model and hand crafted model. The obtained scores are then fused together to yield further improvements in the performance. Score level fusion is chosen attributing to its low complexity and no need to know about the feature extraction models. Moreover, it also avoids any crucial problem related with the dimensionality as is seen in feature-level fusion. The score-level fusion has aided in augmenting the performance of the models by improving the model's accuracy, EER, etc. Out of all the different ways to fuse the scores, we advanced with average fusion as it produced best results for our model.

4 Experiments and Results

4.1 Database

The database used for the experimentation is the standard periocular database called CrossEyed database [11,12]. The database consists of left and right iris and periocular region images of 120 subjects. Each of the 120 subjects have 8 images in Near Infrared Region (NIR) and 8 images in visible wavelength (VW). The data is split in training data, validation data and testing data with training data consisting of 5 images per subject, validation data with 1 image per subject, and training data with 2 images per subject. The model is trained on training data and evaluated on validation and testing data. The model is tested on 960 images of visible and NIR images for both left and right hand sides. The reason for choosing this dataset is due to huge difference in age of the subjects and the distance at which the images are captured. The sample images of the database are shown below in Fig. 2.

4.2 Results and Discussion

To evaluate our approach, we have used popular performance metrics like equal error rate (EER), genuine acceptance rate (GAR), false acceptance rate (FAR) and decidability index (DI). FAR gives an estimate of number of unauthorized users getting accepted as genuine users, as a percentage of total sum of unauthorized users. The percentage of authorized users getting rejected as unauthorized users is FRR. The point at which FAR and FRR becomes equal produces EER. GAR is presented as total accuracy for the model and decidability index is measure of separability between distribution of genuine and imposter scores. Genuine scores are obtained by matching one images of a subject with other images of same subject and imposter scores are obtained by matching an image of a subject with other images of different subjects. We have followed all-to-all matching

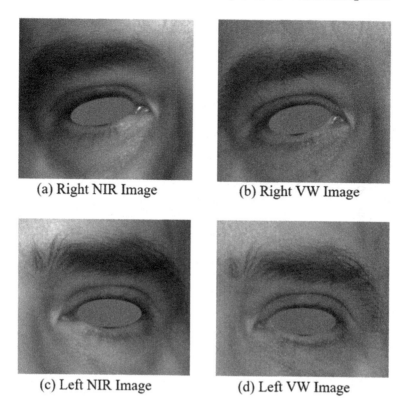

(a) Right NIR Image   (b) Right VW Image

(c) Left NIR Image   (d) Left VW Image

Fig. 2. Sample images from CrossEyed database

protocol [16], which is the most difficult protocol among the available protocol, and in the all-to-all matching protocol we match the images in the database with every other image. Due to the matching protocol followed, the number of genuine and imposter scores obtained are 3,360 and 4,56,960.

We use the averaging technique for performing score level fusion of hand-crafted and deep features. After calculating the genuine and imposter scores for both the approaches, DTLBP and ResNet, we calculate the average of the genuine and imposter scores and finally obtain the performance metrics for the Fusion approach. To depict a graphical comparison among the performances of the hand-crafted features (DTLBP), deep features (ResNet), and fusion features (Fusion), Receiver Operating Characteristics (ROC) curves are plotted for each dataset in Fig. 3. In general, the ROC curves are plotted against FAR and GAR calculated at different thresholds. The legend of the ROC curves in Fig. 3 shows the values of EER, DI, and GAR. Notably, all the GAR values are measured at an FAR of 1%. It could be easily observed that the plot for Fusion is placed higher than the plots of DTLBP and ResNet, which suggests that Fusion outperforms the other two approaches.

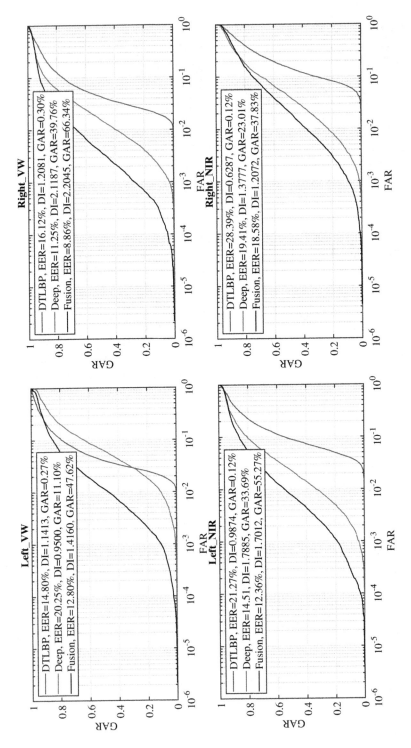

Fig. 3. Comparative ROC curves

Table 1. Comparison table of the performance results

Subset	Approach	EER (%)	GAR (%)	DI
Left-VW	DTLBP	14.80	0.27	1.1413
	Deep	20.25	11.10	0.9500
	Fusion	12.80	47.62	1.4160
Right-VW	DTLBP	16.12	0.30	1.2081
	Deep	11.25	39.76	2.1187
	Fusion	8.86	66.34	2.2045
Left-NIR	DTLBP	21.27	0.12	0.9874
	Deep	14.51	33.69	1.7885
	Fusion	12.36	55.27	1.7012
Right-NIR	DTLBP	28.39	0.12	0.6287
	Deep	19.41	23.01	1.3777
	Fusion	18.58	37.83	1.2072

It is clearly visible from Table 1 that there is significant improvement in EERs and GARs for all cases. When compared to DTLBP, Fusion results in improvement of 13.51%, 45.04%, 41.89% and 34.55% for Left VW, Right VW, Left NIR, and Right NIR subsets, respectively. And when compared to ResNet, Fusion yields improvement of 36.79%, 21.24%, 14.82% and 4.28% in EER Left VW, Right VW, Left NIR, and Right NIR, respectively. Similar improvements can be observed in other metrics (GAR and DI), especially the momentous improvement in GAR values which resulted from the fusion leading to more accurate recognition capability. Concurrently, the DI values are also improved which indicate sublime separation between the genuine and imposter score distributions. Hence, it is verified that the fusion of the two approaches surpasses the individual ones considerably.

5   Conclusion

In this paper, we presented a combinational approach of amalgamating the individual performances of handcrafted and deep features, for the application of periocular recognition. The proposed approach was built upon multiresolution analysis of the periocular images for handcrafted features, and state-of-the-art nature of the CNN model. Experiments conducted with a benchmark periocular database revealed that the proposed approach has high potential to yield outperforming results for all the four underlying subsets (for both eyes of subjects, and with both illumination wavelengths of VW and NIR). The huge relative improvements in EER and GAR as a result of proposed fusion-based methodology, have validated its promising nature. At future avenues, the proposed methodology could be extended to get improvements in the cross-spectral matching scenario.

Acknowledgement. Authors would like to acknowledge the organizers of "2nd Cross-Spectrum Iris/Periocular Recognition Competition" for making their periocular database publicly available for research purpose.

References

1. Behera, S.S., Mishra, S.S., Mandal, B., Puhan, N.B.: Variance-guided attention-based twin deep network for cross-spectral periocular recognition. Image Vis. Comput. **104**, 104016 (2020)
2. Boutros, F., Damer, N., Raja, K., Ramachandra, R., Kirchbuchner, F., Kuijper, A.: Iris and periocular biometrics for head mounted displays: segmentation, recognition, and synthetic data generation. Image Vis. Comput. **104**, 104007 (2020)
3. Toledo Ferraz, C., et al.: A comparison among keyframe extraction techniques for CNN classification based on video periocular images. Multimedia Tools Appl. **80**(8), 12843–12856 (2021)
4. He, K., Zhang, X., Ren, S., Sun, J.: Deep residual learning for image recognition. In: 2016 IEEE Conference on Computer Vision and Pattern Recognition (CVPR). IEEE (2016)
5. Hernandez-Diaz, K., Alonso-Fernandez, F., Bigun, J.: Cross-spectral periocular recognition with conditional adversarial networks. In: 2020 IEEE International Joint Conference on Biometrics (IJCB). IEEE (2020)
6. Kumar, K.C., Lala, A., Vyas, R., Sharma, M.: Periocular recognition via effective textural descriptor. In: 2020 IEEE 7th Uttar Pradesh Section International Conference on Electrical, Electronics and Computer Engineering (UPCON). IEEE (2020)
7. Mallat, S.G.: A theory for multiresolution signal decomposition: the wavelet representation. In: Fundamental Papers in Wavelet Theory, pp. 494–513. Princeton University Press (2009)
8. Proenca, H., Neves, J.C.: Deep-PRWIS: periocular recognition without the iris and sclera using deep learning frameworks. IEEE Trans. Inf. Forensics Secur. **13**(4), 888–896 (2018)
9. Raja, K.B., Raghavendra, R., Busch, C.: Collaborative representation of deep sparse filtered features for robust verification of smartphone periocular images. In: 2016 IEEE International Conference on Image Processing (ICIP). IEEE (2016)
10. Rattani, A., Derakhshani, R., Saripalle, S.K., Gottemukkula, V.: ICIP 2016 competition on mobile ocular biometric recognition. In: 2016 IEEE International Conference on Image Processing (ICIP). IEEE (2016)
11. Sequeira, A., et al.: Cross-eyed - cross-spectral iris/periocular recognition database and competition. In: 2016 International Conference of the Biometrics Special Interest Group (BIOSIG). IEEE (2016)
12. Sequeira, A.F., et al.: Cross-eyed 2017: cross-spectral iris/periocular recognition competition. In: 2017 IEEE International Joint Conference on Biometrics (IJCB). IEEE (2017)
13. Shao, H., Li, J., Zhang, J., Yu, H., Sun, J.: Eye-based recognition for user identification on mobile devices. ACM Trans. Multimedia Comput. Commun. Appl. **16**(4), 1–19 (2021)
14. Tabatabaei, S.M., Chalechale, A.: Noise-tolerant texture feature extraction through directional thresholded local binary pattern. Vis. Comput. **36**(5), 967–987 (2019)
15. Umer, S., Sardar, A., Dhara, B.C., Rout, R.K., Pandey, H.M.: Person identification using fusion of iris and periocular deep features. Neural Netw. **122**, 407–419 (2020)

16. Vyas, R., Kanumuri, T., Sheoran, G., Dubey, P.: Towards ocular recognition through local image descriptors. In: Nain, N., Vipparthi, S.K., Raman, B. (eds.) CVIP 2019. CCIS, vol. 1147, pp. 3–12. Springer, Singapore (2020)
17. Zanlorensi, L.A., Laroca, R., Lucio, D.R., Santos, L.R., Britto Jr, A.S., Menotti, D.: UFPR-periocular: a periocular dataset collected by mobile devices in unconstrained scenarios. arXiv preprint arXiv:2011.12427 (2020)
18. Zanlorensi, L.A., Proenca, H., Menotti, D.: Unconstrained periocular recognition: using generative deep learning frameworks for attribute normalization. In: 2020 IEEE International Conference on Image Processing (ICIP). IEEE (2020)
19. Zhao, Z., Kumar, A.: Improving periocular recognition by explicit attention to critical regions in deep neural network. IEEE Trans. Inf. Forensics Secur. **13**(12), 2937–2952 (2018)

Kernels for Incoherent Projection and Orthogonal Matching Pursuit

Himanshu Kandiyal$^{(\boxtimes)}$ and C. S. Sastry

Department of Mathematics, Indian Institute of Technology,
Hyderabad, Sangareddy 502284, India
{MA19MSCST11007,csastry}@iith.ac.in

Abstract. In compressed sensing, Orthogonal Matching Pursuit (OMP) is one of the most popular and simpler algorithms for finding a sparse description of the system Ax = b. The recovery guarantees of OMP depend on the coherence parameter (maximum off-diagonal entry - in magnitude - in the Gram matrix of normalized columns of A). Nevertheless, when A has a bad coherence (being close to 1), the OMP algorithm is likely to provide a pessimistic performance numerically, which is indeed the case in many applications where one uses the data-driven sensing matrices. With a view to improving the coherence of a highly coherent system $Ax = b$, we transform the columns of A as well as b via a map ϕ and formulate a new system $\phi(b) = \phi(A)x_0$. Here $\phi(A)$ is understood in column-wise sense. We show that the execution of OMP on new system can be carried out using kernels, requiring thereby no explicit expression of ϕ. We use some standard kernels and show that the new system is highly incoherent (possessing reduced coherence) and better behaved (possessing improved condition number) compared to the original system. Notwithstanding the fact that both the systems have different sets of solutions, we demonstrate that the kernel-based OMP significantly improves the performance in the classification of heart-beats for their normal and abnormal patterns.

Keywords: Compressed sensing · Kernels · ECG classification

1 Introduction

Electrocardiogram signals are examined for diagnosing the heart abnormalities accurately. Cardiac arrhythmia is a term used for any of a large and heterogeneous group of conditions in which there is abnormal electrical activity in the heart. The heart beat may be too fast or too slow, and may be regular or irregular [4,5].

Different signal processing techniques like Fourier transform, wavelets, compressive sensing and fractal analysis etc. have been applied on these signals to

Second author is grateful to CSIR, India (No. 25(0309)/20/EMR-II) for its support.

interpret and detect the heart diseases [6]. The problem of classifying ECG signals into normal and anomalous categories has widely been investigated [4,5]. In the general context, wavelet-based techniques have been used for estimating the characteristic points of ECG signals (P, Q, R, S and T). These parameters have been further exploited to identify the heart related anomalies [4–6].

Of late the techniques based on compressed sensing (CS) have become popular for analyzing and classifying ECG signals [2,5]. The dictionary learning methods, being data driven, especially have gained traction owing to their superior classification performance [6]. The sensing matrices when generated from ECG signals are often plagued with issues such as poor conditioning and high coherence etc. (these are discussed in detail in a later section and demonstrated in the simulation section). Motivated by this, in this paper, we discuss a new kernel based method for the classification of ECG signals for their normal and abnormal patterns.

The paper is organized in terms of 7 sections. In Sect. 2, we discuss necessary mathematical details pertaining to compressed sensing and kernels, followed by motivation and contribution in Sect. 3. In Sects. 4 and 5, we present kernel OMP and a new classification method based on it. We provide our experimental setup and simulation results in last two sections respectively.

2   Basics of Compressed Sensing and Kernels

In this section, we discuss the necessary details of compressed sensing and kernel trick that are relevant to the current work.

2.1   Compressed Sensing

For data that can be sparsely generated, one can obtain good reconstructions from reduced number of measurements. A wealth of recent developments in applied mathematics, by the name of Compressed Sensing (CS) aim at achieving this objective. The basic philosophy behind such recoveries is sparse modeling of underlying data by the elements of a given system function.

The objective of Compressive sensing (CS) is to reconstruct a sparse object, a signal or an image, $x \in \mathbb{R}^n$ from a few of its linear measurements $y \in \mathbb{R}^m$ via stable and efficient reconstruction methods [2]. For a given measurement-vector y and a sensing matrix A, one forms a linear system of equations $y = Ax$, where A is of size $m \times n$ with $m < n$ and x is the object to be reconstructed. The meaning of the pair (y, A) is dependent on the application at hand. For instance, in under-sampled magnetic resonance imaging (MRI), A is the row-restricted matrix of discrete Fourier transform while y is the vector of Fourier frequencies of underlying image. The under-determined system $y = Ax$ has infinitely many solutions when A has full row rank. The representation of y in terms of a sensing matrix A is sparse if y is represented by a very few columns of A. In other words, there exists x with a very few nonzero coefficients such that $y = Ax$ holds and such a vector x is called sparse. Sparsity is measured by $\|\cdot\|_0$ norm and is defined as $\|x\|_0 = |\{i \in \{1, 2, 3, \ldots, n\} : x_i \neq 0\}|$. Even though $\| \cdot \|_0$ fails to satisfy the absolute homogeneity[1] of norm properties, one calls $\| \cdot \|_0$ as zero norm out of convenience.

The sparsest solution (the solution which has fewer non-zero entries, implying the least value for $\| \cdot \|_0$-norm) can be obtained from the following optimization problem:

$$\mathcal{P}_1 : min_x \|x\|_0 \text{ subject to } y = Ax, \tag{1}$$

provided A and its size satisfy some properties [2]. This problem can be adopted to the noisy case as well. A convex relaxation of (1) via $\|.\|_1$ norm has been proposed in the literature.

The OMP is a popular method that solves (1) heuristically. OMP being an iterative and greedy algorithm selects at each step a column of the sensing matrix A, which has the maximum correlation with the current residuals. This column is then added to the set of selected columns. The algorithm updates the residuals by projecting the observation onto the linear subspace spanned by the columns that have already been selected and the algorithm then iterates until a convergence criterion is satisfied. Compared with other alternative methods, a major advantage of the OMP lies in its simplicity and fast execution. The pseudo-code of OMP is provided in Algorithm 1.

Algorithm 1. OMP

1: **Data** : $\mathbf{A}, \mathbf{y}$
2: Result: x such that $y \approx Ax$
3: *Initialisation* $\Lambda_0 = \{\}, l = 1, r_0 = y$, Normalise columns of A
4: **while** $l \leq k$ **do**
5:     $z(j) = |A^T r_{l-1}|$
6:     $\Lambda_l = \Lambda_{l-1} \cup \{argmax_j \, z(j)\}$
7:     $x_{\Lambda_l} = argmin_{\eta \in R^{|\Lambda_l|}} \|y - A_{\Lambda_l}\eta\|_2^2$
8:     $r_l = y - A_{\Lambda_l} x_{\Lambda_l}$
9:     $l = l + 1$
10: **end while** $= 0$

---

3   Motivation for Present Work and Contribution

The recovery guarantees of OMP have been established in terms of coherence parameter of the associated sensing matrix [2]. In this section, we discuss the notion of coherence briefly.

Definition 1 (Coherence:). *The coherence of a matrix A is defined as follows:*

$$\mu(A) = \max_{i \neq j, 1 \leq i, j \leq n} \frac{|\langle a_i, a_j \rangle|}{\|a_i\|_2 \|a_j\|_2},$$

---

[1] Absolute homogeneity: $\forall \alpha \neq 0$ and $\forall x \neq 0, \|\alpha x\| = |\alpha| \|x\|$.

where a_i denotes the ith column of A. It is known that the coherence satisfies $\mu(A) \geq \sqrt{\frac{n-m}{m(n-1)}}$, which is called the Welch bound on $\mu(A)$.

Theorem 1. *Given $b \in \mathbf{R}^m, A \in \mathbf{R}^{m \times n}$, for $Ax = b$, $x \in \mathbf{R}^n$ can be recovered using OMP if A and x satisfy*

$$\|x\|_0 < \frac{1}{2\mu(A)} + \frac{1}{2}. \tag{2}$$

The above theorem implies that, for better recovery guarantees of OMP, the sensing matrix A with small coherence (μ) gains importance. This is because a small value for μ gives a larger bound on the sparsity (k) in (2). In view of the least square technique being incorporated in the execution of OMP, better conditioning of associated sensing matrix also attains importance. Often times in such applications as classification, nevertheless, the data driven matrices possess both high coherence (being close to 1) and bad conditioning, implying thereby an unreliable and/or poor classification performance via the sparse solvers like OMP, which is demonstrated in the simulation section.

Motivated by this, the present work looks at the kernel trick with a different perspective (in the sense of better coherence and good conditioning of associated sensing matrix) than in [7,8] and proposes a kernel based OMP for the classification of ECG signals for their normal and abnormal patterns.

3.1 Kernel Trick

In machine learning, in general, the data which are not linearly separable in a dimension m are projected to a higher dimension M, via a feature map

$$\phi : \mathbb{R}^m \longrightarrow \mathbb{R}^M$$

in such a way that the projected data in M dimensional space are linearly separable. In the feature space, the inner-product of feature vectors is given [1] by a kernel function k as

$$k(x,y) = \langle \phi(x), \phi(y) \rangle. \tag{3}$$

There are well established results [1] that talk about the conditions which imply the existence of a kernel k and a feature map ϕ satisfying (3). Thus knowing a kernel function k, one may do the calculations in the feature space without knowing the map ϕ explicitly. Some of the well-known examples of the kernels are as follows:

Polynomial Kernel

$$k(x,y) = \langle x, y \rangle^m.$$

Gaussian kernel

$$k(x, y) = exp\left(-\frac{||x - y||^2}{2\sigma^2}\right), \text{ where } \sigma > 0.$$

Remark: In view of (4), the coherence of $\phi(A)$ can be computed as follows:

$$\mu(\phi(A)) = \max_{i \neq j} \frac{|k(a_i, a_j)|}{\sqrt{k(a_i, a_i).k(a_j, a_j)}}. \tag{4}$$

4   Kernel OMP

This section emphasises how (i). the kernel trick can be applied to the under-determined system $Ax = y$ and (ii). the orthogonal matching pursuit (OMP) can be used in finding the sparse solution in the updated feature space.

4.1   Theory

Let $\phi : \mathbb{R}^m \longrightarrow \mathbb{R}^M$ be the feature map. The original matrix equation $y = Ax$ is converted via the map ϕ as,

$$\phi(y) = \phi(A)\tilde{x}, \text{ where } \phi(A) = [\phi(a_1), \phi(a_2), \ldots, \phi(a_n)], \tag{5}$$

where $a_1, a_2, \ldots, a_n$ are the columns of the original matrix A. The sparse $\tilde{x}$ can be obtained via OMP in kernel domain. The execution of new method, referred to as kernel OMP, is highlighted in Algorithm-2. In view of (3), the steps 5 and 7 of Algorithm-2 can be executed in kernel domain as described below:

Algorithm 2. Kernel OMP

1: **Data** : $\phi(\mathbf{A}), \phi(\mathbf{y})$ given in the form $\kappa(a_i, a_j)$ and $\kappa(a_i, y)$
2: Result: $\tilde{x}$ $s.t$ $\phi(y) \approx \phi(A)\tilde{x}$
3: *Initialisation* $\tilde{\Lambda}_0 = \{\}, l = 1$
4: **while** $l \leq k$ **do**
5:     $\tilde{z}(j) = [\kappa(a_j, y)] - \sum_i (\kappa(a_j, a_i).\tilde{x}(i)$
6:     $\tilde{\Lambda}_l = \tilde{\Lambda}_{l-1} \cup \{argmax_j |\tilde{z}(j)|\}$
7:     $\tilde{x} = [\kappa(a_i, a_j)]^{-1}.[\kappa(a_i, y)]$
8:     $l = l + 1$
9: **end while** $= 0$

– **STEP 5**

$$\begin{aligned}
\tilde{z}(j) &= [\phi(A)^T \tilde{r}_{l-1}](j) \\
&= [\phi(A)^T \phi(y) - \phi(A)^T \phi(A)\tilde{x}(i)] \\
&= [\kappa(a_j, y)] - \sum_i (\kappa(a_j, a_i)\tilde{x}(i),
\end{aligned} \tag{6}$$

where, $r_{l-1} = \phi(y) - \phi(A)\tilde{x}$.

– **STEP 7**

$$\tilde{x} = argmin_{\tilde{\eta}:supp(\tilde{\eta})\subset\tilde{\Lambda}_l}||\phi(y) - \phi(A_{\tilde{\Lambda}_l})\tilde{\eta}||_2^2$$

$$= [\phi(A_{\tilde{\Lambda}_l})^T\phi(A_{\tilde{\Lambda}_l})]^{-1}[\phi(A_{\tilde{\Lambda}_l})^T\phi(y)] \qquad (7)$$

$$= [\kappa(a_i, a_j)]^{-1}[\kappa(a_i, y)].$$

In the above equation (7), $\phi(A_{\tilde{\Lambda}_l})$ refers to the submatrix of $\phi(A)$ restricted to the index set $\tilde{\Lambda}_l$, and $[k(a_i, a_j)]$ denotes the matrix whose (i, j)th entry is $k(a_i, a_j)$, which is equal to $\langle\phi(a_i), \phi(a_j)\rangle$. Finally, $[k(a_i, y)]$ represents the column vector whose i^{th} element is $k(a_i, y)$.

From (6) and (7), it can be concluded that ϕ is not needed explicitly in the execution of Algorithm-2.

5 Classification of ECG Signals via OMP

Without Kernels

Suppose $nb_1, nb_2, \ldots, nb_p$ stand for the normal beats so extracted from the ECG signals and $vb_1, vb_2, \ldots, vb_q$ refer to the abnormal (ventricular) beats. Further consider that the matrix A is formed with these vectors as its columns, that is,

$$A = [nb_1, nb_2, \ldots, nb_p, vb_1, vb_2, \ldots, vb_q].$$

We assign a label 1 to the normal beats and -1 to the ventricular beats. Given a beat y of an unknown label, we solve the system

$$min_x||x||_0 \text{ subject to } y = Ax,$$

for a k-sparse solution x using the OMP. From the magnitude corresponding to the maximum term in the recovered x, we classify whether or not y is normal. For this we calculate

$$\delta(i) = ||A[i].x[i] - y||. \qquad (8)$$

Suppose

$$d = argmin\{\delta(i) : i \in support(x)\}.$$

Then the label of the column of A corresponding to d gives the label of y. Though this is a straight-forward way of classifying data, obtaining sparse x via a method often runs into some numerical problems. For instance, the entries in Tables 1 and 2 indicate poor condition number and high coherence of A. As a result, the classification accuracy gets dented seriously.

With Kernels

In order to alleviate the stated problem, we resort to the kernel setting and consider the following system

$$\phi(y) = [\phi(nb_1), \phi(nb_2), \ldots, \phi(nb_p), \phi(vb_1), \phi(vb_2), \ldots, \phi(vb_q)]\tilde{x}, \qquad (9)$$

which we solve using Kernel OMP. It can be seen in Tables 1 and 2 that the kernel setting results in an improved condition number as well as a fall in coherence. Consequently, the OMP applied on the new system in (9) is expected to result in a good classification performance, which is vindicated by our simulation results.

6   Extraction of Beats and Experimental Setup

In this section, we discuss the issues pertaining to the extraction of beats and data selection for experimental set up.

6.1   Extraction of Beats

The MIT-BIH Arrhythmia Database [3] has contained 48 half-hour excerpts of two-channel ambulatory ECG recordings, obtained from 47 subjects studied by the BIH Arrhythmia Laboratory between 1975 and 1979. Twenty-three recordings have been chosen at random from a set of 4000 24-h ambulatory ECG recordings collected from a mixed population of inpatients (about 60%) and outpatients (about 40%) at Boston's Beth Israel Hospital, the remaining 25 recordings have been selected from the same set to include less common but clinically significant arrhythmia that would not be well-represented in a small random sample. The recordings have been digitized at 360 samples per second per channel with 11-bit resolution over a 10 mV range [3]. Examples of normal and abnormal (of ventricular fibrillation type) beats are shown in Figs. 1 and 2. We have designed the sensing matrix consisting of 1000 beats as training data in 3 different ways with following compositions:

1. 50% Normal beats and 50% Ventricular beats.
2. 33% Normal beats and 67% Ventricular beats.
3. 67% Normal beats and 33% Ventricular beats.

For the test data, however, we have considered 120 random beats. Further, we have executed both normal OMP and kernel-OMP to identify the label of a given testing signal. We have obtained the accuracy by comparing the original labels with the ones calculated using the OMP based methods.

7   Simulation Work and Conclusion

We have discussed in previous sections that OMP's performance is typically tied to the smaller value of the coherence of underlying matrix. Further, for better numerical stability, one expects the condition number of the sensing matrix to be small. In this section, in addition to comparison of performances of OMP and kernel-OMP, we report that the kernels do have a bearing on the coherence and condition numbers. The fall in coherence and an improvement in condition number being resulted in by kernels can be seen in Tables 1 and 2.

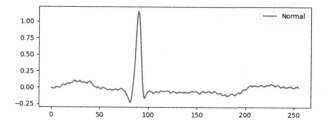

Fig. 1. Normal beat

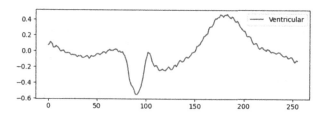

Fig. 2. Abnormal (ventricular) beat

Table 1. This table reports a fall in coherence via Gaussian kernel

Sensing matrix	Without k	With polynomial k	With Gaussian k
33% normal- 67% ventricular	0.99902	0.9975	0.66672
50% normal-50% ventricular	0.99896	0.9979	0.68095
67% normal-33% ventricular	0.99880	9980	0.69508

We now turn to the classification accuracy. The results reported in Table 3 imply that the kernel based OMP outperforms in providing better classification performance. From the afore-stated results we make the following observations:

1. The coherence of sensing matrix decreases in kernel setting, providing thereby a better bound on the sparsity of the signal to be recovered.
2. The condition number of A decreases in the kernel setting.
3. The classification accuracy increases significantly in kernel setting.

Table 2. This table reports a significant improvement in condition number via Gaussian kernel.

Sensing matrix	Without k	With polynomial k	With Gaussian k
33% normal-67% ventricular	168705.59	25844.11	9.339
50% normal-50% ventricular	188746.8	30025.15	11.8124
67% normal-33% ventricular	210884.27	28599.61	14.0216

Table 3. This table demonstrates that the kernel based OMP provides better classification accuracy compared to the OMP without any kernel.

Sensing matrix	Without k	With polynomial k	With Gaussian k
33% normal-67% ventricular	0.69875	0.9200	0.964583
50% normal-50% ventricular	0.71916	0.892	0.97500
67% normal-33% ventricular	0.72416	0.876	0.96

The work reported in this paper has made use of kernel trick and proposed a kernel-based OMP technique for the classification of normal and abnormal ECG beats. Further, our work has demonstrated that kernels can be used to improve upon the numerical properties (such as the coherence and condition number) of the sensing matrices in sparsity based classification methods. In the current work we have demonstrated our results by considering the standard kernels. In future work, however, we will attempt to propose data-driven kernels which are likely to improve further the classification performance.

References

1. Scholkopf, B., Smola, A.J.: Learning with Kernels: Support Vector Machines, Regularization, Optimization, and Beyond. MIT Press, Cambridge (2001/2018)
2. Foucart, S., Rauhut, H.: A Mathematical Introduction to Compressive Sensing. Birkhauser, Basel 2013
3. Moody, G.B., Mark, R.G.: The impact of the MIT-BIH Arrhythmia database. IEEE Eng. Med. Biol. **20**(3), 45–50 (2001)
4. Chandra, S., Sastry, C.S., Jana, S.: Robust heartbeat detection from multimodal data via CNN-based generalizable information fusion. IEEE Trans. Biomed. Eng. **66**, 710–717 (2019)
5. Chandra, S., Sastry, C.S., Jana, S.: Reliable resource-constrained telecardiology via compressive detection of anomalous ECG signals. Comput. Biol. Med. **66**, 144–153 (2015)
6. Chandra, B.S., Sastry, C.S., Anumandla, L., Jana, S.: Dictionary-based monitoring of premature ventricular contractions: an ultra-low-cost point-of-care service. Artif. Intell. Med. **87**, 91–104 (2018)
7. Zhang, L., et al.: Kernel sparse representation-based classifier. IEEE Trans. Signal Process. **60**(4), 1684–1695 (2012)
8. Jian, M., Jung, C.: Class-discriminative kernel sparse representation-based classification using multi-objective optimization. IEEE Trans. Signal Process. **61**(18), 4416–4427 (2013)

AAUNet: An Attention Augmented Convolution Based UNet for Change Detection in High Resolution Satellite Images

P. S. Patil[1]([✉]), R. S. Holambe[1], and L. M. Waghmare[2]

[1] Shri Guru Gobind Singhji Institute of Engineering and Technology, Nanded, Maharashtra 431606, India
patilparam25@gmail.com, rsholambe@sggs.ac.in
[2] Swami Ramanand Marathwada University, Nanded, Maharashtra 431606, India
lmwaghmare@sggs.ac.in

Abstract. Infrastructure surveillance, topographic map-making, urban dynamics, and town planning applications all use high resolution satellite (HRS) imagery to detect changes. Change detection (CD) in these images is critical due to the large amount of information and challenging data. However, the high computing complexity of the network, related to dense convolution layers and an abundance of data to discourage the researcher from designing an efficient and precise CD architecture. The algorithm used to design this architecture must not only be correct, but also efficient in terms of speed and accuracy. Hence, we focus on developing computationally efficient self attention-mechanism-based Attention Augmented Convolution with the backbone of UNet (AAUNet) architecture for CD tasks. Two image pairs, each with a channel-C, can be layered together to create a channel-2C image as an input to train this architecture. The novelty of this method is the standard convolution of original UNet is replaced by a self-attention mechanism based attention augmented (AA) convolution layer in the proposed network. This attention augmented convolutional operation is used to capture long-range global information, however, the standard convolution layer has a significant weakness in that it only works on local information. Therefore, we use attention augmented convolutional layer as an alternative to standard convolution layers. It is allowing us to design network with fewer parameters, speedup training, less computation complexity, and enhance segmentation performance of the model. Test results on LEVIR-CD, SZATKI AirChange (AC), and Onera Satellite Change Detection (OSCD), benchmark datasets demonstrated that the proposed approach beats its predominance as far as Intersection over Union (IoU), number of parameters, and deduction of inference time over the current techniques.

Supported by organization SGGSIET, Nanded.

Keywords: Change detection · Self-attention mechanism · Attention augmented convolution · UNet Architecture · High resolution satellite images

1 Introduction

The goal of image change detection is to identify particular differences between bitemporal images of the same scene or region. Because it is a key approach in many application scenarios, such as land use management, resource monitoring, and urban expansion tracking, it has prompted interest in the field of remote sensing image analysis [1]. The objectives of this work is to detect highly statistically significant changes in bi-temporal multi-sensory remotely sensed images of the same area. In the literature, alternate detection algorithms usually follow three techniques. First, they observe the pixel-based totally analysis [2]. This methods applied the pixel as the important thing characteristic in photo evaluation, thinking about complete use of spectral and statistical functions with out using the spatial contextual records. Pixel-primarily based analysis especially generate a change map by without delay comparing the spectral or texture facts of the pixels and reap the very last end result map via threshold classification or semantic segmentation [3,4]. However, this method is easy to perform, it avoid the spatial context information and produces a essential amount of noise during implementation. In [5] has designed Bayesian algorithms and theory for change detection in stochastic techniques. Although, this algorithm was detection of irregularity problems in cyber-physical and biology applications. In [6], semi-supervised deep learning technique motivated from Bayesian theorem for detecting change map. The performance of the pixel-based technique degrades; secondly, object-based methods were devoloped for change detection purpose. In [7], satellite images are cropped into small objects and utilize the textural, spectral, geometric, and structural features in the image to analyze the differences of bi-temporal images. However, the spatial contextual information of high-resolution remote sensing images is used in these object-based approaches. Lastly, follows the patch-based analysis. For the detection of changes, the author [8] developed an unsupervised model that calculates the similarity between non-local patches of heterogeneous images. For determining the distances of optical images or SAR images, this approach only considers two commonly used noise distribution models; additional noise distributions are not considered. For change detection between optical and SAR images, Liu et al. [9] presented a symmetric convolution coupling network (SCCN). This approach obtains a change detection by translating the given feature into a patch subspace. The network SCCN is learnt and trained by refining the coupling method, which is exclusively dependent on feature points that are not altered. Hand-crafted characteristics were utilised in the above literature, which are complicated and have low robustness.

Deep learning networks are now often utilized to obtain features directly from source images. For change detection applications, the derived characteristics are the most robust and dependable [10]. To reduce the training parameters, in [11] suggested a deep (DDSCN)-depthwise separable convolution network in place of the original UNet, although this DDSCN design is not as efficient as the standard convolution approach. The author of [12] developed a basic 4-layered completely convolutional siamese architecture based on the k-nn technique to improve change detection accuracy. The k-nn, but at the other end, only contributes if their parameterized k-margin is below the level. As a result, analysing the unbalanced data classes that have changed and those that have not changed is wrong. In [13], The author established three siamese FCN extensions: FC-EF (early fusion), FC-Siam-conc (concatenating), and EF-Siam-diff (difference). These three FCN models were developed from the scratch, with no post-processing. The author has built a siamese extension version of FCN networks in [14] (EF-Siam-diff-Att). In this network attention-gate mechanism is used for improving the spatial accuracy. However, this attention mechanism extract discriminative feature form local information of image. Most of the above semantic segmentation techniques can achieve complete segmentation, but its achieved accuracy and speed is comparatively low. However, the convolutional filter's local information prevents it from obtaining global information in an image [15], which is important for improved change detection in segmentation.

2   Related Work

Self-attention, on the other side, is a relatively new technique for capturing long-range dependencies that is often used in generative and sequential model applications [16]. By taking the advantage of this techniques, we propose the AAUNet for change detection semantic segmentation task. The fundamental technique is to apply an Attention Augmented Convolution operation based on a self-attention mechanism to find the altered regions from long-range global information and produce more discriminating feature representations, which makes the learnt features more resistant to changes. The main objective of self-attention is to determine the weighted average values from concealed perceptions. The weights created in the weighted average values are computed similarity between hidden units via dynamically using the convolutional or pooling operator. As a result, rather than being assessed by their associated position as in typical convolutions, the correlation between input features is determined by the feature itself [17]. In further detail, this permits self-attention to obtain long-range dependencies without increasing the number of [18] parameters. We identify the use of self-attention as an alternative to standard convolutions for discriminant feature representations in this paper. We do this by employing a two-dimensional corresponding self-attention mechanism that maintains translation equivalence while being inspired by corresponding position dependencies, making it ideal for image segmentation [19]. The self-attention formulation achieves competitive for combining both attention and standard convolution rather than replacing standard convolutions entirely. However, it is not discard the complete idea of standard convolutions, but instead to propose an Attention Augmented Convolution (AAConv) with this self-attention mechanism. Therefore, we use self-attention mechanism with AAConv operation as an alternative to standard convolution

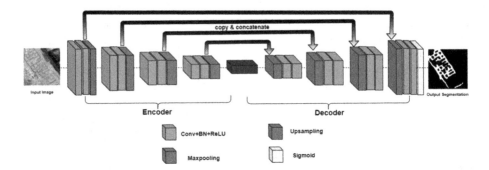

Fig. 1. Semantic segmentation encoder-decoder structure.

layers to obtain more discriminant feature representations. It is allowing us to design architecture with fewer parameters [18].

The change detection is belong to the part of semantic segmentation. In perspective of the advantages and disadvantages of deep learning-based methods, we introduce a novel method to provides a promising solution in the change detection segmentation task to predict the small changes, precisely, accurately, and quickly. This method uses the most efficient deep learning technology for semantic segmentation, which is different from conventional model construction methods. We design efficient deep convolutional network can reduces the computation complexity and improving the speed of semantic segmentation of roads with ensuring high accuracy. Specifically, we design a novel architecture based on self-attention mechanism and improving the UNet network construct by using some approach to improve detection accuracy, speed, and reducing computation complexity of the network. Additionally, main contributions are as follows:

- We design a novel architecture, named AAUNet, which adopts self-attention mechanism with backbone of UNet structure for change detection task. In self-attention mechanism use attention augmented convolutional (AAConv) operation [16] to capture long range global information, however traditional convolution operation has a denoting weakness in this it only perform on a local information [18].
- In proposed framework, we use attention augmented convolutional operation as an alternative to standard convolution layers inside original UNet architecture [20]. The stacked input image is directly given to the input of our proposed network, where the corresponding training labels are the change of the stacked input image.
- Our proposed network uses the depthwise separable convolutions (DSC) operations to speedup training, lower number of parameters, reduction of computational complexity, and enhance segmentation performance with ensuring the segmentation accuracy of the network. The presented approach outperforms the current approaches in form of (IoU) Intersection over Union, inference time, and training parameters on the LEVIR-CD [21], SZATKI (AC) AirChange [22], and (OSCD)-Onera Satellite Change Detection [23] datasets.

The remaining work is organized as follows: Sect. 2 described the proposed framework, and training parameter. Section 3 contains the experimental results and discussion. Finally, Sect. 4 concludes the work.

3   Proposed Framework

In this part, we will briefly discuss the UNet structure based on depthwise separable convolution (DSC) to regain a volume of information with increase training speed, and change segmentation performance of the network. Self-attention mechanisms in architecture to capture long range global interpretation and attention augmented convolution operation with reduction of number of parameter as compare to traditional convolutions.

3.1   Dataset Description

Change Detection Dataset-LEVIR-CD: The LEVIR-CD is a recently massive-scale faraway capturing constructing change detection dataset [21]. This will be an new baseline dataset for testing CD methods based on deep learning. It comprises of 637 high resolution satellite images at a resolution of 0.5 m per pixel area. Google Earth imagery sets having a 1024 × 1024 -pixel resolution. The architectural development of urban changes, in particular, produces bitemporal imagery with a time difference of 5 to 14 years. Experts in the field of remote sensing binary labeled these bitemporal pictures (0-unchanged and 1-changed). To acquire high-quality labeled data, each labeled image is marked (annotated) by one annotator and then validated by other expert. As a result, the LEVIR-CD has a totally of 31,345 unique CD instances.

AirChange Benchmark Dataset-SZATKI: We use the SZATKI AC Dataset to develop the suggested algorithm and evaluate the proposed method. [11–13], and [22] have all used this dataset. This AC dataset comprises 3-sets of optical aerial images collected with a large time difference and under a variety of unusual circumstances. The analytical indexes TISZADOB, SZADA, and ARCHIVE, include 5, 7, and 1 imagery matches with a 23-year time gap, respectively. The GTs got manually labeled by the experts. Each image has a size of 952 × 640 pixels and 1.5m per pixel resolution, as well as binary change mask images. The 3rd-pair of the TISZADOB dataset and the 1st-pair of the SZADA dataset have been used for evaluating our algorithm.

Onera Satellite Change Detection Dataset-OSCD: We evaluate and assessed our results using the Onera Satellite Change Detection (OSCD) [23] image dataset in the presented paper. The OSCD dataset, which is an accessible and standardized approach for examining the efficacy of CD segmentation, was proposed by the remote sensing scientific researcher. Twenty-four locations of roughly 600 × 600 resolution at 10-meter size with differing extents of urbanisation changes have been selected from throughout the world for this dataset

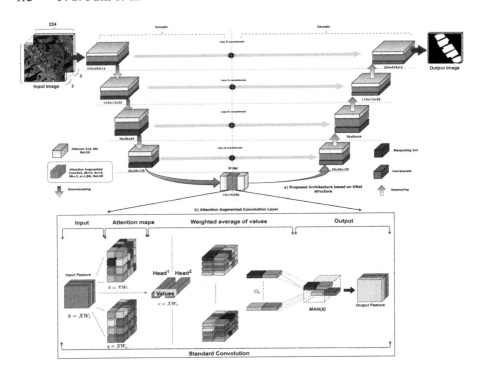

Fig. 2. (a) A schematic representation of the proposed architecture for change detection based on Attention Augmented (AA) Convolution and Depthwise Separable Convolution (DSC) with a UNet foundation. The stacked image pair is fed straight into the proposed network's input. (b) In each stage of the proposed architecture, an Attention Augmented Convolution layer is used to capture long-range global information. It's used to improve segmentation performance by obtaining more discriminative relevant features.

(10-image for testing and 14- image for training set). A total of 24 training image pairs are shown in the dataset. The genuine image visuals for every location on each set have been manually contrasted to generate Categorized GT. This data is more appropriate by using supervised methods to solve the change detection task.

3.2   Implementation Details

For CD, the proposed method based on the original structure of an encoder-decoder-based UNet network with defined size on source and resulting imagery [20]. We crop the left-top region to right bottom region of each image pair to 224×224 scale of the above mentioned datasets to develop overlapped down-scaled patches for testing sets and training sets; here the area are cropped to be 30% overlapped and some space at the horizontal and vertical to remove any room if any. Since the characteristics points are cover in multi-resolution imagery, it is not essential that the proportion of overlapping will give excellent outcomes. Nevertheless, it is possible that they will generate misinterpretation.

The degree of statistical and geographical information in the images is then used to determine the proportion of overlap. By supplementing cropped images, each cropped image is vertically, horizontally flipped, and rotated by 90°, 180°, and 270°, this method substantially extends the range of training data available for the model. For training and testing, we used the AirChange SZATAKI [22], OSCD [23], and LEVIR-CD dataset [21]. We merge the two satellite data of $H \times W \times C$ along the 3rd-channel to generate a channel-2C image for input with a new dimension of $H \times W \times 2C$. The prediction output of the CD map can be produced directly utilizing the proposed model to obtain the output image.

3.3   UNet Structure Based on Encoder-Decoder for Semantic Segmentation

The semantic segmentation task requires the Unet structure in specifically. As shown in Fig. 1, a UNet [20] consists of a convolution layer as an contraction, bridge, and extraction part. The encoder in the UNet is used to convert source images into activation illustrations using multiple convolution layers with max-pooling operation. To extract rich features from the source image, the image is gradually downsampled and the resolution of the feature points is reduced [24]. This is done using current CNN architectures such as ResNet [25], and XceptionNet [26], etc., decoder. To create the final feature map, these CNN architectures demonstrates the scale of the input images. Reconstructing the original size segmentation result from a reduced resolution feature map is a hard process. Deconvolution is used in the decoder to upsample the encoder's feature maps, which restores and refine target information during deconvolution. UNet transfers and concatenates rich feature information from encoder levels to feature information in the decoder's equivalent level.

3.4   Self-attention Mechanisms in Architecture

An attention mechanism is originating from the human visual task [27] which replicates the dependencies between input and output features sequences of networks. This attention mechanism has quickly gain attention over the years with improvement in the deep learning for their specific benefits to capture long rage distance interactions [28]. Bahdanau et al. has firstly designed Recurrent Neural Network with combine attention for Machine Translation alignment [29]. Vaswani et al. [16] was further extended into self-attention Transformer architecture to achieve natural machine translation results on state-of-the-art methods. Self-attention mechanism expresses the different location of a single sequence to measure the representation of each location of the sequence in the input feature. Squeeze-and-Excitation (SE) [30] rethink channel features from entire feature maps by using signals aggregate, while Bottleneck Attention Module (BAM) [31] and Convolutional Block Attention Module (CBAM) [32]. Additionally, various attention structure have been designed for deep learning applications to demonstrate the weaknesses of traditional convolutions [30–33].

In this paper, we use attention augmented convolution, which employ self-attention over the entire model. However, it is not depends on pre-training of convolutional architectures. The multi-head attention (MHA) permit the model to use spatial as well as channel feature together. Additionally, we improve the feature representation of self-attention mechanism over images by approaching corresponding self-attention [17] to two dimensional attention augmented convolution. It is permitting us to model construction equivalence in a principled manner. Finally, we use self-attention mechanism based attention augmented convolution operation inside original UNet as a alternative to standard convolution to extract long range interactions. This mechanism allows us to design networks with fewer parameters as compare to state-of-the-art methods which is discussed in Sect. 3.6.

3.5   Attention Augmented Convolution in Network

Previously discussed different attention mechanisms over images propose that the convolution operator has significant weakness in its locality and inadequacy in understanding of global information [30–32]. In attention augmented convolution operation, to get long-range interactions by straighten out the convolutional feature maps. In contradict to these approaches, firstly we use spatial information and feature spaces (each head related to a feature map) attention mechanism together. Secondly, produces concatenating convolutional and attentional feature maps rather than refining them. Figure 2(b) shows a detailed conceptual representation. We explain three factors to interpret the main idea of the self-attention process [16]: key, value, and query. Include these case: we have a feature map with numerous value or key items. For a new query, we must find the feature map in the key or value features map which has the best similarity. We can get this information by comparing the key to all of the queries in the feature map. This approach is used in the self-attention approach to measure the relationship between the different variables [34]. In the self-attention approach, three separate convolutional operations are used to extract the value, key, and query feature tensors (attention maps) from the input tensor map.

The major aim of the multi-head attention (MHA) factor is to find an attention function that converts a query tensor and a collection of value-key tensor pairs into an output convolutional feature [18]. The weight assigned to each value tensor is determined by the associated key and a learning function of query, and the output feature map is found by value tensor from weighted sum. The outputs are resized, concatenated, and combined with a pointwise convolution process to match the original input feature map size.Lastly, MHA is concurrently with a conventional convolution operation, and the results are combined in attention enhanced convolution [18]. Figure 2(b) shows a conceptual illustration. In addition, Sect. 3.6 contains a full discussion of Attention Augmented Convolution over images.

3.6   Attention Augmented Convolution over Image

The input feature map of dimension $(h \times w \times D_{in})$ is transform into a matrix $I \in \mathbb{R}^{(h \times w \times D_{in})}$ and then perform multi-head attention as explained in the Transformer network [16]. where, width w, height h, and number of input filters

D_{in} of an input feature map respectively. The result of the attention augmented convolution for a one head *head* is expressed as:

$$O_{hd} = Softmax\left(\frac{(I * W_q)(I * W_k)^T}{\sqrt{d_k^{hd}}}\right)(I * W_v) \tag{1}$$

where d_k^{hd} refer to the depth of keys. $W_q/W_k \in \mathbb{R}^{(D_{in} \times d_k^{hd})}$ and $W_v \in \mathbb{R}^{(D_{in} \times d_k^{hd})}$ are determined transformations of linear that assign the I as an input to $q = I * W_q$ queries, $k = I * W_k$ keys, and $v = I * W_v$ values. Then all heads (MHA) outputs are recalculated and concatenated as follows:

$$MHA(I) = Concatenat[O_1, O_2, ..., O_{N_{hd}}] W_o \tag{2}$$

where N_{hd} refer to the number of heads. $W_o \in \mathbb{R}^{(d_v \times d_v)}$ is determined linear transformations. Then *MHA(X)* feature map is reshaped into a dimension ($h \times w \times d_v$) to map the fundamental input feature dimensions. We notice that MHA acquire a computation cost of $O((h * W)^2 * dk)$ and a memory size $O((h * W)^2 * N_{head}$ as It must keep count of each head's attention maps.

Lastly, multi-head attention is run in parallel with a regular convolution process, with the outputs mixed in attention augmented convolution. An ordinary convolution operator with a filter size of K, input filters of D_{in}, and output filters of D_{out}. The formula for correlated attention enhanced convolution is as follows:

$$AAConv(I) = Concatenat[MHA(I), Conv(I)] \tag{3}$$

We consider $v = \frac{d_v}{D_{out}}$ is the ratio of number of attention channels by number of output channels and $k = \frac{d_k}{D_{out}}$ is the ratio of depth of key value by output channels. Compare to the standard convolution. The (AA) convolution is the equal of translational, and it works well with inputs of various spatial resolutions.

Reduction on Number of Parameters:

In multi-head attention, to compute the queries, keys, values by performing pointwise (1×1) convolution with input filters D_{in} and output filters $D_{out} = \frac{(2d_k + d_v)}{(2K + v)}$. Suppose, In the conventional convolutional part, the number of filters is reduced, resulting in the following changes in parameters:

$$\triangle^{params} = D_{in} D_{out}(2K + (1 - (K \times K))v + \frac{D_{in}}{D_{out}} v^2) \tag{4}$$

As per Eq. 4, when replacing 3×3 standard convolution will decrease in parameters [18]. Hence, the attention augmented convolution minimize the computational parameters as compare to the standard convolutions computational cost. Therefore, AAUNet used attention augmented convolution as an alternative

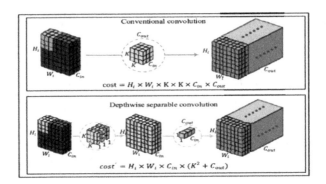

Fig. 3. Traditional convolution and depthwise separable convolution operations are demonstrated in this diagram.

to standard convolution layers inside original UNet [20] architecture to obtain more discriminant feature representations. However, this is very profitable in terms of parameter as explain in Eq. 4.

3.7   Depthwise Separable Convolution

In place of traditional convolution, depthwise separable convolution utilises two steps: depthwise and pointwise convolution [26]. For each input channel, we employ depthwise convolutions to apply a single filter. We apply simple 1×1 convolution on the output of depthwise convolution to obtain a linear combination output of the depthwise layer in pointwise convolution. Traditional convolution and depthwise separable convolution procedures are displayed in Fig. 3.

In depthwise convolution, one filter per input channel is written as:

$$\emptyset_{(p,q,r)} = \sum_{x,y} k_{x,y,r} * N_{(p+x-1),(q+y-1),r} \tag{5}$$

The depthwise convolutional filter of size k is called k. To produce the r_{th} depth of the output of convolution activation map $\emptyset$, the r_{th} channel in P is convoluted with the r_{th} filter in k.

To calculate the parameters of two convolution, we considering that both convolutions are performed on the activation map li of dimension $Hm \times Wm \times Din$ and that a activation map $lout$ of resolution $Hm \times Wm \times Dout$ is obtained. The parameter calculation of the normal convolution with filter $k \times k$ size is given by Eq. 6.

$$cost_{stand} = H_m \times W_m \times k \times k \times D_{in} \times D_{out} \tag{6}$$

The addition of depthwise and pointwise operations is the parameter cost of depthwise separable convolution. Divide the input images into the number of channels Din, filter k into distinct channels, then convolve with every channel using a convolution $k \times k$ of convolution kernel. The parameter counts for the procedure are listed below:

$$cost_{depth} = H_m \times W_m \times D_{in} \times k \times k \times 1 \tag{7}$$

The result of depthwise convolution is then processed using a 1×1 pointwise convolution procedure with a D_{out} number of convolution filters. The total number of parameters is:

$$cost_{point} = H_m \times W_m \times D_{in} \times 1 \times 1 \times D_{out} \tag{8}$$

Then, using Eqs. (7) and (8), sum the depthwise and pointwise convolution parameters to get the parameter count of depthwise separable convolution:

$$cost_{depthwise} = H_m \times W_m \times D_{in} \times (k^2 + D_{out}) \tag{9}$$

We can calculate the ratio of depthwise separable convolution parameter cost to standard convolution parameter cost using Eqs. (6) and (9).

$$\frac{cost_{depthwise}}{cost_{stand}} = \frac{H_m \times W_m \times D_{in} \times (k^2 + D_{out})}{H_m \times W_m \times D_{in} \times k \times k \times D_{out}}$$

$$= \frac{1}{D_{out}} + \frac{1}{k^2}$$

As a result, the DSC reduces the parameter calculation by k^2 compared to the ordinary convolution. To minimise the parameter of network by 9 times that of normal convolution, AAUNet used depthwise separable convolution of $k = 3$ with AAConv in each block. This is quite profitable and greatly speeds up segmentation.

3.8 Proposed Attention Augmented Convolution Based UNet Architecture

In this approach, we employ a UNet architecture for semantic segmentation neural network that is based on attention augmented (AA) convolution and depthwise separable convolution (DSC), as demonstrated in Fig. 2. This semantic segmentation neural network is specially designed for change detection, which uses the backbone of UNet structure. In this segmentation, to obtain a refined output, it is significant to use low level features, although regaining high level segmentation features [35]. An UNet uses skip connections to transfer low-level spatial information to equivalent high-level spatial information, allowing for easy backward propagation during training while also taking care of low-level neat details to high-level segmentation features [20]. This network address the problem of degradation and facilitate training process. This network has benefit of both AAConv and DSC. This combination brings us the following benefits:

1. Self-attention based AA convolution operation as an alternative to standard convolution layers inside original UNet architecture to obtain more discriminant feature representations and also allowing us to design network with fewer parameters, as explain in Sect. (3.5)–(3.6).

Table 1. Model summary of the proposed architecture based on Attention Augmented Convolution (AttAugConv) and Depthwise Separable Convolution (DWConv) with backbone of UNet structure

Path	Stages	Layers	Dimentions	No. of filters	Parameters
Encoder	Level 1	DWConv 3 × 3	256 × 256 × 16	16	150
		AttAugConv 3 × 3	256 × 256 × 16		3816
		Maxpooling	112 × 112 × 16		0
	Level 2	DWConv 3 × 3	112 × 112 × 32	32	656
		AttAugConv 3 × 3	112 × 112 × 32		9528
		Maxpooling	56 × 56 × 32		0
	Level 3	DWConv 3 × 3	56 × 56 × 64	64	2336
		AttAugConv 3 × 3	56 × 56 × 64		36120
		Maxpooling	28 × 28 × 64		0
	Level 4	DWConv 3 × 3	28 × 28 × 128	128	8768
		AttAugConv 3 × 3	28 × 28 × 128		145272
		Maxpooling	14 × 14 × 128		0
Bridge	Middle	DWConv 3 × 3	14 × 14 × 256	256	33920
		AttAugConv 3 × 3	14 × 14 × 256		585096
		DWConv 3 × 3	14 × 14 × 256		67840
Decoder	Level 4	Upsampling & Concate	28 × 28 × 384	128	0
		AttAugConv 3 × 3	28 × 28 × 128		32968
		DWConv 3 × 3	28 × 28 × 128		2192
	Level 3	Upsampling & Concate	56 × 56 × 192	64	0
		AttAugConv 3 × 3	56 × 56 × 64		17832
		DWConv 3 × 3	56 × 56 × 64		1168
	Level 2	Upsampling & Concate	112112 × 96	32	0
		AttAugConv 3 × 3	112 × 112 × 32		10680
		DWConv 3 × 3	112 × 112 × 32		656
	Level 1	Upsampling & Concate	224 × 224 × 48	16	0
		AttAugConv 3 × 3	224 × 224 × 16		7658
		DWConv 3 × 3	224 × 224 × 16		400
	Output Layer	Conv 1 × 1, sigmoid	224 × 224 × 1		17
Total number of parameters					**1492335**

2. The DSC improves the efficiency of convolution and significantly reduces the model training parameters, as explain in Sect. 3.7. Therefore we replace the traditional convolution in standard UNet by the DSC along with AA convolution, to make the entire network lightweight.

3. To understand the profit of AA convolution and DSC, it speedup the training process, lower the number of parameters, reduction of computational complexity, and enhancing the segmentation performance of the proposed AAUNet. Figure 2 shows the detailed representation of proposed architecture.

Table 2. Comparison of Inference Time, parameters, IoU, and Evaluation Matrices between Proposed Method with state-of-the-art methods

Methods	Inf. Time (sec)	Param(M)	Szada/1				Tiszadob/3				OSCD/3ch.				LEVIR-CD			
			Pr.	Rec.	F1_s	IoU	Pr.	Rec.	F1_s	IoU	Pr.	Rec.	F1_s	IoU	Pr.	Rec.	F1_s	IoU
FC-Siam-Con [13]	1.79	2.43	40.9	65.6	50.4	0.69	72.0	75.1	82.6	0.71	44.7	47.9	53.9	0.84	49.8	52.1	65.3	0.52
FC-Siam-Diff [13]	1.68	2.17	41.3	52.3	52.9	072	42.8	49.7	57.3	0.67	69.5	53.1	65.8	0.71	69.3	62.5	67.9	0.68
FC_Siam-Con-Att. [14]	1.71	1.81	57.8	65.1	51.3	0.58	36.3	53.2	47.9	0.74	52.3	61.9	47.4	0.89	65.2	81.9	69.2	0.72
FC-Siam-Diff-Att. [14]	1.63	1.64	75.2	69.7	71.1	0.71	47.4	51.2	64.3	0.72	81.2	76.2	65.3	0.87	75.7	82.4	79.3	0.83
UNet [20]	1.81	7.76	61.4	53.2	69.4	0.68	51.2	79.8	53.2	0.69	75.7	69.4	67.8	0.67	49.4	59.2	53.7	0.81
DDSCN [11]	1.67	1.51	48.2	62.9	76.6	0.75	68.2	59.2	65.4	0.80	63.2	69.8	72.5	0.85	43.5	51.2	59.9	0.76
STANet [38]	1.61	1.74	79.2	81.3	**83.4**	0.79	71.1	72.6	83.5	0.84	83.1	84.6	79.6	0.86	71.3	87.8	70.2	0.89
AAUNet (proposed)	**1.57**	**1.49**	**82.9**	**85.2**	81.5	**0.82**	**79.3**	77.1	**85.3**	**0.88**	**85.6**	**88.3**	**91.7**	0.88	71.9	**89.6**	76.5	**0.92**

In proposed architecture, we use the standard UNet architecture [20] due to of its outspread application and its strength to efficiently scale across several computational resources for semantic segmentation task. The basic layers in standard UNet contains all traditional convolutions of 3 × 3 follows batch normalization (BN) with ReLU activations in encoder and decoder path. We modify all layer of UNet by AA convolution and DSC layers with filter size of 3 × 3 in each layer. We apply AA Convolution and DSC layers in the all stages of the UNet architecture. All attention augmented convolution parameters set $k = 4$, $v = 4$, and the attention heads is set to $N_{hd} = 2$ [18]. All the parameters were chosen based on memory constraints of $N_{head} \left(H \times W^2 \right)$.

Encoder, bridge, and decoder are the three parts of the proposed network. To encode the input images, the AAUNet encoder successively downsampled the image and reduced the resolution of the feature points in order to extract high-level features from the image. Encoding part has four level. In each level, max pooling is used for downsampling the feature map by $\frac{h \times w}{2}$. The central path makes the connection between the encoding and decoding sections. Correspondingly, there are four levels in the decoding section. Before each level, deconvolution is used to upsample the encoder's feature maps, restoring and improving object details along the process. Transfers and concatenates detailed feature information from encoder levels to feature information in the decoder's appropriate level. A 1 × 1 convolution and a sigmoid activation function have been used to predict feature regions into the fined segmentation map after the last layer of decoding path. All level includes a BN [36] and ReLU6 [37] activation function. In addition, ReLu6 has better stability than ReLu in the field of improving the accuracy and speed of the network. Table 1 summarizes our proposed model summery.

3.9 Training Parameters

With 16 images as the batch size, an Adam (adaptive moment estimation) optimizer was used in the training phase as a refinement of the stochastic gradient descent optimization. We employ binary cross-entropy as a loss function to train the proposed model. The Adam optimizer was chosen since it only needed a few

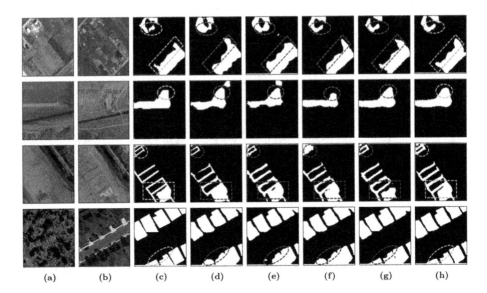

(a)   (b)   (c)   (d)   (e)   (f)   (g)   (h)

Fig. 4. Results from the Szada/1, Tiszadob/3, and OSCD-3ch datasets, as well as the LEVIR-CD dataset. Display the two image pairs in (a) and (b). Ground Truth (c) (d) UNet's result. (g) STANet (e) DDSCN (f) FC-Siam-Diff-Att (g) The proposed approach produced the following result.

parameters to tune [39]. To reduce the risk of overfitting during the training process, we used data augmentation techniques such as horizontal and vertical flips, contrast, and brightness. In our model, we prefer the decaying learning rate, which decreases by a factor of 0.1 every 20 epochs. The learning rate is set to 0.001 as the final value. The model is trained for 100 epochs. The variables given above were chosen based on their acceptable experimental performance. The proposed method's performance can be improved further by altering the training algorithm's parameters.

4   Results and Discussion

In this part, the proposed work presents experimental findings for evaluating the method's validity. We tested the proposed approach using three accessible to the public change detection benchmark datasets, which are provided in the Sect. 3.1. The accuracy of the change detection findings is measured using three assessment measures. The first one is Precision ($Pr.$), which is the proportion of positive (TP) pixels across all positive pixels. The second measurement is recall ($Rec.$), which is the TP fraction of pixels across all GT pixels, and the third is F1 score ($F1\text{-}s$), which is the percent average of precision and recall. Intersection over union (IoU) is a new indication added to the above three evaluation metrics for the recognition of change outcomes to measure the effectiveness of our proposed approach. The IoU measure, which is stated as follows, is used to compute the percent overlap between the actual image and the expected output image:

$$IoU = \frac{TP}{Tp + FP + FN}$$

Here FN, TP, FP denote a certain amount of False Negatives, True Positives, and False Positive pixels. For this segmentation of change detection task, we tested several state-of-the-art approaches, and the findings are summarized in Table 2. As described in Sect. 3, in the proposed network architecture, the attention enhanced convolution, when compared to conventional convolution and DSC, may potentially reduce the calculations of the architecture and has a smaller number of parameters. In this part, we compare the training parameter and inference time (in second) of proposed model with standard convolution and DSC based UNet, which are analyzed in Table 2. It is proved that the parameters of AA convolution are **6x times** and slightly lower than the standard convolution and DSC based UNet architecture respectively. Also, inference time on test images is less than the existing methods. This is proved that, the computational complexity and execution time of AAUNet are much lower than others. Lower parameter can fit the training data much better, then we conform its capability on test dataset through experiments. For fair comparison, we compare proposed method with different standard convolution, depthwise separable, and attention based existing methods and described the results in Table 2. For the OSCD-3ch, SZADA/1, TISZADOB/3, and LEVIR-CD datasets, the AAUNet achieves better results than the original convolution based methods on most of the evaluation matrices. Due to atmospheric light variations, complex statistics properties, some of the existing methods performed better than proposed method in few evaluation matrices. For the all datasets, proposed method achieve better IoU and other matrices due to attention augmented convolution. It obtain the long range global information and achieving better segmentation performance. Different Network Architecture Results (Fig. 4) an example of our results, which are higher in performance and have a greater calming effect on the qualitatively change map.

5   Conclusion

In this paper, we designed change detection architecture based on attention augmented convolution UNet (AAUNet) for high spatial resolution satellite images, which needs very few training parameters, low computation complexity, and less inference time. To capture long range global information, we used self-attention mechanism based attention augmented convolution operation for better feature representation and describe the local features of changes in the model. In training process, an input image pair is combined them together, and then it was fed into the network. This approach, allow the network to fed input image pairs directly, rather than provide the input image pairs to the network individually. This architecture do not require the generation of pre-processing procedure and reduce execution time in change detection task. We design, a novel two-dimensional attention augmented convolution based fully self-attention change detection model on image segmentation task. We propose to attention augmented convolution operator with this self-attention technique and conform the superiority of this method over the other traditional convolution, separable convolution, and other attention based state-of-the-art methods. Thorough research has shown that the proposed AAUNet may improve change detection semantic segmentation applications over a wide range of architectures, execution times, and computational complexity. On benchmark datasets, the proposed approach outperforms multiple network topologies in terms of inference time and intersection of union (IoU) in the identification of urban changes. Our methodology outperforms existing approaches and enhances the spatial accuracy of change detection outputs, according to the findings of the studies. The outcomes of the recommended technique will next be evaluated on multiclass segmentation datasets.

References

1. Chughtai, A.H., Abbasi, H., Ismail, R.K.: A review on change detection method and accuracy assessment for land use land cover. Remote Sensing Applications: Society and Environment, p. 100482 (2021)
2. Patil, P.W., Dudhane, A., Kulkarni, A., Murala, S., Gonde, A.B., Gupta, S.: An unified recurrent video object segmentation framework for various surveillance environments. IEEE Trans. Image Process. **30**, 7889–7902 (2021)
3. Bruzzone, L., Prieto, D.: Automatic analysis of the difference image for unsupervised change detection. IEEE Trans. Geosci. Remote Sens. **38**(3), 1171–1182 (2000)
4. Patil, P.W., Dudhane, A., Chaudhary, S., Murala, S.: Multi-frame based adversarial learning approach for video surveillance. Pattern Recogn. **122**, 108350 (2022)
5. Banerjee, T., Gurram, P., Whipps, G.T.: A bayesian theory of change detection in statistically periodic random processes. IEEE Trans. Inf. Theory **67**(4), 2562–2580 (2021)
6. Lucas, B., Pelletier, C., Schmidt, D., Webb, G.I., Petitjean, F.: A bayesian-inspired, deep learning-based, semi-supervised domain adaptation technique for land cover mapping. Machine Learning, pp. 1–33 (2021)
7. Zhang, Y., Peng, D., Huang, X.: Object-based change detection for VHR images based on multiscale uncertainty analysis. IEEE Geosci. Remote Sens. Lett. **15**(1), 13–17 (2018)
8. Sun, Y., Lei, L., Li, X., Sun, H., Kuang, G.: Nonlocal patch similarity based heterogeneous remote sensing change detection. Pattern Recogn. **109**, 107598 (2021)
9. Liu, J., Gong, M., Qin, K., Zhang, P.: A deep convolutional coupling network for change detection based on heterogeneous optical and radar images. IEEE Trans. Neural Networks Learning Syst. **29**(3), 545–559 (2016)
10. Chaudhary, S., Murala, S.: Tsnet: deep network for human action recognition in hazy videos. In: 2018 IEEE International Conference on Systems, Man, and Cybernetics (SMC), pp. 3981–3986 (2018)
11. Liu, R., Jiang, D., Zhang, L., Zhang, Z.: Deep depthwise separable convolutional network for change detection in optical aerial images. IEEE J. Sel. Topics Appl. Earth Observ. Remote Sensing **13**, 1109–1118 (2020)

12. Zhan, Y., Fu, K., Yan, M., Sun, X., Wang, H., Qiu, X.: Change detection based on deep siamese convolutional network for optical aerial images. IEEE Geosci. Remote Sens. Lett. **14**(10), 1845–1849 (2017)
13. Daudt, R.C., Le Saux, B., Boulch, A.: Fully convolutional siamese networks for change detection. In: 2018 25th IEEE International Conference on Image Processing (ICIP), pp. 4063–4067. IEEE (2018)
14. Heidary, F., Yazdi, M., Dehghani, M., Setoodeh, P.: Urban change detection by fully convolutional siamese concatenate network with attention. arXiv preprint arXiv:2102.00501 (2021)
15. Patil, P.S., Holambe, R.S., Waghmare, L.M.: Effcdnet: transfer learning with deep attention network for change detection in high spatial resolution satellite images. Digital Signal Process. **118**, 103250 (2021)
16. Vaswani, A., et al.: Attention is all you need, arXiv preprint arXiv:1706.03762 (2017)
17. Shaw, P., Uszkoreit, J., Vaswani, A.: Self-attention with relative position representations, arXiv preprint arXiv:1803.02155 (2018)
18. Bello, I., Zoph, B., Vaswani, A., Shlens, J., Le, Q.V.: Attention augmented convolutional networks. In: Proceedings of the IEEE/CVF International Conference on Computer Vision, pp. 3286–3295 (2019)
19. Ramachandran, P., Parmar, N., Vaswani, A., Bello, I., Levskaya, A., Shlens, J.: Stand-alone self-attention in vision models, arXiv preprint arXiv:1906.05909 (2019)
20. O. Ronneberger, P. Fischer, and T. Brox, "U-net: Convolutional networks for biomedical image segmentation," in International Conference on Medical image computing and computer-assisted intervention. Springer, 2015, pp. 234–241
21. H. Chen and Z. Shi, "A spatial-temporal attention-based method and a new dataset for remote sensing image change detection," Remote Sensing, vol. 12, no. 10, 2020
22. Singh, A., Singh, K.K.: Unsupervised change detection in remote sensing images using fusion of spectral and statistical indices. The Egyptian Journal of Remote Sensing and Space Science **21**(3), 345–351 (2018)
23. R. C. Daudt, B. Le Saux, A. Boulch, and Y. Gousseau, "Urban change detection for multispectral earth observation using convolutional neural networks," in IGARSS 2018–2018 IEEE International Geoscience and Remote Sensing Symposium. IEEE, 2018, pp. 2115–2118
24. Phutke, S.S., Murala, S.: Diverse receptive field based adversarial concurrent encoder network for image inpainting. IEEE Signal Process. Lett. **28**, 1873–1877 (2021)
25. Zhang, Z., Liu, Q., Wang, Y.: Road extraction by deep residual u-net. IEEE Geosci. Remote Sens. Lett. **15**(5), 749–753 (2018)
26. Chollet, F.: Xception: deep learning with depthwise separable convolutions. In: Proceedings of the IEEE Conference on Computer Vision and Pattern Recognition, pp. 1251–1258 (2017)
27. Treisman, A.M., Gelade, G.: A feature-integration theory of attention. Cogn. Psychol. **12**(1), 97–136 (1980)
28. Bello, I., Pham, H., Le, Q.V., Norouzi, M., Bengio, S.: Neural combinatorial optimization with reinforcement learning, arXiv preprint arXiv:1611.09940, 2016
29. Bahdanau, D., Cho, K., Bengio, Y.: Neural machine translation by jointly learning to align and translate, arXiv preprint arXiv:1409.0473 (2014)
30. Hu, J., Shen, L., Sun, G.: Squeeze-and-excitation networks. In: Proceedings of the IEEE Conference on Computer Vision and Pattern Recognition, pp. 7132–7141 (2018)

31. Park, J., Woo, S., Lee, J.-Y., Kweon, I.S.: Bam: bottleneck attention module. arXiv preprint arXiv:1807.06514 (2018)
32. Woo, S., Park, J., Lee, J.-Y., Kweon, I.S.: CBAM: convolutional block attention module. In: Ferrari, V., Hebert, M., Sminchisescu, C., Weiss, Y. (eds.) ECCV 2018. LNCS, vol. 11211, pp. 3–19. Springer, Cham (2018). https://doi.org/10.1007/978-3-030-01234-2_1
33. Zhang, H., Goodfellow, I., Metaxas, D., Odena, A.: Self-attention generative adversarial networks. In: International conference on machine learning. PMLR, pp. 7354–7363 (2019)
34. Noori, M., Bahri, A., Mohammadi, K.: Attention-guided version of 2d unet for automatic brain tumor segmentation. In: 2019 9th International Conference on Computer and Knowledge Engineering (ICCKE), pp. 269–275. IEEE (2019)
35. Long, J., Shelhamer, E., Darrell, T.: Fully convolutional networks for semantic segmentation. In: Proceedings of the IEEE Conference on Computer Vision and Pattern Recognition, pp. 3431–3440 (2015)
36. Ioffe, S., Szegedy, C.: Batch normalization: Accelerating deep network training by reducing internal covariate shift, arXiv preprint arXiv:1502.03167 (2015)
37. Xu, B., Wang, N., Chen, T., Li, M.: Empirical evaluation of rectified activations in convolutional network, arXiv preprint arXiv:1505.00853 (2015)
38. Chen, H., Shi, Z.: A spatial-temporal attention-based method and a new dataset for remote sensing image change detection. Remote Sensing 12(10), 1662 (2020)
39. Kingma, D.P., Ba, J.: Adam: a method for stochastic optimization, arXiv preprint arXiv:1412.6980 (2014)

A Large Volume Natural Tamil Character Dataset

M. Arun[(⊠)], S. Arivazhagan, and R Ahila Priyadharshini

Centre for Image Processing and Pattern Recognition, Mepco Schlenk Engineering College,
Sivakasi, Tamil Nadu, India
`{arun,sarivu,rahila}@mepcoeng.ac.in`

Abstract. This paper focuses on recognizing the individual Tamil characters in images of natural scenes. Even though natural character dataset are available publicly for different languages, no specific standardized dataset is available for natural Tamil characters. In this work, we present a publicly available Tamil character dataset "Mepco-TamNatChar" for natural Tamil character recognition. This research work presents the preliminary results on natural Tamil character recognition using spatial and machine learnt features. We report an accuracy of 87.50 ± 1.42% for a train test ratio of 50:50 using machine learnt features.

Keywords: Tamil · Natural image · Characters · HOG · Zoning · CNN

1 Introduction

Character Recognition is a field of pattern recognition which replicates the human capability of recognizing the printed forms of text. In recent days, the character recognition systems are useful in many places but not limited to identifying the vehicle registration number from the number plate images which helps in controlling traffic [1], converting printed academic records into text for storing in an electronic dataset, decoding ancient scripture, automatic data entry by scanning of cards, checks, application forms etc...., making the electronic images of printed documents searchable, extracting information from the documents such as passport, business cards etc. Research works are done on character recognition in different languages such as English [2], Arabic [3], Devanagari [4], Chinese [5] and Tamil [6] etc....Many researchers have worked on recognizing only the numeric digits also [7, 8].

This research work focuses on the recognition of natural Tamil characters. Tamil is one of the longest-surviving classical languages in the world. A. K. Ramanujan described it as "the only language of contemporary India which is recognizably continuous with a classical past [1]. In olden days Tamil script was based on the Grantha alphabet, later modified by Chola, Pallava and Pandian dynasty.

B. Raman et al. (Eds.): CVIP 2021, CCIS 1567, pp. 425–438, 2022.
https://doi.org/10.1007/978-3-031-11346-8_37

Tamil language contains 247 characters in which 12 vowels and 18 consonants form the base letters. These base letters combine with each other to form 216 (12 × 18) compound characters. There is also one special character (Aaytha Ezhuthu, " ஃ"), making a total of 247 characters. In 1978, the Government of Tamil Nadu reformed certain syllables of the modern Tamil script with,view to simplify the written script [9]. Even though 247 characters are in Tamil, only 124 symbolic representations are required for denoting all the characters of Tamil language.

12 vowels can be represented in 11 symbolic characters as the character " ஔ" (au) is a compound representation of the characters " ஒ" and " ள" (a consonant character). 18 consonants have 18 symbolic characters for representation. The compound characters created by the combination of consonants and these specific vowels such as "ஆ", "எ", "ஏ", "ஐ", "ஒ", "ஓ"and " ஔ" can be visualized by adding prefix/postfix with Consonants + "அ". So, the 216 compound characters can be represented by 94 symbolic characters (90 individual symbols and 4 prefix/postfix symbolic characters). Figure 1 depicts some of the examples of the segmented representations of the compound characters. For an example, the compound character " கோ" (kö) can be segmented as the prefix " ே◌", character " க" and postfix " ◌ா" (The dotted O is a representation of empty space). The special character " ஃ" (akk) requires 1 symbolic character representation.

Designing a system for recognizing Tamil characters is a difficult task because of its complexities due to its cursive nature and the similar structure of characters. For example, the characters " க" and "த", "எ" and "ஏ", & "ஒ"and " ஓ" are more or less similar except the tail shape in the second character. This research work focuses on recognizing the 124 symbolic character representations.

Many research works are found in the literature for recognizing the Tamil characters. Bhattacharya et al. used a two stage recognition scheme for Tamil character recognition where the first stage involves unsupervised clustering and second stage, a supervised classification [11]. Kannan and Prabhakar used octal graph conversion to improve the slant correction for recognizing off-line handwritten Tamil characters [12]. Antony and Abirami used structural and statistical properties based features for recognizing Tamil handwritten characters [13].

Compound Characters	Segmented Characters		
	Prefix	Character	Postfix
கா	-	க	◌ா
கெ	ெ◌	க	-
கே	ே◌	க	-
கை	ை◌	க	-
கொ	ெ◌	க	◌ா
கோ	ே◌	க	◌ா
கௌ	ெ◌	க	◌ள

Fig. 1. Segmented Representations of the compound characters

Table 1. Details of Mepco-TamilNatChar dataset.

Characters	Symbolic Representations						Character Count
Vowels	அ	ஆ	இ	ஈ	உ	ஊ	1179
	எ	ஏ	ஐ	ஒ	ஓ		
Consonants	க்	ங்	ச்	ஞ்	ட்	ண்	3891
	த்	ந்	ப்	ம்	ய்	ர்	
	ல்	வ்	ள்	ழ்	ற்	ன்	
Consonants + "அ"	க	ங	ச	ஞ	ட	ண	5738
	த	ந	ப	ம	ய	ர	
	ல	வ	எ	ழ	ற	ன	
Consonants + "இ"	கி	ஙி	சி	ஞி	டி	ணி	2484
	தி	நி	பி	மி	யி	ரி	
	லி	வி	ளி	ழி	றி	னி	
Consonants + "ஈ"	கீ	ஙீ	சீ	ஞீ	டீ	ணீ	1393
	தீ	நீ	பீ	மீ	யீ	ரீ	
	லீ	வீ	ளீ	ழீ	றீ	னீ	
Consonants + "உ"	கு	ஙு	சு	ஞு	டு	ணு	2429
	து	நு	பு	மு	யு	ரு	
	லு	வு	ளு	ழு	று	னு	
Consonants + "ஊ"	கூ	ஙூ	சூ	ஞூ	டூ	ணூ	1352
	தூ	நூ	பூ	மூ	யூ	ரூ	
	லூ	வூ	ளூ	ழூ	றூ	னூ	
Prefix/Postfix, Special Characters	ொ	ெ	ே	ை	ஃ		2162
Total Count							**20,628**

Junction point based procedure has been applied to pre-extract the features of offline Tamil handwritten character recognition by Antony and Abirami [14]. Prakash and Preethi designed a convolutional neural network for recognizing Tamil characters [15]. Kowsalya and Periasamy used modified neural network with aid of elephant herding optimization for recognizing the Tamil characters [16]. Lincy and Gayathri designed a convolutional neural network for Tamil Handwritten Character Recognition and optimized the network using lion optimization model [17]. Raj and Abirami used junction point elimination and then extracted the features for Tamil character recognition [6]. Most of the research works mentioned here uses their own custom dataset or the Offline Isolated Handwritten Tamil Character Dataset collected by HP Labs India used in International Workshop on Frotiers in Handwriting Recognition (IWFHR 2006).

This research work specifically focuses on recognizing the isolated Tamil characters in natural images. Despite many research works on natural English character recognition [18–20], this task is still considered as a complicated and unresolved problem because of its complex backgrounds, font style and dimensions, irregular illumination, resolution problems, occlusions, distortions created by camera angles. According to our knowledge, no research work has been carried out for the recognition of Tamil characters in Natural

Images because of the non-availability of the data. To address the problem of data collection for Tamil Characters in Natural images, we have collected the Natural Tamil Characters Image dataset named as Mepco-TamNatChar (https://www.kaggle.com/pmk arun/mepcotamildatabase) as part of the Kaggle Open Data Research 2020. This research work focuses on introducing the Mepco-TamNatChar dataset and to highlight the initial research findings using different feature extraction methods.

2 Materials and Methods

2.1 Natural Image Tamil Character Dataset

The Mepco-TamNatChar dataset consists of 20628 images spanned across 124 classes. The total 124 symbolic characters used to frame 247 Tamil characters and their corresponding count are represented in Table 1. The sample source images of the natural image characters used in this dataset are shown in Fig. 2. The source images are captured using the mobile camera under different illuminations and viewing angles. A total of 1677 images were taken and each image is cropped to form the isolated character dataset.

Fig. 2. Sample Source Images of Mepco-TamNatChar Dataset

Mostly the images were book titles, shop flex boards, wall written advertisements, name boards of city names, color advertisements in newspapers, etc.… which ensures the difficulties mentioned for the natural image character recognition. In Tamil language few characters like "ஙி", "ஞி", "ஞீ", "ஙீ", "ஙூ", "ஜூ"are not used to form any words. Also, few characters like "ணீ", "ஞ", "டூ", "ற"etc. are rarely used in word formation. Finding a suitable natural image for these characters was difficult. So, for these characters, we synthetically created a natural image by changing the background, font, thickness etc.… to match the criteria of natural image characters. The sample images of the isolated characters of the dataset are shown in Fig. 3 and the synthetically created sample images are shown in Fig. 4.

2.2 Feature Extraction Methods

Feature extraction is a special form of dimensionality reduction, as it obtains the most significant information from the original data and represents the information in a lower dimensionality space. In this research work, we experiment different spatial features and machine extracted features for recognizing the Tamil characters. Spatial features of an image, exploit location/spatial information which can be characterized by its gray levels. Here we have extracted the zoning features, moment features and the Histogram of Gradients (HoG) features and classified using SVM classifier with linear kernel. Also we have experiment the recognition based on the machine learnt features by using the convolutional neural network architecture used in DIGI-Net [8] with slight modifications.

Fig. 3. Sample images of Mepco-TamNatChar dataset

Fig. 4. Synthetically created sample images

Preprocessing

First, the images are converted into binary images using Otsu's thresholding algorithm [21]. Then, smoothening on the images is done using median filter with a kernel size of 5 × 5. This ensures the connectivity of unconnected edges in the images. Now the images are resized to 64 × 64 pixels to maintain uniformity. The sample images of the preprocessing stage are depicted in Fig. 5.

430   M. Arun et al.

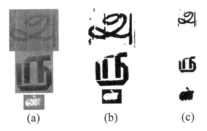

(a)   (b)   (c)

Fig. 5. Preprocessed images (a) Original Image (b) Smoothened Image after thresholding and median filtering (c) Resized smoothened Image

Before feature extraction, the resized images are skeletonized to obtain the outer structure and the inner structure using Zhang's thinning algorithm [12]. The outer structure and the inner structure of the characters are depicted in Fig. 6. It can be observed that the similar character structures "எ", "ஏ", &"ஒ", "ஓ" and "க", "த", are differentiated by their outer structures and inner structures.

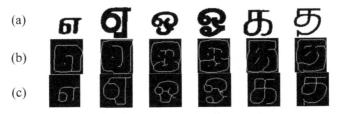

Fig. 6. Sketonized Images (a) Smoothened Image (b) Outer Skeleton (c) Inner Skeleton

Zoning Features

In Zoning, the character image is usually divided into zones of predefined size. After splitting the image into grids, the white pixels in each box is counted and are taken as feature vector. The zones 4×4 and 8×8 results in a feature vector of dimension 16 and 64 respectively. The Zoning is performed both on the outer and inner skeleton of the characters. Figure 7 shows the uniform sampling of skeletonized image using a grid of size 8×8.

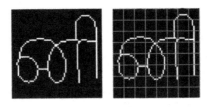

Fig. 7. Uniform sampling of skeletonized image using a grid of size 8×8

Moment Features

After the preprocessing of images, the features are extracted from the images. First the geometric moment features are extracted from the images. Image moments are a weighted average of the image pixels' intensities and these moments have attractive property/interpretation. The regular moment m_{ij} of an image $F(x, y)$ is calculated as given in Eq. 1

$$m_{ij} = \sum_x \sum_y x^i y^j F(x, y) \tag{1}$$

where, $i + j$ denotes the order of the moment. Regular moments are sensitive to (x, y) making it sensitive to the position of the object in the image. The central moment is invariant to the positions and is calculated by Eq. 2.

$$cm_{ij} = \sum_x \sum_y (x - \overline{x})^i (y - \overline{y})^j F(x, y) \tag{2}$$

where $\overline{x} = \frac{m_{10}}{m_{00}}$ and $\overline{y} = \frac{m_{01}}{m_{00}}$.

The normalized central moments are calculated by the Eq. 3.

$$nm_{ij} = \frac{cm_{ij}}{m_{00}^{\left(\frac{i+j}{2}+1\right)}} \tag{3}$$

Regular, central and normalized central moments of various orders are extracted from the preprocessed resized image, outer skeleton and inner skeleton images.

HoG Features

Gradients of an image are extremely useful in recognizing the image as the magnitude of gradients is very high around the edges where abrupt intensity changes are occurring. Edges and corners have more information about the character shape than the flat regions. Local object appearance and shape within an image can be described by the distribution of intensity gradients or edge directions. This is the basic idea behind the HoG feature descriptor. The steps involved in computing the HoG features are as follows:

Step-1: Compute the gradient of the pixel along horizontal and vertical direction

$$G(x, y) = \begin{bmatrix} g_x \\ g_y \end{bmatrix} = \begin{bmatrix} F(x + 1, y) - F(x - 1, y) \\ F(x, y + 1) - F(x, y - 1) \end{bmatrix}$$

Step-2: Compute the magnitude and the direction of the gradient

$$|G(x, y)| = \sqrt{g_x^2 + g_y^2}$$

$$\theta = arctan\left(\frac{g_y}{g_x}\right)$$

Step-3: Divide the image into sub images (cells) of size $N \times N$.

Step-4: Accumulate the magnitude values of each cell cumulatively into B bins of unsigned directions (0–180°). If the direction of the gradient vector of a pixel is between two bin values, its magnitude is split proportionally between the two bins.
Step-4: Normalize the gradients by considering a block of size M × M over the cells.
Step-5: Repeat Step-3 and Step-4 till the entire image is completed.

Figure 8 shows the representation of the HoG features applied on the original images of the dataset. From Fig. 8, it is clear that the HoG features are capturing the information of edges as gradients and directions.

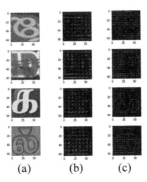

(a)   (b)   (c)

Fig. 8. HoG Features (a) Original Image (b) HoG features using cell size 4 × 4 (c) HoG features using cell size 8 × 8

Recent research works rely on the machine learnt features rather than hand crafted features for various applications such as leaf disease classification [23], segmentation [24], human recognition [25], digit recognition [8] etc.... These research works make use of the convolutional neural network (CNN) for learning the auto generated features. To observe the feature extraction capability of the CNN, the Digi-Net architecture [8] is used with slight modifications in this work. The input size of the original Digi-Net architecture is 128 × 128 and in this work the input size is modified as 64 × 64 to have a better comparison among the feature extraction methods. Also the final output layer in Digi-Net was 10 as it was recognizing numeral digits and here it's changed to 124 to fit the classification problem.

CNN is responsible for sparse interactions, parameter sharing and equivariant representations. Sparse interactions are implemented by the kernels of convolutional layers. The kernel weights are randomly initialized and their values get updated during the learning process. Parameter sharing is used to control the number of parameters in CNN. In contrast to traditional neural networks, CNN's one feature detector is useful to compute many spatial positions; hence parameters are shared across CNN, reducing the number of parameters to be learnt as well as the computational needs. Equivariant representation means that the object can be detected invariant of illumination and translation because of pooling layers. The architecture used in this research work is shown in Fig. 9.

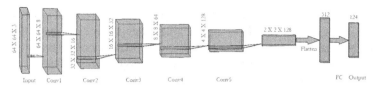

Fig. 9. Digi-Net architecture

The feature maps obtained at the various convolution layers from the deep learning model are given in Fig. 10. From Fig. 10, it is observed that the machine learnt features at the first and second convolutional layers act as a combination of multiple edge detectors. The activations in the first two layers are mostly retaining all of the information present in the initial picture, except the channels 2, 4 in first layer and channel 12 in second layer, where the activations are sparser. The activations in convolutional layer 3 and convolutional layer 4 become more abstract and less interpretable visually. It can be noted that the machine learnt features have learnt a complicated observation about the characters. It is observed that the irrelevant information gets filtered out and also the relevant information gets refined in the upper level layers of the CNN as human vision system perceives.

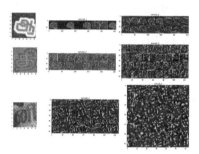

Fig. 10. Sample images and their respective feature maps at various convolutional layers

3   Results and Discussion

The entire experimentation is carried out using the natural Tamil image dataset which has 20628 images in 124 classes with a minimum of 50 images per class. For the entire experimentation a train test ratio maintained is 50:50 and the experimentation is repeated over 10 times with different train and test sets and the average accuracy is reported in this work.

First the experimentation is carried out by extracting the zoning features splitting the preprocessed, outer skeleton and inner skeleton images into 4 × 4 and 8 × 8 zones. The extracted features are then classified using SVM classifier with linear kernel. Table 2 depicts the accuracy of the natural Tamil image character recognition using Zoning features.

Feature_Image_Size is the taxonomy used to represent the features in all tables. Features can be Z, BM, CM, NM, HoG representing Zoning, Basic Moments, Centralized Moments, Normalized Moments and Histogram of Gradients respectively. Image can be ORI, PP, S1 and S2 which indicates that the features extracted from original image, preprocessed image, outer skeleton image and inner skeleton image respectively. Similarly, Size can be 7, 10, 16, 64, 36, and 324 which denotes the number of features. ' +' symbol indicates the concatenation of features.

Table 2. Performance measure of individual zoning features.

Zoning Features	4 × 4 Zone			8 × 8 Zone		
	Z_PP_16	Z_S1_16	Z_S2_16	Z_PP_64	Z_S1_64	Z_S2_64
Accuracy (%)	50.17 ± 0.51	43.40 ± 0.60	46.70 ± 0.60	56.21 ± 0.64	53.78 ± 0.43	52.47 ± 1.17

From Table 2 it is observed that the zoning features obtained using the 8 × 8 zones are better than 4 × 4 zones. Further experimentations are done using the zoning features obtained from 8 × 8 zones. Also it is noted that the zoning features obtained on preprocessed images are better than the skeletonized images. Table 3 shows the performance measure of combinational zoning features obtained on the preprocessed, outer skeleton and inner skeleton images. It is clear from Table 3 that the combinational zoning features yield better accuracy than the individual features.

Table 3. Performance measure of combinational zoning features.

Zoning features	Z_PP_64 + Z_S1_64	Z_PP_64 + Z_S2_64	Z_S1_64 + Z_S2_64	Z_PP_64 + Z_S1_64 + Z_S2_64
Accuracy (%)	63.74 ± 0.57	60.80 ± 0.98	63.05 ± 0.79	67.06 ± 0.67

The experimentation is continued by extracting 10 different basic moments, 7 centralized moments and 7 normalized moment features individually on the preprocessed (PP), outer skeleton and inner skeleton images. As the individual features don't perform well, the experimentation is carried out using the combined moment features. The results are tabulated in Table 4 and it is noted that moment features are not suitable for the classification of Natural Tamil characters.

Table 4. Performance measure of Moment features.

Zoning features	BM_PP_10 + BM_S1_10 + BM_S2_10	CM_PP_7 + CM_S1_7 + CM_S2_7	NM_PP_7 + NM_S1_7 + NM_S2_7	Moments_All*
Accuracy (%)	43.43 ± 0.56	48.66 ± 0.85	51.25 ± 1.01	57.22 ± 0.44

* Moments_All denotes BM_PP_10 + BM_S1_10 + BM_S2_10 + CM_PP_7 + CM_S1_7 + CM_S2_7 + NM_PP_7 + NM_S1_7 + NM_S2_7

In continuation of the experimentation, next the HoG features are extracted from the original, preprocessed, outer skeleton and inner skeleton images with a cell size of 4 × 4 and 8 × 8 yielding 36 and 324 features respectively. Table 5 denotes the performance of the HoG features.

Table 5. Performance measure of HoG features

HoG features	Accuracy (%)
ORI_HOG_36	66.01 ± 0.72
PP_HOG_36	58.29 ± 0.56
S1_HOG_36	48.23 ± 0.97
S2_HOG_36	47.47 ± 0.47
ORI_HOG_36 + PP_HOG_36 + S1_HOG_36 + S2_HOG_36	71.90 ± 0.74
ORI_HOG_324	84.30 ± 0.46
PP_HOG_324	78.00 ± 0.75
S1_HOG_324	69.02 ± 0.79
S2_HOG_324	67.43 ± 0.90
ORI_HOG_324 + PP_HOG_324 + S1_HOG_324 + S2_HOG_324	**85.83 ± 0.34**

From Table 5, it is noted that, the HOG features extracted from the original images outperforms the HoG features extracted from preprocessed and skeletonized images. Even though the combined HoG features extracted from original, preprocessed and skeletonized images yields an accuracy of 85.83%, further experimentations are carried out using HoG features extracted from original image. The 1.5% increase in accuracy is due to the drastic increase in the feature dimension (4 times). To improve the accuracy further, the above extracted features are then combined and classified. The accuracy of the combinational features is tabulated in Table 6. From Table 6, it is evident that the combination of HOG features with the Zoning features yields better accuracy compared to other combinations. Also, it is observed that moment features do not have significant contribution in natural Tamil character recognition.

To investigate, how machine learnt features work on Mepco-TamNatChar dataset, the experimentation is carried out using Digi-Net architecture [8]. During this experimentation, the images are fed into CNN directly without any other preprocessing except resizing the image to match the input size of the CNN architecture. The computational parameter set up of this architecture are as mentioned: Activation function – ReLu, Pooling –Max pool, $\eta = 0.001$, Loss function- Cross entropy, Optimizer- RMS prop and Batch size $= 16$. The performance of the Digi-Net architecture on recognizing natural Tamil characters for various epochs is tabulated in Table 7.

Table 6. Performance measure of combinational features

Combinational features	Accuracy (%)
Z_PP_64 + Z_S1_64 + Z_S2_64 + Moments_All	68.39 ± 0.52
Z_PP_64 + Z_S1_64 + Z_S2_64 + ORI_HOG_324	**86.17 ± 0.40**
Moments_All + ORI_HOG_324	85.64 ± 0.47
Z_PP_64 + Z_S1_64 + Z_S2_64 + Moments_All + ORI_HOG_324	86.05 ± 0.54

Table 7. Performance measure of Machine learnt features.

Epochs	10	20	50	75	100
Accuracy (%)	84.83	85.53	87.42	87.71	87.93

It is observed that the increase in epoch over 50 doesn't improve the accuracy significantly. So, the experimentation is repeated with different train - test images over 10 times for 50 epochs. After exhaustive experimentation using Digi-Net architecture, we report an accuracy of 87.50 ± 1.42%. The maximum confusions for the natural characters yielding less than 50% classification accuracy are tabulated in Table 8. Because of these maximum confusions, the overall accuracy is pulled down to 87.50 ± 1.42%.

Table 8. Confusions for the natural characters

Character	Misclassified as	Accuracy
ஜ	ஜா, மூ	37.83
யி	வி	44.44
து	டு, ஹு,ஞு, ல், ள்	42.42
யு	வி, ட, தி, பீ	48.64
மு	ச, ட, ற, து	47.22
ஞு	து, வீ, யு, ச, வ்	28.12
கு	னீ, மு, ஜு	42.85

4 Conclusion

In this work, we have introduced a publicly available Tamil Character dataset "Mepco-TamNatChar" for natural Tamil Character recognition. Also, we have studied the performance of spatial features such as Zoning, Moments and HOG feature descriptors and machine learnt features for Tamil character recognition in natural images. The maximum accuracy obtained for a train test ratio of 50:50 is $87.50 \pm 1.42\%$ using deep learnt features. We have benchmarked the preliminary results on recognizing Tamil characters in natural images, but the problem is extremely challenging and could possibly promote the research community for further experimentations to explore the discriminative features.

Acknowledgement. This research is done as a part of Kaggle's Open Data Research Grant 2020.

References

1. Li, H., Yang, R., Chen, X.: License plate detection using convolutional neural network. In: 2017 3rd IEEE International Conference on Computer and Communications (ICCC), Chengdu, 2017, pp. 1736–1740 (2017). https://doi.org/10.1109/CompComm.2017.8322837
2. Chandio, A.A., Asikuzzaman, M., Pickering, M.R.: Cursive character recognition in natural scene images using a multilevel convolutional neural network fusion. IEEE Access **8**, 109054–109070 (2020). https://doi.org/10.1109/ACCESS.2020.3001605
3. Altwaijry, N., Al-Turaiki, I.: Arabic handwriting recognition system using convolutional neural network. Neural Comput. Appl. (2020). Doi: https://doi.org/10.1007/s00521-020-050 70-8
4. Deore, S.P., Pravin, A.: Devanagari handwritten character recognition using fine-tuned deep convolutional neural network on trivial dataset. Sādhanā **45**(1), 1–13 (2020). https://doi.org/10.1007/s12046-020-01484-1
5. Cao, Z., Lu, J., Cui, S., Zhang, C.: Zero-shot handwritten Chinese character recognition with hierarchical decomposition embedding. Pattern Recogn. **107**, 107488 (2020). https://doi.org/10.1016/j.patcog.2020.107488
6. Raj, M.A.R., Abirami, S.: Junction point elimination based Tamil handwritten character recognition: an experimental analysis. J. Syst. Sci. Syst. Eng. **29**(1), 100–123 (2019). https://doi.org/10.1007/s11518-019-5436-6
7. Ahlawat, S., Choudhary, A., Nayyar, A., Singh, S., Yoon, B.: Improved handwritten digit recognition using convolutional neural networks (CNN). Sensors **20**, 3344 (2020)
8. Madakannu, A., Selvaraj, A.: DIGI-Net: a deep convolutional neural network for multiformat digit recognition. Neural Comput. Appl. **32**(15), 11373–11383 (2019). https://doi.org/10.1007/s00521-019-04632-9
9. Zvelebil, K.: The Smile of Murugan, BRILL, pp. 11–12 (1973). ISBN 978-90-04-03591-1
10. Kesavan, B.S., Venkatachari, P.N.: History of printing and publishing in India: a story of cultural re-awakening, vol. 1. National Book Trust. p. 82 (1984)
11. Bhattacharya, U., Ghosh, S.K., Parui, S.: A two stage recognition scheme for handwritten Tamil characters. In: Ninth International Conference on Document Analysis and Recognition (ICDAR 2007), Parana, 2007, pp. 511–515 (2007). https://doi.org/10.1109/ICDAR.2007.437 8762
12. Kannan, R., Prabhakar, R.: An improved handwritten tamil character recognition system using octal graph. J. Comput. Sci. **4**, 509–516 (2008)

13. Robert, A., Raj, M., Abirami, S.: Analysis of statistical feature extraction approaches used Tamil handwritten OCR. In: 12th Tamil Internet Conference-INFITT, pp. 114–150 ((2013)
14. Robert, A., Raj, M., Abirami, S.: Offline Tamil handwritten character recognition using chain code and zone based features. In: 13th Tamil Internet Conference- INFITT, pp. 28–34 (2014)
15. Prakash, A.A., Preethi, S.: Isolated offline tamil handwritten character recognition using deep convolutional neural network. In: 2018 International Conference on Intelligent Computing and Communication for Smart World (I2C2SW), Erode, India, 2018, pp. 278–281. https://doi.org/10.1109/I2C2SW45816.2018.8997144
16. Kowsalya, S., Periasamy, P.S.: Recognition of Tamil handwritten character using modified neural network with aid of elephant herding optimization. Multimed. Tools Appl. **78**(17), 25043–25061 (2019). https://doi.org/10.1007/s11042-019-7624-2
17. Lincy, R.B., Gayathri, R.: Optimally configured convolutional neural network for Tamil Handwritten Character Recognition by improved lion optimization model. Multimed. Tools Appl. **80**(4), 5917–5943 (2020). https://doi.org/10.1007/s11042-020-09771-z
18. Campos, D.T., Babu, B.R., Varma, M.: Character recognition in natural images. In: Ranchordas, A., Araújo, H. (eds.) VISAPP 2009—Proceedings of the Fourth International Conference on Computer Vision Theory and Applications, Lisboa, Portugal, 5–8 February, 2009, vol. 2, pp. 273–280. INSTICC Press (2009)
19. Akbani, O., Gokrani, A., Quresh, M., Khan, F.M., Behlim, S.I., Syed, T.Q.: Character recognition in natural scene images. In: 2015 International Conference on Information and Communication Technologies (ICICT), Karachi, 2015, pp. 1–6. https://doi.org/10.1109/ICICT.2015.7469575
20. Ali, M.: A study of holistic strategies for the recognition of characters in natural scene images. Electronic Theses and Dissertations, 2004–2019. 5066 (2016). https://stars.library.ucf.edu/etd/5066
21. Otsu, N.: A threshold selection method from gray-level histograms. IEEE Trans. Syst. Man Cybern. **9**(1), 62–66 (1979). https://doi.org/10.1109/TSMC.1979.4310076
22. Zhang, T.Y., Suen, C.Y.: A fast parallel algorithm for thinning digital patterns. Commun. ACM **27**(3), 236–239 (1984)
23. Ahila Priyadharshini, R., Arivazhagan, S., Arun, M. et al.: Maize leaf disease classification using deep convolutional neural networks. Neural Comput. Appl. **31**, 8887–8895 (2019). https://doi.org/10.1007/s00521-019-04228-3
24. Saha, O., Sathish, R., Sheet, D.: Fully Convolutional Neural Network for Semantic Segmentation of Anatomical Structure and Pathologies in Colour Fundus Images Associated with Diabetic Retinopathy. arXiv:1902.03122
25. Ahila Priyadharshini, R., Arivazhagan, S., Arun, M.: A deep learning approach for person identification using ear biometrics. Appl. Intell. (2020). https://doi.org/10.1007/s10489-020-01995-8

Datasets of Wireless Capsule Endoscopy for AI-Enabled Techniques

Palak Handa[2], Nidhi Goel[1(✉)], and S. Indu[2]

[1] Department of ECE, IGDTUW, Delhi, India
nidhi.iitr1@gmail.com
[2] Department of ECE, DTU, Delhi, India

Abstract. High-quality, open-access and free wireless capsule endoscopy (WCE) data act as a catalyst for on-going state-of-the-art (SOTA) Artificial Intelligence (AI) research works in management of various gastro-intestinal tract related diseases such as Crohn's disease, colorectal cancer, gastro-intestinal (GI) bleeding, motility disorders, celiac disease, inflammation, polyps, and hookworms *etc.* This paper presents widely used, open and downloadable WCE datasets to perform various AI-enabled techniques like video summarization, segmentation, disease detection, classification and prediction. A brief comparison and discussion of open and private WCE datasets has also been done. Such WCE datasets will help in development and evaluation of AI powered, computer-aided system for different anomalies in gastroenterology.

Keywords: Image frames · Videos · Datasets · Evaluation · Wireless capsule endoscopy

1 Introduction

Wireless Capsule Endoscopy (WCE) is a non-invasive, painless, novel imaging method to effectively visualize the digestive system of our body [1]. It requires little or no hospitalization and specialized care. However, it takes long hours to develop a differential diagnosis based on 6–8 h WCE video [2]. Specialized health experts evaluate the anomalies, in a frame-by-frame manner which is not only time-consuming but is also prone to human error [1]. Since the camera moves along the tract, it is prone to poor light, motion artefacts, blurring and missed abnormalities at the back side of the camera and may get stuck in narrow areas of the GI tract [2].

Recent advancements in Artificial Intelligence (AI) techniques have enabled automation in personalized medicine and healthcare [3]. Researchers have focused on different problems related to WCE like anomaly detection, video summarization, noise and artefact removal, and processing *etc.* Each problem requires unique, high-quality data for analysis.

The authors acknowledges the SMDP-C2SD project, Ministry of Electronics and Information Technology, Government of India for the research grant.

B. Raman et al. (Eds.): CVIP 2021, CCIS 1567, pp. 439–446, 2022.
https://doi.org/10.1007/978-3-031-11346-8_38

The WCE videos are captured using varying resolution (256×256, 320×320) pill cameras which are about 11 mm $\times$ 26 mm in size (diameter $\times$ length) and can be swallowed from mouth. It travels the GI tract for 6–8 h depending upon the need and application [2]. There are several FDA approved WCE cameras like PillCam, MicroCam, and EndoCapsule1 *etc.* [2]. The WCE data can be obtained as a video or as image frames (sequential or non-sequential) [2].

High quality data which contains variety of anomalies, artefacts, different light intensities, pill camera angle and view variations, and depth is needed to develop an end-to-end AI based systems to reduce the time of evaluation and aid in early diagnosis in gastroenterology field.

Several researchers have come forward and released their WCE datasets for research purpose wherein KID project remains the benchmark dataset for WCE image and video analysis [3]. Medically verified annotation masks play a vital role in segmentation, and classification process of different polyps, ulcers, and lesions.

The WCE datasets mentioned in the Sect. 2 are freely available, redistributable for research purposes. Section 3 discusses all the existing private WCE datasets for various tasks such as segmentation, detection, video summarization, prediction, classification, *etc.* Table 1 shows a comparison of existing open and private WCE datasets. Finally, in Sect. 4 concluding remarks have been presented.

The source and availability of these were verified on 20-08-2021, which may change in the future. All the dataset web links have been given in their respective sub-sections. The datasets were found using different keywords like 'open wireless capsule endoscopy datasets', 'private WCE data', 'free WCE datasets', and 'available WCE data' on popular search engines such as mendeley, zenodo, pub med and google scholar.

2   Open WCE Datasets

This section discusses about the publically available datasets in WCE. They have been used for several AI techniques for video and image frames such as segmentation, video summarization, and detection [4–9].

2.1   Kvasir-Capsule [4]

It is the largest and most diverse, publically available video capsule endoscopy (VCE) dataset which contains 4,741,504 normal and abnormal image frames extracted from 117 anonymous videos. It was collected from Norwegian Hospital using Olympus EC-S10 endocapsule. It was released in 2020 on OSF home, a free website to share research works.

The findings are divided into two categories *i.e.*, anatomy and luminal findings. 47,238 video frames are labelled and contains a bounding box for each frame. Rest of the images frames are unlabelled. Both video and images which are labelled and unlabelled are available for download. All the annotations have been medically verified by four specialized hospital doctors. Available link.

2.2   Red Lesion Endoscopy Dataset [5]

It is the first publically available VCE dataset which contains red lesions like angioectasias, angiodysplasias, and bleeding only. It is freely available on INESCTEC data repository since 2018 and contains two sets. Set 1 and 2 consists of about 3295 non-sequential and 600 sequential frames respectively with manually annotated masks. The videos were recorded using different cameras like MiroCam, Pill-Cam SB1, SB2 and SB3. Available link.

2.3   Annotated Bleeding Dataset [6]

This dataset was released in 2016 for automatic segmentation of 50 bleeding and non-bleeding capsule endoscopy (CE) images. The ground truth images are also available. No other information is available for this dataset. Available link.

2.4   EndoSLAM [7]

EndoSLAM dataset contains different types of endoscopic recordings of porcine GI tract organs, synthetic data generated through VR caps and phantom recordings of the colon and other GI tract organs with CT scan ground truth. The recordings have been acquired using conventional endoscopes like Olympus colonoscope and newer WCE cameras like MicroCam, Pillcam colon, high and low resolution cameras. 42,700 image frames distributed in 35 sub-datasets have been developed which aims to provide 6D depth pose, 3D ground truths, image frames from different cameras views, angles and light conditions. A virtual environment has also been released on the similar area of interest known as VR caps. Both of them are available freely on Github. EndoSLAM dataset and VR caps software.

2.5   KID Project [8]

This project was originally launched as an internet-based digital video atlas for WCE in 2017 [8]. It contains more than 2500 annotated image and 47 videos and was collected from six centers. All the videos were acquired using MiroCam (IntroMedic Co, Seoul, Korea) capsule endoscope. KID data is bifurcated into two datasets, three videos and its parts.

Dataset 1 consists of 77 WCE images which has various anomalies like angioectasias, apthae, chylous cysts, polypoid lesions, villous oedema, bleeding, lymphangiectasias, ulcers and stenoses. Dataset 2 consists of 2371 WCE images. Several polypoids, vascular and, inflammatory lesions observed in small bowel region are included in this dataset along with normal images from the GI tract.

It was developed with a high standard image quality, protocols and standard annotations for SOTA research purposes. The datasets were first available on the original website and then shifted to Kaggle, a machine learning and data science community website. A similar dataset named as 'Capsule endoscope tracking dataset' was released by the authors. No direct source was found to download these datasets. Both the data are now available on request from the authors. Original website and Kaggle link.

Table 1. Comparison of existing open and private wireless capsule endoscopy datasets

Ref.	Availability	Year	Acquisition	Image resolution	Total no. of image frames	Ground truths
[4]	Free	2017	Olympus EC-S10	336 × 336	4,741,504	Yes
[5]	Free	2018	MiroCam, Pill-Cam SB1, SB2 and SB3	512 × 512 or 320 × 320	3,895	Yes
[6]	Free	2016	-	-	100	Yes
[7]	Free	2021	MicroCam, Pillcam colon	320 × 320 256 × 256	3,294	Yes
[8]	On request	2017	MiroCam	-	2,500	Yes
[9]	On request	2020	Pillcam SB3	-	25,124	Yes
[10]	On request	2014	MicroCam	320 × 320	1,370	Yes
[11]	On request	2020	PillCam3	-	3,218	Yes
[12]	Private	2021	PillCam	-	71,191	-
[13]	Private	2018	PillCam SB, SB1, SB2 and EndoCapsule1 (Olympus)	256 × 256	8,872	-
[14]	Private	2021	PillCam SB3	-	102,346	Yes
[15]	Private	2019	PillCam SB2 and SB3	576 × 576	-	-
[16]	Website based	2018	-	-	2,300	Yes
[18]	Website based	2017	-	243 × 424	2,333	-
[19]	Website based	2020	-	-	-	-
[20]	Website based	2019	-	256 × 256	1,875	-

3   Private WCE Datasets

This section discusses various WCE datasets that are not publically available for research purposes. Some of the datasets are available upon request to the authors [9–11].

3.1   CAD-CAP [9]

It is a multi-center WCE dataset which was recorded at thirteen french hospitals using Pillcam SB3 system, Medtronic. Both normal and abnormal image frames containing anomalies like different type of lesions, ulcers, fresh blood, *etc.* were extracted from 4000 WCE videos. The database was split into two datasets *i.e.,* one for the development of SOTA AI pipeline and another for testing and validation of the pipeline. The training and testing data contains 2562 abnormal images and 10K normal images. It was released as a part of the MICCAI challenge in 2017 and further continued in 2018.

3.2   Lesion Detection Dataset [10]

It contains 1370 WCE images frames which were collected from 252 WCE videos at Royal Infirmary of Edinburgh, United Kingdom, and the Technological Educational Institute of Central Greece, Lamia, Greece. It contains various anomalies like polyps, ulcers, stenoses, apthae, hemorrhage *etc.* with annotation masks for each image frame. It was previously available at link. However, it can be made available on request from the authors.

3.3   Crohn IPI [11]

This dataset contains 3498 WCE image frames from different pathological findings and normal images collected using PillCam3 at Nantes University Hospital. All the abnormal videos were taken from patients suffering from Crohn's disease. The annotations were medically verified by three independent medical experts. Various anomalies like ulcers, lesions, erythema, edema, and stenosis *etc.* The data is available on request through this website.

3.4   Cleansing Small Bowel Capsule Endoscopy [12]

This dataset was collected from 2016 to 2020 using PillCam SB3 system at three University hospitals, South Korea. It contains 3500, 2500 and 1000 images frames in training, validation and testing sets. Small bowel preparation scale (cleansing score) and clinical grading like Grade A, B, and so on were given to each still cut image frame. It contains different anomalies such as ulcer, bleeding, angioectasia, erosions, and mass *etc.*

3.5   Bleeding Dataset [13]

This dataset contains image frames and videos collected from a and b. The videos were captured through PillCam SB, SB1 and SB2 and EndoCapsule1 (Olympus). A total of 8872 image frames are available wherein 2467 image frames are bleeding images and rest are non-bleeding images.

3.6   WCE-2019-Video [14]

This dataset contains 30 WCE videos with anatomical and pathological markings of the human GI tract and is supported by Chongqing Jinshan Science and Technology (Group) Co., Ltd. It is the first dataset for video summarization and also contains annotations. 102,346 image frames were extracted from these videos and contains different anatomical markings such as from stomach, colon, duodenum *etc.*

3.7   Celiac Disease WCE Dataset [15]

This dataset was recorded for 13 celiac and healthy control patients using two WCE cameras *i.e.,* PillCam SB2 and SB3 at Columbia University Medical Center, New York. Different anatomical markings such as from jejunum, distal jejunum, and proximal ileum *etc.* are present in this data.

3.8 AIIMS WCE Dataset

Our research team is developing the AIIMS WCE dataset. It contains video segments of 20 s duration for more than seven patient's data with different anatomical and pathological findings such as angioectasia, polyps and uclers in duodenum, small bowel, and terminal ileum region *etc.* The image dataset comprises of 8942 images wherein 7259 images are normal WCE images and 1683 images are abnormal WCE images. The image resolution is of 576×576.

4 Miscellaneous

All the WCE datasets mentioned in this section were not found online but mentioned as available/downloadable datasets by various works and hence were put in miscellaneous wce datasets.

Studies have mentioned data available at website as publically available dataset [16, 17]. According to the studies, the dataset contains 2300 WCE images out of which 450 contains bleeding events. Out of total 32 WCE videos, 20 contain non-bleeding events and 12 videos contain bleeding events. Ulcer dataset contains 2333 WCE images which were extracted from 16 ucler and 7 normal individuals WCE videos. According to the study done in [18], it was downloaded from website.

GastroLab dataset discussed in [19] contains several conventional endoscopy and WCE videos of various anomalies since 1996 at website. Work done in [20] has taken the WCE dataset from website. It contains 1875 ulcer and non-ulcer image frames from esophagus and gastric part of the digestive system of diseased individuals.

5 Conclusion

Diagnosis, treatment and management of diseases like colorectal cancer, gastrointestinal bleeding, motility disorders, and celiac disease *etc.* which are related to the digestive system of our body are still a challenging task in healthcare. Wireless capsule endoscopy method is a novel imaging method to effectively visualize the GI tract of humans which requires little or no hospitalization. AI techniques are enabling automation of WCE image processing, disease detection and video summarization. This paper has focused on presenting open and private WCE datasets used for various research purposes. Such datasets motivate scientific research in early diagnosis of GI tract related diseases and effective management and processing of WCE through robust techniques.

References

1. Goenka, M.K., Majumder, S., Goenka, U.: Capsule endoscopy: present status and future expectation. World J. Gastroenterol. WJG **20**(29), 10024 (2014)
2. Wang, A., et al.: Wireless capsule endoscopy. Gastrointest. Endosc. **78**(6), 805–815 (2013)
3. Atsawarungruangkit, A., et al.: Understanding deep learning in capsule endoscopy: can artificial intelligence enhance clinical practice?. Artif. Intell. Gastrointest. Endosc. **1**(2), 33–43 (2020)
4. Smedsrud, P.H., et al.: Kvasir-Capsule, a video capsule endoscopy dataset. Sci. Data **8**(1), 1–10 (2021)
5. Coelho, P., Pereira, A., Leite, A., Salgado, M., Cunha, A.: A deep learning approach for red lesions detection in video capsule endoscopies. In: Campilho, A., Karray, F., ter Haar Romeny, B. (eds.) ICIAR 2018. LNCS, vol. 10882, pp. 553–561. Springer, Cham (2018). https://doi.org/10.1007/978-3-319-93000-8_63
6. Deeba, F., Bui, F.M., Wahid, K.A.: Automated growcut for segmentation of endoscopic images. In: 2016 International Joint Conference on Neural Networks (IJCNN). IEEE (2016)
7. Ozyoruk, K.B., et al.: EndoSLAM dataset and an unsupervised monocular visual odometry and depth estimation approach for endoscopic videos. Med. Image Anal. **71**, 102058 (2021)
8. Koulaouzidis, A., et al.: KID project: an internet-based digital video atlas of capsule endoscopy for research purposes. Endosc. Int. Open **5**(06), E477–E483 (2017)
9. Leenhardt, R., et al.: CAD-CAP: a 25,000-image database serving the development of artificial intelligence for capsule endoscopy. Endosc. Int. Open **8**(03), E415–E420 (2020)
10. Iakovidis, D.K., Koulaouzidis, A.: Automatic lesion detection in capsule endoscopy based on color saliency: closer to an essential adjunct for reviewing software. Gastrointest. Endosc. **80**(5), 877–883 (2014)
11. Vallée, R., et al.: CrohnIPI: an endoscopic image database for the evaluation of automatic Crohn's disease lesions recognition algorithms. In: Medical Imaging 2020: Biomedical Applications in Molecular, Structural, and Functional Imaging, vol. 11317. International Society for Optics and Photonics (2020)
12. Nam, J.H., et al.: Development of a deep learning-based software for calculating cleansing score in small bowel capsule endoscopy. Sci. Rep. **11**(1), 1–8 (2021)
13. Deeba, F., et al.: Performance assessment of a bleeding detection algorithm for endoscopic video based on classifier fusion method and exhaustive feature selection. Biomed. Sig. Process. Control **40**, 415–424 (2018)
14. Lan, L., Ye, C.: Recurrent generative adversarial networks for unsupervised WCE video summarization. Knowl.-Based Syst. **222**, 106971 (2021)
15. biKoh, J.E.W., et al.: Automated diagnosis of celiac disease using DWT and non-linear features with video capsule endoscopy images. Future Gener. Comput. Syst. **90**, 86–93 (2019)
16. Kundu, A.K., Fattah, S.A., Rizve, M.N.: An automatic bleeding frame and region detection scheme for wireless capsule endoscopy videos based on interplane intensity variation profile in normalized RGB color space. J. Healthc. Eng. **2018** (2018)
17. Ghosh, T., Fattah, S.A., Wahid, K.A.: CHOBS: color histogram of block statistics for automatic bleeding detection in wireless capsule endoscopy video. IEEE J. Transl. Eng. Health Med. **6**, 1–12 (2018)

18. Charfi, S., El Ansari, M.: Computer-aided diagnosis system for ulcer detection in wireless capsule endoscopy videos. In: 2017 International Conference on Advanced Technologies for Signal and Image Processing (ATSIP). IEEE (2017)
19. Muhammad, K., et al.: Vision-based personalized wireless capsule endoscopy for smart healthcare: taxonomy, literature review, opportunities and challenges. Future Gener. Comput. Syst. **113**, 266–280 (2020)
20. Alaskar, H., et al.: Application of convolutional neural networks for automated ulcer detection in wireless capsule endoscopy images. Sensors **19**(6), 1265 (2019)

Moving Objects Detection in Intricate Scenes via Spatio-Temporal Co-occurrence Based Background Subtraction

Shweta Singh[1] and Srikanth Vasamsetti[2]($\boxtimes$)

[1] Indian Institute of Technology, Delhi, India
[2] CSIR-Central Scientific Instruments Organisation, Chandigarh 160030, India
srikanth.vasamsetti@csio.res.in

Abstract. Moving object detection using single feature-based techniques often fails in intricate scenes such as complex background, illumination variation, camouflage, moving background objects etc. In this letter, a novel feature descriptor, Multi-frame spatio-temporal co-occurrence (MSC) descriptor is proposed for moving object detection. The MSC descriptor collects the information from the 3D lattice which is formed by neighborhood (typically five) frames in a video. Co-occurrence matrix is computed from the collected 3D grid values. Then, Statistical textural features are calculated from MSC descriptor. Further, the background models are constructed by using Statistical textural features extracted from MSC descriptor, Gray scale intensity value and R, G, B values. Stability of adaptive feature (SoAF) model is modified by applying gaussian distribution with introduction of dynamic weights for proximity calculation. The performance of the proposed algorithm is validated on Change Detection dataset. Qualitative and quantitative analysis are carried out on benchmark datasets. The results after investigation, the proposed method outperforms the state-of-the-art techniques for moving object detection in terms of PR curves and F- measure.

Keywords: Co-occurrence matrix · Statistical textual features · Background modelling · And multi-feature

1 Introduction

Detection of moving objects in video sequences is a fundamental step in a wide range of applications like automated video surveillance, object tracking, action recognition, human computer interaction etc. Immense research has been carried out in this field and great success has been achieved in the case of static or near static backgrounds. This doesn't limit the need to improve the accuracy in real-world scenarios which offer many challenges like: dynamic backgrounds (swaying vegetation, fountain, water bodies, blizzard etc.), rapid illumination changes, shadows, motion of camera, poor textured small objects, low framerate etc. or foreground.

In literature, background subtraction methods are classified based on the number and type of features and procedure used for feature extraction [1]. The single-feature based approaches [2–5] only reflect single characteristics of a pixel whereas, pixel properties varies over time. Multi-feature based approaches [6–8] exploit different characteristics of a pixels by drawing the merit of each feature.

To construct feature vector, mostly three types of procedures, i.e., spatial [9, 10], temporal [11] and spatio-temporal [12, 13] were used in background modelling. In literature, spatio-temporal features were collected from two or more consecutive frames [13–16].

Background modelling is another crucial step in moving object detection techniques. Simple background model is effective in dealing constrained environment whereas it will fail in intricate scenes. For dealing dynamic backgrounds, more than one background model is used in literature [17, 18].

The present work focuses on multi-feature-based background subtraction technique for moving object detection. This uses stability of features in background pixels as the basis of classification of a pixel as background. Proposed work is inspired by a recent technique [18] in which, gray, colour and texture (R-SILTP) features were used. The major contributions and modification as compared to [18] are: A novel Multi-frame Spatio-temporal Co-occurrence descriptor is proposed for moving object detection. Gaussian distribution is used instead of simple histogram (considers peak of the bin) which is used for judging how strongly pixel lies in background. Dynamic weights are

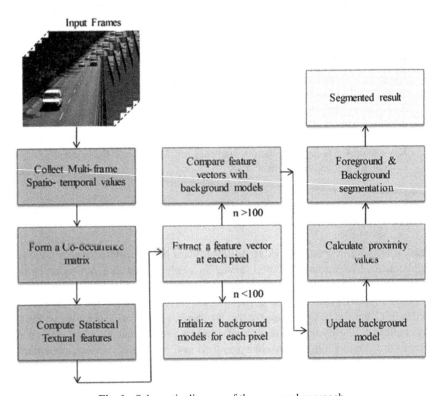

Fig. 1. Schematic diagram of the proposed approach.

used in gaussian models for background proximity calculation by giving more weightage to feature value which is closer to the mean and less weightage for the feature value which is far away from the mean (explained in Fig. 4).

2 Proposed System Framework

The proposed moving object detection framework (shown in Fig. 1) in challenging environments contains of following steps:

- Multi-frame spatio-temporal values are computed for horizontal and vertical directions. Co-occurrence matrix is calculated from these collected 3D grid values. Thus, MSC descriptor is generated for each pixel.
- Statistical textural features are calculated from MSC descriptor. A histogram is formed for each feature for each pixel, from the feature vectors of F frames.
- Background models are updated by comparing incoming frame feature vector with previously constructed background models.
- Proximity value is calculated followed by pixel classification as foreground/background.

2.1 Multi-frame Spatio-Temporal Co-occurrence (MSC) Descriptor

The MSC descriptor collects the information from the 3D lattice which is formed by collecting f, f − 3, f − 5, f + 3 and f + 5 frames in a given video. Figure 2 shows pixel arrangement of neighbourhood for a given frame f and possible directions for collection of spatio-temporal information. After forming the 3D lattice for a reference frame f, the spatio-temporal information is collected for vertical and horizontal directions as given in Eqs. (1) and (2).

$$
S^{\beta=2}\Big|_{N=24} = \begin{bmatrix}
K^{f-5}(N-\beta^2), K^{f-5}(N-9\beta), K^{f-5}(C), K^{f-5}(N-11\beta), K^{f-5}(N-6\beta); \\
K^{f-3}(N-\beta^2), K^{f-3}(N-9\beta), K^{f-3}(C), K^{f-3}(N-11\beta), K^{f-3}(N-6\beta); \\
K^{f}(N-\beta^2), K^{f}(N-9\beta), K^{f}(C), K^{f}(N-11\beta), K^{f}(N-6\beta); \\
K^{f+3}(N-\beta^2), K^{f+3}(N-9\beta), K^{f+3}(C), K^{f+3}(N-11\beta), K^{f+3}(N-6\beta); \\
K^{f+5}(N-\beta^2), K^{f+5}(N-9\beta), K^{f+5}(C), K^{f+5}(N-11\beta), K^{f+5}(N-6\beta);
\end{bmatrix}
\tag{1}
$$

$$
S^{\beta=4}\Big|_{N=24} = \begin{bmatrix}
K^{f-5}(N-2\beta), K^{f-5}(N-5\beta), K^{f-5}(C), K^{f-5}(N-6\beta), K^{f-5}(N-\beta^2); \\
K^{f-3}(N-2\beta), K^{f-3}(N-5\beta), K^{f-3}(C), K^{f-3}(N-6\beta), K^{f-3}(N-\beta^2); \\
K^{f}(N-2\beta), K^{f}(N-5\beta), K^{f}(C), K^{f}(N-6\beta), K^{f}(N-\beta^2); \\
K^{f+3}(N-2\beta), K^{f+3}(N-5\beta), K^{f+3}(C), K^{f+3}(N-6\beta), K^{f+3}(N-\beta^2); \\
K^{f+5}(N-2\beta), K^{f+5}(N-5\beta), K^{f+5}(C), K^{f+5}(N-6\beta), K^{f+5}(N-\beta^2);
\end{bmatrix}
\tag{2}
$$

where, N represents the number of neighbours and represents the direction for spatio-temporal neighbours collection.

An example of horizontal and vertical spatio-temporal values calculation for a given center pixel having intensity value 227 highlighted with green colour is depicted in Fig. 3.

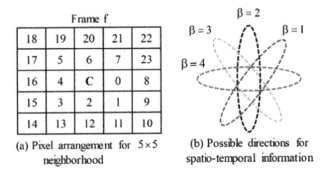

Frame f

18	19	20	21	22
17	5	6	7	23
16	4	C	0	8
15	3	2	1	9
14	13	12	11	10

(a) Pixel arrangement for 5×5 neighborhood

(b) Possible directions for spatio-temporal information

Fig. 2. Pixel arrangement of neighborhood for a given frame f and possible directions for spatio-temporal information collection.

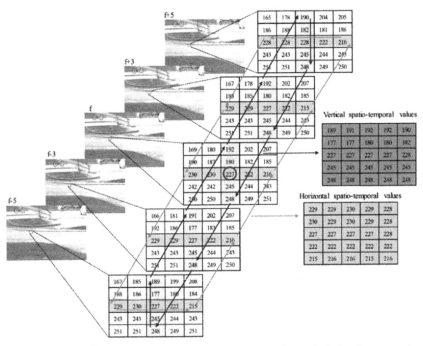

Fig. 3. An example of horizontal and vertical spatio temporal values calculation from two selected directions in Pedestrians video sequence.

It is used for calculating co-occurrence matrix K. $K_{\theta,d}$ computes the frequency of occurrences of two gray levels in matrix M at a distance d and angle θ. In this work $d = 2$ and $\theta = 45°$ were used to take into effect both the spatial and temporal characteristics. Dimensionality of matrix K is $l \times l$, where l is the no. of levels into which intensity values have been quantized. Matrix K is now converted into a symmetric matrix, $K_s = K + K'$

and then normalized into matrix C given as

$$C = \frac{K_s}{\sum\limits_{i=1}^{l} l \sum\limits_{j=1}^{l} K_s(i,j)} \qquad (3)$$

where $K_s(i,j)$ are the values of the symmetric co-occurrence matrix.

2.2 Feature Vector Generation

Feature vector (D) is computed for every pixel in each frame of the video sequence, comprising of seven features – Gray scale intensity value; R, G, B values; statistical textural features: Contrast, Correlation and Entropy. Feature vector (D) of $(i,j)^{th}$ pixel is represented as $D_{ij} = \{d_I, d_R, d_G, d_B, d_{contrast}, d_{corr}, d_{entropy}\}$. Statistical textural features are calculated from MSC descriptor are given as follows.

$$d_{contrast} = \sum_{i=0}^{l-1}\sum_{j=0}^{l-1} |i-j|^2 \, c(i,j) \qquad (4)$$

$$d_{corr} = \sum_{i=0}^{l-1}\sum_{j=0}^{l-1} c(i,j) \qquad (5)$$

$$d_{entropy} = -\sum_{i=0}^{l-1}\sum_{j=0}^{l-1} c(i,j) \log(1 + c(i,j)) \qquad (6)$$

where $c(i,j)$ are the values of the normalized symmetric co-occurrence matrix.

2.3 Background Modelling

Background model constructed for each pixel comprises of seven unimodal gaussian distributions, each representing distribution of a feature characterising that pixel. But as distribution of features with time can be multimodal because of changes in the background, four background models have been created for each pixel. Let us consider one background model $B = \{B_{d1}, B_{d2}, B_{d3}, B_{d4}, B_{d5}, B_{d6}, B_{d7}\}$ for pixel p, where $B_{di} = \{\mu_i, \sigma_i, h_i, w_i\}$, i represents i-th feature. B is actually a collection of seven background feature models corresponding to each feature in D extracted from pixel p. All these feature models are unimodal gaussian distributions characterised by mean value (μ), standard deviation (σ) and height (h). Weights of feature models are equal to the height of corresponding Gaussians. Feature model with a higher weight is more stable and hence is more dominant in classification of the pixel as a background or foreground.

For background model initialization, a histogram is made showing the distribution of each feature over some initial set of frames and a gaussian is fitted to its height and weight equal to the height of the histogram. The height of the histogram represents the number of frames in which the feature value of the pixel was nearly equal to the mean

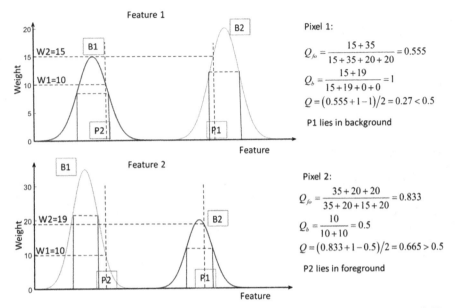

Fig. 4. Process of foreground detection for two background models having two features each. Two gaussians in each graph represent two different background models for the respective features. P1 and P2 are two pixels to be classified.

of distribution and is an also a measure of stability. And as we know that lesser is the variation in feature value of a pixel (or more is its stability), more are the chances of that pixel belonging to the background. Hence more is the height of the histogram, higher should be the weight of that feature model in determining the proximity of that pixel to the background. For faster convergence, while initializing background models for a given pixel, one model is initialized with corresponding pixel value and the rest are initialized with the neighbourhood pixels.

After initialization of background models for all pixels using F initial frames, we update them with each incoming frame. Updation is dependent on the feature vector of pixels in the incoming frame. Background updation procedure is exactly same for all pixels and feature component models. Hence, let's discuss the updation procedure for any one pixel, say P. Feature vector for P is denoted as $D_P = \{p_I, p_R, p_G, p_B, p_{contrast}, p_{corr}, p_{entropy}\}$. For each j-th feature gaussian model of i-th background model, $B_{ij} = \{\mu_{ij}, \sigma_{ij}, w_{ij}\}$ belonging to P, calculated the distance (e_{ij}) between feature and mean of the gaussian μ_{ij}. If $|p_{ij} - \mu_{ij}| < \sigma_{ij}$, then that pixel belongs to the background according to B_{ij} and it is updated as follows:

$$\mu_{ij} = a_m \times \mu_{ij} + (1 - a_m) \times \mu_{ij} \tag{7}$$

$$\sigma_{ij} = a_s \times \sigma_{ij} + (1 - a_s) \times \sigma_{ij} \tag{8}$$

$$w_{ij} = w_{ij} + 1, h_{ij} = w_{ij} \tag{9}$$

If $\left| p_{ij} - \mu_{ij} \right| > \sigma_{ij}$, then the background model with the least weight is updated as follows:

$$\mu_{ij} = a_{mfo} \times \mu_{ij} + \left(1 - a_{mfo}\right) \times \mu_{ij} \tag{10}$$

$$\sigma_{ij} = a_{sfo} \times \sigma_{ij} + \left(1 - a_{sfo}\right) \times \sigma_{ij} \tag{11}$$

where $a_{sfo} < a_s$ & $a_{mfo} < a_m$.

2.4 Foreground Detection

It was studied in [19], that a single feature can't characterise every pixel in a video frame because different features represent different characteristics. Motivated from [18], used the concept of dominant and secondary features for foreground detection. Figure 4 describes a classic example of calculating dynamic weights which are used in gaussian models for background proximity calculation by giving more weightage to feature value if the pixel feature value is closer to the mean and less weightage if the feature value is far away from the mean.

The proximity between a given pixel and background is calculated as The proximity between a given pixel and background is calculated as $Q_b = \theta_{mb} / \theta_{sb}$. θ_{mb} is the sum of weights of the feature components which match the background in all the models and it is given by $\theta_{mb} = \sum_{i=1}^{L} \sum_{j \in G} w_{ij}$ where L is number of background models and G is the set of features p_j for which $\left| p_j - \mu_{ij} \right| < \sigma_{ij}$. θ_{sb} is the sum of weights of all feature components in all the models and is given by $\theta_{sb} = \sum_{i=1}^{L} \sum_{j=1}^{D} w_{ij}$ where D is the number of features. For calculation of proximity between the pixel and background, weights used are dynamic and not statically equal to the height of the gaussian feature model.

$$w_{ij} = h_{ij} \times \exp\left(\left(p_j - \mu_{ij}\right)^2 \Big/ 2 \times \sigma_{ij}^2\right) \tag{12}$$

The proximity between a given pixel and foreground is calculated as $Q_{fo} = \theta_{mfo} / \theta_{sfo}$. θ_{mfo} is the sum of weights of the feature components which do not match the background in all the models and it is given by $\theta_{mfo} = \sum_{i=1}^{L} \sum_{j \in G} h_{ij}$ where G is the set of features p_j for which $\left| p_j - \mu_{ij} \right| < \sigma_{ij}$. $\theta_{sfo} = \sum_{i=1}^{L} \sum_{j=1}^{D} h_{ij}$ where h_{ij} is the height of j-th feature model in background model i. Net probability of the given pixel belonging to foreground is $\left(Q_{fo} + (1 - Q_b)\right) / 2$.

3 Experimental Results

The performance of the proposed method is evaluated on Changedetection dataset [20]. Precision, Recall and F-measure are used as quantitative measures for analysis. The proposed algorithm is implemented in MATLAB R2013a, 64-bit Windows8 platform with Intel Xenon CPU@2.80 GHz and 16 GB of RAM.

Table 1 shows the performance of the proposed method with the state-of-the-art methods (MST [21], MoG [22], IMoG [23], RMoG [24], SoAF [18]) in terms of F-measure values on Baseline, Dynamic Background, Camera Jitter, Shadow and Thermal video categories. Figure 6 illustrates the qualitative comparison of the proposed method with existing methods on ChangeDetection dataset. Further, the performance of the proposed method is also analyzed with PR curve as shown in Fig. 5.

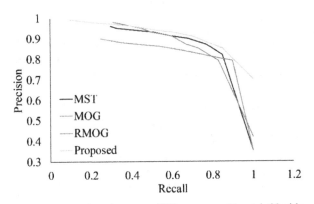

Fig. 5. Performance comparison in terms of PR curves on Fountain02 video sequences.

There are four types of videos in the Baseline, in which proposed method performed well in Pedestrians sequences, whereas comparable performance in PET2006. However low F-score value in Highway and Office video sequences is due to holes produced in detected objects. In Dynamic Background scenes, proposed method outperforms various techniques in Canoe, Fall and Fountain02 video sequences.

Table 1. F-measure values of various techniques on change detection dataset [20]

Videos	MST [21]	MoG [22]	IMoG [23]	RMoG [24]	SoAF [18]	Proposed
Baseline						
Highway	0.87	**0.92**	0.90	0.86	0.81	0.78
Office	0.80	0.59	0.66	0.59	**0.90**	0.76
Pedestrians	0.95	0.95	0.96	0.94	0.89	**0.97**
PETS2006	0.75	0.86	0.83	0.75	**0.92**	0.89
Dynamic Background						
Canoe	0.88	0.88	0.89	0.94	0.90	**0.98**
Fall	0.41	0.44	0.42	0.67	0.46	**0.96**

(continued)

Table 1. (*continued*)

Videos	MST [21]	MoG [22]	IMoG [23]	RMoG [24]	SoAF [18]	Proposed
Fountain02	0.82	0.80	0.79	0.87	0.87	**0.99**
Camera Jitter						
Traffic	0.48	0.66	0.61	0.75	NA	**0.89**
Shadow						
Backdoor	0.85	0.64	0.63	0.78	**0.87**	0.65
Bungalows	0.78	0.80	0.79	0.81	**0.93**	0.84
Busstation	0.70	0.80	0.79	0.78	0.84	**0.87**
Peopleinshade	0.86	0.89	0.88	0.77	0.93	**0.98**
Thermal						
Park	0.58	0.71	0.70	0.57	0.00	**0.93**

Table 2. Average processing time per frame on ChangeDetection dataset [20]

Methods	MST [21]	MoG [22]	IMoG [23]	RMoG [24]	Proposed
Time (sec.)	0.10	0.47	0.20	0.158	0.36

The proposed method does better in Busstation and Peopleinshade video categories. However, it has low F-scores in Backdoor and Bungalows video sequences of Shadow category. From Table 1, Fig. 5 and Fig. 6, it is evident that the proposed method outperforms the state-of-the-art methods on Change Detection Dataset. Table 2 illustrates the average processing time per frame of various methods on Changedetection dataset. From Table 2, it is observed that the proposed method faster than MoG and comparable to remaining techniques.

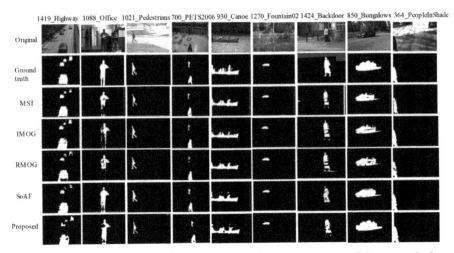

Fig. 6. Qualitative Comparison of the proposed technique with state-of-the-art methods on Change detection dataset

4 Conclusion

In this work, a new Multi-frame spatio-temporal co-occurrence (MSC) texture feature has been proposed. MSC collects the multidirectional spatio-temporal information from neighborhood (typically five) frames in a video by forming 3D structure. A Co-occurrence matrix is derived from collected spatio-temporal values. Further, statistical textural features were calculated from MSC descriptor. Texture, gray scale and colour features are used for background model construction. Proximity values are computed by using modified Stability of adaptive feature (SoAF) model. The proposed method performed better in detecting moving objects as compared to state-of-the-art methods under various scenarios.

For citations of references, we prefer the use of square brackets and consecutive numbers. Citations using labels or the author/year convention are also acceptable. The following bibliography provides a sample reference list with entries for journal articles [1], an LNCS chapter [2], a book [3], proceedings without editors [4], as well as a URL [5].

References

1. Bouwmans, T., Silva, C., Marghes, C., et al.: On the role and the importance of features for background modeling and foreground detection. Comput. Sci. Rev. **28**, 26–91 (2018)
2. Hati, K.K., Sa, P.K., Majhi, B.: Intensity range based background subtraction for effective object detection. IEEE Signal Process. Lett. **20**(8), 759–762 (2013)
3. Kim, W., Kim, C.: Background subtraction for dynamic texture scenes using fuzzy color histograms. IEEE Signal Process. Lett. **19**(3), 127–130 (2012)
4. Panda, D.K., Meher, S.: Detection of moving objects using fuzzy color difference histogram based background subtraction. IEEE Signal Process. Lett. **23**(1), 45–49 (2016)

5. Kim, W., Kim, Y.: Background subtraction using illumination-invariant structural complexity. IEEE Signal Process. Lett. **23**(5), 634–638 (2016)
6. Ji, Z., Wang, W.: Detect foreground objects via adaptive fusing model in a hybrid feature space. Pattern Recogn. **47**(9), 2952–2961 (2014)
7. Han, H., Zhu, J., Liao, S., et al.: Moving object detection revisited: Speed and robustness. IEEE Trans. Circuits Syst. Video Technol. **25**(6), 910–921 (2015)
8. Vasamsetti, S., Setia, S., Mittal, N., et al.: Automatic underwater moving object detection using multi-feature integration framework in complex backgrounds. IET Computer Vision (2018)
9. Spampinato, C., Palazzo, S., Kavasidis, I.: A texton-based kernel density estimation approach for background modeling under extreme conditions. In: Computer Vision and Image Understanding, vol. 122, pp. 74–83, May 2014
10. Han, B., Davis, L.S.: Density-based multifeature background subtraction with support vector machine. IEEE Trans. Pattern Anal. Mach. Intell. **34**(5), 1017–1023 (2012)
11. Wang, Z., Liao, K., Xiong, J., et al.: Moving object detection based on temporal information. IEEE Signal Process. Lett. **21**(11), 1403–1407 (2014)
12. Boulmerka, A., Allili, M.S.: Foreground segmentation in videos combining general Gaussian mixture modeling and spatial information. IEEE Trans. Circuits Syst. Video Technol. **28**(6), 1330–1345 (2018)
13. Lin, L., Xu, Y., Liang, X., et al.: Complex background subtraction by pursuing dynamic spatio-temporal models. IEEE Trans. Image Process. **23**(7), 3191–3202 (2014)
14. Zhang, B., Gao, Y., Zhao, S., et al.: Kernel similarity modeling of texture pattern flow for motion detection in complex background. IEEE Trans. Circuits Syst. Video Technol. **21**(1), 29–38 (2011)
15. Yoshinaga, S., Shimada, A., Nagahara, H., et al.: Object detection based on spatiotemporal background models. Comput. Vis. Image Underst. **122**, 84–91 (2014)
16. Vasamsetti, S., Mittal, N., Neelapu, B.C., Sardana, H.K.: 3D local spatio-temporal ternary patterns for moving object detection in complex scenes. Cogn. Comput. **11**(1), 18–30 (2018). https://doi.org/10.1007/s12559-018-9594-5
17. Sajid, H., Cheung, S.-C.S.: Universal multimode background subtraction. IEEE Trans. Image Process. **26**(7), 3249–3260 (2017)
18. Yang, D., Zhao, C., Zhang, X., et al.: Background modeling by stability of adaptive features in complex scenes. IEEE Trans. Image Process. **27**(3), 1112–1125 (2018)
19. Goyette, N., Jodoin, P.-M., Porikli, F., et al.: Changedetection. net: a new change detection benchmark dataset, pp. 1–8
20. Bouwmans, T.: Traditional and recent approaches in background modeling for foreground detection: an overview. Comput. Sci. Rev. **11**, 31–66 (2014)
21. Lu, X.: A multiscale spatio-temporal background model for motion detection, pp. 3268–3271
22. Stauffer, C., Grimson, W.E.L.: Adaptive background mixture models for real-time tracking, pp. 2246
23. Zivkovic, Z.: Improved adaptive Gaussian mixture model for background subtraction, pp. 28–31
24. Varadarajan, S., Miller, P., Zhou, H.: Spatial mixture of Gaussians for dynamic background modelling, pp. 63–68

Script Identification in Natural Scene Text Images by Learning Local and Global Features on Inception Net

Kalpita Dutta$^{(\boxtimes)}$, Shuvayan Ghosh Dastidar, Nibaran Das, Mahantapas Kundu, and Mita Nasipuri

Department of Computer Science and Engineering, Jadavpur University, Kolkata, India
dutta.kalpita@gmail.com, nibaran.das@jadavpuruniversity.in

Abstract. In a multi script environment Script identification is essential prior to text recognition. Compared to document images, Script identification in natural scene images becomes a more challenging task due to complex backgrounds, intricate font styles, poor image quality etc. All this is in addition to the common problem of script recognition, related to similar layouts of characters found for certain scripts. The proposed work involves fine tuning of a pretrained model of Inception net V3 on a combination of word and the constituent character images extracted from the sample images of the scene text. In this model, the relu activation function originally used with Inception net is replaced by an experimentally selected Mish activation function and a softmax layer is added at the output to have a probability distribution for possible scripts of the input word images. To identify the script of an input word image, maximum of the sums of the weighted probability values for the word image and the images of its constituent characters is considered for all the script categories. The proposed method is tested on MLe2e and CVSI-2015 datasets showing encouraging results by slightly crossing the existing benchmarks.

Keywords: Script identification · Natural scene text · Mish activation function · Histogram projection profile · Inception net · Transfer learning

1 Introduction

In a multi script environment script identification is necessary prior to Optical Character Recognition (OCR) of text character images. This is because of the fact that OCR systems [2] are always script dependant. In the last few decades, many research studies [2,10] were reported to identify scripts from document images. Identifying scripts of embedded text in natural scene images and videos

---

Jadavpur University.

B. Raman et al. (Eds.): CVIP 2021, CCIS 1567, pp. 458–467, 2022.
https://doi.org/10.1007/978-3-031-11346-8_40

[1, 9, 12] using deep neural networks has attracted the attention of the researchers in the recent past. Few samples of natural scene text images of different scripts are shown in the Fig. 1. Apart from the varying writing styles, different curvatures and shapes appearing in different scripts, natural scene text images may not be free from blurred and haze affects as illustrated in Fig. 2 with some sample images taken from CVSI-2015 [11] dataset. All these make the problem of script identification in natural scene text images complex.

Scripts	Example Images	
English	DEAL	MATCH
Bengali	সক্রিয়	সমাধান
Gujrati	રાહુલ	વારંવાર
Kannada	ಸಂಪೂರ್ಣ	ತಂಡದ
Hindi	मिल	सीएम
Oriya	ଗାମିଲ	ଯାର୍
Punjabi	ਜਗੀਰ	ਹੇਠੀ
Tamil	கஎர்	தெழ
Telugu	శ్రీదే	ఈ్ఠ
Arabic	برشی	مرشد

(CVSI 2015 Dataset)

Scripts	Example Images	
Chinese	未经登记	空车驶入
Korean	홍길동	계룡고실
Latin	Carib	BANK
Kannada		

(MLe2e Dataset)

Fig. 1. Few sample of natural scene text images of multi-lingual script, taken from MLe2e & CVSI 2015 dataset

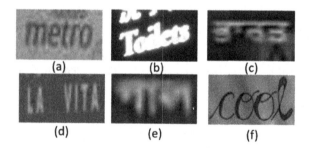

(a)   (b)   (c)

(d)   (e)   (f)

Fig. 2. Example of some input images with various difficulties. Figure (a), (c), (d), (e) shows some example of hazy and blur images and figure (b) and (f) is also blur with complex font style image of CVSI-2015 dataset

1.1   The Past Work

Ghosh et al. [2] made a detailed survey dealing with the various aspects of problem of script identification. The ICDAR2015 Competition on Video Script Identification(CVSI) [11] presented the problem of script identification over superimposed text in videos where the best four participants used Convolutional Neural

Networks (Cnns). In the work of Bhunia et al. [1], a CNN-LSTM framework has been introduced to identify scripts in videos and document images. The framework is used for extraction of local and global features from input image patches. A softmax layer is added after the LSTM to obtain attention based patch weights. Then to obtain local features for individual patches, product of the weights and feature vector obtained from the corresponding CNN is computed. Additionally global features are also extracted from the last cell state of the LSTM. Finally a fusion technique is employed to dynamically assign weights to local and global features for each individual patch. In the work of Shi et al. [12], an attempt has been made to learn certain discriminative local regions in the scripts, where the visual differences between different scripts are observed. In this work, a mid level representation and a deep feature map, densely callected from a CNN model (pretrained with local patches extracted from training images), are jointly optimized in a deep network, called Discriminative Convolutional Neural Network (DCNN). To find the mid level representation, Discriminative clustering is performed on the local image patches, densely collected from the CNN model. This is to discover patches that are both representative and discriminative for the script classes under consideration. Based on these learned discriminative pathes(codebook), the local features are encoded to produce the said midlevel representation. In the work of Gomez et al. [3] ensembles of conjoined networks are employed to learn discriminative stroke-parts of different scripts and their relative importance in a patch-based classification scheme. The work has been extended by using a global horizontal pooling strategy [6] to identify scripts.

1.2   The Present Work

One major focus of all these contemporary research efforts is to develop methodologies to learn local and global script specific features to achieve a judicious combination of the two for state-of-the-art script detection. In this context, pretrained Inception Net V3 [13] model, fine tuned with training data, is used here for achieving state-of-the-art script detection. The Inception Net is featured by its low parameter count and improved utilization of the computing reasources inside the network. Two publicly available datasets, CVSI 2015 [11] and MLe2e [4], are used here. To ensure enough labeled data for training with script specific global features as well as character specific in-script local features, a new data augmentation technique is proposed here. All word images, based on their vertical histogram profiles, are segmented into constituent characters. The training set is finally made up of word sample images together with their possible constituent character sample images. The data set so prepared is used for fine tuning of Inception Net V3 model pretrained on ImageNet data. The softmax layer at the output of the model is updated here to have a probability distribution for all possible scripts under consideration. Before final script identification, the probability values for all scripts are recorded for an input word image as well as for its all constituent character images. Maximum of the sums of the weighted probability values for an input word image and the images of its constituent characters is considered to identify the script of the input word image. Relu activation function originally used for Inception Net V3 is replaced here from 151th layer by Mish activation function [8], chosen experimentally. This experimental selection of Mish activation function in Inception Net V3 on the task of script identification. Once again confirms the observation, "Mish still provides under most experimental conditions, better empirical results than Swish, ReLU, and Leaky ReLU", made by Misra et al. [8]. It also fulfills a part of the objective of evaluating the performance of the Mish activation function in a state-of-the-art model, viz. Inception Net V3, on the task of script detection, previously not considered by Misra et al. [8].

The remaining portion of this paper is structured as follows: The proposed work has been described in Sect. 2. The dataset description, experimental results, and a comparative assessment of the work are presented in Sect. 3. The work is concluded in Sect. 4.

1.3   Contribution

Briefly Speaking, the major contributions of this work come from a data augmentation technique by including constituent character sample images with their respective word images, and a methodology to learn local (character level) and global (word level) features through fine tuning of an Inception Net V3 model to achieve benchmark results on standard datasets. Lastly the work also contributes in providing some empirical results relating to performances of Mish activation function in Inception Net V3 on script identification.

2   Methodology

The methodology of the present work is illustrated in Fig. 3 and Algorithm 1. Scene extracted word images of various scripts are supplied as input here. Considering their vertical histogram profiles, the word images are segmented into possible constituent character images and supplied to the Inception Net V3 model. The pretrained model is fine tuned with training data, both word images and constituent character images, from 151th layer. ReLU activation function originally used in Inception Net is replaced here with Mish Activation function, also from the same layer. For final Script Identification, the probability values for all scripts, obtained at the Softmax layer of the Inception Net V3, are collected by Script Identification Module for each word and its Constituent Character images. The Script Identification Module finally determines the script of an input word image by considering the maximum of the sums of the weighted probability values for the word image and the images of its constituent characters.

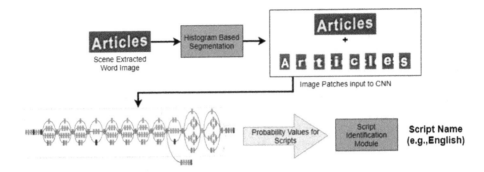

Fig. 3. Flowchart of our proposed work

3   Experiments

The proposed method is tested here on Mle2e and CVSI-2015 datasets, mentioned before. Scripts of sample text images in Mle2e include Chinese, Korean, Latin, Kannada. Out of these, Latin is in use mostly in Europe and the rest, including Chinese, Korean Latin and Kannada in South East Asia. Sample text images in the CVSI-2015 consists of scripts of ten Indian languages, e.g., English, Hindi, Bengali etc. The proposed method is implemented here in PyTorch on a machine with Nvidia GeForce GTX 1600 GPU, 6 GB RAM and 1408 Cuda Cores.

All the image samples, containing scene text or segmented characters are resized in 224×224 image patches. For fine tuning of Inception Net V3 model, pretrained on ImageNet data, 151th and successive layers, starting from input layer, are considered for training here. Parameters for first 150 layers of the model are freezed to transfer already learned low level image features to the model, fine tuned with training scene text and constituent character images from 151th layer. Training is done for 100 epochs here, using cross-entropy loss [5] and Adagrad optimizer [7] with learning rate of 0.001. With Early Stopping enabled, the training process has stopped at around 400 epochs. In the proposed method, learning of global (word level) and local (character level) features are done by including the images of the constituent characters with the natural scene text images. For this, scene text images are segmented here with their vertical pixel density Histogram. Some results of this segmentation are shown in Fig. 4. It has already been mentioned that Activation functions play a crucial role in the performance and training dynamics in neural networks. This is why, before the final experiment, utility of Mish function, compared to ReLU originally used in Inception Net V3 and others, such as Swish, PreLU, and ELU, is emperically tested on scene text data. For quick results in shorter training time, the model is trained for 100 epochs each time. Performances of the model so tested with various activation functions are given in Table 1. It can be observed from the Table 1 that Mish activation function excels all others for both the datasets, Mle2e and CVSI-2015. So, Mish function is chosen here for the subsequent experiment. For script detection, the maximum of the weighted sums of the probability values obtained from the softmax layer of the proposed model for different scripts with an input text image and the images of its constituent characters is to be determined. For this, appropriate weight values for a word image and its constituent character images are determined here from an experimentally drawn Bar Chart, shown in Fig. 5. In this Figure, the accuracy of script determination is computed by providing unity weight value for both script and character images. The subsequent bars are drawn by increasing the associated weight value for text image one by one, keeping the weight value for character images fixed to unity. In this process, it has been observed that the maximum accuracy is obtained with 5 weight value for text images. By increasing weight values over 5, no gain is observed. So weight values for text images and character images are chosen in a ratio of 5:1. Assigning a higher weight value to text images is justified because text images contain more local and global script features compared to character images.

After the final experiment, the fine tuned Inception Net V3 yields test accuracies of 98.72% and 96.72% on CVSI-2015 and MLe2e respectively. Confusion matrices formed with CVSI-2015 and MLe2e are shown in Fig. 6. Test accuracies obtained by different methods on MLe2e are shown in Table 4 for a comparative assessment. The values obtained for Precision, Recall, F-score on various scripts of the two datasets are given in Table 2. It can be observed from Table 2 that performances of the proposed method on Kannada are closed on both the datasets. Script wise accuracies obtained by different methods, including the proposed one, on CVSI-2015 are shown in Table 3. It has been observed that the proposed method achieved an accuracy, on CVSI-2015, slightly higher than the last bench mark one obtained Google.

Algorithm 1. Script identification in natural scene text images

1: Input: P number of character image patches generated from Natural scene text word images.
2: Output: Identified script.
3: **procedure**
4:     **For** each patch I_p of $I_1 \dots I_P$ **do**
5:     convert the image into gray scale image
6:     Resize the image patch into $\min(I_h, I_w)/2$, where (h, w) is the height and width of the input image using a Gaussian Filter.
7:     Apply Adaptive Thresholding.
8:     Segment the word image patches using vertical histogram based method in Fig. 4.
9:     Modify the Inception Net V3 by freezing the 150 initial layers and fine tuned ReLU activation function with Mish from 151th layer.
10:     Feed patches into modified Inception Net V3 and obtain feature vector O_p as output
11:     Classify each input as a different script by taking the argmax.

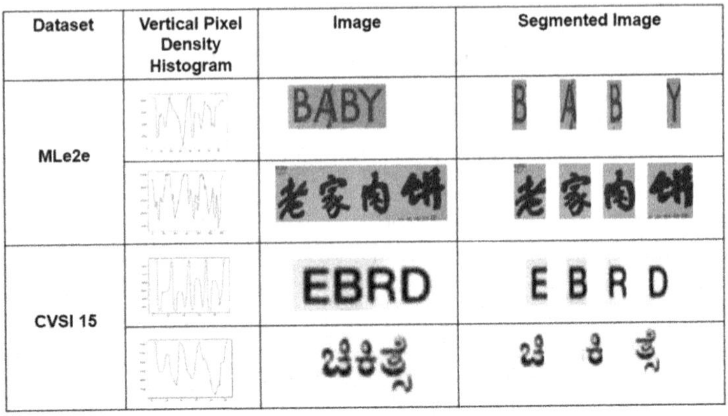

Dataset	Vertical Pixel Density Histogram	Image	Segmented Image
MLe2e		BABY	B A B Y
		老家肉饼	老 家 肉 饼
CVSI 15		EBRD	E B R D
		ಚಿತ್ರ	ಚಿ ತ್ರ

Fig. 4. Character segmentation results using vertical project profile

Table 1. Performance of different activation functions on two different dataset with respect to accuracy on test dataset after training for 100 epochs on the train dataset without segmenting the images into their character level patches.

Dataset	Accuracy				
	ReLU	Mish	Swish	PreLU	ELU
MLe2e	94.82	**95.01**	93.99	92.23	91.74
CVSI-2015	96.92	**97.33**	97.13	96.33	96.34

Table 2. Script wise results of CVSI 2015 and Mle2e dataset

Scripts	Precision	Recall	F-Score
Arabic	0.99	1.00	0.99
Bengali	0.97	0.99	0.98
English	0.98	0.99	0.99
Gujrathi	1.00	0.99	0.99
Hindi	0.99	0.99	0.99
Kannada	0.99	0.92	0.95
Oriya	0.99	0.99	0.99
Punjabi	0.99	0.97	0.98
Tamil	0.99	0.99	0.99
Telegu	0.93	0.99	0.96

Scripts	Precision	Recall	F-Score
Latin	0.94	0.95	0.95
Chinese	0.95	0.98	0.97
Kannada	0.98	0.98	0.98
Korean	0.99	0.94	0.96

Table 3. Script wise accuracy results comparison with other methods of CVSI-2015 dataset

Methods	English	Hindi	Bengali	Oriya	Gujrati	Punjabi	Kannada	Tamil	Telugu	Arabic	Final accuracy
CUK	65.69	61.66	68.71	79.14	73.39	92.09	71.66	82.55	57.89	89.44	74.06
C-DAC	68.33	71.47	91.61	88.04	88.99	90.51	68.47	91.90	91.33	97.69	84.66
CVC-2	88.86	96.01	92.58	98.16	98.17	96.52	97.13	99.69	93.80	99.67	96.00
HUST	93.55	96.31	95.81	98.47	97.55	97.15	92.68	97.82	97.83	**100.00**	96.69
Attention based CNN-LSTM	94.20	96.50	95.60	98.30	98.70	99.10	98.60	99.20	97.70	99.60	97.75
ECN	–	–	–	–	–	–	–	–	–	–	97.2
Proposed methods	**99.71**	**99.39**	**100.00**	**100.00**	**99.69**	98.73	92.68	**99.38**	**100.00**	**100.00**	**98.97**
Google	97.95	99.08	99.35	98.47	98.17	**99.38**	**97.77**	**99.38**	**99.69**	**100.00**	98.91

Table 4. Results comparison chart of MLe2e dataset

Methods	Accuracy
CVC-2 [11]	88.16
Gomez [3]	91.12
ECN [1]	94.40
Attention based CNN-LSTM [1]	96.70
Baseline Sequence-based CNN	89.80
Proposed method	**96.72**

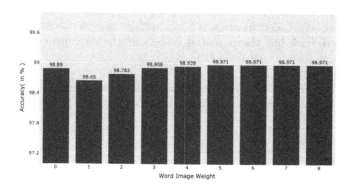

Fig. 5. The results of CVSI dataset after weight increase

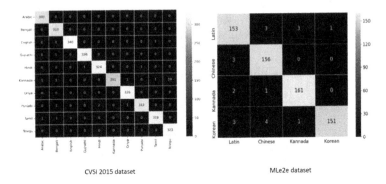

CVSI 2015 dataset   MLe2e dataset

Fig. 6. Confusion matrix of CVSI 2015 and MLe2e dataset

4   Conclusion and Future Scope

In this paper, we propose a deep-learning based approach to identify scripts from natural scene images and video scripts embedded with a data augmentation technique by including weight on image patches (both word and character level of text images). Inspired by the methodologies to learn local and global script-specific features, our training set comprises word sample images and their possible constituent character sample images. To identify the script of an input word image, the maximum of the sums of the weighted probability values for an input word image and the images of its constituent characters is considered. For this, a popular deep learning module i.e. Inception net V3 is used with MISH activation function instead of ReLU in some layer to boost the performance. The main novelty of the proposed network is lying on the proposed weight to each image patches (both word and character) along with ReLu replacement with MISH function to improvise the performance. Experiments have performed in two datasets (CVSI 2015 and Mle2e dataset) exhibit state of the art accuracy rates in comparison to a number of previous state-of-the-art methods. In future, an end to end system from detection to recognition task can be implemented where script identification is also a middle task to execute with the flow. The proposed work has the potential to benefit the document image research community.

Acknowledgements. This work was supported by Rashtriya Uchchatar Shiksha Abhiyan (RUSA) 2.0, Government of India, Ministry of Human Resource Development project.

References

1. Bhunia, A.K., Konwer, A., Bhunia, A.K., Bhowmick, A., Roy, P.P., Pal, U.: Script identification in natural scene image and video frames using an attention based convolutional-LSTM network. Pattern Recogn. **85**, 172–184 (2019)

2. Ghosh, D., Dube, T., Shivaprasad, A.: Script recognition–a review. IEEE Trans. Pattern Anal. Mach. Intell. **32**(12), 2142–2161 (2010)

3. Gomez, L., Karatzas, D.: A fine-grained approach to scene text script identification. In: 2016 12th IAPR Workshop on Document Analysis Systems (DAS), pp. 192–197. IEEE (2016)

4. Gomez, L., Nicolaou, A., Karatzas, D.: Improving patch-based scene text script identification with ensembles of conjoined networks. Pattern Recogn. **67**, 85–96 (2017)

5. Gordon-Rodriguez, E., Loaiza-Ganem, G., Pleiss, G., Cunningham, J.P.: Uses and abuses of the cross-entropy loss: case studies in modern deep learning. In: Forde, J.Z., Ruiz, F., Pradier, M.F., Schein, A. (eds.) Proceedings on "I Can't Believe It's Not Better!" at NeurIPS Workshops. Proceedings of Machine Learning Research, vol. 137, pp. 1–10. PMLR, 12 December 2020. https://proceedings.mlr.press/v137/gordon-rodriguez20a.html

6. Lu, L., Yi, Y., Huang, F., Wang, K., Wang, Q.: Integrating local CNN and global CNN for script identification in natural scene images. IEEE Access **7**, 52669–52679 (2019)

7. Lydia, A., Francis, S.: Adagrad—an optimizer for stochastic gradient descent. Int. J. Inf. Comput. Sci. **6**(5), 566–568 (2019)

8. Misra, D.: Mish: a self regularized non-monotonic activation function. arXiv preprint arXiv:1908.08681 (2019)

9. Nayef, N., Yin, F., Bizid, I., et al.: ICDAR 2017 robust reading challenge on multilingual scene text detection and script identification-RRC-MLT. In: 2017 14th IAPR International Conference on Document Analysis and Recognition (ICDAR), vol. 1, pp. 1454–1459. IEEE (2017)

10. Obaidullah, S.M., Santosh, K.C., Das, N., Halder, C., Roy, K.: Handwritten Indic script identification in multi-script document images: a survey. Int. J. Pattern Recognit. Artif. Intell. **32**(10), 1856012:1–1856012:26 (2018)

11. Sharma, N., Mandal, R., Sharma, R., Pal, U., Blumenstein, M.: ICDAR 2015 competition on video script identification (CVSI 2015). In: 2015 13th International Conference on Document Analysis and Recognition (ICDAR), pp. 1196–1200. IEEE (2015)

12. Shi, B., Bai, X., Yao, C.: Script identification in the wild via discriminative convolutional neural network. Pattern Recogn. **52**, 448–458 (2016)

13. Szegedy, C., Vanhoucke, V., Ioffe, S., Shlens, J., Wojna, Z.: Rethinking the inception architecture for computer vision. In: Proceedings of the IEEE Conference on Computer Vision and Pattern Recognition, pp. 2818–2826 (2016)

Survey of Leukemia Cancer Cell Detection Using Image Processing

Tulasi Gayatri Devi[1(✉)] (iD), Nagamma Patil[1], Sharada Rai[2] (iD),
and Cheryl Sarah Philipose[2] (iD)

[1] Department of Information Technology, National Institute of Technology
Karnataka, Surathkal, Mangalore, Karnataka, India
{177it003tulasi,nagammapatil}@nitk.edu.in
[2] Department of Pathology, Kasturba Medical College, Mangalore, Manipal
Academy of Higher Education, Manipal, Karnataka, India
{sharada.rai,cheryl.philipose}@manipal.edu

Abstract. Cancer is the development of abnormal cells that divide at
an abnormal pace, uncontrollably. Cancerous cells have the ability to
destroy other normal tissues and can spread throughout the body. Cancer cells can develop in various parts of the body. The paper focuses on
leukemia which is a type of blood cancer. Blood cancer usually start in
the bone marrow where the blood is produced in the body. The types
of blood cancer are: Leukemia, Non-Hodgkin lymphoma, Hodgkin lymphoma, and Multiple myeloma. Leukemia is a type of blood cancer that
originates in the bone marrow. Leukemia is seen when the body produces
an abnormal amount of white blood cells that hinder the bone marrow
from creating red blood cells and platelets. Several detection methods
to identify the cancerous cells have been proposed. Identification of the
cancer cells through cell image processing is very complex. The use of
computer aided image processing allows the images to be viewed in 2D
and 3D making it easier to identify the cancerous cells. The cells have
to undergo segmentation and classification in order to identify the cancerous tumours. Several papers propose segmentation methods, classification methods and some propose both. The purpose of this survey is to
review various papers that use either conventional methods or machine
learning methods to detect the cells as cancerous and non-cancerous.

Keywords: Cancer cell detection · Classification · Deep learning
approaches · Image processing · Leukemia disease · Machine learning ·
Segmentation

1 Introduction

The human body is a complex mixture of various organs, tissues, cells, and other
components. There are many disorders, ailments and diseases that can affect the

---

Supported by National Institute of Technology Karnataka.

B. Raman et al. (Eds.): CVIP 2021, CCIS 1567, pp. 468–488, 2022.
https://doi.org/10.1007/978-3-031-11346-8_41

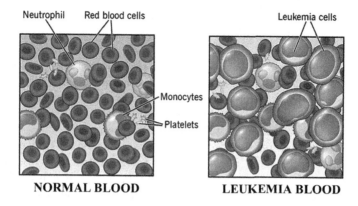

Fig. 1. Normal blood versus Leukemia infected blood [7].

normal functioning of the human body. Cancer is one such disease. Cancer is a genetic disease that occurs when the cells in the body divide at an abnormal rate and spread to other tissues as well. The cells in the human body divide when there is a need to form new cells, but cancerous cells divide uncontrollably and without stop causing harm to the body. The uncontrolled division of the cells forms tissue masses called tumors [8]. There are three kinds of tumors:

- Benign: A benign tumor is not cancerous. These tumors do not spread to other parts of the body and multiply at a slow rate. The chances of return after removal are less.
- Pre-malignant: The pre-malignant tumors are not cancerous at first but have the potential to become cancerous.
- Malignant: The malignant tumors are cancerous in nature. The cells in this kind of tumor multiply and spread to other parts of the body [17].

Blood is a circulating connective tissue that consists of mainly three components: Red blood cells (RBC), White blood cells (WBC), and Platelets. Blood cancer is of four types: Leukemia, Non-Hodgkin lymphoma, Hodgkin lymphoma, and Multiple myeloma. Leukemia is a hematological disease that forms abnormal amount of white blood cells that have proliferation, in the bone marrow. The cancerous WBC hinders the production of other RBCs and platelets. Leukemia further attacks the other tissues as well. There are four major types of leukemia: Acute myeloid leukemia (AML), Acute lymphocytic leukemia (ALL), Chronic myelogenous leukemia (CML), and Chronic lymphocytic leukemia (CLL). The detection of leukemia is different from other types of cancers as the cancerous cells of leukemia does not form tumors that can be detected through imaging [7].

Medical imaging is a vast field. There are several approaches and mechanisms used to detect the differences and distinguish the features of cells for medical purposes. It is important to review the history of cell segmentation before comparing the available techniques and approaches. Automatic cell detection, which is a major interest to a wide range of medical imaging and clinical practices, is intended to find and localize the presence of certain type of cells in an input microscopic image. For example, a breast cancer patient' sprognosis depends on important biomarkers indicative of tumor proliferation speed, that is tumor growth. In a sensible state, the most common technique is habitually performed by pathologists, who examine microscopic anatomy slides beneath a magnifier. The assessments made by the pathologists may be correct in many cases, however, typically is slow and liable to fatigue-induced errors.

Cell detection and localization present various challenges that merit attention. First, clutters represented by complex histological structures like capillaries, collagen and adipocytes etc. surrounding the target cells. It can be difficult to distinguish the target cell from the aforementioned clutter since its size is small in many cases. Second, the appearance of the target cells may be moderately dense, very sparse, or highly dense in microscopic images of high resolution. Labeling of tissue as normal or abnormal is done once image features are identified. Combination of histopathological image features, prior experience, and diagnostic criteria helps in making a final diagnosis [42].

Classification of different types of smears in exfoliated cells was the first started in the first half of 1950 when cell analysis was done using automated methods [31]. The first use of an automated system was to screen for cervical cancer in the same decade. Decision rules were used and thresholding was the common factor in several screening methods that check for different one-dimensional lines in the images. It was in the next decade, during the 1960s, the two-dimensional images were considered for processing. The automation of image processing for 2D images could provide the details of the number of white blood cells that belong to the leukocytes category. It was not until the next decade, around 1975 when the commercial application of 2D image processing for medical purposes was available. It was not until the 1980s, 3-D image processing was possible. However, computerized 3D image processing techniques could provide significant details and analysis if the computer hardware were powerful enough to handle the complex patterns of histopathology. The research in the field of medical image processing gained momentum around the year 2000, when maximum numbers of papers were published on the subject.

Digital pathology involves image segmentation that is partitioning the image into biologically- relevant tissue, or cellular structures allowing for quantification and extraction of specific features for further usage in prognosis or diagnosis. Quantitative histomorphometry defines the process of applying image analysis techniques to extract features related to histological aspects. Histologic primitives should be considered as the first priority for the features that have varying powers (predictive) especially with respect to the context in the tissue. Segmentation is therefore performed before histomorphometry. This concept can be understood well with an example. Usually, perivascular regions have the presence of stroma in the cardiac tissues. Segmentation of cells using manual methods is not usually practiced in this context although it is an important pre-requisite for the histomorphometry process. Predictive modeling also has similar situation with respect to cardiac tissues. It is therefore necessary to design and develop automated techniques that can segment the tissues in different contexts [27].

A large number of applications for cell segmentation and classification use conventional methods as well as advanced methods such as deep learning [18]. Classification using automated classifiers and detectors is the next step of conventional thresholding methods. Feature extraction and transformations were introduced later in the cell classification field [30,37]. Different features of the image such as shape, size or other parameters were considered to extract the features before they could be input to the classifiers. Deep learning methods are the latest techniques used in this field.

This paper performs a thorough survey of various research papers which focus on classifying and segmenting cancerous leukemia cells. The papers reviewed makes use of conventional methods or machine learning and deep learning methods to either segment, classify, or perform both the functions in order to identify leukemia images. This review benefits researchers who would wish to investigate this field, in coming up with improvements based on the drawbacks of the reviewed papers. Researchers can steer the research in new paths based on new technology and methods. Existing research can be modified by rectifying the drawbacks to enhance the model. This paper also provides information on various publicly available datasets that can be used by researchers to train and test their models to detect, segment, and classify the images into cancerous and non-cancerous. Practitioners in the medical field can benefit from this review by checking out the various methods that can be used to perform segmentation and classification and utilizing the best one suited to their purposes.

Pre-processing Steps

Pre-processing image data allows the model to process the input data uniformly [38]. Image processing is a technique used to extract desired features and enhance useful information in the image data. Some of the image parameters are: Dimension, size, color scale, and no. of pixels.

Following are the steps that are involved in image pre-processing.

1. The input images are in an RGB (Red-Green-Blue) scale which can be transformed into gray-scale images.
2. The base dimension of the images has to be same. The images are brought to the same ratio by cropping the images.
3. The images are resized by upscaling or downscaling.
4. The pixel values of the images are normalized to provide a similar data distribution.

Data augmentation is also a process which is used to zoom, rotate, or change the brightness of the input images. Data augmentation increases the dataset variation through image conversion [11]. The images undergo another process called feature extraction. Feature extraction is performed by separating gray values and putting them together. The types of feature extraction performed on an image are:

- Textural features: The inter pixel relationship is defined by the texture feature. The inter pixel relationship is the relationship between a number of pixels in the image. The texture feature extraction process extracts the sharpness, smoothness, roughness, and textures of the image.
- Gray level correlation matrix features: GLCM features are very powerful and are texture features that correspond to contrast, entropy, homogeneity, and the correlation of the pixels in an image. GLCM is useful for detection and classification in the image processing field.
- Morphological features: The morphological feature extraction process extracts from binary images. The features contain a no. of connected components, perimeters, andarea of the image. The images have sharp features and edge features [35]

2   Literature Review

This section throws light on approaches based on conventional methods and machine learning methods to detect the presence of cancer cell in the microscopic images. Traditional methods are without the use of machine learning models and use the traditional computer vision techniques. The literature review segregates the papers according to conventional methods of segmentation and classification, machine learning methods of segmentation and classification, and deep learning methods of segmentation and classification. The papers for the review are chosen according to certain criteria like the paper should focus on leukemia type of cancer, the proposed model should use either conventional methods, machine learning methods, or deep learning methods, the paper should either segment the image, classify the image, or perform both the operations to help detect the types of leukemia in a sample.

2.1   Conventional Methods

Conventional methods of detecting leukemia are through blood tests (Complete Blood Count where the results show abnormality raising the suspicion of leukemia), cytomorphology, flow cytometry, and Leukemia Associated Immunophenotype (LAIP) [3]. The image processing techniques have become a benefit for identifying cancerous cells. There are many conventional techniques that help in the recognition of cancerous cells in classical image processing.

The paper with the dataset obtained from the Leukemia laboratory at the Helwan University [22] takes two groups of samples for the experiment conduction; one is a normal blood sample group, and the other is the blood sample group that has Leukemia (ALL). The paper designs a model using the Rohde & Schwarz ZVB14 VNA (Vector Network Analyzer) that has two patch antennas and a 50 Ω microstrip to feed the sample to the device. The paper searches for scattering parameters to differentiate between the two blood sample groups by using the UWB (Ultra-Wide Band) in the frequency range of 3.1–10.6 GHz. The paper classifies the blood sample as either cancerous (ALL) or non-cancerous.

The results show that the healthy blood sample peaked at 4.4 GHz with 21.6 Ω, while the leukemia blood sample peaked at 17.9 Ω at the same frequency. With a distribution of impedance, the normal blood sample peaked at 7.8 Ω at 9.724 GHz, while the leukemia blood sample peaked at 6.61 Ω at 9.65 GHz. With a phase shift between the two samples, the normal one peaked at 7.79 GHz, while the leukemia one peaked at 7.85 GHz. This concludes that the leukemia blood sample peaks at a higher point than that of a normal blood sample.

The paper, [33], performs the experiment with the dataset obtained from ALL-IDB. The pre-processing method taken to filter the noise in the images is Weiner filtering by enhancing the contrast with a histogram equalizer. The paper performs the classification of the microscopic images into normal blood and ALL blood by using DCT (Discrete Cosine Transformation). The paper uses a marker based watershed algorithm to segment the images. The paper uses a PC of 3.40 GHz Core-i7 processor with 4 GB RAM and Windows 8 operating system to carry out the experiment while simulation is performed in the MATLAB 2013 toolbox. The paper takes 59 normal blood images and 49 ALL affected blood images. The DCT coefficients are taken as the features for the classification. The optimum accuracy obtained for classifying the samples is 89.76% with sensitivity of 84.67% and specificity of 94.61%.

The paper, [44], performs the experiment with the dataset obtained from the department of haematology laboratory at Saidu Medical college, Pakistan. The process starts by converting the images into HSV colour scheme. The component S is processed to obtain better results during segmentation. Different threshold values are found according to the L1, L2, and L3 types of ALL according to the morphological structure seen in the lymphoblasts. MATLAB's command Imfill holes is used to restore any lost information. According to the threshold values, the segmentation of the images was performed. As a result, the proposed system was able to identify with 100% accuracy L1 type, 100% accuracy L2 type, and 93.3% accuracy L3 type.

2.2   Machine Learning Methods

Machine learning offers a wide range of techniques and algorithms that aid in the classification and segmentation of images into normal non-cancerous and ALL affected [38]. Some of the algorithms are reviewed in this paper. The Fig. 2 represents a taxonomy of microscopy cell features, image correction, image separation, segmentation, and classification.

K-means Clustering

The paper, [29], performs the experiment with samples obtained from Dr. RML Awadh Hospital, Lucknow. In the pre- processing process, the image is applied with the Wiener filter, histogram equalization, and Gray-scale transformation to obtain a noise free binary image. The paper segments the images to nucleus and cytoplasm by using the K-means clustering algorithm. The ALL is mainly associated with the lymphocytes therefore the other components of the WBC are not considered. The paper classifies the images into cancerous and non-cancerous by using the K-NN (K-Nearest Neighbour) and the Naïve Bayes classifier. The accuracy obtained is 92.8%.

The paper, [12], performs the experiment with samples obtained from the pathology labs at Isfahan Al-Zahra and Omid hospital. In the pre-processing process, the images are exposed and a histogram equalization on the V band is applied for the colour space HSV channels. The segmentation of the nucleus is performed by the K-means clustering algorithm whose equation is given in Eq. 1. The paper uses SVM classifier to classify the images into cancerous (ALL) and non-cancerous. The paper obtains the results with accuracy of 97%, sensitivity of 98%, and specificity of 95%.

$$J = \sum_{j=1}^{k} \sum_{i=1}^{n} ||x_i^j - c_j||^2 \tag{1}$$

where, J = objective function; k = no. of clusters; n = no. of cases; x_i = case i ; c_j = centroid for the cluster j.

This paper, [10], performs the experiment taking four different datasets namely ALL-IDB, ASH, Shuttershock image bank, and a collection taken from Pathpedia.com. Pre-processing of the images is performed by converting the images to L*a*b colour space. The Otsu's method is used for segmentation of the image. Noise removal is done using the morphological operations of flood-fill, dilation, and opening. In order to segregate the nucleus various methods like watershed segmentation, k-means clustering, and morphological operation were applied. The nucleus and cytoplasm are separated, and the nucleus is analysed using k-means clustering. The overall segmentation accuracy obtained by the proposed model is 96% for normal and blast cells, 93% for nuclei region.

K-nearest Neighbour

The paper, [43], performs the experiment with samples obtained from Sains Malaysia Hospital's haematology department. The paper utilizes pre-processed images which highlight the size, shape, and colour base. The paper conducts the experiment to detect both ALL and AML from the set of images chosen for the experiment. The paper uses the K-NN algorithm to classify the images into either ALL, AML, or non-cancerous. The paper identifies that when the value of k = 4, an accuracy of 86% was observed.

The paper, [34], performs the experiment with samples obtained from the ALL-IDB2 dataset. The pre-processing process of the images the Median filter is utilized to discard noise. The paper conducts the experiment to detect ALL and classify the cells into cancerous or non-cancerous with the K-NN algorithm. The paper identifies that when the value of k = 7, the accuracy, sensitivity, and specificity obtained is 90%.

$$[d(p,q) = d(q,p) = \sqrt{\sum_{i=1}^{n} (q_i - p_i)^2}] \tag{2}$$

Naïve Bayes Classifier

The paper, [40], performs the experiment with the samples obtained from ALL-IDB2 dataset. The paper utilizes pre-processed images for the experiment. The paper uses the k-means clustering method to segment the nucleus as normal and abnormal. The paper proposes the use of the Naïve Bayes Classification method to classify the images as either a normal lymphocyte image or an abnormal lymphocyte image. The result obtained by the paper is an accuracy of 75%, sensitivity of 77.78%, and specificity of 72.72%.

The paper, [19], performs the experiment with the samples obtained from ALL-IDB1 dataset. The pre-processing process of the images are performed by applying hue transformation, thresholding, and morphological opening. The paper performs segmentation using adaptive thresholding which is preceded by the LUV colour transformation techniques. The paper proposes the use of Gini index based fuzzy naïve bayes classification technique to determine whether the cells in the image are ALL cancerous or non-cancerous. The paper obtains an accuracy of 95.91%, specificity of 95.99%, and sensitivity of 100% when classifying the images into cancerous and non-cancerous.

Artificial Neural Network

The paper, [21], performs the experiment with samples obtained from the paper [24]. The paper utilizes pre-processed images for the experiment. The paper utilizes the multilayer perception artificial neural network to classify the cells as cancerous or non-cancerous. The paper compares the functioning of the proposed method against SVM, classification trees, logistic regression, K-NN, and Naïve Bayes algorithms. The paper obtains a classification accuracy of 98% using ANN to classify the cells of the dataset into cancerous and non-cancerous.

The paper, [13], performs the experiment with samples captured from human bone marrow. The experiment captures 75 blood sample images. The pre-processing process of the images are cropping and resizing as the paper wants to preserve the cytoplasm of the blood cell images. The paper applies back propagation neural network to classify the images into ALL or AML type leukemia. Along with back propagation neural network, the paper also employs blood cell imagery extraction to classify the images. The paper achieves an accuracy of 86.6% in classifying the images as either ALL or AML.

Support Vector Machine

The paper, [39], performs the experiment with samples obtained from the Hayatabad Medical Complex, Peshawar, Pakistan. The pre-processing process was carried out using MATLAB to fit to the requirements of the experiment. The images are sharpened using an un-sharp mask Gaussian mask and converted to the HIS colour space. The segmentation of the images is done using k-means, FCM (Fuzzy C-Means) clustering, watershed method, Otsu binarization, active contours, and simple thresholding. The paper classifies the samples into cancerous and non-cancerous using multiclass support vector machine driven classification. The paper tries to implement the model in the mobile-cloud storage linked to smartphone The paper achieves an accuracy of 98.6% for classification.

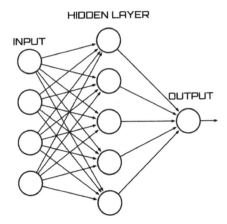

Fig. 2. Artificial neural network data flow [14]

The paper, [26]), performs the experiment with samples obtained from St. Jude Children's Research Hospital. The paper utilizes microarray data that contain ALL mRNA expression from all the samples. The data has 958 features but only 248 samples which may result in high computational cost. Therefore, the paper performs a feature selection using MSVM-RF (Multiclass Support Vector Machine Recursive Feature Elimination). The paper utilizes One Multiclass Support Vector Machine (OAO-MSVM) with RBF-Kernel and Polynomial-Kernel. The result of the experiment is an accuracy of 94%, precision of 95%, and recall of 95%. Figure 3 shows the simple working of a support vector machine (SVM). This paper, [32], performs the experiment by taking the blood samples of 7 normal patients and 14 ALL patients at the Isfahan university of medical sciences. The pre-processing of the images is performed by changing the RGB colour space to HSV colour space and histogram equalization is applied. Nucleus segmentation is performed using the fuzzy c-means clustering method. The proposed model is

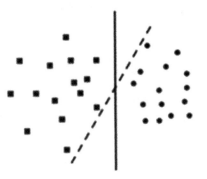

Fig. 3. SVM model [2]

used to classify the images into the three types of ALL(L1, L2, and L3) along with normal. Multi-SVM classifier is used for the selection of important features. The random forest classifier is used to classify the images into ALL type L1, L2, L3, and normal cells. The accuracy achieved by the random forest classifier is 98.22%.

2.3   Deep Learning Methods

The paper, [41], performs the experiment with the sample obtained from ALL-IDB2 and Google. The pre-processing process is data augmentation. The images are applied with image rotation and mirroring to obtain a data that is not overfitted. The data augmentation process yielded 760 images where 260 images were normal, and the rest 500 images were leukemia affected. The paper uses AlexNet for the detection of ALL. The model is trained on a system having NVIDIA Geforce GTX960M with a DDR5 of 4096 MB. The paper utilizes a pretrained CNN for the detection of ALL and classifying it into its sub types. The paper obtained a result with an accuracy of 99.50%, sensitivity of 100%, and specificity of 98.11%.

The paper, [28], performs the experiment with the samples merged from patients having B-Lineage Acute Lymphoblastic Leukemia and patients having Multiple Myeloma. The pre-processing process of the images is done by applying feature selection as it is very important in deep leaning. The paper adopts the univariate feature selection process to obtain the processed images. The processed images are divided into train and test datasets where 75% of the images are taken as train data and 25% of the images are taken as test data. The model is built using TensorFlow platform. The overall accuracy obtained as a result is 97.2%.

The paper, [16], performs the experiment with samples obtained from ALL-IDB and ASH image bank. The pre-processing process the images undergo is data augmentation. The images are rotated, horizontally flipped, sheared, and shifted horizontally and vertically. The no. of images obtained after augmentation are 3277 of ASH image bank and 2359 from ALL-IDB. The paper uses Dense convolutional neural network DenseNet-121 and Residual convolutional neural network ResNet-34 to identify ALL, AML, CLL, and CML types of leukemia. The accuracy of DenseNet-121 is 99.91%, and ResNet-34 is 99.56%.

This paper, [20], performs the experiment with images obtained from the ALL-IDB1 and ALL-IDB2 datasets. Pre-processing of the images are performed through data augmentation in order to avoid overfitting the data onto the model. The test data and train data are selected randomly. The proposed model is a deep convolutional neural network which is considered as a hybrid transfer learning method, is devised from MobileNetV2 and ResNet18 CNN which are hybridised according to the weight that benefits the two approaches. The proposed model provides an accuracy of 99.33% for ALL-IDB1 dataset and 97.18% for ALL-IDB2 dataset.

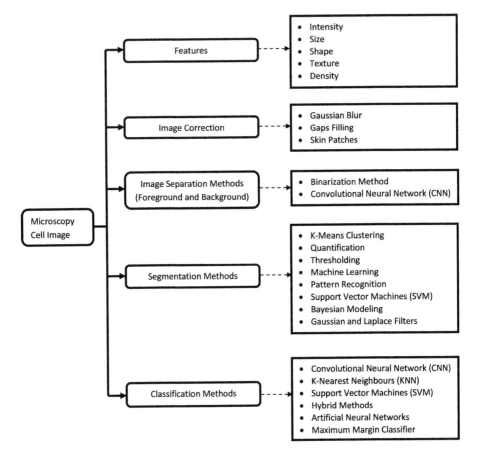

Fig. 4. Taxonomy of microscopy cell features, image correction, image separation, segmentation and classification

This paper, [9], performs the experiment taking images from the blood smears of 15 leukemia patients in the VIN hospital laboratory. After processing the images, a dataset of 1870 images were created. The model uses CNN in the form of a pre-trained model by applying the framework You Only Look Once version 2(YOLOv2). The model makes use of two Computer Aided Diagnosis Models, CADM1 and CADM2. CADM1 divides the input images to separate the white blood cells. CADM2 further divides the white blood cells and classifies into ALL or non-ALL. The CADM1 provides an output of 56% accuracy for class1 images, 69% for class2 images, and 72% for class3 images where classes 1, 2, and 3 correspond to the white blood cell types. The mean accuracy of CADM1 is 65.6%. CADM2 provides a detection accuracy of 94.1% and classification output of 92.4%.

Summary of the Literature Review

Table 1 contains a summary of the important points of the literature reviewed in this paper. The table is segregated into three parts which confer to the three types of paper surveyed in the literature review section. The table is divided into conventional method based, machine learning based, and deep learning based. The conventional methods offer less accurate results when compared to the machine learning and deep learning methods. The accuracy is higher in the machine learning and deep learning methods, in the range of 90% and above overall. The machine learning methods and deep learning methods are better when compared with the conventional methods according to the papers surveyed in the literature review.

3   Datasets

Publicly available datasets are discussed in brief. These datasets are exclusively designed and made public to check the performance and efficiency of segmentation and classification systems.

ALL_IDB1 Dataset

This publicly available dataset collected during September 2005 is composed of 108 images taken with different microscope magnifications ranging from 300 to 500, and contains 39000 blood elements, where expert oncologists have labeled the lymphocytes [1].

ALL_IDB2 Dataset

This collection of images was designed to test the efficiency of classification systems and is publicly available. ALL-IDB2 version 1.0 is a collection of normal and blast cell cropped area of interest which belongs to the ALL-IDB1 dataset. ALL-IDB2 images without the image dimensions have identical gray level properties to the ALL-IDB1 images [1].

C_NMC_2019 B-ALL Dataset

This dataset contains 118 individual subjects having 69 ALL subjects and 49 Normal subjects. It contains total of 15,135 images and is publicly available. Microscopic images of patients diagnosed with B-lineage acute lymphoblastic leukemia (B-ALL) were taken from bone marrow aspirate slides. Jenner-Giemsa stain was used to stain slides and lymphoblasts, which are cells of interest, were measured. Photos were obtained with a resolution of 2560×1920 pixels in raw BMP format using a Nikon Eclipse-200 microscope fitted with a 100x digital camera magnification [4]. The images were taken at various lighting settings to activate the process of gathering data from the real world. A professional human oncologist has done the collection of cells of interest from captured images.

TCIA Cancer Imaging Archive(SN-AM)

This website provides publicly available datasets on medical images of cancer. It contains various types of cancer image datasets. The website consists of datasets for all types of leukemia images. The images on the website can be downloaded

Table 1. Summary of the literature review

Author & Year	Dataset	Technique used		Limitations	Result
		Segmentation	Classification		
Conventional methods					
Eldosoky et al., 2012 [22]	Private dataset	NA	Ultra-Wide Band	Cannot distinguish other types of Blood cancer	The leukemia blood sample peaks at a higher range than the normal one
Mishra et al., 2017 [33]	ALL-IDB 59 Normal 49 ALL	Marker controlled watershed	Discrete Cosine Transformation	Computational overhead is high	Optimum accuracy is 89.76%
Rahman et al., 2021 [44]	Private dataset with 230 RGB images	Threshold based segmentation	NA	Segmentation accuracy for L3 type is low	Accuracy 100% for l1 and L2 type of ALL and 93.3% for L3 type ALL
Machine learning					
Supradi et al., 2012 [43]	Private dataset with 1500 samples	Not mentioned	K-nearest neighbour	Accuracy decreases with a larger dataset	When k = 4, accuracy is 86%
Amin et al., 2015 [12]	Private dataset 14 ALL 7 normal	K-means clustering	SVM classifier	Cytoplasm segmentation and extraction cannot be performed	Accuracy of 97%
Selvaraj et al., 2015 [40]	ALL-IDB220 normal 20 cancerous	K-means clustering	Naïve Bayes Classifier	The accuracy depends on the training dataset	Accuracy is 75%
Dwivedi et al., 2018 [21]	Private dataset with 32 ALL and 14 AML samples	Not mentioned	Artificial Neural Network	Error in classifying other types of Leukemia types	Classification accuracy of 98%
Purwanti et al., 2017 [34]	ALL-IDB2 60 Normal 60 ALL	Otsu's thresholding	K-nearest neighbour	No. of abnormal leukocytes is not calculated to detect the type of leukemia	When k = 7, accuracy is 90%
Sajjad et al., 2017 [39]	Private dataset with 1030 blood smear samples	K-means, FCM clustering, watershed method, Otsu binarization, active contours, and simple thresholding	Support vector machine	Computational overhead is not practical for operating in smartphones	Accuracy is 98.6%
Asadi et al., 2017 [13]	Private dataset with 75 samples	Not mentioned	Back propagation neural network	Classification is not overall successful for AML	Accuracy is 86.66%

(continued)

Table 1. (*continued*)

Author & Year	Dataset	Technique used		Limitations	Result
		Segmentation	Classification		
Kumar et al., 2018 [29]	Private dataset with 60 samples	K-means clustering	K-NN and Naïve Bayes	Overlapping cell segmentation cannot be performed	Accuracy achieved is 92.8%
Das et al., 2020 [19]	ALL-IDB1 With 108 samples	Adaptive thresholding	Naïve Bayes classifier	Accuracy is based on the training dataset	Accuracy is 95.91%
Hamidah et al., 2020 [26]	Private dataset with 248 samples	Multiclass Support Vector Machine Recursive Feature Elimination	One Multiclass Support Vector Machine	High accuracy cannot be obtained if there is more data	Accuracy of 94%
Abdullah et al., 2021 [10]	ALL-IDB, ASH, Shuttershock image bank, Pathpedia.com with 132 samples	K-means classification	NA	Normal cell segmentation accuracy is low	Accuracy 96% for normal and blast cell segmentation and 93% for nuclei segmentation
Mir et al., 2021 [32]	Private dataset with 312 images	Fuzzy c-means and multi-SVM classifiers	Random forest	Can only be used to classify ALL	98.22% accuracy
Deep learning					
Shafique et al., 2018 [41]	ALL-IDB2 260 Normal 130 ALL 50 Google images	Does not require segmentation	Convolutional Neural Network	Computation is slow	Accuracy is 99.05%
Kumar et al., 2020 [28]	Private dataset with 90 B-ALL samples and 100 MM samples	Not specified	Convolutional Neural Network	Computation speed is slow	Accuracy of 97.2%
Bibi et al., 2020 [16]	ALL-IDB 51, 52 samples and ASH image bank 50 samples	Not specified	Dense CNN(DenseNet-121) and Residual CNN(ResNet-34)	Computation is slow	DenseNet-121 accuracy is 99.91% and ResNet-34 accuracy is 99.56%
Das et al., 2021 [20]	ALL-IDB1 108 samples and ALL-IDB2 260 samples	Not specified	Hybrid transfer learning method	Sensitivity % is low when for ALL-IDB2 dataset	99.33%-ALL-IDB1 and 97.18%-ALL-IDB2
Abas et al., 2021 [9]	Private dataset with 1870 samples	Not specified	YOLOv2 and CNN	CADM1 showed low performance	CADM1- 65.6%, CADM2-94.1%(detection) and 92.4%

and used as it is publicly available. The SN-AM dataset contains images for B-ALL and MM types of leukemia. Images are from the bone marrow, which are captured with a Nikon Eclipse-200 microscope fitted out with a digital camera at 100x magnification. The Jenner-Giemsa stain is used to stain the slides. The images have a size of 2560×1920 pixels. There are 90 images for B-ALL and 100 images for MM [25].

ASH Image Bank
The American Society Of Hematology operates an image bank which contains a large collection of images related to hematology topics. The website offers a wide range of images related to the different types of leukemia like ALL [5].

Kaggle Codalabs Dataset
The Kaggle codalabs dataset is a multidisciplinary website that offers data and codes for various fields. The website has over 50,000 public datasets. In the leukemia classification dataset, which is publicly available, there are 15,135 images which correspond to both normal cells and leukemia blast calls. The cancer type specified is ALL type of leukemia. The images are segmented but contain some noise and errors due to illumination [6].

4   Evaluation Model

The interpretation on analysis of data is important for the evaluation of a model. There are set evaluation metrices in place to evaluate machine learning and deep learning techniques.

– Confusion matrix: A confusion matrix is a summary of the results obtained from the model. A confusion matrix describes the results of a model's performance in a simple way. The parameters of a confusion matrix are: True Positive (It is a correct and positive prediction), True Negative (It is a correct and negative prediction), False Positive (It is an incorrect but positive prediction), and False Negative (It is an incorrect and negative prediction).
– Classification report: The classification report is used to explain and measure the quality of the problem.
– Accuracy: The effective measure of a classifier which can correctly classify the values in a set. It is the number of accurate predictions made to the total predictions.

$$Accuracy = \frac{(TP + TN)}{(TP + TN + FP + FN)} \tag{3}$$

– Recall: The calculation of the total number of true positives divided by the sum of the total number of true positives and false negatives. Recall score is the calculation of how correctly the model predicts positive results.

$$Recall = \frac{TP}{(TP + FN)} \tag{4}$$

- Precision: A calculation of the total correct predictions made by the classification technique is its precision. If the model is spilt between A and B classes, precision score is how correctly the model calculates both A and B classes.

$$Precision = \frac{TP}{(TP + FP)} \tag{5}$$

- F1-score: It is a harmonic mean of the values of precision and recall.

$$F1 - score = \frac{2 * Recall * Precision}{Recall + Precision} \tag{6}$$

- Validation: The validation process where the proportion of the test model is evaluated with the trained model. This process is performed after a model is trained and then testing the performance of the model.
- Logarithmic loss: The logarithmic loss is a loss classification function based on the theory of probability. Logarithmic loss determines the performance of a model prediction where the values of probability are between 0 and 1. The accuracy of a classifier in increased when the value of logarithmic loss is nearer to 0 (Ali, 2020).

5   Research Problem

Cell classification is the subset of image processing which is popular in the recent times as the computerized tools became popular. The blood disorders could be identified using cell classification. Cell classification with highest accuracy is the first step to come to a conclusive decision in case of blood disorders. The major challenge in cell identification and segmentation is that the normal and malignant cells look alike. There are similar features for both the cells except that malignant cells change in the advanced stages of cancer only to be detected by medical expertise to observe the irregular growth, and not due to image processing techniques. It is therefore important to identify the malignant cells in the early stages so that there are better chances for treatment. Flow cytometry and similar methods are proven to be efficient; however, they are expensive and do not offer the required services for different cases. These methods are also not available as widely as required. Computerized solutions are easy and inexpensive because they are not complex and can be implemented everywhere. The hypothesis is that the medical image processing methods can identify the normal and cancerous cells efficiently. Automated classifier is the proposed work of this research study.

It is necessary to develop advanced but inexpensive computerized methods so that the medical professionals and experts can decide sooner with the help of the results of automated methods. The challenges of similar looking cells, cost, complexity, and subject expertise are addressed by the proposed system. Misclassification of blood cells can be minimized by accurate segmentation and detection of object boundaries. These regions or objects are further used for the classification and diagnosis of disease. Every classic automated blood cell microscopic image analysis system is comprised of three major stages i.e. a) image segmentation, b) feature extraction and c) classification. Image segmentation is used to identify certain structures like glands, cancer nuclei, and lymphocytes and is one of the pre-requisites in the diagnosis of disease. Certain features like shape,structure, morphological appearances, and shape of these segmented objects act as vital indicators for knowing the presence of disease.

6   Challenges in Cell Segmentation and Classification

The following list of points explains the current state of research in the field of cell segmentation based on the literature survey.

- The research in the field of medical image processing is advancing on a daily basis. The ongoing research requires authentication from medical professionals before they can be implemented in hospitals [23].
- Research has to be conducted in the field of automatic segmentation for fine parameters with the help of medical experts [36]. There is no standard procedure for cell classification and segmentation [15]. Therefore, the comparison of existing methods for one parameter is a challenging task.
- Dataset plays a vital role in all the approaches of cell classification and segmentation. The datasets are available in the public domain or not sufficient for improving the accuracy of complex algorithms in research. The accuracy can only be improved if the training and testing data set are large.
- There is no uniformity in the samples related to the features or the parameters such as devices, lighting conditions, medical condition of the patient, adjustments in the device, human intervention, and error, etc. These parameters can cause significant variation in the images of the same data set. Hence, there would be a large deviation in the results.
- Most of the datasets used for evaluation are private and belongs to foreign laboratories or hospitals which deny public access and less work is carried out on Indian hospital datasets. Hence, there is need to work on Indian datasets and make it available publicly for evaluating the performance of other algorithms.
- Due to staining, lighting, and human preparation variations there is no consistency in images across the dataset. This creates anomaly as there is variation in creating sample by different institutions. Hence, there is a need to build system that can handle aforementioned issues.
- Multiclass classification is less focused in cell classification. Major works are on binary classification for example detecting only cancer and non-cancer cell. Microscopy images contain vast information. Hence, there is need for multi-class classification model.

7   Ideas for Further Research

Complete Blood Cell is considered for the laboratory test that provides several details of the sample including the presence of cancerous cells. This process is challenging and complex. The process of microscopy and image processing is supported by image processing and other advanced technologies, making it a suitable alternative in the first stages to detect cancer using image processing techniques. An automated cell analysis system using microscopy is the requirements for the current trends in the field of medical diagnosis.

Image orientation is a major issue that is ignored in the research studies analysed. The orientation of the image with respect to classification is an issue that is considered as a research gap. Systems use machine learning techniques that get trained with the dataset and then provide accurate results. Image orientation and machine learning are considered to be research gaps and need to be addressed.

8 Analysis

The research in the field of Medical Image Processing is complex and requires in-depth knowledge of several fields and processes. A large amount of information hidden in the medical image cannot be decoded and understood using manual methods. Cell classification and segmentation methods have existed for a long time. Computer tools have significantly improved the quality and accuracy of the process using different approaches and mechanisms. This paper provides a detailed survey of different approaches used in cell segmentation and classification in a generic sense.

9 Conclusion

Cancer is a degenerative disease of the body where the cells abnormally and rapidly multiply without stop. Blood cancer is a type of cancer that affects the generation of healthy blood cells in the bone marrow. Leukemia is a type of blood cancer that affects the white blood cells, where the WBCs produced in the nucleus are cancerous. Early detection of leukemia is very important. Research has developed overtime so that the blood sample images can be used to detect and classify the type of leukemia. Image processing techniques are helpful in identifying the type of leukemia so that proper action can be taken towards treatment of the cancer. This paper performs a thorough survey of the various research studies dedicated to the detection, segmentation, and classification of Acute Lymphoblastic Leukemia (ALL). The paper surveys conventional, machine learning, and deep learning techniques that segment and classify the cells as normal and cancerous. This paper also throws light on publicly available datasets that can be used for the research purpose by other researchers for training and validation of their proposed methodologies on segmentation and classification.

References

1. ALL-IDB Acute Lymphoblastic Leukemia Image Database for Image Processing (2011). https://homes.di.unimi.it/scotti/all/

2. Support Vector Machines (SVM)—An Overview—by Rushikesh Pupale—Towards Data Science (2018). https://towardsdatascience.com/https-medium-com-pupalerushikesh-svm-f4b42800e989

3. Chapter 1 - Diagnosis and classification of leukaemias—OncologyPRO (2021). https://oncologypro.esmo.org/education-library/essentials-for-clinicians/leukaemia-and-myeloma/chapter-1-diagnosis-and-classification-of-leukaemias

4. C_NMC_2019 Dataset: ALL Challenge dataset of ISBI 2019 - The Cancer Imaging Archive (TCIA) Public Access - Cancer Imaging Archive Wiki, February 2021. https://wiki.cancerimagingarchive.net/display/Public/C_NMC_2019Dataset%3AALLChallengedatasetofISBI2019

5. ImageBank—Home—Regular Bank (2021). https://imagebank.hematology.org/

6. Leukemia Classification—Kaggle (2021). https://www.kaggle.com/andrewmvd/leukemia-classification

7. Leukemia: Symptoms, Types, Causes & Treatments (2021). https://my.clevelandclinic.org/health/diseases/4365-leukemia

8. What is Cancer? - National Cancer Institute, May 2021. https://www.cancer.gov/about-cancer/understanding/what-is-cancer

9. Abas, S.M., Abdulazeez, A.M.: Detection and classification of leukocytes in Leukemia using YOLOv2 with CNN. Asian J. Res. Comput. Sci. 64–75 (2021). https://doi.org/10.9734/ajrcos/2021/v8i330204

10. Abdullah, N.A.A., Ibrahim, M.A.M., Haider, A.S.M.: Automatic segmentation for Acute Leukemia Cells from Peripheral Blood Smear images. Int. J. Creative Res. Thoughts 9(4), 2248–2264 (2021)

11. Ali, N.O.: A Comparative study of cancer detection models using deep learning (2020). http://hdl.handle.net/2043/32148

12. Amin, M.M., Kermani, S., Talebi, A., Oghli, M.G.: Recognition of acute lymphoblastic leukemia cells in microscopic images using K-means clustering and support vector machine classifier. J. Med. Sign. Sens. 5(1), 49 (2015). https://www.ncbi.nlm.nih.gov/pmc/articles/PMC4335145/

13. Asadi, F., Putra, F.M., Sakinatunnisa, M.I., Syafria, F., Okfalisa, Marzuki, I.: Implementation of backpropagation neural network and blood cells imagery extraction for acute leukemia classification. In: 5th International Conference on Instrumentation, Communications, Information Technology, and Biomedical Engineering (ICICI-BME), pp. 106–110. IEEE, November 2017. https://doi.org/10.1109/ICICI-BME.2017.8537755

14. Asanka, D.: No Title. Implement Artificial Neural Networks (ANNs) (2021)

15. Bengtsson, E., Wählby, C., Lindblad, J.: Robust cell image segmentation methods. Pattern Recogn. Image Anal. 14(2), 157–167 (2004). http://citeseerx.ist.psu.edu/viewdoc/download?doi=10.1.1.464.5405&rep=rep1&type=pdf

16. Bibi, N., Sikandar, M., Ud Din, I., Almogren, A., Ali, S.: IoMT-based automated detection and classification of leukemia using deep learning. J. Healthc. Eng. 2020, 1–12 (2020). https://doi.org/10.1155/2020/6648574

17. Brazier, Y.: Tumors: benign, premalignant, and malignant, August 2019. https://www.medicalnewstoday.com/articles/249141

18. Chen, C.L., et al.: Deep learning in label-free cell classification. Sci. Rep. 6(1), 21471 (2016). https://doi.org/10.1038/srep21471

19. Das, B.K., Dutta, H.S.: GFNB: Gini index-based Fuzzy Naive Bayes and blast cell segmentation for leukemia detection using multi-cell blood smear images. Med. Biol. Eng. Comput. 58(11), 2789–2803 (2020). https://doi.org/10.1007/s11517-020-02249-y

20. Das, P.K., Meher, S.: An efficient deep Convolutional Neural Network based detection and classification of Acute Lymphoblastic Leukemia. Expert Syst. Appl. **183**, 115311 (2021). https://doi.org/10.1016/j.eswa.2021.115311
21. Dwivedi, A.K.: Artificial neural network model for effective cancer classification using microarray gene expression data. Neural Comput. Appl. **29**(12), 1545–1554 (2018). https://doi.org/10.1007/s00521-016-2701-1
22. Eldosoky, M.A., Moustafa, H.M.: Experimental detection of the leukemia using UWB. In: Proceedings of the 2012 IEEE International Symposium on Antennas and Propagation, pp. 1–2, July 2012. https://doi.org/10.1109/APS.2012.6349100
23. Goel, N., Yadav, A., Singh, B.M.: Medical image processing: a review. In: 2016 Second International Innovative Applications of Computational Intelligence on Power, Energy and Controls with their Impact on Humanity (CIPECH), pp. 57–62, November 2016. https://doi.org/10.1109/CIPECH.2016.7918737
24. Golub, T.R., et al.: Molecular classification of cancer: class discovery and class prediction by gene expression monitoring. Sci. **286**(5439), 531–537 (1999). https://doi.org/10.1126/science.286.5439.531
25. Gupta, A., Gupta, R.: SN-AM Dataset: white blood cancer dataset of B-ALL and MM for stain normalization (2019). https://doi.org/10.7937/tcia.2019.of2w8lxr
26. Hamidah, Rustam, Z., Utama, S., Siswantining, T.: Multiclass classification of acute lymphoblastic leukemia microarrays data using support vector machine algorithms. J. Phys. Conf. Ser. **1490**, 012027 (2020). https://doi.org/10.1088/1742-6596/1490/1/012027
27. Hayes, J., Peruzzi, P.P., Lawler, S.: MicroRNAs in cancer: biomarkers, functions and therapy. Trends Molecular Med. **20**(8), 460–469 (2014). https://doi.org/10.1016/j.molmed.2014.06.005
28. Kumar, D., et al.: Automatic detection of white blood cancer from bone marrow microscopic images using convolutional neural networks. IEEE Access **8**, 142521–142531 (2020). https://doi.org/10.1109/ACCESS.2020.3012292
29. Kumar, S., Mishra, S., Asthana, P., Pragya: Automated detection of acute leukemia using K-mean clustering algorithm. In: Automated Detection of Acute Leukemia using K-mean Clustering Algorithm, pp. 655–670 (2018). https://doi.org/10.1007/978-981-10-3773-_64
30. Loey, M., Naman, M., Zayed, H.: Deep transfer learning in diagnosing leukemia in blood cells. Computers **9**(2), 29 (2020). https://doi.org/10.3390/computers9020029
31. Meijering, E.: Cell segmentation: 50 years down the road [life sciences]. IEEE Signal Process. Mag. **29**(5), 140–145 (2012). https://doi.org/10.1109/MSP.2012.2204190
32. Mirmohammadi, P., Ameri, M., Shalbaf, A.: Recognition of acute lymphoblastic leukemia and lymphocytes cell subtypes in microscopic images using random forest classifier. Phys. Eng. Sci. Med. **44**(2), 433–441 (2021). https://doi.org/10.1007/s13246-021-00993-5
33. Mishra, S., Sharma, L., Majhi, B., Sa, P.K.: Microscopic image classification using DCT for the detection of acute lymphoblastic leukemia (ALL). In: Advances in Intelligent Systems and Computing, pp. 171–180 (2017). https://doi.org/10.1007/978-981-10-2104-6_16
34. Purwanti, E., Calista, E.: Detection of acute lymphocyte leukemia using k-nearest neighbor algorithm based on shape and histogram features. J. Phys. Conf. Ser. **853**, 012011 (2017). https://doi.org/10.1088/1742-6596/853/1/012011
35. Ratley, A., Minj, J., Patre, P.: Leukemia disease detection and classification using machine learning approaches: a review. In: 2020 First International Conference on Power, Control and Computing Technologies (ICPC2T), pp. 161–165. IEEE, January 2020. https://doi.org/10.1109/ICPC2T48082.2020.9071471

36. Rengier, F., et al.: 3D printing based on imaging data: review of medical applications. Int. J. Comput. Assisted Radiol. Surg. **5**(4), 335–341 (2010). https://doi.org/10.1007/s11548-010-0476-x

37. Rovithakis, G., Maniadakis, M., Zervakis, M.: A hybrid neural network/genetic algorithm approach to optimizing feature extraction for signal classification. IEEE Trans. Syst. Man Cybern. Part B (Cybernetics) **34**(1), 695–703 (2004). https://doi.org/10.1109/TSMCB.2003.811293

38. Sahlol, A.T., Abdeldaim, A.M., Hassanien, A.E.: Automatic acute lymphoblastic leukemia classification model using social spider optimization algorithm. Soft Comput. **23**(15), 6345–6360 (2019). https://doi.org/10.1007/s00500-018-3288-5

39. Sajjad, M., et al.: Leukocytes classification and segmentation in microscopic blood smear: a resource-aware healthcare service in smart cities. IEEE Access **5**, 3475–3489 (2017). https://doi.org/10.1109/ACCESS.2016.2636218

40. Selvaraj, S., Kanakaraj, B.: Naïve Bayesian classifier for acute lymphocytic leukemia detection. ARPN J. Eng. Appl. Sci. **10**(16) (2015). http://www.arpnjournals.com/jeas/research_papers/rp_2015/jeas_0915_2495.pdf

41. Shafique, S., Tehsin, S.: Acute lymphoblastic leukemia detection and classification of its subtypes using pretrained deep convolutional neural networks. Technol. Cancer Res. Treatment **17**, 153303381880278 (2018). https://doi.org/10.1177/1533033818802789

42. Su, H., Xing, F., Kong, X., Xie, Y., Zhang, S., Yang, L.: Robust cell detection and segmentation in histopathological images using sparse reconstruction and stacked denoising autoencoders. Lecture Notes In Computer Science, pp. 383–390 (2015). https://doi.org/10.1007/978-3-319-24574-4_46

43. Supardi, N.Z., Mashor, M.Y., Harun, N.H., Bakri, F.A., Hassan, R.: Classification of blasts in acute leukemia blood samples using k-nearest neighbour. In: 2012 IEEE 8th International Colloquium on Signal Processing and its Applications, pp. 461–465, March 2012. https://doi.org/10.1109/CSPA.2012.6194769

44. Ur Rahman, S.I., Jadoon, M., Ali, S., Khattak, H., Huang, J.: Efficient segmentation of lymphoblast in acute lymphocytic leukemia. Sci. Programm. 2021, 1–7 (2021). https://doi.org/10.1155/2021/7488025

MS-Net: A CNN Architecture for Agriculture Pattern Segmentation in Aerial Images

Sandesh Bhagat[1]($\boxtimes$), Manesh Kokare[1], Vineet Haswani[1], Praful Hambarde[2], and Ravi Kamble[1]

[1] SGGS Institute of Engineering and Technology, Nanded 431606, India
2018pec901@sggs.ac.in
[2] Indian Institute of Technology, Ropar 140001, India

Abstract. Computer vision for crop sciences is overgrowing with the advancement in pattern recognition and deep learning. Agriculture pattern segmentation is an important application such as segmentation of cloud shadow, waterway, standing water, weed cluster, planter skip, double plant, etc. However, the segmentation of agriculture patterns is challenging due to multi-scale variations of patterns and considerable overlap between classes. Furthermore, size and shape variation, unclear boundaries, and missing edges make this task more complex. To address this problem, we proposed the encoder-decoder architecture with input as a multi-scale image pyramid to improve the multi-scale feature extraction of agriculture patterns. EfficientNetB7 is utilized as an encoder for efficient feature extraction. In addition, the proposed Lateral-output layer shows rich semantic features by aggregating low level and high level features from the decoder, shows improvement in dice score. The proposed research uses the Agriculture Vision dataset with aerial farmland images. The proposed method outperformed different state-of-the-art methods in the literature for six agricultural patterns segmentation with a mean dice score of 74.78, 68.11, and 84.23 for RGB, NIR, and RGB + NIR images, respectively.

Keywords: Computer vision · CNN · Aerial images · Segmentation

1 Introduction

Agriculture is a significant source of revenue in most countries, accounting for a considerable percentage of the overall economy. Agriculture contributes 18% of the gross domestic product of India [28]. The high population demands enhanced agricultural productivity [38]. Thus Smart farming is a key component of long-term sustainability and production. Smart farming may help to improve the yield by optimizing resources. Farming challenges can be effectively overcome by perpetual observation and analysis of different physical aspects.

B. Raman et al. (Eds.): CVIP 2021, CCIS 1567, pp. 489–500, 2022.
https://doi.org/10.1007/978-3-031-11346-8_42

Remote sensing is a widely used technique for analysis and assessment of farmlands [31]. Pattern segmentation of aerial images is a significant aspect of agricultural image analysis. Pattern detection is the process of identifying agricultural patterns in images [7]. This study investigates several field agriculture patterns vital to farmers and significantly impacts the farmland yield potential. It is vital to locate them appropriately. Effective field pattern detection algorithms will enable prompt response and planning to reduce costly losses and increase output. Several field anomaly patterns have a significant influence on the potential yield of farmlands [19]. Segmentation of agriculture patterns in the aerial images is a challenging task due to multi-scale variation in size, shape, unclear boundaries, and overlap between classes makes this task more complex [40].

The economic potential of visual agriculture pattern recognition on aerial farmland images is significant; the development has been hampered by an absence of publicly available large datasets. The first Agriculture-Vision dataset is made publicly available in CVPR 2020, consist of Red Green Blue (RGB) images and Near Infrared (NIR) images for research work [6,40]. The proposed study uses the same dataset for agriculture pattern segmentation.

The following are the significant contributions of this work:

1. For agriculture pattern segmentation, the proposed method utilized a Multi-scale image pyramid as multi-level inputs help to extract multi-scale feature context of complex agricultural patterns.
2. The EfficientNetB7 is utilized as an encoder for efficient feature extraction of agricultural patterns.
3. The proposed Lateral-output layer enhanced features at different scales show rich semantic features by aggregating low level and high level features from the decoder.

The remainder of this paper is organised as follows: The second section examines the literature work. The proposed methodology for agriculture pattern segmentation is introduced in Sect. 3. The experimental results and discussion are described in Sect. 4, and the paper is concluded with future scope in Sect. 5.

2 Related Work

In the literature, several agricultural studies have been presented to extract useful information from pictures. Since the last decades, several studies have presented image processing-based techniques utilizing machine learning to advance deep learning. [37] Provides an overview of different machine learning approaches such as Support Vector Machines, Bayesian networks, etc., and image processing-based approaches such as histogram equalization and contrast enhancement used in agriculture applications. CNN has boosted the performance in image classification, segmentation and object detection other applications [2,3,9,12–14,33–35].

The transfer learning principle is used in computer vision-based agriculture applications that use unmanned aerial vehicle images for land cover classification [26]. In [29], computationally complex ensemble of Convolution Neural

Table 1. Agriculture-Vision dataset

Classes	Number of training Images	Number of validation images	Resolution	Annotations type
Double plant	1761	442	512×512	Pixel level
Planter skip	270	52	512×512	Pixel level
Cloud shadow	931	209	512×512	Pixel level
Weed cluster	8890	3164	512×512	Pixel level
Standing water	815	105	512×512	Pixel level
Waterway	1769	558	512×512	Pixel level

Network (CNN) model for crop and weed segmentation is proposed. In [20], a maize segmentation method based on region growth is presented utilizing R-CNN deep network. Multispectral data, NIR and RGB images improve crop and weed classification [15,25,30]. Agricultural visual identification, aerial picture segmentation is a crucial challenge [21]. The standard semantic segmentation technique is used for agriculture pattern segmentation. Two early deep learning-based semantic segmentation architectures, Fully Convolutional Neural Network [24] and SegNet [1], outperformed state-of-the-art approaches. Dilated convolution is employed in the Deeplab serieso to increase the receptive field of neurons and collect multiscale information [4]. In order to increase speed, SPGNet [5] used multiscale context modules. In [36], a U-shaped fully convolutional network with medical applications is suggested. Encoder and decoder are the two fundamental components of segmentation models. For extracting useful features from the source data, many state-of-the-art image classification architectures are commonly utilized. The decoder takes on the difficult task of upsampling a low-resolution feature map into an accurate segmentation map. The goal of the research is to design efficient encoder and decoder architecture design for improving segmentation performance.

A wide range of object classes are represented in existing segmentation datasets in the literature. [8,10,23], which focuses on simple objects or street scenes. In recent years, a few datasets for aerial agricultural image visual recognition studies have been proposed [16,32]. However, they have fewer high-resolution pictures and fewer class labels. The disparity between agricultural datasets and the previously described common picture datasets hampered progress in this sector [27]. Agriculture Vision is the first large-scale collection with high-quality, multi-band pictures and different field patterns annotated by agronomy specialists that are freely available.

3 Materials and Methods

Although many approaches have been proposed in past, but their performance is often not optimal. This paper investigates the uses of recent advanced deep learning models for the accurate agriculture pattern segmentation from aerial images.

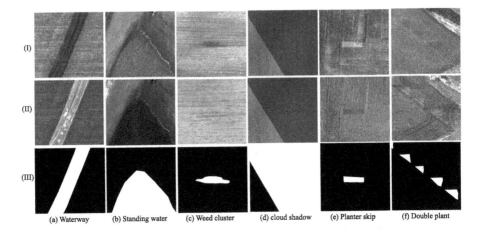

(a) Waterway   (b) Standing water   (c) Weed cluster   (d) cloud shadow   (e) Planter skip   (f) Double plant

Fig. 1. Agriculture-Vision dataset (I) RGB Images, (II) NIR images (III) Binary mask of respective classes

3.1   Dataset

The Agriculture Vision dataset with aerial farmland images is proposed as part of the CVPR 2020 challenge [6,19]. The images are taken between 2017 and 2019 throughout the growing season in a variety of rural regions around the United States. Four-channel input image, NIR, and RGB with the ground truth of the agriculture pattern are represented by a binary mask. Large aerial farmland images are not suitable for training segmentation models. Thus the farmland images crop with the size of 512×512 patches.

Double plant, Planter skip, Cloud shadow, Weed cluster, Standing water, and Waterway are six of the most relevant agriculture field pattern images and annotations in the dataset. These patterns as classes have a great effect on the agriculture field and the eventual yield. Figure 1 shows each agriculture pattern's image with RGB and NIR image and ground truth binary mask. The original dataset was split into 12901 images, 4431 images, and 3729 images for training, validation, and test set, respectively. Ground truth binary mask of six agriculture patterns classes We collected the Agriculture Vision dataset from the Agriculture-Vision challenge competition on the codalab platform. As the ground truth of the test dataset is not publicly available, the validation dataset is used as an independent test dataset for performance evaluation.

4   Proposed Method

In this section, we provide details of the proposed method; the task of agriculture pattern segmentation is considered as pixel-wise classification problem. Encoder-Decoder architecture is utilized for agriculture pattern segmentation.

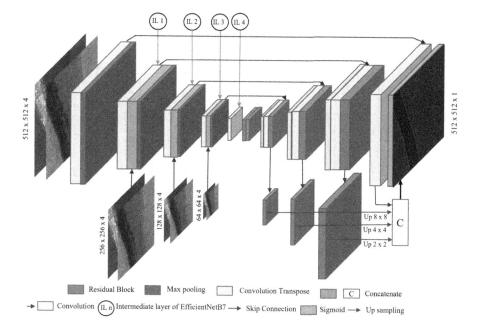

Fig. 2. Proposed MS-Net architecture.

4.1 MS-Net Architecture

The proposed MS-Net end-to-end multi-scale deep network consists of three main parts. First, a multi-scale input layer is used to create an input image pyramid and accomplish multi-level receptive field fusion. The second, The EfficientNetB7, is utilized as an encoder for agricultural pattern feature ex-traction from images efficiently. The third, Lateral-output layer enhance features at different scales shows rich semantic features by aggregating low level feature and high level features from decoder.

Multi-scale Input. The quality of segmentation is improved with multi-scale input [11]. Multi-scale image pyramid as multi-level inputs helps to extract multi scale feature con-text of complex agricultural patterns [11],[?]. The proposed MS-Net uses an average pooling layer to effectively downsample the image and generate a multi-scale input in the encoder route. Multi-scale input $RGB + NIR$ images as $MS_1 \rightarrow (512 \times 512 \times 4)$, $MS_2 \rightarrow (256 \times 256 \times 4)$, $MS_3 \rightarrow (128 \times 128 \times 4)$, and $MS_4 \rightarrow (64 \times 64 \times 4)$. Each input is passed through convolution operation and concatenate with encoder as show in Fig. 2. Multi-scale input helps to accurately segment multi scale agriculture patterns in aerial images.

Efficient-Net as Encoder. In recent deep learning technology, EfficientNet outperformed recent state-of-the-art techniques for classification tasks on the

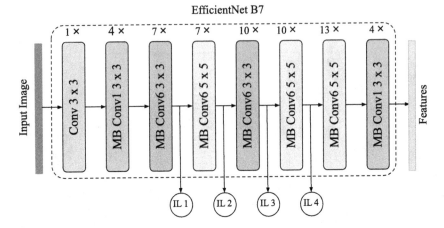

Fig. 3. EfficientNetB7 architecture is composed using MBconv blocks intermediate layers extracted as IL_1, IL_2, IL_3, and IL_4 with shape as $256 \times 256 \times 156$, $128 \times 128 \times 228$, $64 \times 64 \times 480$, and $32 \times 32 \times 960$ respectively.

ImageNet dataset. We investigated the usage of an EfficientNet [39] in the proposed MS-Net architecture as a feature extraction encoder. The EfficientNet model has been pre-trained on ImageNet, is capable of distinguishing between different agriculture patterns features. EfficientNetB0 to EfficientNetB7 are the eight versions in the EfficientNet family. Mobile reversed bottleneck convolution (MBConv) is the basic block of the EfficientNet network. The number of these MBConv blocks varies with each EfficientNet network family. EfficientNet proposed by Tan and Le [39], employs a compound scaling method to increase accuracy and efficiency by scaling up the CNN model across width, depth, and resolution. We utilised EfficientNetB7 as backbone in MS-Net architecture it consist of 7 blocks which downscale the input 512×512 to 7×7. The intermediate feature maps from four blocks of EfficientNet as IL1 ($256 \times 256 \times 156$), IL2 ($128 \times 128 \times 228$), IL2 ($64 \times 64 \times 480$) and, IL4 ($32 \times 32 \times 960$) were extracted at different scales from encoder as shown in Fig. 3 and then it is passed to the encoder where it is combined with multi-scale inputs as shown in MS-Net architecture Fig. 2.

Lateral-Output Layer. We introduce the lateral-output layer for aggregating low-level and high-level features from the decoder. Decoder consists of residual blocks after convolution transpose layer Let, P indicate all of the typical convolutional layers' parameters, and N signifies the number of lateral-output layers in the network. Where, $w = (w^{(1)}, ..., w^{(N)})$ denotes the relevant weights. Function for the lateral output layer is given as:

$$L_s(P, w) = [U_r L_s^{(n)}(P, w)]_{n=1}^N \tag{1}$$

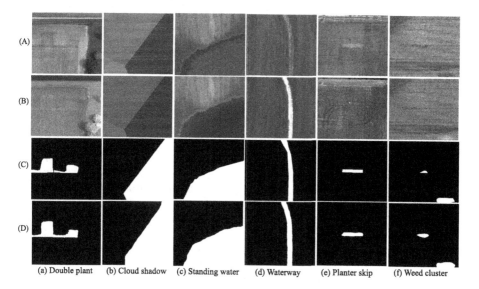

(a) Double plant   (b) Cloud shadow   (c) Standing water   (d) Waterway   (e) Planter skip   (f) Weed cluster

Fig. 4. Qualitative results on validation dataset from Agriculture Vision. The (A) RGB images for agriculture pattern, (B) NIR Images, (C) Ground truth mask for agriculture patterns and (D) Predicted mask for each agriculture patterns.

where, U_r is upsampling layer with r as upsamplig rate, $L_s^{(n)}$ denotes the nth lateral-output layer, [ ] denotes the concatenated operation. Four lateral-output layer from decoder extracted as L^1, L^2, L^3 and L^4 each layer upsampled to spatial dimension 256×256 with diffrent upsamplig rates as $L^1 \to U_{8 \times 8}$, $L^2 \to U_{4 \times 4}$, $L^3 \to U_{2 \times 2}$ and $L^4 \to U_{1 \times 1}$. Further, these upsampled outputs concatenated and perform upsampling and 1×1 convolutions followed by sigmoid activation to get the final agriculture pattern segmented image ($512 \times 512 \times 1$).

5 Experimental Results

5.1 Evaluation Metric

For quantitative performance evaluation, we use Dice as an evaluation metric for agriculture pattern segmentation. Dice measure an overlap among samples. This measure stages from 0 to 1, in which a Dice coefficient of 1 denotes best and entire overlap.

$$Dice = \frac{2 \times TP}{(TP + FN) + (TP + FP)} \tag{2}$$

Wheare, FN, FP and TP shows number of False Negative, False Positive and True Positive classified pixels.

Table 2. Comparison with state-of-the-art methods with input RGB images

Methods	Dice						Mean dice
	Cloud Shadow	Double plant	Planter skip	Standing water	Waterway	Weed cluster	
Deeplab V3+(ResNet50) [4]	64.29	66.68	68.23	72.77	70.08	73.86	69.31
DeeplabV3+(MobileNet) [4]	69.16	62.44	62.6	64.73	66.24	69.06	65.71
Res-U-Net [19]	61.59	66.05	67	65.74	66.37	61.36	64.68
Mobile-U-Net [19]	65.11	60.95	62.53	61.09	71.25	62.44	63.89
Eff-U-Net [19]	63.78	68.85	69.62	73.63	68.68	62.16	67.78
Res-FPN [19]	71.42	67.97	75.2	78.1	63.32	74.77	71.79
Mobile-FPN [19]	76	62.1	73	66.38	73.02	60.78	68.55
Eff-PN [19]	60.98	68.15	63.49	64.66	76.48	73.54	67.88
Fuse-PN [19]	66.3	74.15	73.19	76.32	72.96	76.63	73.26
Proposed	**68.7**	**74.88**	**74.21**	**77.36**	**71.36**	**77.21**	**74.78**

Table 3. Comparison with state-of-the-art methods input with NIR images

Methods	Dice						Mean dice
	Cloud Shadow	Double plant	Planter skip	Standing water	Waterway	Weed cluster	
Deeplab V3+(ResNet50) [4]	67.86	63.34	64.13	62.39	63.97	68.12	64.97
DeeplabV3+(MobileNet) [4]	59.88	52.38	56.48	56.32	57.66	64.25	57.83
Res-U-Net [19]	55.92	48.27	58.01	56.89	62.48	66.27	57.97
Mobile-U-Net [19]	52.86	55.28	42.85	59.66	54.91	63.82	54.90
Eff-U-Net [19]	53.61	56.71	54.97	51.05	60.59	66.08	57.17
Res-FPN [19]	58.31	59.96	50.39	57.18	64.31	67.06	59.54
Mobile-FPN [19]	57.02	55.31	56.55	60.99	47.2	54.85	55.32
Eff-PN [19]	59.68	57.21	59.55	63.33	64.25	67.88	61.98
Fuse-PN [19]	63.35	66.23	61.42	66.8	69.1	69.65	66.09
Proposed	**64.46**	**70.38**	**62.72**	**68.39**	**71.26**	**71.45**	**68.11**

Table 4. Comparison with state-of-the-art methods input with RGB + NIR images

Methods	Dice						Mean dice
	Cloud Shadow	Double plant	Planter skip	Standing water	Waterway	Weed cluster	
Deeplab V3+(ResNet50) [4]	78.43	77.51	78.45	78.51	79.28	81.2	78.90
DeeplabV3+(MobileNet) [4]	67.61	74.17	68.57	67.09	70.05	76.63	70.68
Res-U-Net [19]	75.14	78.87	77.02	75.69	77.54	81.28	77.59
Mobile-U-Net [19]	71.53	69.53	69.71	71.78	69.69	73.27	69.25
Eff-U-Net [19]	74.81	70.67	71.79	69.57	70.58	75.08	72.08
Res-FPN [19]	79.76	69.2	71.14	74.01	77.76	78.29	75.03
Mobile-FPN [19]	72.83	70.75	72.81	73.62	68.3	74.57	72.15
Eff-PN [19]	78.64	73.81	79.41	70.32	73.12	73.57	74.81
Fuse-PN [19]	85.91	81.69	79.83	82.34	81.85	84.59	82.71
Proposed	**86.53**	**82.76**	**81.82**	**84.32**	**83.76**	**86.21**	**84.23**

5.2   Results and Discussion

The proposed MS-Net end-to-end segmentation model is implemented using Keras and Tensorflow 2.0.0 as a deep learning framework for the training purpose. The proposed MS-Net network is trained by combining RGB and NIR images as input spatial dimension is $512 \times 512 \times 4$ with experimental environment Ubuntu 16.04 operating system, NVIDIA P100 GPU. Adam optimization algorithm used for optimization network, all convolution filters used 3×3 with the same padding with ReLU activation function. Combination of Dice loss and Binary cross-entropy loss used as loss function. The training was carried out with a batch size of 4, and the learning rate was initially set to 0.001 and reduced by a factor of 0.3 when there is no change in validation loss for consecutive five epochs; otherwise, it is kept constant. The complete network is trained for 100 epochs.

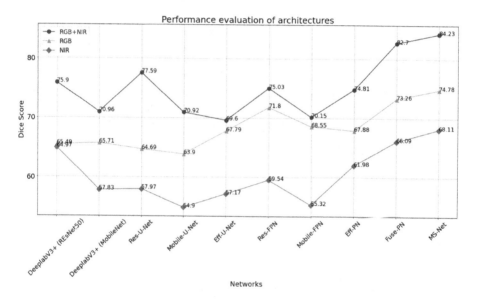

Fig. 5. Results comparison on the Agriculture-Vision Dataset on multiple architectures with various input RGB, NIR, and RGB+NIR Images.

To overcome the problem of overlap between the different class labels in Agriculture Vision dataset training a several CNN model approach is utilised that segments each agriculture pattern class separately. MS-Net Architecture is trained for each class category with multi-scale input of RGB and NIR images. The model is trained using three images: RGB, NIR, and RGB + NIR. Results are shown in Table 2, Table 3, and Table 4 respectively. We compared the proposed MS-Net architecture with various other state-of-art methods from literature like, Fuse-PN [19], UNet [36], FPN [22], ResNet [17], DeeplabV3+ [4], MobileNet [18] and EfficientNet [39]. Multi-scale input shows improvement in dice score of the agriculture patterns like Weed Cluster, Planter Skip, Waterway, Double , Standing Water and Cloud Shadow as shown in Table 2, 3, and 4. Multi-scale input constructs an image pyramid to fed a multi-level input. These pyramids are useful to extract multi-scale features of complex agricultural patterns at multiple levels. While the lateral output Layer enables the low to high-level feature aggregation from the decoder shows significant improvement in dice score. Qualitative results for agriculture pattern segmentation are shown in Fig. 4. The performance of several architectures is compared using RGB, NIR, and RGB+NIR as input images shown in Fig. 5.

6   Conclusion

Agriculture pattern segmentation for aerial farmland images utilizing the Agriculture Vision dataset is discussed in the proposed study. A CNN architecture MS-Net is implemented to extract the multi-scale features of agriculture patterns in aerial images. The proposed deep learning-based Multi-Scale input architecture (MS-Net) outperformed the state-of-the-art methods. The multiscale image pyramid input helps extract different scale features to analyze the complex agricultural scenes. The lateral output layer shows low level and high level feature aggregation. Proposed MS-Net outperformed state-of-the-art methods achieves a mean dice score of 74.78, 68.11, and 84.23 for RGB, NIR, and RGB with NIR images as input, respectively, over six agriculture patterns. MS-Net has proven to be effective in segmenting agricultural patterns and can be used in various other applications.

References

1. Badrinarayanan, V., Kendall, A., Cipolla, R.: SegNet: a deep convolutional encoder-decoder architecture for image segmentation. IEEE Trans. Pattern Anal. Mach. Intell. **39**(12), 2481–2495 (2017)
2. Bhagat, S., Kokare, M., Haswani, V., Hambarde, P., Kamble, R.: WheatNet-Lite: a novel light weight network for wheat head detection. In: Proceedings of the IEEE/CVF International Conference on Computer Vision (ICCV) Workshops, pp. 1332–1341, October 2021
3. Bhagat, S., Kokare, M., Haswani, V., Hambarde, P., Kamble, R.: Eff-UNet++: a novel architecture for plant leaf segmentation and counting. Eco. Inform. **68**, 101583 (2022)
4. Chen, L.C., Zhu, Y., Papandreou, G., Schroff, F., Adam, H.: Encoder-decoder with atrous separable convolution for semantic image segmentation. In: Proceedings of the European Conference on Computer Vision (ECCV), pp. 801–818 (2018)
5. Cheng, B., et al.: SPGNet: semantic prediction guidance for scene parsing. In: Proceedings of the IEEE/CVF International Conference on Computer Vision, pp. 5218–5228 (2019)
6. Chiu, M.T., et al.: Agriculture-vision: a large aerial image database for agricultural pattern analysis. In: Proceedings of the IEEE/CVF Conference on Computer Vision and Pattern Recognition, pp. 2828–2838 (2020)

7. Christiansen, P., Nielsen, L.N., Steen, K.A., Jørgensen, R.N., Karstoft, H.: Deep-Anomaly: combining background subtraction and deep learning for detecting obstacles and anomalies in an agricultural field. Sensors **16**(11), 1904 (2016)
8. Cordts, M., et al.: The cityscapes dataset for semantic urban scene understanding. In: Proceedings of the IEEE Conference on Computer Vision and Pattern Recognition, pp. 3213–3223 (2016)
9. Dudhane, A., Biradar, K.M., Patil, P.W., Hambarde, P., Murala, S.: Varicolored image de-hazing. In: proceedings of the IEEE/CVF Conference on Computer Vision and Pattern Recognition, pp. 4564–4573 (2020)
10. Everingham, M., Van Gool, L., Williams, C.K., Winn, J., Zisserman, A.: The pascal visual object classes (VOC) challenge. Int. J. Comput. Vis. **88**(2), 303–338 (2010)
11. Fu, H., Cheng, J., Xu, Y., Wong, D.W.K., Liu, J., Cao, X.: Joint optic disc and cup segmentation based on multi-label deep network and polar transformation. IEEE Trans. Med. Imaging **37**(7), 1597–1605 (2018)
12. Hambarde, P., Dudhane, A., Murala, S.: Single image depth estimation using deep adversarial training. In: 2019 IEEE International Conference on Image Processing (ICIP), pp. 989–993. IEEE (2019)
13. Hambarde, P., Dudhane, A., Patil, P.W., Murala, S., Dhall, A.: Depth estimation from single image and semantic prior. In: 2020 IEEE International Conference on Image Processing (ICIP), pp. 1441–1445. IEEE (2020)
14. Hambarde, P., Murala, S.: S2DNet: depth estimation from single image and sparse samples. IEEE Trans. Computat. Imaging **6**, 806–817 (2020)
15. Haug, S., Michaels, A., Biber, P., Ostermann, J.: Plant classification system for crop/weed discrimination without segmentation. In: IEEE Winter Conference on Applications of Computer Vision, pp. 1142–1149. IEEE (2014)
16. Haug, S., Ostermann, J.: A crop/weed field image dataset for the evaluation of computer vision based precision agriculture tasks. In: Agapito, L., Bronstein, M.M., Rother, C. (eds.) ECCV 2014. LNCS, vol. 8928, pp. 105–116. Springer, Cham (2015). https://doi.org/10.1007/978-3-319-16220-1_8
17. He, K., Zhang, X., Ren, S., Sun, J.: Deep residual learning for image recognition. In: Proceedings of the IEEE Conference on Computer Vision and Pattern Recognition, pp. 770–778 (2016)
18. Howard, A., Zhmoginov, A., Chen, L.C., Sandler, M., Zhu, M.: Inverted residuals and linear bottlenecks: mobile networks for classification, detection and segmentation (2018)
19. Innani, S., Dutande, P., Baheti, B., Talbar, S., Baid, U.: Fuse-PN: a novel architecture for anomaly pattern segmentation in aerial agricultural images. In: Proceedings of the IEEE/CVF Conference on Computer Vision and Pattern Recognition, pp. 2960–2968 (2021)
20. Jin, S., et al.: Deep learning: individual maize segmentation from terrestrial lidar data using faster R-CNN and regional growth algorithms. Front. Plant Sci. **9**, 866 (2018)
21. Kamilaris, A., Prenafeta-Boldú, F.X.: Deep learning in agriculture: a survey. Comput. Electron. Agric. **147**, 70–90 (2018)
22. Lin, T.Y., Dollár, P., Girshick, R., He, K., Hariharan, B., Belongie, S.: Feature pyramid networks for object detection. In: Proceedings of the IEEE Conference on Computer Vision and Pattern Recognition, pp. 2117–2125 (2017)
23. Lin, T.-Y., et al.: Microsoft COCO: common objects in context. In: Fleet, D., Pajdla, T., Schiele, B., Tuytelaars, T. (eds.) ECCV 2014. LNCS, vol. 8693, pp. 740–755. Springer, Cham (2014). https://doi.org/10.1007/978-3-319-10602-1_48

24. Long, J., Shelhamer, E., Darrell, T.: Fully convolutional networks for semantic segmentation. In: Proceedings of the IEEE Conference on Computer Vision and Pattern Recognition, pp. 3431–3440 (2015)
25. Lottes, P., Hörferlin, M., Sander, S., Stachniss, C.: Effective vision-based classification for separating sugar beets and weeds for precision farming. J. Field Robot. **34**(6), 1160–1178 (2017)
26. Lu, H., Fu, X., Liu, C., Li, L.G., He, Y.X., Li, N.W.: Cultivated land information extraction in UAV imagery based on deep convolutional neural network and transfer learning. J. Mountain Sci. **14**(4), 731–741 (2017)
27. Lu, Y., Young, S.: A survey of public datasets for computer vision tasks in precision agriculture. Comput. Electron. Agric. **178**, 105760 (2020)
28. Madhusudhan, L.: Agriculture role on Indian economy. Bus. Econ. J. **6**(4), 1 (2015)
29. McCool, C., Perez, T., Upcroft, B.: Mixtures of lightweight deep convolutional neural networks: applied to agricultural robotics. IEEE Robot. Autom. Lett. **2**(3), 1344–1351 (2017)
30. Milioto, A., Lottes, P., Stachniss, C.: Real-time blob-wise sugar beets vs weeds classification for monitoring fields using convolutional neural networks. ISPRS Ann. Photogramm. Remote Sens. Spatial Inf. Sci. **4** (2017)
31. Mouret, F., Albughdadi, M., Duthoit, S., Kouamé, D., Rieu, G., Tourneret, J.Y.: Detecting anomalous crop development with multispectral and SAR time series using unsupervised outlier detection at the parcel-level: application to wheat and rapeseed crops (2020)
32. Olsen, A., et al.: DeepWeeds: a multiclass weed species image dataset for deep learning. Sci. Rep. **9**(1), 1–12 (2019)
33. Patil, P.W., Biradar, K.M., Dudhane, A., Murala, S.: An end-to-end edge aggregation network for moving object segmentation. In: proceedings of the IEEE/CVF Conference on Computer Vision and Pattern Recognition, pp. 8149–8158 (2020)
34. Patil, P.W., Dudhane, A., Kulkarni, A., Murala, S., Gonde, A.B., Gupta, S.: An unified recurrent video object segmentation framework for various surveillance environments. IEEE Trans. Image Process. **30**, 7889–7902 (2021)
35. Phutke, S.S., Murala, S.: Diverse receptive field based adversarial concurrent encoder network for image inpainting. IEEE Signal Process. Lett. **28**, 1873–1877 (2021)
36. Ronneberger, O., Fischer, P., Brox, T.: U-net: convolutional networks for biomedical image segmentation. In: International Conference on Medical image computing and computer-assisted intervention. pp. 234–241. Springer (2015). https://doi.org/10.1007/978-3-319-24574-4_28
37. Shah, J.P., Prajapati, H.B., Dabhi, V.K.: A survey on detection and classification of rice plant diseases. In: 2016 IEEE International Conference on Current Trends in Advanced Computing (ICCTAC), pp. 1–8. IEEE (2016)
38. Singh, A., Ganapathysubramanian, B., Singh, A.K., Sarkar, S.: Machine learning for high-throughput stress phenotyping in plants. Trends Plant Sci. **21**(2), 110–124 (2016)
39. Tan, M., Le, Q.: EfficientNet: rethinking model scaling for convolutional neural networks. In: International Conference on Machine Learning, pp. 6105–6114. PMLR (2019)
40. Chiu, M.T., et al.: The 1st agriculture-vision challenge: methods and results. arXiv e-prints pp. arXiv-2004 (2020)

Vision Transformer for Plant Disease Detection: *PlantViT*

Poornima Singh Thakur$^{(\boxtimes)}$ⒾⒹ, Pritee KhannaⒾⒹ, Tanuja SheoreyⒾⒹ, and Aparajita OjhaⒾⒹ

Indian Institute of Information Technology, Design and Manufacturing,
Jabalpur 482001, India
poornima@iiitdmj.ac.in

Abstract. With the COVID-19 pandemic outbreak, most countries have limited their grain exports, which has resulted in acute food shortages and price escalation in many countries. An increase in agriculture production is important to control price escalation and reduce the number of people suffering from acute hunger. But crop loss due to pests and plant diseases has also been rising worldwide, inspite of various smart agriculture solutions to control the damage. Out of several approaches, computer vision-based food security systems have shown promising performance, and some pilot projects have also been successfully implemented to issue advisories to farmers based on image-based farm condition monitoring. Several image processing, machine learning, and deep learning techniques have been proposed by researchers for automatic disease detection and identification. Although recent deep learning solutions are quite promising, most of them are either inspired by ILSVRC architectures with high memory and computational requirements, or light convolutional neural network (CNN) based models that have a limited degree of generalization. Thus, building a lightweight and compact CNN based model is a challenging task. In this paper, a transformer-based automatic disease detection model *"PlantViT"* has been proposed, which is a hybrid model of a CNN and a Vision Transformer. The aim is to identify plant diseases from images of leaves by developing a Vision Transformer-based deep learning technique. The model takes the capabilities of CNNs and the Vision Transformer. The Vision Transformer is based on a multi-head attention module. The experiment has been evaluated on two large-scale open-source plant disease detection datasets: PlantVillage and Embrapa. Experimental results show that the proposed model can achieve 98.61% and 87.87% accuracy on the PlantVillage and Embrapa datasets, respectively. The *PlantViT* can obtain significant improvement over the current state-of-the-art methods in plant disease detection.

Keywords: Plant disease · Vision transformer · Convolutional neural network · PlantVillage

© The Author(s), under exclusive license to Springer Nature Switzerland AG 2022
B. Raman et al. (Eds.): CVIP 2021, CCIS 1567, pp. 501–511, 2022.
https://doi.org/10.1007/978-3-031-11346-8_43

1   Introduction

As per the survey by the Department of Economic and UN Social Affairs, food security is a vital concern for many countries. In 2050, the world population will reach around 10 billion [1], which is an alarming condition for the world's ability to meet the food demand. To avoid food shortages and price spikes in this COVID-19 scenario, FAO, WHO, and WTO issue a public statement to maintain the world's food supply chain [2]. As per a report by the United Nations on the State of Food Security and Nutrition in the World, around 720–811 million people suffered from hunger in 2020, with a rise of 118 million people facing chronic hunger compared to the figures in 2019. This year, the number of people at the risk of acute food insecurity is estimated to go up further. Therefore, domestic food security and agricultural supply chain management are of the utmost priority for governments. But crop production is also damaged by pests and plant diseases. Plant diseases are affecting crops worldwide on a large scale. The top five cash crops are destroyed by 10–40% because of plant diseases [3]. Hence, appropriate measures need to be taken to timely identify the disease and control its further spread.

The manifestation of various plant diseases has adverse effect on crop growth and yield. Presently, agriculture field experts and farmers are the concern source to identify the plant diseases. But, due to limited numbers of field experts, time and cost; it is not possible to observe the entire disease affected field. Hence, there is an imperative necessity of fast, accurate and compact system for plant disease detection. With the development and availability of digital cameras; there is a trend of digital images-based disease detection systems. Researchers have started working with traditional image processing by the color, shape and texture features of images for disease identification. Due to diversity in diseases and limitations of traditional image processing methods; machine learning based classifier SVM, decision tree, random forest etc. have attracted attention of researchers. Traditional machine learning-based application required manual intervention for image feature extraction which make the process tedious.

In recent years, deep learning has provided promising solutions in various fields, including medical, automotive, finance, environmental and others. With the breakthrough performance of convolutional neural networks (CNNs) when AlexNet won the ILSVRC challenge in 2010 [4], a series of CNN architectures came into existence and demonstrated their capabilities at the ILSVRC challenge. With the development of CNNs in different fields, researchers started using them for image-based plant disease detection problems. The initial work using a large dataset was pillared in 2016 by Mohanty et al. [5], who compared the performance of AlexNet and GoogLeNet architectures on the PlantVillage [6] dataset. After that, a variety of methods have been developed for plant disease detection (see, for example, [7–12]).

CNNs have extraordinary performance on image data using the concept of parameter sharing. Deeper CNNs are more efficient in extracting high-level features. With the introduction of the attention mechanism in processing sequential data, several new CNN architectures have also been proposed, leveraging the concept of spatial and channel-wise attention. As per some recent studies, transformers are shown to outperform natural language processing (NLP) tasks such as machine translation and text summarization for large-sized input sequences. Vision Transformers (ViT) are designed to incorporate transformer capabilities for image data. CNN-based ViT has recently emerged as a powerful architecture for many problems, [13].

In this work, a Vision Transformer based CNN model *"PlantViT"* has been proposed for plant disease detection. The architecture is a hybrid of convolutional layers and the Vision Transformer. Initially, three convolution layers are used to process the input image for the generation of convolutional image embedding. In the second step, multi-head attention is applied to the unfolded image embedding. The proposed model *"PlantViT"* demonstrates good performance for plant disease detection in two publicly available datasets. It has been shown to outperform some recent plant disease detection methods. The main contributions of the present paper are as follows.

1. *"PlantViT"* is the first Vision Transformer-based model for plant disease detection problem.
2. It is a very lightweight model with only 0.4 million trainable parameters.

The rest of the paper is arranged as follows. Section 2 includes related work in the area of plant disease classification. In Sect. 3, the proposed work is presented; Sect. 4 presents results and discussion, and Sect. 5 concludes the work.

2   Related Work

For the past decade, digital image processing-based plant disease detection has been a significant area of research for developing smart agriculture solutions. As a result, several approaches based on image processing, machine learning, and deep learning techniques are introduced. This section discusses some of the approaches relevant to the current work.

Initially, traditional machine learning and image processing approaches were used by researchers to identify plant diseases. Barbedo et al. [14] applied color and intensity histogram transformation for plant disease detection. Johannes et al. [15] used colour constancy transformation and simple linear iterative clustering (SLIC) for super pixel segmentation. Furthermore, Naïve Bayes and Random Forest classifiers were applied to segmented images for wheat disease detection. Kumar et al. [10] applied a subtractive pixel adjacency model (SPAM) with exponential spider monkey optimization for image feature extraction. With the help of the SVM classifier, their model attained an accuracy of 92.12% on 1000 images of the PlantVillage dataset. In another work, Sharif et al. [16] employed SVM for citrus disease detection in six categories and reported 97% accuracy.

Mohanty et al. [5] made another breakthrough in plant disease detection problems when they compared the performances of deep learning models AlexNet [4] and GoogLeNet [17] on the PlantVillage dataset with 54,305 images in 38 classes using training from scratch, transfer learning, and fine-tuning methods on the PlantVillage dataset. They achieved 99.35% accuracy on the GoogLeNet model with transfer learning. Later, many researchers have employed transfer learning techniques for plant disease detection on state-of-the-art ILSVRC models. Too et al. [9] extended the work by comparing VGG 16, Inception, ResNet, and DenseNet on the same dataset and reported 99.75% accuracy on the DenseNet architecture. Ferentinos [7] categorized the extended PlantVillage dataset with 87,848 images into 58 classes using transfer learning. They analyzed VGG16, AlexNet, OverFeat, and GoogLeNet and reported that VGG16 achieved the highest accuracy of 99.53%. Finally, Lee et al. [11] compared the performance of GoogleNet, VGG, and Inception networks on PlantVillage, IPM, and Bing datasets. They have reported VGG16 as the best performing model. Liang et al. [18] presented a modified ResNet architecture with custom residual blocks and reported 98% accuracy on the PlantVillage dataset.

In some recent approaches, multiple training paradigms have been incorporated for disease detection. For example, Argüeso et al. [12] have used the concept of Few-Shot Learning (FSL) on the PlantVillage dataset for disease detection. They have trained Inception V3 on 32 classes of PlantVillage, and then in the remaining six classes, knowledge transfer is performed. They have also developed a Siamese network using Inception V3. Karthik et al. [19] have developed a residual attention based CNN model and have attained 98% accuracy for tomato disease detection. Sambasivam and Opiyo [20] have trained a three-layer CNN model on cassava disease classification with SMOTE as a class balancing technique. The last two years have witnessed the use of attention mechanisms in CNNs for image classification. Many researchers have combined attention mechanism capability with CNN for disease detection tasks. Chen et al. [21] have applied an attention mechanism with depthwise separable convolution to dense blocks and classified maize diseases. In another work by them [22], a detection mechanism has been applied to the MobileNet v2 architecture for rice disease detection.

Although numerous efficient models have been proposed by researchers to improve plant disease classification performance, each model has its own merits and limitations. Many models have a large number of trainable parameters. Such models are not suitable for mobile and embedded device-based solutions. The lightweight models, on the other hand, are shown to perform well mostly on specific small datasets like wheat or rice disease datasets. Their performance has not been evaluated on large datasets with a variety of diseases.

In this work, a lightweight CNN-based Vision Transformer network is introduced that alleviates the problem of a large number of parameters. The model outperforms some recently introduced lightweight models.

3   Plant Vision Transformer: *PlantViT*

The objective of the present work is to develop a Vision Transformer [23] with convolutional layers for plant disease classification problems. The architecture integrates three convolutional layers and a multi-head attention mechanism on the top of the Vision Transformer. The Vision Transformer-based plant disease detection system *"PlantViT"* is proposed by combining the capabilities of the convolutional layer with the Vision Transformer. The structure of the *"PlantViT"* is shown in Fig. 1. It accepts input of the size 224 × 224 × 3. The model consists of two parts: CNN and a transformer.

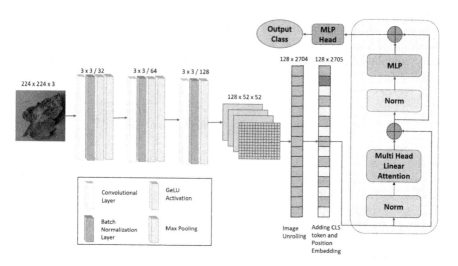

Fig. 1. Overall architecture of *PlantViT*: vision transformer based plant disease detection

In the CNN part, a shallow network with three convolutional blocks has been created to identify low level image features. The initial two blocks consist of a convolutional layer with a filter of size 3 × 3, a batch normalization layer, GELU activation layer, and a max pooling layer. In the last block, a convolutional layer, batch normalization and a GELU activation layer are present. In the next step, the feature maps generated by the last GELU activation layer are divided into patches. The size of each patch is set as a unit so that each individual pixel can contribute to token building. The idea is that each pixel pays attention to other pixels in the image. Finally, the token sequence is generated by unrolling the entire image based on the patches. The idea behind this arrangement is to mimic large-sized image sequences similar to the language transformers.

Position embedding is applied to each patch to maintain the relative positional information. It consists of a rotation matrix and the self-attention mechanism [24]. An extra classification token is added at the beginning of the sequence to retain the class information for further prediction. The sequence is then passed onto the transformer encoder using a linear projection. The transformer encoder includes multi-head attention (MHA) blocks and multi-layer perceptron (MLP) blocks. Each block is preceded by a normalization layer and residual connection at the end of the block.

MHA includes self-attention, which is applied to each patch individually. Self-attention is calculated with the help of Query, Key, and Value. These are generated by multiplying patch embedding, which acts like a weight matrix and is updated while training. The output of this sequence is passed to a dense layer. There can be any number of self-attention and dense layers in an MHA. In this work, the self-attention and dense layer are of depth four. Finally, the output vector is passed to the SoftMax layer for classification. A dot-product of Q and K values is taken to generate a scoring matrix based on the attention of patch embedding. Then, the SoftMax activation is applied to the score matrix for probability calculation. Further, the output is multiplied into V values to generate the self-attention result as shown in Eq. 1 where d_k represents the dimension of the K vector.

$$SelfAttention(Q, K, V) = SoftMax(\frac{QK^T}{\sqrt{d_k}}) * V \qquad (1)$$

Finally, self-attention matrices are combined and passed onto a linear layer followed by a regression head. Self-attention enables the selection of relevant semantic features at image locations for classification. There can be any number of self-attentions present in the transformer encoder, so-called multi-head attention. An MLP head is added with GELU non-linearity to the transformer encoder to generate the classification output. The GELU activation is calculated by multiplying the input by its Bernoulli distribution.

To develop the proposed model *PlantViT*, it was initially trained on 60,000 images of the ImageNet dataset, which has 50 classes. Then the pretrained model was further fine-tuned on plant disease datasets. The model has been trained with a learning rate of 0.0001 on the Adam optimizer for 30 epochs for each dataset.

4   Result and Discussion

4.1   Dataset

The *PlantViT* has been trained and evaluated on two public datasets: PlantVillage and Embrapa. Both the datasets have been generated with different capturing conditions. PlantVillage contains leaf images in a fixed background condition, whereas Embrapa has the leaf disease portion cropped from actual images. In Fig. 2, some sample images from both the datasets are presented with class information.

1. PlantVillage Dataset - It is the most frequently used public dataset for plant disease detection developed by Penn State University [6]. In the dataset, 54,305 leaf images of 14 species in 38 categories are present in three types: color, gray scale, and segmented. It is captured in a fixed background condition in the laboratory.

2. Embrapa Dataset - Barbedo et al. [25] have developed a plat disease databased(PDDB) dataset which has plant diseases from different portions of the plant. Further, extended database(XDB) has been generated by extending PDDB and cropping disease portions from leaves. It has 46,376 images in 93 categories, from 18 species. As in the actual dataset, there are some classes with very few images, so data augmentation is performed in the present work on the classes with less than ten images.

| Apple Scab | Grape Leaf Blight | Northern Leaf Blight | Cassava Bacterial Blight |

(a) PlantVillage [6]   (b) Embrapa [25]

Fig. 2. Sample images from the datasets used in the experiment

Both the datasets have been divided into training, validation, and test sets. Initially, training and test sets were created by dividing the datasets in a 4:1 ratio., the training dataset is split into a ratio of 4:1 to generate training and validation sets.

4.2 Evaluation Metrics

Accuracy. Accuracy is a widely used performance metric for the image classification task. It defines the relationship between the actual class value and the predicted class value. The higher the accuracy value achieved by the algorithm, the better performance is attained. Accuracy is defined as follows.

$$Accuracy = \frac{(TP + TN)}{Total \# of Samples} \qquad (2)$$

A true positive (TP) is the count of the samples belonging to a particular class A and predicted correctly in class A. Class true negative (TN) is the count of the samples that belong to class B and are predicted as class B. False-positive (FP) is the count of the samples that belong to class B but are predicted as A, and false-negative (FN) is the count of the samples that belong to class A but are predicted as class B.

Precision. It is the ratio of true positives to all predicted positives. It is in between the range of 0 and 1. The precision value should be as high as possible to define the preciseness of the algorithm.

$$Precision = \frac{TP}{(TP + FP)} \tag{3}$$

Recall. It defined the ratio between the true positive labels to all the actual positive labels. The value of recall lies in between 0 to 1.

$$Recall = \frac{TP}{(TP + FN)} \tag{4}$$

F1-Score. It relates Precision and Recall by calculating the harmonic mean between them.

$$F1 - Score = 2 * \frac{(Precision * Recall)}{(Precision + Recall)} \tag{5}$$

Loss. Another parameter is categorical cross-entropy loss, which is defined as follows.

$$Loss = -\frac{1}{n} \sum_{i=1}^{n} y_i \, log\hat{y}_i \tag{6}$$

Loss for all the n samples has been calculated by y_i as the true value and $\hat{y}_i$ as the predicted value of i-th sample.

4.3   Results

All the training and validations have been performed on the NVIDIA DGX A100 system. It has four NVIDIA DGX A100 GPU cards, each with 40 GB of memory. The model contains only 0.4 million trainable parameters. The model is fine-tuned on ImageNet trained weights for 30 epochs with a learning rate of 0.0001 and the Adam optimizer. Figure 3 presents the epoch-wise training and validation performance. It resulted in 98.61% and 87.87% accuracy on the PlantVillage and Embrapa datasets. The result observations are presented in Table 1 and Table 2. It is found that the proposed *PlantViT* model is able to converge faster than other recent state-of-the-art models for disease detection.

4.4   Discussion

In this work, a Vision Transformer with convolutional layers has been analyzed for plant disease detection. The observation of the experiment has reported in Table 1 and Table 2. The results show that the proposed transformer based system performs better for disease detection with an accuracy of 98.61% and 87.87% on PlantVillage and Embrapa datasets, respectively. Furthermore, the performance of the *PlantViT* model is compared against three recent works reported

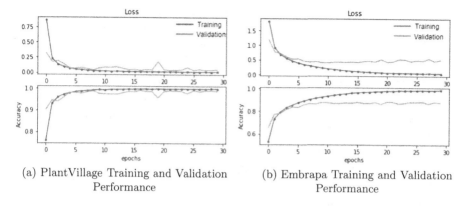

(a) PlantVillage Training and Validation   (b) Embrapa Training and Validation
Performance   Performance

Fig. 3. Loss and Accuracy for training and validation dataset

Table 1. Results on PlantVillage dataset

Approach	No of parameters	Loss	Accuracy	Precision	Recall	F1-score
Karthik et al. [19], 2020	0.7 M	0.1599	95.83	96.20	95.60	95.89
Chen et al. [21], 2021	0.8 M	0.4044	87.94	89.59	86.71	88.07
Chen et al. [22], 2021	4 M	0.1735	96.68	97.49	95.83	96.64
PlantViT	**0.4 M**	**0.0484**	**98.61**	**98.24**	**98.33**	**98.28**

in the literature. In the tables, accuracy, precision, recall, f1-score and loss values for all three works has been tabulated, and the best performing metrics have been highlighted.

It may be observed that the proposed model has the least number of trainable parameters. *PlantViT* consists of 0.4 millions of trainable parameters whereas in [21] 0.8 million has been present. For the PlantVillage dataset, the model reached categorical cross-entropy loss of 0.0484, accuracy of 98.61%, precision as 98.24%, recall as 98.33% and f1-score as 98.28%. When considering other approaches, [19,21] and [22]. None of the models have attain accuracy more than 96.68%. Similarly, on Embrapa dataset Karthik et al. [19] achieved an accuracy of 80.95% which is less than *PlantViT* with an accuracy of 87.87%. The *PlantViT* model attained loss as 0.4954, precision as 84.70%, recall as 80.75% and f1-score as 82.52%. As per the results, on Embrapa dataset precision score of Chen et al. [21] is little higher then the proposed approach.

Table 2. Results on Embrapa dataset

Approach	Loss	Accuracy	Precision	Recall	F1-score
Ramamurthy et al. [19], 2020	0.7652	80.29	83.07	78.38	80.60
Chen et al. [21], 2021	0.6018	80.95	**85.08**	76.02	80.01
Chen et al. [22], 2021	1.1153	74.88	82.93	66.06	73.18
PlantViT	**0.4954**	**87.87**	**84.70**	**80.75**	**82.52**

5   Conclusion and Future Work

In this paper a Vision Transformer based CNN is proposed to classify plant diseases. To the best of our knowledge, this is the first attempt to employ the Vision Transformer concept for plant disease detection. The main contribution of the proposed work is to integrate the convolutional layers with the Vision Transformer for effective image feature extraction and classification. The initial three layers of the model are convolutional layers for better low level feature extraction. Later, multi-head attention based transformer has appended to extract high level features. The proposed model has around 0.4 million trainable parameters, which is comparatively less than other recently introduced disease detection approaches reported in the results and discussion section. Experimental results indicate that the proposed Vision Transformer based model *PlantViT* can detect plant diseases with accuracies of 98.61% and 87.87% on the PlantVillage and Embrapa datasets, respectively. Further the work will be extended to localize the diseases for in-field datasets.

References

1. Department of Economic and United Nation Social Affairs Population. World population prospects 2019. https://www.un.org/development/desa/publications/world-population-prospects-2019-highlights.html (2019). Accessed 30 May 2020
2. Food and Agriculture Organization of the United Nation. Mitigating impacts of covid-19 on food trade and markets (2019). http://www.fao.org/news/story/en/item/1268719/icode/. Accessed 30 Aug 2020
3. Savary, S., Willocquet, L., Pethybridge, S.J., Esker, P., McRoberts, N., Nelson, A.: The global burden of pathogens and pests on major food crops. Nat. Ecol. Evol. **3**(3), 430–439 (2019)
4. Krizhevsky, A., Sutskever, I., Hinton, G.E.: ImageNet classification with deep convolutional neural networks. Adv. Neural Inf. Process. Syst. **25**, 1097–1105 (2012)
5. Mohanty, S.P., Hughes, D.P., Salathé, M.: Using deep learning for image-based plant disease detection. Front. Plant Sci. **7**, 1419 (2016)
6. Hughes, D., Salathé, M., et al.: An open access repository of images on plant health to enable the development of mobile disease diagnostics. arXiv preprint arXiv:1511.08060 (2015)
7. Ferentinos, K.P.: Deep learning models for plant disease detection and diagnosis. Comput. Electron. Agric. **145**, 311–318 (2018)

8. Kamal, K.C., Yin, Z., Wu, M., Wu, Z.: Depthwise separable convolution architectures for plant disease classification. Comput. Electron. Agric. **165**, 104948 (2019)
9. Too, E.C., Yujian, L., Njuki, S., Yingchun, L.: A comparative study of fine-tuning deep learning models for plant disease identification. Comput. Electron. Agric. **161**, 272–279 (2019)
10. Kumar, S., Sharma, B., Sharma, V.K., Sharma, H., Bansal, J.C.: Plant leaf disease identification using exponential spider monkey optimization. Sustain. Comput. Inform. Syst. **28**, 100283 (2020)
11. Lee, S.H., Goëau, H., Bonnet, P., Joly, A.: New perspectives on plant disease characterization based on deep learning. Comput. Electron. Agric. **170**, 105220 (2020)
12. Argüeso, D., et al.: Few-shot learning approach for plant disease classification using images taken in the field. Comput. Electron. Agric. **175**, 105542 (2020)
13. Jeevan, P., Sethi, A.: Vision Xformers: efficient attention for image classification. arXiv preprint arXiv:2107.02239 (2021)
14. Barbedo, J.G.A., Koenigkan, L.V., Santos, T.T.: Identifying multiple plant diseases using digital image processing. Biosyst. Eng. **147**, 104–116 (2016)
15. Johannes, A., et al.: Automatic plant disease diagnosis using mobile capture devices, applied on a wheat use case. Comput. Electron. Agric. **138**, 200–209 (2017)
16. Sharif, M., Khan, M.A., Iqbal, Z., Azam, M.F., Lali, M.I.U., Javed, M.Y.: Detection and classification of citrus diseases in agriculture based on optimized weighted segmentation and feature selection. Comput. Electron. Agric. **150**, 220–234 (2018)
17. Szegedy, C., et al.: Going deeper with convolutions. In: Proceedings of the IEEE Conference on Computer Vision and Pattern Recognition, pp. 1–9 (2015)
18. Liang, Q., Xiang, S., Yucheng, H., Coppola, G., Zhang, D., Sun, W.: PD2SE-Net: computer-assisted plant disease diagnosis and severity estimation network. Comput. Electron. Agric. **157**, 518–529 (2019)
19. Karthik, R., Hariharan, M., Anand, S., Mathikshara, P., Johnson, A., Menaka, R.: Attention embedded residual CNN for disease detection in tomato leaves. Appl. Soft Comput. **86**, 105933 (2020)
20. Sambasivam, G., Opiyo, G.D.: A predictive machine learning application in agriculture: cassava disease detection and classification with imbalanced dataset using convolutional neural networks. Egyptian Inform. J. **22**(1), 27–34 (2021)
21. Chen, J., Wang, W., Zhang, D., Zeb, A., Nanehkaran, Y.A.: Attention embedded lightweight network for maize disease recognition. Plant Pathol. **70**(3), 630–642 (2021)
22. Chen, J., Zhang, D., Zeb, A., Nanehkaran, Y.A.: Identification of rice plant diseases using lightweight attention networks. Expert Syst. Appl. **169**, 114514 (2021)
23. Vaswani, A., et al.: Attention is all you need. In: Advances in Neural Information Processing Systems, pp. 5998–6008 (2017)
24. Su, J., Lu, Y., Pan, S., Wen, B., Liu, Y.: RoFormer: enhanced transformer with rotary position embedding. arXiv preprint arXiv:2104.09864 (2021)
25. Barbedo, J.G.A., et al.: Annotated plant pathology databases for image-based detection and recognition of diseases. IEEE Latin Am. Trans. **16**(6), 1749–1757 (2018)

Evaluation of Detection and Segmentation Tasks on Driving Datasets

Deepak Singh[1]([✉]), Ameet Rahane[2], Ajoy Mondal[1], Anbumani Subramanian[3], and C. V. Jawahar[1]

[1] International Institute of Information Technology, Hyderabad, India
deepak.singh@research.iiit.ac.in, {ajoy.mondal,jawahar}@iiit.ac.in
[2] University of California, Berkeley, Berkeley, USA
ameetrahane@berkeley.edu
[3] Intel, Bangalore, India
anbumani.subramanian@intel.com

Abstract. Object detection, semantic segmentation, and instance segmentation form the bases for many computer vision tasks in autonomous driving. The complexity of these tasks increases as we shift from object detection to instance segmentation. The state-of-the-art models are evaluated on standard datasets such as PASCAL-VOC and MS-COCOC, which do not consider the dynamics of road scenes. Driving datasets such as Cityscapes and Berkeley Deep Drive (BDD) are captured in a structured environment with better road markings and fewer variations in the appearance of objects and background. However, the same does not hold for Indian roads. The Indian Driving Dataset (IDD) is captured in unstructured driving scenarios and is highly challenging for a model due to its diversity. This work presents a comprehensive evaluation of state-of-the-art models on object detection, semantic segmentation, and instance segmentation on-road scene datasets. We present our analyses and compare their quantitative and qualitative performance on structured driving datasets (Cityscapes and BDD) and the unstructured driving dataset (IDD); understanding the behavior on these datasets helps in addressing various practical issues and helps in creating real-life applications.

Keywords: Object detection · Semantic segmentation · Instance segmentation

1 Introduction

In computer vision, the granularity of the label increases as we move from object detection to instance segmentation. We perform classification and localization of the objects of interest in object detection, but in semantic segmentation, we also consider the boundary of each object during classification. Further in instance segmentation, we differentiate each instance of the object during segmentation. Figure 1 captures the increasing complexity in each of the tasks.

B. Raman et al. (Eds.): CVIP 2021, CCIS 1567, pp. 512–524, 2022.
https://doi.org/10.1007/978-3-031-11346-8_44

For autonomous driving applications, datasets like Cityscapes [8], BDD [34] and IDD [27] are collected in structured and unstructured driving conditions respectively. Academic datasets such as PASCAL-VOC [9] and MS-COCO [19] are commonly used for benchmark object detection, semantic segmentation, and instance segmentation.

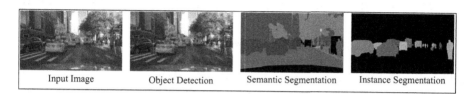

Input Image   Object Detection   Semantic Segmentation   Instance Segmentation

Fig. 1. Illustrates popular tasks of computer vision on road scenes. We can notice that the granularity of the label becomes more complex as we move from Object Detection to Instance Segmentation. (Best viewed in color and zoomed). (Color figure online)

Our **contributions** in this work comprise of evaluation and analyses of various state-of-the-art deep learning models on object detection, semantic segmentation, and instance segmentation with structured datasets - Cityscapes [8] and BDD [34], and an unstructured driving dataset - IDD [27]. We evaluate the performances with:

(i) four object detectors: Faster R-CNN [25], SSD [20], RetinaNet [18], and YOLOv3 [24],
(ii) three semantic segmentation architectures: PSPNet [37], ERFNet [26], and DRN [35], and
(iii) three instance segmentation techniques—Mask R-CNN [12], Cascade Mask R-CNN [4], and Mask Scoring R-CNN [14].

To our knowledge, this is the first comprehensive work to use driving datasets instead of standard academic datasets such as PASCAL-VOC [9] and MS-COCO [19], to perform quantitative and qualitative analyses of various deep learning models on multiple tasks. Understanding the behavior of state-of-the-art object detection, semantic segmentation, and instance segmentation techniques on driving sequences play a vital role in creating real-life applications.

2   Related Work

Object Detection: Existing Deep Convolutional Neural Network (DCNN) based object detectors are of two categories: (i) two-stage detectors and (ii) one-stage detectors. The two-stage detectors comprises of a region-proposal step, region classification and regression step. Some popular works include [10,11,25], several modified architectures [4,12] have also been developed to improve detection accuracy. Though two-stage detectors produce high accuracy, they cannot be used for real-time applications due to their high computation time. In contrast, one-stage detectors predict boxes from input images directly without a region proposal step and hence are time efficient, lending their use for real-time applications. The notable work of Redmon *et al.* in YOLO [22] laid the foundation for several other versions such as YOLOv2 [23] and YOLOv3 [24]. Other popular one-stage object detectors are SSD [20], MT-DSSD [1], RetinaNet [18], M2Det [38], and RefineDet [36].

Semantic Segmentation: Deep Convolutional Neural Network (DCNN) based semantic segmentation techniques demonstrate improvements by replacing the fully-connected layer in image classification network with convolution layers, calling it Fully Convolutional Network (FCN) [21]. Several methods [6,37] have been developed to overcome the limitations of FCN [21]. While methods [7,21,37] have been developed by combining multi-scale features to improve the segmentation performance, another approaches [2,6] involve semantic segmentation based on structure prediction. Running DCNNs on mobile platforms (e.g., drones, robots, and smartphones) requires networks to work in real-time on embedded devices with space and memory constraints. Some lightweight networks in real-time semantic segmentation do exist [26,29,30] in the literature.

Instance Segmentation: Instance segmentation assigns different labels to each instance of an object belonging to the same category. Pose estimation, surveillance, robotics, and self-driving cars are areas where instance segmentation plays a key role. Instance segmentation techniques are of two categories: (i) two-stage, and (i) one-stage. Some of the latest works for two-stage approaches constitutes Mask R-CNN [12], Cascade Mask R-CNN [4], Mask Scoring R-CNN [14], CenterMask [16], BCNet [15]. The popular examples of one-stage methods are PolarMask [32], YOLOACT [3], and SOLO [28].

3   Experiments

3.1   Datasets

We aim to understand the effects of various state state-of-the-art models on diverse road scene datasets for our experiments. We considered two structured driving datasets; Cityscapes and Berkeley DeepDrive (BDD). In these two datasets, there is low variation in the appearance of objects and also in the background, the road infrastructure is well delineated with proper markings on the road. The same assumptions do not hold for Indian driving conditions. For unstructured driving sequences, we consider the Indian Driving Dataset (IDD) dataset.

Cityscapes [8]*:* is a large scale dataset with urban scenes collected in 50 different cities across Europe. It provides 5000 frames of high-quality pixel-level (fine) annotations and a large set of 20000 weakly (coarse) annotated frames. There are 30 labeled classes, and each image can consist of multiple instances of each class.

Berkeley DeepDrive (BDD) [34]: is a diverse and large-scale dataset of visual driving scenes. It consists of over 100K video clips. Each video is about 40 seconds long, 720p, and 30 fps. The videos are recorded using mobile phones, under different weather conditions and are collected from multiple cities in the United States. The dataset is split into training (70K), validation (10K), and testing (20K) sets.

Indian Driving Dataset (IDD) [27]: is a dataset of road scenes from unstructured environments in India. It consists of 10004 images, finely annotated with 34 classes collected from 182 drive sequences on Indian roads. A four-level label hierarchy provides varying degrees of complexity. It also has the fallback class to accommodate unknown road objects.

3.2   Setup

For object detection and instance segmentation, we use the popular frameworks Detectron2 [31] and mmdetection [5]. The code is written in PyTorch and executed on a machine with 4 NVIDIA's GeForce GTX 1080 Ti GPUs with CUDA 10.2, CUDNN 7.6.5. Each detector model is trained with a batch of 8 images, learning rate of 0.02, momentum of 0.9, and weight decay factor of 0.0001.

Each instance segmentation model is trained on a base learning rate of 0.01 with other hyper-parameters being the same as the object detection training. For instance segmentation, we train Mask R-CNN [12] model on a ResNet-50 [13] backbone with a base learning rate of 0.01 for 24000 iterations. In Cascaded Mask R-CNN [4] model, we use base learning rate of 0.02 for 27000 iterations. While Mask Scoring R-CNN [14] model has the backbone of ResNeXt-101 [33] with base learning rate of 0.02. We use momentum of 0.9, weight decay of 0.0001, and batch size of 8 for all models.

In the case of semantic segmentation, we use the hyper-parameters as defined in the literature of the respective models. We use two NVIDIA's GeForce GTX 1080 TI GPUs in a Xeon server in order to train the models.

3.3   Performance Metric

We evaluate object detection performance with the widely used mean Average Precision (mAP) [18, 20, 24, 25] metric. We denote AP for bounding box as AP_{box} and mask as AP_{mask}. We also provide class-wise AP_{box} and AP_{mask} for class-wise analysis at a threshold of 0.5. For semantic segmentation evaluation, we use the common metric of mIoU [21, 26, 37]. For instance segmentation evaluation, we use the Average Precision (AP) metric [4, 12, 17]. As in [19], we calculate AP by varying the Intersection over Union (IoU) threshold from 0.5 to 0.95 with a step of 0.05.

4 Results

4.1 Object Detection

Baselines: We choose Faster R-CNN [25] as a two-stage detector, and SSD [20], YOLOV3 [24], and RetinaNet [18] as one-stage detectors for the object detection task.

Table 1. Shows results of object detection: Class-wise Average Precision (AP) on Cityscapes, BDD, and IDD datasets using Faster R-CNN, SSD, YOLOv3, and RetinaNet. The last row indicates mean Average Precision (mAP). m. cycle: indicates motorcycle, t. light: indicates traffic-light, t. sign: indicates traffic-sign, and veh. flbk: indicates vehicle-fallback. FR, Y3, and RN: indicates Faster R-CNN, YOLOv3, and RetinaNet, respectively. The bold values indicate the category wise best result among all the methods on respective datasets.

Class	Cityscapes				BDD				IDD			
	FR	SSD	Y3	RN	FR	SSD	Y3	RN	FR	SSD	Y3	RN
person	49.9	30.8	43.5	**51.0**	62.2	45.8	59.1	**65.0**	55.9	41.6	50.2	**57.2**
truck	35.2	32.4	30.9	**38.8**	61.9	59.7	58.7	**63.2**	**68.4**	61.3	57.8	66.8
m. cycle	36.4	32.4	34.8	**41.0**	45.5	34.7	46.0	**46.5**	**70.6**	62.8	63.1	68.6
rider	55.9	37.1	51.3	**56.9**	**48.3**	33.3	47.7	46.8	**59.5**	49.0	54.3	58.1
bus	**63.7**	58.3	58.3	60.9	61.7	60.2	59.4	**62.5**	**74.1**	69.5	67.3	73.5
bicycle	47.4	39.7	44.6	**50.7**	50.0	39.8	46.9	**51.7**	**54.8**	39.3	41.3	52.8
car	67.0	65.0	66.4	**69.8**	79.4	75.9	76.2	**80.6**	71.0	65.6	64.5	**71.0**
train	40.9	**47.6**	39.5	45.5	0.0	0.0	**3.3**	0.0	0.0	0.0	0.0	0.0
t. light	-	-	-	-	64.3	53.9	57.1	63.1	28.5	13.8	25.5	**29.4**
t. sign	-	-	-	-	69.8	64.6	66.5	69.2	**39.5**	27.6	27.3	38.3
caravan	-	-	-	-	-	-	-	-	0.0	0.0	0.0	0.0
auto	-	-	-	-	-	-	-	-	**74.1**	66.9	67.9	73.6
trailer	-	-	-	-	-	-	-	-	0.0	0.0	0.0	0.5
animal	-	-	-	-	-	-	-	-	26.4	20.1	20.2	**28.1**
veh. flbk	-	-	-	-	-	-	-	-	**10.0**	7.9	6.7	**10.0**
mAP	49.6	42.9	46.2	**51.8**	54.3	46.8	52.1	**54.8**	**42.2**	35.0	36.4	41.9

Discussion: Table 1 presents object detection results using Faster R-CNN, SSD, YOLO3, and RetinaNet on Cityscapes, BDD, and IDD datasets. From the table, we observe that RetinaNet performs better than all other detectors on the structured driving datasets: Cityscapes and BDD. While Faster R-CNN obtains the best detection results among all the used models on the unstructured driving dataset: IDD. In the case of IDD, we also observe that all the used methods completely fail to detect objects like *train, caravan,* and *trailer* (AP very close to 0). It happens because of fewer amount of annotated images for those categories and unstructured road conditions. For a similar reason, all the methods obtain less than 30% AP scores for object categories such as *traffic-light, traffic-sign, animal,* and *vehicle-fallback.* We also observe from the table that all models perform better on Cityscapes than IDD and BDD datasets for the object category *train.* This is because of domain shift and ubiquitous presence of the object in Cityscapes than on IDD and BDD. We find similar observation for object categories *traffic-light* and *traffic-sign* on which all the used models perform better on BDD than IDD due to geographic domain shift.

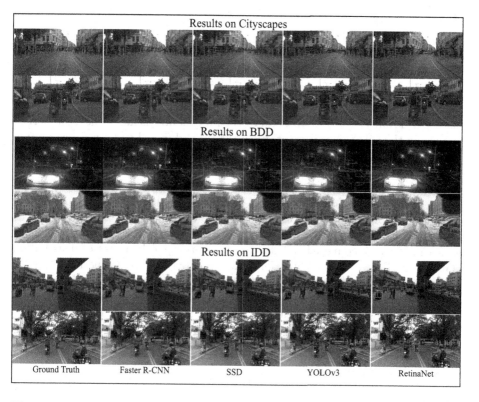

Fig. 2. Presents some qualitative results of object detection on Cityscapes, BDD, and IDD datasets. (Best viewed in color and zoomed). (Color figure online)

We present some qualitative results on few selected frames of Cityscapes, BDD, and IDD using the models: Faster R-CNN, SSD, YOLOv3, and RetinaNet in Fig. 2. We choose frames under various complex conditions to establish the robustness of the used models. In Cityscapes, one of the selected frames is an empty road with multiple pedestrians walking on the left and right sides of the road, and another image of dense traffic. We notice that Faster R-CNN, YOLOv3, and SSD detect accurate boundaries of all motorcycles and cars. But RetinaNet fails to detect the boundaries of a few cars. In the case of BDD, the selected frames are of moving cars on the road at nighttime and during snowfall. In both cases, YOLOv3 and SSD detect all cars accurately. While Faster R-CNN and RetinaNet fail to detect cars that are far away from the camera. In nighttime scenarios, we notice some false detection of *traffic-light* and *traffic-sign* caused due to headlights of vehicles. Notice that even in such challenging scenarios, all the models detect all trainable classes. However, Faster R-CNN and RetinaNet fail to detect a few people accurately due to heavy occlusions caused by crowded vehicles and the shadows cast by the trees.

4.2   Semantic Segmentation

Baselines: We choose three popular models, PSPNet, ERFNet, and DRN to benchmark semantic segmentation task on driving sequences.

Discussion: Quantitative score (mIoU) produced by the models are given in Table 2. We train and evaluate a model on various pair-wise combinations of datasets. From the table, we observe that all models achieve the best performance on the Cityscapes dataset. Even the trained model on Cityscapes is often considered a baseline for the segmentation of driving sequences.

It is also interesting to note that the trained model on Cityscapes does not generalize well. Using the model trained on Cityscapes to infer on BDD and IDD (data distribution is different from Cityscapes) resulted in lower performance (almost half of original). From the table, we also infer that Cityscapes is the simplest to learn while IDD is slightly more difficult, and BDD is the most difficult to learn. The trained model on Cityscapes performs poorly on out-of-distribution data points (i.e., IDD and BDD). The trained model on IDD also performs poorly on out-of-distribution data (i.e., BDD and Cityscapes), but it is relatively better than the model trained on Cityscapes. The trained model on BDD performs the best on out-of-distribution data (i.e., IDD and Cityscapes).

Table 2. Shows quantitative results on semantic segmentation: results of three different models: PSPNet, ERFNet, and DRN. The model is trained on one dataset but evaluated on all other three datasets. Values in bold indicates best result among all the methods on respective test dataset.

Training set	Test set								
	Cityscapes			BDD			IDD		
	PSP Net	ERF Net	DRN	PSP Net	ERF Net	DRN	PSP Net	ERF Net	DRN
Cityscapes	**76.99**	72.20	71.35	35.06	29.37	38.72	38.46	31.37	40.30
BDD	43.75	33.95	50.77	47.40	37.84	**56.34**	39.70	30.10	46.19
IDD	42.69	28.31	46.43	39.51	28.89	41.91	62.95	59.39	**74.69**

Figure 3 shows visual results of semantic segmentation on Cityscapes, BDD, and IDD datasets using DRN. In the case of Cityscapes, the example images shown are (i) of a road with few moving cars and has adjacent buildings on both sides, (ii) a road with a single car and dense buildings and trees on both

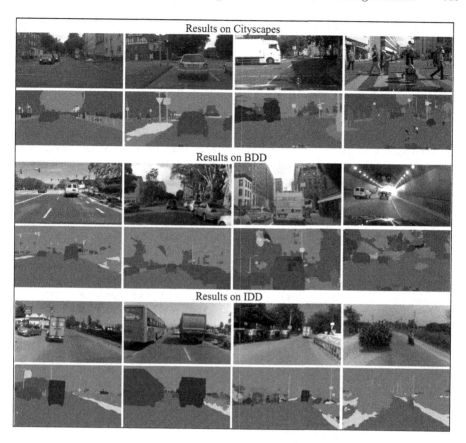

Fig. 3. Presents some qualitative results of semantic segmentation on few selected frames of Cityscapes, BDD, and IDD datasets using DRN-D 38. (Best viewed in color and zoomed). (Color figure online)

sides, (iii) a big truck is crossing a road with shadow cast by road side's trees and buildings, and (iv) multiple people are crossing a road. DRN produces few false segmentation for all images. While the example images of BDD are of (i) a clean road with few moving cars, (ii) a road with many cars and shadow cast by the roadside adjacent trees, (iii) moving trucks and cars on a road with dense adjacent big buildings, and (iv) car moving under the tunnel. In this case, DRN segments well on the first two images. However, due to dense adjacent buildings and lights in the tunnel, it produces few false segmentation for the third and fourth images. The selected images from IDD contain (i) a clean road with two cars, (ii) road with a bus and a truck, overtaking each other, (iii) a road with dense autos and dense trees on the road's side, and (iv) road with one moving motorcycle. DRN performs reasonably well for all images except the third image where the performance drops due to dense vehicles and adjacent roadside trees.

4.3   Instance Segmentation

Baselines: We use three popular existing models—Mask R-CNN (MR), Cascade R-CNN (CR), and Mask Scoring R-CNN (MSR) to benchmark instance segmentation tasks on driving datasets.

Table 3. Shows results on instance segmentation: Class-wise AP_{box} and AP_{mask} scores on Cityscapes, BDD, and IDD datasets. **MR, CM, MSR:** indicates Mask R-CNN, Cascaded Mask R-CNN, and Mask Scoring R-CNN, respectively. Values in bold indicates the best results among all the methods on respective datasets.

Class	Metric	Cityscapes			BDD			IDD		
		MR	CM	MSR	MR	CM	MSR	MR	CM	MSR
person	AP_{box}	**41.6**	32.3	33.8	31.0	**37.3**	32.7	**35.6**	31.2	29.1
	AP_{mask}	**34.0**	23.9	25.7	25.3	**32.7**	30.2	**31.5**	27.1	25.2
truck	AP_{box}	**35.2**	23.7	25.7	28.8	**34.0**	28.2	**54.1**	52.7	49.5
	AP_{mask}	**35.7**	23.6	26.8	27.9	**33.4**	27.9	**53.1**	50.3	49.6
motorcycle	AP_{box}	**29.5**	18.4	23.7	25.3	28.7	**28.9**	39.9	38.5	35.1
	AP_{mask}	**22.5**	12.6	15.5	15.5	16.8	**17.8**	32.2	30.6	28.2
rider	AP_{box}	**43.7**	36.9	37.6	21.0	20.5	**21.6**	39.5	37.4	34.3
	AP_{mask}	**29.2**	21.0	21.8	08.8	11.7	**11.8**	29.4	27.3	24.4
bus	AP_{box}	**60.1**	52.5	42.5	30.8	**35.5**	27.7	**49.5**	48.1	43.4
	AP_{mask}	**58.8**	49.5	42.0	30.0	**35.4**	28.9	**47.9**	45.3	43.8
bicycle	AP_{box}	**34.7**	25.9	30.4	11.5	**13.5**	10.7	**24.3**	20.5	20.4
	AP_{mask}	**22.9**	15.7	15.8	05.6	**08.3**	07.9	**14.3**	12.1	11.7
train	AP_{box}	**28.8**	14.7	9.5	0.0	0.0	0.0	-	-	-
	AP_{mask}	**42.1**	25.2	13.2	0.0	0.0	0.0	-	-	-
car	AP_{box}	**58.4**	50.8	52.6	48.0	**52.4**	47.6	**54.1**	51.9	48.6
	AP_{mask}	**52.5**	44.2	45.1	44.1	**48.6**	45.4	**50.2**	47.1	45.4
autorickshaw	AP_{box}	-	-	-	-	-	-	**55.5**	53.9	50.0
	AP_{mask}	-	-	-	-	-	-	**52.4**	48.9	47.1
vehicle-fallback	AP_{box}	-	-	-	-	-	-	**04.5**	03.8	02.8
	AP_{mask}	-	-	-	-	-	-	**03.9**	03.2	02.5
Average	AP_{box}	**41.5**	31.9	31.9	24.5	**27.7**	24.6	**39.7**	37.5	34.8
	AP_{mask}	**37.2**	26.9	25.7	19.7	**23.3**	21.2	**34.9**	32.4	30.9

Discussion: Table 3 shows the class-wise AP_{box} and AP_{mask} scores on Cityscapes, BDD, and IDD datasets. We notice that for all object categories, Mask R-CNN obtains the best AP_box and AP_mask scores among all methods for Cityscapes and IDD. While Cascade Mask R-CNN obtains the best AP_{box} and AP_{mask} scores for majority of object classes (except *motorcycle* and *rider*) in case of BDD. For Cityscapes, Mask Scoring R-CNN produces the worse AP_{box} and AP_{mask} scores which are 9.5% and 11.4% lower than that of Mask R-CNN.

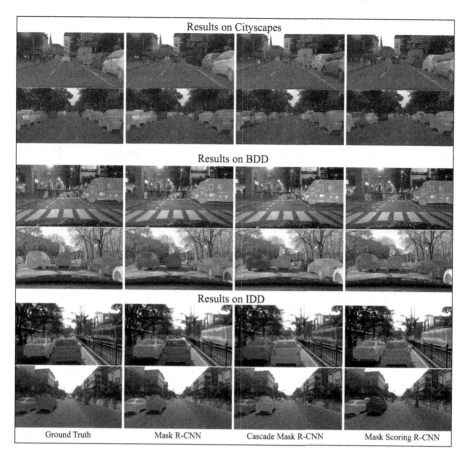

Fig. 4. Shows some qualitative results on instance segmentation showing both mask and bounding boxes of a few selected frames from Cityscapes, BDD, and IDD datasets. (Best viewed in color and zoomed). (Color figure online)

For *motorcycle* and *train* object categories of Cityscapes, the performances of the two techniques—Cascade Mask R-CNN and Mask Scoring R-CNN drops more than 10% compared to Mask R-CNN. In BDD, we notice that for the object category car, all methods obtain AP_{box} and AP_{mask} scores more than 44%. We also notice that Cascade Mask R-CNN obtains the best average AP_{box} and AP_{mask} and Mask R-CNN obtains the worse results among the used methods. In case of IDD, we notice that the AP_{box} score is higher (more than 39%) for commonly found road objects such as *autorickshaw, truck, bus*, and *car*. While the AP_{mask} score for *person* and *rider* classes is very alike due to similar looking visual features. Among the object categories, all methods achieve the lowest AP_{box} and AP_{mask} for *vehicle-fallback*. MR obtains the best AP_{box} and AP_{mask} scores compared to other techniques. While MSR produces the worse average AP_{box} and AP_{mask} scores which are 4.8% and 4%, respectively less than MR.

From the table, we also observe that the performances of all methods are worse on BDD as compared to Cityscapes and IDD. This is because sequences of BDD are captured under several complex conditions. The quantitative results highlight that BDD is more complex than IDD and Cityscapes for instance segmentation. While IDD is more complex than Cityscapes for the same task.

Figure 4 shows the qualitative results of a few randomly selected frames. Images of the first and second rows are from Cityscapes. Both images show multiple cars moving on the left and right sides of the road. From the figure, we notice that Mask R-CNN produces better results on overlapping cars. However, both Cascade Mask R-CNN and Mask Scoring R-CNN fail to segment instances of a car far away from the camera. The image in the third row shows a crowded traffic junction and multiple pedestrians are crossing the road in BDD. We notice that Cascade Mask R-CNN can accurately segment instances of small pedestrians than Mask R-CNN and Mask Scoring R-CNN. Images of the fourth row present multiple moving cars on a road, with shadows cast by roadside trees. In this case, Mask Scoring R-CNN obtains the best results. Images of fifth and sixth rows are taken from IDD and include multiple overlapping vehicles of varying scales on a road with dense buildings on both sides. In both the cases, Mask R-CNN produces better results than Cascade Mask R-CNN and Mask scoring R-CNN.

5   Summary

In this work, we used various state-of-the-art models for object detection, semantic segmentation, and instance segmentation tasks and evaluate their characteristics on structured and unstructured driving datasets: Cityscapes, BDD, and IDD. To our knowledge, this work is the first comprehensive report on analyses of models for tasks with driving datasets. All the methods performed significantly better on object category *train* in Cityscapes than on BDD and IDD in the object detection task. Due to the unstructured nature, object detection tasks on IDD performed lower compared to Cityscapes and BDD. Cityscapes is the easiest dataset for object detection tasks among the three datasets being used. In semantic segmentation, we notice that all models perform better on Cityscapes than on BDD and IDD. We also notice that the DRN model performs consistently well across all the driving datasets compared to other models. In instance segmentation, we observe that Mask R-CNN performs better than all other models on Cityscapes and IDD, while Cascade Mask R-CNN performs better for the majority of the object categories of BDD. Looking at the complexity of the dataset for different tasks, we notice that for instance segmentation and semantic segmentation tasks, BDD is a more complex dataset than Cityscapes and IDD.

A further study on identifying and addressing the problems inherent in road scene datasets can help in a better generalization. An empirical study on domain adaptation and domain generalization can be performed to further understand the behavior of the models in different geographic and environmental settings.

Acknowledgements. This work was partly funded by IHub-Data at IIIT-Hyderabad.

References

1. Araki, R., Onishi, T., Hirakawa, T., Yamashita, T., Fujiyoshi, H.: MT-DSSD: deconvolutional single shot detector using multi task learning for object detection, segmentation, and grasping detection. In: ICRA (2020)
2. Arnab, A., Jayasumana, S., Zheng, S., Torr, P.H.: Higher order Conditional Random Fields in deep neural networks. In: ECCV (2016)
3. Bolya, D., Zhou, C., Xiao, F., Lee, Y.: YOLACT: real-time instance segmentation. In: ICCV (2019)
4. Cai, Z., Vasconcelos, N.: Cascade R-CNN: High quality object detection and instance segmentation. IEEE Trans. PAMI (2019)
5. Chen, K., et al.: MMDetection: Open MMLab detection toolbox and benchmark. arXiv (2019)
6. Chen, L.C., Papandreou, G., Kokkinos, I., Murphy, K., Yuille, A.L.: Deeplab: Semantic image segmentation with deep convolutional nets, atrous convolution, and fully connected CRFs. IEEE Trans. PAMI (2018)
7. Chen, L.C., Yang, Y., Wang, J., Xu, W., Yuille, A.L.: Attention to scale: scale-aware semantic image segmentation. In: CVPR (2016)
8. Cordts, M., et al.: The Cityscapes dataset for semantic urban scene understanding. In: CVPR (2016)
9. Everingham, M., Van Gool, L., Williams, C.K., Winn, J., Zisserman, A.: The pascal visual object classes (voc) challenge. IJCV (2010)
10. Girshick, R.: Fast R-CNN. In: ICCV (2015)
11. Girshick, R., Donahue, J., Darrell, T., Malik, J.: Rich feature hierarchies for accurate object detection and semantic segmentation. In: CVPR (2014)
12. He, K., Gkioxari, G., Dollár, P., Girshick, R.: Mask R-CNN. In: CVPR (2017)
13. He, K., Zhang, X., Ren, S., Sun, J.: Deep residual learning for image recognition. In: CVPR (2016)
14. Huang, Z., Huang, L., Gong, Y., Huang, C., Wang, X.: Mask Scoring R-CNN. In: CVPR (2019)
15. Ke, L., Tai, Y.W., Tang, C.K.: Deep occlusion-aware instance segmentation with overlapping bilayers. In: CVPR (2021)
16. Lee, Y., Park, J.: Centermask: Real-time anchor-free instance segmentation. In: CVPR (2020)
17. Liang, X., Lin, L., Wei, Y., Shen, X., Yang, J., Yan, S.: Proposal-free network for instance-level object segmentation. IEEE Trans. PAMI (2017)
18. Lin, T.Y., Goyal, P., Girshick, R., He, K., Dollár, P.: Focal loss for dense object detection. In: ICCV (2017)
19. Lin, T.Y., et al.: Microsoft COCO: common objects in context. In: ECCV (2014)
20. Liu, W., Anguelov, D., Erhan, D., Szegedy, C., Reed, S., Fu, C.Y., Berg, A.C.: SSD: Single shot multibox detector. In: ECCV (2015)
21. Long, J., Shelhamer, E., Darrell, T.: Fully convolutional networks for semantic segmentation. In: CVPR (2015)
22. Redmon, J., Divvala, S., Girshick, R., Farhadi, A.: You only look once: Unified, real-time object detection. In: CVPR (2016)
23. Redmon, J., Farhadi, A.: YOLO9000: Better, faster, stronger. In: CVPR (2017)
24. Redmon, J., Farhadi, A.: YOLOv3: An incremental improvement. arXiv (2018)
25. Ren, S., He, K., Girshick, R., Sun, J.: Faster R-CNN: Towards real-time object detection with region proposal networks. In: NeurIPS (2015)

26. Romera, E., Alvarez, J.M., Bergasa, L.M., Arroyo, R.: ERFNet: efficient residual factorized convnet for real-time semantic segmentation. IEEE Trans. Intell. Transp. Syst. (2018)

27. Varma, G., Subramanian, A., Namboodiri, A., Chandraker, M., Jawahar, C.: IDD: A dataset for exploring problems of autonomous navigation in unconstrained environments. In: WACV (2019)

28. Wang, X., Kong, T., Shen, C., Jiang, Y., Li, L.: SOLO: segmenting objects by locations. In: ECCV (2020)

29. Wang, Y., Zhou, Q., Xiong, J., Wu, X., Jin, X.: ESNet: an efficient symmetric network for real-time semantic segmentation. In: PRCV (2019)

30. Wu, T., Tang, S., Zhang, R., Cao, J., Zhang, Y.: CGNet: a light-weight context guided network for semantic segmentation. IEEE Trans. Image Process. (2020)

31. Wu, Y., Kirillov, A., Massa, F., Lo, W.Y., Girshick, R.: Detectron2. https://github.com/facebookresearch/detectron2 (2019)

32. Xie, E., et al.: Polarmask: Single shot instance segmentation with polar representation. In: CVPR (2020)

33. Xie, S., Girshick, R., Dollár, P., Tu, Z., He, K.: Aggregated residual transformations for deep neural networks. In: CVPR (2017)

34. Yu, F., et al.: BDD100k: a diverse driving dataset for heterogeneous multitask learning. In: CVPR (2020)

35. Yu, F., Koltun, V., Funkhouser, T.A.: Dilated residual networks. arXiv (2017)

36. Zhang, S., Wen, L., Bian, X., Lei, Z., Li, S.Z.: Single-shot refinement neural network for object detection. In: CVPR (2018)

37. Zhao, H., Shi, J., Qi, X., Wang, X., Jia, J.: Pyramid scene parsing network. In: CVPR (2017)

38. Zhao, Q., et al.: M2Det: a single-shot object detector based on multi-level feature pyramid network. In: AAAI (2019)

Classification of Gender in Celebrity Cartoon Images

S. Prajna[1]([⊠]), N. Vinay Kumar[2], and D. S. Guru[1]

[1] Department of Studies in Computer Science, Manasagangotri, University of Mysore, Mysuru 570006, India
prajna.s63@gmail.com, dsg@compsci.uni-mysore.ac.in
[2] NTT Data Services, Bangalore, India

Abstract. This paper presents a model by integrating deep architecture-based feature extraction with classical learning algorithms for the effective gender classification of celebrity cartoon images. The proposed model makes use of colored celebrity cartoon images. For face representation, we have extracted features using various conventional approaches such as Scale-Invariant Feature Transform (SIFT), Fast Fourier Transform (FFT), and Discrete Cosine Transform (DCT), and the deep approach using deep features from a pre-trained architecture. After extracting the features to classify the gender of celebrity cartoon images, we have used conventional classifiers. Here in this work, we have recommended the integration of random forest (RF) with deep features extracted from FaceNet pre-trained architecture. We have used an existing dataset, the Cartoon Faces in the wild (IIIT-CFW) database of celebrity cartoon faces consisting of 8928 cartoon images. At the same time, we segregate it into two distinct classes, male and female, comprising 4594 and 2073, respectively. There is an imbalance in the proportion of the dataset; we have attempted to balance the unbalanced data using the SMOTE technique. Lastly, to classify the gender of celebrity cartoon images, we have adopted distinct supervised conventional learning models. The classification results are validated using classification metrics such as accuracy, precision, recall, f-measure. We show that our approach model establishes a state-of-the-art F1-score of 95% on the task of gender recognition of cartoons faces. The model has been compared against other existing contemporary models for its effectiveness.

Keywords: Cartoon images · Feature extraction · Deep features · Classifiers

1 Introduction

Due to immense growth in digital multimedia, cartoons have become a highly noticeable part of the entertainment. Cartoons have got a wide range of applications in entertainment, education, advertisement, and others. Usually, cartoons are used in newspapers, comics, and instant messages mode of communicating information humorously. Thus nowadays, extensive usage of cartoons has drawn research attention in computer graphics and multimedia. Recognition of cartoons characters is challenging meantime to recognize the celebrity in a cartoon is still more demandingly contrasting to original images due to its heterogeneous features within the class. In this direction, categorizing the gender using cartoon images is still more expected to motivate us to classify gender as a binary class problem, which carries a highly distinguished information concern to gender-specific. It aims to recognize the gender of a person based on the characteristics that differentiate between masculinity and femininity. Human beings need to classify gender to have successful communication, and it turns out to be relatively easy for individuals but highly challenging for a computer. Concurrently, when we consider original images, visual information from human faces provides one of the more important sources of information. relating to cartoons, we have vast variation among them due to their design, modeling, and structural representation as it differs from another. Figure 1 Demonstrates the modeling gap between the original images and cartoon images (a) shows the cartoon images of Aishwarya Rai Bachchan limited to the female class (b) illustrates original images conflicting with cartoon images of Aishwarya Rai Bachchan (c) represents cartoon images of Aamir Khan specific to male class (d) original images concern cartoon of Aamir Khan. Subsequently, the facial interpretation of cartoons is highly challenging due to its heterogeneous features specific to the class intangible structural representation and appearance. The approaches used to handle detection and recognition of an original face using facial characteristics may not be so complex as those of cartoons.

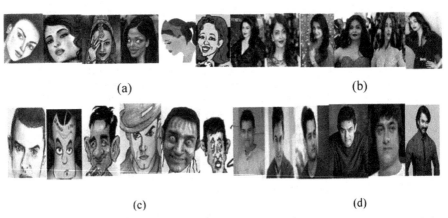

(a)   (b)

(c)   (d)

Fig. 1. Illustration of original and cartoon images (a) Cartoon images of Aishwarya Rai Bachchan (b) Original images of Aishwarya Rai Bachchan (c) Cartoon images of Aamir Khan (d) Original images Aamir Khan

Hence we have attempted to integrate the approaches to handle these cartoon images using conventional classifiers. Due to class imbalance, we have focused on F1-score as a metric for classification than the accuracy score, which tends to bias the majority class. Class imbalance is a quite frequently occurring problem. If we fail to handle it might have a powerful impact on the performance of the model. We have a few techniques to overcome the class imbalance problem, such as re-sampling [12], the training set, k-fold cross-validation, cluster the abundant class is a widely adopted technique for dealing with highly unbalanced datasets. Addressing the re-sampling technique to balance the imbalanced data, we come across two distinct approaches, removing samples from the majority class as under-sampling or adding samples to the minority class as over-sampling. We find a few limitations in the classical over-sampling technique, which tends to duplicate the minority data from a particular minority data population. Meanwhile, it increases data by number, although it does not give new information but tends to over-fit it. While handling the under-sampling, it tends to remove the samples from the majority class, where we may lose some of the relevant information. Thus we have adopted a well-known technique below oversampling of data called SMOTE. To balance the unbalanced data, generate new synthetic samples for the minority class using the k-nearest neighbors algorithm (KNN). To demonstrate all the explored algorithmic models for their effectiveness dataset is a primary requirement for system design and testing. We have demanded a reasonably large dataset of celebrity cartoon images. However, one can trace an attempt towards creating a dataset [4] addition to these celebrity cartoon images, animations, and sketches are determined. This work integrates deep architecture-based feature extraction with classical learning algorithms to classify gender using celebrity cartoon images. We have focused on deep features to recognize the face cartoon images using deep convolutional network architecture [14], a pertained architecture. We have trained cartoon face images from scratch and extracted deep features for facial representation, which outperforms classical learning algorithms.

The following are the contributions of this paper.

- A model by integrating deep architecture-based feature extraction with classical learning algorithms for effective gender classification of celebrity cartoon images
- Exploiting SMOTE technique for balancing the unbalanced data.

1.1 Related Works

In literature, we find a couple of works on detecting and recognizing celebrity cartoon images. Primarily, these works mainly rely on cartoon character images. In [1], face detection of cartoon characters was explored using primitive features such as skin color regions and edges extracted from the given cartoon character images. In [2] have explored the image retargeting techniques for mobile comics by adopting the comic contents to mobile screens for better visualization. Contextual contours depict its structural outline, where this is one of the significant features to be studied. In [3], for face detection, they have incorporated the multitask cascaded convolutional network (MTCNN) architecture and contrasting it to that conventional methods. For face recognition, our two-fold contributions include:(i) an inductive transfer learning approach combining the feature learning capability of the Inception v3 network and the feature recognizing capability of support vector machines (SVMs), (ii) a proposed hybrid convolutional neural network (HCNN) framework trained over a fusion of pixel values and 15 manually located facial key points, shown that the Inception + SVM model establishes a state-of-the-art (SOTA) F1 score on the task of gender recognition of cartoon faces. In [4], an attempt to detect and recognize celebrity cartoon images, the IIIT Hyderabad (IIIT-CFW) database. Also, there a few works are available for the gender classification of celebrity cartoons. Keeping this in mind, we thought of addressing the classification of the gender of celebrity cartoon images. This paper mainly concentrates on only classification. In the literature, there exist some conventional classifiers. Hence we make use of conventional classifiers to classify the gender of celebrity cartoon images. Finally, the proposed system is compared with either model viz., To check the robustness, we have compared our model with the existing dataset. Our system has outperformed the former and latter models in terms of classification metrics. This paper is structured as follows: In Sect. 2, the framework of the proposed model is explained. The Experiments and observations have been presented in Sect. 3. Further, comparison to the proposed model against the existing conventional models are given. Finally, the conclusion remarks are given in Sect. 5.

2 Proposed Model

The proposed model is designed with three stages such as pre-processing, feature extraction, and decision making. The general architecture of the proposed model is presented in Fig. 2. The different stages of the proposed model are explained in the following subsections.

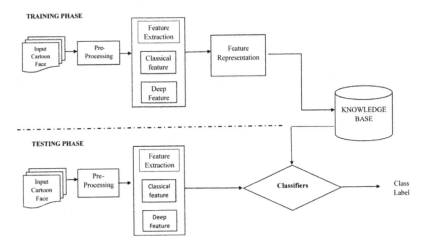

Fig. 2. General architecture of proposed model

2.1 Pre-processing

2.1.1 Face Detection and Cropping

A Common Pre-processing technique considered detecting and cropping the face is also an important task. Regarding this, we manually detect face parts and physically align them based on gender-specific. However, the automation of this task kept beyond the current work.

2.1.2 Class Balancing Through SMOTE Technique

In this sub-section, a unique pre-processing technique is performed with an appropriate procedure for balancing the unbalanced dataset. We use SMOTE oversampling techniques to balance the unbalanced data, which is adapted during the training stage. The SMOTE [12] technique uses a k-nearest neighbors algorithm to create synthetic data points. It identifies the minority class vector and decides the nearest neighbors (k) is considered. Compute a line between the minority data points and any of its neighbors and place a synthetic point. We repeated the process until the unbalanced data was balanced for all minority data points and their k-neighbors.

2.2 Feature Extraction

2.2.1 Classical Features

In this work, we have extracted distinct classical features to classify the gender of celebrity cartoon images. Due to uncompromising structural representation and high variations among the cartoon images, it is highly challenging to extract the most discriminating feature using the conventional approach. Therefore, we explore feature engineering for gender classification by using the classical features as added work. Accordingly, we have used classical features, such as Scale-Invariant Feature Transform (SIFT), Fast Fourier Transform (FFT), Discrete Cosine Transform (DCT) [11] for feature extraction.

2.2.2 Deep Features

In this work, we have used a pre-trained network to extract features for the face representation of cartoon images using a deep network [14]. We train the network using the IIIT-CFW dataset and directly train its output to be a compact 128-D embedding using a triplet-based loss function based on a large nearest neighbors margin. Our triplets consist of two matching faces and nonmatching face images; Loss aims to separate the positive pair from the negative by a distance margin.

2.3 Classifiers

To test the effectiveness of the proposed classification system, we have used five distinct supervised conventional learning models. In the literature, there are plenty of learning models used for face recognition, viz. Support Vector Machines (SVM), K-Nearest Neighbors (K-NN), Decision Tree (DT), Random Forest (RF), Gaussian Naive Bayes (GNB), [5], and so on associated with this ensemble decision tree outperforms well in terms of classification metrics.

2.4 Integrated Model

We propose an integrated model using deep features extracted from FaceNet pre-trained architecture. Deep features extracted from deep architecture [15] perform more efficiently than any classical approach for face recognition. Using deep features from a pertained deep architecture with a Random Forest (RF) classifier [13], We recommend that our model outperforms all the other combinations of classifiers for robust classification (Fig. 3).

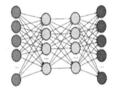

Fig. 3. Depicts the integrated framework of deep features with random forest classifier

3 Experiment Results

3.1 Dataset

Dataset plays a vital role in cartoon celebrity gender classification, the creation of a suitable dataset is crucial for any machine learning application. However, we find an attempt to create the dataset [4]. We have evaluated our model using the existing dataset. The dataset consists of 8928 cartoon faces of 100 public celebrity figures. Simultaneously, we segregate it into two distinct classes, male and female, including 4594 and 2073.

3.2 Experimental Setup

During the stage of pre-processing step, celebrity's cartoon face image is detected and cropped manually, followed by feature extraction: classical features such as Scale Invariant Feature Transform (SIFT), Fast Fourier Transform (FFT), Discrete Cosine Transform DCT, and deep features using Face Net, that directly learns a mapping from face images to a compact Euclidean space where distances directly correspond to a measure of face similarity. We train the network using cartoon images from scratch; these features are extracted from celebrity cartoon images as discussed in Sect. 2.2. Further, the samples of the feature matrix are divided into training samples and testing samples. Due to the unbalanced data distribution, the SMOTE over-sampling technique for the minority class is performed during the training stage. In our proposed classification system, the dataset is divided randomly into training by varying numbers as 60%,70%,80% of cartoon images, respectively, and testing use the remaining 40%, 30%, and 20% cartoon images, respectively, for classifying them as any one of the two classes. The experimentation in testing is repeated for 20 different trials. During testing, the classification results are presented by the confusion matrix. The performance of the classification system is evaluated using classification accuracy, precision, recall, and F-Measure computed from the confusion matrix [13]. However, we concentrate more on other related parameters than accuracy due to accuracy paradoxes to handle the unbalanced data.

3.3 Experimental Results

The performance of the proposed classification system is evaluated based on classification metrics such as accuracy, precision, recall, and F-Measure computed from the confusion matrix. The classification results are obtained for different training and testing splits. These results are measured in terms of accuracy (average), precision (average), recall (average), F-measure (average). To handle the unbalanced data, we focus primarily on the f1-score and recall of the model than the accuracy (Tables 1, 2, 3 and 4, Fig. 4).

Table 1. Performance measures for **sift as a conventional feature** and different classifiers under varied training and testing percentage of samples on Cartoon Faces in the wild (IIIT-CFW) dataset.

Classifiers	Splits	Gender	Precision	Recall	F1-score	Accuracy
SIFT + SVM	60–40	Female	0.60	0.63	0.62	0.61
		Male	0.61	0.58	0.59	
	70–30	Female	0.61	0.63	0.62	0.61
		Male	0.61	0.59	0.60	
	80–20	Female	0.61	0.65	0.63	0.62
		Male	0.63	0.59	0.61	
SIFT + KNN	60–40	Female	0.53	0.97	0.69	0.56
		Male	0.87	0.15	0.26	
	70–30	Female	0.54	0.97	0.69	0.57
		Male	0.89	0.17	0.29	
	80–20	Female	0.53	0.97	0.69	0.57
		Male	0.88	0.16	0.27	
SIFT + DT	60–40	Female	0.67	0.69	0.68	0.67
		Male	0.68	0.66	0.67	
	70–30	Female	0.67	0.70	0.69	0.68
		Male	0.69	0.66	0.68	
	80–20	Female	0.69	0.72	0.70	0.70
		Male	0.70	0.68	0.69	
SIFT + RF	60–40	Female	0.87	0.74	0.80	0.81
		Male	0.77	0.88	0.83	
	70–30	Female	0.86	0.75	0.80	0.81
		Male	0.78	0.88	0.82	
	80–20	Female	0.87	0.75	0.80	0.82
		Male	0.78	0.88	0.83	
SIFT + GNB	60–40	Female	0.63	0.65	0.64	0.63
		Male	0.64	0.61	0.63	
	70–30	Female	0.62	0.63	0.63	0.63
		Male	0.63	0.62	0.62	
	80–20	Female	0.63	0.62	0.62	0.62
		Male	0.62	0.63	0.63	

Table 2. Performance measures for **FFT as a conventional feature** and different classifiers under varied training and testing percentage of samples on Cartoon Faces in the wild (IIIT-CFW) dataset.

Classifiers	Splits	Gender	Precision	Recall	F1-Score	Accuracy
FFT + SVM	60–40	Female	0.40	0.45	0.43	0.75
		Male	0.86	0.83	0.84	
	70–30	Female	0.41	0.46	0.43	0.76
		Male	0.86	0.83	0.84	
	80–20	Female	0.40	0.43	0.41	0.76
		Male	0.85	0.84	0.84	
FFT + KNN	60–40	Female	0.42	0.44	0.43	0.76
		Male	0.85	0.84	0.85	
	70–30	Female	0.40	0.48	0.44	0.75
		Male	0.86	0.81	0.84	
	80–20	Female	0.45	0.58	0.51	0.77
		Male	0.88	0.82	0.85	
FFT + DT	60–40	Female	0.30	0.40	0.34	0.70
		Male	0.83	0.77	0.80	
	70–30	Female	0.31	0.33	0.32	0.72
		Male	0.83	0.81	0.82	
	80–20	Female	0.30	0.41	0.35	0.69
		Male	0.84	0.76	0.80	
FFT + RF	60–40	Female	0.63	0.58	0.10	0.80
		Male	0.80	0.99	0.89	
	70–30	Female	0.50	0.22	0.42	0.80
		Male	0.80	0.99	0.88	
	80–20	Female	0.63	0.11	0.19	0.81
		Male	0.81	0.98	0.89	
FFT + GNB	60–40	Female	0.22	0.54	0.31	0.53
		Male	0.82	0.53	0.64	
	70–30	Female	0.22	0.54	0.31	0.53
		Male	0.82	0.53	0.64	
	80–20	Female	0.22	0.53	0.32	0.54
		Male	0.82	0.55	0.66	

Table 3. Performance measures for **dct as a conventional feature** and different classifiers under varied training and testing percentage of samples on Cartoon Faces in the wild (IIIT-CFW) dataset.

Classifiers	Splits	Gender	Precision	Recall	F1-Score	Accuracy
DCT + SVM	60–40	Female	0.43	0.40	0.42	0.77
		Male	0.85	0.86	0.86	
	70–30	Female	0.47	0.44	0.45	0.78
		Male	0.86	0.87	0.86	
	80–20	Female	0.36	0.36	0.36	0.74
		Male	0.84	0.84	0.84	
DCT + KNN	60–40	Female	0.48	0.35	0.41	0.79
		Male	0.84	0.90	0.87	
	70–30	Female	0.54	0.43	0.48	0.81
		Male	0.86	0.91	0.88	
	80–20	Female	0.54	0.5	0.52	0.81
		Male	0.87	0.89	0.88	
DCT + DT	60–40	Female	0.38	0.42	0.40	0.75
		Male	0.85	0.83	0.84	
	70–30	Female	0.35	0.45	0.40	0.72
		Male	0.85	0.79	0.82	
	80–20	Female	0.31	0.35	0.33	0.71
		Male	0.83	0.80	0.82	
DCT + RF	60–40	Female	0.75	0.025	0.048	0.80
		Male	0.80	0.99	0.89	
	70–30	Female	0.4	0.022	0.042	0.79
		Male	0.80	0.99	0.88	
	80–20	Female	0.2	0.016	0.030	0.79
		Male	0.80	0.98	0.88	
DCT + GNB	60–40	Female	0.20	0.6	0.30	0.46
		Male	0.81	0.43	0.56	
	70–30	Female	0.20	0.57	0.30	0.46
		Male	0.80	0.43	0.56	
	80–20	Female	0.20	0.58	0.30	0.47
		Male	0.81	0.45	0.58	

Table 4. Performance measures for **Deep Feature** and different classifiers under varied training and testing percentage of samples on Cartoon Faces in the wild (IIIT-CFW) dataset.

Classifiers	Splits	Gender	Precision	Recall	F1-score	Accuracy
SVM	60–40	Female	0.94	0.91	0.9	0.93
		Male	0.91	0.94	0.93	
	70–30	Female	0.94	0.92	0.93	0.93
		Male	0.92	0.94	0.93	
	80–20	Female	**0.93**	**0.93**	**0.93**	**0.93**
		Male	**0.93**	**0.93**	**0.93**	
KNN	60–40	Female	0.87	0.99	0.93	0.92
		Male	0.99	0.86	0.92	
	70–30	Female	0.87	0.99	0.92	0.92
		Male	0.98	0.85	0.92	
	80–20	Female	0.86	0.99	0.92	0.91
		Male	0.99	0.84	0.91	
DT	60–40	Female	0.88	0.89	0.89	0.89
		Male	0.89	0.88	0.89	
	70–30	Female	0.89	0.88	0.88	0.88
		Male	0.88	0.89	0.88	
	80–20	Female	0.89	0.90	0.89	0.89
		Male	0.89	0.89	0.89	
RF	60–40	Female	0.95	0.93	0.94	0.94
		Male	0.94	0.95	0.94	
	70–30	Female	**0.95**	**0.95**	**0.95**	**0.95**
		Male	**0.95**	**0.95**	**0.95**	
	80–20	Female	0.95	0.94	0.94	0.94
		Male	0.94	0.95	0.94	
GNB	60–40	Female	0.93	0.87	0.90	0.90
		Male	0.87	0.94	0.91	
	70–30	Female	0.93	0.85	0.89	0.89
		Male	0.86	0.94	0.90	
	80–20	Female	0.93	0.85	0.88	0.89
		Male	0.86	0.93	0.89	

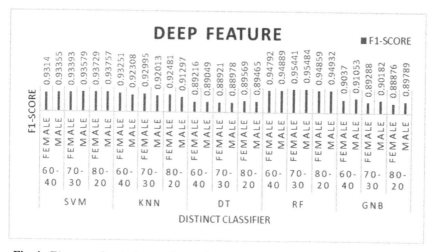

Fig. 4. F1-score of each class under varying percentage of training and testing samples

4 Comparative Analyses

To check the robustness of our proposed model, we embedded it on the IIIT-(CFW) dataset. Our approach outperforms, corresponding to the same set of classifiers used. And in addition to that, "We have demonstrated" the other set of classifiers too. The below table shows the efficiency of the proposed model against the IIIT-CFW dataset. Our model performs well with 93% of F1-score for the Deep feature + Conventional Classifiers (SVM) and 95% of the result concerning the deep feature + Conventional classifier (RF). Table 5 depicts the performance of the models on the task of gender classification of celebrity cartoon faces. Our model outperforms all three metrics on the IIT-(CFW) dataset with a 95% f1-score, recall, and precision, respectively. In the literature [4], data augmentation is performed to handle the imbalanced data, which may not be as effective as our model using the SMOTE technique. Meanwhile, the deep pre-trained architecture used FaceNet is more promising than Inception v3 + SVM for recognition of celebrities in cartoon images, which has been demonstrated using the statistical data in the above tables. Thus, we believe that the scores hold a state-of-the-art (Fig. 5).

Table 5. Performance comparison of our model with respect to other existing models on IIIT-(CFW) Dataset for classification of gender in celebrity cartoon images.

Models		Precision	Recall	F1-score
Proposed model Conventional classifiers on IIIT-(CFW)	**MAX**	**0.95**	**0.95**	**0.95**
	MIN	0.89	0.88	0.88
Inception v3 + SVM on IIIT-(CFW) dataset (Jha et al., 2018)		0.927	0.894	0.91
HCNN on IIIT-(CFW) dataset (Jha et al., 2018)		0.622	0.680	0.516

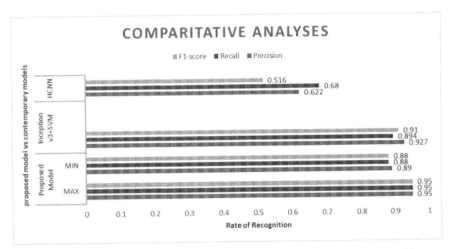

Fig. 5. Graphical Representation of Performance comparison of our proposed model with respect to contemporary models on IIIT-(CFW) Dataset for classification of gender in celebrity cartoon images

5 Conclusion

The study aims to present a model by integrating deep architecture-based feature extraction with classical learning algorithms for the effective gender classification of celebrity cartoon images. Finally, we recommend emphasizing the integration of deep features with a random forest classifier, which outperforms all three metrics. Finally, the work concludes with an understanding that better classification results are obtained from our proposed model compared to other models. We conclude that our model establishes a state-of-the-art F1-score of 0.95% on the classification of Gender in celebrity cartoon images.

References

1. Takayama, K., Johan, H., Nishita, T.: Face detection and face recognition of cartoon characters using feature extraction. In: Image, Electronics and Visual Computing Workshop, p. 48 (2012)
2. Gao, X., Liu, J., Lin, J., Liao, M., Xiang, L.: Contour-preserved retargeting of cartoon images. In: IEEE 17th International Conference on Computational Science and Engineering, pp. 1772–1778, Chengdu (2014)
3. Jha, S., Agarwal, N., Agarwal, S.: Bringing Cartoons to Life: Towards Improved Cartoon Face Detection and Recognition Systems (2018). arXiv preprint arXiv:1804.01753
4. Mishra, A., Rai, S.N., Mishra, A., Jawahar, C.V.: IIIT-CFW: a benchmark database of cartoon faces in the wild. In springer European Conference on Computer Vision, pp. 35–47 (2016)
5. Kotsiantis, S.B., Zaharakis, I.D., Pintelas, P.E.: Machine learning: a review of classification and combining techniques. Artif. Intell. Rev. **26**, 159–190 (2006). https://doi.org/10.1007/s10 462-007-9052-3
6. Arai, Masayuki: Feature extraction methods for cartoon character recognition. IEEE Trans. Image Signal Process., 445–448 (2012)

7. Chen, Y., Lai, Y.-K., Liu, Y.-J.: Cartoongan: generative adversarial networks for photo cartoonization. In: IEEE Conference on Computer Vision and Pattern Recognition, pp. 9465–9474 (2018)

8. Wu, Y., Zhou, X., Lu, T., Mei, G., Sun, L.: EvaToon: a novel graph matching system for evaluating cartoon drawings. In: IEEE 23rd International Conference on Pattern Recognition (ICPR), pp. 1119–1124 (2016)

9. Yu, J., Wang, M., Tao, D.: Semi supervised Multiview distance metric learning for cartoon synthesis. IEEE Trans. Image Process., 4636–4648 (2012)

10. Duda, O.R., Hart, E.P., Stork, G.D.: Pattern Classification, 2nd edn. Wiley-Interscience (2000)

11. Ghorbani, R., Ghousi, R.: Comparing different resampling methods in predicting students' performance using machine learning techniques. IEEE Access 8, 67899–67911 (2020). https://doi.org/10.1109/ACCESS.2020.2986809

12. Nassih, B., et al.: An efficient three-dimensional face recognition system based random forest and geodesic curves. Comput. Geom. 97, 101758 (2021)

13. Powers, D.M.W.: Evaluation: From Precision, Recall and F-Measure to ROC, Informedness, Markedness & Correlation. J. Mach. Learn. Tech. 2(1), 37–63 (2011)

14. Schroff, F., Kalenichenko, D., Philbin, J.: FaceNet: a unified embedding for face recognition and clustering, 815–823 (2015). https://doi.org/10.1109/CVPR.2015.7298682

15. Ben Fredj, H., Bouguezzi, S., Souani, C.: Face recognition in unconstrained environment with CNN. Vis. Comput. 37(2), 217–226 (2021). https://doi.org/10.1007/s00371-020-01794-9

Localization of Polyps in WCE Images Using Deep Learning Segmentation Methods: A Comparative Study

Samir Jain[✉], Ayan Seal, and Aparajita Ojha

PDPM Indian Institute of Information Technology, Jabalpur, India
{samirjain,ayan,aojha}@iiitdmj.ac.in

Abstract. Wireless capsule endoscopy (WCE) is a promising technology for the investigation of gastrointestinal (GI) tracts. Long WCE video pose a challenge before the field experts and therefore automatic identification of anomalous video frames and localization of anomalies is an important research problem. Various segmentation models based on deep learning techniques for object localization have been suggested for different type of applications including biomedical applications. Recently, some researchers have applied these methods for the analysis of WCE images. In this paper four popular deep learning-based segmentation models UNet, SegNet, PSPNet, and Fully Convolutional Network (FCN) are analyzed for their suitability in localization of anomaly. Popular CNN architectures like VGG16, MobileNet, and ResNet50 are used as the base architecture to create the segmentation models. In this work two well known polyp datasets namely ETIS-Larib and CVC-ClinicDB are considered. The outcomes show that UNet and SegNet developed using MobilenetV1 architecture are performing relatively better than other architectures. Mean IoU of 0.910 and 0.883 is achieved using MobileNet-UNet whereas using MobileNet-SegNet it reaches 0.894 and 0.885 on CVC-ClinicDB and ETIS-Larib datasets respectively.

Keywords: Wireless capsule endoscopy · Polyp · Segmentation · Deep learning

1 Introduction

In the medical imaging domain, computer-aided detection (CAD) systems are becoming more popular due to more accurate and precised outcomes with the advent of technologies like artificial intelligence (AI) and computer vision. In today's scenario, medical imaging techniques like X-ray, MRI, ultrasound, endoscopy are getting the aid of AI based CAD systems for the identification of abnormality. WCE is one of the latest development and in the field of endoscopy is explored. WCE helps in the examination of those regions of the GI tracts where conventional endoscopic procedures are unreachable. WCE is a non-invasive GI investigation technique in which a capsule is swallowed by a patient that records

B. Raman et al. (Eds.): CVIP 2021, CCIS 1567, pp. 538–549, 2022.
https://doi.org/10.1007/978-3-031-11346-8_46

a video of the GI system. Computer vision-based WCE analysis tools help in identifying those frames in the video that probably contain anomalies with them and possible location in video frames.

Colorectal cancer also known as colon cancer, rectal cancer, or bowel cancer is one of the most common cancers found in both men and women [16]. Tumor in the form of colonic polyps (CP) appear as abnormal growth on the surface of the colon. Mostly CP's are harmless but they can develop into a cancer with time. These situations can be avoided by regular screening tests where WCE plays an important role. For accurate detection of polyps in WCE images, a CAD-based automatic diagnostic system is quite beneficial. Since the appearance of CP vary in texture, color, and size, manual examination can be a difficult task [22]. Moreover, a complete WCE video, can contain more than $80,000$ frames [11] and scrutinizing the anomalous frames is a tedious task for a physician. Hence, a CAD-based system can assist the physician in diagnosing the CPs from endoscopic images.

Several schemes have been proposed for the detection and segmentation of polyps. Methods incorporating image processing techniques and machine learning algorithms are quite popular. Researchers have suggested the use of various feature descriptors like Grey-Level-Co-Occurrence matrix (GLCM) and Local-Binary-Patterns (LBP) [2] for identification of different types of anomalies in WCE images. Frequently used classifiers like ANN, SVM, KNN are trained on these features for identification of anomalous regions or frames. Recently, deep learning (DL) based methods have come up with better solutions employing convolutional neural networks (CNNs) [1], autoencoder [22], and generative adversarial networks (GANs) [17], etc. In this paper, a comparative study of DL-based pixelwise segmentation methods is performed for the localization of polyps. Four popular models namely PSPNet [23], UNet [14], SegNet [3], FCN [12] are considered for performance comparison. The purpose of the study is to identify the best performing model on the available datasets. Main highlights of the present work are as follows:

- A comparative study is done to record the segmentation performance of DL-based segmentation methods on localization of polyps in WCE images.
- Four popular segmentation methods namely SegNet, UNet, PSPNet, and FCN are considered in this paper.
- Each of the above segmentation method is developed on three popular CNN models, that are VGG16, ResNet50, and MobileNetV1.
- Experiments are performed on two publicly available polyp datasets and the best performing segmentation model is identified based on the localization results.

The paper is organized as follows: a brief survey on the available polyp segmentation methods is contained in Sect. 2. The principle architectures of segmentation models are discussed in Sect. 3. In Sect. 4, experimental results are discussed. Finally, Sect. 5 concludes the paper.

2   Related Work

The existing literature for the segmentation of polyp can be broadly grouped into three categories. First category belongs to the methods that involve primarily the conventional image processing techniques. These include region-based and contour-based techniques. In region-based methods, the whole image is divided into homogeneous regions. Like Bernal et al. [7] suggested a polyp segmentation technique employing a watershed algorithm that divides the image into clusters or regions after which region merging is done based on morphological gradients. Hwang et al. [10] made use of the watershed algorithm with the ellipse fitting method that creates an ellipse along a polyp boundary utilizing the edge information in each region formed by watershed. Active contour (AC) based methods are very common in literature for polyp segmentation. Sasmal et al. [15] projected the idea of the principal component pursuit algorithm, that identifies specular regions, on which the AC method is applied.

The second category is related to researches involving handcrafted feature extraction from images and the application of ML algorithms on those features. As in [20], Tajbakhsh et al. made use of shape features by extracting the edges using discrete cosine transform. After which the shape featured information was utilized for discarding non-polyp edges from the image. Polyp edges were retained by using a voting scheme centered on information related to curve of extracted edges. A voting scheme was suggested followed by a probabilistic candidate selection scheme for the identification of polyps. Prasath et al. [13] suggested a polyp localization technique using vascularization features where textural information was extracted from principle curvatures exploiting information associated with image surface and multiscale directional vesselness stamping.

The final category consists of DL-based techniques. DL-based methods encompasses the capability of automatic feature extraction. Convolutional neural networks (CNN) are quite popular in the field of computer vision and has been extensively used in the medical imaging domain. Various methods suggesting DL-based solutions have been devised for abnormality detection in WCE images. Recently, a CNN-based polyp segmentation model Polyp-Net was proposed by Banik et al. [5]. In Polyp-Net dual-tree wavelet pooled mechanism and a modified level set method, termed as local gradient weighting-embedded level set method was adopted for segmentation of polyps. A 3D-fully convolutional network was proposed by Yu et al. [21] that extracts spatio-temporal features to identify polyp regions. A sliding window mechanism was used to mark the polyp regions. Shin et al. [16] employed region-based CNN model (Inception-ResNet) exploiting transfer learning to highlight polyp regions. A two-stage polyp segmentation method was proposed by Akbari et al. [1] wherein the first stage a variant of FCN, FCN-8S was exploited for segmenting polyp regions. The FCN-8S segmented candidate regions based on extracted features after which post-processing wass performed using Otsu's thresholding method that extracted a binary image. Finally, the largest connected component was taken out that predicted the possible polyp locations.

Table 1. Summary of some state-of-the-art polyp detection and segmentation and methods.

Author	Year	Method	Results	Dataset
Hwang et al. [10]	2007	ML	SE: 93%, SP: 98%	MAYO-CLINIC
Bernal et al. [7]	2011	IP	AC: 72.33%, 70.26%	CVC-COLON, CVC-CLINIC
Tajbaksh et al. [20]	2015	ML	SE: 88%, 48%	CVC-COLON, ASU-MAYO
Prasanth et al. [13]	2015	ML	Qualitative	Private
Yu et al. [21]	2016	CNN	F1: 78.6%	ASU-MAYO
Akbari et al. [1]	2018	FCN	DC:81%	CVC-COLON
Sasmal et al. [15]	2018	PCA	Qualitative	CVC-CLINIC
Shin et al. [16]	2018	CNN	PR: 91.4%	ASU-MAYO
Banik et al. [5]	2020	CNN	DC: 81%	CVC-COLON

3 Methodology

Pixel-based segmentation methods developed on deep learning platform are quite popular when medical imaging is concerned. Before deep learning various methods have been proposed based on independent classification of pixel using handcrafted features. In these conventional methods the image needs to be pre-processed primarily to identify the region of interest (ROI). The candidate patches are extracted from the extracted ROI, and finally the prediction is made. In 2015, Long et al. introduced FCN [12], which was an encoder-decoder architecture, designed for pixel-based segmentation of images. The encoder network produced low-resolution representations of the input image. Decoder in the FCN tries to learn upsampling of the input feature map for generation of class segments. Inspired from this architecture as shown in Fig. 1, various segmentation models have been suggested in the literature. In this work four popular CNN-based segmentation models namely SegNet [3], UNet [14], FCN [12], and PSPNet

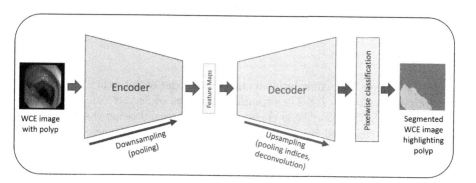

Fig. 1. Block diagram of a typical encoder-decoder network for pixelwise segmentation of images.

[23] are considered and a comparative study is done related to the localization performance on the WCE polyp dataset.

3.1 FCN

An FCN [12] is a deep CNN that performs subsampling and upsampling operations, that is generally employed for semantic segmentation tasks. FCNs extend the architecture of deep CNNs pretrained for classification that are fine tuned entirely convolutionally from whole image inputs and ground truths (see Fig. 2). Outputs from are taken from the convolutional layers of the available classification networks (e.g. VGG16, ResNet32, MobilenetV1) which are passed through upsampling layers added with a mechanism for pixelwise prediction. In a traditional convnet each layer of data is a three-dimensional array of size a × b × f, where a and b correspond to the spatial dimensions, and d refers to the number of features. These features refer to the coarse output maps. Since the repeated application of convolutional layers downsamples the input, upsampling is performed on the feature maps generated by the last convolutional layer. It is achieved by reshaping and adding the deconvolution layers. A pixelwise prediction layer is appended to the tail of the network that finds the relation of points in the output of upsampling layer to the pixels for generation of segmentation mask.

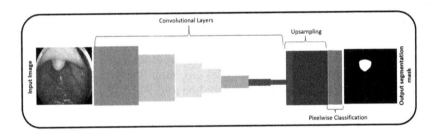

Fig. 2. Simplified block diagram of a typical FCN.

3.2 SegNet

SegNet is a deep fully convolutional encoder-decoder architecture for pixel-wise semantic segmentation [3]. The overall architecture of SegNet can be sliced into three parts. The first part is an encoder network, second being the decoder network which is followed by a final pixel-wise classification layer. The encoder network is used to extract the feature maps (FM) that identify the prominent locations in the input image. Since the encoder network gets narrower with depth, the decoder plays the role of turning low-resolution FMs to higher resolution to meet the size of the input image. The reconstructed image is then fed to the final pixel-wise classification that categorize the pixels to a particular class. SegNet gained popularity with the unique upsampling operation in decoder part.

Specifically, the pooling indices computed in the max-pooling step of the corresponding encoder are used by the decoder to perform non-linear upsampling as displayed in Fig. 3.

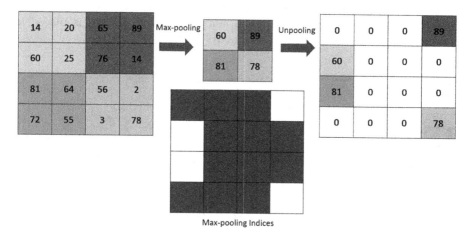

Fig. 3. Max-pooling indices used by SegNet decoder to upsample the input feature map.

3.3 UNet

UNet [14] is also an encoder-decoder architecture just like SegNet discussed above. It is a fully convolutional network without any fully-connected layer. The encoder in UNet is a simple CNN with max-pooling layers. The difference lies in the upsampling part as compared to the SegNet. In UNet there are large number of FM during upsampling. UNet makes use of transposed convolution for upsampling in contrast to SegNet where max-pooling indices are used. UNet concatenates the FM after upsampling with the FMs in the corresponding encoder layer and passes it to the next layer in the decoder network. Hence the concatenation allows more feature maps during upsampling.

3.4 PSPNet

In addition to SegNet and UNet, the pyramid scene parsing network (PSPNet) is also one of the popular networks used for pixel-level segmentation of images [23]. It consists of three different modules, a base CNN, a pyramid pooling module, and a final per-pixel classification layer. The pyramid pooling (PP) mechanism helps in reducing context information loss between different sub-regions. PP takes the input from the final convolution layer of base CNN. In PP features are fused under four different bin sizes of $1 \times 1, 2 \times 2, 3 \times 3, 6 \times 6$. In a 4-level pyramid, the pooling kernels cover the whole, half of, and small portions of the image. The different size of pooling filters produces feature maps of varying sizes. A 1×1

convolution is performed after each pyramid level to reduce the dimension of context representation to 1/N where N is the total feature maps before pyramid pooling. After which bi-linear interpolation (upsampling) is performed to get the same size feature as the original feature map. Finally, features generated at different levels are concatenated with the original feature map as the final pyramid pooling global feature. In the end, a convolution layer is placed to generate the pixel-wise final prediction map (Fig. 4).

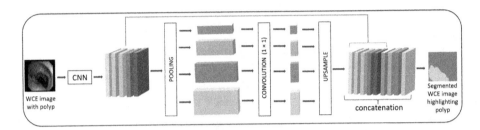

Fig. 4. Schematic block diagram of PSPNet.

4   Results

In this section, the segmentation performance of the adopted models is reported. The encoder-decoder architectures are developed on three popular CNNs that are ResNet50 [8], VGG16 [19], and MobileNetV1 [9]. An empirical study is performed to identify the best method with a particular CNN architecture on the WCE polyp dataset. In this study, two popular WCE polyp datasets are used that are CVC-ClinicDB [6] and ETIS-Larib [18]. CVC-ClinicDB contains 612 images of size 384×288 whereas the ETIS-Larib dataset encompasses a total of 196 images of size 1225×966. Images of both the datasets are reshaped to the size of 512×512 before experimentation. Both datasets are divided into training and test sets in the ratio of $80 : 20$. As discussed above, three popular CNN architectures ResNet50, VGG16, and MobileNetV1 are adopted each as the corresponding encoder-decoder for SegNet, UNet, PSPNet and FCN. The depth of encoder and decoder is taken as 5 that is first five CNN layers of each architecture are considered in both encoder and decoder networks to make the model lighter. Since there are two categories of pixels in the segmentation masks (normal and polyp), binary cross-entropy loss is employed to train the segmentation models. Each model is trained for 200 epochs using Adam optimizer with learning rate of 0.01. The results are shown in Tables 1 and 2 where IoU corresponds to intersection over union and $F_w IoU$ is frequency weighted IoU.

Table 2. Localization performance of adopted segmentation models on CVC-ClinicDB dataset.

Model	UNet		PSPNet		SegNet		FCN	
	$F_w IoU$	$MIoU$	$F_w IoU$	$MIoU$	$F_w IoU$	$MIoU$	$F_w IoU$	$MIoU$
VGG16	0.938	0.830	0.940	0.831	0.920	0.781	0.872	0.772
ResNet50	0.953	0.869	0.938	0.829	0.961	0.892	0.882	0.801
MobilenetV1	0.968	0.910	0.950	0.698	0.961	0.894	0.910	0.854

Table 3. Localization performance of adopted segmentation models on ETIS-Larib dataset.

Model	UNet		PSPNet		SegNet		FCN	
	$F_w IoU$	$MIoU$	$F_w IoU$	$MIoU$	$F_w IoU$	$MIoU$	$F_w IoU$	$MIoU$
VGG16	0.942	0.639	0.936	0.620	0.942	0.645	0.862	0.604
ResNet50	0.970	0.813	0.960	0.770	0.955	0.744	0.875	0.658
MobilenetV1	0.980	0.883	0.950	0.698	0.981	0.885	0.895	0.692

The empirical study aims to find out the segmentation model that fits best to a particular dataset. In both the datasets it is noticeable that the performance of both SegNet and UNet is nearly the same when crafted with MobileNet architecture as encoder-decoder. Therefore, we can consider both the models, and they can be used interchangeably. In this work, cross-validation is also done to check the performance of both models in a way that the trained model on one of the datasets is tested on the another one. The results of cross-validation are shown in Table 3 (Fig. 5).

Table 4. Performance comparison of suggested segmentation models with state-of-the-art methods on CVC-CLINIC dataset

Method	Train dataset	Test dataset	$F_w IoU$	$MIoU$
MobileNet-SegNet	CVC-ClinicDB	ETIS-Larib	0.938	0.693
MobileNet-UNet	CVC-ClinicDB	ETIS-Larib	0.940	0.662
MobileNet-SegNet	ETIS-Larib	CVC-ClinicDB	0.892	0.704
MobileNet-SegNet	ETIS-Larib	CVC-ClinicDB	0.877	0.665

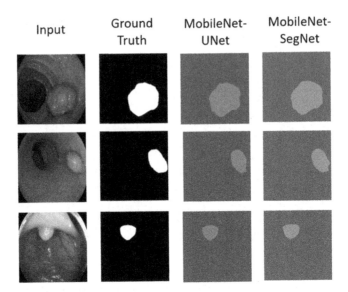

Fig. 5. Few samples of segmentation results on ETIS-Larib dataset using UNet and SegNet.

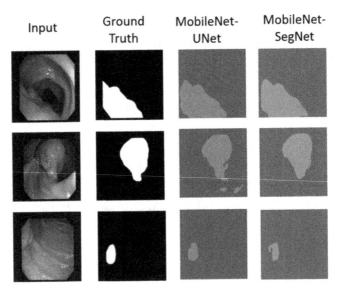

Fig. 6. Some examples of segmentation results on CVC-ClinicDB dataset employing UNet and SegNet.

The performance of these networks is also compared with two state-of-the-art methods proposed by Banik et al. [4] and Akbari et al. [1]. Banik et al. suggested a pair of CNNs that extract local and global features form the WCE images. The local and global patches of size 34 × 34 and 68 × 68 are extracted from images using a sliding window and are fed to the CNNs with 3 convolutional layers and 2 fully connected layers. Patches of different scales for the same center pixel enables learning shape-invariant features on different scales. Akbari et al. [1] framed the solution for segmentation of polyps using an FCN with the upsampling scale of 8 termed as FCN-8. After segmentation of the image, post processing is performed using Otsu's thresholding method. The results are reported in Table 4. It can be inferred from the results that the MobileNet-SegNet produces better results with a dice score of 0.882 (Fig. 6, Table 5).

Table 5. Performance comparison of suggested segmentation models with state-of-the-art methods on CVC-CLINIC dataset

Method	Dice score	Precision	Recall
Patch CNN [4]	0.813	0.809	0.786
FCN-8 [1]	0.850	0.893	0.839
MobileNet-SegNet	**0.882**	**0.912**	**0.913**
MobileNet-UNet	0.872	0.901	0.898

5   Conclusion

In this work, an empirical study on polyp segmentation performance of four popular segmentation models namely UNet, SegNet, PSPNet, and FCN is performed. Since all these models can be developed on any CNN architecture, three popular CNN's are utilized for experimentation those are VGG16, ResNet50, and MobileNetV1. It can be extrapolated form the segmentation outcomes that the UNet and SegNet on MobileNetV1 are performing relatively close. Also these two models are performing better than the other deep learning state-of-the-art methods [1,4] considered in the study. The present study can be extended by developing a more robust and light CNN architecture that can be used with the idea of UNet and SegNet.

References

1. Akbari, M., et al.: Polyp segmentation in colonoscopy images using fully convolutional network. In: 2018 40th Annual International Conference of the IEEE Engineering in Medicine and Biology Society (EMBC), pp. 69–72. IEEE (2018)
2. Ameling, S., Wirth, S., Paulus, D., Lacey, G., Vilarino, F.: Texture-based polyp detection in colonoscopy. In: Bildverarbeitung für die Medizin 2009, pp. 346–350. Springer, Heidelberg (2009)
3. Badrinarayanan, V., Kendall, A., Cipolla, R.: Segnet: a deep convolutional encoder-decoder architecture for image segmentation. IEEE Trans. Pattern Anal. Mach. Intell. **39**(12), 2481–2495 (2017)

4. Banik, D., Bhattacharjee, D., Nasipuri, M.: A multi-scale patch-based deep learning system for polyp segmentation. In: Chaki, R., Cortesi, A., Saeed, K., Chaki, N. (eds.) Advanced Computing and Systems for Security. AISC, vol. 1136, pp. 109–119. Springer, Singapore (2020). https://doi.org/10.1007/978-981-15-2930-6_9

5. Banik, D., Roy, K., Bhattacharjee, D., Nasipuri, M., Krejcar, O.: Polyp-net: a multimodel fusion network for polyp segmentation. IEEE Trans. Instrum. Meas. **70**, 1–12 (2020)

6. Bernal, J., Sánchez, F.J., Fernández-Esparrach, G., Gil, D., Rodríguez, C., Vilariño, F.: Wm-dova maps for accurate polyp highlighting in colonoscopy: Validation vs. saliency maps from physicians. Computerized Medical Imaging and Graphics **43**, 99–111 (2015)

7. Bernal, J., Sánchez, J., Vilariño, F.: A region segmentation method for colonoscopy images using a model of polyp appearance. In: Vitrià, J., Sanches, J.M., Hernández, M. (eds.) IbPRIA 2011. LNCS, vol. 6669, pp. 134–142. Springer, Heidelberg (2011). https://doi.org/10.1007/978-3-642-21257-4_17

8. He, K., Zhang, X., Ren, S., Sun, J.: Deep residual learning for image recognition. corr abs/1512.03385 (2015) (2015)

9. Howard, A.G., et al.: Mobilenets: efficient convolutional neural networks for mobile vision applications. arXiv preprint arXiv:1704.04861 (2017)

10. Hwang, S., Oh, J., Tavanapong, W., Wong, J., De Groen, P.C.: Automatic polyp region segmentation for colonoscopy images using watershed algorithm and ellipse segmentation. In: Medical Imaging 2007: Computer-Aided Diagnosis. vol. 6514, p. 65141D. International Society for Optics and Photonics (2007)

11. Jain, S., Seal, A., Ojha, A., Krejcar, O., Bureš, J., Tachecí, I., Yazidi, A.: Detection of abnormality in wireless capsule endoscopy images using fractal features. Comput. Biol. Med. **127**, 104094 (2020)

12. Long, J., Shelhamer, E., Darrell, T.: Fully convolutional networks for semantic segmentation. In: Proceedings of the IEEE Conference on Computer Vision and Pattern Recognition, pp. 3431–3440 (2015)

13. Prasath, V.S., Kawanaka, H.: Vascularization features for polyp localization in capsule endoscopy. In: 2015 IEEE International Conference on Bioinformatics and Biomedicine (BIBM), pp. 1740–1742. IEEE (2015)

14. Ronneberger, O., Fischer, P., Brox, T.: U-Net: convolutional networks for biomedical image segmentation. In: Navab, N., Hornegger, J., Wells, W.M., Frangi, A.F. (eds.) MICCAI 2015. LNCS, vol. 9351, pp. 234–241. Springer, Cham (2015). https://doi.org/10.1007/978-3-319-24574-4_28

15. Sasmal, P., Iwahori, Y., Bhuyan, M., Kasugai, K.: Active contour segmentation of polyps in capsule endoscopic images. In: 2018 International Conference on Signals and Systems (ICSigSys), pp. 201–204. IEEE (2018)

16. Shin, Y., Qadir, H.A., Aabakken, L., Bergsland, J., Balasingham, I.: Automatic colon polyp detection using region based deep CNN and post learning approaches. IEEE Access **6**, 40950–40962 (2018)

17. Shin, Y., Qadir, H.A., Balasingham, I.: Abnormal colon polyp image synthesis using conditional adversarial networks for improved detection performance. IEEE Access **6**, 56007–56017 (2018)

18. Silva, J., Histace, A., Romain, O., Dray, X., Granado, B.: Toward embedded detection of polyps in WCE images for early diagnosis of colorectal cancer. Int. J. Comput. Assist. Radiol. Surg. **9**(2), 283–293 (2014)

19. Simonyan, K., Zisserman, A.: Very deep convolutional networks for large-scale image recognition. arXiv preprint arXiv:1409.1556 (2014)

20. Tajbakhsh, N., Gurudu, S.R., Liang, J.: Automated polyp detection in colonoscopy videos using shape and context information. IEEE Trans. Med. Imaging **35**(2), 630–644 (2015)
21. Yu, L., Chen, H., Dou, Q., Qin, J., Heng, P.A.: Integrating online and offline three-dimensional deep learning for automated polyp detection in colonoscopy videos. IEEE J. Biomed. Health Inform. **21**(1), 65–75 (2016)
22. Yuan, Y., Meng, M.Q.H.: Deep learning for polyp recognition in wireless capsule endoscopy images. Med. Phys. **44**(4), 1379–1389 (2017)
23. Zhao, H., Shi, J., Qi, X., Wang, X., Jia, J.: Pyramid scene parsing network. In: Proceedings of the IEEE Conference on Computer Vision and Pattern Recognition, pp. 2881–2890 (2017)

Evaluation of Deep Architectures for Facial Emotion Recognition

B. Vinoth Kumar, R. Jayavarshini, Naveena Sakthivel$^{(\boxtimes)}$, A. Karthiga, R. Narmadha, and M. Saranya

Department of Information Technology, PSG College of Technology, Coimbatore, India
bvk@psgtech.ac.in, naveenaks.2000@gmail.com

Abstract. Facial expressions play an important role in identifying the emotional state of an individual. Individuals can have different reactions to the same stimuli. Various emotions (anger, disgust, fear, joy, sadness, surprise or neutral) are detected while the user plays a game and their facial expressions are analyzed through a live web camera. Implementing the Haar Algorithm, the frames are cropped and the face alone is procured on which grey scaling and resizing process is carried out. Now the most necessary features of the face are extracted by a neural network model which will encode motion and facial expressions to predict emotion. In this paper, a linear model along with ResNeXt and PyramidNet models are analyzed side by side to identify the algorithm which gives the best accuracy.

Keywords: Facial emotion recognition · Convolutional neural network · Res-NeXt · PyramidNet · Haar-cascade algorithm

1 Introduction

Human emotion recognition plays a crucial role within the interpersonal relationship. Extracting and understanding emotions has a high importance of the interaction between human and machine communication. Emotional state of a person may greatly influence problem solving, thinking capability, reasoning, ability to remember things, decision-making skills and so on. Computer system must be able to recognize and influence human emotions in order to enhance productivity and effectiveness. Several models that recognize facial expressions with high accuracy have been performed in real-time systems for several applications (behavioral analysis, machine vision and video gaming) are already available. Currently, lot of growth is being displayed in the field of improving human-machine interaction.

Convolutional neural-network based architectures are widely used for facial emotion recognition. The facial emotion of the person is detected using a live webcam. Once the webcam is turned off, all the detected emotions are stored in excel sheets with time frames and also the video is recorded. Different architectures are implemented to analyze which model provides the most efficient result for this scenario. The quantity of training and testing datasets are also varied to see how they affect the model.

© The Author(s), under exclusive license to Springer Nature Switzerland AG 2022
B. Raman et al. (Eds.): CVIP 2021, CCIS 1567, pp. 550–560, 2022.
https://doi.org/10.1007/978-3-031-11346-8_47

The objective of this paper is to provide real time data of emotions experienced by users throughout the span of the live video feed. This data will be stored as an.xlwt file, which can be used as a dataset in itself in various medical practices. We have experimented with multiple hybrid models for the first time and have analyzed it to see which is the most effective. This paper would contribute to upcoming backend data collection projects and would act as the base proof of concept (POC).

This paper is organized in various sections as follows. The outline of Neural network architectures for emotion recognition are explained in Sect. 2. Section 3 illustrates the proposed methodology. Experiment and result analysis is available in Sect. 4. Section 5 contains the conclusions on the topic.

2 Deep Learning Architectures

2.1 Visual Geometry Group (VGG)

VGG is a linear model and is one of the most used image-recognition architectures. VGG is an object-recognition model that can consist up to 19 layers. VGG being built as a deep convolutional neural network (CNN) can outperform many tasks and datasets outside of ImageNet.

This network is characterized by its simplicity, using only 3 × 3 convolutional layers stacked on top of every other in increasing depth.

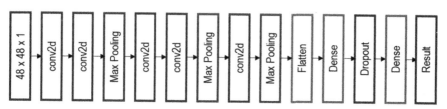

Fig. 1. VGG architecture

The 48 × 48 grayscale image is given as input to the first convolutional layer. The image is passed through a stack of five convolutional layers each with a kernel size of 3 × 3 as shown in Fig. 1. Each convolution layer results with the output of feature maps of that image which is fed as input to the next layer. Every convolutional layer is followed by the rectified linear activation function (ReLU). The down-sampling of feature maps is done using a max-pooling layer over a 2 × 2 pixel window. Flattening layer is used to convert 2-dimensional features maps into single long feature vector, which is connected to the final classification model. Following these layers, two fully connected layers with a dropout of 50% are added to get the final output of 7 neurons indicating seven possible outputs which represents the emotions.

The disadvantages of VGG architecture are as follows,

• Training takes lot of time.
• Weights of this architecture is quite large.

- Based on the number of layers of nodes it requires more memory. So, development of this model is difficult and small network architectures like VGG are often more desirable.

2.2 Pyramid Neural Network (PyramidNet)

A PyramidNet is a type of convolutional neural network (CNN) architecture and it basically focuses on the feature map dimension. Here the feature map dimension is increased gradually rather than increasing it sharply. In addition, the PyramidNet is a combination of the previous linear convolution neural network model (VGG) and the residual neural network (ResNet) model (Fig. 2).

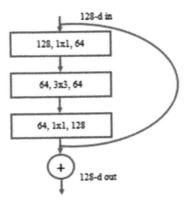

Fig. 2. ResNet architecture

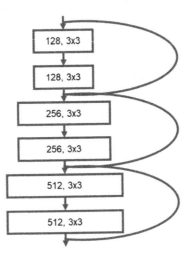

Fig. 3. PyramidNet architecture

A residual neural network (ResNet) is an artificial neural network (ANN) which makes use of the skip connections or shortcuts to jump over the layers. PyramidNet is a combination of both linear and ResNet models. It is more suitable for emotion recognition. PyramidNet is basically an improvement of the ResNet architecture. In ResNet, the number of channels increases greatly only at the special residual blocks. Whereas in PyramidNet, instead of these special residual blocks the number of channels increases step by step on each residual block which helps in improving the accuracy (Fig. 3).

2.3 Extended Residual Neural Network (ResNeXt)

ResNeXt is a homogeneous neural network and an extended version of ResNet. ResNeXt requires low number of hyperparameters than conventional ResNet. It also makes use of cardinality which is an additional dimension on top of the depth and width of ResNet. Cardinality defines the number of blocks. ResNeXt follows the "split-transform-merge" strategy. The input of the block is projected into a series of lower dimensional representations instead of performing convolutions over the entire input feature map. A few convolutional filters are then applied before merging the results. The separate groups in grouped convolution focused on different characteristics of the input image which led grouped convolutions to a degree of specialization among groups. Hence the accuracy is improved by this grouped convolution technique.

For each convolution path, Conv1 × 1–Conv3 × 3–Conv1 × 1 is done. The internal dimension for every path is denoted as d (d = 4). The cardinality C (C = 32) is the number of parallel paths that appear in a block. The same transformation is applied 32 times, and the result is aggregated at the end. The sum of the dimension of each Conv3 × 3 (i.e., d × C = 4 × 32) gives the dimension of 128. An increase in dimension from 4 to 256 happens abruptly, and then added together, and also added with the skip connection path (Fig. 4).

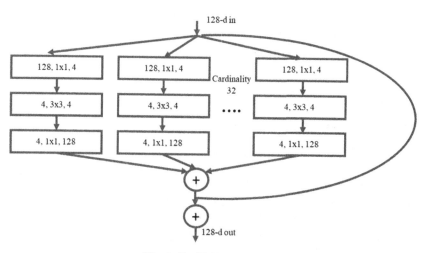

Fig. 4. ResNeXt architecture

3 Methodology

The proposed system is explained in the following four steps – data collection, data preprocessing, model creation and emotion detection.

3.1 Data Collection

The dataset used in the paper is fer2013 from Kaggle. The dataset consists of 48x48 pixel grayscale images of the face of different persons. Each face is categorized based on the emotion shown in the facial expression into one of the seven categories (0 = Angry, 1 = Disgust, 2 = Fear, 3 = Happy, 4 = Sad, 5 = Surprise, 6 = Neutral).

The data set contains three columns, "emotion", "pixels" and "usage". The "emotion" column contains a number which ranges from 0 to 6, indicating the corresponding emotion of the image. The "pixels" column contains the 48 x 48 space separated pixels of the image in row order. The "Usage" column specifies whether the particular data is used for training or testing.

The summary of the fer2013 dataset is given in Table 1. It shows that the dataset is imbalanced as the number of samples for each emotion varies.

Table 1. Summary of fer2013 dataset

Label	Emotion	Number of samples
0	Angry	4953
1	Disgust	547
2	Fear	5121
3	Happy	8989
4	Sad	6077
5	Surprise	4002
6	Neutral	6198
Total number of samples		35887

3.2 Data Preprocessing

The data is split into testing and training sets. The split data is converted into NumPy arrays. Then normalization is applied to speed up the convergence. Oversampling of data is then done to adjust the class distribution in the dataset.

Table 2 shows the balanced dataset as the number of samples for each emotion are the same after oversampling. The dataset is increased by two folds. The training and testing dataset are split randomly in a defined ratio.

Table 2. Summary of fer2013 dataset after oversampling

Label	Emotion	Number of samples
0	Angry	8989
1	Disgust	8989
2	Fear	8989
3	Happy	8989
4	Sad	8989
5	Surprise	8989
6	Neutral	8989
Total number of samples		62923

3.3 Model Creation

The neural network models for emotion detection are build using the architectures mentioned in Sect. 3. These three models are then trained with the pre-processed dataset for about 100 epochs using the computing service provided by the GPU of Google Colab.

3.4 Emotion Detection

After the model is created using the architecture, the data is read from json and weights are loaded from the.h5 file. Using OpenCV live web camera is automatically turned on. The image frames are captured from the video and converted into gray images. Using the Haar-Cascade algorithm, the faces are detected from the image within the angle of 45° on either side from the front. Emotions can be detected even when the user is wearing makeup, contacts or glasses. Then the images are resized and converted into image pixels. The image pixels are then passed to the model to predict the emotion. The predicted emotion is displayed on the screen. Along with the emotions, the time frame of each emotion will also get recorded and stored.

4 Experimental Result

Oversampled dataset provides better results than the original dataset in terms of both loss and accuracy.

The accuracy of the oversampled dataset increases drastically whereas the accuracy of the original dataset saturates within a few epochs as shown in Fig. 5.

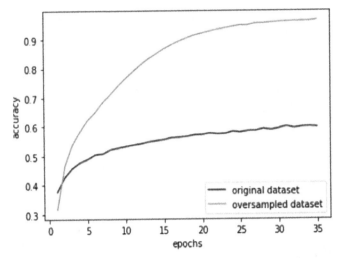

Fig. 5. Accuracy of original dataset and oversampled dataset for 35epochs

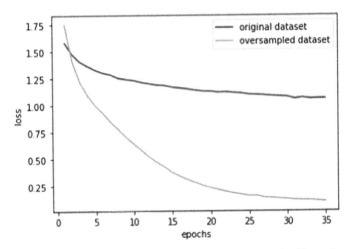

Fig. 6. Loss of original dataset and oversampled dataset for 35 epochs

Also, Fig. 6 shows that the loss of the oversampled dataset is very low compared to the original dataset.

The performances of the VGG, ResNeXt, and PyramidNet architecture are measured in terms of four evaluation metrics: accuracy, F-score, recall and precision. The performance of network models is compared for an original dataset and oversampled dataset where the 90% of the dataset is taken as training and 10% of the dataset for testing. The oversampled dataset was split as training to testing datasets in three ratios as 90:10, 80:20, 70:30.

For the three different ratios, the accuracy, recall, precision and F-score values of VGG, ResNeXt and PyramidNet Architectures are listed in Table 3, Table 4, and Table 5 respectively.

Table 3. Performance of VGG architecture

Evaluation metrics	Split size		
	Training size = 90% Testing size = 10%	Training size = 80% Testing size = 20%	Training size = 70% Testing size = 30%
Precision (%)	83.86	82.00	81.43
Recall (%)	82.86	80.28	80.14
F1 score (%)	83.43	81.00	80.86
Train accuracy (%)	97.60	97.31	97.85
Test accuracy (%)	83.08	80.83	80.56

Table 4. Performance of ResNeXt architecture

Evaluation metrics	Split size		
	Training size = 90% Testing size = 10%	Training size = 80% Testing size = 20%	Training size = 70% Testing size = 30%
Precision (%)	79.43	78.28	75.14
Recall (%)	77.57	76.43	73.14
F1 score (%)	78.14	76.85	73.85
Train accuracy (%)	98.67	97.69	97.81
Test accuracy (%)	78.04	76.68	73.81

Table. 5. Performance of pyramidNet architecture

Evaluation metrics	Split size		
	Training size = 90% Testing size = 10%	Training size = 80% Testing size = 20%	Training size = 70% Testing size = 30%
Precision (%)	83.00	81.00	79.00
Recall (%)	81.43	77.85	77.14
F1 score (%)	82.28	79.43	77.85
Train accuracy (%)	97.98	97.33	98.82
Test accuracy (%)	81.96	79.01	77.72

No variation is noticeable in the VGG model (Table 3) on altering the ratio of testing and training dataset. It provides more or less a uniform result with slight alterations. The

ResNeXt (Table 4) and PyramidNet (Table 5) models however help us visualize a clear-cut image when it comes to the change in dataset ratio alterations. Though Res-NeXt provides a lower accuracy than PyramidNet, it still shows a huge leap in precision after applying an oversampled dataset.

Table. 6. Comparing the performance of all three architectures for original dataset and oversampled dataset

Evaluation metrics	VGG		ResNeXt		PyramidNet	
	Original dataset	Oversample dataset	Original dataset	Oversample dataset	Original dataset	Oversample dataset
Precision (%)	61.42	83.86	47.28	79.43	56.85	83.00
Recall (%)	53.14	82.86	47.28	77.57	47.57	81.43
F1 Score (%)	56.00	83.43	50.00	78.14	50.14	82.28
Train accuracy (%)	98.93	97.60	96.88	98.67	96.41	97.98
Test accuracy (%)	56.95	83.08	51.38	78.04	53.41	81.96

For all three models, accuracy, recall, precision and F-score values of both original dataset and oversampled dataset are listed in Table 6.

The various emotions detected by testing the model in real-time using a webcam is shown in the Fig. 7.

These detected emotions are then stored in a.xsl file which can be viewed once the webcam is turned off.

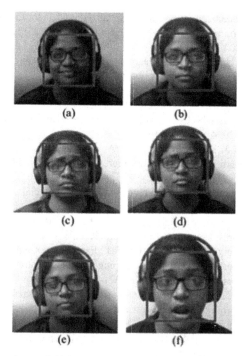

Fig. 7. Emotions detected (a) happy (b) angry (c) fear (d) sad (e) neutral (f) surprise

5 Conclusion

Manual recordings of these emotions are hard and inaccurate to maintain. Identification of emotions through a live webcam using Neural network models helps an individual to go back and review their progress as they always have a detailed record of emotion. An oversampled dataset proved to provide a better accuracy in all the three models implemented. The PyramidNet model provides the most efficient result pertaining to our initial objective. If at all different datasets are used, PyramidNet model will provide the accuracy in same range due it's more reliable model design. Though VGG provides the highest precision, it seems to provide a saturated result, which questions whether it works well with all types of datasets. Hence, PyramidNet provides a high training accuracy of 97.98%.

Acknowledgement. We express our sincere thanks to PSG College of Technology for providing constant support and guidance throughout the project. We also acknowledge Google for providing a Colab platform for training and testing the Neural Network models for facial emotion recognition using deep learning.

References

1. Mehendale, N.: Facial emotion recognition using Convolutional neural networks (FERC), Ninad's Research Lab, Thane, India, 18 February 2020

2. Rescigno, M., Spezialetti, M., Rossi, S.: Personalized models for facial emotion recognition through transfer learning. Multimed. Tools Appl. **79**(47–48), 35811–35828 (2020). https://doi.org/10.1007/s11042-020-09405-4

3. Verma, G., Verma, H.: Hybrid-deep learning model for emotion recognition using facial expressions. Rev. Socionetwork Strat. **14**(2), 171–180 (2020). https://doi.org/10.1007/s12626-020-00061-6

4. Rutkowski, L., Korytkowski, M., Scherer, R., Tadeusiewicz, R., Zadeh, L.A., Zurada, J.M. (eds.): ICAISC 2012. LNCS (LNAI), vol. 7267. Springer, Heidelberg (2012). https://doi.org/10.1007/978-3-642-29347-4

5. Anjani Suputri Devi, D., Satyanarayana, Ch.: An efficient facial emotion recognition system using novel deep learning neural network-regression activation classifier. Multimed. Tools Appl. (2021)

6. Rani, P.I., Muneeswaran, K.: Emotion recognition based on facial components. Sadhana **43**, 48 (2018)

7. González-Lozoya, S.M., de la Calleja, J., Pellegrin, L., et al.: Recognition of facial expressions based on CNN features. Multimed. Tools Appl. **79**, 13987–14007 (2020)

8. Li, K., Jin, Y., Akram, M.W., Han, R., Chen, J.: Facial expression recognition with convolutional neural networks via a new face cropping and rotation strategy. Vis. Comput. **36**(2), 391–404 (2019). https://doi.org/10.1007/s00371-019-01627-4

9. Caroppo, A., Leone, A., Siciliano, P.: Comparison between deep learning models and traditional machine learning approaches for facial expression recognition in ageing adults. J. Comput. Sci. Technol. **35**(5), 1127–1146 (2020). https://doi.org/10.1007/s11390-020-9665-4

10. Lai, Z., Chen, R., Jia, J. et al. Real-time micro-expression recognition based on ResNet and atrous convolutions. J. Ambient Intell. Human. Comput. (2020)

11. Gruber, I., Hlavac, M., Zelezny, M., Karpov, A: Facing Face Recognition with Res-Net (2017)

12. Wang, Z., Zhou, X., Wang, W., Liang, C.: Emotion recognition using multimodal deep learning in multiple psychophysiological signals and video. Int. J. Mach. Learn. Cybern. **11**(4), 923–934 (2020). https://doi.org/10.1007/s13042-019-01056-8

13. Cui, R., Plested, J., Liu, J.: Declarative Residual Network for Robust Facial Expression Recognition (2020)

14. Do, L.-N., Yang, H.-J., Nguyen, H.-D., Kim, S.-H., Lee, G.-S., Na, I.-S.: Deep neural network-based fusion model for emotion recognition using visual data. J. Supercomputing **77**, 10773–10790 (2021)

15. Jie, S., Yongsheng, Q.: Multi-view facial expression recognition with multi-view facial expression LightWeight Network. Pattern Recognit. Image Anal. **30**, 805–814 (2020)

Adaptive Rough-Fuzzy Kernelized Clustering Algorithm for Noisy Brain MRI Tissue Segmentation

Rudrajit Choudhuri and Amiya Halder$^{(\boxtimes)}$

St. Thomas College of Engineering and Technology, 4 D. H. Road, Kolkata, India
amiya.halder77@gmail.com

Abstract. Image Segmentation is a crucial processing technique for segregating regions in medical images for analysis and abnormality detection. In this paper, an adaptive rough-fuzzy set based kernelized C means clustering algorithm is presented which is aimed at robust segmentation of brain magnetic resonance imaging (MRI) data. The algorithm is developed by amalgamating fuzzy set and rough set theory along with an adaptive substructure based kernelized distance metric to form a reliable clustering approach for seamless segmentation. Rough and fuzzy sets help in dealing with uncertainties caused due to vagueness, imperceptibility, ambiguities, and overlappingness while clustering data points. Incorporation of an adaptive substructure into the algorithm compensates for noise corruptions and inhomogeneities of intensity values in the image by taking the local neighborhood features and spatial information into consideration. The kernelized distance metric leverages linear separability and allows for easy segregation by mapping data points to a higher dimensional space while preserving fine details and spatial features. Upon experimentation, the proposed approach is proved to be reliable and manages to achieve superior performance when compared to the state of the art methods, especially when segmenting images corrupted by noise or any other artifacts.

Keywords: Magnetic resonance imaging · Image segmentation · Rough set · Unsupervised clustering · Kernel method

1 Introduction

Segmentation has a major contribution in biomedical applications of image processing and helps in the quantification of various regions, partitioning and automated detection. Several radiology tools and techniques including X-Rays, Magnetic Resonance Imaging (MRI), Computer/Positron Emission Tomography (CT/PET) have emerged over decades out of which MRIs provide significant advantage when it comes to studying the human brain and for early detection of anomalies in tissues and organs [14]. Acquisition of multimodal images of tissues with varying contrasts is made possible with the help of brain MR imaging. Due

B. Raman et al. (Eds.): CVIP 2021, CCIS 1567, pp. 561–573, 2022.
https://doi.org/10.1007/978-3-031-11346-8_48

to these reasons, a wide variety of algorithms for brain MRI segmentation have been proposed in order to partition and highlight several regions of a human brain so as to perform meticulous diagnosis.

Several techniques based on deep learning [16], pattern recognition [1], and image processing [4] are often applied for ease in anomaly detection. Segmentation becomes a challenging problem to tackle mainly due to the complex structure of the human brain. Various segmentation paradigms such as thresholding [13], edge detection [12], and pixel classification [11] leverage the performance of automated diagnosis. Clustering of image data points proves to be a decent approach for medical image segmentation but its performance faces a sheer drop in the presence of noise corruptions, intensity inhomogeneities, and other artifacts. Noise corruptions in medical images including Gaussian Noise [9], Rician Noise [5], and Salt and Pepper Noise are common and they degrade the image to such an extent that segmentation or any further image processing task fails to achieve desired results. The reason for these corruptions lies in the faulty acquisition, storage, or transmission of an MR Image.

Thus arises the need for a robust algorithm that can achieve significant performance even in the presence of noise and other artifacts. One of the earliest conventional clustering approach is the hard K Means [17]. A major drawback of the algorithm is that it forces pixels to belong to one class and does not allow any flexibility. Introduction of fuzzy sets [7] in the domain tackles this drawback and makes the clustering approach more flexible towards uncertainties. However, the Fuzzy C Means algorithm (FCM) neglects any kind of spatial information which makes it sensitive to noise. Kernel induced metrics [18] improve the performance of the FCM algorithm but an improper kernel choice can lead to unwanted results arising due to convergence issues. To accelerate the performance of the FCM algorithm, clustering techniques including an enhanced FCM (ENFCM) [15], and a fast generated fuzzy algorithm (FGFCM) [2] were proposed. Introduction of rough sets into the domain of image segmentation has paved a new paragon for image segmentation. Rough Fuzzy C Means (RFCM) [10], Contextual Kernelized Rough Fuzzy C Means (KRFCMSC) [6] are some of the methods that are based on rough set substructure. In 2021, Khosravanian proposed a local intensity based Fuzzy Clustering model (FLICM) [8] which is aimed at automatic segmentation of images. These techniques are quite efficient when it comes to image segregation but the quality of results and the performance degrade drastically when images are corrupted with various types of noise and are subjected to a high level of inhomogeneity.

In this paper, an adaptive rough-fuzzy set based kernelized C means clustering algorithm is presented in order to overcome these drawbacks and improve upon the performance of clustering based unsupervised segmentation. The reliability of the algorithm is highlighted by its ability in handling uncertainties due to imperceptible class definitions and in dealing with noise corruptions and inhomogeneities by harmonizing spatial information during data point clustering. For performance comparison, three different T1-weighted MRI data volumes each containing 51 images are obtained from the McConnell Brain Imaging Centre of the Montreal Neurological Institute. Different regions including white matter (WM), gray matter (GM), and cerebrospinal fluid (CSF) are prominent in these images. The images are corrupted by different noise types to check the fault tolerance of algorithms across a wide spectrum of use cases. On rigorous experimentation, the proposed algorithm is found to be efficient mainly for noisy and inhomogeneous image segmentation and it achieves superior performance than all its peers on all mentioned datasets.

2 Ground Work

2.1 Fuzzy Set Theory

Fuzzy set theory had been introduced to treat uncertainties arising due to incompleteness, ambiguity, or vagueness. Incorporation of fuzzy logic into systems leverages its ability to treat uncertainties arising due to imprecise decisions or where selection of more than one option among a set is involved in order to obtain satisfactory conclusions. In the domain of image segmentation, assimilating fuzzy sets allow data points to belong in a particular cluster upto a certain degree. Partial membership allowance to a data point and accounting for respective importance of each class is a major benefit of amalgamating fuzzy sets in a clustering algorithm. A fuzzy set mapping for a set L is an $L \rightarrow [0, 1]$ mapping, and depending on the use case, the membership function can be designed.

2.2 Fuzzy C Means Clustering (FCM)

FCM is an iterative optimization algorithm used for clustering data points to different classes. It incorporates fuzzy set logic for membership computation which is necessary for assigning a category to a data point. Consider $Y = (y_1, y_2 \ldots y_n)$ to be an image consisting of N pixels which are to be segmented into C clusters, where image pixels in Y denote multispectral features. The cost function that needs to be optimized is defined in Eq. 1.

$$J = \sum_{q=1}^{c} \sum_{p=1}^{N} \mu_{qp}^m ||y_p - v_q||^2 \tag{1}$$

where μ_{qp}, v_q denote the membership value of pixel y_p and the cluster centroid corresponding to the qth cluster respectively, and m is a fuzziness control parameter. FCM iteratively minimizes the cost function by assigning higher membership values to pixels that are nearer to the cluster centroid. The membership degree acts as a probabilistic measure that represents the probability of a pixel to belong in a specified cluster. The fuzzy membership function is defined in Eq. 2 and the membership values are bounded by the constraints $\sum_{q=1}^{c} \mu_{qp} = 1$, $\mu_{qp} \in [0, 1]$.

$$\mu_{qp} = \frac{1}{\sum_{j=1}^{c} (\frac{||y_p - v_q||}{||y_p - v_j||})^{\frac{2}{m-1}}} \tag{2}$$

$$v_q = \frac{\sum_{p=1}^{N} \mu_{qp}^m y_p}{\sum_{p=1}^{N} \mu_{qp}^m} \tag{3}$$

The cluster centroids are computed using Eq. 3 after taking the fuzzy membership values into account. The algorithm begins with an initial assumption for cluster centroids and iteratively converges values to generate solutions that are effectively minimal saddle points of the defined objective function.

2.3 Kernel Methods

Kernel methods are a commonly used trick in the domain of pattern recognition. The reason behind using kernel methods is due to the ease of structuring and separating data points by mapping them to a higher dimensional space. Using kernel methods assimilated with vector algebra is a smarter alternative to the rigorous computations involved in mapping functions. It bridges the gap between linearity and non-linearity for any algorithm that can be represented in the form of scalar products between vectors. The basic intuition behind is that after mapping the data into a higher dimensional space, any linear function in the augmented space acts as a non-linear one in the original space. The trick works by replacing the scalar product with a Kernel function. A kernel function represents a scalar product in a feature space and is of the form as defined in Eq. 4.

$$K(x, y) = \langle \psi(x), \psi(y) \rangle \tag{4}$$

where $\langle \psi(x), \psi(y) \rangle$ represents the scalar product of the vectors. Commonly used kernel functions include the Gaussian Radial Basis Function Kernel (GRBF), the sigmoid kernel, polynomial kernel, and the circular kernel.

2.4 Rough Set Theory

Rough set theory is based on approximation space substructure, which in effect is a pair $< U, R >$ where U is a non-empty set and R denotes an equivalence relation on U (satisfying reflexivity, symmetricity, and transitivity). Using the relation R, the set U is decomposed into disjoint categories such that two data points (x, y) are in the same category iff xRy holds. Consider $U/R = \{X_1, X_2, \ldots, X_n\}$ to be the quotient set of the set U by relation R, where X_i denotes an equivalence class of R. This implies that two elements (x, y) in U are indistinguishable if they belong to the same equivalence class. It might not be possible to describe an arbitrary set accurately in $< U, R >$. Let an arbitrary set $X \in 2^U$, now it may be possible to characterize the set X by a pair of lower and upper approximations as defined in Eq. 5.

$$\underline{R}(X) = \bigcup_{X_i \subseteq X} X_i$$
$$\overline{R}(X) = \bigcup_{X_i \cap X \neq \phi} X_i \tag{5}$$

$\underline{R}(X)$ is the lower approximation which is essentially the union of every elementary set that are subsets of X, whereas $\overline{R}(X)$ denotes the upper approximation, i.e. the union of every elementary set having non-empty intersections with X. Given the lower and upper approximations, the $[\underline{R}(X), \overline{R}(X)]$ interval is the representation of X in the approximation space $< U, R >$ and is known as the rough set of X. The reason for such an approximation is to interpret a set of elements of U that may or may not belong to X.

3   Proposed Methodology

In this section, an Adaptive Rough Fuzzy Set Based Kernelized C Means Clustering Algorithm (ARFKCM) is proposed for robust human brain MR Image segmentation. This technique integrates the theories of fuzzy sets and rough sets along with an adaptive kernel induced distance metric to form a reliable clustering algorithm. Fuzzy set helps in dealing with overlapping partitions and imprecise data points, while rough sets allow for seamless handling of uncertainties caused due to ambiguities, vagueness, incompleteness, and imperceptibility in class definitions. The adaptive substructure method amalgamated with possibilistic and probabilistic measures in the membership value computation prudently includes the influence of spatial features and neighborhood details while clustering data points thus compensating for noise corruptions and inhomogeneities of intensity values in the image. The Kernel method is responsible for the ascendancy of linear separability and allows smooth segregation via a higher dimensional mapping of data points.

3.1   Adaptive Kernelized Distance Metric

The proposed approach considers spatial information around an image pixel along with its intensity value as a feature. In order to achieve this, a 3×3 window centered at the concerned pixel (y_i) is picked and the average pixel intensity value $(\overline{y_i})$ of the window is computed and is used as a data point for clustering. The adaptive substructure accounts for local spatial information during segmentation which compensates for inhomogeneities leading to efficient segregation. The proposed approach uses a circular kernel as defined in Eq. 6.

$$K(x,y) = \frac{2}{\pi} cos^{-1}(\frac{-||x-y||}{\sigma}) - \frac{2}{\pi}\frac{||x-y||}{\sigma}\sqrt{1 - (\frac{||x-y||}{\sigma})^2} \qquad (6)$$

where σ is the tuning parameter for adjusting the kernel. The reason behind using the kernel lies in its ability in dramatically improving the performance of the algorithm and leading to faster convergences when compared to its peers and with other kernel methods.

3.2   Objective Function

Consider $\underline{R}(\xi_i), \overline{R}(\xi_i)$ to be the lower approximation and upper approximation of the cluster (ξ_i), and $H(\xi_i) = \{\overline{R}(\xi_i) - \underline{R}(\xi_i)\}$ to be the boundary region corresponding to the cluster(ξ_i). The objective function that the proposed method aims to optimize is defined in Eq. 7.

$$J_{ARKFCM} = \begin{cases} \omega \times J_L + (1 - \omega) \times J_B & \text{if } \underline{R}(\xi_i) \neq \phi, H(\xi_i) \neq \phi \\ J_L, & \text{if } \underline{R}(\xi_i) \neq \phi, H(\xi_i) = \phi \\ J_B, & \text{if } \underline{R}(\xi_i) = \phi, H(\xi_i) \neq \phi \end{cases} \quad (7)$$

where

$$J_L = \sum_{k=1}^{c} \sum_{\overline{y_i} \in \underline{R}(\xi_i)} \mu_{ki}^q (1 - K(\overline{y_i}, v_k)) + \sum_{k=1}^{c} \lambda_i \sum_{\overline{y_i} \in \underline{R}(\xi_i)} (1 - \mu_{ki}) \quad (8)$$

$$J_B = \sum_{k=1}^{c} \sum_{\overline{y_i} \in H(\xi_i)} \mu_{ki}^q (1 - K(\overline{y_i}, v_k)) + \sum_{k=1}^{c} \lambda_i \sum_{\overline{y_i} \in H(\xi_i)} (1 - \mu_{ki}) \quad (9)$$

λ_i is a scale parameter that represents the influence of the concerned cluster, ω and $(1-\omega)$ correspond to the relative importance of lower approximation space and boundary region respectively. In the presented technique, each cluster has a crisp lower approximation space along with a defined fuzzified boundary region. Lower approximation is responsible for the final partition fuzziness. According to the rough set theory, if a data point is in the lower approximation space, it definitely belongs to the concerned cluster. Therefore, the weights of these data points should be independent of the influence of other clusters and should not be coupled with other clusters based on similarity measures. On the contrary, if a data point lies in the boundary region, it has a potential chance of belonging to a different cluster. Therefore, the data points lying in the boundary region should not directly influence the centroid of the cluster. Effectively, the presented technique bifurcates data points into two different classes - lower approximation space and boundary region. The technique only fuzzifies data points that are in the boundary region.

3.3 Membership Function and Cluster Centroid Computation

The cost function defined in Eq. 7 on optimization with respect to the membership function and cluster centroid succeeded by equating the expression to zero under the constraint imposed by $\sum_{q=1}^{c} \mu_{qp} = 1$ leads to necessary and sufficient conditions for the membership function and the cluster centroid of the cost function to be at the minimal saddle point. Equating the partial derivative of J_B with respect to the membership function to zero we get:

$$\frac{\partial J_B}{\partial \mu_{ki}} = 0$$
$$=> q\mu_{ki}^{q-1}(1 - K(\overline{y_i}, v_k)) - \lambda_i = 0 \quad (10)$$
$$=> \mu_{ki} = (\frac{\lambda_i}{q})^{\frac{1}{q-1}} \times [\frac{1}{1-K(\overline{y_i}, v_k)}]^{\frac{1}{q-1}}$$

From the constraint $\sum_{q=1}^{c} \mu_{qp} = 1$, we get

$$\sum_{j=1}^{c} (\frac{\lambda_i}{q})^{\frac{1}{q-1}} \times [\frac{1}{1-K(\overline{y_i}, v_k)}]^{\frac{1}{q-1}} = 1$$
$$=> (\frac{\lambda_i}{q})^{\frac{1}{q-1}} = \frac{1}{\sum_{j=1}^{c} (\frac{1}{1-K(\overline{y_i}, v_k)})^{\frac{1}{q-1}}} \quad (11)$$

From Eq. 10 and Eq. 11, we get

$$\mu_{ki} = \frac{(1 - K(\overline{y_i}, v_k))^{-\frac{1}{q-1}}}{\sum_{j=1}^{c}(1 - K(\overline{y_i}, v_k))^{-\frac{1}{q-1}}} \tag{12}$$

Similarly, equating the partial derivative of J_B with respect to the cluster centroid to zero we get:

$$\frac{\partial J_B}{\partial v_k} = 0$$
$$\Rightarrow \sum_{i=1}^{N} \mu_{ki}^q (1 - K(\overline{y_i}, v_k))(\overline{y_i} - v_k)(-1) = 0$$
$$\Rightarrow \sum_{i=1}^{N} \mu_{ki}^q (1 - K(\overline{y_i}, v_k))v_k = \sum_{i=1}^{N} \mu_{ki}^q \overline{y_i}(1 - K(\overline{y_i}, v_k)) \tag{13}$$
$$\Rightarrow v_k = \frac{\sum_{i=1}^{N} \mu_{ki}^q \overline{y_i}(1 - K(\overline{y_i}, v_k))}{\sum_{i=1}^{N} \mu_{ki}^q (1 - K(\overline{y_i}, v_k))}$$

Equating partial derivatives of J_L with respect to cluster centroids and membership functions to zero yield similar results. Therefore, on incorporating rough set theory into adaptive kernel induced fuzzy clustering, the centroid computation is done based on Eq. 14.

$$v_k' = \begin{cases} \omega \times \frac{\sum_{\overline{y_i} \in \underline{R}(\xi_i)} \mu_{ki}^q \overline{y_i} K(\overline{y_i}, v_k)}{\sum_{\overline{y_i} \in \underline{R}(\xi_i)} \mu_{ki}^q K(\overline{y_i}, v_k)} + (1 - \omega) \times \frac{\sum_{\overline{y_i} \in H(\xi_i)} \mu_{ki}^q \overline{y_i} K(\overline{y_i}, v_k)}{\sum_{\overline{y_i} \in H(\xi_i)} \mu_{ki}^q K(\overline{y_i}, v_k)} & \text{if } \underline{R}(\xi_i) \neq \phi, H(\xi_i) \neq \phi \\[2ex] \frac{\sum_{\overline{y_i} \in \underline{R}(\xi_i)} \mu_{ki}^q \overline{y_i} K(\overline{y_i}, v_k)}{\sum_{\overline{y_i} \in \underline{R}(\xi_i)} \mu_{ki}^q K(\overline{y_i}, v_k)}, & \text{if } \underline{R}(\xi_i) \neq \phi, H(\xi_i) = \phi \\[2ex] \frac{\sum_{\overline{y_i} \in H(\xi_i)} \mu_{ki}^q \overline{y_i} K(\overline{y_i}, v_k)}{\sum_{\overline{y_i} \in H(\xi_i)} \mu_{ki}^q K(\overline{y_i}, v_k)}, & \text{if } \underline{R}(\xi_i) = \phi, H(\xi_i) \neq \phi \end{cases} \tag{14}$$

where ω tunes the influence of the lower approximation space. The proposed algorithm is summarized in Algorithm 1.

Algorithm 1: PROPOSED ALGORITHM

Input: Brain MRI Image
Output: Segmented MRI Image

1 Initialize number of clusters(C), maximum iterations (M), fuzziness control parameter (q) $[q > 1]$, and threshold $T > 0$
2 Set initial membership values μ^0 is 0 and select C distinct data points as cluster centroids, set iteration counter (IC) as 1.
3 **while** $IC < M$ **do**
4   Compute membership values μ_{ki} using Eq. 12 for all pixels and all clusters
5   **for** $i = 1...N$ **do**
6   Maximum Membership value is assigned to each pixel y_i as follows:
7          $\mu_{gi} = max(\mu_{ji})$
8          $g = j$ corresponding to $max(\mu_{ji})$
9   **for** $j = 1...C$ **do**
10   **if** $|\mu_{ji} - \mu_{gi}| \leq T$ **then**
11   assign y_i to upper approximation spaces $\overline{R}(\xi_g)$ and $\overline{R}(\xi_j)$
12   **if** $y_i \notin$ *upper approximation spaces* **then**
13   assign y_i to lower approximation space $\underline{R}(\xi_g)$

14   Compute cluster centroids based on Eq. 14.
15   **if** $|v_k' - v_k| < T$ **then**
16   Stop
17      $IC = IC + 1$

---

4   Performance Comparison and Results

In this section, the performance of the algorithm is tested on Brain MRI images that are obtained from the McConnell Brain Web dataset [3]. Three different T1-weighted data volumes have been collected containing 51 images each. In these images, different regions like white matter (WM), gray matter (GM), and cerebrospinal fluid (CSF) are prominent. The first, second, and third image volumes contain 7% Gaussian noise, 8% salt and pepper noise, and 9% noise with 40% inhomogeneity respectively. All collected images have a fixed size of 1 mm × mm × 1 mm and the resolutions of the images are $181 \times 217 \times 181$ voxels. For qualitative and quantitative comparative study, we compare performances of the proposed algorithm (Prop) with FCM, KFCM, ENFCM, FGFCM, RFCM, RKFCMSC, and FLICM approaches.

For quantitative evaluation purposes, we have presented cluster validity indices: (i) Partition coefficient (Vpc), (ii) Partition entropy (Vpe) and tissue segmentation accuracy (TSA). Partition coefficient and partition entropy are the important indicators of fuzzy partition. Higher partition coefficient values (tending to 1) and lower partition entropy values (tending to 0) correspond to better segmentation results. Tissue segmentation accuracy measures the precision of the approach in segmenting various regions/tissues of the human brain. partition coefficient, partition entropy, and tissue segmentation accuracy values are computed as follows:

$$V_{pc} = \frac{\sum_{k=1}^{c} \sum_{i=1}^{N} \mu_{ki}^2}{N} \tag{15}$$

$$V_{pe} = -\frac{\sum_{k=1}^{c} \sum_{i=1}^{N} \mu_{ki} * log(\mu_{ki})}{N} \tag{16}$$

$$TSA = \frac{TP + TN}{TP + FP + TN + FN} \tag{17}$$

where TP, TN, FP, and FN correspond to true positive, true negative, false positive, and false negative respectively. Qualitative evaluation helps in understanding the quality of the output images and brings out the inefficiencies of an approach. The presented technique stands out in terms of performance when compared to the other existing algorithms, especially when segmenting images corrupted with noise and other artifacts.

Figure 1 and Fig. 2 show the segmented outputs of the proposed and compared algorithms for T1-weighted MRI images with 7% Gaussian noise (F80 slice) and 8% salt and pepper noise (F90 slice). Also, Fig. 3 gives the segmented output image for 9% noise with 40% inhomogeneity (F95 slice). Additionally, it presents the segmented tissue (CSF, GM, and WM) regions using all of the mentioned methods. It can be clearly noticed that the presented technique is better than its peers and produces reliable results. Quantitative evaluation serves as an important gauging criterion for judging the performance of various algorithms. Tables 1, 2, 3, 4, 5 and 6 bring up the performance results of the listed algorithms using cluster validity functions (Vpc, Vpe) and Tables 7, 8 and 9 demonstrate the

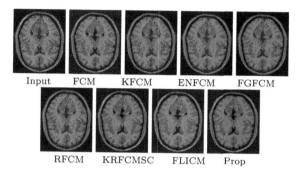

Input   FCM   KFCM   ENFCM   FGFCM

RFCM   KRFCMSC   FLICM   Prop

Fig. 1. Brain MRI segmented images (F80 slice) corrupted by 7% Gaussian noise

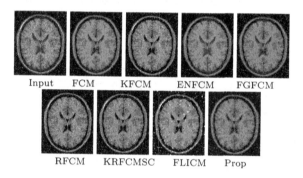

Input   FCM   KFCM   ENFCM   FGFCM

RFCM   KRFCMSC   FLICM   Prop

Fig. 2. Brain MRI segmented images (F90 slice) corrupted by 8% Salt and Pepper noise.

Table 1. Comparative V_{pc} values for different algorithms over 7% Gaussian noisy Brain MRI images.

Algorithm	50	55	60	65	70	75	80	85	90	95	100
FCM	0.8113	0.8188	0.8241	0.8278	0.813	0.8246	0.819	0.8351	0.8424	0.8457	0.8481
KFCM	0.806	0.8139	0.8196	0.8231	0.8216	0.8266	0.8224	0.8305	0.8379	0.8273	0.8404
ENFCM	0.8152	0.8248	0.8353	0.8404	0.8398	0.8454	0.8408	0.8511	0.8603	0.8646	0.8674
FGFCM	0.8168	0.8261	0.8362	0.8414	0.8413	0.8474	0.8425	0.853	0.8619	0.8662	0.8634
RFCM	0.7947	0.815	0.8196	0.8222	0.8245	0.8278	0.8242	0.8305	0.8385	0.8379	0.8494
KRFCMSC	0.8021	0.8278	0.8236	0.7958	0.8121	0.8133	0.8199	0.8408	0.7963	0.8487	0.8587
FLICM	0.8225	0.831	0.8094	0.8223	0.8171	0.8331	0.8263	0.832	0.8578	0.866	0.8642
MRKFCM	0.8959	0.9018	0.9021	0.9016	0.9041	0.9065	0.9036	0.9137	0.9161	0.9164	0.9261

tissue segmentation accuracy corresponding to T1-weighted MRI images with 7% Gaussian noise, 8% salt and pepper noise, and 9% noise with 40% inhomogeneity. The results corresponding to the presented technique prove its robustness in segmenting images with noise corruptions and inhomogeneities. The better results for each of the cases defend the observations made from qualitative evaluations and the reliability of the presented approach for brain MRI segmentation.

Table 2. Comparative V_{pe} values for different algorithms over 7% Gaussian noisy Brain MRI images.

Algorithm	50	55	60	65	70	75	80	85	90	95	100
FCM	0.366	0.352	0.3418	0.3348	0.3614	0.3407	0.3507	0.3215	0.3091	0.3026	0.2984
KFCM	0.3781	0.3633	0.3526	0.3459	0.3482	0.3393	0.3467	0.3324	0.3202	0.3416	0.3167
ENFCM	0.3552	0.3379	0.3186	0.3088	0.3091	0.2993	0.3079	0.289	0.2717	0.2636	0.2586
FGFCM	0.3522	0.3353	0.3167	0.3066	0.306	0.2954	0.3044	0.2854	0.2685	0.2601	0.2657
RFCM	0.3901	0.3595	0.35	0.345	0.34	0.3344	0.3411	0.3303	0.3163	0.3196	0.2971
KRFCMSC	0.393	0.3348	0.3505	0.3969	0.3625	0.3927	0.3498	0.3142	0.4204	0.3034	0.2747
FLICM	0.3453	0.3293	0.3682	0.3464	0.3539	0.3263	0.3386	0.3301	0.2775	0.2632	0.2667
Prop	0.1904	0.1821	0.1817	0.1823	0.1698	0.1695	0.1702	0.1683	0.1679	0.1677	0.1631

Table 3. Comparative V_{pc} values for different algorithms over 8% salt-and-pepper noise density Brain MRI images.

Algorithm	50	55	60	65	70	75	80	85	90	95	100
FCM	0.8559	0.8558	0.8318	0.8476	0.8438	0.8505	0.8463	0.8557	0.865	0.8666	0.8731
KFCM	0.8036	0.8461	0.8375	0.8381	0.8341	0.8398	0.8289	0.8474	0.8566	0.8615	0.865
ENFCM	0.775	0.7877	0.7989	0.8008	0.7923	0.7949	0.7957	0.7993	0.8012	0.8174	0.8098
FGFCM	0.7707	0.7809	0.7921	0.7924	0.7905	0.7978	0.7955	0.8003	0.8083	0.8102	0.8155
RFCM	0.8101	0.8303	0.845	0.8351	0.8351	0.8393	0.8478	0.8579	0.8668	0.8515	0.8521
KRFCMSC	0.8093	0.8118	0.8283	0.8376	0.8294	0.8386	0.8392	0.8242	0.8607	0.861	0.8596
FLICM	0.8187	0.8374	0.8478	0.8488	0.8404	0.8478	0.8501	0.855	0.8612	0.8625	0.8705
Prop	0.866	0.8695	0.8814	0.8825	0.8767	0.8748	0.8726	0.8708	0.8817	0.8788	0.8845

Table 4. Comparative V_{pe} values for different algorithms over 8% salt-and-pepper noise density Brain MRI images.

Algorithm	50	55	60	65	70	75	80	85	90	95	100
FCM	0.2823	0.2834	0.3251	0.289	0.2963	0.2842	0.2921	0.2749	0.2576	0.2552	0.2423
KFCM	0.3774	0.3058	0.3146	0.3131	0.3211	0.3093	0.3414	0.297	0.2796	0.2695	0.2636
ENFCM	0.4234	0.4024	0.3821	0.3781	0.3908	0.384	0.3878	0.3917	0.3836	0.3699	0.3557
FGFCM	0.4364	0.4182	0.3994	0.3979	0.4011	0.3878	0.3917	0.3836	0.3699	0.3649	0.3557
RFCM	0.3568	0.3216	0.2946	0.3185	0.3181	0.3094	0.291	0.2726	0.2558	0.2893	0.2833
KRFCMSC	0.3721	0.3595	0.3345	0.3221	0.3432	0.3164	0.3172	0.3488	0.2769	0.278	0.2761
FLICM	0.3452	0.3112	0.2913	0.289	0.3042	0.2913	0.2879	0.2787	0.2667	0.2647	0.2496
Prop	0.2632	0.2582	0.2435	0.2431	0.2509	0.2517	0.2526	0.2532	0.2433	0.2499	0.2414

Table 5. Comparative V_{pc} values for different algorithms over 9% noise density and 40% inhomogeneity Brain MRI images.

Algorithm	50	55	60	65	70	75	80	85	90	95	100
FCM	0.7946	0.8	0.8062	0.8073	0.806	0.8067	0.809	0.8149	0.822	0.8263	0.8305
KFCM	0.7906	0.7961	0.8024	0.8032	0.8013	0.803	0.805	0.8105	0.8175	0.8215	0.8255
ENFCM	0.81	0.8161	0.8245	0.8313	0.828	0.8322	0.8314	0.8399	0.8455	0.8512	0.8563
FGFCM	0.8105	0.8185	0.8252	0.8323	0.8288	0.8333	0.8324	0.8407	0.8461	0.8519	0.8569
RFCM	0.793	0.7976	0.8036	0.6455	0.8029	0.7963	0.7991	0.8148	0.8214	0.8253	0.8291
KRFCMSC	0.7696	0.7931	0.7993	0.8097	0.805	0.8181	0.8198	0.7615	0.802	0.8422	0.8568
FLICM	0.8153	0.8213	0.8203	0.8264	0.8238	0.8272	0.8282	0.8358	0.8434	0.8483	0.8446
Prop	0.8912	0.8976	0.894	0.8979	0.8946	0.8997	0.8986	0.9005	0.9076	0.9126	0.9156

Table 6. Comparative V_{pe} values for different algorithms over 9% noise density and 40% inhomogeneity Brain MRI images.

Algorithm	50	55	60	65	70	75	80	85	90	95	100
FCM	0.3962	0.3865	0.3751	0.3727	0.3738	0.3716	0.3689	0.3582	0.3458	0.3376	0.331
KFCM	0.4056	0.3956	0.3841	0.3823	0.3846	0.3808	0.3787	0.3686	0.3565	0.3489	0.3426
ENFCM	0.3655	0.3544	0.3395	0.3271	0.3321	0.3239	0.3264	0.3109	0.3007	0.2898	0.2806
FGFCM	0.3643	0.3501	0.3379	0.325	0.3304	0.3214	0.3243	0.3092	0.299	0.2881	0.2789
RFCM	0.3991	0.391	0.3792	0.592	0.3793	0.391	0.3872	0.358	0.3465	0.339	0.3329
KRFCMSC	0.4455	0.3955	0.3839	0.3653	0.3724	0.3485	0.3471	0.4328	0.3765	0.3112	0.2816
FLICM	0.3588	0.3475	0.3469	0.3365	0.3399	0.3334	0.3317	0.319	0.305	0.2961	0.3068
Prop	0.1945	0.1963	0.1928	0.1861	0.1916	0.1854	0.1847	0.1813	0.1686	0.1594	0.1689

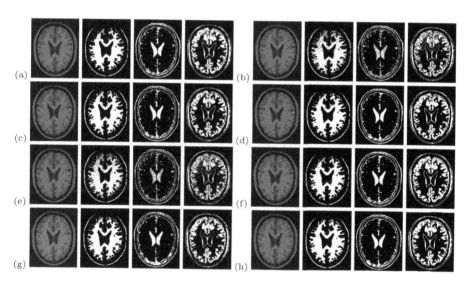

Fig. 3. Segmented results of the original image, CSF, GM, WM (from left to right) using different methods (a) FCM, (b) KFCM, (c) ENFCM, (d) FGFCM, (e) RFCM, (f) RKFCMSC, (g) FLICM, and (h) Prop on a T1-weighted Brain MRI image (F95 slice) corrupted by 9% Noise with 40% inhomogeneity.

Table 7. Different TSA values for the slice number F95 MRI image using different algorithms for 7% Gaussian noise.

Algorithm	CSF	WM	GM
FCM	75.011	75.764	65.692
KFCM	73.817	75.304	66.741
ENFCM	86.926	86.022	80.248
FGFCM	86.959	86.114	80.309
RFCM	83.608	82.304	74.874
KRFCMSC	85.64	85.907	75.985
FLICM	86.44	86.206	80.673
Prop	87.415	88.336	81.948

Table 8. Different TSA values for the slice number F95 MRI image using different algorithms for 8% salt-and-pepper noise

Algorithm	CSF	WM	GM
FCM	80.785	76.981	69.028
KFCM	86.903	83.003	80.543
ENFCM	77.702	83.614	78.171
FGFCM	77.623	84.006	77.979
RFCM	84.39	82.735	77.555
KRFCMSC	83.442	83.822	79.447
FLICM	80.677	81.908	78.69
Prop	87.171	85.877	82.822

Table 9. Different TSA values for the slice number F95 MRI image using different algorithms for 9% noise with 40% inhomogeneity.

Algorithm	CSF	WM	GM
FCM	86.575	86.565	79.864
KFCM	86.343	85.302	79.28
ENFCM	86.743	86.323	80.004
FGFCM	86.893	86.305	80.019
RFCM	86.343	85.302	79.28
KRFCMSC	86.679	86.478	79.889
FLICM	86.868	86.442	80.307
Prop	87.076	87.211	81.377

5   Conclusion

In this paper, an Adaptive Rough Fuzzy Set Based Kernelized C Means Clustering algorithm is proposed for unsupervised Brain MRI tissue segmentation. Experimental results demonstrate the efficiency of the proposed method in the domain of segmentation. The algorithm is straightforward, it requires less computation time, its wide scale application and reliable performance for various use cases (segmentation of normal image, corrupted image with various noise types) makes it a rightful candidate to be integrated with hardware to form an embedded system for real time computer aided diagnosis. In future, the algorithm can be scaled with different pre and post processing techniques for better performance and applications in domains of star region clustering, remote sensing, and others.

References

1. Bishop, C.M.: Pattern recognition. Mach. Learn. **128**(9) (2006)

2. Cai, W., Chen, S., Zhang, D.: Fast and robust fuzzy c-means clustering algorithms incorporating local information for image segmentation. Pattern Recogn. **40**(3), 825–838 (2007)

3. Cocosco, C.A., Kollokian, V., Kwan, R.K.S., Pike, G.B., Evans, A.C.: Brainweb: Online interface to a 3D MRI simulated brain database. In: NeuroImage. Citeseer (1997)

4. Gonzalez, R.C., Woods, R.E., et al.: Digital Image Processing (2002)

5. Gudbjartsson, H., Patz, S.: The Rician distribution of noisy MRI data. Magn. Reson. Med. **34**(6), 910–914 (1995)

6. Halder, A., Talukdar, N.A.: Brain tissue segmentation using improved kernelized rough-fuzzy c-means with Spatio-contextual information from MRI. Magn. Reson. Imaging **62**, 129–151 (2019)

7. Havens, T.C., Bezdek, J.C., Leckie, C., Hall, L.O., Palaniswami, M.: Fuzzy c-means algorithms for very large data. IEEE Trans. Fuzzy Syst. **20**(6), 1130–1146 (2012)

8. Khosravanian, A., Rahmanimanesh, M., Keshavarzi, P., Mozaffari, S.: Fuzzy local intensity clustering (flic) model for automatic medical image segmentation. Vis. Comput. **37**, 1185–1206 (2021). https://doi.org/10.1007/s00371-020-01861-1

9. Liu, W., Lin, W.: Additive white gaussian noise level estimation in SVD domain for images. IEEE Trans. Image Process. **22**(3), 872–883 (2012)

10. Maji, P., Pal, S.K.: Maximum class separability for rough-fuzzy C-means based brain MR image segmentation. In: Peters, J.F., Skowron, Aj., Rybiński, H. (eds.) Transactions on Rough Sets IX. LNCS, vol. 5390, pp. 114–134. Springer, Heidelberg (2008). https://doi.org/10.1007/978-3-540-89876-4_7

11. Rajapakse, J.C., Giedd, J.N., Rapoport, J.L.: Statistical approach to segmentation of single-channel cerebral MR images. IEEE Trans. Med. Imaging **16**(2), 176–186 (1997)

12. Singleton, H.R., Pohost, G.M.: Automatic cardiac MR image segmentation using edge detection by tissue classification in pixel neighborhoods. Magn. Reson. Med. **37**(3), 418–424 (1997)

13. Subudhi, B.N., Thangaraj, V., Sankaralingam, E., Ghosh, A.: Tumor or abnormality identification from magnetic resonance images using statistical region fusion based segmentation. Magn. Reson. Imaging **34**(9), 1292–1304 (2016)

14. Suetens, P.: Fundamentals of Medical Imaging. Cambridge University Press, Cambridge (2017)

15. Szilagyi, L., Benyo, Z., Szilágyi, S.M., Adam, H.: Mr brain image segmentation using an enhanced fuzzy c-means algorithm. In: Proceedings of the 25th Annual International Conference of the IEEE Engineering in Medicine and Biology Society (IEEE Cat. No. 03CH37439), vol. 1, pp. 724–726. IEEE (2003)

16. Theodoridis, S., Koutroumbas, K.: Pattern recognition and neural networks. In: Paliouras, G., Karkaletsis, V., Spyropoulos, C.D. (eds.) ACAI 1999. LNCS (LNAI), vol. 2049, pp. 169–195. Springer, Heidelberg (2001). https://doi.org/10.1007/3-540-44673-7_8

17. Wagstaff, K., Cardie, C., Rogers, S., Schrödl, S., et al.: Constrained k-means clustering with background knowledge. In: Icml. vol. 1, pp. 577–584 (2001)

18. Zhang, D.Q., Chen, S.C.: A novel kernelized fuzzy c-means algorithm with application in medical image segmentation. Artif. Intell. Med. **32**(1), 37–50 (2004)

On the Prospects of Latent Masterprints

Mahesh Joshi$^{(\boxtimes)}$ (ID), Bodhisatwa Mazumdar (ID), and Somnath Dey (ID)

Department of Computer Science & Engineering, Indian Institute of Technology
Indore, Simrol, Khandwa Road, Indore 453552, Madhya Pradesh, India
{phd1701101004,bodhisatwa,somnathd}@iiti.ac.in

Abstract. Latent fingerprints are the prime evidence for forensic offi-
cers investigating a criminal case. Subsequently, the legislative procedure considers the forensic department's reports as authentic document
to support their judgment. Hence, an automated latent fingerprint identification system must produce accurate results to ensure only culprits
are punished instead of innocent individuals. Recent research confirmed
the existence of a *MasterPrint* as a partial fingerprint identifying more
than four distinct subjects enrolled with the database. Usually, latent
fingerprints are partial impressions, i.e. fingerprints cover small portion
of full finger. Hence, it presents a scope to examine the possibility of a
Latent MasterPrint. We investigate the feasibility of the Latent Master-
Print in this article using the Multi-sensor Optical and Latent Fingerprint (MOLF) DB4 dataset. The identification results using the NIST
Biometric Image Software (NBIS) reveal the possibility of Latent MasterPrints.

Keywords: Latent fingerprint identification · Latent MasterPrint ·
Biometrics · Forensics

1 Introduction

Fingerprints are considered a unique trait every individual as no incidence of any
two persons with similar patterns is reported to date [2]. Even though biometric
systems employing other traits such as ear, face, voice etc., are commercially
available, fingerprint-based biometric systems gained popularity due to conve-
nience, high accuracy and low-cost devices. Hence, numerous government and
private organizations extensively employ them as an identification and authoriza-
tion mechanism at airports, educational institutions, access control, and border
security applications [13]. The biometric system usually enhances the impression
captured by its sensor to divide the whole fingerprint into a dark portion known
as ridges and a white region comprising valleys for accurate feature extraction.
Moreover, minutia is the most widely used feature formed by the location where
a ridge terminates, or three ridges emerge [7].

A fingerprint recognition system uses features extracted from a user's fingerprint to conclude if he is a legitimate user of the system. The input to such
a system can be a full fingerprint or a small portion of the user fingerprint,

B. Raman et al. (Eds.): CVIP 2021, CCIS 1567, pp. 574–581, 2022.
https://doi.org/10.1007/978-3-031-11346-8_49

i.e., a partial fingerprint. Such systems can thus act as a security mechanism for automatic identification and authentication of an individual. In the *identification* process, we assume that the user is already enrolled, but his identity is unknown. We compare the user's fingerprint with all the enrolled records from the database. The system declares the anonymous user with the identity associated with the entry having the highest similarity score, usually a numeric value. For a biometric *authentication* system, the user reveals his identity while submitting the fingerprint called an input fingerprint. Subsequently, the system compares the freshly acquired fingerprint against the records of the claimed user and declares if he's what he claimed or trying to impersonate the alleged user. University attendance systems, government offices, housing societies, smartphone screen lock apps usually employ biometric-based *authentication systems*. However, civilian and criminal identification systems, airports, railways, border security applications, military access control systems, and fin-tech organizations use a biometric-based *identification system* to reveal user identity.

2 Latent Fingerprint Identification

The finger impressions unwittingly left behind at a crime scene are referred to as *latent fingerprints*. Forensics agencies try to identify a probable suspect based on the evidence collected at a crime scene. In such a case, the agency might collect the culprit's latent fingerprint impressions on various surfaces at the site. Such latent fingerprints are usually partial and also lack clarity in terms of ridge patterns. Hence, an automated fingerprint identification system (AFIS) is employed to process and analyse such blurry and ambiguous digital data. The forensic investigators employ AFIS for acquiring latent fingerprints, marking features like minutiae, and comparing enhanced latent fingerprints [13].

An overview of different steps involved in a latent fingerprint identification system is shown in Fig. 1. Forensic investigators visit the crime scene to identify probable locations of latent fingerprints left behind by the criminal. Latent fingerprints are formed using sweat and oil secreted from the finger pores. The experts employ different powders based on the surface material to develop such prints [15]. Since these leftover impressions are distorted, they require preprocessing to enhance the quality before extracting features. Yoon et al. [16] proposed a metric Latent Fingerprint Image Quality (LFIQ) to distinguish good quality and bad quality (i.e., requiring human intervention for processing the latent fingerprint) latent fingerprints. The authors employed parameters related to ridges and minutiae to decide the LFIQ of a latent fingerprint.

The latent fingerprint image is segmented into foreground and background regions for clearly visualizing the ridge pattern. SegFinNet is a convolutional neural network (CNN) based automatic latent fingerprint segmentation approach [9]. The segmentation process follows normalization, orientation estimation, ridge frequency estimation to reconstruct broken ridges and curve patterns [6]. Further, latent fingerprint enhancement is performed using Canny Edge Detection Filter, Laplacian Filter, Gaussian Low Pass Filter, etc., for improving the latent fingerprint quality.

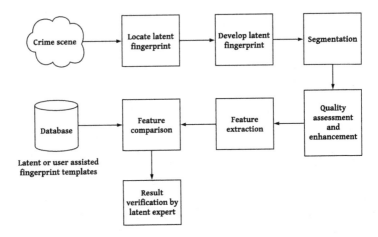

Fig. 1. Overview of various steps involved in a latent fingerprint identification system.

A fingerprint comprises features that can be classified into three categories [5]. Level 1 features are the ridge flow pattern. In general, fingerprint ridges are classified using 17 characteristic features [15]. Minutiae come under Level 2 features. However, minute level details from the ridges are categorized as Level 3 features. As the latent fingerprints usually possess a low minutiae count, most approaches for latent fingerprint identification employ correlation-based matching, or non-minutiae feature-based matching [4]. However, Krish et al. [8] proposed an approach based on extended minutiae types suitable for automated latent fingerprint identification. When combined with the existing minutiae-based approach, the results show that the approach can improve its accuracy.

3   MasterPrint Vulnerability

Recent research by Roy et al. [10] revealed the *MasterPrint* vulnerability associated with fingerprint identification systems. MasterPrints are the fingerprints that can identify at least 4% distinct subjects from the enrolled dataset. The authors conducted the experiments on FVC 2002 dataset using commercial VeriFinger SDK. The demonstration results conclude that a dictionary of the top five MasterPrints generated from partially cropped fingerprints could disclose the identity of more than 60% unique subjects. Even though the vulnerability existed for the partial dataset, there is a probability that employing a robust approach for full fingerprint identification may lead to MasterPrint generation if the pre-processing stage employs inappropriate thresholding and skeletonization methods. We define a *Latent MasterPrint* as a latent fingerprint identifying at least 4% subjects within the enrolled database. The existence of Latent MasterPrint is a severe concern. A criminal with a technical background can misuse such MasterPrints to prove an innocent as a criminal. In this paper, we investigate the possibility of a Latent MasterPrint and present the experimental results.

4 Experimental Setup

During our experiment to identify Latent MasterPrint, we followed a closed-set identification setup. In this scenario, we assume that every input has a corresponding matching fingerprint in the database. We compare each probe with every other template from the dataset and compute the similarity score for each comparison during the *identification test* [1]. If the highest score corresponds to the actual subject sample, we call it a *correct detect and identify* (CDI). In the scenario of a *false alarm* (FA), the highest score belongs to some other subjects' template. Rejection rate (RR) reports the percentage of latent fingerprints that have shown no similarity with any of the enrolled templates. During the identification test, we measure the *detect and identification rate* (DIR) based on CDI count, the *false alarm rate* (FAR) based on FA count, and the number of MasterPrints generated during the experiment. An identification system producing very low MasterPrints at higher DIR and lower FAR would become ideal for practical use in the fingerprint biometric system. The identification test results are computed for threshold value 0, 5, 15, 25, 35 and 45.

A *cumulative matching characteristic* (CMC) curve shows the rank-k performance of an identification system, which depicts the identification of the correct subject at different ranks [3]. The results from the identification test make up the data for each dataset's CMC curve. Suppose we have k subjects enrolled with a system; ideally, the rank-k identification rate should be 100%. The best approach is expected to reach 100% performance at the earliest. Hence, the CMC plots presented here show the DIR performance till rank-10.

MOLF DB4 dataset consists of 4400 latent fingerprints cropped from simultaneous prints [12]. The dataset contains 2 samples of thumb and little finger, 4 samples of the ring finger, 6 samples of the middle finger, and 8 samples of index finger from left and right hand collected from 100 subjects. The latent fingerprints size is variable. The dataset contains more than 96% latent fingerprints with an NFIQ (NBIS Fingerprint Image Quality) score of 5, i.e. these are the worst quality images [11].

5 Minutiae Detection and Minutiae Matching

The existing literature on fingerprint recognition includes several approaches employing various schemes to locate and detect a minutia. These approaches use a gray-scale fingerprint, a binarized image, or a thinned image. Moreover, the performance of a matching algorithm is highly dependent on the minutiae detection method employed. Hence, we require a scheme wherein the algorithms for minutiae detection and matching are tuned and blended to deliver high accuracy. The NIST Biometric Image Software (NBIS) is a standardized software bundled with the MINDTCT algorithm for minutiae detection and the BOZORTH3 algorithm for minutiae matching [14]. Therefore, we employed these algorithms for our experiments.

6 Result Analysis

We present the results for various thresholds on MOLF DB4 dataset using Table 1. We started experimenting without any threshold and increased the threshold at a step size of 5 until zero MasterPrints are observed. We observed that till threshold of 15, there are $64\% - 84\%$ MasterPrints generated and the largest MasterPrint at each threshold identifies all the subjects from the dataset. Moreover, the DIR is between $36 - 38\%$, and the FAR is $40 - 50\%$ under this scenario. The DIR decreases gradually as we increase the threshold, but the percentage of MasterPrints generated and the number of subjects identified by the largest MasterPrint reduces drastically. We observed zero MasterPrints at a threshold of 50. The DIR, in this case, was 18.1%. However, the alarming situation arises here as all other latent fingerprints are rejected while showing zero FAR.

The CMC plots for the MOLF DB4 dataset at various thresholds is shown in Fig. 2. It is observed that the rank-10 performance at the lower thresholds is above 75%, wherein NBIS rejected around 13% of latent fingerprints. As we raised the threshold, the DIR reaches below 22% while generating zero Master-Prints. Moreover, there is no increase in the DIR for higher ranks at thresholds above 25. The situation signifies that we have above 75% rejection rate at higher thresholds as we try to lower the probability of Latent MasterPrint.

7 Future Work

The results from the experiments show the possibility of Latent MasterPrints. As the latent fingerprints are usually low-quality impressions, there is a possibility that its small portion may overlap with some other individual's fingerprints. Hence, in our future work, we would target devising a novel approach to extract unique features from latent fingerprints to identify an individual accurately and minimize the possibility of Latent MasterPrint. We would be employing more latent datasets during our experiments and compare the results with existing latent fingerprint identification approaches. We would also be experimenting with comparing the latent fingerprints with a user-assisted good quality fingerprint dataset.

Table 1. Results on MOLF DB4 dataset for various thresholds. DIR=Detect and Identification Rate, FAR = False Accept Rate, RR = Rejection Rate, MPs = percentage of MasterPrints generated, LMPs = No. of subjects identified by the largest MasterPrint at a given threshold.

Threshold	DIR	FAR	RR	MPs	LMPs
0	38.2%	48.94%	12.86%	87.14%	100
5	38%	49.02%	12.98%	85.89%	100
15	36.4%	41.96%	21.64%	64.23%	100
25	31.4%	27.3%	41.3%	7.86%	91
35	26.8%	5.09%	68.11%	0.16%	47
45	21.4%	0.6%	78%	0.04%	13

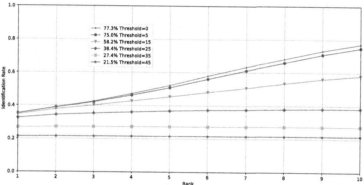

Fig. 2. CMC plots. Rank-10 performance on MOLF DB4 dataset at various thresholds

8 Conclusion

The MasterPrint vulnerability associated with the partial fingerprint identification system has shown another loophole in the fingerprint identification system. As a latent fingerprint usually covers a partial finger region, we investigated the possibility of a Latent MasterPrint. The results on MOLF DB4 latent dataset using NBIS's minutiae detection and fingerprint matching modules prove the presence of Latent MasterPrints. We observed around 8% Latent MasterPrints at a threshold of 25 wherein the largest MasterPrint has identified above 90 subjects. The existing approaches from the literature showed their performance using CMC curves, but this work depicts the need of including the Latent MasterPrint metric in future research on latent fingerprint identification. Also, our work demonstrates the importance of developing resilient approaches to thwart Latent MasterPrint vulnerability.

References

1. Blackburn, D., Miles, C., Wing, B., Shepard, K.: Biometric testing and statistics. Tech. rep., National Science and Technology Council (NSTC), Washington, D.C. (2006). http://www.nws-sa.com/biometrics/testing/BioTestingAndStats.pdf
2. Cao, K., Jain, A.K.: Automated latent fingerprint recognition. IEEE Trans. Pattern Anal. Mach. Intell. 41(4), 788–800 (2019). https://doi.org/10.1109/TPAMI.2018.2818162
3. DeCann, B., Ross, A.: Relating ROC and CMC curves via the biometric menagerie. In: IEEE Sixth International Conference on Biometrics: Theory, Applications and Systems, BTAS 2013, Arlington, VA, USA, September 29 - October 2, 2013, pp. 1–8. IEEE (2013). https://doi.org/10.1109/BTAS.2013.6712705
4. Deshpande, U.U., Malemath, V.S., Patil, S.M., Chaugule, S.V.: Latent fingerprint identification system based on a local combination of minutiae feature points. SN Comput. Sci. 2(3), 1–17 (2021). https://doi.org/10.1007/s42979-021-00615-7
5. Ezhilmaran, D., Adhiyaman, M.: A review study on latent fingerprint recognition techniques. J. Inf. Optim. Sci. 38(3–4), 501–516 (2017). https://doi.org/10.1080/02522667.2016.1224468
6. Himanshi, Kaur, A., Verma, A.: Latent fingerprint recognition using hybridization approach of partial differential equation and exemplar inpainting. Indian J. Sci. Technol. 9(45), December 2016. https://doi.org/10.17485/ijst/2016/v9i45/101871
7. Joshi, M., Mazumdar, B., Dey, S.: A comprehensive security analysis of match-in-database fingerprint biometric system. Pattern Recognit. Lett. 138, 247–266 (2020). https://doi.org/10.1016/j.patrec.2020.07.024
8. Krish, R.P., Fierrez, J., Ramos, D., Alonso-Fernandez, F., Bigun, J.: Improving automated latent fingerprint identification using extended minutia types. Inf. Fusion 50, 9–19 (2019). https://doi.org/10.1016/j.inffus.2018.10.001
9. Nguyen, D., Cao, K., Jain, A.K.: Automatic latent fingerprint segmentation. In: 9th IEEE International Conference on Biometrics Theory, Applications and Systems, BTAS 2018, Redondo Beach, CA, USA, October 22–25, 2018, pp. 1–9. IEEE (2018). https://doi.org/10.1109/BTAS.2018.8698544
10. Roy, A., Memon, N.D., Ross, A.: Masterprint: exploring the vulnerability of partial fingerprint-based authentication systems. IEEE Trans. Inf. Forensics Secur. 12(9), 2013–2025 (2017). https://doi.org/10.1109/TIFS.2017.2691658
11. Sankaran, A., Vatsa, M., Singh, R.: Latent fingerprint matching: a survey. IEEE Access 2, 982–1004 (2014). https://doi.org/10.1109/ACCESS.2014.2349879
12. Sankaran, A., Vatsa, M., Singh, R.: Multisensor optical and latent fingerprint database. IEEE Access 3, 653–665 (2015). https://doi.org/10.1109/ACCESS.2015.2428631
13. Singla, N., Kaur, M., Sofat, S.: Automated latent fingerprint identification system: a review. Forensic Sci. Int. 309, 110187 (2020). https://doi.org/10.1016/j.forsciint.2020.110187
14. Watson, C.I., et al.: User's Guide to NIST Biometric Image Software (NBIS). NIST Interagency/Internal Report (NISTIR) - 7392 (2007). https://doi.org/10.6028/NIST.IR.7392

15. Win, K.N., Li, K., Chen, J., Fournier-Viger, P., Li, K.: Fingerprint classification and identification algorithms for criminal investigation: a survey. Future Gener. Comput. Syst. **110**, 758–771 (2020). https://doi.org/10.1016/j.future.2019.10.019
16. Yoon, S., Cao, K., Liu, E., Jain, A.K.: LFIQ: latent fingerprint image quality. In: IEEE Sixth International Conference on Biometrics: Theory, Applications and Systems, BTAS 2013, Arlington, VA, USA, September 29–2 October 2013, pp. 1–8. IEEE (2013). https://doi.org/10.1109/BTAS.2013.6712750

Correction to: *Signature2Vec* - An Algorithm for Reference Frame Agnostic Vectorization of Handwritten Signatures

Manish Kumar Srivastava⬤, Dileep Reddy, Bhargav Kurma, and Kalidas Yeturu⬤

Correction to:
Chapter "*Signature2Vec* - An Algorithm for Reference Frame Agnostic Vectorization of Handwritten Signatures" in: B. Raman et al. (Eds.): *Computer Vision and Image Processing*, CCIS 1567, https://doi.org/10.1007/978-3-031-11346-8_12

In the originally published version of the chapter 12, the name of one of the co-authors was erroneously missed out. The author's name "Bhargav Kurma" has been added to the list of authors.

The updated version of this chapter can be found at
https://doi.org/10.1007/978-3-031-11346-8_12

Author Index

Printed in the United States
by Baker & Taylor Publisher Services